SOURCES OF OUR LIBERTIES

SOURCES OF OUR LIBERTIES

Documentary Origins of Individual Liberties in
the United States Constitution and Bill of Rights

Revised Edition

Edited by
RICHARD L. PERRY
Under the general supervision of
JOHN C. COOPER
Former Administrator, American Bar Foundation

William S. Hein & Co., Inc.
Buffalo, NY
1991

ISBN 0-89941-752-3 (reprint)

Printed in the United States of America

This volume is printed on acid-free paper by
William S. Hein & Co., Inc.

SOURCES OF OUR LIBERTIES

Documentary Origins of Individual Liberties in
the United States Constitution and Bill of Rights

Edited by
RICHARD L. PERRY
Under the general supervision of
JOHN C. COOPER
Former Administrator, American Bar Foundation

Revised Edition
Chicago • *AMERICAN BAR FOUNDATION*
1978

© *1978 by the American Bar Foundation*

Library of Congress Catalog Card Number: 78-67316

Revised Edition, 1978

Grateful acknowledgment is made for permission to quote passages from the following publications:

Carl Becker, *The Declaration of Independence.* (Copyright 1922, 1942, Alfred A. Knopf, Inc.)

William Haller and Godfrey Davies, *The Leveller Tracts, 1647-53.* (Copyright 1944, Columbia University Press.)

William S. Holdsworth, *A History of English Law.* (Copyright 1931, Little, Brown and Company.)

ISBN 0-910058-90-3

AMERICAN BAR FOUNDATION
1155 East 60th Street
Chicago, Illinois

BOARD OF DIRECTORS (August 1978)

Bernard G. Segal, *President*, of the Pennsylvania Bar
Robert W. Meserve, *Vice-President*, of the Massachusetts Bar
Phil C. Neal, *Secretary*, University of Chicago Law School
J. David Andrews, *Treasurer*, of the Washington State Bar

John J. Creedon, of the New York Bar
Hon. Erwin N. Griswold, of the District of Columbia Bar
Hon. Patricia Roberts Harris, Department of Housing and Urban Development, Washington, D.C.
Seth M. Hufstedler, of the California Bar
F. Wm. McCalpin, of the Missouri Bar
Hon. Vincent L. McKusick, Supreme Judicial Court, Maine
Maynard J. Toll, of the California Bar
David E. Ward, Jr., of the Florida Bar

ex officio

S. Shepherd Tate, *President, American Bar Association*
Leonard S. Janofsky, *President-Elect, American Bar Association*
John C. Shepherd, *Chairman, House of Delegates, American Bar Association*
Gibson Gayle, Jr., *President, American Bar Endowment*
Hon. Charles W. Joiner, *Chairman, The Fellows of the American Bar Foundation*
John Gavin, *Vice-Chairman, The Fellows of the American Bar Foundation*

ADMINISTRATION

Spencer L. Kimball, *Executive Director*
Barbara A. Curran, *Associate Executive Director*
Donald M. McIntyre, *Associate Executive Director*
Louis B. Potter, *Assistant Executive Director*
Benjamin S. Jones, *Accounting Officer*
Bette H. Sikes, *Director of Publications*
Olavi Maru, *Librarian*

CONTENTS

Foreword	ix
I. Magna Carta, 1215	1
II. Confirmatio Cartarum, 1297	23
III. The First Charter of Virginia, 1606	32
IV. Ordinances for Virginia, 1618	47
V. Mayflower Compact, 1620	55
VI. Petition of Right, 1628	62
VII. The Charter of Massachusetts Bay, 1629	76
VIII. The Charter of Maryland, 1632	97
IX. Fundamental Orders of Connecticut, 1639	115
X. Abolition of the Star Chamber, 1641	125
XI. Massachusetts Body of Liberties, 1641	143
XII. Charter of Rhode Island and Providence Plantations, 1663	162
XIII. Concessions and Agreements of West New Jersey, 1677	180
XIV. Habeas Corpus Act, 1679	189
XV. Frame of Government of Pennsylvania, 1682	204
XVI. Bill of Rights, 1689	222

CONTENTS

XVII. Pennsylvania Charter of Privileges, 1701	251
XVIII. Resolutions of the Stamp Act Congress, 1765	261
XIX. Declaration and Resolves of the First Continental Congress, 1774	272
XX. Declaration of the Causes and Necessity of Taking Up Arms, 1775	290
XXI. Constitution of Virginia, 1776	301
XXII. Declaration of Independence, 1776	314
XXIII. Constitution of Pennsylvania, 1776	323
XXIV. Delaware Declaration of Rights, 1776	332
XXV. Constitution of Maryland, 1776	341
XXVI. Constitution of North Carolina, 1776	352
XXVII. Constitution of Vermont, 1777	358
XXVIII. Constitution of Massachusetts, 1780	368
XXIX. Constitution of New Hampshire, 1784	379
XXX. Northwest Ordinance, 1787	387
XXXI. The Constitution of the United States, 1787	399
XXXII. The First Ten Amendments to the Constitution, 1791	418
Appendix	435
Bibliography	443
Postscript 1978: Bibliographical Note	449
Index	457

FOREWORD

The purpose of this book is to present in a single usable volume the historic documents constituting the major legal sources of our individual liberties. As Mr. Perry, the editor, says in his introductory note to the text of Magna Carta on page 1: "The liberties of the American citizen depend upon the existence of established and known rules of law limiting the authority and discretion of men wielding the power of government."

The United States Constitution and Bill of Rights assert the existence of certain of these liberties as part of the fundamental law on which our government rests. But these great documents are not the only original sources. The rights there stated were established through generations of conflict and struggle. The great drama goes far back into English and American political history. It appears and reappears in documentary form, step by step, sometimes years apart, in royal concessions, in legislation, attempted legislation, popular compacts, colonial charters—all culminating finally, for the American citizen, in the Declaration of Independence, the Constitution and the Bill of Rights.

Believing that too little is known of the solid foundation on which the structure of our individual liberties has long stood, the Committee on American Citizenship of the American Bar Association recommended that the major documents be re-examined and published as a single volume. The task was assigned to the American Bar Foundation, the research affiliate of the American Bar Association. This book is the result.

The Foundation was fortunate to secure the services of Mr. Richard L. Perry, now of the District of Columbia Bar, to direct the research project and to act as editor. How well he fulfilled his task is evidenced by his excellent introduction to each document, by the careful, readable and scholarly annotations, by the list of reference works following each document, and by the general bibliography at the end of the book.

FOREWORD

Plan of the Book

The plan of the book is simple. Each document is preceded by an introductory editorial note on its political background, its effectiveness in its own time in meeting the problems which it sought to solve, its ultimate influence in the final establishment of our liberties. These introductions, with the notes and bibliographies, tie together the documents as part of a single long political process. But, at the same time, each document within itself represents an absorbing segment of history. Few if any stage, television or radio productions of our time can rival the tense human drama behind Magna Carta (1215), the First Charter of Virginia (1606), the Mayflower Compact (1620), the British Petition of Right (1628), the Abolition of the Star Chamber (1641), the British Bill of Rights (1689), the Resolutions of the Stamp Act Congress (1765), the debates preceding the signing of the Declaration of Independence (1776), to name but a few.

The first problem facing Mr. Perry and the Administrator of the Foundation was the choice of documents. Some were finally omitted which might have been useful but not deemed vital. In the case of colonial charters, only a few could be included due to space limitations. Those presented are believed to be of particular importance as original sources. In the case of state constitutions adopted after the outbreak of the Revolution, and before the adoption of the United States Constitution, it was again found necessary to include only the several state declarations or bills of rights. It is believed that every document eventually included directly or indirectly contributes to the establishment of those rules of law in our Constitution and Bill of Rights which now state and guarantee our liberties.

The documents are presented in order of time. This arrangement emphasizes the important part played by the founding and growth of the American colonies. Some readers will undoubtedly be surprised to learn that important contributions to individual liberties were made by the Virginia Charter (1606) and the Mayflower Compact (1620), which preceded in time the historic struggle in England between king and Parliament culminating in the Petition of Right (1628), the first great British constitutional document since Magna Carta (1215). Also of special significance is the primary place which must be assigned to the all but forgotten, but important and dramatic Resolutions of the Stamp Act Congress (1765), Declaration and Resolves of the First Continental Congress (1774), and Declaration of the Causes and Necessity of Taking Up Arms (1775). These were the courageous acts of English colonists in far-off America, still seeking a basis for remaining loyal

FOREWORD

to the land of their fathers but insisting on the recognition of the liberties of the individual, the "rights of Englishmen" guaranteed in the colonial charters.

Perhaps, however, the most important result of the research project is the evidence that the colonists always sought unequivocal statements of the existence and extent of their liberties. No uncertainty could be hazarded. The germ of a written constitution was always present. It may well be that the final adoption of the United States Constitution and its Bill of Rights is very akin to the acceptance of Magna Carta forced on King John more than five and a half centuries earlier. The liberties of the individual are formally stated in each, and contrary acts of arbitrary governments shall be of no avail.

The Documents

The documents included in the book, with certain of the reasons for their inclusion, are:

I. *Magna Carta (1215)*. The text here presented is an English translation of the original Latin text accepted by King John. It is believed that the primary source of our liberties was the actual acceptance of this document. Few scholars, and fewer practicing lawyers, realize that the Magna Carta of the British Statutes (9 Hen. 3, cc 1-37) is in fact a later reissue of the original document. The text here presented shows in the footnotes the changes made by the three reissues of Henry III, successor to King John.

The law of the land, due process, trial by jury—these certainly may be traced back directly or indirectly to Magna Carta. If it were nothing more than the source of these liberties, it should be required reading in every school and college. As Mr. Perry points out, one of the ablest of our founder statesmen, John Adams, when attacking the Stamp Act, cited Magna Carta in support of the principle of "no taxation without representation." To the men of that day, Magna Carta was a living document.

II. *Confirmatio Cartarum (1297)*. This great document is now practically unknown to students and lawyers. Enacted as a statute (25 Edw. 1, c 1), it served as a confirmation by Edward I that the terms of Magna Carta "shall be kept in every point without breach." It went further. In section 2, the king agreed that "if any judgement be given from henceforth contrary to the points of the charters aforesaid by the justices, or by any other our ministers that hold plea before them against the points of the charters, it shall be undone, and holden for nought." Mr. Perry's excellent analysis of the influence of this document is recommended for careful study. The Confirmatio Cartarum goes far to aid the principle that the rights asserted by Magna Carta are a form of higher law which shall override judgments and even legislation to the contrary. The germ of a written constitution was beginning to emerge, affecting the American colonists years later.

III. *First Charter of Virginia (1606)*. Short-lived though it was, replaced in 1609 and 1612 by later royal charters, the First Charter of Virginia is a milestone in the history of individual liberties. It stated the principle that the colonists in Virginia "shall have and enjoy all Liberties, Franchises, and Immunities . . . to all Intents and Purposes as if they had been abiding and born, within this our Realm of England, or any other of our said Dominions." The individual rights of Englishmen, as stated in Magna Carta and developed by custom during the intervening four hundred years, traveled with the colonists to North America. This charter was signed by the Stuart king, James I, certainly himself not a proponent of individual liberties. The principle, however, did not originate with him. The quoted language is adapted from the 1578 and 1584 charters granted by the more liberal and farsighted Queen Elizabeth to Sir Humphrey Gilbert and Sir Walter Raleigh, respectively, for their ill-starred colonial expeditions to America. The principle was never abrogated. It was in fact repeated in the later Virginia charters and in other colonial charters. Whatever individual rights were held by Englishmen, these the colonists would continue to enjoy. As Mr. Perry points out, Patrick Henry so stated before the Virginia House of Burgesses in 1765 when opposing the Stamp Act, insisting that the Virginia charters guaranteed to the colonists the rights of Englishmen, including the right of representation in the levy of taxes.

IV. *Ordinances for Virginia (1618)*. The actual text of the "Ordinances for Virginia" included here is not the 1618 Ordinance but one adopted by the Virginia Company on July 24, 1621. The original Ordinance of 1618 is lost, but most scholars are convinced that it was practically identical with the 1621 Ordinance. Certainly the proof is ample that the Virginia Company did in 1618 adopt and put into effect an ordinance granting to the colonists participation in the conduct of their local government through the right to elect burgesses to the newly created General Assembly. While the legal basis for this assembly may have been technically destroyed when the Virginia Company's charter was revoked in England in 1624, representative government had taken a firm foothold from which it was never entirely dislodged. The claimed rights of the colonist to participation in government through his duly elected representatives continued until independence became a fact, and the principle took its place in the structure of our liberties inherent in the Constitution.

FOREWORD

V. *Mayflower Compact* (*1620*). No collection of political documentary sources of our individual liberties would be complete without the Mayflower Compact, signed on board ship not long before the landing of the Pilgrims in America. In the background of its single paragraph and few sentences lies the principle of freedom of religion. On its face stands the assumption that men may covenant together as to how they shall be governed. While Plymouth never succeeded in its desire to be granted a charter as a separate colony, the spirit of its founders will not leave us while individual liberties continue as a sacred heritage.

VI. *Petition of Right* (*1628*). The scene returns from America to England. James I was dead, his twenty-two years on the throne marked by the collection of revenues not authorized by the Parliament. Charles I had come to the throne in 1625, dissolving a recalcitrant Parliament in 1626. In Virginia the colonists claimed to have the "rights of Englishmen." At home in England these rights were at stake when the Parliament met in 1628. Troops had been quartered in private homes. Citizens had been imprisoned for failure to pay forced loans to the crown. Mr. Perry's introduction to this great document, the Petition of Right, is a noteworthy restatement of the struggle which ensued. One of the greatest of English lawyers, Sir Edward Coke, then in his late seventies, led the parliamentary battle for individual liberties. The Petition of Right emerged. Drafted in the House of Commons by a group headed by Coke, finally agreed to by the House of Lords, grudgingly accepted by the King, this document is part of our charter of liberties. Imprisonment without a show of cause was condemned, trials by court-martial of civilians were declared illegal, quartering soldiers in private homes was stopped, habeas corpus was strengthened, the principles of due process and trial by jury were sustained.

Of equal importance was the historic first clause of section X that "no man hereafter be compelled to make or yield any gift, loan, benevolence, tax, or such-like charge without common consent by act of parliament." The principle of "no taxation without representation" was thus formally affirmed as one of the "rights of Englishmen." Admittedly King Charles ignored this prohibition in the eleven disastrous years from 1629 when he ruled without Parliament. But no legal question could properly be raised after 1628 that the colonists had a valid claim to this great constitutional privilege.

The Petition of Right is a catalogue of some of our most cherished liberties. The student, lawyer, judge or legislator, when construing our fundamental law, should have a clear concept of the principles for which Coke and his associates risked their political future, their fortunes and, perhaps, their lives.

FOREWORD

VII. *Charter of Massachusetts Bay (1629).* The charter included in this book is the formal confirmation by Charles I of the grant made by the Council for New England (an organization created by James I having its seat at Plymouth in England) to the members of what became the "Governor and Company of Mattachusetts Bay in Newe-England," more familiarly the Massachusetts Bay Company. Local history, geography, ancient lineage, legal precedents, royal prerogatives—all have their place in this great document useful to the student particularly concerned. Of paramount importance, however, are the provisions of the charter granting powers to the company to admit new freemen to its membership, to elect officers for its governing purposes, and to make laws not inconsistent with the laws of England. Mr. Perry has outlined the practical and political effects of these provisions. His introductory note makes it clear that representative government had come to New England in the North as it had come to Virginia in the South. It is doubtful whether Charles I was any more aware of the effect of this grant than James I had been of the implications of the liberal Virginia charters and the ordinances which followed. Whatever may have been the intent of the king in confirming the wide grant of powers to the Massachusetts Bay Company, the fact remains that one more step had been taken in the New World toward the Declaration of Independence and complete self-government which came into existence thereafter, and was finally evidenced by the adoption of the Constitution.

VIII. *Charter of Maryland (1632).* The Maryland Charter was granted by Charles I to Cecil Calvert, the second Lord Baltimore, as a result of the efforts of his father, George Calvert, first Lord Baltimore, who had died just before the charter was issued. Leonard Calvert, the first governor, and the first colonists landed in 1634. The charter, strictly construed, was a direct grant of title to the proprietor and his heirs, including both the lands and broad powers of political government. It must have reflected theories of autocratic government then prevalent at the court of Charles I where the Calverts were well entrenched. But the results in the colony were far different. Article IV of the charter granted sweeping jurisdiction "and royal rights and temporal franchises" to the proprietor. But Article VII, while granting the proprietor the power to enact laws of every kind, qualified this right with the celebrated provision that such laws should be "with the Advice, Assent, and Approbation of the Free-Men of the same Province, or the greater Part of them, or of their Delegates or Deputies, whom We will shall be called together for the framing of Laws, when, and as often as Need shall require, by the aforesaid now Baron of Baltimore, and his Heirs..."

FOREWORD

The charter is included in this book primarily to illustrate the vigor with which the colonists used this loophole to establish the third representative legislative body in America.

Mr. Perry's introductory note details the extent and success of their continued efforts. Article X of the charter had granted to the colonists the rights of Englishmen in language similar to the Virginia Charter. In 1639 the "Act for the Liberties of the People" was adopted. Various articles of the charter dealt in somewhat ambiguous terms with the freedom of religion. In 1649 the Toleration Act was adopted, for which Maryland became famous. The principle of religious liberty is a cornerstone of our existing theory of government, evidenced by the First Amendment to the Constitution.

The continued struggle of Maryland from its founding to revolutionary times, insisting on broad powers of local self-government and individual freedoms, is an important source of the liberties which we enjoy today.

IX. *Fundamental Orders of Connecticut (1639)*. The "Inhabitants and Residents of Windsor, Harteford and Wethersfield" then "dwelling in and uppon the River of Conectecotte," having come from Massachusetts, met together and adopted with due formality this covenant for their future government. As Mr. Perry shows, Bryce called it "the oldest truly political Constitution in America." It provided careful regulations for popular elections of the officers and legislators to rule the "Publike State or Comonwelth" created by its terms. Its "Generall Courts shall consist the supreme power of the Comonwelth, and they only shall have power to make laws or repeale" them. Freedom of speech was guaranteed at meetings of the General Court which alone had power to levy taxes. The spirit of representative government had moved to the settlements in Connecticut in form even more liberal than in its old home. This tradition never left Connecticut. It was one of the sources of our liberties.

X. *The Abolition of the Star Chamber (1641)*. The document here included is in fact the great British Statute, 16 Car. 1, c 10. Charles I was still on the throne in England. After eleven years he had recalled Parliament in 1640 to seek new taxes. Of the period immediately preceding, Macaulay has said that "this was the conjuncture at which the liberties of the nation were in the greatest peril" and that "many looked to the American wilderness as the only asylum in which they could enjoy civil and spiritual freedom." But the battle to preserve the spirit of Magna Carta and the "rights of Englishmen" was not dead.

The Parliament of 1640 was soon dismissed. But more money was needed. The celebrated Long Parliament was convened within a few months. One of its first reforms was the abolition of the Star Chamber Court, long an instrument of arbitrary autocratic power. The statute that accomplished this will repay the most thorough study. It opens with a recital of the provisions of Magna Carta (referred to simply as the great charter) that condemnation of a freeman shall only be "by lawful judgment of his peers, or by the law of the land." It then recites later statutes requiring "due process," and certain procedural statutes. It charges that the judges "have undertaken to punish where no law doth warrant, and to make decrees for things having no such authority, and to inflict heavier punishments than by any law is warranted." The court was then abolished; the king and his Privy Council were prohibited from taking jurisdiction as to matters affecting the property of individuals unless the matter "be tried and determined in the ordinary courts of justice, and by the ordinary course of the law"; the right to writs of habeas corpus was carefully stated. As Mr. Perry says in his introductory note to the text, a notable advance was made in the development of the principle of due process of law as administered by the ordinary courts; also that the abolition of the Star Chamber opened the way for later establishment of the privilege against self-incrimination, now part of our fundamental law.

This statute was perhaps the turning point in the long battle to protect the individual liberties of the British citizen. In so doing it added strength to the claims of our forefathers to similar protection.

XI. *Massachusetts Body of Liberties (1641)*. Five months after the British Parliament reaffirmed Magna Carta in abolishing the Star Chamber, the General Court in Massachusetts approved a code of conduct and rights which had been under consideration since 1635. In final form this "coppie of the Liberties of the Massachusets Colonie in New England," was accepted not as a statute, but with the recommendation that those in authority treat it as law. This amazing document is a fascinating mixture of civil liberties, religious principles and penal law. Perhaps it is the first real bill of rights. Certainly it was the carefully considered, but entirely spontaneous, expression of the colonists' claims to individual liberties. While Charles I was ruling in England, without a Parliament, the Massachusetts General Court had been codifying the citizen's personal freedoms. As Mr. Perry's analysis shows, the articles of the final codification cover such basic privileges as trial by jury, freedom of speech in courts and public assemblies, adequate compensation for goods taken, and others.

While the document was not technically a statute, its influence on subsequent thinking is certain. None of the major individual liberties which it asserted were thereafter abandoned. The colonists were moving forward, not backward.

XII. *Charter of Rhode Island (1663).* The charter here included is that obtained from Charles II of England after the Restoration. The founder of Rhode Island, Roger Williams, had in fact obtained a patent in 1644 from the Long Parliament in England. This patent had provided for a large degree of self-government. Under it a General Court had functioned as a representative body. That patent, as a matter of political expediency, was replaced by the royal charter of 1663.

Its primary reason for inclusion here is that it was, as Mr. Perry has stated, the first fundamental law applicable to a colony in which religious liberty was guaranteed. The Maryland Toleration Act of 1649 was a legislative enactment which could have been modified by the local body which adopted it. But not so in Rhode Island. Religious freedom was part of the basic framework of government, a principle reflected in our Bill of Rights. The ultimate influence of the Rhode Island Charter cannot be denied. It became part of the American scene, as it is today.

XIII. *Concessions and Agreements of West New Jersey (1677).* This document is included primarily to illustrate how great was the influence of the principles of Magna Carta in the aspirations of the American colonists for individual freedoms. It is further evidence of the continued approach toward the principle of fundamental law to which the citizen might look as written proof of his rights and liberties.

XIV. *Habeas Corpus Act (1679).* From the time of Magna Carta, the British citizen sought legal means to protect his liberties. The writ of habeas corpus developed. Strengthened by the Petition of Right, asserted and broadened in the act abolishing the Star Chamber, the writ, by the act of 1679, was further strengthened through the stated procedure governing the courts. Mr. Perry's introductory note outlines this long process, as well as the efforts of the American colonists to enjoy its protection. These efforts finally bore fruit in Article I, section 9 of the Constitution as it stands today. The Congress of the United States is specifically denied the power to suspend "the Privilege of the Writ of Habeas Corpus . . . unless when in Cases of Rebellion or Invasion the public Safety may require it."

XV. *Frame of Government of Pennsylvania (1682).* If no other reason existed for the inclusion of William Penn's great contribution to the development of representative government in America, it would be found in his statement in the preface to this document. Discussing the choice between monarchy, aristocracy and democracy, he said: "But I chuse to solve the controversy with this small distinction, and it belongs to all three: *Any government is free to the people under it* (whatever be the frame) *where the laws rule, and the people are a party to those laws,* and more than this is tyranny, oligarchy, or confusion."

The document itself is in substance a colonial constitution promulgated by Penn as sole proprietor. Under it, representative government came to another part of America. It was superseded by a somewhat similar Frame of Government of 1683 and eventually by the Charter of Privileges, also included in this book. But the basic approach toward the freedom of the individual in a representative government never disappeared. Much of the spirit of William Penn is in our Constitution and Bill of Rights today.

XVI. *The Bill of Rights (1689).* This is the British Act of December 16, 1689 (I Will. and Mary, Sess. 2, c 2), entitled: "An act for declaring the rights and liberties of the Subject, and Settling the Succession of the Crown." It became law as part of the agreement under which William and Mary succeeded to the British throne after the fall of James II. It is one of the important documents of American as well as British constitutional history. Mr. Perry's excellent analysis of its provisions and effects on our liberties is summed up in his quotation from Macaulay:

"The Declaration of Right, though it made nothing law which had not been law before, contained the germ of the law which gave religious freedom to the Dissenter, of the law which secured the independence of the Judges, of the law which limited the duration of Parliaments, of the law which placed the liberty of the press under the protection of juries, of the law which prohibited the slave trade, of the law which abolished the sacramental test, of the law which relieved the Roman Catholics from civil disabilities, of the law which reformed the representative system, of every good law which had been passed during more than a century and a half, of every good law which may hereafter, in the course of ages, be found necessary to promote the public weal, and to satisfy the demands of public opinion."

XVII. *Pennsylvania Charter of Privileges (1701).* This document, approved by William Penn, and accepted formally by the Pennsylvania Assembly, superseded earlier provisions for the colonial government. It was a written constitution in every sense. No amendment was permitted except by six-sevenths of the Assembly. Freedom of conscience, religious liberty, representative government, right of the accused to counsel and witnesses, due process, were among the liberties protected. It closes with a striking statement guaranteeing the inhabitants the "Liberties, Priveleges, and Benefits" stated in the Charter, "any Law, Usage, or Custom of this Government

FOREWORD

heretofore made and practised, or any Law made and passed by this General Assembly, to the Contrary hereof, notwithstanding." Thus speaks our Constitution today. No arbitrary nor capricious legislation may take away the liberties which it guarantees to the American citizen.

XVIII. *Resolutions of the Stamp Act Congress (1765)*. With the passage of these stirring resolutions, the form of the revolution ten years later began to emerge. Nine of the colonies were represented at the New York meeting, held at the suggestion of Massachusetts. Faced with the impositions of the Stamp Tax, already passed by the British Parliament, the colonists took direct issue on major constitutional points. They contended that the colonists were individually entitled to the "inherent rights and priveleges" of natural-born "subjects within the United Kingdom." They insisted that the "rights of Englishmen" included the privilege "that no taxes should be imposed on them, but with their own consent, given personally, or by their representatives," and that the colonists' only representatives were their own legislatures. In addition they challenged the provisions of the Stamp Act giving jurisdiction to the admiralty courts as being in violation of the right of trial by jury. Ten years later it became apparent to all the world that the American colonists were prepared to go to war to defend these liberties.

XIX. *Declaration and Resolves of the First Continental Congress (1774)*. This sometimes forgotten declaration was an American national bill of rights. Its background is fully stated in Mr. Perry's introductory note. For the first time the law of nature was recognized as one of the foundations of the rights of the colonists, together with the Constitution, foreshadowing the Declaration of Independence to be drafted two years later. In the minds of the able and courageous men who sat in the 1774 Congress, the "inhabitants of the English colonies in North-America, by the immutable laws of nature, the principles of the English Constitution, and the several charters or compacts" had certain rights which are carefully detailed, beginning with the right to "life, liberty, and property." These were rights of the citizens of all the colonies for whom the Congress spoke—not as separate communities. The rights of citizens of what is now the United States were set forth. The American citizen was emerging from a colonial status. Certainly this document is a major source of our present liberties.

XX. *Declaration of the Causes and Necessity of Taking up Arms (1775)*. If we in the United States are ever tempted to surrender our liberties, then this document should be published in every village, town and city. War had broken out; the colonies were prepared to continue it. As the Declaration of the Continental Congress says in timeless language:

FOREWORD

"Our cause is just. Our union is perfect. . . . With hearts fortified with these animating reflections, we most solemnly, before God and the world, *declare,* that, exerting the utmost energy of those powers, which our beneficent Creator hath graciously bestowed upon us, the arms we have been compelled by our enemies to assume, we will, in defiance of every hazard, with unabating firmness and perseverence, employ for the preservation of our liberties; being with one mind resolved to die freemen rather than to live slaves."

XXI. *Virginia Bill of Rights (1776).* On June 12, 1776, three weeks before the Declaration of Independence was signed, the Virginia Convention, meeting in Williamsburg, adopted a declaration of rights. It contains such ringing phrases as: "That all men are by nature equally free and independent, and have certain inherent rights . . . That all power is vested in, and consequently derived from the people; . . . That government is, or ought to be, instituted for the common benefit, protection, and security of the people, nation, or community; . . . That the legislative and executive powers of the State should be separate and distinct from the judiciary; . . ."

This declaration, as Mr. Perry points out, was one of the most important forerunners of the first ten amendments (our Federal Bill of Rights) and directly influenced similar declarations by six of the original thirteen states, and also that of Vermont. These later documents are included in this book.

The Virginia document is particularly noteworthy for its constitutional leadership in establishing freedom of the press as one of the liberties of a free people. Taken as a whole, the declaration is of major interest.

XXII. *Declaration of Independence (1776).* Anything said here as to why the Declaration is a source of our liberties would be inadequate. It speaks for itself, as it has during the more than one hundred eighty years since it came into being. It then represented the spirit of America. It still speaks today with the same voice.

XXIII to XXIX *(inclusive).* These documents are the Declarations of Rights, or Bills of Rights, adopted before the Federal Constitution by Pennsylvania, Delaware, Maryland, North Carolina, Vermont, Massachusetts, and New Hampshire. As Mr. Perry states, in his introductory note to the Virginia declaration, the new constitutions adopted by New Jersey (1776), South Carolina (1776), New York (1777), and Georgia (1777) were not prefaced with formal bills of rights, but each adhered to the principle that rights should be stated as the fundamental law of the land. Connecticut and Rhode Island continued under their old liberal charters.

Each of these state declarations adds to the overwhelming evidence that

FOREWORD

the first citizens of an independent United States were prepared to assert and defend their individual liberties, then and always.

XXX. *Northwest Ordinance (1787)*. This act of the Congress, adopted in July, 1787, before the Constitution was approved in September of the same year, contains, as Mr. Perry says, "the first bill of rights enacted by the federal government in the United States." The ordinance provided for the future of the great territory west of the Appalachian Mountains. Its effect on the future of every new state and its inhabitants is unquestioned, but not always understood. Its Bill of Rights included provisions for religious liberty, habeas corpus, trial by jury, preservation of rights and property, republican form of government in new states, and the prohibition of slavery. The effect of this document on the subsequent history of individual rights has not always been appreciated.

XXXI and XXXII. These documents are the Constitution of the United States and the Bill of Rights (the first ten amendments). Together they are the sources to which every American citizen has looked since 1791 for a statement of his historic liberties. For completeness, particularly because of the historic importance of Amendments XIII, XIV and XV, all of the amendments adopted after the Bill of Rights are included in an appendix.

It was my good fortune, as chairman of the American Bar Association's Committee on American Citizenship, to be associated with this project when it was first suggested, and later, as administrator of the American Bar Foundation, when the research and preparation of the book were under way. This research could not have been done nor the book now published without the aid of two generous grants from the Alfred P. Sloan Foundation, Inc., of New York. As a former administrator of the American Bar Foundation, I wish to express my thanks and appreciation to the Sloan Foundation for their assistance, to Mr. Perry for the painstaking and able research and editorial work which made this book possible, to Mr. John C. Leary, Acting Administrator and Librarian for the Foundation, and Mr. James E. Holton of the Department of Political Science, University of Chicago, for their assistance in the final stages of preparing the manuscript, and to the members of the Board of Directors and Research Committee of the American Bar Foundation for their continued advice and encouragement. I should also like to express my sincere thanks for the invaluable assistance of Mr. Harold J. Gallagher of New York, former President of the American Bar Association,

FOREWORD

who was instrumental in arranging for the grants from the Sloan Foundation and in conducting the final negotiations for publication.

It is my hope that the completed work will be found of value to students, lawyers, judges, legislators, and other public officials—in fact to every American citizen who, having inherited the liberties, rights and privileges stated in these historic documents, has also inherited the responsibility to protect their continued enjoyment.

JOHN COBB COOPER

Princeton, New Jersey
January, 1959

SOURCES OF OUR LIBERTIES

I. MAGNA CARTA
1215

The liberties of the American citizen depend upon the existence of established and known rules of law limiting the authority and discretion of men wielding the power of government. Magna Carta announced the rule of law; this was its great contribution. It is this characteristic which has provided throughout the years the foundation on which has come to rest the entire structure of Anglo-American constitutional liberties.

General Significance

Magna Carta was the culmination of a protest against the arbitrary rule of King John, who was using governmental powers which had been established by the great builders of the English nation, William the Conqueror, Henry I, and Henry II, for selfish and tyrannical purposes.[1] In general, these abuses took the pattern of increasing customary feudal obligations and decreasing established feudal rights and privileges. The barons were forced to pay taxes above the usual rate, and their right to hold court for their tenants was restricted. The king exerted pressure in order to influence church elections. The merchants of London were burdened by heavy taxes, and their trading privileges were curtailed. To a limited extent even the lowest of King John's subjects suffered because his confiscation of church property destroyed

Origins
King John

---

[1] By King John's time the struggle for orderly government in England had been substantially won. William the Conqueror (1066-87) was able to assert his authority over many scattered and warring Anglo-Saxon and Danish tribes not only by reason of armed conquest but also by reason of his election by a body claiming to represent the old Witenagemot, his alleged nomination by his kinsman Edward the Confessor, and by the renunciation of Harold in his favor. Under Henry I (1100-35) the monarchy was strengthened at the expense of feudal power by the introduction within the King's Council of a class of administrators dependent upon the king, and by the organization of the Exchequer whose traveling officers from the first held pleas in the course of their financial duties. Henry II (1154-89) repaired much of the damage to monarchical power that occurred during the incompetent reign of Stephen. The writ process was developed, and judicial business was diverted from the manorial courts to the central courts. See William S. McKechnie, *Magna Carta* (2d ed.; Glasgow, 1914), 1-16.

the only available source of poor relief.² In addition, John's administration was disorganized and inefficient, and he employed unscrupulous foreign adventurers as royal officers and as sheriffs and bailiffs in every county of the land.

King John's reign may be divided into three periods, each of which was marked by failure brought about by his own misgovernment: The unsuccessful war with France (1199-1206); the quarrel with the church (1206-13); and the crisis with the barons (1213-16).³ His attempt to regain the lands of his Norman ancestors led him into war with the king of France, and he was decisively defeated. His oppression of the church brought opposition from Pope Innocent III, and to gain the church's support he was forced to receive Stephen Langton as Archbishop of Canterbury. He even went through the form of surrendering the crown of England to Rome, receiving it back as the Pope's feudatory.

The charter   The final crisis of the reign began in 1213 when John sought to revive the war with the king of France. The barons refused to follow their king to battle,⁴ and John prepared to march against them to compel obedience.⁵ The barons rallied around Stephen Langton, who produced in their midst a copy of Henry I's Charter of Liberties.⁶ The barons then resolved to fight

---

² *Ibid.*, 24, 50. This fact affords some basis for the theory, often advanced, that Magna Carta was the product of a popular uprising. William Stubbs, for example, described the charter as "the act of the united nation, the church, the barons, and the commons, for the first time thoroughly at one." William Stubbs, *The Constitutional History of England* (6th ed.; Oxford, 1897), I, 583. Although the commons may have suffered from the king's oppression, they had little, if anything, to do with obtaining the charter or dictating its terms. Other writers have characterized it as a class document in both origin and effect. Sir Edward Jenks has pointed out that none of the chroniclers mentioned anything resembling a popular uprising. His view is that Magna Carta is not in any sense the work of the "nation" or the "people," and that there is evidence "that such faint popular manifestation as appeared was on the side of the king." "The Myth of Magna Carta," *The Independent Review*, IV (1904), 261, 263, 265. It is clear that the lower classes got little benefit from Magna Carta. It protected the villein, not as the possessor of legal rights but as a valuable chattel of the lord, who was the real party in interest. McKechnie, *op. cit.*, 125-26.

³ *Ibid.*, 22.

⁴ At first the barons refused to serve on the ground that John was still under the ban of excommunication ordered by Innocent III because of his depredations against church property. After John was absolved, the barons based their refusal on the ground that their tenures did not require service abroad. Stubbs, *op. cit.*, I, 563-64; McKechnie, *op. cit.*, 27-28.

⁵ This fact has an important bearing upon the significance of chapter 39, the clause of Magna Carta which has led to many disputes of interpretation. It is believed that this clause was intended to forbid John's practice of attacking his barons with forces of mercenaries, seizing their persons, families and property, and otherwise ill-treating them, without first convicting them of some offense in his court. McKechnie, *op. cit.*, 381, 387-88; Charles H. McIlwain, "Due Process of Law in Magna Carta," *Columbia Law Review*, XIV (January, 1914), 41.

⁶ Latin text in William Stubbs (ed.), *Select Charters and Other Illustrations of English Constitutional History* (8th ed.; Oxford, 1900), 99-102; English text in George B. Adams and H. Morse Stephens (eds.), *Select Documents of English Constitutional History* (New York, 1935), 4-6. This

for those liberties "even unto death." Langton, whose sympathies were with the barons, tried to obtain a peaceable solution if possible. The king promised Langton that he would give the barons a trial in his court to determine whether their disobedience was justified, but this promise was never fulfilled. To the barons' demands for restoration of the ancient laws and liberties of the realm, John answered contemptuously, "Why do not the barons, with these unjust exactions, ask my kingdom?" [7]

On May 5, 1215, the barons formally renounced their allegiance and chose as their leader Robert Fitz-Walter, who became "Marshal of the army of God and Holy Church." John's last hope of success disappeared when the merchants of London turned against him and opened the gates to the insurgents. With only a small band of supporters remaining, John at last agreed to meet the demands of the barons.[8] The dramatic meeting occurred on June 15 at Runnymede, along the banks of the Thames, where John found himself confronted by the armed barons, arrayed in a warlike host. The articles presented by the barons were agreed to and sealed, and during the next few days copies of Magna Carta were drawn up in final form and sealed by the king.[9]

John assented to the charter with tongue in cheek. He affixed his seal only because of the threat of armed might. In fact he had never intended to comply with the charter and had even begun his preparations for repudiating it before the historic meeting at Runnymede. He gained the support of the

Effects

---

charter was one of the models for Magna Carta. It was published by Henry I at his coronation and was probably reissued by him from time to time. In form it is an amplification of the coronation oath and is considered to be the price which Henry paid for the support he required in his candidature for the crown. McKechnie, *op. cit.*, 104.

[7] On January 6, 1215, a deputation from the insurgents met the king at London where they demanded a confirmation of the laws of King Edward together with the liberties set forth in the Charter of Liberties of Henry I. On April 27 the barons presented John with a schedule of their demands. These consisted mainly of the ancient laws and customs of the realm with an added threat that if the king did not immediately consent to the demands the rebels would seize his castles, lands, and goods. This schedule is regarded as a rough draft of the Articles of the Barons, the document from which the text of Magna Carta was immediately derived. *Ibid.*, 32-33, 37-38.

[8] Stubbs classifies the barons of the charter into four groups: Those who refused to follow John to France in 1213 and who led the rebellion; those who joined the first group after the councils at St. Alban's and St. Paul's; those who deserted the king in the spring of 1215; and those few who remained with the king to the last. The fourth group were mostly of foreign origin, and "had everything to fear and nothing to hope from the victory of the confederates." *Constitutional History*, I, 580-83. See also Sidney Painter, *The Reign of King John* (Baltimore, 1949), 303-4. It is possible that a large number of barons remained neutral during the rebellion. *Ibid.*, 296-97.

[9] Magna Carta was probably not sealed until June 19, the date on which John in more than one writ stated that peace had been concluded. In that age elaborate charters, which required a considerable time to prepare, usually bore the date on which agreement was reached instead of the date on which they were formally executed. The charter is thus dated June 15. McKechnie, *op. cit.*, 40-41.

Pope by arguing that the hostility of the rebels interfered with the vow of crusade which he had taken three months earlier. On August 24, 1215, a papal bull declared Magna Carta void. The barons were reminded that Innocent III was lord of all England and that nothing could be done without his consent. Excommunication was decreed for those who had persecuted "John, King of England, crusader and vassal of the Church of Rome."[10]

The barons would not surrender their hard-won liberties. They invited Prince Louis of France to replace John on the English throne—in much the same way as their descendants, more than four centuries later, invited William of Orange to replace James II. Death, however, removed the two men who stood in the barons' way and another crisis was averted. Innocent III died June 2, 1216, and King John died October 19. Magna Carta was reissued by the advisers of the young King Henry III with the consent of Innocent's successor.

The charter was issued three times by Henry III, and many changes were made. The reissues completely replaced John's charter, which had actually been in force only seventeen months. It is the last reissue, that of 1225, which appears in the English statute books and most legal treatises.[11] The substance of the text presented here is that of the document assented to

---

[10] William S. McKechnie, "Magna Carta (1215-1915)," *Magna Carta Commemoration Essays*, ed. Henry E. Malden (Aberdeen, 1917), 7. The action of the Pope was probably based on his ecclesiastical rights acquired March 4, 1215, when John took the vow of crusade and not upon his rights as a feudal overlord. Under feudal law the vassal might do nothing with his fief which reduced its value to himself to such an extent as to endanger his ability to perform the service by which he held it. Since John held England by money payments, and because the grant of Magna Carta would not substantially have affected his ability to continue those payments, this ground for annulling the charter would have been insufficient, and both John and the Pope realized it. By taking the cross, John gained the extensive privileges of the crusader which included relief from contracts and other interferences which would prevent him from carrying out his vows. *Magna Carta Commemoration Essays*, 26, 35. It may be said in defense of Innocent's actions that he was dependent for his information as to the merits of the struggle in England mainly upon information given him by John. *Ibid.*, 35n.

[11] McKechnie, *Magna Carta*, 155. Some scholars believe that with the first reissue on November 12, 1216, John's charter was deprived of all validity. Arthur J. Collins, "The Documents of the Great Charter of 1215," *Proceedings of the British Academy*, XXXIV (1948), 274. The second reissue was dated November 6, 1217, and the third February 11, 1225. McKechnie, *Magna Carta*, 146, 154. The name "Magna Carta" was first applied only to the third reissue, and the charter of King John was called simply *carta libertatum*. Max Radin, *Handbook of Anglo-American Legal History* (St. Paul, 1936), 153. Until the middle of the thirteenth century, the title "Magna Carta" meant "little charter" instead of "great charter" and was used to distinguish it from the Charter of the Forest, 1217, of Henry III, which was called *parva carta*. *Ibid.*; cf. Jencks, *op. cit.*, 261. The seventeenth-century interpretation of the name, which is the one that has come down to us, was stated by Sir Edward Coke as follows: "It is called *Magna Charta*, not that it is great in quantity, for there be many voluminous charters commonly passed, specially in these later times, longer then this is; nor comparatively in respect that it is greater than Charta de Foresta, but in respect of the great importance, and weightinesse of the matter, as hereafter shall appear: and likewise for the same cause *Charta de Foresta*, is called *Magna Charta de Foresta*, and both of them are called *Magnae Chartae libertatum Angliae*." *The Second Part of the Institutes of the Laws of England* (London, 1809 ed.), Proeme.

by King John, and the principal changes made by the reissues are shown in the footnotes.

Later Significance

The amazing vitality of Magna Carta has given it an importance in the protection of individual liberties far transcending its role in the dispute between King John and the barons. Time after time it has been called upon when liberty has been threatened by despotic power, and its provisions have been linked with some of the most essential liberties now embodied in American constitutional law. The fact that this has not always been done with complete historical accuracy does not diminish the debt owed to Magna Carta. The establishment of certain principles of liberty in our law was greatly assisted by the prestige of Magna Carta. During the fourteenth century it was relied upon by Parliament as a guarantee that definite limitations existed upon the power of the king and his council. A number of statutes in support of Magna Carta were passed during that century and these furnished many of the materials on which later interpretations were based. In the seventeenth century the lawyers in Parliament answered the Stuarts' claimed "divine right of kings" by pointing to Magna Carta as a declaration that substantial restrictions upon monarchical power existed. Sir Edward Coke's *Second Institute*, a detailed treatise on Magna Carta completed in 1628, set forth that great lawyer's interpretation of the document. His work influenced not only the legal thinking of his own day but also helped shape the constitutional theories which developed in America during the seventeenth and eighteenth centuries. The American colonists, looking at the document itself, its many supporting statutes, and the writings of commentators like Coke, viewed Magna Carta as a written constitution limiting the power of government and securing to the individual the rights of trial by jury, the protection of the writ of habeas corpus, and the guarantee that no person could be deprived of life, liberty, or property without due process of law.

Due process of law

No clause of Magna Carta has been cited more often as a guarantee of the liberties of the citizen than chapter 39, which became chapter 29 in the reissue of Henry III in 1225. This chapter provides that no freeman shall be imprisoned, dispossessed, banished, or destroyed "except by the legal judgment of his peers or by the law of the land." This phrase has been traced back through English lawbooks of the twelfth century to documents of the Holy Roman Empire in the eleventh century.[12] Although there has been much scholarly dispute on the subject, it appears that this phrase was

---

[12] Rodney L. Mott, *Due Process of Law* (Indianapolis, 1926), 1-2.

intended by the barons to enunciate a concept very similar to the principle found in the fifth and fourteenth amendments to the Constitution of the United States that no person may be deprived of life, liberty, or property without due process of law.[13]

As early as the fourteenth century the "law of the land" provision was considered to be identical with the concept of "due process of law." In addition, the protection of this provision was extended to all subjects, instead of just to the "freemen," who were a very limited group in medieval England. These things occurred in 1354 when Parliament declared:

> That no man of what estate or condition that he be, shall be put out of land or tenement, nor taken nor imprisoned, nor disinherited, nor put to death, without being brought in answer by due process of the law.[14]

A number of other statutes passed during the fourteenth century further expanded the principles of Magna Carta. These attempted to strengthen the administration of justice by the common law courts by limiting the powers of the King's Council; judgments were required to be rendered in accordance

---

[13] The authorities are summarized in William S. Holdsworth, *A History of English Law* (4th ed.; Boston, 1931), I, 60-63. The theory that chapter 39 was intended to guarantee due process of law is developed at length by McIlwain, *op. cit.*, 27-51. It is pointed out that Magna Carta was based on the Charter of Liberties of Henry I, which promised to restore the old laws of the realm. In addition, Roger of Wendover stated that when John was absolved from excommunication in 1213 he promised: ". . . that he would restore the good laws of his ancestors, and especially the laws of King Edward, that he would remove abuses, and would judge all his men according to the just judgments of his court and restore to each his rights." Quoted in *ibid.*, 36-37. Of the meeting in London in 1215 between John and the barons, Roger of Wendover stated: "Coming there to the king in full military array, the aforesaid magnates demanded the confirmation of certain liberties and laws of King Edward along with other liberties conceded to them and the realm of England and the English Church, as contained in writing in the charter of King Henry I and the laws aforesaid. Besides, they asserted that at the time of his absolution at Winchester he had promised those laws and ancient liberties, and had become bound to an observance of them by a personal oath." Quoted in *ibid.*, 38.

In May, 1215, John referred to the fact that he had conceded to the barons "that we will neither arrest nor disseize them or their men, and we will not go upon them by force or by arms, except according to the law of the realm or pursuant to the judgment of their peers in our court." Quoted in *ibid.*, 39. This phraseology was similar to that appearing in the Articles of the Barons, on which Magna Carta was directly based. McIlwain concludes: "We are not assuming too much in saying, therefore, that chapter 39 was in 1215 the most important chapter in the Charter, as it is today; and that it is identical in aim with the absolution oath of 1213, and designed as a fulfillment of it." *Ibid.*, 41.

Another interpretation is suggested by McKechnie, who states that the clause refers primarily, although perhaps not exclusively, to the form of "proof" such as battle, ordeal, compurgation, or recognition. He states that this was the technical meaning of "lex" in that day and is apparently what is meant by the term as used elsewhere in the charter. He admits, however, that much weight must be given the view that the clause was intended to secure recognition of the "law of the land" as that phrase is used in popular speech. *Magna Carta*, 379-81.

A third view is that "per legem terrae" means almost the opposite of "the law of the land," and that it refers instead to local and very exceptional forms of procedure followed in place of the *judicium parium*. The phrase is "merely a lawyer's qualification, added *ex abundanti cautela*." Radin, *op. cit.*, 165-67.

[14] 28 Edw. 3, c. 3.

with Magna Carta; and it was established that no one might be charged with crime except by indictment or presentment rendered by men of the neighborhood.[15]

It is sometimes said that Magna Carta was "invented" in the seventeenth century and that the "myth of Magna Carta" came into being as a result of historical distortions. The blame for departing from the "true" interpretation of chapter 39 is usually given to seventeenth-century lawyers like Sir Edward Coke and John Selden. It is true these men held Magna Carta in the highest esteem. Coke said in reference to chapter 39:

> As the goldfiner will not out of the dust, threds, or shreds of gold, let passe the least crum, in respect of the excellency of the metall: so ought not the learned reader to let passe any syllable of this law, in respect of the excellency of the matter.[16]

It is doubtful, however, that Coke ever "invented" any significant or completely novel interpretation of Magna Carta.[17] Instead, he and other seventeenth-century lawyers based their interpretation of the document upon statutes and decisions since the fourteenth century which had already established an effective link between it and the requirement that no person shall be deprived of life, liberty, or property without due process of law.[18]

Trial by jury

The demand of Magna Carta for a judgment of peers is based on one of the oldest principles of English law, namely that a man who is to be judged should be judged by his equals. Thus a noble should not be judged by a vassal and a vassal should not be judged by a subvassal. Like the right of the individual to be protected by due process of law, the origins of trial by jury extend to Continental sources earlier than Magna Carta. One of the important prerogatives of Norman dukes which was carried to England by William the Conqueror was the right to compel the sworn evidence of reliable men of the neighborhood to answer questions put to them. This procedure was used by William to collect the laws and customs of the people

---

[15] See 2 Edw. 3, c. 8; 5 Edw. 3, c. 9; 25 Edw. 3, stat. 5, c. 4; 37 Edw. 3, c. 18; and 42 Edw. 3, c. 3.

[16] *Op. cit.*, 56.

[17] Faith Thompson, *Magna Carta* (Minneapolis, 1948), 356.

[18] Coke himself said: ". . . our expositions or commentaries upon Magna Charta, and other statutes are the resolutions of judges in courts of justice in judiciall courses of proceeding, either related and reported in our books, or extant in judiciall records, or in both, and therefore being collected together, shall (as we conceive) produce certainty, the mother and nurse of repose and quietnesse, and are not like to the waves of the sea, but *Statio bene fida peritis:* for *Judicia sunt tanquam juris dicta.*" *Op. cit.*, Proeme.

Selden stated that Magna Carta, like other statutes, was to be interpreted "as it is clearly taken in continual practice, and in the books, according to the known use of the legal proceedings, and not by literal interpretation of words." Quoted in Thompson, *op. cit.*, 241-42.

after England had been conquered. It was also the procedure used in compiling the Domesday Book, which listed landholdings in England. Later on it came to be used generally as a method of gathering information for taxing purposes, and by the time of King John's reign it had become a form of trial which was competing in importance with trial by battle and by ordeal.[19] The judgment of peers required by chapter 39 of Magna Carta, however, did not refer to this body of men of the neighborhood. It referred instead to the men who presided over trials and who decided the manner in which the trial was to be conducted. This might be trial by battle, trial by ordeal, trial by jury, or one of several other forms of proof.[20]

As the ancient forms of trial became obsolete and trial by jury assumed greater prominence, the judgment of peers required by Magna Carta came to be looked upon as a guarantee of that right.[21] It was probably William Lambarde, writing in the sixteenth century, who first connected trial by jury, which he described as "the antiente libertie of the Lande," with the provisions of Magna Carta.[22] American constitutional law has come to equate trial by jury with the guarantees of Magna Carta, and the references of some state constitutions to the judgment of peers are considered to establish that right. The traditional view was stated by Mr. Justice Story as follows:

> It seems hardly necessary in this place to expatiate upon the antiquity or importance of the trial by jury in criminal cases. It was from very early times insisted on by our ancestors in the parent country, as the great bulwark of their civil and political liberties, and watched with an unceasing jealousy and solicitude. The right constitutes one of the fundamental articles of Magna Charta in which it is declared, *"nullus homo capiatur, nec imprisonetur, aut exulet, aut aliquo modo destruatur, etc.; nisi per legale judicium parium suorum, vel per legem terrae"*; no man shall be arrested, nor imprisoned, nor banished, nor deprived of life, etc., but by the judgment of his peers, or by the law of the land. The judgment of his peers here alluded to, and commonly called, in the quaint language of former times, a trial *per pais*, or trial by the country, is the trial by a jury,

---

[19] McKechnie, *Magna Carta*, 134-38.

[20] *Ibid.*, 377-79.

[21] The confusion of the "judgment of peers" with "trial by peers" ignores the fact that under medieval law the judgment preceded the trial. The only important judgment in the case was that which determined the form of "proof" to which the parties were to be put. *Ibid.*, 84-88. The barons would have scorned the verdict of men from the neighborhood and would have chosen instead trial by combat as the "proof." See also Holdsworth, *op. cit.*, I, 59; McIlwain, *op. cit.*, 31, 51; F. W. Maitland, *The Constitutional History of England* (Cambridge, 1909), 169.

[22] Thompson, *op. cit.*, 185-86. The earliest identification of judgment by peers with trial by jury occurred during the fourteenth century, although Magna Carta was not cited in support of this conclusion. *Ibid.*, 70.

who are called the peers of the party accused, being of the like condition and equality in the state. When our more immediate ancestors removed to America, they brought this great privilege with them, as their birthright and inheritance, as a part of that admirable common law, which had fenced round and interposed barriers on every side against the approaches of arbitrary power.[23]

Nearly all the rights listed in the sixty-three chapters of Magna Carta relate to the feudal system which was becoming obsolete even in King John's time. Because many of its provisions sought to restore the old feudal relationships it was, to this extent, a conservative document. The only other individual liberty of modern constitutional law at all related to Magna Carta is the writ of habeas corpus. This relationship, however, is only indirect, and rests solely upon Magna Carta's general guarantee protecting the liberty of the freeman.[24] The development of the writ of habeas corpus as an instrumentality for the protection of individual liberty came at a later date.[25]

Other rights

It is difficult to fit Magna Carta into any particular category of modern jurisprudence. It was not a formal constitution because it did not set up the organs of government and define their powers; these things were all assumed by the document. It cannot be considered as a treaty because it was not the contract of two sovereign and independent powers. It was not an ordinary legislative enactment because it was not adopted in the manner customary for legislation in that day. It is probably most accurately described as a bargain agreed to by the king and the barons for the purpose of settling the immediate issues at hand. The barons, for their part, promised to renew their oaths of fealty and homage, and the king, in return, agreed to recognize their liberties.[26] It was a practical document and aimed at obtaining the recognition of certain very specific rights which had been violated by the king. Because it recognized that the existence of these rights imposed limitations on the power of the king, it has been termed "the exemplar of the Bill of Rights."[27]

General position of Magna Carta

Magna Carta played an essential part in the history of American constitutional development. It came to be regarded by the colonists as a generic term for all documents of constitutional significance. Among the documents framed by the colonists as counterparts of Magna Carta were the Massachu-

Magna Carta in American constitutional development

---

[23] *Commentaries on the Constitution of the United States* (4th ed.; Boston, 1873), II, 540-41.
[24] Holdsworth, *op. cit.*, IX, 112-13.
[25] See pp. 190-95.
[26] See McKechnie, *op. cit.*, 104-108.
[27] Max Radin, "The Myth of Magna Carta," *Harvard Law Review*, LX (September, 1947), 1072.

setts Body of Liberties,[28] the New York Charter of Liberties and Privileges, the Pennsylvania Charter of Privileges,[29] the instructions to Sir George Yeardley, popularly known as "The Great Charter," and the Carolina "Great Deed of Grant."[30] In addition, the colonists frequently embodied the provisions of Magna Carta, particularly chapter 39, into their own legislation. Although these enactments were often vetoed by King George III, who feared that his prerogative would be threatened by any concession, the colonists always claimed the rights which they considered were to be found in Magna Carta.[31] Thus the Stamp Act was denounced by John Adams as a violation of Magna Carta, and its provisions were cited in support of the principle "no taxation without representation."[32] The Constitution of the United States was considered by many to have been framed to serve the purposes that Magna Carta was thought to serve in England. Tom Paine said of it, when he proposed the calling of a Continental Conference, "The conferring members being met, let their business be to frame a *CONTINENTAL CHARTER,* or Charter of the United Colonies, answering to what is called the Magna Charta of England . . ."[33]

The present-day significance of Magna Carta may be summed up by the language of Mr. Justice Johnson, who said:

> As to the words from Magna Charta . . . after volumes spoken and written with a view to their exposition, the good sense of mankind has at length settled down to this: that they were intended to secure the individual from the arbitrary exercise of the powers of government, unrestrained by the established principles of private rights and distributive justice.[34]

[28] See pp. 143-61.

[29] See pp. 251-60.

[30] H. D. Hazeltine, "Magna Carta in the American Colonies," *Magna Carta Commemoration Essays*, ed. Henry E. Malden (Aberdeen, 1917), 199-200.

[31] *Ibid.*, 198-99.

[32] "We cannot help asserting, therefore, that this part of the act will make an essential change in the constitution of juries, and it is directly repugnant to the Great Charter itself; for, by that charter, 'no amerciament shall be assessed, but by the oath of honest and lawful men of the vicinage'; and, 'no freeman shall be taken, or imprisoned, or disseized of his freehold, or liberties of free customs, nor passed upon, nor condemned, but by lawful judgment of his peers, or by the law of the land.'" "Instructions of the Town of Braintree," October 14, 1765, Charles F. Adams (ed.), *The Works of John Adams* (Boston, 1851), III, 467.

[33] *Common Sense* (London, 1844 ed.), 21.

[34] *Bank of Columbia v. Okely*, 4 Wheat. 235, 244 (1819).

MAGNA CARTA[35]

June 15, 1215

John, by the grace of God, king of England, lord of Ireland, duke of Normandy *Preamble*
and Aquitaine, count of Anjou, to the archbishops, bishops, abbots, earls, barons,
justiciars, foresters, sheriffs, reeves, servants, and all bailiffs and his faithful people
greeting. Know that by the inspiration of God and for the good of our soul and those
of all our predecessors and of our heirs, to the honor of God and the exaltation of holy
church, and the improvement of our kingdom, by the advice of our venerable fathers
Stephen, archbishop of Canterbury, primate of all England and cardinal of the holy
Roman church, Henry, archbishop of Dublin, William of London, Peter of Winchester,
Jocelyn of Bath and Glastonbury, Hugh of Lincoln, Walter of Worcester, William of
Coventry, and Benedict of Rochester, bishops; of Master Pandulf, sub-deacon and
member of the household of the lord Pope, of Brother Aymeric, master of the Knights
of the Temple in England; and of the noblemen William Marshall, earl of Pembroke,
William, earl of Salisbury, William, earl of Warren, William, earl of Arundel, Alan of
Galloway, constable of Scotland, Warren Fitz-Gerald, Peter Fitz-Herbert, Hubert
de Burgh, steward of Poitou, Hugh de Nevil, Matthew Fitz-Herbert, Thomas Bassett,
Alan Bassett, Philip d'Albini, Robert de Roppelay, John Marshall, John Fitz-Hugh,
and others of our faithful.[36]

1. In the first place, we have granted to God, and by this our present charter *Liberties of*
confirmed, for us and for our heirs forever, that the English church shall be free, and *the church*
shall hold its rights entire and its liberties uninjured; and we will that it be thus observed; which is shown by this, that the freedom of elections, which is considered to
be most important and especially necessary to the English church, we, of our pure
and spontaneous will, granted, and by our charter confirmed, before the contest
between us and our barons had arisen; and obtained a confirmation of it by the lord

---

[35] *Translations and Reprints from the Original Sources of European History*, "English Constitutional Documents," ed. Edward P. Cheyney (Philadelphia, n.d.), I, No. 6, 6-17, based on Stubbs' reprint of the Latin text. The charter was reissued by Henry III with substantial changes and omissions in 1216, 1217, and 1225. The name "Magna Carta" technically applies only to the last reissue, 9 Hen. 3, c. 1. See p. 4n.

[36] The barons whose names appear in the preamble and who are again referred to as witnesses in chapter 63, were those who were most sympathetic to King John. It is believed that they may have been named in the hope of binding them to support the liberties announced by the document. The preamble was altered in the reissues.

Pope Innocent III.; which we shall observe and which we will shall be observed in good faith by our heirs forever.[37]

We have granted moreover to all free men of our kingdom for us and our heirs forever all the liberties written below, to be had and holden by themselves and their heirs from us and our heirs.

Inheritance 2. If any of our earls or barons, or others holding from us in chief by military service shall have died, and when he has died his heir shall be of full age and owe relief,[38] he shall have his inheritance by the ancient relief; that is to say, the heir or heirs of an earl for the whole barony of an earl a hundred pounds; the heir or heirs of a baron for a whole barony a hundred pounds; the heir or heirs of a knight for a whole knight's fee a hundred shillings at most; and who owes less let him give less according to the ancient custom of fiefs.

Same 3. If moreover the heir of any one of such shall be under age, and shall be in wardship, when he comes of age he shall have his inheritance without relief and without a fine.[39]

Rights of wards 4. The custodian of the land of such a minor heir shall not take from the land of the heir any except reasonable products, reasonable customary payments, and reasonable services, and this without destruction or waste of men or of property; and if we shall have committed the custody of the land of any such a one to the sheriff or to any other who is to be responsible to us for its proceeds, and that man shall have caused destruction or waste from his custody we will recover damages from him, and the land shall be committed to two legal and discreet men of that fief, who shall be responsible for its proceeds to us or to him to whom we have assigned them; and if we shall have given or sold to any one the custody of any such land, and he has caused destruction or waste there, he shall lose that custody, and it shall be handed over to two legal

---

[37] Compare with Coronation Charter of Henry I, 1101, which provided: ". . . I . . . make the holy church of God free, so that I will neither sell nor place at rent, nor, when archbishop, or bishop, or abbot is dead, will I take anything from the domain of the church, or from its men, until a successor is installed into it. . . ." *Translations and Reprints*, I, No. 6, 3.

The second Charter of Stephen, 1136, promised that simony should not be allowed and gave the bishops power over ecclesiastical persons and the distribution of ecclesiastical goods. George B. Adams and H. Morse Stephens (eds.), *Select Documents of English Constitutional History* (New York, 1935), 8. During the reign of Henry II (1154-89), an attempt was made in the Constitutions of Clarendon, 1164, to define the spheres of lay and ecclesiastical authority. *Ibid.*, 11-14. By the time of John's reign the freedom of the church was more restricted than during Stephen's. McKechnie, *Magna Carta*, 193. The right of canonical election had been confirmed by John in a separate charter issued in 1214. *Ibid.*, 194. Magna Carta's declaration of the church's freedom had no counterpart in the Articles of the Barons. *Ibid.*, 191. The declaration was repeated in chapter 63. In the reissues the part of the paragraph following "uninjured" was omitted.

[38] "Relief" was payment owed by the heir to the king for obtaining the estate of his ancestor.

[39] A "fine" was an agreement or composition involving payment by the heir. The reissue of 1225 provided: "But if the heir of any such be within age, his Lord shall not have the ward of him, nor of his land, before that he hath taken of him homage. . . . And after that such an heir hath been in ward (when he is come to full age) that is to say, to the age of one and twenty years, he shall have his inheritance without Relief, and without Fine: so that if such an heir being within age, be made Knight, yet nevertheless his land shall remain in the keeping of his Lord unto the term aforesaid." 9 Hen. 3, c. 3.

and discreet men of that fief who shall be in like manner responsible to us as is said above.

5. The custodian moreover, so long as he shall have the custody of the land, must keep up the houses, parks, warrens, fish ponds, mills, and other things pertaining to the land, from the proceeds of the land itself; and he must return to the heir, when he has come to full age, all his land, furnished with ploughs and implements of husbandry according as the time of wainage requires and as the proceeds of the land are able reasonably to sustain.[40] *Same*

6. Heirs shall be married without disparity, so nevertheless that before the marriage is contracted, it shall be announced to the relatives by blood of the heir himself.[41] *Marriage of heirs*

7. A widow, after the death of her husband, shall have her marriage portion and her inheritance immediately and without obstruction, nor shall she give anything for her dowry or for her marriage portion, or for her inheritance, which inheritance her husband and she held on the day of the death of her husband; and she may remain in the house of her husband for forty days after his death, within which time her dowry shall be assigned to her.[42] *Rights of widows*

8. No widow shall be compelled to marry so long as she prefers to live without a husband, provided she gives security that she will not marry without our consent, if she holds from us, or without the consent of her lord from whom she holds, if she holds from another. *Same*

9. Neither we nor our bailiffs will seize any land or rent for any debt, so long as the chattels of the debtor are sufficient for the payment of the debt;[43] nor shall the pledges of a debtor be distrained so long as the principal debtor himself has enough for the payment of the debt; and if the principal debtor fails in the payment of the debt, not having the wherewithal to pay it, the pledges shall be responsible for the debt; and if they wish, they shall have the lands and the rents of the debtor until they shall have been satisfied for the debt which they have before paid for him, unless the principal debtor shall have shown himself to be quit in that respect towards those pledges. *Debtors*

[40] The reissue of 1225 provided: "The keeper, so long as he hath the custody of the land of such an heir, shall keep up the houses, parks, warrens, ponds, mills and other things pertaining to the same land, with the issues of the said land; and he shall deliver to the Heir, when he cometh to his full age, all his land stored with ploughs, and all other things, at the least as he received it. All these things shall be observed in the custodies of Archbishopricks, Bishopricks, Abbeys, Priories, Churches, and Dignities vacant, which appertain to us; except this, that such custody shall not be sold." 9 Hen. 3, c. 5.

[41] The purpose of this provision was to restrict John's practice of selling his wards in marriage. McKechnie, *Magna Carta*, 212-14. Only the first clause appeared in the reissue.

[42] The reissue of 1225 added here: ". . . (if it were not assigned her before) or that the house be a castle; . . . and if she depart from the castle, then a competent house shall be forthwith provided for her, in the which she may honestly dwell, until her dower be to her assigned, as it is aforesaid; and she shall have in the mean time her reasonable estovers of the common; . . . and for her dower shall be assigned unto her the third part of all the lands of her husband, which were his during coverture, except she were endowed of less at the Church-door. . . . No widow shall be distrained to marry herself; nevertheless she shall find surety, that she shall not marry without our licence and assent (if she hold of us) nor without the assent of the Lord, if she hold of another." 9 Hen. 3, c. 7.

[43] The reissue added: "and the debtor himself be ready to satisfy therefore." 9 Hen. 3, c. 8.

Interest on debts

10.[44] If any one has taken anything from the Jews, by way of a loan, more or less, and dies before that debt is paid, the debt shall not draw interest so long as the heir is under age, from whomsoever he holds; and if that debt falls into our hands, we will take nothing except the chattel contained in the agreement.

Heirs of debtors

11.[45] And if any one dies leaving a debt owing to the Jews, his wife shall have her dowry, and shall pay nothing of that debt; and if there remain minor children of the dead man, necessaries shall be provided for them corresponding to the holding of the dead man; and from the remainder shall be paid the debt, the service of the lords being retained. In the same way debts are to be treated which are owed to others than the Jews.

Taxation

12.[46] No scutage or aid[47] shall be imposed in our kingdom except by the common council of our kingdom, except for the ransoming of our body, for the making of our oldest son a knight, and for once marrying our oldest daughter, and for these purposes it shall be only a reasonable aid; in the same way it shall be done concerning the aids of the city of London.

Liberties of the City of London

13. And the city of London shall have all its ancient liberties and free customs, as well by land as by water. Moreover, we will and grant that all other cities and boroughs and villages and ports shall have all their liberties and free customs.[48]

Assent to taxation by common council of the kingdom

14.[49] And for holding a common council of the kingdom concerning the assessment of an aid otherwise than in the three cases mentioned above, or concerning the assessment of a scutage, we shall cause to be summoned the archbishops, bishops, abbots, earls, and greater barons by our letters under seal; and besides we shall cause to be summoned generally, by our sheriffs and bailiffs all those who hold from us in chief, for a certain day, that is at the end of forty days at least, and for a certain place; and in all the letters of that summons, we will express the cause of the summons, and when the summons has thus been given the business shall proceed on the appointed day, on the advice of those who shall be present, even if not all of those who were summoned have come.

Taxation of subtenants

15.[50] We will not grant to any one, moreover, that he shall take an aid from his free men, except for ransoming his body, for making his oldest son a knight, and for once

---

[44] Omitted from the reissues.

[45] Omitted from the reissues.

[46] Omitted from the reissues.

[47] A "scutage" was a money payment in lieu of knight's service. An "aid" was a grant by the tenant to his lord in times of distress.

[48] The reissue of 1225 provided: "The city of *London* shall have all the old liberties and customs, which it hath been used to have. Moreover we will and grant, that all other Cities, Boroughs, Towns, and the Barons of the Five Ports and all other Ports, shall have all their liberties and free customs." 9 Hen. 3, c. 9. The principal liberties of the citizens of London were the right to appoint a mayor and the right to choose sheriffs. McKechnie, *Magna Carta*, 241.

[49] Omitted from the reissues.

[50] Omitted from the reissues.

marrying his oldest daughter; and for these purposes only a reasonable aid shall be taken.

16. No one shall be compelled to perform any greater service for a knight's fee, or for any other free tenement than is owed from it. *Knights' services*

17. The common pleas shall not follow our court, but shall be held in some certain place. *Justice available at a fixed place*

18. The recognitions[51] of *novel disseisin*,[52] *mort d'ancestor*,[53] and *darrein presentment*[54] shall be held only in their own counties and in this manner: we, or if we are outside of the kingdom our principal justiciar, will send two justiciars through each county four times a year, who with four knights of each county, elected by the county, shall hold in the county and on the day and in the place of the county court the aforesaid assizes[55] of the county.[56] *Courts to be held regularly to determine land disputes*

19.[57] And if the aforesaid assizes cannot be held within the day of the county court, a sufficient number of knights and free-holders shall remain from those who were present at the county court on that day to give the judgments, according as the business is more or less. *Same*

20. A free man shall not be fined for a small offence, except in proportion to the measure of the offence; and for a great offence he shall be fined in proportion to the magnitude of the offence, saving his freehold; and a merchant in the same way, saving his merchandise; and the villain shall be fined in the same way, saving his wainage,[58] if he shall be at our mercy; and none of the above fines shall be imposed except by the oaths of honest men of the neighborhood. *Assessment of fines*

21. Earls and barons shall be fined only by their peers, and only in proportion to their offence. *Same*

22. A clergyman shall be fined, like those before mentioned, only in proportion to his lay holding, and not according to the extent of his ecclesiastical benefice.[59] *Same*

23. No manor or man shall be compelled to make bridges over the rivers except those which ought to do it of old and rightfully. *Duty to provide bridges*

24. No sheriff, constable, coroners, or other bailiffs of ours shall hold pleas of our crown. *Unauthorized persons not to administer justice*

[51] Trials.
[52] An action to recover land following dispossession.
[53] An action involving a disputed right to inherit land.
[54] An action involving the right to ecclesiastical benefit.
[55] Trials.
[56] In the reissue of 1225 justices were required to be sent to the counties only once a year, and matters which could not be concluded by the justices either at the locality or on circuit were to be submitted to the "Justices of the Bench," a court which later became known as Common Pleas. Assizes of *darrein presentment* were to be taken before the Justices of the Bench. 9 Hen. 3, cc. 12, 13.
[57] Omitted from the reissues.
[58] "Wainage" refers to agricultural instruments.
[59] "Benefice" refers to office and dignities.

Rents

25.[60] All counties, hundreds, wapentakes, and trithings[61] shall be at the ancient rents and without any increase, excepting our demesne manors.[62]

Attachments of decedents' goods for debt

26. If any person holding a lay fief from us shall die, and our sheriff or bailiff shall show our letters-patent of our summons concerning a debt which the deceased owed to us, it shall be lawful for our sheriff or bailiff to attach and levy on the chattels of the deceased found on his lay fief, to the value of that debt, in the view of legal men, so nevertheless that nothing be removed thence until the clear debt to us shall be paid; and the remainder shall be left to the executors for the fulfilment of the will of the deceased; and if nothing is owed to us by him, all the chattels shall go to the deceased, saving to his wife and children their reasonable shares.

Goods of intestates

27. If any free man dies intestate,[63] his chattels shall be distributed by the hands of his near relatives and friends, under the oversight of the church, saving to each one the debts which the deceased owed to him.[64]

Payment for goods taken by officers

28. No constable or other bailiff of ours shall take anyone's grain or other chattels, without immediately paying for them in money, unless he is able to obtain a postponement at the good will of the seller.[65]

Castleguard

29. No constable shall require any knight to give money in place of his ward of a castle[66] if he is willing to furnish that ward in his own person or through another honest man, if he himself is not able to do it for a reasonable cause; and if we shall lead or send him into the army he shall be free from ward in proportion to the amount of time by which he has been in the army through us.

Horses and carriages of freemen

30. No sheriff or bailiff of ours or any one else shall take horses or wagons of any free man for carrying purposes except on the permission of that free man.

Taking of timber

31. Neither we nor our bailiffs will take the wood of another man for castles,[67] or for anything else which we are doing, except by the permission of him to whom the wood belongs.

Lands of felons

32. We will not hold the lands of those convicted of a felony for more than a year and a day, after which the lands shall be returned to the lords of the fiefs.

---

[60] Omitted from the reissues.

[61] "Hundreds, wapentakes, and trithings" were subdivisions of counties.

[62] "Demesne manors" were the lands reserved by a lord for his private use.

[63] "Intestate" means without a will.

[64] In the thirteenth century a will was valid as to personal property but not as to land. The church courts had jurisdiction over the probate of wills and their administration. In John's reign crown officers interfered with the testator's right to make a will and with the church's control over the distribution of the property in accordance with the will. This provision was omitted from the reissues.

[65] The reissue of 1225 provided: "No Constable, nor his Bailiff, shall take corn or other chattels of any man, if the man be not of the Town where the Castle is, but he shall forthwith pay for the same, unless that the will of the seller was to respite the payment; . . . and if he be of the same Town, the price shall be paid unto him within forty days." 9 Hen. 3, c. 19.

[66] "Ward of a castle" refers to the duty of a knight to guard the castle near which he lived.

[67] The reissue of 1225 provided: "No Sheriff nor Bailiff of ours, or any other, shall take the Horses or Carts of any man to make carriage, except he pay the old price limited, that is to say, for carriage with two horse, x.d. a day; for three horse, xiv.d. a day . . . No demesne Cart of any Spiritual person or Knight, or any Lord, shall be taken by our Bailiffs . . ." 9 Hen. 3, c. 21.

MAGNA CARTA

33. All the fish-weirs in the Thames and the Medway, and throughout all England shall be done away with, except those on the coast.[68] — *Fishweirs*

34. The writ which is called *praecipe* shall not be given for the future to any one concerning any tenement by which a free man can lose his court.[69] — *Writ of praecipe*

35. There shall be one measure of wine throughout our whole kingdom, and one measure of ale, and one measure of grain, that is the London quarter, and one width of dyed cloth and of russets and of halbergets, that is two ells within the selvages; of weights, moreover, it shall be as of measures. — *Uniform measures*

36. Nothing shall henceforth be given or taken for a writ of inquisition concerning life or limbs,[70] but it shall be given freely and not denied. — *Writ of life and limb*

37. If any one holds from us by fee farm[71] or by soccage[72] or by burgage,[73] and from another he holds land by military service, we will not have the guardianship of the heir or of his land which is of the fief of another, on account of that fee farm, or soccage, or burgage, nor will we have the custody of that fee farm, or soccage, or burgage, unless that fee farm itself owes military service. We will not have the guardianship of the heir or of the land of any one, which he holds from another by military service on account of any petty serjeanty[74] which he holds from us by the service of paying to us knives or arrows, or things of that kind. — *Rights of wards*

38. No bailiff for the future shall place any one to his law on his simple affirmation, without credible witnesses brought for this purpose. — *Proof of indictments*

39. No free man shall be taken or imprisoned or dispossessed, or outlawed, or banished, or in any way destroyed, nor will we go upon him, nor send upon him, except by the legal judgment of his peers or by the law of the land.[75] — *Procedure against freemen*

40. To no one will we sell, to no one will we deny, or delay right or justice. — *Sale, denial or delay of justice*

41. All merchants shall be safe and secure in going out from England and coming into England and in remaining and going through England, as well by land as by

---

[68] The fishweirs referred to were bulky contrivances which interfered with navigation on the rivers.

[69] Much of the administration of justice was conducted in the lords' courts ("free man" here means a lord). By the writ of *praecipe* the king could deprive the lord's court of jurisdiction, and the case would be handled by the royal courts. Had this provision been strictly observed, the development of the common law, which was the law administered by the royal courts, would have been hindered. McKechnie, *Magna Carta*, 346-55.

[70] This is also known as the writ *de odio et atia*.

[71] Tenure whereby land was held of another at a yearly rent.

[72] Tenure whereby land was held of another in consideration of certain inferior services of husbandry.

[73] Tenure whereby houses and lands which were formerly the site of houses in an ancient borough were held of some lord by a certain rent.

[74] Tenure whereby land was held of the king in consideration of rendering him some small implement of war such as a sword, arrow, or lance.

[75] *"Nullus liber homo capiatur, vel imprisonetur, aut dissaisiatur, aut utlagetur, aut exuletur, aut aliquo modo destruatur, nec super eum ibimus, nec super eum mittemus, nisi per legale judicium parium suorum vel per legem terrae."* Stubbs, *Select Charters*, 301.
The Charter of Liberties of Henry I contained the following language: "A firm peace in my whole kingdom I establish and require to be kept from henceforth. The law of King Edward I give to you again with those changes with which my father changed it by the counsel of his barons." Adams and Stephens, *op. cit.*, 6.

SOURCES OF OUR LIBERTIES

Liberties of merchants

water, for buying and selling, free from all evil tolls, by the ancient and rightful customs, except in time of war, and if they are of a land at war with us; and if such are found in our land at the beginning of war, they shall be attached without injury to their bodies or goods, until it shall be known from us or from our principal justiciar in what way the merchants of our land are treated who shall then be found in the country which is at war with us; and if ours are safe there, the others shall be safe in our land.

Liberty to leave and enter the kingdom

42.[76] It is allowed henceforth to any one to go out from our kingdom, and to return, safely and securely, by land and by water, saving their fidelity to us, except in time of war for some short time, for the common good of the kingdom; excepting persons imprisoned and outlawed according to the law of the realm, and people of a land at war with us, and merchants, of whom it shall be done as is before said.

Escheats

43. If any one holds from an escheat, as from the honor of Wallingford, or Nottingham, or Boulogne, or Lancaster, or from other escheats which are in our hands and are baronies, and he dies, his heir shall not give any other relief, nor do to us any other service than he would do to the baron, if that barony was in the hands of the baron; and we will hold it in the same way as the baron held it.[77]

Administration of forest laws

44. Men who dwell outside the forest shall not henceforth come before our justiciars of the forest, on common summons, unless they are in a plea of, or pledges for any person or persons who are arrested on account of the forest.[78]

Qualifications of officers

45.[79] We will not make justiciars, constables, sheriffs or bailiffs except of such as know the law of the realm and are well inclined to observe it.

Custody of abbeys

46. All barons who have founded abbeys for which they have charters of kings of England, or ancient tenure, shall have their custody when they have become vacant, as they ought to have.

Forest boundaries

47. All forests which have been afforested in our time shall be disafforested immediately; and so it shall be concerning river banks which in our time have been fenced in.[80]

Forest customs

48.[81] All the bad customs concerning forests and warrens and concerning foresters and warreners, sheriffs and their servants, river banks and their guardians shall be inquired into immediately in each county by twelve sworn knights of the same county, who shall be elected by the honest men of the same county, and within forty days after the inquisition has been made, they shall be entirely destroyed by them, never to be restored, provided that we be first informed of it, or our justiciar, if we are not in England.

---

[76] Omitted from the reissues.

[77] The reissue of 1225 added: ". . . neither shall we have, by occasion of any Barony or Eschete, any Eschete or keeping of any of our men, unless he that held the Barony or Eschete elsewhere held of us in chief." 9 Hen. 3, c. 31.

[78] Although this provision was omitted from the reissues of Magna Carta, it was re-enacted as section 2 of the Charter of the Forest issued by Henry III in 1217. Stubbs, *Select Charters*, 348.

[79] Omitted from the reissues.

[80] Part of this provision was incorporated into the Charter of the Forest. Stubbs, *Select Charters*, 349.

[81] Omitted from the reissues.

49.[82] We will give back immediately all hostages and charters which have been liberated to us by Englishmen as security for peace or for faithful service.

Securities for peace

50.[83] We will remove absolutely from their bailiwicks the relatives of Gerard de Athyes, so that for the future they shall have no bailiwick in England; Engelard de Cygony, Andrew, Peter and Gyon de Chancelles, Gyon de Cygony, Geoffrey de Martin and his brothers, Philip Mark and his brothers, and Geoffrey his nephew and their whole retinue.

Ouster of foreign favorites

51.[84] And immediately after the re-establishment of peace we will remove from the kingdom all foreign-born soldiers, crossbow men, servants, and mercenaries who have come with horses and arms for the injury of the realm.

Disbandment of troops

52.[85] If any one shall have been dispossessed or removed by us without legal judgment of his peers, from his lands, castles, franchises, or his right, we will restore them to him immediately; and if contention arises about this, then it shall be done according to the judgment of the twenty-five barons, of whom mention is made below concerning the security of the peace. Concerning all those things, however, from which any one has been removed or of which he has been deprived without legal judgment of his peers by King Henry our father, or by King Richard our brother, which we have in our land, or which others hold, and which it is our duty to guarantee, we shall have respite till the usual term of crusaders; excepting those things about which the suit has been begun or the inquisition made by our writ before our assumption of the cross; when, however, we shall return from our journey or if by chance we desist from the journey, we will immediately show full justice in regard to them.

Restoration of rights

53.[86] We shall, moreover, have the same respite and in the same manner about showing justice in regard to the forests which are to be disafforested or to remain forests, which Henry our father or Richard our brother made into forests; and concerning the custody of lands which are in the fief of another, custody of which we have until now had on account of a fief which any one has held from us by military service; and concerning the abbeys which have been founded in fiefs of others than ourselves, in which the lord of the fee has asserted for himself a right; and when we return or if we should desist from our journey we will immediately show full justice to those complaining in regard to them.

Grant of respite

54. No one shall be seized nor imprisoned on the appeal of a woman concerning the death of any one except her husband.[87]

Prosecutions by women

55.[88] All fines which have been imposed unjustly and against the law of the land,

[82] Omitted from the reissues.
[83] Omitted from the reissues.
[84] Omitted from the reissues.
[85] Omitted from the reissues.
[86] Omitted from the reissues.
[87] At this point the reissue of 1225 added three chapters regulating the time for holding county courts, sheriffs' tourns, and views of frankpledge, prohibiting the giving of land in mortmain, and providing that scutage shall be taken as it was in the time of Henry II. 9 Hen. 3, cc. 35, 36, 37.
[88] Omitted from the reissues.

Illegal judgments invalidated and all penalties imposed unjustly and against the law of the land are altogether excused, or will be on the judgment of the twenty-five barons of whom mention is made below in connection with the security of the peace, or on the judgment of the majority of them, along with the aforesaid Stephen, archbishop of Canterbury, if he is able to be present, and others whom he may wish to call for this purpose along with him. And if he should not be able to be present, nevertheless the business shall go on without him, provided that if any one or more of the aforesaid twenty-five barons are in a similar suit they should be removed as far as this particular judgment goes, and others who shall be chosen and put upon oath, by the remainder of the twenty-five shall be substituted for them for this purpose.

Rights of Welshmen 56.[89] If we have dispossessed or removed any Welshmen from their lands, or franchises, or other things, without legal judgment of their peers, in England, or in Wales, they shall be immediately returned to them; and if a dispute shall have arisen over this, then it shall be settled in the borderland by judgment of their peers, concerning holdings of England according to the law of England, concerning holdings of Wales according to the law of Wales, and concerning holdings of the borderland according to the law of the borderland. The Welsh shall do the same to us and ours.

Same 57.[90] Concerning all those things, however, from which any one of the Welsh shall have been removed or dispossessed without legal judgment of his peers, by King Henry our father, or King Richard our brother, which we hold in our hands, or which others hold, and we are bound to warrant to them, we shall have respite till the usual period of crusaders, those being excepted about which suit was begun or inquisition made by our command before our assumption of the cross. When, however, we shall return or if by chance we shall desist from our journey, we will show full justice to them immediately, according to the laws of the Welsh and the aforesaid parts.

Same 58.[91] We will give back the son of Lewellyn immediately, and all the hostages from Wales and the charters which had been liberated to us as a security for peace.

Rights of Alexander, King of Scots 59.[92] We will act toward Alexander, king of the Scots, concerning the return of his sisters and his hostages, and concerning his franchises and his right, according to the manner in which we shall act toward our other barons of England, unless it ought to be otherwise by the charters which we hold from William his father, formerly king of the Scots, and this shall be by the judgment of his peers in our court.

Liberties of subtenants 60. Moreover, all those customs and franchises mentioned above which we have conceded in our kingdom, and which are to be fulfilled, as far as pertains to us, in respect to our men; all men of our kingdom as well clergy as laymen, shall observe as far as pertains to them, in respect to their men.

61.[93] Since, moreover, for the sake of God, and for the improvement of our king-

---

[89] Omitted from the reissues.
[90] Omitted from the reissues.
[91] Omitted from the reissues.
[92] Omitted from the reissues.
[93] Omitted from the reissues.

MAGNA CARTA

dom, and for the better quieting of the hostility sprung up lately between us and our barons, we have made all these concessions; wishing them to enjoy these in a complete and firm stability forever, we make and concede to them the security described below; that is to say, that they shall elect twenty-five barons of the kingdom, whom they will, who ought with all their power to observe, hold, and cause to be observed, the peace and liberties which we have conceded to them, and by this our present charter confirmed to them; in this manner, that if we or our justiciar, or our bailiffs, or any of our servants shall have done wrong in any way toward any one, or shall have transgressed any of the articles of peace or security; and the wrong shall have been shown to four barons of the aforesaid twenty-five barons, let those four barons come to us or to our justiciar, if we are out of the kingdom, laying before us the transgression, and let them ask that we cause that transgression to be corrected without delay. And if we shall not have corrected the transgression or, if we shall be out of the kingdom, if our justiciar shall not have corrected it within a period of forty days, counting from the time in which it has been shown to us or to our justiciar, if we are out of the kingdom; the aforesaid four barons shall refer the matter to the remainder of the twenty-five barons, and let these twenty-five barons with the whole community of the country distress and injure us in every way they can; that is to say by the seizure of our castles, lands, possessions, and in such other ways as they can until it shall have been corrected according to their judgment, saving our person and that of our queen, and those of our children; and when the correction has been made, let them devote themselves to us as they did before. And let whoever in the country wishes take an oath that in all the above-mentioned measures he will obey the orders of the aforesaid twenty-five barons, and that he will injure us as far as he is able with them, and we give permission to swear publicly and freely to each one who wishes to swear, and no one will we ever forbid to swear. All those, moreover, in the country who of themselves and their own will are unwilling to take an oath to the twenty-five barons as to distressing and injuring us along with them, we will compel to take the oath by our mandate, as before said. And if any one of the twenty-five barons shall have died or departed from the land or shall in any other way be prevented from taking the above mentioned action, let the remainder of the aforesaid twenty-five barons choose another in his place, according to their judgment, who shall take an oath in the same way as the others. In all those things, moreover, which are committed to those five and twenty barons to carry out, if perhaps the twenty-five are present, and some disagreement arises among them about something, or if any of them when they have been summoned are not willing or are not able to be present, let that be considered valid and firm which the greater part of those who are present arrange or command, just as if the whole twenty-five had agreed in this; and let the aforesaid twenty-five swear that they will observe faithfully all the things which are said above, and with all their ability cause them to be observed. And we will obtain nothing from any one, either by ourselves or by another by which any of these concessions and liberties shall be revoked or diminished; and if any such thing shall have been obtained, let it be invalid and void, and we will never use it by ourselves or by another.

Enforcement of liberties by committee of twenty-five barons to keep the peace

Infringement of liberties to be invalid and void

Pardon of transgressions

62.[94] And all ill-will, grudges, and anger sprung up between us and our men, clergy and laymen, from the time of the dispute, we have fully renounced and pardoned to all. Moreover, all transgressions committed on account of this dispute, from Easter in the sixteenth year of our reign till the restoration of peace, we have fully remitted to all, clergy and laymen, and as far as pertains to us, fully pardoned. And moreover we have caused to be made for them testimonial letters-patent of lord Stephen, archbishop of Canterbury, lord Henry, archbishop of Dublin, and of the aforesaid bishops and of master Pandulf, in respect to that security and the concessions named above.

Oath to observe liberties

63.[95] Wherefore we will and firmly command that the Church of England shall be free, and that the men in our kingdom shall have and hold all the aforesaid liberties, rights and concessions, well and peacefully, freely and quietly, fully and completely, for themselves and their heirs, from us and our heirs, in all things and places, forever, as before said. It has been sworn, moreover, as well on our part as on the part of the barons, that all these things spoken of above shall be observed in good faith and without any evil intent. Witness the above named and many others. Given by our hand in the meadow which is called Runnymede, between Windsor and Staines, on the fifteenth day of June, in the seventeenth year of our reign.

[94] Omitted from the reissues.
[95] Omitted from the reissues.

REFERENCES

Barrington, Boyd C. *The Magna Charta and Other Great Charters of England.* Philadelphia: William S. Campbell, 1900.

Corwin, Edward S. "The 'Higher Law' Background of American Constitutional Law," *Harvard Law Review,* XLII (1928-29), 149-85, 365-409.

Fox, John C. "The Originals of the Great Charter of 1215," *English Historical Review,* XXXIX (1924), 321-36.

Jenks, Edward. "The Myth of Magna Carta," *The Independent Review,* IV (1904), 260-73.

Malden, Henry E. (ed.). *Magna Carta Commemoration Essays.* Aberdeen: The University Press, 1917.

McIlwain, Charles H. "Due Process of Law in Magna Carta," *Columbia Law Review,* XIV (1914), 27-51.

McKechnie, William S. *Magna Carta.* 2d ed. Glasgow: James Maclehose and Sons, 1914.

Mullett, Charles F. *Fundamental Law and the American Revolution, 1760-1776.* New York: Columbia University Press, 1933.

Painter, Sidney. "Magna Carta," *American Historical Review,* LIII (1947-48), 42-49.

———. *The Reign of King John.* Baltimore: Johns Hopkins Press, 1949.

Radin, Max. "The Myth of Magna Carta," *Harvard Law Review,* LX (1947), 1060-91.

Thompson, Faith. *Magna Carta.* Minneapolis: University of Minnesota Press, 1948.

II. CONFIRMATIO CARTARUM
1297

A recurrent problem of constitutional law is how the fundamental law of the land, once established, is to be enforced against officials of the government for the time being. King John promised, in chapter 61 of Magna Carta, that anything done contrary to the charter should be considered invalid and void. To enforce this promise and protect the liberties established by the document, Magna Carta authorized a committee of twenty-five barons to take action against the king by armed might if necessary. This cumbersome and violent machinery was never used, and chapter 61 was one of the provisions omitted from the reissues of the charter under Henry III.[1] Compliance with Magna Carta was not at once achieved. Abuses crept into the administration of justice, royal officers exceeded their customary powers, and illegal commercial practices were allowed to flourish. The demand for reform always centered on Magna Carta.

Establishment of fundamental law

Confirmatio Cartarum attempted to secure enforcement of Magna Carta by declaring judgments given contrary to that document to be void. This method of enforcing its terms recognized Magna Carta as a "higher law," and made it similar to the Constitution of the United States, the terms of which are enforced by the courts, which declare subordinate acts of government contrary to it to be void and of no legal effect.

Forty-seven confirmations of Magna Carta are found in the records to the time of Henry V.[2] Some of these occurred at the opening of Parliament

Confirmations of Magna Carta

---

[1] See pp. 20-21.

[2] By reigns the numbers are as follows: Henry III (1216-72), one; Edward I (1272-1307), two; Edward III (1327-77), twenty-three; Richard II (1377-99), thirteen; Henry IV (1399-1413), six; Henry V (1413-22), two. There were other confirmations which appear on neither the statute rolls nor the Parliament rolls on which this list is based. Faith Thompson, *Magna Carta* (Minneapolis, 1948), 9-12.

when the entire body of ancient customary law, together with Magna Carta and all other statutes, was confirmed. In some cases the confirmation was obviously something bought and paid for, usually by the barons and the clergy. Confirmatio Cartarum was only one enactment in this long series, but its special provisions gave it a significance not possessed by the other confirmations.

Origins
Development of Parliament

The events leading up to Confirmatio Cartarum, like those which led up to Magna Carta, show that the king's violation of established laws oppressed the community as a whole and caused the barons and clergy to unite in demanding the observance of the law. As was also true of Magna Carta, this oppression often took the form of illegal and unreasonable taxation. Magna Carta had sought to deal with this problem in chapters 12 and 14, which provided for the summoning of a feudal assembly to assent to the king's demands for new taxes. These clauses, however, were omitted from the reissues of the charter under Henry III.[3] The outlines of the modern Parliament began to appear, therefore, by custom and not by any express requirement contained in either Magna Carta or any other major constitutional document. This development was motivated by the fact that the crown's increasing needs for revenue forced the king to negotiate with all classes of the community. By 1254 knights of the shire were summoned to consider new taxes, and the word "parliamentum" had come into use. By 1265 the right of the cities and boroughs to be represented in Parliament was established.[4] The essential character of Parliament was completely developed in 1295, only two years before the granting of Confirmatio Cartarum, when representatives of the commons and inferior clergy were admitted.[5]

Grievances of the barons and clergy

Edward I's need for money became pressing when he decided in 1294 to wage war against France to regain the domain which English kings had considered their inheritance since the time of William the Conqueror. Despite

---

[3] Modern historians generally believe that the omission of chapters 12 and 14 of Magna Carta actually promoted the development of parliamentary government. The feudal assembly was intended to protect only crown tenants from arbitrary aids and scutages imposed by the king in his capacity as a feudal lord. "The Runnymede Charter was a very special document which, had it been followed, would have reduced England to a feudal oligarchy." Max Radin, "The Myth of Magna Carta," *Harvard Law Review*, LX (September, 1947), 1063; F. W. Maitland, *The Constitutional History of England* (Cambridge, 1909), 69-70, 75.

[4] *Ibid.*, 72-73, 95.

[5] *Ibid.*, 95-96; William Stubbs, *The Constitutional History of England* (4th ed.; Oxford, 1896), II, 133-34.

repeated levies, Edward's needs remained unfulfilled.[6] His problems were increased by the refusal of the leading barons to serve abroad on the ground that their feudal obligations did not compel such service.[7] In addition, Pope Boniface VIII forbade the clergy to submit to the taxing power of the king.[8] In desperation, Edward seized the wool and leather of the merchants and the money in the sacristies of the monasteries and cathedrals. These seizures were in the nature of forced loans and occurred both in 1294 and 1297.[9]

In August, 1297, the barons formally presented their grievances to the king. They complained of the requirements of foreign military service; they said that they could render no further contributions to the king because they had been impoverished by heavy taxes. They objected that they were not being governed in accordance with the laws and customs of the land, that their liberties were being taken from them by arbitrary means, and that the guarantees of Magna Carta were, for the most part, being infringed. They objected to the seizure of the wool, and ended with a petition that the king should abandon or defer his expedition in Flanders.[10] Because the barons were preparing to arm against him, and because of his desperate need of money, Edward agreed to confirm Magna Carta and the Charter of the Forest. The confirmation was sealed by the king November 5, 1297.[11] The barons met the king's demands for money, and the threat of outright revolution was averted.

Confirmatio Cartarum has had two principal effects upon the development of the liberties of the citizen. First, it established Parliament as a truly representative organ of government by providing in section 6 that the taxes must be raised by the common assent of the realm. The imposition of direct

Effects

In general

---

[6] Fourteen levies made by Edward I between May, 1294, and August, 1297, are listed by J. G. Edwards, "Confirmatio Cartarum and Baronial Grievances in 1297," *English Historical Review*, LVIII (1943), 158-59.

[7] The king proposed to take command in Flanders, while the barons fought in Gascony. The barons asserted the technicality that, although they were willing to serve with the king, they were not obliged to serve abroad without him. The real motive for refusing to serve, however, was a lack of sympathy with the objectives of the expedition. Stubbs, *op. cit.*, II, 136-39.

[8] The bull *Clericis laicos*, issued February 24, 1296, forbade the clergy to pay, and the secular powers to exact, under penalty of excommunication, contributions or taxes from the revenues or goods of the churches or their ministers. Its purpose was to prevent oppression of the clergy and to check the wars which were waged largely at their cost. *Ibid.*, 135.

[9] Edwards, *op. cit.*, 158-59; Stubbs, *op. cit.*, II, 131-39.

[10] Edwards, *op. cit.*, 153-61.

[11] The confirmation was issued by Prince Edward, as the king's lieutenant, on October 10, while the king himself was in France, and later was issued in identical terms by the king. *Ibid.*, 162.

taxes without the consent of the people's representatives in Parliament was now against the very letter of the law. Because the representative character of Parliament had been established in 1295, the "common assent of all the realm" required by Confirmatio Cartarum was no vague phrase, but had its appropriate organ in a Parliament of the three estates.[12] Second, Confirmatio Cartarum helped to establish Magna Carta as the fundamental law of the land by declaring judgments contrary to that document to be null and void.[13]

Later English statutes   The declaration contained in section 2 of Confirmatio Cartarum that judgments contrary to Magna Carta should be "undone, and holden for nought" provides an idea capable of being enforced against the government when its own laws are brought into question.[14] It thus goes far toward the establishment of Magna Carta as a "higher law," with a status superior to all other laws of the kingdom. Later enactments sought to strengthen this provision. The so-called statute *de Tallagio non Concedendo*, 1306, provided:

> We will and grant for us and our heirs, that all clerks and laymen of our land shall have their laws, liberties, and free customs, as largely and wholly as they have used to have the same at any time when they had them best; . . . and if any statutes have been made by us or our ancestors, or any customs, brought in contrary to them, or any manner of article contained in this present charter, we will and grant, that such manner of statutes and customs shall be void and frustrate for evermore.[15]

[12] Maitland, *op. cit.*, 96.

[13] Other provisions of Confirmatio Cartarum which tended to impart a fundamental character to Magna Carta were sections 1 and 3, which required the charters to be published throughout the land and read before the people twice a year, and section 4, which ordered the sentence of excommunication to be imposed upon violators. General excommunications were issued against violators of Magna Carta in 1253 and 1297, and violators were punished as late as 1489. Radin, *op. cit.*, 1065 and note. The provision of section 1 allowing the charters to be pleaded before royal officers greatly increased the influence of Magna Carta by establishing its provisions as part of the common law. Max Radin, *Handbook of Anglo-American Legal History* (St. Paul, 1936), 156, 161n. In addition, the very fact that Magna Carta was repeatedly confirmed undoubtedly did much to impart to it a fundamental and especially sacrosanct character. See Charles H. McIlwain, "Magna Carta and Common Law," *Magna Carta Commemoration Essays*, ed. Henry E. Malden (Cambridge, 1917), 141-42, 165.

[14] Possibly the word "judgments" was meant to include legislative enactments, as the word *"jugementz"* had a very inclusive meaning in that day. Charles H. McIlwain, *The High Court of Parliament and Its Supremacy* (New Haven, 1910), 59n.

[15] The authenticity of this statute is questionable. It has variously been considered to be an authoritative document actually sealed by the king, a kind of abstract or translation of Confirmatio Cartarum and of the accompanying pardon of the two earls, and as a statement of the demands of the barons in the form of a draft charter. These views are discussed in Edwards, *op. cit.*, 147-48; Harry Rothwell, "The Confirmation of the Charters, 1297," *English Historical Review*, LX (September, 1945), 300-15. It was considered to be a valid statute, however, in the seventeenth century. It is cited as controlling law in the Petition of Right (see p. 73) and was considered "without question" to be a statute in the *Ship-Money Case* (1637), *State Trials* (T. B. Howell, comp.), III, 825, 1081. It appears in the *Statutes at Large* dated 1306. 34 Edw. I, stat. 4, c. 1.

CONFIRMATIO CARTARUM

A further development of the same idea is found in the statute of 1368 which declared that "the Great Charter, and the Charter of the Forest be holden and kept in all points; . . . and if any statute be made to the contrary, that shall be holden for none."[16] The effect of this statute was probably to nullify statutes previously passed that were contrary to Magna Carta, and not to declare invalid any such statutes which might be made in the future.[17] Under English law, the attempt of one Parliament to limit the power of all later Parliaments is both illogical and ineffective because the later bodies possess a sovereignty equal to that of the earlier Parliament. These statutes, however, contain the idea, found in the Constitution of the United States, that there is a supreme law of the land, embodied in a written document, which is of greater force and effect than the ordinary laws.

When the power of the courts to declare acts of Parliament unconstitutional was first asserted, it was the common law generally and the principles of common right and reason which constituted the "higher law" appealed to and not the specific provisions of Magna Carta. This step was taken early in the seventeenth century when Lord Coke said in his famous dictum in *Bonham's Case:*

Bonham's Case

> And it appears in our books, that in many cases, the common law will controul acts of parliament, and sometimes adjudge them to be utterly void; for when an act of parliament is against common right and reason, or repugnant, or impossible to be performed, the common law will controul it, and adjudge such act to be void.[18]

The concept of a "higher law," similar to the idea found in Confirmatio Cartarum and the later English statutes, appeared in the Charter of Privileges of William Penn, 1701, which provided that the document might, in general, be amended with the consent of the governor and six-sevenths of the assembly. The article relating to liberty of conscience, however, was not to be amended and was to be kept and remain inviolable forever.[19] The intention of this provision was clearly to establish the charter as the fundamental law of the colony. The clause relating to religious liberty was to be treated as especially sacrosanct. The effectiveness of this clause, however,

Colonial laws

---

[16] 42 Edw. 3, c. 1.

[17] J. W. Gough, *Fundamental Law in English Constitutional History* (Oxford, 1955), 16.

[18] 8 Coke's Reports 107, 118 (1610). See also Edward S. Corwin, "The 'Higher Law' Background of American Constitutional Law," *Harvard Law Review*, XLII (January, 1929), 367; Gough, *op. cit.*, 31-40; S. E. Thorne, "The Constitution and the Courts: a Re-examination of the Famous Case of Dr. Bonham," ed. Conyers Read, *The Constitution Reconsidered* (New York, 1938), 15-24.

[19] See pp. 256, 259.

rested solely upon the proprietor's will, and the problem of enforcing even the right of religious liberty of the individual still remained. The desire to establish certain rights of the citizen as part of the supreme law of the land, coupled with a keen awareness of the difficulty of providing effective governmental machinery to protect those rights, was shown in the Virginia Statute of Religious Liberty of 1786, drafted by Thomas Jefferson. Article III of that statute provided:

> And though we well know that this assembly elected by the people for the ordinary purposes of legislation only, have no power to restrain the acts of succeeding assemblies, constituted with powers equal to our own, and that therefore to declare this act to be irrevocable would be of no effect in law; yet as we are free to declare, and do declare, that the rights hereby asserted are of the natural rights of mankind, and that if any act shall be hereafter passed to repeal the present, or to narrow its operation, such act will be an infringement of natural right.[20]

During their struggle against oppressive British legislation, the American colonists began to look to the courts to check what they considered to be violations of their fundamental rights. In 1761 James Otis, relying on Coke's opinion in *Bonham's Case*, challenged the constitutionality of the writs of assistance issued by the Massachusetts Superior Court, saying that they were contrary to the English constitution and the principles of natural law:

> As to Acts of Parliament. An Act against the Constitution is void; an act against natural equity is void; and if an act of Parliament should be made, in the very words of this petition, it would be void. The executive Courts must pass such acts into disuse. 8 Rep. 118 from Viner. Reason or the common law to control an act of Parliament.[21]

Samuel Adams argued that the Stamp Act, "I take it, is utterly void, and of no binding force upon us; for it is against our Rights as Men and our Privileges as Englishmen. An act made in defiance of the first principles of Justice . . . There are certain Principles fixed unalterably in Nature."[22] The same idea was repeated in 1768 in a number of letters drawn up by Adams for the Massachusetts Assembly and sent to prominent British statesmen.[23]

Judicial review

When the Constitution of the United States was framed, it was believed by most of the influential members at the convention that the courts would

---

[20] W. W. Hening (ed.), *Statutes at Large* (Richmond, 1823), XII, 86.

[21] Charles F. Adams (ed.), *The Works of John Adams* (Boston, 1850), II, 522.

[22] Quoted in Andrew C. McLaughlin, *The Foundations of American Constitutionalism* (New York, 1932), 127.

[23] Henry S. Commager (ed.), *Documents of American History* (6th ed.; New York, 1958), I, 65.

have power to declare void any act of Congress contrary to the Constitution.[24] The legal machinery for the enforcement of the higher law embodied in the Constitution is now called judicial review. By applying the essential idea found in Confirmatio Cartarum to the Constitution of the United States, this principle was established by Mr. Chief Justice Marshall in 1803 in the case of *Marbury* v. *Madison*. "Certainly all those who have framed written constitutions," he stated, "contemplate them as forming the fundamental and paramount law of the nation, and, consequently, the theory of every such government must be, that an act of the legislature, repugnant to the constitution, is void."[25]

[24] Citations to the statements of the framers both in and out of the convention are given in Edward S. Corwin (ed.), *The Constitution of the United States: Analysis and Interpretation*, 82d Cong., 2d Sess., 1953, Senate Doc. 170, 556n. But see Learned Hand, *The Bill of Rights* (Cambridge, Mass., 1958), 1-30.

[25] 1 Cranch 137, 177 (1803).

CONFIRMATIO CARTARUM[26]

November 5, 1297

Confirmation of the charters

EDWARD, *by the grace of God, King of* England, *Lord of* Ireland, *and Duke of* Guian,[27] *to all those that these present letters shall hear or see, greeting.* Know ye that we, to the honour of God and of Holy Church, and to the profit of our realm, have granted for us and our heirs, that the Charter of liberties, and the Charter of the forest,[28] which were made by common assent of all the realm, in the time of King HENRY our father, shall be kept in every point without breach. (2) And we will that the same charters shall be sent under our seal, as well to our justices of the forest, as to others, and to all sheriffs of shires, and to all our other officers, and to all our cities throughout the realm, together with our writs, in the which it shall be contained, that they cause the foresaid charters to be published, and to declare to the people that we have confirmed them in all points; (3) and that our justices, sheriffs, mayors, and other ministers, which under us have the laws of our land to guide, shall allow the said charters pleaded before them in judgement in all their points, that is to wit, the Great Charter as the common law, and the Charter of the forest, for the wealth of our realm.

Publication of the charters

Charters allowed as common law

Judgments contrary to charters are void

2. AND we will, That if any judgement be given from henceforth contrary to the points of the charters aforesaid by the justices, or by any other our ministers that hold plea before them against the points of the charters, it shall be undone, and holden for nought.

Charters sent to churches

3. AND we will, That the same charters shall be sent, under our seal, to cathedral churches throughout our realm, there to remain, and shall be read before the people two times by the year.

Excommunication of violators

4. AND that all archbishops and bishops shall pronounce the sentence of excommunication against all those that by word, deed, or counsel do contrary to the foresaid charters, or that in any point break or undo them. (2) And that the said curses be twice a year denounced and published by the prelates aforesaid. (3) And if the said prelates, or any of them, be remiss in the denunciation of the said sentences, the arch-

---

[26] 25 Edw. 1, c. 1. Danby Pickering (ed.), *Statutes at Large* (Cambridge, 1726-1807), I, 273-75.

[27] Aquitaine, the territory in southwestern France.

[28] The Charter of the Forest was issued in 1217, early in the reign of Henry III, as a supplement to Magna Carta. It was confirmed by him in 1225. Some of the provisions omitted in the reissues of Magna Carta which relate to forest matters appeared in the Charter of the Forest.

CONFIRMATIO CARTARUM

bishops of *Canterbury* and *York* for the time being shall compel and distrein them to the execution of their duties in form aforesaid.

5. AND *for so much as divers people of our realm are in fear that the aids and tasks*[29] *which they have given to us beforetime towards our wars and other business, of their own grant and good will (howsoever they were made) might turn to a bondage to them and their heirs, because they might be at another time found in the rolls, and likewise for the prises taken throughout the realm by our ministers:* (2) We have granted for us and our heirs, that we shall not draw such aids, tasks, nor prises into a custom, for any thing that hath been done heretofore, be it by roll or any other precedent that may be founden.

Limitation of aids, tasks, and prises

6. Moreover we have granted for us and our heirs, as well to archbishops, bishops, abbots, priors, and other folk of holy church, as also to earls, barons, and to all the communalty of the land, that for no business from henceforth we shall take such manner of aids, tasks, nor prises, but by the common assent of the realm, and for the common profit thereof, saving the ancient aids, and prises due and accustomed.

Common assent of realm required in taxation

7. AND *for so much as the more part of the communalty of the realm find themselves sore grieved with the maletent of woolls, that is to wit, a toll of forty shillings for every sack of wool, and have made petition to us to release the same;* We at their requests have yearly released it, and have for granted us and our heirs, that we shall not take such things without their common assent and good will, saving to us and our heirs the custom of wools, skins, and leather, granted before by the communalty aforesaid. In witness of which things we have caused these our letters to be made patents. Witness EDWARD our son at *London* the tenth day of *October,* the five and twentieth year of our reign.

Tax on wool

[29] "Aids," "tasks," and "prises" were forms of taxation.

REFERENCES

See also references on p. 22.

Edwards, J. G. "Confirmatio Cartarum and Baronial Grievances in 1297," *English Historical Review,* LVIII (1943), 147-71, 273-300.

Mullett, Charles F. *Fundamental Law and the American Revolution, 1760-1776.* New York: Columbia University Press, 1933.

Rothwell, Harry. "The Confirmation of the Charters, 1297," *English Historical Review,* LX (1945), 16-35, 177-91, 300-15.

Thompson, Faith. "Parliamentary Confirmations of the Great Charter," *American Historical Review,* XXXVIII (1933), 659-72.

III. THE FIRST CHARTER OF VIRGINIA
1606

Origins   By this charter the rights of the English subject were transported to the New World where they later developed into the rights of the American citizen. Although the charter was granted by James I (1603-25), the Stuart king was not the originator of the policy that the protection of the laws of England should follow the subject who settled in remote lands. This policy, which distinguished English colonial administration from that of other nations, was established during the more liberal reign of Queen Elizabeth. The

Charters to Gilbert and Raleigh   charters issued to Sir Humphrey Gilbert in 1578 and Sir Walter Raleigh in 1584 contained the same guarantee.[1] Permanent colonies were never established, however, under either of these charters.

During the sixteenth century, explorations and colonizing efforts were conducted by individual adventurers largely at private expense. Later colonization owed much to these adventurers—particularly Raleigh, who established an unsuccessful colony at Roanoke. By the beginning of the seventeenth century, however, it had become clear that the purses of individuals were

---

[1] The letters patent to Gilbert provided: "And wee doe graunt to the sayd sir Humfrey, his heires and assignes, and to all and every of them, and to all and every other person and persons, being of our allegiance, whose names shall be noted or entred in some of our courts of Record, within this our Realme of England, and that with the assent of the said sir Humfrey, his heires or assignes, shall nowe in this journey for discoverie, or in the second journey for conquest hereafter, travel to such lands, countries and territories as aforesaid, and to their and every of their heires: that they and every or any of them being either borne within our sayd Realmes of England or Ireland, or within any other place within our allegiance, and which hereafter shall be inhabiting within any the lands, countreys and territories, with such licence as aforesayd, shall and may have, and enjoy all the priveleges of free denizens and persons native of England, and within our allegiance: any law, custome, or usage to the contrary notwithstanding." Francis N. Thorpe (ed.), *The Federal and State Constitutions, Colonial Charters, and Other Organic Laws* (Washington, 1909), I, 50-51.

Gilbert was also given power to make laws for the government of the people: "So always that the sayd statutes, laws and ordinances may be as neere as conveniently may, agreeable to the forme of lawes & pollicy of England..."

These provisions appeared in almost identical terms in the charter to Raleigh. *Ibid.*, 55.

THE FIRST CHARTER OF VIRGINIA

inadequate to meet the vast expenses involved.[2] For this reason companies were formed to establish colonies and carry on trade. The first successful colonies were established by these companies. Their corporate charters had an important effect on the governmental institutions which were developed.[3] The charter of the East India Company, which was organized in 1600, was probably the model on which the Virginia Charter of 1606 was framed.[4] Although colonization was undertaken by a company organized for private profit, broad considerations of national policy also motivated the colonial movement. The primary motives were the desire to spread Christianity to the heathens, to establish England as a national power able to compete with Spain and France in commercial activity as well as in naval warfare, and to relocate some of England's surplus population.[5]

The Virginia Charter of 1606 was drawn up by the chief legal officers of England. The first draft was probably prepared by Sir John Popham, Lord Chief Justice. The charter was then drawn by Sir Edward Coke, Attorney General, and Sir John Dodderidge, Solicitor General. It was sealed by Sir Thomas Egerton, Lord Chancellor, on April 10.[6] The charter created the London and Plymouth companies and gave them separate territorial

---

[2] In 1616 His Majesty's Council for Virginia wrote: "When first it pleased God to move his Maiesties minde, at the humble suit of Sundry his loving subjects, to yeild unto them his gracious Priviledge for the Virginia Plantation, it was a thing seeming strange and doubtfull in the eye of the World, that such and so few Under-takers should enterprise a charge of that waight, as rather beseemed a whole State and Commonwealth to take in hand." Alexander Brown, *The Genesis of the United States* (Boston, 1891), I, 49.
  Gilbert's voyage in 1578 was financially a failure. His losses so embarrassed him that in 1581 he complained of "daily arrests, executions and outlawries." Herbert L. Osgood, *The American Colonies in the Seventeenth Century* (New York, 1904), I, 8-10. Raleigh spent £40,000 in his efforts to colonize Virginia. For financial reasons he consented in 1589 to assign a right to trade in Virginia to Sir Thomas Smith, John White, Richard Hakluyt and others, reserving a fifth of all gold and silver extracted. Lyon G. Tyler, *England in America, 1580-1652*, Vol. IV of *The American Nation: A History*, ed. A. B. Hart (28 vols.; New York, 1904-18), 31.

[3] English commercial activity developed at a rapid rate after 1550. The trading companies of the latter half of the sixteenth century were not, however, entirely novel forms of commercial organization. The Society of Merchants Adventurers, whose origins go back at least as far as the fifteenth century, furnished a model for the sixteenth-century companies. Edward P. Cheyney, *European Background of American History, 1300-1600*, Vol. I of *The American Nation: A History*, 140. The Muscovy Company, established in 1554, was the first of some fifty or sixty companies chartered by England, Holland, France, Sweden, and Denmark in the sixteenth and seventeenth centuries. *Ibid.*, 135-39.

[4] Tyler, *op. cit.*, 36.

[5] In "Reasons for Raising a Fund," presented to Parliament in 1605, the following reasons were stated: (1) To promote trade and navigation, (2) to stimulate the building of ships for defense purposes, (3) to obtain a source of masts, cordage, pitch, tar, and resin, which were not available in England, (4) to give employment to mariners, (5) to provide a market for English goods, and (6) to protect the English interest in discovered lands. Brown, *op. cit.*, I, 36-40.

[6] Alexander Brown, *The First Republic in America* (Boston, 1898), 6; Brown, *Genesis*, I, 47.

jurisdictions. The document is a landmark in the history of territorial boundaries because of its claim of England's right to colonize American lands between the thirty-fourth and forty-fifth parallels of latitude, to which the name "Virginia" was given.[7]

General Effect

Form of government

The government of the colonies was neither wholly private nor wholly royal but was a mixture of the two forms.[8] The government of both colonies was under the Royal Council of Virginia, whose members were appointed by the king and who could be removed at his pleasure. The Royal Council nominated subordinate councils for each of the colonies, and they were to govern according to laws, ordinances and instructions issued by the king. Because there was no local self-government it has been said that the charter contains "not one ray of popular rights."[9]

The king's Instructions for the government of the colony were issued on November 20, 1606.[10] In the Instructions he appointed fourteen members to the Royal Council, which was given power to appoint the members of the first colonial councils and to issue directions to those councils. The colonial councils were to have power to nominate the first president for one year "unless he shall in the mean time dye or be removed from that office." The Christian religion was to be "preached, planted, and used" both within the plantations and among the savages "according to the doctrine, rights, and religion now professed and established within our realme of England." Land was to descend as like estates in England. The president and the council were given power to hear and determine all offenses with a jury, except that no jury was required in civil cases nor for minor offenses such as drunkenness

---

[7] Edward Channing, *A History of the United States* (New York, 1928), I, 157-58. No specific boundaries were mentioned in the charter to Raleigh, 1584. Instead he was given "all the soile of all such lands, territories, and Countreis, so to bee discouered." Thorpe, *op. cit.*, I, 54.

[8] Osgood, *op. cit.*, I, 29.

[9] Brown, *First Republic*, 7; Tyler, *op. cit.*, 37; George Bancroft, *History of the United States of America* (New York, 1892), I, 87. The Royal Council afforded a special protecting and connecting link with the crown. The direction of the company was under a treasurer and a deputy treasurer (members of the Royal Council); sixteen directors (a majority to be of the Royal Council); seven auditors (two, at least, to be of the Royal Council); a secretary; bookkeeper; husband; beadle; and cashier. The bookkeeper was clerk to the auditors; the cashier was clerk to the treasurer; the husband was special manager of the concerns of the ships and kept records of the voyages. In addition, there were several courts: the Court of the Committees, which had general direction of the affairs of the company; the Ordinary Courts, which included some of the generality of the company; the Preparative Courts of the Directors, which were held before the Great Quarter Courts to prepare business to be submitted to those courts; and the Great Quarter Courts, which elected officers, made laws, and considered other business. Brown, *Genesis*, I, vii-ix. Whether so elaborate a governmental superstructure was either necessary or desirable is highly questionable. See Channing, *op. cit.*, I, 163.

[10] Brown, *Genesis*, I, 65-75.

and idleness. Tumults, rebellion, conspiracies, mutiny, sedition, murder, manslaughter, incest, rape, and adultery were all punishable by death; but in these cases the jury was to be bound by the evidence. The colonists were required to take the oath of obedience. The president and the council had power to make laws consistent with the laws of England. These were subject to revision by the Royal Council.

The Charter's guarantee in the fifteenth paragraph that the colonists should enjoy the rights of Englishmen was simply declaratory of the principle that the colonists who settled on the territory claimed by England and who recognized their allegiance to the English crown carried with them, whether the king willed it or not, so much of the English constitutional and legal system as was applicable to their situation. From a strictly legal point of view, therefore, this guarantee was not absolutely essential in the charter.[11] Although this guarantee was designed merely to distinguish English colonization from that of other countries, which viewed their colonists as persons outside the protection of the constitutional and legal system of the home country, it was destined to play an important role in the struggles of the American colonists against oppressive rulers in England particularly during the period preceding the American Revolution.

Rights of Englishmen

The same guarantee is found in the Charter of New England, 1620; the Charter of Massachusetts Bay, 1629; the Charter of Maryland, 1632; the Charter of Maine, 1639; the Charter of Connecticut, 1662; the Charter of Rhode Island, 1663; the Charter of Carolina, 1663; and the Charter of Georgia, 1732.[12] The Virginia Charter of 1606 was thus the first of a long series of documents which stated unequivocally that the colonists were entitled to the rights of Englishmen.

In the early seventeenth century there existed no statement of just what were the rights of Englishmen.[13] Magna Carta, together with its confirma-

---

[11] H. D. Hazeltine, "The Influence of Magna Carta on American Constitutional Development," *Magna Carta Commemoration Essays*, ed. Henry E. Malden (Aberdeen, 1917), 188-89; Channing, *op. cit.*, I, 162.

[12] See the following documents in Thorpe's *Charters*: Virginia, 1609, VII, 3800; Virginia, 1612, VII, 3804-05, 3806, 3810; Charter of New England, 1620, III, 1839; Massachusetts Bay, 1629, III, 1856-57; Maryland, 1632, III, 1681; Maine, 1639, III, 1635; Connecticut, 1662, I, 533; Rhode Island, 1663, VI, 3220; Carolina, 1663, V, 2747; Georgia, 1732, II, 773.

[13] It has been said that, although the liberties, franchises, and immunities of the subject under English law included trial by jury, benefit of clergy, and rights of land tenure and inheritance, the words have nothing to do with civil liberty, self-government, or democracy. Instead, they were strictly "legal, tenurial, and financial" in their application. Charles M. Andrews, *The Colonial Period of American History* (New Haven, 1934), I, 86n.

tions and other supporting statutes, certainly constituted the primary source of the rights of the subject; but in 1606 Magna Carta was almost four hundred years old, and most of its provisions related to the feudal order which had become obsolete.

The Virginia Charter did not at once bring the entire body of English laws to the colonies. In the words of Mr. Justice Story:

> The common law of England is not to be taken, in all respects, to be that of America. Our ancestors brought with them its general principles, and claimed it as their birthright; but they brought with them and adopted only that portion which was applicable to their situation.[14]

At first there was a period of popular, untechnical law in which only the barest outlines of English justice can be discerned. There were no written laws until the arrival of Lord Delaware in 1610.[15] The absence of settled governmental institutions and the desperate struggle for survival waged against disease, the elements, and the Indians caused many deviations from procedures and principles observed in England.[16] The power of life and death over the colonists was often held by one or two councilors,[17] private property was unknown, and a code of martial law was in force for a number of years.[18] This code established rigid military discipline and restricted free-

---

[14] *Van Ness* v. *Pacard*, 2 Peters 137, 144 (1829). The more simple, popular, and general parts of the common law from the first had great influence in the colonies. "This is, however, very far from declaring the common law of England a subsidiary system in actual force from the beginning of colonization." Paul S. Reinsch, "The English Common Law in the Early American Colonies," *Select Essays in Anglo-American Legal History* (Boston, 1907), I, 369.

[15] Osgood, *op. cit.*, I, 69.

[16] In the instructions to Sir Thomas Gates, appointed governor in 1609, it was provided that "in all matters of Civill Justice you shall finde it properest and usefullest for your government to proceede rather as a Chancellor than as a Judge, rather upon the naturall right and equity than upon the nicenesse and lettre of the lawe, which perplexeth in this tender body rather than dispatcheth all Causes; so that a summary and arbitrary way of Justice discreetly mingled with those gravities and fourmes of magistracy as shall in your discrecon seeme aptest for you and that place, will be of most use both for expedicon and for example." Quoted in *ibid.*, 63.

[17] During the winter of 1609, when John Smith was the only surviving member of the council, he had the letters patent read to the colonists once a week so they would know the extent of his powers over them. He stated that "there are no more councils to protect you, nor curb my endeavors," and he told them that every offender could "assuredly expect his due punishment." *Ibid.*, 53-54.

[18] This was a combined civil and martial code. The civil part was prepared by William Strachey and the martial part was probably borrowed from the regulations in force in the Netherlands. *Ibid.*, 69. The laws sent over by Gates in June, 1609, were established May 24, 1610. Additions were made by Dale, June 22, 1611. Although these laws seem terrible, "they were not much, if any, more severe than the Draconic Code, which then obtained in England, in which nearly three hundred crimes, varying from murder to keeping company with a gypsy, were punishable with death." Brown, *Genesis*, II, 528-29. For text see Peter Force (comp.), *Tracts and Other Papers* (Washington, 1844), III, No. 2, 9-62.

THE FIRST CHARTER OF VIRGINIA

dom of action to a minimum. Strict religious observance was required. Punishments for offenders were severe, and some twenty crimes were made punishable by death. These even included such offenses as unlicensed trading with Indians, the killing of cattle and poultry without a license, the destruction of growing crops, extortion practiced by seamen in the sale of goods, the stealing of boats or vessels of the colony, escape from the colony, persistent refusal to attend church, and embezzlement by the keeper of the store.

The instability of government under the Charter of 1606 caused it to be replaced by the royal charters of 1609 and 1612.[19] Sir Edwin Sandys played a leading role in obtaining these charters,[20] and his ideals had much to do with the establishment of the first democratic government in the colonies.[21] The charter granted May 23, 1609, established the London Company as a corporation separate from the Plymouth Company. Additional territorial rights were granted. The colonists were to be free from customs for twenty-one years, and were to be free from certain taxes forever. The government of the colony was taken from the Royal Council and placed under the treasurer and the council of the company, which was given power to fill vacancies in its own body.[22] The effect of this was to grant the company a large measure

Charters of 1609 and 1612

---

[19] For texts see Thorpe, *op. cit.*, VII, 3790, 3802.

[20] Sandys prepared the first draft of the Charter of 1609 which was then revised by the king and his Council. The final draft is based on a warrant issued by Sir Robert Cecil, Secretary of State, and it was prepared by Sir Henry Hobart, Attorney General, and Sir Francis Bacon, Solicitor General. Brown, *Genesis*, I, 207.

[21] See p. 48. "Sir Edwin Sandys was then the leader of the independent party in Parliament. He had already aided in drawing up 'with great force of reasoning and Spirit of Liberty' the remonstrance against the conduct of James I. towards his first Parliament; had contended that all prisoners should have the assistance of counsel; had been an advocate of the freedom of trade, an opponent of the monopolies held by companies; had frequently appealed for a correction of the grievances of the people and against the impositions upon them by the crown; and had already 'learned to raise his voice for the toleration of those with whom he did not wholly agree.' He had in mind a well-matured plan for the future good of Englishmen, and when drafting the Virginia Company charters he inserted therein the authority which would enable him to put this plan in execution when the proper time arrived." Brown, *First Republic*, 75, 408.

[22] The charter of 1609 provided: "And further, of our special Grace, certain Knowledge, and mere Motion, for Us, our Heirs and Successors, we do, by these Presents, GIVE and GRANT full Power and Authority to our said Council here resident, as well at this present time, as hereafter from time to time, to nominate, make, constitute, ordain and confirm, by such Name or Names, Stile or Stiles, as to them shall seem good, And likewise to revoke, discharge, change, and alter, as well all and singular Governors, Officers, and Ministers, which already have been made, as also which hereafter shall be by them thought fit and needful to be made or used for the Government of the said Colony and Plantation:

"AND also to make, ordain, and establish all Manner of Orders, Laws, Directions, Instructions, Forms and Ceremonies of Government and Magistracy, fit and necessary for and concerning the Government of the said Colony and Plantation; And the same, at all Times hereafter, to abrogate, revoke, or change, not only within the Precincts of the said Colony, but also upon the Seas, in going and coming to and from the said Colony, as they in their good Discretion, shall think to be fittest for the Good of the Adventurers and inhabitants there." Thorpe, *op. cit.*, VII, 3797-98.

of self-government and thus open the way for the enlarged rights of democratic government created by the Ordinance of 1618.[23]

Later Significance   A century and a half after this charter was granted, the colonists turned to it in one of the final attempts before the American Revolution to secure the protection of their rights as Englishmen. On May 29, 1765, Patrick Henry came before the Virginia House of Burgesses, which had met to consider what measures to take against the Stamp Act. Among the measures he urged were the following resolutions which were intended to place the claimed right of representation in the levying of taxes on the solid documentary foundation of the colonial charters:

> That the first Adventurers and Settlers of this His Majesty's Colony and Dominion of *Virginia* brought with them and transmitted to their Posterity, and all other His Majesty's Subjects since inhabiting in this his Majesty's said Colony, all the Liberties, Privileges, Franchieses, and Immunities, that have at any Time been held, enjoyed, and possessed, by the people of *Great Britain*. That by two royal Charters, granted by King *James* the First, the Colonists aforesaid are declared entitled to all Liberties, Privileges, and Immunities of Denizens and natural Subjects, to all Intents and Purposes, as if they had been abiding and born within the Realm of *England*.[24]

The great contribution of the Virginia Charter of 1606, therefore, was to establish the principle that the American colonists were entitled to the "rights of Englishmen." This principle, reiterated in many later colonial documents, shaped the whole course of the development of individual liberties in America.

[23] See pp. 47-54.
[24] *Journal of the House of Burgesses of Virginia, 1761-65,* 360.

THE FIRST CHARTER OF VIRGINIA[25]
April 10, 1606

JAMES, by the Grace of God, King of *England, Scotland, France* and *Ireland,* Defender of the Faith, &c. WHEREAS our loving and well-disposed Subjects, Sir *Thomas Gates,* and Sir *George Somers,* Knights, *Richard Hackluit,* Clerk, Prebendary of *Westminster,* and *Edward-Maria Wingfield, Thomas Hanham,* and *Ralegh Gilbert,* Esqrs. *William Parker,* and *George Popham,* Gentlemen, and divers others of our loving Subjects, have been humble Suitors unto us, that We would vouchsafe unto them our Licence, to make Habitation, Plantation, and to deduce a colony of sundry of our people into that part of *America* commonly called VIRGINIA, and other parts and Territories in *America,* either appertaining unto us, or which are not now actually possessed by any *Christian* Prince or People, situate, lying, and being all along the Sea Coasts, between four and thirty Degrees of *Northerly* Latitude from the Equinoctial Line, and five and forty Degrees of the same Latitude, and in the main Land between the same four and thirty and five and forty Degrees, and the Islands thereunto adjacent, or within one hundred Miles of the Coast thereof; *Names of founders of London and Plymouth companies*

And to that End, and for the more speedy Accomplishment of their said intended Plantation and Habitation there, are desirous to divide themselves into two several Colonies and Companies; the one consisting of certain Knights, Gentlemen, Merchants, and other Adventurers, of our City of *London* and elsewhere, which are, and from time to time shall be, joined unto them, which do desire to begin their Plantation and Habitation in some fit and convenient Place, between four and thirty and one and forty Degrees of the said Latitude, alongst the Coasts of *Virginia,* and the Coasts of *America* aforesaid: And the other consisting of sundry Knights, Gentlemen, Merchants, and other Adventurers, of our Cities of *Bristol* and *Exeter,* and of our Town of *Plimouth,* and of other Places, which do join themselves unto that Colony, which do desire to begin their Plantation and Habitation in some fit and convenient Place, between eight and thirty Degrees and five and forty Degrees of the said Latitude, all alongst the said Coasts of *Virginia* and *America,* as that Coast lyeth: *Origins of the founders*

We, greatly commending, and graciously accepting of, their Desires for the Furtherance of so noble a Work, which may, by the Providence of Almighty God, here- *Propagation of religion*

---

[25] Thorpe, *op. cit.,* VII, 3783-89. This charter was replaced in 1609 and 1612 by the second and third Virginia Charters. *Ibid.,* 3790-3810.

after tend to the Glory of his Divine Majesty, in propagating of *Christian* Religion to such People, as yet live in Darkness and miserable Ignorance of the true Knowledge and Worship of God, and may in time bring the Infidels and Savages, living in those parts, to human Civility, and to a settled and quiet Government: DO, by these our Letters Patents, graciously accept of, and agree to, their humble and well-intended Desires;

Territory of London Company

And do therefore, for Us, our Heirs, and Successors, GRANT and agree, that the said Sir *Thomas Gates,* Sir *George Somers, Richard Hackluit,* and *Edward-Maria Wingfield,* Adventurers of and for our City of *London,* and all such others, as are, or shall be, joined unto them of that Colony, shall be called the *first Colony;* And they shall and may begin their said first Plantation and Habitation, at any Place upon the said Coast of *Virginia* or *America,* where they shall think fit and convenient, between the said four and thirty and one and forty Degrees of the said Latitude; And that they shall have all the Lands, Woods, Soil, Grounds, Havens, Ports, Rivers, Mines, Minerals, Marshes, Waters, Fishings, Commodities, and Hereditaments, whatsoever, from the said first Seat of their Plantation and Habitation by the Space of fifty Miles of *English* Statute Measure, all along the said Coast of *Virginia* and *America,* towards the *West* and *Southwest,* as the Coast lyeth, with all the Islands within one hundred Miles directly over against the same Sea Coast; And also all the Lands, Soil, Grounds, Havens, Ports, Rivers, Mines, Minerals, Woods, Waters, Marshes, Fishings, Commodities, and Hereditaments, whatsoever, from the said Place of their first Plantation and Habitation for the space of fifty like *English* Miles, all alongst the said Coasts of *Virginia* and *America,* towards the *East* and *Northeast,* or towards the *North,* as the Coast lyeth, together with all the Islands within one hundred Miles, directly over against the said Sea Coast; And also all the Lands, Woods, Soil, Grounds, Havens, Ports, Rivers, Mines, Minerals, Marshes, Waters, Fishings, Commodities, and Hereditaments, whatsoever, from the same fifty Miles every way on the Sea Coast, directly into the main Land by the Space of one hundred like *English* Miles; And shall and may inhabit and remain there; and shall and may also build and fortify within any the same, for their better Safeguard and Defence, according to their best Discretion, and the Discretion of the Council of that Colony; And that no other of our Subjects shall be permitted, or suffered, to plant or inhabit behind, or on the Backside of them, towards the main Land, without the Express License or Consent of the Council of that Colony, thereunto in Writing first had and obtained.

Territory of Plymouth Company

And we do likewise, for Us, our Heirs, and Successors, by these Presents, GRANT and agree, that the said *Thomas Hanham,* and *Ralegh Gilbert, William Parker,* and *George Popham,* and all others of the Town of *Plimouth* in the County of *Devon,* or elsewhere, which are, or shall be, joined unto them of that Colony, shall be called the *second Colony;* And that they shall and may begin their said Plantation and Seat of their first Abode and Habitation, at any Place upon the said Coast of *Virginia* and *America,* where they shall think fit and convenient, between eight and thirty Degrees of the said Latitude, and five and forty Degrees of the same Latitude; And that they

THE FIRST CHARTER OF VIRGINIA

shall have all the Lands, Soils, Grounds, Havens, Ports, Rivers, Mines, Minerals, Woods, Marshes, Waters, Fishings, Commodities and Hereditaments, whatsoever, from the first Seat of their Plantation and Habitation by the Space of fifty like *English* Miles, as is aforesaid, all alongst the said Coasts of *Virginia* and *America,* towards the *West* and *Southwest,* or towards the *South,* as the Coast lyeth, and all the Islands within one hundred Miles, directly over against the said Sea Coast; And also all the Lands, Soils, Grounds, Havens, Ports, Rivers, Mines, Minerals, Woods, Marshes, Waters, Fishings, Commodities, and Hereditaments, whatsoever, from the said Place of their first Plantation and Habitation for the Space of fifty like Miles, all alongst the said Coast of *Virginia* and *America,* towards the *East* and *Northeast,* or towards the *North,* as the Coast lyeth, and all the Islands also within one hundred Miles directly over against the same Sea Coast; And also all the Lands, Soils, Grounds, Havens, Ports, Rivers, Woods, Mines, Minerals, Marshes, Waters, Fishings, Commodities, and Hereditaments, whatsoever, from the same fifty Miles every way on the Sea Coast, directly into the main Land, by the Space of one hundred like *English* Miles; And shall and may inhabit and remain there; and shall and may also build and fortify within any the same for their better Safeguard, according to their best Discretion, and the Discretion of the Council of that Colony; And that none of our Subjects shall be permitted, or suffered, to plant or inhabit behind, or on the back of them, towards the main Land, without express Licence of the Council of that Colony, in Writing thereunto first had and obtained.

Provided always, and our Will and Pleasure herein is, that the Plantation and Habitation of such of the said Colonies, as shall last plant themselves, as aforesaid, shall not be made within one hundred like *English* Miles of the other of them, that first began to make their Plantation, as aforesaid. *Colonies at least one hundred miles apart*

And we do also ordain, establish, and agree, for Us, our Heirs, and Successors, that each of the said Colonies shall have a Council, which shall govern and order all Matters and Causes, which shall arise, grow, or happen, to or within the same several Colonies, according to such Laws, Ordinances, and Instructions, as shall be, in that behalf, given and signed with Our Hand or Sign Manual, and pass under the Privy Seal of our Realm of *England;* Each of which Councils shall consist of thirteen Persons, to be ordained, made, and removed, from time to time, according as shall be directed and comprised in the same instructions; And shall have a several Seal, for all Matters, that shall pass or concern the same several Councils; Each of which Seals, shall have the King's Arms engraven on the one Side thereof, and his Portraiture on the other; And that the Seal for the Council of the said first Colony shall have engraven round about, on the one Side, these Words; *Sigillum Regis Magnae Britanniae, Franciae, & Hiberniae;* on the other Side this Inscription round about; *Pro Concilio primae Coloniae Virginiae.* And the Seal for the Council of the said second Colony shall also have engraven, round about the one Side thereof, the aforesaid Words; *Sigillum Regis Magnae Britanniae, Franciae, & Hiberniae;* and on the other Side; *Pro Concilio secundae Coloniae Virginiae:* *Colonial councils, their membership and powers*

Royal Council, its membership and powers

And that also there shall be a Council, established here in *England,* which shall, in like manner, consist of thirteen Persons, to be, for that Purpose, appointed by Us, our Heirs and Successors, which shall be called our *Council of Virginia;* And shall, from time to time, have the superior Managing and Direction, only of and for all Matters that shall or may concern the Government, as well of the said several Colonies, as of and for any other Part or Place, within the aforesaid Precincts of four and thirty and five and forty Degrees abovementioned; Which Council shall, in like manner, have a Seal, for Matters concerning the Council or Colonies, with the like Arms and Portraiture, as aforesaid, with this inscription, engraven round about on the one Side; *Sigillum Regis Magnae Britanniae, Franciae, & Hiberniae;* and round about on the other Side, *Pro Concilio suo Virginiae.*

Reservation of mineral rights by the crown

And moreover, we do GRANT and agree, for Us, our Heirs and Successors; that that the said several Councils of and for the said several Colonies, shall and lawfully may, by Virtue hereof, from time to time, without any Interruption of Us, our Heirs or Successors, give and take Order, to dig, mine, and search for all Manner of Mines of Gold, Silver, and Copper, as well within any Part of their said several Colonies, as of the said main Lands on the Backside of the same Colonies; And to HAVE and enjoy the Gold, Silver, and Copper, to be gotten thereof, to the Use and Behoof of the same Colonies, and the Plantations thereof; YIELDING therefore to Us, our Heirs and Successors, the fifth Part only of all the same Gold and Silver, and the fifteenth Part of all the same Copper, so to be gotten or had, as is aforesaid, without any other Manner of Profit or Account, to be given or yielded to Us, our Heirs, or Successors, for or in Respect of the same:

Authority to coin money

And that they shall, or lawfully may, establish and cause to be made a Coin, to pass current there between the people of those several Colonies, for the more Ease of Traffick and Bargaining between and amongst them and the Natives there, of such Metal, and in such Manner and Form, as the said several Councils there shall limit and appoint.

Authority to bring colonists

And we do likewise, for Us, our Heirs, and Successors, by these Presents, give full Power and Authority to the said Sir *Thomas Gates,* Sir *George Somers, Richard Hackluit, Edward-Maria Wingfield, Thomas Hanham, Ralegh Gilbert, William Parker,* and *George Popham,* and to every of them, and to the said several Companies, Plantations, and Colonies, that they, and every of them, shall and may, at all and every time and times hereafter, have, take, and lead in the said Voyage, and for and towards the said several Plantations, and Colonies, and to travel thitherward, and to abide and inhabit there, in every the said Colonies and Plantations, such and so many of our Subjects, as shall willingly accompany them or any of them, in the said Voyages and Plantations; With sufficient Shipping, and Furniture of Armour, Weapons, Ordinance, Powder, Victual, and all other things, necessary for the said Plantations, and for their Use and Defence there: PROVIDED always, that none of the said Persons be such, as shall hereafter be specially restrained by Us, our Heirs, or Successors.

THE FIRST CHARTER OF VIRGINIA

Moreover, we do, by these Presents, for Us, our Heirs, and Successors, GIVE AND GRANT Licence unto the said Sir *Thomas Gates,* Sir *George Somers, Richard Hackluit, Edward-Maria Wingfield, Thomas Hanham, Ralegh Gilbert, William Parker,* and *George Popham,* and to every of the said Colonies, that they, and every of them, shall and may, from time to time, and at all times forever hereafter, for their several Defences, encounter, expulse, repel, and resist, as well by Sea as by Land, by all Ways and Means whatsoever, all and every such Person or Persons, as without the especial Licence of the said several Colonies and Plantations, shall attempt to inhabit within the said several Precincts and Limits of the said several Colonies and Plantations, or any of them, or that shall enterprise or attempt, at any time hereafter, the Hurt, Detriment, or Annoyance, of the said several Colonies or Plantations: *Defense of colonies*

Giving and granting, by these Presents, unto the said Sir *Thomas Gates,* Sir *George Somers, Richard Hackluit, Edward-Maria Wingfield, Thomas Hanham, Ralegh Gilbert, William Parker,* and *George Popham,* and their Associates of the said second Colony, and to every of them, from time to time, and at all times for ever hereafter, Power and Authority to take and surprise, by all Ways and Means whatsoever, all and every Person and Persons, with their Ships, Vessels, Goods, and other Furniture, which shall be found trafficking, into any Harbour or Harbours, Creek or Creeks, or Place, within the Limits or Precincts of the said several Colonies and Plantations, not being of the same Colony, until such time, as they, being of any Realms, or Dominions under our Obedience, shall pay, or agree to pay, to the Hands of the Treasurer of that Colony, within whose Limits and Precincts they shall so traffick, two and a half upon every Hundred, of any thing so by them trafficked, bought, or sold; And being Strangers, and not Subjects under our Obeysance, until they shall pay five upon every Hundred, of such Wares and Merchandises, as they shall traffick, buy, or sell, within the Precincts of the said several Colonies, wherein they shall so traffick, buy, or sell, as aforesaid; WHICH Sums of Money, or Benefit, as aforesaid, for and during the Space of one and twenty Years, next ensuing the Date hereof, shall be wholly emploied to the Use, Benefit, and Behoof of the said several Plantations, where such Traffick shall be made; And after the said one and twenty Years ended, the same shall be taken to the Use of Us, our Heires, and Successors, by such Officers and Ministers as by Us, our Heirs, and Successors, shall be thereunto assigned or appointed. *Customs*

And we do further, by these Presents, for Us, our Heirs and Successors, GIVE AND GRANT unto the said Sir *Thomas Gates,* Sir *George Somers, Richard Hackluit,* and *Edward-Maria Wingfield,* and to their Associates of the said first Colony and Plantation, and to the said *Thomas Hanham, Ralegh Gilbert, William Parker,* and *George Popham,* and their Associates of the said second Colony and Plantation, that they, and every of them, by their Deputies, Ministers, and Factors, may transport the Goods, Chattels, Armour, Munition, and Furniture, needful to be used by them, for their said Apparel, Food, Defence, or otherwise in Respect of the said Plantations, out of our Realms of *England* and *Ireland,* and all other our Dominions, from time to time, for and during the Time of seven Years, next ensuing the Date hereof, for the *Same*

43

better Relief of the said several Colonies and Plantations, without any Customs, Subsidy, or other Duty, unto Us, our Heirs, or Successors, to be yielded or payed for the same.

Liberties of inhabitants   Also we do, for Us, our Heirs, and Successors, DECLARE, by these Presents, that all and every the Persons being our Subjects, which shall dwell and inhabit within every or any of the said several Colonies and Plantations, and every of their children, which shall happen to be born within any of the Limits and Precincts of the said several Colonies and Plantations, shall HAVE and enjoy all Liberties, Franchises, and Immunities, within any of our other Dominions, to all Intents and Purposes, as if they had been abiding and born, within this our Realm of *England*, or any other of our said Dominions.[26]

Forfeiture of illegal exports   Moreover, our gracious Will and Pleasure is, and we do, by these Presents, for Us, our Heirs, and Successors, declare and set forth, that if any Person or Persons, which shall be of any of the said Colonies and Plantations, or any other, which shall traffick to the said Colonies and Plantations, or any of them, shall, at any time or times hereafter, transport any Wares, Merchandises, or Commodities, out of any of our Dominions, with a Pretence to land, sell, or otherwise dispose of the same, within any the Limits and Precincts of any of the said Colonies and Plantations, and yet nevertheless, being at Sea, or after he hath landed the same within any of the said Colonies and Plantations, shall carry the same into any other Foreign Country, with a Purpose there to sell or dispose of the same, without the Licence of Us, our Heirs, and Successors, in that Behalf first had and obtained; That then, all the Goods and Chattels of such Person or Persons, so offending and transporting, together with the said Ship or Vessel, wherein such Transportation was made, shall be forfeited to Us, our Heirs, and Successors.

Punishment of robbers   Provided always, and our Will and Pleasure is, and we do hereby declare to all Christian Kings, Princes, and States, that if any Person or Persons which shall hereafter be of any of the said several Colonies and Plantations, or any other, by his, their, or any of their Licence and Appointment, shall, at any Time or Times hereafter, rob or spoil, by Sea or Land, or do any Act of unjust and unlawful Hostility to any the Subjects of Us, our Heirs, or Successors, or any the Subjects of any King, Prince, Ruler, Governor, or State, being then in League or Amitie with Us, our Heirs, or Successors, and that upon such Injury, or upon just Complaint of such Prince, Ruler, Governor, or State, or their Subjects, We, our Heirs, or Successors, shall make open Proclamation, within any of the Ports of our Realm of *England*, commodious for that purpose, That

[26] The Second Charter of Virginia, 1609, provided: "ALSO we do for Us, our Heirs and Successors, DECLARE by these Presents, that all and every the Persons being our Subjects, which shall go and inhabit within the said Colony and Plantation, and every their Children and Posterity, which shall happen to be born within any of the Limits thereof, shall HAVE and ENJOY all Liberties, Franchizes, and Immunities of Free Denizens and natural Subjects within any of our other Dominions to all Intents and Purposes, as if they had been abiding and born within this our Realm of *England*, or in any other of our Dominions." *Ibid.*, 3800. The Third Charter, 1612, provided that persons newly admitted to the company were to have "all and singular Freedoms, Liberties, Franchizes, Privileges, Immunities, Benefits, Profits, and Commodities whatsoever" as present members. *Ibid.*, 3806.

the said Person or Persons, having committed any such robbery, or Spoil, shall, within the term to be limited by such Proclamations, make full Restitution or Satisfaction of all such Injuries done, so as the said Princes, or others so complaining, may hold themselves fully satisfied and contented; And, that if the said Person or Persons, having commited such Robery or Spoil, shall not make, or cause to be made Satisfaction accordingly, within such Time so to be limited, That then it shall be lawful to Us, our Heirs, and Successors, to put the said Person or Persons, having committed such Robbery or Spoil, and their Procurers, Abettors, and Comforters, out of our Allegiance and Protection; And that it shall be lawful and free, for all Princes, and others to pursue with hostility the said offenders, and every of them, and their and every of their Procurers, Aiders, abettors, and comforters, in that behalf.

And finally, we do for Us, our Heirs, and Successors, GRANT and agree, to and with the said Sir *Thomas Gates*, Sir *George Somers, Richard Hackluit, Edward-Maria Wingfield,* and all others of the said first colony, that We, our Heirs and Successors, upon Petition in that Behalf to be made, shall, by Letters Patent under the Great Seal of *England,* GIVE and GRANT, unto such Persons, their Heirs and Assigns, as the Council of that Colony, or the most part of them, shall, for that Purpose nominate and assign all the lands, Tenements, and Hereditaments, which shall be within the Precincts limited for that Colony, as is aforesaid, TO BE HOLDEN of Us, our heirs and Successors, as of our Manor at *East-Greenwich,* in the County of *Kent,* in free and common Soccage only, and not in Capite: *Tenure of lands of London Company*

And do in like Manner, Grant and Agree, for Us, our Heirs and Successors, to and with the said *Thomas Hanham, Ralegh Gilbert, William Parker,* and *George Popham,* and all others of the said second Colony, That We, our Heirs, and Successors, upon Petition in that Behalf to be made, shall, by Letters-Patent, under the Great Seal of *England,* GIVE and GRANT, unto such Persons, their Heirs and Assigns, as the Council of that Colony, or the most Part of them, shall for that Purpose nominate and assign, all the Lands, Tenements, and Hereditaments, which shall be within the Precincts limited for that Colony, as is aforesaid, to BE HOLDEN of Us, our Heires, and Successors, as of our Manor of *East-Greenwich,* in the County of *Kent,* in free and common Soccage only, and not in Capite. *Tenure of lands of Plymouth Company*

All which Lands, Tenements, and Hereditaments, so to be passed by the said several Letters-Patent, shall be sufficient Assurance from the said Patentees, so distributed and divided amongst the Undertakers for the Plantation of the said several Colonies, and such as shall make their Plantations in either of the said several Colonies, in such Manner and Form, and for such Estates, as shall be ordered and set down by the Council of the said Colony, or the most part of them, respectively, within which the same Lands, Tenements, and Hereditaments shall lye or be; Although express Mention of the true yearly Value or Certainty of the Premises, or any of them, or of any other Gifts or Grants, by Us or any of our Progenitors or Predecessors, to the aforesaid Sir *Thomas Gates,* Knt. Sir *George Somers,* Knt. *Richard Hackluit, Edward-Maria Wingfield, Thomas Hanham, Ralegh Gilbert, William Parker,* and *George* *Distribution of land*

Popham, or any of them, heretofore made, in these Presents, is not made; Or any Statute, Act, Ordinance, or Provision, Proclamation, or Restraint, to the contrary hereof had, made, ordained, or any other Thing, Cause, or Matter whatsoever, in any wise notwithstanding. IN WITNESS whereof, we have caused these our Letters to be made Patent; Witness Ourself at *Westminster,* the tenth Day of *April,* in the fourth Year of our Reign of *England, France,* and *Ireland,* and of *Scotland* the nine and thirtieth.

LUKIN
Per breve de privato Sigillo.

REFERENCES

Andrews, Charles M. *The Colonial Period of American History.* 3 vols. New Haven: Yale University Press, 1934.
Brown, Alexander. *The First Republic in America.* Boston: Houghton Mifflin Co., 1898.
———. *The Genesis of the United States.* 2 vols. Boston: Houghton Mifflin Co., 1891.
Channing, Edward. *A History of the United States.* 6 vols. New York: Macmillan Co., 1927-30.
Cheyney, Edward P. *European Background of American History, 1300-1600* (Vol. I of *The American Nation: A History*). New York: Harper & Bros., 1904.
Osgood, Herbert L. *The American Colonies in the Seventeenth Century.* 3 vols. New York: Macmillan Co., 1904-7.
Reinsch, Paul S. "The English Common Law in the Early American Colonies," *Select Essays in Anglo-American Legal History.* Boston: Little, Brown and Co., 1907. I, 367-415.
Tyler, Lyon G. *England in America, 1580-1652* (Vol. IV of *The American Nation: A History*). New York: Harper & Bros., 1904.

IV. ORDINANCES FOR VIRGINIA
1618

The right of the American settlers to participate in the conduct of government by means of a legislative assembly was first established in 1618 in Virginia. That this right was not considered to be one of the "rights of Englishmen" secured by the Virginia Charters of 1606 and 1609 is hardly surprising. In the early part of the seventeenth century the relative unimportance of Parliament in comparison with the Privy Council and the Star Chamber and the property qualifications imposed upon electors made the right to vote much less important to the average citizen than it is today.

Origins

By 1618 it had become clear that, if the colony at Jamestown was ever to prosper, the government would have to be drastically reformed. The administration of Sir Thomas Dale as Deputy Governor was particularly overbearing. The colonists were governed by a code of martial laws,[1] and were cruelly treated in various ways. They considered the punishments inflicted by Dale for minor violations of the law to be "extraordinary." These included shooting, hanging, burning, breaking on the wheel, and starving to death in chains for such offenses as obtaining food from the Indians, stealing food, and attempting to return to England. Lesser offenses were punished by whippings and sentences to slavery in irons for terms of years.[2] It was hoped that Captain Samuel Argall, who replaced Dale in 1616, would govern more justly, but he proved to be completely unscrupulous.[3]

Administrations of Dale and Argall

---

[1] See pp. 36-37.

[2] "A Breife Declaration of the Plantation of Virginia Duringe the First Twelve Years," *Colonial Records of Virginia*, Senate Document (Extra) (Richmond, 1874), 74.

[3] Lyon G. Tyler, *England in America, 1580-1652*, Vol. IV of *The American Nation: A History*, ed. A. B. Hart (28 vols.; New York, 1904-18), 77-78.

Yeardley and the Great Charter

In April, 1618, steps were taken by the company officials in England to have Argall arrested and removed from office, and Sir George Yeardley was sent over as governor a year later. "From the moment of Yeardley's arrival dates the real life of Virginia."[4] He abolished the cruel laws of the former administrations, and put into effect a new code of laws which, among other things, called for the establishment of a legislative assembly. This document, issued by the company November 28, 1618, was called by the colonists the "Great Charter" because of its importance and the respect in which they held it.[5]

Sandys' influence

It was the political philosophy of Sir Edwin Sandys, one of the most influential members of the Virginia Company, which guided the movement for reform. His ideals of government included greater religious toleration, the abolition of the relics of feudalism, the establishment of freedom of trade together with the overthrow of monopolies, and the limitation of monarchical institutions, particularly the king's prerogative.[6] As a member of the parliamentary opposition in England, Sandys was having little success in making his views prevail against the monarchical absolutism of James I (1603-25). These views, however, found expression in Virginia in 1618 when the faction of the London Company to which he belonged secured control of the direction of the colony. To promote the growth of the colony and the welfare of the settlers Sandys favored the abandonment of monopolistic policies together with the plantation system which accompanied it; he encouraged the establishment of private plantations, the granting of land on easy conditions, freedom of trade, and more emigration to the colony. To promote these reforms he realized that it would be necessary to elicit the fullest cooperation of the colonists themselves, and the establishment of a popular assembly proved to be an effective means to this end.[7]

Effects

Elections had been held in the summer of 1619, and on July 30 the first legislative assembly to be convened on the American continent met in the church at Jamestown. The assembly consisted of the governor, six councilors, and twenty burgesses. The right of suffrage was broader than in England,

---

[4] George Bancroft, *Colonial Records of Virginia*, Introductory Note, vi.

[5] Edward Channing, *History of the United States*, Vol. I: *The Planting of a Nation in the New World, 1000-1660* (New York, 1928), 203-4; Charles M. Andrews, *The Colonial Period of American History* (New Haven, 1934), I, 180-84.

[6] Channing, *op. cit.*, I, 191-93.

[7] Herbert L. Osgood, *The American Colonies in the Seventeenth Century* (New York, 1904), I, 91-92; Channing, *op. cit.*, I, 196-98.

ORDINANCES FOR VIRGINIA

and possibly even indentured servants were allowed to vote for the burgesses.[8] The assembly remained in session for six days and made substantial accomplishments. It was then prorogued by Governor Yeardley until March 1 because of the intemperate weather and the sickness of many of the members. Before it adjourned, however, it passed two important resolutions. One of these requested the company that laws passed by the assembly should continue in force until disapproved by the company, "for otherwise this people (who nowe at length have gotte the raines of former servitude into their owne swindge) would in shorte time growe so insolent, as they would shake off all government, and there would be no living among them."[9] The second request was that the assembly should be given power to approve or disapprove the orders of the company's Quarter Court.[10]

Once the colonists had been freed from the oppression of the Dale and Argall administrations, there was a remarkable improvement in their condition. The colonists themselves regarded the new assembly as the major cause of their prosperity, and for several years it seemed as though Sandys' dream of a prosperous self-governing community would be realized.[11]

The Virginia Company's charter, however, was revoked in 1624 because of its many failures in the past and because its weakened condition made the likelihood of improved management doubtful.[12] This action destroyed

Dissolution of the Virginia Company

---

[8] It was not until 1670 that the voting laws of Virginia were brought into accord with the law of England, which extended the franchise only to property owners. Andrews, *op. cit.*, I, 184-85.

[9] *Colonial Records of Virginia*, 31.

[10] *Ibid.*, 31-32.

[11] A declaration of the colonists in 1624 stated: "And that they might have a hande in the governinge of themselves, it was granted that a general assemblie should be helde yearly once, wherat were to be present the Govr and Counsell with two Burgesses from each Plantation freely to be elected by the inhabitants thereof; this assembly to have power to make and ordaine whatsoever lawes and orders should by them be thought good and proffittable for our subsistance. The effect of which proceedinge gave such incouragement to every person heere that all of them followed their perticular labours with singular alacrity and industry, soe that, through the blessinge of God uppon our willinge labors, within the space of three yeares, our countrye flourished with many new erected Plantations, from the head of the River to Kicoughtan, beautifull and pleasant to the spectators, and comfortable for the releife and succor of all such as by occasion did travaile by land or by water; every man giveinge free entertainment, both to frendes or others. The plenty of these times likewise was such that all men generally were sufficiently furnished with corne, and many alsoe had plenty of cattle, swine, poultry and other good provisions to nourish them. Monethly courtes were held in every precinct to doe justice in redressinge of all small and petty matters, others of more consequence beinge referred to the Govr, Counsell and Generall Assemblie. Now alsoe were begunne and sett a foote the erectinge of Iron Workes, plantinge of vines and mulberrie trees for the nourishinge of silke wormes; a trial made for silke grasse tillage for English graine, gardeninge, and the like, which gave great hopes of present and future plenty in their severall perticulars, wherein no doubt but much more had been effected had not great sicknes and mortalitie prevented." "A Breife Declaration," *Colonial Records of Virginia*, 81-82.

[12] Other factors of a political nature also played a part in deciding the case against the company. Wesley F. Craven, *Dissolution of the Virginia Company* (New York, 1932), 292-95.

49

SOURCES OF OUR LIBERTIES

the legal basis of the legislative assembly, but the desire of the colonists for self-government continued. Shortly before the company was dissolved, the assembly requested that the royal governors that were to be sent over should not be given overpowering authority; that the right of the local council to act in an advisory capacity should be recognized; and that a general assembly should be allowed, "then wch nothing can more conduce to our satisfaction or the publique utilitie." It was also requested that the governor should not be allowed to levy taxes upon the colony without the consent of the assembly.[13] Between 1624 and 1639 there was no authorization for a colonial lawmaking body. Several assemblies were convened, however, to consider special matters during that period. In the instructions to Governor Wyatt in 1639 and those to Governor Berkeley in 1641 royal consent for a regular assembly was given.[14] These developments in Virginia became a precedent for the other colonies and the legislative assemblies became one of the principal features of colonial administration.[15]

Later Significance By the beginning of the eighteenth century the colonial assemblies were regarded as having functions and powers very similar to those exercised by Parliament in England. The assemblies regarded themselves as smaller replicas of the British House of Commons, having all the rights and prerogatives of that house, especially in matters of taxation. Writing in 1724, Hugh Jones said that the Virginia burgesses

> meet, chose a Speaker, &c. and proced in most Respects as the *House of Commons* in *England*, who with the *Upper House*, consisting of the *Governor and Council*, make Laws exactly as the *King* and *Parliament* do; the Laws being passed there by the *Governor*, as by the *King* here.[16]

The development of the legislative assembly thus began with the government established by the London trading company. It was the Quarter Court, a gathering of the generality of the company for the purpose of making im-

---

[13] Andrews, *op. cit.*, I, 190-91.

[14] The instructions to Wyatt ordered him: "as formerly once a year or oftener, if urgent occasion shall require, to summon the burgesses of all and singular plantations there, which together with the governor and council shall have power to make acts and laws for the government of that plantation, correspondent as near as may be to the laws of England, in which assembly the governor was to have a negative voice as formerly." Quoted in *ibid.*, 204.

[15] Assemblies were established in the other colonies in the following years: Massachusetts, 1634; Connecticut, 1639; Maryland, 1639; Rhode Island, 1647; North Carolina, 1667; New Jersey, 1668; South Carolina, 1674; New Hampshire, 1680; Pennsylvania, 1682; Delaware, 1682; New York, 1683; Georgia, 1754. Richard Frothingham, *The Rise of the Republic of the United States* (Boston, 1890), 18n.

[16] *The Present State of Virginia* (London, 1724), 63.

portant decisions, which furnished the immediate model for the assembly of 1619. From these beginnings in Virginia and elsewhere the colonial assemblies eventually became the dominant factor in American government, and the right of the people to representative government became one of the most cherished landmarks of American liberties.

ORDINANCES FOR VIRGINIA[17]
(*November 28, 1618*)
July 24, 1621

Preamble

TO all People, to whom these Presents shall come, be seen, or heard, The Treasurer, Council, and Company of Adventurers and Planters for the City of *London* for the first Colony of *Virginia,* send Greeting. KNOW YE, that we, the said Treasurer, Council, and Company, taking into our careful Consideration the present State of the said Colony of *Virginia,* and intending, by the Divine Assistance, to settle such a Form of Government there, as may be to the greatest Benefit and Comfort of the People, and whereby all Injustice, Grievances, and Oppression may be prevented and kept off as much as possible from the said Colony, have thought fit to make our Entrance, by ordering and establishing such Supreme Councils, as may not only be assisting to the Governor for the time being, in the Administration of Justice, and the executing of other Duties to this office belonging, but also, by their vigilant care and Prudence, may provide, as well for a Remedy of all Inconveniences, growing from time to time, as also for advancing of Increase, Strength, Stability, and Prosperity of the said Colony:

Establishment of two supreme councils

II. WE therefore, the said Treasurer, Council, and Company, by Authority directed to us from his Majesty under the Great Seal, upon mature Deliberation, do hereby order and declare, that, from hence forward, there shall be TWO SUPREME COUNCILS in *Virginia,* for the better Government of the said Colony aforesaid.

Council of State

III. THE one of which Councils, to be called THE COUNCIL OF STATE (and whose Office shall chiefly be assisting, with their Care, Advise, and Circumspection, to the said Governor) shall be chosen, nominated, placed and displaced, from time to time, by Us, the said Treasurer, Council, and Company, and our Successors: Which Council of State shall consist, for the present, only of these Persons, as are here inserted, *viz.* Sir *Francis Wyat,* Governor of *Virginia,* Captain *Francis West,* Sir *George Yeardley,* Knight, Sir *William Neuce,* Knight Marshal of *Virginia,* Mr. *George Sandys,* Treasurer, Mr. *George Thorpe,* Deputy of the College, Captain

---

[17] Francis N. Thorpe (ed.), *The Federal and State Constitutions, Colonial Charters, and Other Organic Laws* (Washington, 1909), VII, 3810-12. Articles 1-5 of the Ordinances of July 24, 1621, are believed to be almost identical to some of the provisions of a lost document issued November 28, 1618, under which the first Assembly of Virginia was convened by Governor Yeardley. The text of the Ordinances of 1621 is given here. Channing, *op. cit.,* 203-4; Andrews, *op. cit.,* I, 180-84.

ORDINANCES FOR VIRGINIA

Thomas Neuce, Deputy for the Company, Mr. *Pawlet*, Mr. *Leech*, Captain *Nathaniel Powel*, Mr. *Christopher Davison*, Secretary, Doctor *Pots*, Physician to the Company, Mr. *Roger Smith*, Mr. *John Berkeley*, Mr. *John Rolfe*, Mr. *Ralph Hamer*, Mr. *John Pountis*, Mr. *Michael Lapworth*, Mr. *Harwood*, Mr. *Samuel Macock.* Which said Counsellors and Council we earnestly pray and desire, and in his Majesty's Name strictly charge and command, that (all Factions, Partialities, and sinister Respect laid aside) they bend their Care and Endeavours to assist the said Governor; first and principally, in the Advancement of the Honour and Service of God, and the Enlargement of his Kingdom amongst the Heathen People; and next, in erecting of the said Colony in due obedience to his Majesty, and all lawful Authority from his Majesty's Directions; and lastly, in maintaining the said People in Justice and *Christian* Conversation amongst themselves, and in Strength and Ability to withstand their Enemies. And this Council, to be always, or for the most Part, residing about or near the Governor. *Its powers*

IV. THE other Council, more generally to be called by the Governor, once yearly, and no oftener, but for very extraordinary and important occasions, shall consist, for the present, of the said Council of State, and of two Burgesses out of every Town, Hundred, or other particular Plantation, to be respectively chosen by the Inhabitants: Which Council shall be called THE GENERAL ASSEMBLY, wherein (as also in the said Council of State) all Matters shall be decided, determined, and ordered, by the greater Part of the Voices then present; reserving to the Governor always a Negative Voice. And this General Assembly shall have free Power to treat, consult, and conclude, as well of all emergent Occasions concerning the Publick Weal of the said Colony and every Part thereof, as also to make, ordain, and enact such general Laws and Orders, for the Behoof of the said Colony, and the good Government thereof, as shall, from time to time, appear necessary or requisite; *General Assembly*

V. WHEREAS in all other Things, we require the said General Assembly, as also the said Council of State, to imitate and follow the Policy of the Form of Government, Laws, Customs, and Manner of Trial, and other Administration of Justice, used in the Realm of *England*, as near as may be, even as ourselves, by his Majesty's Letters Patent, are required. *Applicability of English laws*

VI. PROVIDED, that no Law or Ordinance, made in the said General Assembly, shall be or continue in Force or Validity, unless the same shall be solemnly ratified and confirmed, in a General Quarter Court of the said Company here in England and so ratified, be returned to them under our Seal; It being our Intent to afford the like Measure also unto the said Colony, that after the Government of the said Colony shall once have been well framed, and settled accordingly, which is to be done by Us, as by Authority derived from his Majesty, and the same shall have been so by us declared, no Orders of Court afterwards shall bind the said Colony, unless they be ratified in like Manner in the General Assemblies. IN WITNESS whereof we have hereunto set our Common Seal, the 24th of *July* 1621, and in the Year of the Reign of our Sovereign Lord, JAMES, King of *England*, &c., the *** and of Scotland the ***. *Ratification of laws by the company* *By the General Assembly*

REFERENCES

See also references on p. 46.

Andrews, Charles M. *The Colonial Period of American History.* 3 vols. New Haven: Yale University Press, 1934. I, chaps. 8, 9.

Channing, Edward. *A History of the United States.* 6 vols. New York: Macmillan Co., 1928. I, chap. 7.

Craven, Wesley F. *Dissolution of the Virginia Company.* New York: Oxford University Press, 1932.

Neill, Edward D. *History of the Virginia Company of London.* Albany: Joel Munsell, 1869.

V. MAYFLOWER COMPACT
1620

The Mayflower Compact was one of the most significant political products of the great religious struggles which rocked the world during the sixteenth and seventeenth centuries. It is famous not only for the ideas contained in its few lines but also for the ideas which lie behind the document. One of the most important of these, and the one which furnished the original motive for the action of the Pilgrim Fathers, was the objection of the Pilgrims to the institution of a state religion as had been established in England during the reigns of Elizabeth I and James I.[1]

The Pilgrim Fathers were among the Separatists, who had long suffered persecution for their religious beliefs.[2] As early as 1593 some of the Separatists had fled to Holland, which was the only country at that time sufficiently enlightened to open its doors to all religions. The Pilgrim Fathers came from a later group which was first formed at Scrooby, in central England. Before long their teachings brought them into conflict with the authorities. Some

Origins

---

[1] The government's policy was fixed shortly after the accession of Elizabeth by the Act of Supremacy, 1 Eliz. 1, c. 1, which required all clergymen and officeholders to renounce both the spiritual and the temporal jurisdiction of foreign princes and prelates, and by the Act of Uniformity, 1 Eliz. 1, c. 2, which required ministers to use the form of service established by Parliament. These statutes were directed primarily against the Catholic Church, and were supplemented and extended in later years by additional legislation. See Edward P. Cheyney, *European Background of American History, 1300-1600*, Vol. I of *The American Nation: A History*, ed. A. B. Hart (28 vols.; New York, 1904-18), 200-9. With the accession of James I there arose a strong hope that the minority Protestant groups would be able to obtain relaxation of the rigid forms of worship which had previously been required. These hopes, however, were shattered early in the reign. *Ibid.*, 209-11; Edward Channing, *A History of the United States* (New York, 1928), I, 273-77, 283.

[2] Channing divides the Puritan groups into the Nonconformists, who continued to attend church services but sought to gain control for the church and mold it to their will; the Independents, who were turned out of the church and had little interest in the beliefs of others; and the Brownists or Separatists, who opposed the existence of the established church. *Ibid.*, 272-73, 283-84. Cf. Kenneth S. Latourette, *A History of Christianity* (New York, 1953), 813-16.

were jailed and others were fined by the Court of High Commission for disobedience in matters of religion. The Scrooby congregation fled to Holland in 1608 under the leadership of John Robinson.[3] They stayed there together during the twelve years' truce between Spain and Holland.

In order to improve their circumstances and preserve their identity as a religious body, they decided to emigrate to Virginia. John Carver and Robert Cushman went to London where Sir Edwin Sandys, who had been instrumental in the granting of the Virginia Ordinance of 1618,[4] aided them in obtaining patents for this purpose from the London Company.[5] In June, 1620, a patent was issued in the name of John Pierce and his associates, and the Pilgrims started their long voyage, going first from Holland to England where they joined friends from London. They experienced some difficulty in getting underway, but finally left Plymouth aboard the "Mayflower" on September 16, 1620 with 149 persons aboard.[6]

Most of the passengers aboard the "Mayflower" were not Pilgrims. The Pilgrims, however, were the dominant group, and their manner of governing reflected the forms of church organization to which they were accustomed. The "Mayflower's" destination was a point south of the Hudson River, within the Virginia patent; but they missed their course and found themselves in Cape Cod Bay. Their leaders probably knew that area, and so it is not likely that strenuous objections were made to the decision to settle there instead of proceeding south to Virginia.[7] The compact was drawn

[3] They had attempted to escape in 1607 in a ship hired at Boston, Lincolnshire, but were betrayed by the captain to the police, who rifled them of their money and goods and confined them in jail. When they did succeed in making good their escape, some members of the group were left behind because a band of soldiers approached the ship just as the passengers were boarding. Some gave up all thought of escape at this time. The rest made their way to Holland by the summer of 1608. Lyon G. Tyler, *England in America, 1508-1652*, Vol. IV of *The American Nation: A History*, ed. A. B. Hart (28 vols.; New York, 1904-18), 156; George F. Willison, *Saints and Strangers* (New York, 1945), 55-58.

[4] See pp. 48, 52-54.

[5] Sandys was not only willing but even anxious to have the Pilgrims settle in Virginia, and he wished to give them the privileges of civil and political liberty. The emigration of the Pilgrims has been said to be as much a result of the popular policy under the Virginia Charter as was the creation of the House of Burgesses. Alexander Brown, *The First Republic in America* (Boston, 1898), 262-63.

[6] Some 30 of the 238 members of the Leyden church participated in the voyage. They purchased the "Speedwell" aboard which they sailed to Southampton where they were joined by Carver and Cushman, who had recently come from London in the "Mayflower." The "Mayflower" had been hired by Weston and the merchants adventurers who were financially supporting the journey. The Pilgrims left Southampton on August 5, but were forced to turn back because the "Speedwell" proved unseaworthy. The "Mayflower" was not able to carry all the passengers, and those left behind returned to London. Charles M. Andrews, *The Colonial Period of American History* (New Haven, 1934), I, 267-69.

[7] *Ibid.*, 272n.

up and signed while the Pilgrims were still aboard the "Mayflower" at anchor in the bay.

The compact's simplicity in form and language is deceptive. Its true significance and the purposes it was intended to fulfill are really complex and somewhat obscure. It was much more than an extemporaneous solution advanced under circumstances which were unforeseen. The patent granted to John Pierce in 1620 by the Virginia Company was of no legal value to the Pilgrims because they settled outside the territorial boundaries over which the Virginia Company had jurisdiction. It is significant, however, that the Pierce patent authorized the Pilgrims to form their own government. It is possible, therefore, to view the compact as the fulfillment of what had been contemplated at the time the Pilgrims sailed.[8] The origins of the compact, however, go even deeper than this. The document represents the application to the affairs of civil government of the philosophy of the church covenant which was the basis of Puritan theology. This theology found in the Scriptures the right of men to associate and covenant to form a church and civil government and to choose their own officers to administer both religious and civil affairs. Each member of the congregation had a vote in the election of officers, and each congregation was considered as independent and autonomous of every other and not subject to the authority of any centralized church hierarchy.[9] The compact may also be viewed as an extension of the old sea law under which it was customary for the passengers on long voyages to agree upon a rudimentary government of their own during the long weeks aboard ship.[10] Another motive which had some influence

General Significance

The Pierce patent

The church covenant

The sea law

---

[8] The second Pierce patent, which was obtained from the Council for New England in 1621, provided: ". . . Yt shalbe lawfull for the said John Peirce his Associates Vndertakers and Planters their heires and assignes by consent of the greater part of them to establish such Lawes and ordynaunces as are for their better governem[en]t, and the same by such Officer or Officers as they shall by most voyces elect and choose to put in execūcon." Quoted in William Bradford, *History of Plymouth Plantation, 1620-1647* (Massachusetts Historical Society, 1912), I, 249-50. This language was probably also used in the first Pierce patent. Andrews, *op. cit.*, I, 279-80, 292.

[9] The relationship between the church covenant and the Mayflower Compact is developed at length in Andrew C. McLaughlin, *The Foundations of American Constitutionalism* (New York, 1932), chap. 1. Behind the compact lie the Puritan beliefs in the word of God as a higher law, the establishment of the higher law in written documents, and the formation of government by the consent of individuals. Each of these doctrines played an important role in the development of American constitutional theories. In this connection, it is significant that one of the reasons for the compact assigned by Bradford is "that shuch an acte by them done (this their condition considered) might be as firme as any patent, and in some respects more sure." *Op. cit.*, I, 190.

[10] This explanation of the Mayflower Compact does not rest upon either the patent from the Virginia Company or the religious philosophy of the Separatists. Some support for this theory is given by the fact that Bradford, after describing the drawing of the compact, said, "After this they chose, or rather confirmed, Mr. John Carver (a man godly and well approved amongst them) their Governour

The threat-ened rebellion when the compact was drawn was the desire of the leaders to avoid a rebellion threatened by some of the passengers by obtaining their assent before going ashore to whatever government might be established.[11]

Effects The administration of justice and other functions of government were handled entirely by the governor and the council. The freemen were entitled to vote at elections, but were not convened by the governor for other purposes except where especially weighty questions were concerned. The first major deviation from the Pilgrim ideal of a single covenanted body of Christians, united for civil as well as spiritual purposes, occurred in 1643 when a representative system replaced the old meeting of the freemen.[12] Trial by jury was introduced as early as 1623,[13] and in 1624 a long step toward private ownership of land was taken when permanent allotments of one acre each were made to the settlers.[14]

The plantation covenants The Mayflower Compact was the earliest of a long series of plantation covenants which formed the basis for the earliest governments in New England.[15] These covenants had a special importance for many years because the Council for New England never established a central government as had been done in Virginia.[16] Although the Pilgrims made several attempts to secure a royal charter, they were unsuccessful. Their right to exist as a self-governing state, therefore, always rested upon the Mayflower Compact.[17]

With the new colonial and commercial policy instituted by England after 1660 and with the rising dominance of Plymouth's northern neighbor, the

for that year." *Op. cit.*, I, 192. The reference to Carver's being "confirmed" may have meant that Carver had been governor aboard ship under the sea law. See McLaughlin, *op. cit.*, 24n.

[11] Bradford said: ". . . occasioned partly by the discontented and mutinous speeches that some of the strangers amongst them had let fall from them in the ship; That when they came a shore they would use their owne libertie; for none had power to command them, the patente they had being for Virginia, and not for New england, which belonged to an other Goverment, with which the Virginia Company had nothing to doe." *Op. cit.*, I, 189.

[12] Andrews, *op. cit.*, I, 296.

[13] Before that time there is no record of any order concerning judicial administration. Herbert L. Osgood, *The American Colonies in the Seventeenth Century* (New York, 1904), I, 294.

[14] Andrews, *op. cit.*, I, 284.

[15] These covenants were framed in Dover, Exeter, Providence, New Haven, Portsmouth, Newport, and in many other towns. McLaughlin, *op. cit.*, 25-29; Osgood, *op. cit.*, I, 291.

[16] Andrews, *op. cit.*, I, 280-81.

[17] The compact was, of course, buttressed by the Pierce patents, and the patent which Allerton later obtained for Bradford and his associates. *Ibid.*, 294-95. Text in Francis N. Thorpe (ed.), *The Federal and State Constitutions, Colonial Charters, and Other Organic Laws* (Washington, 1909), III, 1841-46.

Massachusetts Bay Colony, the absence of a legal right to exist proved to be the undoing of the colony, and in 1691 Plymouth was annexed to Massachusetts. By that time, however, the Mayflower Compact had firmly established its place in history as one of the earliest examples of the right of self-government to be found in America.

MAYFLOWER COMPACT[18]

November 11, 1620

IN THE NAME OF GOD, AMEN. We, whose names are underwritten, the Loyal Subjects of our dread Sovereign Lord King *James,* by the Grace of God, of *Great Britain, France,* and *Ireland,* King, *Defender of the Faith,* &c. Having undertaken for the Glory of God, and Advancement of the Christian Faith, and the Honour of our King and Country, a Voyage to plant the first Colony in the northern Parts of *Virginia;* Do by these Presents, solemnly and mutually, in the Presence of God and one another, covenant and combine ourselves together into a civil Body Politick, for our better Ordering and Preservation, and Furtherance of the Ends aforesaid: And by Virtue hereof do enact, constitute, and frame, such just and equal Laws, Ordinances, Acts, Constitutions, and Officers, from time to time, as shall be thought most meet and convenient for the general Good of the Colony; unto which we promise all due Submission and Obedience. IN WITNESS whereof we have hereunto subscribed our names at *Cape-Cod* the eleventh of *November,* in the Reign of our Sovereign Lord King *James, of England, France,* and *Ireland,* the eighteenth, and of *Scotland,* the fifty-fourth, *Anno Domini,* 1620.

Mr. John Carver,	Mr. Samuel Fuller,	Edward Tilly,
Mr. William Bradford,	Mr. Christopher Martin,	John Tilly,
Mr. Edward Winslow,	Mr. William Mullins,	Francis Cooke,
Mr. William Brewster,	Mr. William White,	Thomas Rogers,
Isaac Allerton,	Mr. Richard Warren,	Thomas Tinker,
Myles Standish,	John Howland,	John Ridgdale,
John Alden,	Mr. Steven Hopkins,	Edward Fuller,
John Turner,	Digery Priest,	Richard Clark,
Francis Eaton,	Thomas Williams,	Richard Gardiner,
James Chilton,	Gilbert Winslow,	Mr. John Allerton,
John Craxton,	Edmund Margesson,	Thomas English,
John Billington,	Peter Brown,	Edward Doten,
Joses Fletcher,	Richard Bitteridge,	Edward Liester.
John Goodman,	George Soule,	

[18] *Ibid.,* III, 1841. The original list of signers has disappeared. Nathaniel Morton, writing in 1669, listed forty-one signers of the document. Channing, *op. cit.,* I, 308.

REFERENCES

See also references on p. 96.

Andrews, Charles M. *The Colonial Period of American History.* 3 vols. New Haven: Yale University Press, 1934. I, chaps. 13, 14.

Bancroft, George. *History of the United States of America.* 3 vols. Author's last revision; New York: Appleton and Co., 1892. I, chap. 12.

Channing, Edward. *A History of the United States.* 6 vols. New York: Macmillan Co., 1928. I, chap. 11.

McLaughlin, Andrew C. *The Foundations of American Constitutionalism.* New York: New York University Press, 1932. Chap. 1.

Osgood, Herbert L. *The American Colonies in the Seventeenth Century.* 3 vols. New York: Macmillan Co., 1904. I, chap. 5.

Tyler, Lyon G. *England in America, 1580-1652* (Vol. IV of *The American Nation: A History*). New York: Harper & Bros., 1904. Chaps. 9, 10.

Willison, George F. *Saints and Strangers.* New York: Reynal and Hitchcock, 1945.

VI. PETITION OF RIGHT
1628

General Significance By recourse to ancient principles of the English constitution, the Petition of Right announced important restrictions upon government by prerogative as practiced by Charles I (1625-49) in violation of the principles of individual liberty. It struck at prerogative taxation, which was the power of the king to exact taxes without the consent of Parliament; it provided that prisoners committed at the king's command should be freed on bail before trial; it declared illegal the quartering of troops in private houses; and it forbade the trial of civilians under the martial law. Parliament presented the grievances of the people in the form of a petition to the king, asserting that no more was asked than the observance of existing laws. Although no change in the law was intended, several important points were clarified by the document. Once the royal assent had been secured, these points became established as part of the law of the land.

The Petition of Right was "the first of those great constitutional documents since Magna Carta, which safeguard the liberties of the people by securing the supremacy of the law."[1] It has also been called "the second Great Charter of the liberties of England"[2] and "the first great official interpretation of Magna Carta since the time of Edward III."[3]

Origins
Reign of Elizabeth I The Tudor monarchs had assumed powers for the protection of the middle classes against the great landowners and for the support of the national church against foreign ecclesiastical organizations. Elizabeth I had generally acted with sagacity and moderation, but such matters as the power of the

---

[1] William Holdsworth, *A History of English Law* (Boston, 1937), V, 449.
[2] Thomas Macaulay, *The History of England*, ed. Charles H. Firth (London, 1913-15), I, 74.
[3] Rodney L. Mott, *Due Process of Law* (Indianapolis, 1926), 81. See also Samuel R. Gardiner (ed.), *The Constitutional Documents of the Puritan Revolution, 1625-1660* (Oxford, 1906), xx.

crown to levy impositions, which were customs duties not voted by Parliament, the power to remove judges, and the increasing importance of prerogative courts such as the Court of Star Chamber and the Court of High Commission all contained germs of oppression.

Reign of James I

Abuses occurred when these powers came into the hands of less scrupulous rulers. These potentialities became manifest during the reign of James I (1603-25). Twice during his reign he raised a benevolence by means of "privy seals," which were strongly worded invitations for donations to the crown conveyed in letters from the Privy Council. James also levied heavy impositions. This form of taxation was upheld by the Court of Exchequer in 1607 in *Bates' Case*.[4] James at once began to use this almost unlimited source of revenue not only to meet the expenditures of the kingdom but also to satisfy the lavish generosity he customarily bestowed upon court favorites. As the result of parliamentary protests to the exactions, a noteworthy compromise was attempted in 1610 between James and the Commons whereby the king agreed not to levy the impositions without the consent of Parliament.[5] Had the compromise been successful, it is possible that the Petition of Right would never have been necessary. It fell through, however, and later protests by the Commons against the impositions proved unavailing.

Reign of Charles I

Problems arising in the reign of James I continued, and even became intensified, during that of Charles I (1625-49). Parliament was dissatisfied with the conduct of the war with Spain under the management of the king's chief

---

[4] *State Trials* (T. B. Howell, comp.), II, 371. In 1606 John Bates, a merchant, refused to pay a duty on the ground that the king had no legal power to take it without a grant from Parliament. Judgment was given for the king. In the course of his opinion, Baron Clark said, ". . . in these cases of prerogative the judgment shall not be according to the rules of the common law, but according to the precedents of this court, wherein these matters are disputable and determinable." *Ibid.*, 383. The precedents were found to be in favor of the power. In addition, it was pointed out that because the king had complete power to permit or forbid imports and exports he might tax them.

Of this decision it has been said that no judges could be "more peremptory in resisting an attempt to overthrow the most established precedents than were these barons of King James's Exchequer in giving away those fundamental liberties which were the inheritance of every Englishman." Henry Hallam, *The Constitutional History of England* (5th ed.; New York, 1847), 185. On the other hand, it has been pointed out that "Whatever may have been the value of the statutes and precedents quoted, at the bar and on the bench . . . the judges were the only authorised exponents of the law, and the judges had decided that James's claim was legal." Gardiner, *op. cit.*, xiv-xv.

[5] In 1608 James had raised the value of the impositions to £75,000, a sum that would increase in future years with the increasing trade of the country. Under the compromise James agreed to strike off about a third of the new impositions, and the remainder was to be sanctioned by act of Parliament. It was also agreed that neither James nor his successors would again levy duties without the consent of Parliament. This compromise, however, was dependent on a larger bargain, known as the Great Contract, by which all military tenures were to be converted into free socage, and wardship and other feudal dues were to be given up in exchange for a grant of £200,000 to the king as a permanent revenue. When the Great Contract failed, the compromise on the impositions also failed. *Ibid.*, xiv; Samuel R. Gardiner, *History of England* (3d ed.; London, 1889), II, 63-87, 106-8.

adviser, the Duke of Buckingham. The first Parliament of Charles' reign showed its discontent by failing to grant supplies to the king. In retaliation the king dissolved Parliament. By 1626 the king's need for money had become pressing, but the Commons remained adamant. They focused all their hostilities upon the Duke of Buckingham, whom they proceeded to impeach. The king again dissolved Parliament and was soon forced to resort to various forms of prerogative taxation in order to raise the money he needed. In July, 1626, he issued a letter requesting his subjects to make a free gift of money. This appeal to the good will of the people failed, so he immediately issued a commission for the collection of tonnage and poundage, a duty on exports and imports. In September, 1626, he issued a commission for the collection of a forced loan, which was a compulsory grant to the king in accordance with the subject's ability to pay, for which the lender had only the king's promise to repay at a later time.

Five Knights' Case

A number of persons refused to pay the forced loan, and were imprisoned by order of the king. Among these were five men of ancient families and great influence. They brought the question of the legality of their imprisonment before the Court of King's Bench on a writ of habeas corpus. This proceeding is referred to as the *Five Knights' Case*, or sometimes as *Darnel's Case*.[6] The court returned the prisoners to jail, and the case became a

---

[6] *State Trials*, III, 1. The case is noteworthy for several reasons including the fact that the judges had prejudged the case by stating their opinion to the king prior to the hearing and because there was a popular misconception as to the real holding in the case, which influenced some of the debates on the Petition of Right.

The desire of the five knights to have their case brought before the King's Bench led to their application for a writ of habeas corpus. Other prisoners, like John Eliot, submitted a petition for release to the king instead of seeking a writ of habeas corpus. Gardiner, *History of England*, VI, 212. Although the king did not wish to have the legality of the loans tested in court, he consented to the issuance of the writ of habeas corpus after a conference with the judges at which he was "appeased by reasons." Frances H. Relf, *The Petition of Right* (Minneapolis, 1917), 2. The issue in the case was whether upon a return by the warden to a writ of habeas corpus that the prisoners were held *per speciale mandatum Domini Regis*, without any cause expressed, they should be admitted to bail or remanded pending trial. There was no question of their complete discharge. The lawyers for the defense were Bramston, Noy, Selden, and Calthrop. It was argued on behalf of the prisoners that a refusal to bail might result in their perpetual imprisonment and would thus deny to them the benefits of Magna Carta, chapter 39, and 28 Edw. 3, c. 3, which provided that the liberty of the subject should not be taken without due process of law. It was urged that the "law of the land" provision of Magna Carta required either presentment or indictment and that if *per speciale mandatum Domini Regis* were allowed as the law of the land the words of Magna Carta would mean nothing. To this Attorney General Heath answered that not even Magna Carta required presentment or indictment prior to committal, that the law of the land also included commitments by the Privy Council, and that the king on many occasions committed without cause being shown. This power, he said, is essential to unravel and put down conspiracies and assassination plots in which a commitment without charge may be necessary for the safety of the state pending the gathering of evidence and the arrest of co-conspirators. It is said that Heath's last point was probably his strongest from a legal point of view, but his weakest in the eyes of Parliament, inasmuch as there was no question of a conspiracy being involved nor any need to collect additional evidence. Gardiner, *History of England*, VI, 213-17; Relf,

PETITION OF RIGHT

cause célèbre which focused public attention upon the right of personal liberty and led directly to the Petition of Right.

Although the *Five Knights' Case* presented the chief grievance, other matters affecting the rights of the subject also were before Parliament during its momentous session in 1628. Chief among these was the complaint against the quartering of troops in private homes. Like the question of arbitrary imprisonment, this grievance arose indirectly from the lack of sympathy of Parliament with the aims of the war with Spain and its consequent failure to provide sufficient funds for the commanders to billet soldiers in inns, as was the practice when there was sufficient money.[7] The billeting of soldiers in private homes caused many serious abuses. In addition, the martial law was sometimes applied to civilians both as a code governing their right to obtain redress against soldiers who had injured them and as a means for punishing infractions of the law by civilians.

Other matters

When the Commons met in 1628, attention was thus focused upon specific grievances that had arisen since Charles I had come to the throne. On January 2, 1628, seventy-six persons who had been imprisoned for failure to pay the forced loan were released, and a number of these, including some of the parliamentary leaders, were present when the session opened. The members were determined that their actions to remedy these grievances should be based upon the fundamental principles of the English constitution. The opinion of many members was picturesquely phrased by Sir Benjamin Rudyard:

Parliament takes action

> For mine own part, I shall be very glad to see that old decrepit Law *Magna Carta*, which hath been kept so long, and lien bed-rid, as it were, I shall be glad to see it walk abroad again with new vigour and lustre, attended and followed with the other six Statutes:[8] questionless it will be a great heartning to all the People.[9]

The intellectual leader in the House of Commons at that session was Sir Edward Coke, then in his late seventies and at the height of his career. In the Petition of Right are embodied Coke's views of the concept of "due

Coke and personal liberty

---

op. cit., 3. The common belief was that the court had rendered a final judgment approving commitment at the king's pleasure for failure to pay the loan. The matter was not finally cleared up until April 14, 1628, when the judges appeared before the Lords to explain their decision. By that time the five knights had been released and the position of the Commons on the question of arbitrary imprisonment had become established. Gardiner, *History of England*, VI, 256; Relf, *op. cit.*, 8-9.

[7] Gardiner, *History of England*, VI, 247-48.

[8] As to the "six statutes," see Faith Thompson, *Magna Carta* (Minneapolis, 1948), 87-94.

[9] John Rushworth (ed.), *Historical Collections* (London, 1721), I, 552.

process of law" as that right had developed since Magna Carta. On March 21, Coke introduced a bill which provided that, except by the sentence of a court, no person should be detained untried in prison for more than two months if he could find bail or for more than three months if he could not.[10] The next day Sir Thomas Wentworth summarized the most important grievances of the Commons in a manner which later provided much of the substance of the Petition of Right.[11] The case of the Five Knights was debated at length. Coke denounced the idea of imprisonment at the king's command as "the utter subversion of the choice Liberty and Right belonging to every free born Subject of this Kingdom."[12] On April 1 the Commons unanimously adopted three resolutions to establish the writ of habeas corpus as the right of every subject. In addition, taxation without the assent of Parliament was condemned.[13] The resolutions were sent to the House of Lords, where they were taken under consideration. Meanwhile, on April 14, the judges in the case of the Five Knights appeared before the Lords to explain their decision.[14]

[10] Gardiner, *History of England*, VI, 232.

[11] "First, the freedom of them from imprisonment. Secondly, from employment abroad, contrary to the antient Customs: For our Goods, that no Levies be made, but by Parliament. Secondly, no billeting of Soldiers. It is most necessary that these be resolved, that the Subject may be secured in both." Rushworth, *op. cit.*, I, 501. At this time Coke was apparently not prepared to frame a bill to cover all the grievances. "I am not able to fly at all Grievances, but only at Loans." *Ibid.*

[12] *Ibid.*, 509.

[13] "I. That no Freeman ought to be detained or kept in prison, or otherwise restrained by the command of the King or Privy-Council, or any other, unless some cause of the commitment, detainer, or restraint be expressed, for which by Law he ought to be committed, detained, or restrained.

"II. That the Writ of *Habeas Corpus* may not be denied, but ought to be granted to every man that is committed or detained in prison, or otherwise restrained, though it be by the command of the King, the Privy-Council, or any other, he praying the same.

"III. That if a Freeman be committed or detained in prison, or otherwise restrained by the command of the King, the Privy-Council, or any other, no cause of such Commitment, Detainer, or Restraint being expressed, for which by Law he ought to be committed, detained, or restrained, and the same be returned upon a *Habeas corpus*, granted for the said Party, then he ought to be delivered or bailed."

At the same time it was resolved,

"That it is the antient and undubitable right of every Freeman, that he hath a full and absolute property in his Goods and Estate; that no Tax, Tallage, Loan, Benevolence, or other like Charge ought to be commanded, or levied by the King, or any of his Ministers, without common consent by Act of Parliament." *Ibid.*, 513. As to the date of these resolutions, see Gardiner, *History of England*, VI, 245.

[14] *Ibid.*, 256. Judge Whitlock said: "*My Lords*, We are, by your appointment, here ready to clear any Asperosin of the House of Commons in their late Presentment upon the King's Bench, that the Subject was wounded in the Judgment there lately given. If such a thing were, my Lords, your Lordships, not they, have the power to question and judge the same. But, my Lords, I say, there was no Judgment given, whereby either the Prerogative might be enlarged, or the Right of the Subject trenched upon. It is true, my Lords, in *Mich.* Term last, four Gentlemen petitioned for a *Habeas Corpus*, which they obtained, and Counsel was assigned unto them; the Report was, *Per speciale mandatum Domini Regis*, which likewise was made known to us under the hands of Eighteen Privy Counsellers. Now, my Lords, if we had delivered them presently upon this, it must have been, because the King did not show cause

PETITION OF RIGHT

In addition, the Commons prepared a petition protesting the billeting of soldiers which they submitted to the king.[15] He postponed his reply to that petition.

On April 25 the Lords submitted a set of five counterproposals to the Commons.[16] Although the Lords were willing to support the liberty of the subject by affirming the principles of Magna Carta, they insisted, in their fifth proposition, on reserving the right of imprisonment for reasons of state as an essential part of the prerogative. Coke immediately objected because the Lords would make the confirmation of Magna Carta and the liberties of the subject an act of grace on the part of the king instead of matters of right which the subject could demand.[17]

Proposals of the Lords

The king promised

> *That he holdeth the Statute of* Magna Charta, *and the other Six Statutes insisted upon for the Subjects Liberty, to be all in force, and assures you, that he will maintain all his Subjects in the just Freedom of their Persons, and safety of their Estates; and that he will*

---

wherein we should have judged the King had done wrong, and this is beyond our knowledge, for he might have committed them for other matters than we could have imagined; but they might say thus, They might have been kept in Prison all their days: I answer, No, but we did remit them, that we might better advise of the matter; and they the next day might have had a new Writ, if they had pleased. But they say, we ought not to have denied Bail: I answer, If we had done so, it must needs have reflected upon the King, that he had unjustly imprisoned them. . . ." Rushworth, *op. cit.*, I, 509-10.

[15] *Ibid.*, 542-44.

[16] "THat his Majesty would be pleased graciously to Declare, That the good old Law called *Magna Charta*, and the six Statutes conceived to be Declarations and Explanations of that Law, do still stand in force to all intents and purposes.

"2. That his Majesty would be pleased graciously to Declare, That according to *Magna Charta*, and the Statutes afore-named, as also according to the most antient Customs and Laws of this Land, every free Subject of this Realm, hath a fundamental Propriety in his Goods, and a fundamental Liberty of his Person.

"3. That his Majesty would be graciously pleased to Declare, That it is his Royal pleasure to ratify and confirm unto all and every his Loyal and faithful Subjects, all their antient, several, just Liberties, Privileges, and Rights, in as ample beneficial manner to all intents and purposes, as their Ancestors did enjoy the same under the best of his most noble Progenitors.

"4. That his Majesty would be further pleased graciously to Declare, for the good content of his Loyal Subjects, and for the securing them from future fear, That in all Cases within the Cognizances of the Common Law concerning the Liberties of the Subject, his Majesty would proceed according to the Common Law of this Land, and according to the Laws established in the Kingdom, and in no other manner or wise.

"5. As touching his Majesty's Royal Prerogative, intrinsical to his Sovereignty, and betrusted him withal from God, *ad communem totius populi salutem, & non ad destructionem,* That his Majesty would resolve not to use or divert the same, to the prejudice of any his loyal People in the propriety of their Goods, or liberty of their Persons: And in case, for the security of his Majesty's Royal Person, the common safety of his People, or the peaceable Government of this Kingdom, his Majesty shall find just cause for reason of State to imprison or restrain any man's Person, his Majesty would graciously Declare, That within a convenient time he shall, and will express the cause of the Commitment or restraint, either General or Special; and upon a cause so expressed, will leave him immediately to be tried according to the common Justice of the Kingdom." *Ibid.*, 546-47.

[17] Gardiner, *History of England*, VI, 261.

govern according to the Laws and Statutes of this Realm; and that ye shall find as much security in his Majesty's Royal Word and Promise, as in the strength of any Law ye can make . . .[18]

Bill for the liberties of the subject

The Commons were not content to rely on the king's word, and they proceeded to prepare a bill to safeguard the liberties of the subject.[19] The bill was presented for debate by Coke on April 29. During the debate there were many differences of opinion. Some were willing to rely on the king's promise to confirm the ancient laws, and some objected to any bill which would completely deny to the king the power to imprison. Coke urged that they proceed by way of petition to the king instead of by an ordinary bill.[20] This procedure was based on the assumption that all the Commons really desired was a confirmation of the laws as they then stood and not a change in the laws.[21]

The Petition of Right

The Petition of Right was prepared by the same committee which had drawn the earlier bill on the liberties of the subject. It was presented to the Commons on May 8, and the Lords were asked to meet for a conference. The Lords agreed to the substance of the petition. They desired, however, to add a clause protecting the sovereignty of the king.[22] This proposal immediately aroused the opposition of the Commons. Alford said:

[18] Rushworth, *op. cit.*, I, 549.

[19] "*An Act for the better securing of every freeman touching the propriety of his goods and liberty of his person.*

"Whereas it is enacted and declared by Magna Carta that no freeman is to be convicted, destroyed, &c., and whereas by a statute made in E. 7, called *de tallagio non concedendo;* and whereas by the Parliament, 5 E. 3, and 29 E. 3 &c.; and whereas by the said great Charter was confirmed, and that the other laws, &c.

"Be it enacted that Magna Carta and these Acts be put in due execution and that all allegements, awards, and rules given or to be given to the contrary shall be void; and whereas by the common law and statute it appeareth that no freeman ought to be committed by command of the King, &c.; and if any freeman be so committed and the same returned upon a *habeas corpus,* he ought to be delivered or bailed, and whereas by the common law and statutes every freeman hath a propriety of his goods and estate as no tax, tallage, &c., nor any soldier can be billeted in his house, &c.

"Be it enacted that no tax, tallage, or loan shall be levied &c., by the King or any minister by Act of Parliament, and that none be compelled to receive any soldiers into his house against his will." Gardiner, *Constitutional Documents,* 65-66.

[20] Because Parliament proceeded by petition instead of by bill, the Petition of Right is not technically termed a statute. E. R. Adair, "The Petition of Right," *History,* V (July, 1920), 101-2; Relf, *op. cit.,* 27-43.

[21] A petition of right was a request by the individual that the benefit of the law be allowed to him in cases where it was alleged that the king's prerogative had overriden the law. It was distinguished from a petition of grace, which was presented to the king in Parliament praying for an alteration of the law in a particular case. Adair, *op. cit.,* 100.

[22] "We present this our humble Petition to your Majesty, with the care not only of preserving our own Liberties, but with due regard to leave intire that Sovereign Power wherewith your Majesty is trusted for the Protection, Safety, and Happiness of the People." Rushworth, *op. cit.,* I, 561.

PETITION OF RIGHT

Let us look into the Records, and see what they are, what is Sovereign Power? *Bodin* saith, That it is free from any Condition, by this we shall acknowledge a Regal as well as a Legal Power: Let us give that to the King that the Law gives him, and no more.[23]

Coke added:

I know that Prerogative is part of the Law, but Sovereign Power is no Parliamentary word: In my opinion, it weakens *Magna Charta,* and all our Statutes; for they are absolute without any saving of Sovereign Power: And shall we now add it, we shall weaken the Foundation of Law, and then the Building must needs fall; take we heed what we yield unto, *Magna Charta* is such a Fellow, that he will have no Sovereign.[24]

The persistence of the Commons was rewarded. The Lords agreed to the Petition of Right without the clause reserving the king's rights of sovereignty, and the king was placed in the position of either yielding or losing the support of the entire nation. Before Charles gave his consent to the petition, he consulted his judges as to its legal effect.[25] Upon learning that by assenting to the petition he would acknowledge the illegality of his former conduct and agree to a restriction upon powers he had formerly assumed, Charles answered in ambiguous terms.[26] Because his answer amounted to no more than a promise to uphold and follow the laws of the realm, a promise he had already offered to give, the Commons insisted on an acceptance of the petition in clear and unambiguous terms. This was given on June 7 when the king called the Commons before him, had the petition read, and the clerk pronounced the words of approval, *"Soit droit fait comme est desiré,"* let right be done as is desired.[27]

The king's assent

In evaluating the effect of the Petition of Right, it must be remembered

Effects

---

[23] *Ibid.,* 562.

[24] *Ibid.*

[25] To the question of whether the king might in any case commit a subject without showing cause, the judges answered, "We are of opinion that by the general rule of the law the cause of commitment by his Majesty ought to be shown; yet some cases may require such secrecy that the King may commit a subject without showing the cause, for a convenient time." To the question of whether the judges should deliver a prisoner brought before them on a writ of habeas corpus and it appeared that he was being held by order of the king, no special cause being shown, it was answered: ". . . The party ought by the general rule of law to be delivered. But if the case be such that the same requireth secrecy and may not presently be disclosed, the Court in discretion may forbear to deliver the prisoner for a convenient time, to the end the Court may be advertised of the truth thereof." Gardiner, *History of England,* VI, 294-95.

[26] "The King willeth that right be done according to the laws and customs of the realm; and that the statutes be put in due execution, that his subjects may have no cause to complain of any wrong or oppressions, contrary to their just rights and liberties, to the preservation whereof he holds himself as well obliged as of his prerogative." Gardiner, *Constitutional Documents,* 70.

[27] The king attempted to qualify even this answer. He said, "This I am sure is full; yet no more than I granted you on my first answer . . ." Gardiner, *History of England,* VI, 309. As to the nature of the answer, see Relf, *op. cit.,* 48-51.

SOURCES OF OUR LIBERTIES

Unsolved questions

that the document did not attempt to provide a remedy for all the grievances of Parliament against the king. Animosity against the king's favorite, the Duke of Buckingham, continued; religious differences became more serious and widened the breach between Parliament and the king; and the king continued to exact the form of prerogative taxation known as tonnage and poundage. None of these matters was settled by the Petition of Right, although the Commons soon claimed that the question of tonnage and poundage had been.[28] The king dissolved Parliament in 1629, and no other was convened for a period of eleven years—the longest time an English king had ever governed without a Parliament.

Personal liberty

Perhaps the greatest contribution of the Petition of Right is found in its clauses safeguarding the liberty of the individual. The writ of habeas corpus was greatly strengthened as a protection of that right by the provision that no person might be imprisoned at the king's command without cause. The effects of the Petition of Right, however, were not at once apparent. After Parliament had been dissolved, Charles proceeded to govern in the most arbitrary fashion, infringing every right of the subject. The duty of tonnage and poundage and other forms of prerogative taxation were levied regularly, and persons refusing to pay were imprisoned by the Council or by the Court of Star Chamber.[29] During that period, called the "Eleven Years of Tyranny," it is probable that the courts rarely issued writs of habeas corpus in the interest of personal liberty.[30] The question of arbitrary imprisonment was still a major grievance when the Long Parliament met in 1640. Section VIII of the act abolishing the Star Chamber[31] was designed to put the writ of habeas corpus on a firmer basis, but effective means for the enforcement of the right were not fully established until the Habeas Corpus Act of

---

[28] By the Remonstrance against Tonnage and Poundage, June 25, 1628, the Commons declared "That the receiving of Tonnage and Poundage, and other impositions not granted by Parliament, is a breach of the fundamental liberties of this kingdom, and contrary to your Majesty's royal answer to the said Petition of Right." Gardiner, *Constitutional Documents*, 73.

[29] The most famous of the other taxes was the levy of ship money, which was based upon the custom of issuing writs requiring seaports to provide ships for the king's use. Ship money was an exaction of money in lieu of ships. In 1635 the writ was directed to the inland counties as well as to the coastal counties. Under Charles I the writ of ship money became a permanent tax having no relationship to the needs of war. The legality of the levy was tested in 1637 in *Hampden's Case*, *State Trials*, III, 825, and judgment was given for the crown by a narrow margin. It has been said that the case marked the beginning of the collapse of arbitrary government as established by Charles I. J. R. Tanner, *English Constitutional Conflicts of the Seventeenth Century, 1603-1689* (Cambridge, 1928), 76-79, 273-77.

[30] Edward Jenks, "The Story of the *Habeas Corpus*," *Select Essays in Anglo-American Legal History* (Boston, 1908), II, 546.

[31] See pp. 132, 141-43.

PETITION OF RIGHT

1679.[32] The Petition of Right thus stands as the first of a series of enactments in the seventeenth century by which the writ of habeas corpus was made an effective mechanism for the protection of the right of personal liberty.

The Petition of Right strengthened the concept of due process of law by condemning the practice of trying civilians by tribunals erected in accordance with the martial law. The principle that civilians should not be tried by courts-martial had been announced in 1327 when Parliament annulled the attainder of the Earl of Lancaster saying,

Martial law

> (1) That in the time of peace no man ought to be adjudged to death for treason or any other offense, without being arraigned and held to answer; (2) that regularly when the King's courts are opened it is a time of peace in judgment of law; and (3) that no man ought to be sentenced to death by the record of the King without his legal trial *per pares*.[33]

The same principle later appeared in the English Mutiny Act of 1689:

> ... no man may be forejudged of Life or Limb, or subjected to any kind of punishment by Martial Law, or in any other manner than by the judgment of his Peers and according to the known and established Laws of this realm ...[34]

Martial law is thus recognized in England only to the extent that the government has the right to repel force by force in the case of invasion, insurrection, riot, or generally of any violent resistance to the law. As a method of government by military tribunals which supersede the jurisdiction of the ordinary courts, however, martial law is unknown.[35]

In the famous case of Wolfe Tone in 1798 it was argued, *"that martial law and civil law are incompatible; and that the former must cease with the existence of the latter."*[36] The same principle has been carried over to the Constitution of the United States by Article III and Amendments V and VI which guarantee the right of trial by jury and provide that no one shall be deprived of life, liberty, or property without due process of law. The Supreme Court has said,

> As necessity creates the rule, so it limits its duration; for, if this government is continued *after* the courts are reinstated, it is a gross usurpation of power. Martial rule can never

---

[32] See pp. 189-203.

[33] 1 Edw. 3; see Thompson, *op. cit.*, 75-76, 349-50.

[34] 1 Will. and Mary, c. 5.

[35] Albert V. Dicey, *Introduction to the Study of the Law of the Constitution* (8th ed.; London, 1915), 283-90.

[36] *Wolfe Tone's Case, State Trials*, XXVII, 625.

exist where the courts are open, and in proper and unobstructed exercise of their jurisdiction. It is also confined to the locality of actual war.[37]

Quartering of soldiers Although the practice of quartering soldiers in private homes was condemned by the Petition of Right, this oppression became one of the grievances of the American colonists in 1765. The Quartering Act of 1765[38] was passed at the request of General Gage to aid the enforcement of the Stamp Act and the Revenue Act of 1764. The act stated that quarters should be provided for his Majesty's officers and troops

> ... in the barracks provided by the colonies; and if there shall not be sufficient room in the said barracks ... then and in such case only, to quarter and billet the residue ... in inns, livery stables, ale-houses, victualling-houses, and the houses of sellers of wine ... and in case there shall not be sufficient room ... that in such and no other case, and upon no other account, it shall and may be lawful for the governor and council of each respective province in his Majesty's dominions in *America*, to authorize and appoint ... such proper person or persons as they shall think fit, to take, hire and make fit ... such and so many uninhabited houses, outhouses, barns, or other buildings, as shall be necessary, to quarter therein the residue of such officers and soldiers for whom there should not be room in such barracks and publick houses as aforesaid ...

This provision was repeated in the Quartering Act of 1774,[39] one of the "Intolerable Acts." As the result of these statutes, the quartering of troops became one of the major grievances of the colonists. The practice was cited as a grievance by the Declaration and Resolves of the First Continental Congress[40] and by the Declaration of Independence.[41] Provisions against the quartering of soldiers appeared in a number of state constitutions enacted after the Revolution. The Third Amendment to the Constitution of the United States provides that soldiers shall not be quartered in any house without the owner's consent in time of peace, nor in time of war, except as provided by law.[42]

Conclusion The Petition of Right thus contributed much in the establishment of some of the essential personal liberties of the citizen. The king was forbidden to imprison persons without showing cause, the quartering of soldiers and mariners in private homes was stopped, the trial of civilians by courts-martial was declared illegal, and the king's power to levy taxes without the consent of the peoples' representatives in Parliament was restricted.

[37] *Ex Parte Milligan*, 4 Wall. 2, 127 (1866).
[38] 5 Geo. 3, c. 33.
[39] 15 Geo. 3, c. 15.
[40] See p. 289.
[41] See p. 320.
[42] See p. 432.

PETITION OF RIGHT[43]

June 7, 1628

To the King's most excellent majesty.

HUMBLY *shew unto our sovereign lord the King, the lords spiritual and temporal, and commons in parliament assembled, That whereas it is declared and enacted by a statute made in the time of the reign of King* Edward *the First commonly called* Statutum de tallagio non concedendo,[44] *That no tallage or aid shall be laid or levied by the King or his heirs in this realm, without the good will and assent of the archbishops, bishops, earls, barons, knights, burgesses, and other the freemen of the commonalty of this realm;* (2) *and by authority of parliament holden in the five and twentieth year of the reign of King* Edward *the Third, it is declared and enacted, That from thenceforth no person should be compelled to make any loans to the King against his will, because such loans were against reason and the franchise of the land;* (3) *and by other laws of this realm it is provided, That none should be charged by any charge or imposition called a benevolence, nor by such like charge:* (4) *by which the statutes before mentioned, and other the good laws and statutes of this realm, your subjects have inherited this freedom, That they should not be compelled to contribute to any tax, tallage, aid or other like charge not set by common consent in parliament.*

II. *Yet nevertheless, of late divers commissions directed to sundry commissioners in several counties, with instructions, have issued; by means whereof your people have been in divers places assembled, and required to lend certain sums of money unto your Majesty, and many of them, upon their refusal so to do, have had an oath administred unto them not warrantable by the laws or statutes of this realm, and have been constrained to become bound to make appearance and give attendance before your privy council and in other places, and others of them have been therefore imprisoned, confined, and sundry other ways molested and disquieted;* (2) *and divers other charges have been laid and levied upon your people in several counties by lord lieutenants, deputy lieutenants, commissioners for musters, justices of peace and others, by command or direction from your Majesty, or your privy council, against the laws and free customs of the realm.*

Margin notes:
- Recital of statutes
- 34 Edw. 1, stat. 4, c. 1
- 25 Edw. 1, stat. 1, c. 6
- Other statutes
- The forced loans and other levies

---

[43] 3 Car. 1, c. 1. Danby Pickering (ed.), *Statutes at Large* (Cambridge, 1726-1807), VII, 317-20.
[44] See p. 26.

Recital of Magna Carta, c. 29

III. And where also by the statute called The great charter of the liberties of England, it is declared and enacted, That no freeman may be taken or imprisoned, or be disseised of his freehold or liberties, or his free customs, or be outlawed or exiled, or in manner destroyed, but by the lawful judgment of his peers, or by the law of the land.[45]

Recital of 28 Edw. 3, c. 3

IV. And in the eight and twentieth year of the reign of King Edward the Third, it was declared and enacted by authority of parliament, That no man of what estate or condition that he be, should be put out of his land or tenements, nor taken, nor imprisoned, nor disherited, nor put to death without being brought to answer by due process of law:

Personal liberty and habeas corpus

V. Nevertheless against the tenor of the said statutes, and other the good laws and statutes of your realm to that end provided, divers of your subjects have of late been imprisoned without any cause shewed; (2) and when for their deliverance they were brought before your justices by your Majesty's writs of habeas corpus, there to undergo and receive as the court should order, and their keepers commanded to certify the causes of their detainer, no cause was certified, but that they were detained by your Majesty's special command, signified by the lords of your privy council, and yet were returned back to several prisons, without being charged with any thing to which they might make answer according to the law:

Quartering of troops

VI. And whereas of late great companies of soldiers and mariners have been dispersed into divers counties of the realm, and the inhabitants against their wills have been compelled to receive them into their houses, and there to suffer them to sojourn, against the laws and customs of this realm, and to the great grievance and vexation of the people:

Recital of 25 Edw. 3, stat. 5, c. 4 and other laws

VII. And whereas also by authority of parliament, in the five and twentieth year of the reign of King Edward the Third, it is declared and enacted, That no man should be forejudged of life or limb against the form of the great charter and the law of the land; (2) and by the said great charter and other the laws and statutes of this your realm, no man ought to be adjudged to death but by the laws established in this your realm, either by the customs of the same realm, or by acts of parliament:

Application of martial law

(3) and whereas no offender of what kind soever is exempted from the proceedings to be used, and punishments to be inflicted by the laws and statutes of this your realm: nevertheless of late time divers commissions under your Majesty's great seal have issued forth, by which certain persons have been assigned and appointed commissioners with power and authority to proceed within the land, according to the justice of martial law, against such soldiers or mariners, or other dissolute persons joining with them, as should commit any murder, robbery, felony, mutiny or other outrage or misdemeanor whatsoever, and by such summary course and order as is agreeable to martial law, and as is used in armies in time of war, to proceed to the trial and condemnation of such offenders, and them to cause to be executed and put to death according to the law martial:

Trials

VIII. By pretext whereof some of your Majesty's subjects have been by some of

---

[45] See pp. 5-7, 17.

the said commissioners put to death, when and where, if by the laws and statutes of the land they had deserved death, by the same laws and statutes also they might, and by no other ought to have been judged and executed:

IX. *And also sundry grievous offenders, by colour thereof claiming an exemption, have escaped the punishments due to them by the laws and statutes of this your realm, by reason that divers of your officers and ministers of justice have unjustly refused or forborn to proceed against such offenders according to the same laws and statutes, upon pretence that the said offenders were punishable only by martial law, and by authority of such commissions as aforesaid:* (2) *which commissions, and all other of like nature, are wholly and directly contrary to the said laws and statutes of this your realm:* — *Exemptions from punishment*

X. *They do therefore humbly pray your most excellent Majesty, That no man hereafter be compelled to make or yield any gift, loan, benevolence, tax, or such-like charge, without common consent by act of parliament;* (2) *and that none be called to make answer, or take such oath, or to give attendance, or be confined, or otherwise molested or disquieted concerning the same, or for refusal thereof;* (3) *and that no freeman, in any such manner as is before-mentioned, be imprisoned or detained;* (4) *and that your Majesty would be pleased to remove the said soldiers and mariners, and that your people may not be so burthened in time to come;* (5) *and that the aforesaid commissions, for proceeding by martial law, may be revoked and annulled; and that hereafter no commissions of like nature may issue forth to any person or persons whatsoever to be executed as aforesaid, lest by colour of them any of your Majesty's subjects be destroyed, or put to death contrary to the laws and franchise of the land.* — *Taxes / Oaths / Imprisonment / Soldiers and mariners / Martial law*

XI. *All which they most humbly pray of your most excellent Majesty as their rights and liberties, according to the laws and statutes of this realm; and that your Majesty would also vouchsafe to declare, That the awards, doings and proceedings, to the prejudice of your people in any of the premisses, shall not be drawn hereafter into consequence or example;* (2) *and that your Majesty would be also graciously pleased, for the further comfort and safety of your people, to declare your royal will and pleasure, That in the things aforesaid all your officers and ministers shall serve you according to the laws and statutes of this realm, as they tender the honour of your Majesty, and the prosperity of this kingdom. Qua quidem petitione lecta & plenius intellecta per dictum dominum regem taliter est responsum in pleno parliamento, viz. Soit droit fait come est desire.* — *Prayer that rights and liberties be recognized / The king's answer*

REFERENCES

Adair, E. R. "The Petition of Right," *History*, V (new series; July, 1920), 99-103.
Gardiner, Samuel R. *History of England*. 10 vols. New ed.; London: Longmans, Green and Co., 1891. VI.
Relf, Frances H. *The Petition of Right*. Minneapolis: University of Minnesota Press, 1917.
Tanner, J. R. *English Constitutional Conflicts of the Seventeenth Century, 1603-1689*. Cambridge, England: The University Press, 1928.

VII. THE CHARTER OF MASSACHUSETTS BAY
1629

Origins   It has been said that "the disorders of the mother country were the safeguard of the infant liberty of New England."[1] This fact was of crucial significance during the early days in Massachusetts. When the Massachusetts Charter of 1629 was drawn, the greatest figures of England were locked in a life-and-death struggle for the control of their own government and little attention was paid to the colonies. Only two years before the Massachusetts Charter was granted, the contest between the king's prerogative and the liberty of the subject had led to the *Five Knights' Case,* an event which, in turn, led directly to the Petition of Right in 1628.[2] In 1629 Parliament was dissolved by Charles I, who thereupon proceeded to govern in tyrannical fashion for the next eleven years. Meanwhile the Star Chamber and the High Commission, both dominated by Archbishop William Laud, reached the height of their terrible powers. Spurred by these events, colonization of the New World proceeded at a rapid pace. It is little wonder that the absence of firm control by England allowed the colonists to develop forms of government which, although suited to their own circumstances, were both novel and unauthorized. This development is nowhere better illustrated than in Massachusetts.

The founders of Massachusetts received a patent from the Council for New England on March 19, 1628, which gave them all the rights possessed by the Council in the region of Massachusetts Bay. Because of a dispute over trading rights, the patentees soon sought to have their title confirmed by a royal charter. Largely through the influence of Robert Rich, Earl of War-

---
[1] See Edward Channing, *A History of the United States,* Vol. I: *The Planting of a Nation in the New World, 1000-1660* (New York, 1928), 334.
[2] See pp. 64-66, 73-75.

THE CHARTER OF MASSACHUSETTS BAY

wick, a charter was issued March 4, 1629, which confirmed the previous grant and gave the founders corporate status under the title of the "Governor and Company of Massachusetts Bay in New England."

One of the most momentous steps in the history of the colony was taken shortly after the formation of the company. This was the conclusion of the Cambridge Agreement. The agreement grew from the suggestion of Governor Cradock that the control of the company should be transferred to those who were to emigrate to the colony instead of remaining with officials in England. By the Cambridge Agreement twelve wealthy and educated gentlemen, among whom were John Winthrop, Isaac Johnson, Thomas Dudley, and Richard Saltonstall, agreed to go to New England provided that the transfer of government could be legally made.[3] It was found that there was no prohibition to the transfer,[4] and the government was turned over to those who were willing to emigrate, Winthrop and Dudley being chosen governor and deputy governor respectively.

Effects Cambridge Agreement

The men of the company were Nonconformists, and their goal was to found a state based on the principles of the Bible and governed by the laws of God. There were about two thousand emigrants, many of whom did not adhere to Nonconformist tenets. The Puritans in the colony constituted a minority. The others were in general sympathy with Puritan ideals, but often did not see eye to eye with the leaders. A serious problem of governing the colonists was thus presented at the outset.[5]

Representative government

A struggle for control soon began between the officers and the other

---

[3] The propositions of Governor Cradock were read to the assembled shareholders on July 28, 1629. He asked the shareholders to regard the suggestion as confidential and to think it over carefully. The signers of the Cambridge Agreement pledged on August 26 that they and their families would be ready to depart for New England by March 1, 1630, provided that before September 30, 1629, the charter and the government "be first, by an order of court, legally transferred and established to remain with us and others which shall inhabit upon the said plantation." Technically, this decision related to the question of where future meetings of the company should be held. Actually, it amounted to the transfer of the seat of government to New England. It was sanctioned by legal advice; its lawfulness was not questioned by the Privy Council; it was later affirmed by the Attorney General; and in 1677 Chief Justices Rainsford and North still described the "charter as making the adventurers a corporation upon the place." The policy of permitting the colonial governments to reside in the colonies was followed in the charters of Rhode Island and Connecticut, and in those to Baltimore and Penn. Channing, *op. cit.*, I, 329-30; George Bancroft, *History of the United States of America* (New York, 1892), I, 231-32.

[4] Whether the transfer of the government to America was unauthorized and an act of bad faith or whether it was something that had been contemplated from the start has been a subject of dispute. The authorities are cited in Channing, *op. cit.*, I, 353-54. The charter was apparently modeled on the charter to the Council for New England of 1620, and it is possible that the requirement of residence in England, which is contained in that charter, was omitted from the Massachusetts Charter through inadvertence. *Ibid.*, 345-46.

[5] Charles M. Andrews, *The Colonial Period of American History* (New Haven, 1934), I, 67.

colonists. It was several years before the colonists had fully established their right to participate in the government. The composition of the first General Court of Massachusetts, which met October 19, 1630, demonstrated that control of the government was in the hands of only a few. That court was composed of the governor, the deputy governor, eight assistants, and one or two freemen.[6] These were all who possessed the franchise, and it was this group which had the power of admitting additional freemen. The issue of whether Massachusetts was to become an oligarchy or a democracy was squarely presented in October, 1629, when a large number of emigrants applied to be admitted as freemen of the company. The officials, fearing the possibility of a mass exodus of colonists to New Hampshire or New Plymouth, decided to admit the applicants but to restrict their rights so that they could elect only the assistants. The number of assistants to be elected was then limited so that the control of the company by the existing leaders would not be impaired. It was also decided that no one should be admitted in the future as a freeman whose beliefs were not in harmony with those of the officers.[7] Only members of churches who had been formally admitted to freemanship and had taken the freeman's oath could hold office and take part in civic affairs.[8] These restrictions were in violation of the charter, and they were intended to allow a comparatively few men to control. For a number of years there continued to be more nonfreemen than freemen in the colony.

The freemen who were admitted in 1629, unaware of the fact that as members of the General Court they had the right to participate in the legislative process, allowed their powers to lie dormant for several years.[9] During that time the governor, deputy governor, and assistants made and executed the laws and administered justice.[10] In 1634 some of the freemen, dissatisfied

---

[6] Although the charter provided that there should be eighteen assistants, not more than twelve were chosen during the early years. Channing, *op. cit.*, I, 345.

[7] *Ibid.*, 341-43.

[8] Andrews, *op. cit.*, I, 459-60.

[9] The General Court met in each year after 1629, but its records show little activity on the part of the freemen. William H. Whitmore (ed.), *The Colonial Laws of Massachusetts, 1672* (Boston, 1890), 2-3.

[10] The power of the governor, deputy governor, and the assistants to make laws was confirmed by the General Court on October 19, 1630. *Ibid.* There were some practical advantages in this deviation from the terms of the charter. In the General Court the consent of the governor or deputy governor and six assistants was necessary for the transaction of business, whereas in the Court of Assistants seven constituted a quorum and they could act by majority vote. Because there were only seven or eight assistants in the colony at this time, their acting in the Court of Assistants instead of in the General Court relieved them of what amounted to a requirement of virtual unanimity. Channing,

THE CHARTER OF MASSACHUSETTS BAY

with certain laws which had been made, demanded to see the charter. After seeing the document, they insisted that its terms be complied with and that they be allowed full participation in the lawmaking process. The governor, however, insisted that the Court of Assistants should continue to legislate. It was not convenient, he said, for all the freemen to meet together to make laws, first because their number had grown and second because the company could not afford the loss of their time from other pursuits.[11] The freemen, meeting in the General Court in 1634, answered these arguments by instituting a system of representative government.[12] They also declared that only the General Court had power to choose and admit freemen, to make and establish laws, to appoint or remove officers and fix their duties, to raise money and taxes, and to dispose of lands.[13]

Not long after the freemen had first asserted their powers of legislation in the General Court, the claim was advanced that the Massachusetts lawmaking body was not subject to the authority of Parliament. In 1646, when the question was raised of what allegiance was owed to England, some of the magistrates expressed the opinion that the colonial government was subordinate to Parliament. Winthrop and others denied this, however, pointing out that the charter gave the colonists the "power to make laws, to erect all sorts of magistracy, to correct, punish, pardon, govern, and rule the

Legislative sovereignty

---

op. cit., I, 343. The participation of the assistants in the administration of justice led to their being called "magistrates." This resulted from the fact that most of the assistants had at one time or another exercised the office of magistracy in England. It was agreed that they should undertake the functions of the English justice of the peace, or magistrate. *Ibid.*, 340-41.

[11] The freemen had deputed two of their number from each town to consider matters to come before the General Court on May 14, 1634. It was this representative body that demanded to see the patent. Winthrop's account of the answer they received is as follows: "He told them, that, when the patent was granted, the number of freemen was supposed to be (as in like corporations) so few, as they might well join in making laws; but now they were grown to so great a body, as it was not possible for them to make or execute laws, but they must choose others for that purpose: and that howsoever it would be necessary hereafter to have a select company to intend that work, yet for the present they were not furnished with a sufficient number of men qualified for such a business, neither could the commonwealth bear the loss of time of so many as must intend it. Yet this they might do at present, viz., they might, at the general court, make an order, that, once in the year, a certain number should be appointed (upon summons from the governor) to revise all laws, etc., and to reform what they found amiss therein; but not to make any new laws, but prefer their grievances to the court of assistants; and that no assessment should be laid upon the country without the consent of such a committee, nor any lands disposed of." James K. Hosmer (ed.), *Winthrop's Journal* (New York, 1908), I, 122-23.

[12] It was provided: "Such persons as shall be hereafter so deputed by the freemen of the several plantations, to deal in their behalf in the public affairs of the commonwealth, shall have the full power and voices of all the said freemen, derived to them for the making and establishing of laws, granting of lands, etc., and to deal in all other affairs of the commonwealth wherein the freemen have to do, the matter of election of magistrates and other officers only excepted, wherein every freemen is to give his own voice." Whitmore, *op. cit.*, 4.

[13] *Ibid.*

people absolutely...."[14] In 1661 the General Court issued a "Declaration of Liberties" which asserted that the charter was "the first & maine foundation of our civil politye" under which the governor, deputy governor, assistants, and representatives had full power and authority for the government of the people, except that they could not enact laws repugnant to the laws of England.[15] The charter thus provided at an early date the basis for the idea, often voiced by colonial patriots at the time of the American Revolution, that the statutes of England were limited in their application to England and did not reach beyond the seas.

Bicameral legislature

The achievement of the freemen in replacing the oligarchy established by the company with a democratic form of government was a great one. The long struggle between the freemen and the magistrates, however, produced other results of major importance. One of these was the enactment in 1641 of the Body of Liberties, which can be called the earliest American bill of rights;[16] the second was the development of the first American bicameral, or two-chamber, assembly.

Although there is a resemblance between the Senate and House of Representatives in the United States, on the one hand, and the House of Lords and House of Commons in England, on the other, the development of the bicameral assembly in America did not result from conscious imitation of English institutions. It arose instead from the forms of government evolved by the trading companies which established the early colonies of America. The bicameral legislature developed in Massachusetts as a compromise in the struggle for power waged between the freemen of the company and the assistants.

The charter provided that the governor, assistants, and freemen together should constitute the General Court. After the freemen had asserted their right to participate in the General Court, they were able to dominate it because of their superior numbers. There existed considerable uncertainty, however, as to the respective functions of the General Court and the Court of Assistants. Because of friction between the two bodies, a compromise was reached in 1635 by which it was agreed that no law should be passed without the consent of a majority of both the assistants and the freemen.[17] Further

[14] Hosmer, *op. cit.*, II, 290.
[15] Henry S. Commager (ed.), *Documents of American History* (3d ed.; New York, 1943), I, 34.
[16] See pp. 143-61.
[17] "And whereas it may fall out that in some of theis Genall Courts, to be holden by the magistrates & deputies, there may arise some difference of judgemt in doubtfull cases, it is therefore ordered,

opposition between the two branches led to the law of 1644, which provided that the branches should sit apart, that acts agreed upon by one branch should be sent to the other, and that if both should agree, the act should be passed. Thereafter the two bodies sat as separate and coordinate branches of the General Court.[18]

---

that noe lawe, order, or sentence shall passe as an act of the Court, without the consent of the greatr p̄te of the magistrates on the one p̄te, & the greatr number of the deputyes on the other p̄te; & for want of such accorde, the cause or order shalbe suspended, & if either p̄tie thinke it soe materiall, there shalbe forthwith a comittē chosen, the one halfe by the magistrates, & the other halfe by the deputyes, & the comittee soe chosen to elect an umpire, whoe togeather shall have power to heare & determine the cause in question." Nathaniel B. Shurtleff (ed.), *Records of the Governor and Company of Massachusetts Bay in New England* (Boston, 1853), I, 170.

[18] William C. Morey, "The First State Constitutions," *Annals of the American Academy of Political and Social Science*, IV (September, 1893), 213-14. The development of the bicameral system in the colonies under royal councils arose from the division between the governor and council, on the one hand, and the assemblies, on the other. Pennsylvania and Georgia were the only colonies with unicameral systems. *Ibid.*, 214-15.

THE CHARTER OF MASSACHUSETTS BAY[19]

March 4, 1629

Recital of grant by James I to Council for New England

CHARLES, BY THE GRACE OF GOD, Kinge of England, Scotland, Fraunce, and Ireland, Defendor of the Fayth, &c. To ALL to whome theis Presents shall come Greeting. WHEREAS, our most Deare and Royall Father, Kinge James, of blessed Memory, by his Highnes Letters-patents bearing Date at Westminster the third Day of November, in the eighteenth Yeare of his Raigne, HATH given and graunted vnto the Councell established at Plymouth, in the County of Devon, for the planting, ruling, ordering, and governing of Newe England in America, and to their Successors and Assignes for ever, all that Parte of America, lyeing and being in Bredth, from Forty Degrees of Northerly Latitude from the Equinoctiall Lyne, to forty eight Degrees of the saide Northerly Latitude inclusively, and in Length, of and within all the Breadth aforesaid, throughout the Maine Landes from Sea to Sea; together also with all the Firme Landes, Soyles, Groundes, Havens, Portes, Rivers, Waters, Fishing, Mynes, and Myneralls, as well Royall Mynes of Gould and Silver, as other Mynes and Myneralls, precious Stones, Quarries, and all and singular other Comodities, Jurisdiccons, Royalties, Priviledges, Franchesies, and Prehemynences, both within the said Tract of Land vpon the Mayne, and also within the Islandes and Seas adjoining: PROVIDED always, That the saide Islandes, or any the Premisses by the said Letters-patents intended and meant to be graunted, were not then actuallie possessed or inhabited, by any other Christian Prince or State, nor within the Boundes, Lymitts, or Territories of the Southerne Colony, then before graunted by our saide Deare Father, to be planted by divers of his loveing Subiects in the South Partes. TO HAVE and to houlde, possess, and enioy all and singular the aforesaid Continent, Landes, Territories, Islandes, Hereditaments, and Precincts, Seas, Waters, Fishings, with all, and all manner their Comodities, Royalties, Liberties, Prehemynences, and Proffits that should from thenceforth arise from thence, with all and singuler their Appurtenances, and every Parte and Parcell thereof, vnto the saide Councell and their Successors and Assignes for ever, to the sole and proper Vse, Benefitt, and Behoofe of them the saide Councell, and their Successors and Asignes for ever: To be houlden of our saide most Deare and Royall Father, his Heires and Successors, as

---

[19] Francis N. Thorpe (ed.), *The Federal and State Constitutions, Colonial Charters, and Other Organic Laws* (Washington, 1909), III, 1846-60.

of his Mannor of East Greenewich in the County of Kent, in free and comon Soccage, and not in Capite nor by Knight's Service: YEILDINGE and paying therefore to the saide late Kinge, his heires and Successors, the fifte Parte of the Oare of Gould and Silver, which should from tyme to tyme, and at all Tymes then after happen to be found, gotten, had and obteyned in, att, or within any of the saide Landes, Lymitts, Territories, and Precincts, or in or within any Parte or Parcell thereof, for or in Respect of all and all Manner of Duties, Demaunds anr Services whatsoever, to be don, made, or paide to our saide Dear Father the late Kinge his Heires and Successors, as in and by the saide Letters-patents (amongst sundrie and other Clauses, Powers, Priviledges, and Grauntes therein conteyned), more at large appeareth:

AND WHEREAS, the saide Councell established at Plymouth, in the County of Devon, for the plantinge, ruling, ordering, and governing of Newe England in America, have by their Deede, indented vnder their Comon Seale, bearing Date the nyneteenth Day of March last past, in the third Yeare of our Raigne, given, graunted, bargained, soulde, enfeoffed, aliened, and confirmed to Sir Henry Rosewell, Sir John Young, Knightes, Thomas Southcott, John Humphrey, John Endecott, and Symon Whetcombe, their Heires and Assignes, and their Associats for ever, all that Parte of Newe England in America aforesaid, which lyes and extendes betweene a greate River there comonlie called Monomack alias Merriemack, and a certen other River there, called Charles River, being in the Bottome of a certayne Bay there, comonlie called Massachusetts, alias Mattachusetts, alias Massatusetts Bay, and also all and singuler those Landes and Hereditaments whatsoever, lyeing within the Space of three English Myles on the South Parte of the said Charles River, or of any, or everie Parte thereof; and also, all and singuler the Landes and Hereditaments whatsoever, lyeing and being within the Space of three English Myles to the Southward of the Southermost Parte of the saide Bay called Massachusetts, alias Mattachusetts, alias Massatusets Bay; and also, all those Landes and Hereditaments whatsoever, which lye, and be within the space of three English Myles to the Northward of the said River called Monomack, alias Merrymack, or to the Northward of any and every Parte thereof, and all Landes and Hereditaments whatsoever, lyeing within the Lymitts aforesaide, North and South in Latitude and bredth, and in Length and Longitude, of and within all the Bredth aforesaide, throughout the Mayne Landes there, from the Atlantick and Westerne Sea and Ocean on the East Parte, to the South Sea on the West Parte; and all Landes and Groundes, Place and Places, Soyles, Woodes and Wood Groundes, Havens, Portes, Rivers, Waters, Fishings, and Hereditaments whatsoever, lyeing within the said Boundes and Lymitts, and everie Parte and Parcell thereof; and also all Islandes lyeing in America aforesaide, in the saide Seas or either of them on the Westerne or Eastern Coastes or Partes of the said Tractes of Lande, by the saide Indenture mencōed to be given, graunted, bargained, sould, enfeoffed, aliened, and confirmed, or any of them; and also, all Mynes and Myneralls, as well Royall Mynes of Gould and Silver, as other Mynes and Myneralls whatsoeuer, in the

Recital of grant by Council for New England to members of Massachusetts Bay Company

saide Lands and Premisses, or any Parte thereof; and all Jurisdiccons, Rights, Royalties, Liberties, Freedomes, Ymmunities, Priviledges, Franchises, Preheminences, and Comodities whatsoever, which they, the said Councell established at Plymouth, in the County of Devon, for the planting, ruling, ordering, and governing of Newe England in America, then had, or might vse, exercise, or enjoy, in or within the saide Landes and Premisses by the saide Indenture mencōed to be given, graunted, bargained, sould, enfeoffed, and confirmed, or in or within any Parte or Parcell thereof:

TO HAVE and to hould, the saide Parte of Newe England in America, which lyes and extendes and is abutted as aforesaide, and every Parte and Parcell thereof; and all the saide Islandes, Rivers, Portes, Havens, Waters, Fishings, Mynes, and Myneralls, Jurisdiccons, Franchises, Royalties, Liberties, Priviledges, Comodities, Hereditaments, and Premisses whatsoever, with the Appurtenances vnto the saide Sir Henry Rosewell, Sir John Younge, Thomas Southcott, John Humfrey, John Endecott, and Simon Whetcombe, their Heires and Assignes, and their Associatts, to the onlie proper and absolute vse and Behoofe of the said Sir Henry Rosewell, Sir John Younge, Thomas Southcott, John Humfrey, John Endecott, and Simon Whettcombe, their Heires and Assignes, and their Associatts forevermore; TO BE HOULDEN of Us, our Heires and Successors, as of our Mannor of Eastgreenwich, in the County of Kent, in free and comon Soccage, and not in Capite, nor by Knightes Service; YEILDING and payeing therefore vnto Vs, our Heires and Successors, the fifte Parte of the Oare of Goulde and Silver, which shall from Tyme to Tyme, and at all Tymes hereafter, happen to be founde, gotten, had, and obteyned in any of the saide Landes, within the saide Lymitts, or in or within any Parte thereof, for, and in Satisfaccon of all manner Duties, Demaundes and Services whatsoever to be donn, made, or paid to Vs, our Heires or Successors, as in and by the said recited Indenture more at large maie appeare.

Royal confirmation of the grant from the Council for New England to members of Massachusetts Bay Company

NOWE Knoew Ye, that Wee, at the humble Suite and Peticon of the saide Sir Henry Rosewell, Sir John Younge, Thomas Southcott, John Humfrey, John Endecott, and Simon Whetcombe, and of others whome they have associated vnto them, HAVE, for divers good Causes and consideracons, vs moveing, graunted and confirmed, and by theis Presents of our especiall Grace, certen Knowledge, and meere Mocon, doe graunt and confirme vnto the saide Sir Henry Rosewell, Sir John Younge, Thomas Southcott, John Humfrey, John Endecott, and Simon Whetcombe, and to their Associatts hereafter named; (videlicet) Sir Richard Saltonstall, Knight, Isaack Johnson, Samuel Aldersey, John Ven, Mathew Cradock, George Harwood, Increase Nowell, Richard Perry, Richard Bellingham, Nathaniell Wright, Samuel Vassall, Theophilus Eaton, Thomas Goffe, Thomas Adams, John Browne, Samuell Browne, Thomas Hutchins, William Vassall, William Pinchion, and George Foxcrofte, their Heires and Assignes, all the saide Parte of Newe England in America, lyeing and extending betweene the Boundes and Lymytts in the said recited Indenture expressed, and all Landes and Groundes, Place and Places, Soyles, Woods and Wood Groundes, Havens, Portes, Rivers, Waters, Mynes, Minerals, Jurisdiccōns, Rightes, Royalties, Liberties, Freedomes, Immunities, Priviledges, Franchises, Preheminences, Hereditaments, and

THE CHARTER OF MASSACHUSETTS BAY

Comodities whatsoever, to them the saide Sir Henry Rosewell, Sir John Younge, Thomas Southcott, John Humfrey, John Endecott, and Simon Whetcombe, theire Heires and Assignes, and to their Associatts, by the saide recited Indenture, given, graunted, bargayned, solde, enfeoffed, aliened, and confirmed, or mencōed, or intended thereby to be given, graunted, bargayned, sold, enfeoffed, aliened, and confirmed: TO HAVE, and to hould, the saide Parte of Newe England in America, and other the Premisses hereby mencōed to be graunted and confirmed, and every Parte and Parcell thereof with the Appurtennces, to the saide Sir Henry Rosewell, Sir John Younge, Sir Richard Saltonstall, Thomas Southcott, John Humfrey, John Endecott, Simon Whetcombe, Isaack Johnson, Richard Pery, Richard Bellingham, Nathaniell Wright, Samuell Vassall, Theophilus Eaton, Thomas Goffe, Thomas Adams, John Browne, Samuel Browne, Thomas Hutchins, Samuel Aldersey, John Ven, Mathewe Cradock, George Harwood, Increase Nowell, William Vassall, William Pinchion, and George Foxcrofte, their Heires and Assignes forever, to their onlie proper and absolute Vse and Behoofe for evermore; To be holden of Vs, our Heires and Successors, as of our Mannor of Eastgreenewich aforesaid, in free and comon Socage, and not in Capite, nor by Knights Service; AND ALSO YEILDING and paying therefore to Vs, our Heires and Successors, the fifte parte onlie of all Oare of Gould and Silver, which from tyme to tyme, and att all tymes hereafter shalbe there gotten, had, or obteyned, for all Services, Exaccons and Demaundes whatsoever, according to the Tenure and Reservacon in the said recited Indenture expressed.

AND FURTHER, knowe yee, that of our more especiall Grace, certen Knowledg, and meere mocon, Wee have given and graunted, and by theis Presents, doe for Vs, our Heires and Successors, give and graunte vnto the saide Sir Henry Rosewell, Sir John Younge, Sir Richard Saltonstall, Thomas Southcott, John Humfrey, John Endecott, Symon Whetcombe, Isaack Johnson, Samuell Aldersey, John Ven, Mathewe Cradock, George Harwood, Increase Nowell, Richard Pery, Richard Bellingham, Nathaniel Wright, Samuell Vassall, Theophilus Eaton, Thomas Goffe, Thomas Adams, John Browne, Samuell Browne, Thomas Hutchins, William Vassall, William Pinchion, and George Foxcrofte, their Heires and Assignes, all that Parte of Newe England in America, which lyes and extendes betweene a great River there, comonlie called Monomack River, alias Merrimack River, and a certen other River there, called Charles River, being in the Bottome of a certen Bay there, comonlie called Massachusetts, alias Mattachusetts, alias Massatusetts Bay; and also all and singuler those Landes and Hereditaments whatsoever, lying within the Space of Three Englishe Myles on the South Parte of the said River, called Charles River, or of any or every Parte thereof; and also all and singuler the Landes and Hereditaments whatsoever, lying and being within the Space of Three Englishe Miles to the southward of the southenmost Parte of the said Baye, called Massachusetts, alias Mattachusetts, alias Massatusets Bay: And also all those Landes and Hereditaments whatsoever, which lye and be within the Space of Three English Myles to the Northward of the saide River, called Monomack, alias Merrymack, or to the Norward of any and every Parte thereof, and all Landes and Hereditaments whatsoever, lyeing within the Lymitts

Description of lands granted

85

aforesaide, North and South, in Latitude and Bredth, and in Length and Longitude, of and within all the Bredth aforesaide, throughout the mayne Landes there, from the Atlantick and Westerne Sea and Ocean on the East Parte, to the South Sea on the West Parte; and all Landes and Groundes, Place and Places, Soyles, Woodes, and Wood Groundes, Havens, Portes, Rivers, Waters, and Hereditaments whatsoever, lyeing within the said Boundes and Lymytts, and every Parte and Parcell thereof; and also all Islandes in America aforesaide, in the saide Seas, or either of them, on the Westerne or Easterne Coastes, or Partes of the saide Tracts of Landes hereby mencōed to be given and graunted, or any of them; and all Mynes and Mynerals as well Royal mynes of Gold and Silver and other mynes and mynerals, whatsoever, in the said Landes and Premisses, or any parte thereof, and free Libertie of fishing in or within any the Rivers or Waters within the Boundes and Lymytts aforesaid, and the Seas therevnto adjoining; and all Fishes, Royal Fishes, Whales, Balan, Sturgions, and other Fishes of what Kinde or Nature soever, that shall at any time hereafter be taken in or within the saide Seas or Waters, or any of them, by the said Sir Henry Rosewell, Sir John Younge, Sir Richard Saltonstall, Thomas Southcott, John Humfrey, John Endecott, Simon Whetcombe, Isaack Johnson, Samuell Aldersey, John Ven, Mathewe Cradock, George Harwood, Increase Noell, Richard Pery, Richard Bellingham, Nathaniell Wright, Samuell Vassell, Theophilus Eaton, Thomas Goffe, Thomas Adams, John Browne, Samuell Browne; Thomas Hutchins, William Vassall, William Pinchion, and George Foxcrofte, their Heires and Assignes, or by any other person or persons whatsoever there inhabiting, by them, or any of them, to be appointed to fishe therein.

Exception of lands inhabited prior to November 3, 1620, or within the Virginia grant

PROVIDED alwayes, That yf the said Landes, Islandes, or any other the Premisses herein before mencōned, and by theis presents, intended and meant to be graunted, were at the tyme of the graunting of the saide former Letters patents, dated the Third Day of November, in the Eighteenth Yeare of our said deare Fathers Raigne aforesaide, actuallie possessed or inhabited by any other Christian Prince or State, or were within the Boundes, Lymytts or Territories of that Southerne Colony, then before graunted by our said late Father, to be planted by divers of his loveing Subiects in the south partes of America, That then this present Graunt shall not extend to any such partes or parcells thereof, soe formerly inhabited, or lyeing within the Boundes of the Southerne Plantacōn as aforesaide, but as to those partes or parcells soe possessed or inhabited by such Christian Prince or State, or being within the Bounders aforesaide, shal be vtterlie voyd, theis presents or any Thinge therein conteyned to the contrarie notwithstanding. TO HAVE and hould, possesse and enioye the saide partes of New England in America, which lye, extend, and are abutted as aforesaide, and every parte and parcell thereof; and all the Islandes, Rivers, Portes, Havens, Waters, Fishings, Fishes, Mynes, Myneralls, Jurisdiccōns, Franchises, Royalties, Liberties, Priviledges, Comodities, and Premisses whatsoever, with the Appurtenances, vnto the said Sir Henry Rosewell, Sir John Younge, Sir Richard Saltonstall, Thomas Southcott, John Humfrey, John Endecott, Simon Whetcombe, Isaack Johnson, Samuell Aldersey, John Ven, Mathewe Cradock, George Harwood, Increase Nowell, Richard Perry,

THE CHARTER OF MASSACHUSETTS BAY

Richard Bellingham, Nathaniell Wright, Samuel Vassall, Theophilus Eaton, Thomas Goffe, Thomas Adams, John Browne, Samuell Browne, Thomas Hutchins, William Vassall, William Pinchion, and George Foxcroft, their Heires and Assignes forever, to the onlie proper and absolute Vse and Behoufe of the said Sir Henry Rosewell, Sir John Younge, Sir Richard Saltonstall, Thomas Southcott, John Humfrey, John Endecott, Simon Whetcombe, Isaac Johnson, Samuell Aldersey, John Ven, Mathewe Cradocke, George Harwood, Increase Nowell, Richard Pery, Richard Bellingham, Nathaniell Wright, Samuell Vassall, Theophilus Eaton, Thomas Goffe, Thomas Adams, John Browne, Samuell Browne, Thomas Hutchins, William Vassall, William Pinchion, and George Foxcroft, their Heires and Assignes forevermore: TO BE HOLDEN of Vs, our Heires and Successors, as of our Manor of Eastgreenwich in our Countie of Kent, within our Realme of England, in free and comon Soccage, and not in Capite, nor by Knights Service; and also yeilding and paying therefore, to Vs, our Heires and Sucessors, the fifte Parte onlie of all Oare of Gould and Silver, which from tyme to tyme, and at all tymes hereafter, shal be there gotten, had, or obteyned, for all Services, Exaccons, and Demaundes whatsoever; PROVIDED alwaies, and our expresse Will and Meaninge is, that onlie one fifte Parte of the Gould and Silver Oare above mencōed, in the whole, and noe more be reserved or payeable vnto Vs, our Heires and Successors, by Collour or Vertue of theis Presents, the double Reservacōns or rentals aforesaid or any Thing herein conteyned notwithstanding. AND FORASMUCH, as the good and prosperous Successe of the Plantacon of the saide Partes of Newe-England aforesaide intended by the said Sir Henry Rosewell, Sir John Younge, Sir Richard Saltonstall, Thomas Southcott, John Humfrey, John Endecott, Simon Whetcombe, Isaack Johnson, Samuell Aldersey, John Ven, Mathew Cradock, George Harwood, Increase Noell, Richard Pery, Richard Bellingham, Nathaniell Wright, Samuell Vassall, Theophilus Eaton, Thomas Goffe, Thomas Adams, John Browne, Samuell Browne, Thomas Hutchins, William Vassall, William Pinchion, and George Foxcrofte, to be speedily sett vpon, cannot but cheifly depend, next vnder the Blessing of Almightie God, and the support of our Royall Authoritie vpon the good Government of the same, To the Ende that the Affaires and Buyssinesses which from tyme to tyme shall happen and arise concerning the saide Landes, and the Plantation of the same maie be the better mannaged and ordered, WEE HAVE FURTHER hereby of our especial Grace, certain Knowledge and mere Mocōn, Given, graunted and confirmed, and for Vs, our Heires and Successors, doe give, graunt, and confirme vnto our said trustie and welbeloved subiects Sir Henry Rosewell, Sir John Younge, Sir Richard Saltonstall, Thomas Southcott, John Humfrey, John Endicott, Simon Whetcombe, Isaack Johnson, Samuell Aldersey, John Ven, Mathewe Cradock, George Harwood, Increase Nowell, Richard Pery, Richard Bellingham, Nathaniell Wright, Samuell Vassall, Theophilus Eaton, Thomas Goffe, Thomas Adams, John Browne, Samuell Browne, Thomas Hutchins, William Vassall, William Pinchion, and George Foxcrofte: AND for Vs, our Heires and Successors, Wee will and ordeyne, That the saide Sir Henry Rosewell, Sir John Young, Sir Richard Saltonstall, Thomas Southcott, John Humfrey, John Endicott, Symon Whetcombe, Isaack

Formation of Massachusetts Bay Company

Johnson, Samuell Aldersey, John Ven, Mathewe Cradock, George Harwood, Increase Noell, Richard Pery, Richard Bellingham, Nathaniell Wright, Samuell Vassall, Theophilus Eaton, Thomas Goffe, Thomas Adams, John Browne, Samuell Browne, Thomas Hutchins, William Vassall, William Pinchion, and George Foxcrofte, and all such others as shall hereafter be admitted and made free of the Company and Society hereafter mencōed, shall from tyme to tyme, and att all tymes forever hereafter be, by Vertue of theis presents, one Body corporate and politique in Fact and Name, by the Name of the Governor and Company of the Mattachusetts Bay in Newe-England, and them by the Name of the Governour and Company of the Mattachusetts Bay in Newe-England, one Bodie politique and corporate, in Deede, Fact, and Name; Wee doe for vs, our Heires and Successors, make, ordeyne, constitute, and confirme by theis Presents, and that by that name they shall have perpetuall Succession, and that by the same Name they and their Successors shall and maie be capeable and enabled aswell to implead, and to be impleaded, and to prosecute, demaund, and aunswere, and be aunsweared vnto, in all and singuler Suites, Causes, Quarrells, and Accons, of what kinde or nature soever. And also to have, take, possesse, acquire, and purchase any Landes, Tenements, or Hereditaments, or any Goodes or Chattells, and the same to lease, graunte, demise, alien, bargaine, sell, and dispose of, as other our liege People of this our Realme of England, or any other corporacon or Body politique of the same may lawfully doe.

Officers: governor, deputy governor, eighteen assistants to be elected from the freemen of the company

AND FURTHER, That the said Governour and Companye, and their Successors, maie have forever one comon Seale, to be vsed in all Causes and Occasions of the said Company, and the same Seale may alter, chaunge, breake, and newe make, from tyme to tyme, at their pleasures. And our Will and Pleasure is, and Wee doe hereby for Vs, our Heires and Successors, ordeyne and graunte, That from henceforth for ever, there shalbe one Governor, one Deputy Governor, and eighteene Assistants of the same Company, to be from tyme to tyme constituted, elected and chosen out of the Freemen of the saide Company, for the twyme being, in such Manner and Forme as hereafter in theis Presents is expressed, which said Officers shall applie themselves to take Care for the best disposeing and ordering of the generall buysines and Affaires of, for, and concerning the said Landes and Premisses hereby mencōed, to be graunted, and the Plantacion thereof, and the Government of the People there. AND FOR the better Execucon of our Royall Pleasure and Graunte in this Behalf, WEE doe, by theis presents, for Vs, our Heires and Successors, nominate, ordeyne, make, & constitute; our welbeloved the saide Mathewe Cradocke, to be the first and present Governor of the said Company, and the saide Thomas Goffe, to be Deputy Governor of the saide Company, and the saide Sir Richard Saltonstall, Isaack Johnson, Samuell Aldersey, John Ven, John Humfrey, John Endecott, Simon Whetcombe, Increase Noell, Richard Pery, Nathaniell Wright, Samuell Vassall, Theophilus Eaton, Thomas Adams, Thomas Hutchins, John Browne, George Foxcrofte, William Vassall, and William Pinchion, to be the present Assistants of the saide Company, to continue in the saide several Offices respectivelie for such tyme, and in such manner, as in and by theis Presents is hereafter declared and appointed.

Names of first governor, deputy governor, and assistants

THE CHARTER OF MASSACHUSETTS BAY

AND FURTHER, Wee will, and by theis Presents, for Vs, our Heires and Successors, doe ordeyne and graunte, That the Governor of the saide Company for the tyme being, or in his Absence by Occasion of Sicknes or otherwise, the Deputie Governor for the tyme being, shall have Authoritie from tyme to tyme vpon all Occasions, to give order for the assembling of the saide Company, and calling them together to consult and advise of the Bussinesses and Affaires of the saide Company, and that the said Governor, Deputie Governor, and Assistants of the saide Company, for the tyme being, shall or maie once every Moneth, or oftener at their Pleasures, assemble and houlde and keepe a Courte or Assemblie of themselves, for the better ordering and directing of their Affaires, and that any seaven or more persons of the Assistants, togither with the Governor, or Deputie Governor soe assembled, shalbe saide, taken, held, and reputed to be, and shalbe a full and sufficient Courte or Assemblie of the said Company, for the handling, ordering, and dispatching of all such Buysinesses and Occurrents as shall from tyme to tyme happen, touching or concerning the said Company or Plantacon; and that there shall or maie be held and kept by the Governor, or Deputie Governor of the said Company, and seaven or more of the said Assistants for the tyme being, vpon every last Wednesday in Hillary, Easter, Trinity, and Michas Termes respectivelie forever, one greate generall and solempe assemblie, which foure generall assemblies shalbe stiled and called the foure greate and generall Courts of the saide Company; IN all and every, or any of which saide greate and generall Courts soe assembled, WEE DOE for Vs, our Heires and Successors, give and graunte to the said Governor and Company, and their Successors, That the Governor, or in his absence, the Deputie Governor of the saide Company for the tyme being, and such of the Assistants and Freeman of the saide Company as shalbe present, or the greater number of them so assembled, whereof the Governor or Deputie Governor and six of the Assistants at the least to be seaven, shall have full Power and authoritie to choose, nominate, and appointe, such and soe many others as they shall thinke fitt, and that shall be willing to accept the same, to be free of the said Company and Body, and them into the same to admitt; and to elect and constitute such Officers as they shall thinke fitt and requisite, for the ordering, mannaging, and dispatching of the Affaires of the saide Govenor and Company, and their Successors; And to make Lawes and Ordinances for the Good and Welfare of the saide Company, and for the Government and ordering of the saide Landes and Plantacon, and the People inhabiting and to inhabit the same, as to them from tyme to tyme shalbe thought meete, soe as such Lawes and Ordinances be not contrarie or repugnant to the Lawes and Statuts of this our Realme of England. AND, our Will and Pleasure is, and Wee doe hereby for Vs, our Heires and Successors, establish and ordeyne, That yearely once in the yeare, for ever hereafter, namely, the last Wednesday in Easter Tearme, yearely, the Governor, Deputy-Governor, and Assistants of the saide Company and all other officers of the saide Company shalbe in the Generall Court or Assembly to be held for that Day or Tyme, newly chosen for the Yeare ensueing by such greater parte of the said Company, for the Tyme being, then and there present, as is aforesaide. AND, yf it shall happen the present governor,

Governor
May convene the company

Court of Assistants

Quorum

General Court

Admission of freemen

Election of officers
Lawmaking

Annual elections

Special elections Deputy Governor, and assistants, by theis presents appointed, or such as shall hereafter be newly chosen into their Roomes, or any of them, or any other of the officers to be appointed for the said Company, to dye, or to be removed from his or their severall Offices or Places before the saide generall Day of Eleccon (whome Wee doe hereby declare for any Misdemeanor or Defect to be removeable by the Governor, Deputie Governor, Assistants, and Company, or such greater Parte of them in any of the publique Courts to be assembled as is aforesaid) That then, and in every such Case, it shall and maie be lawfull, to and for the Governor, Deputie Governor, Assistants, and Company aforesaide, or such greater Parte of them soe to be assembled as is aforesaide, in any of their Assemblies, to proceade to a new Eleccon of one or more others of their Company in the Roome or Place, Roomes or Places of such Officer or Officers soe dyeing or removed according to their Discrecons, And, ymediately vpon and after such Eleccon and Eleccons made of such Governor, Deputie Governor, Assistant or Assistants, or any other officer of the saide Company, in Manner and Forme aforesaid, the Authoritie, Office, and Power, before given to the former Governor, Deputie Governor, or other Officer and Officers soe removed, in whose Steade and Place newe shabe soe chosen, shall as to him and them, and everie of them, cease and determine.

Oath of office PROVIDED alsoe, and our Will and Pleasure is, That aswell such as are by theis Presents appointed to be the present Governor, Deputie Governor, and Assistants of the said Company, as those that shall succeed them, and all other Officers to be appointed and chosen as aforesaid, shall, before they vndertake the Execucon of their saide Offices and Places respectivelie, take their Corporal Oathes for the due and faithfull Performance of their Duties in their severall Offices and Places, before such Person or Persons as are by theis Presents herevnder appointed to take and receive the same; That is to saie, the saide Mathewe Cradock, whoe is hereby nominated and appointed the present Governor of the saide Company, shall take the saide Oathes before one or more of the Masters of our Courte of Chauncery for the Tyme being, vnto which Master or Masters of the Chauncery, Wee doe by theis Presents give full Power and Authoritie to take and administer the said Oathe to the said Governor accordinglie: And after the saide Governor shalbe soe sworne, then the said Deputy Governor and Assistants, before by theis Presents nominated and appointed, shall take the said severall Oathes to their Offices and Places respectivelie belonging, before the said Mathew Cradock, the present Governor, soe formerlie sworne as aforesaide. And every such person as shallbe at the Tyme of the annuall Eleccon, or otherwise, vpon Death or Removeall, be appointed to be the newe Governor of the said Company, shall take the Oathes to that Place belonging, before the Deputy Governor, or two of the Assistants of the said Company at the least, for the Tyme being: And the newe elected Deputie Governor and Assistants, and all other officers to be hereafter chosen as aforesaide from Tyme to Tyme, to take the Oathes to their places respectivelie belonging, before the Governor of the said Company for the Tyme being, vnto which said Governor, Deputie Governor, and assistants, Wee doe by theis Presents give full Power and Authoritie to give and administer the

THE CHARTER OF MASSACHUSETTS BAY

said Oathes respectively, according to our true Meaning herein before declared, without any Comission or further Warrant to be had and obteyned of our Vs, our Heires or Successors, in that Behalf. AND, Wee doe further, of our especial Grace, certen Knowledge, and meere mocon, for Vs, our Heires and Successors, give and graunte to the said Governor and Company, and their Successors for ever by theis Presents, That it shalbe lawfull and free for them and their Assignes, at all and every Tyme and Tymes hereafter, out of any our Realmes or Domynions whatsoever, to take, leade, carry, and transport, for in and into their Voyages, and for and towardes the said Plantacon in Newe England, all such and soe many of our loving Subjects, or any other strangers that will become our loving Subjects, and live under our Allegiance, as shall willinglie accompany them in the same Voyages and Plantacon; and also Shipping, Armour, Weapons, Ordinance, Municon, Powder, Shott, Corne, Victualls, and all Manner of Clothing, Implements, Furniture, Beastes, Cattle, Horses, Mares, Merchandizes, and all other Thinges necessarie for the saide Plantacon, and for their Vse and Defence, and for Trade with the People there, and in passing and returning to and fro, any Lawe or Statute to the contrarie hereof in any wise notwithstanding; and without payeing or yeilding any Custome or Subsidie, either inward or outward, to Vs, our Heires or Successors, for the same, by the Space of seaven Yeares from the Day of the Date of theis Presents. PROVIDED, that none of the saide Persons be such as shalbe hereafter by especiall Name restrayned by Vs, our Heires or Successors. AND, for their further Encouragement, of our especiall Grace and Favor, Wee doe by theis Presents, for Vs, our Heires and Successors, yeild and graunt to the saide Governor and Company, and their Successors, and every of them, their Factors and Assignes, That they and every of them shalbe free and quitt from all Taxes, Subsidies, and Customes, in Newe England, for the like Space of seaven Yeares, and from all Taxes and Imposicons for the Space of twenty and one Yeares, vpon all Goodes and Merchandizes at any Tyme or Tymes hereafter, either vpon Importacon thither, or Exportacon from thence into our Realme of England, or into any other our Domynions by the said Governor and Company, and their Successors, their Deputies, Factors, and Assignes, or any of them; EXCEPT onlie the five Pounds per Centum due for Custome vpon all such Goodes and Merchandizes as after the saide seaven Yeares shalbe expired, shalbe brought or imported into our Realme of England, or any other of our Dominions, according to the aunciont Trade of Merchants, which five Poundes per Centum onlie being paide, it shall be thenceforth lawfull and free for the said Adventurers the same Goodes and Merchandizes to export and carry out of our said Domynions into forraine Partes, without any Custome, Tax, or other Dutie to be paid to Vs, our Heires or Successors, or to any other Officers or Ministers of Vs, our Heires and Successors. PROVIDED, that the said Goodes and Merchandizes be shipped out within thirteene Monethes, after their first Landing within any Parte of the saide Domynions.

AND, Wee doe for Vs, our Heires and Successors, give and graunte vnto the saide Governor and Company, and their Successors, That whensoever, or soe often as any Custome or Subsedie shall growe due or payeable vnto Vs, our Heires, or Successors,

New colonists

Imports

Customs

according to the Lymittacon and Appointment aforesaide, by Reason of any Goodes, Wares, or Merchandizes to be shipped out, or any Retorne to be made of any Goodes, Wares, or Merchandize vnto or from the said Partes of Newe England hereby moncōed to be graunted as aforesaid, or any the Landes or Territories aforesaide, That then, and soe often, and in such Case, the Farmors, Customers, and Officers of our Customes of England and Ireland, and everie of them for the Tyme being, vpon Request made to them by the saide Governor and Company, or their Successors, Factors, or Assignes, and vpon convenient Security to be given in that Behalf, shall give and allowe vnto the said Governor and Company, and their Successors, and to all and everie Person and Persons free of that Company, as aforesaide, six Monethes Tyme for the Payement of the one halfe of all such Custome and Subsidy as shalbe due and payeable unto Vs, our Heires and Successors, for the same; for which theis our Letters patent, or the Duplicate, or the inrollem^t thereof, shalbe vnto our saide Officers a sufficient Warrant and Discharge. NEVERTHELES, our Will and Pleasure is, That yf any of the saide Goodes, Wares, and Merchandize, which be, or shalbe at any Tyme hereafter landed or exported out of any of our Realmes aforesaid, and shalbe shipped with a Purpose not to be carried to the Partes of Newe England aforesaid, but to some other place, That then such Payment, Dutie, Custome, Imposicōn, or Forfeyture, shalbe paid, or belonge to Vs, our Heires and Successors, for the said Goodes, Wares, and Merchandize, soe fraudulently sought to be transported, as yf this our Graunte had not been made nor graunted. AND, Wee doe further will, and by theis Presents, for Vs, our Heires and Successors, firmlie enioine and comaunde, as well the Treasorer, Chauncellor and Barons of the Exchequer, of Vs, our Heires and Successors, as also all and singuler the Customers, Farmors, and Collectors of the Customes, Subsidies, and Imposts, and other the Officers and Ministers of Vs, our Heires and Successors whatsoever, for the Tyme Being, That they and every of them, vpon the shewing forth vnto them of theis Letters patents, or the Duplicate or exemplificacōn of the same, without any other Writt or Warrant whatsoever from Vs, our Heires or Successors, to be obteyned or sued forth, doe and shall make full, whole, entire, and due Allowance, and cleare Discharge vnto the saide Governor and Company, and their Successors, of all Customes, Subsidies, Imposicōns, Taxes and Duties whatsoever, that shall or maie be claymed by Vs, our Heires and Successors, of or from the said Governor and Company, and their Successors, for or by Reason of the said Goodes, Chattels, Wares, Merchandizes, and Premises to be exported out of our saide Domynions, or any of them, into any Parte of the saide Landes or Premises hereby mencōed, to be given, graunted, and confirmed, or for, or by Reason of any of the saide Goodes, Chattells, Wares, or Merchandizes to be imported from the said Landes and Premises hereby mencōed, to be given, graunted, and confirmed into any of our saide Dominions, or any Parte thereof as aforesaide, excepting onlie the saide five Poundes per Centum hereby reserved and payeable after the Expiracōn of the saide Terme of seaven Yeares as aforesaid, and not before: And theis our Letters-patents, or the Inrollment, Duplicate, or Exemplificacōn of the same shalbe for ever hereafter, from time to tyme, as well to the Treasorer, Chauncellor and Barons of the Exchequer of Vs, our Heires

THE CHARTER OF MASSACHUSETTS BAY

and Successors, as to all and singuler the Customers, Farmors, and Collectors of the Customes, Subsidies, and Imposts of Vs, our Heires and Successors, and all Searchers, and other the Officers and Ministers whatsoever of Vs, our Heires and Successors, for the Time being, a sufficient Warrant and Discharge in this Behalf.

AND, further our Will and Pleasure is, and Wee doe hereby for Vs, our Heires and Successors, ordeyne and declare, and graunte to the saide Governor and Company, and their Successors, That all and every the Subiects of Vs, our Heires or Successors, which shall goe to and inhabite within the saide Landes and Premisses hereby mencōed to be graunted, and every of their Children which shall happen to be borne there, or on the Seas in goeing thither, or retorning from thence, shall have and enjoy all liberties and Immunities of free and naturall Subiects within any of the Domynions of Vs, our Heires or Successors, to all Intents, Construccōns, and Purposes whatsoever, as yf they and everie of them were borne within the Realme of England. And that the Governor and Deputie Governor of the said Company for the Tyme being, or either of them, and any two or more of such of the saide Assistants as shalbe therevnto appointed by the saide Governor and Company at any of their Courts or Assemblies to be held as aforesaide, shall and maie at all Tymes, and from tyme to tyme hereafter, have full Power and Authoritie to minister and give the Oathe and Oathes of Supremacie and Allegiance, or either of them, to all and everie Person and Persons, which shall at any Tyme or Tymes hereafter goe or passe to the Landes and Premisses hereby mencōed to be graunted to inhabite in the same. AND, Wee doe of our further Grace, certen Knowledg and meere Mocōn, give and graunte to the saide Governor and Company, and their Successors, That it shall and maie be lawfull, to and for the Governor or Deputie Governor, and such of the Assistants and Freemen of the said Company for the Tyme being as shalbe assembled in any of their generall Courts aforesaide, or in any other Courtes to be specially sumoned and assembled for that Purpose, or the greater Parte of them (whereof the Governor or Deputie Governor, and six of the Assistants to be alwaies seaven) from tyme to tyme, to make, ordeine, and establishe all Manner of wholesome and reasonable Orders, Lawes, Statutes, and Ordinānces, Direccōns, and Instruccōns, not contrairie to the Lawes of this our Realme of England, aswell for setling of the Formes and Ceremonies of Governm^t and Magistracy, fitt and necessary for the said Plantacōn, and the Inhabitants there, and for nameing and setting of all sorts of Officers, both superior and inferior, which they shall finde needefull for that Governement and Plantacon, and the distinguishing and setting forth of the severall duties, Powers, and Lymytts of every such Office and Place, and the Formes of such Oathes warrantable by the Lawes and Statutes of this our Realme of England, as shalbe respestivelie ministred vnto them for the Execucōn of the said severall Offices and Places; as also, for the disposing and ordering of the Eleccōns of such of the said Officers as shalbe annuall, and of such others as shalbe to succeede in Case of Death or Removeall, and ministring the said Oathes to the newe elected Officers, and for Imposicons of lawfull Fynes, Mulcts, Imprisonment, or other lawfull Correccōn, according to the Course of other Corporacons in this our Realme of England, and for the directing, ruling, and disposeing of all other Matters and

Liberties of colonists

Oath of supremacy

Laws
In general

Forms of government
Officers

Oaths

Elections

Punishments

Other matters

Thinges, whereby our said People, Inhabitants there, may be soe religiously, peaceablie, and civilly governed, as their good Life and orderlie Conversacon, maie wynn and incite the Natives of Country, to the Knowledg and Obedience of the onlie true God and Sauior of Mankinde, and the Christian Fayth, which in our Royall Intencon, and the Adventurers free Profession, is the principall Ende of this Plantacion. WILLING, comaunding, and requiring, and by theis Presents for Vs, our Heires, and Successors, ordeyning and appointing, that all such Orders, Lawes, Statuts and Ordinnces, Instruccons and Direccons, as shalbe soe made by the Governor, or Deputie Governor of the said Company, and such of the Assistants and Freemen as aforesaide, and published in Writing, vnder their comon Seale, shalbe carefullie and dulie observed, kept, performed, and putt in Execucon, according to the true Intent and Meaning of the same; and theis our Letters-patents, or the Duplicate or exemplificacon thereof, shalbe to all and everie such Officers, superior and inferior, from Tyme to Tyme, for the putting of the same Orders, Lawes, Statutes, and Ordinnces, Instruccons, and Direccons, in due Execucon against Vs, our Heires and Successors, a sufficient Warrant and Discharge.

Powers of Officers

AND WEE DOE further, for Vs, our Heires and Successors, give and graunt to the said Governor and Company, and their Successors by theis Presents, that all and everie such Chiefe Comaunders, Captaines, Governors, and other Officers and Ministers, as by the said Orders, Lawes, Statuts, Ordinnces, Instruccons, or Direccons of the said Governor and Company for the Tyme being, shalbe from Tyme to Tyme hereafter ymploied either in the Government of the saide Inhabitants and Plantacon, or in the Waye by Sea thither, or from thence, according to the Natures and Lymitts of their

To punish, pardon, and govern

Offices and Places respectively, shall from Tyme to Tyme hereafter for ever, within the Precincts and Partes of Newe England hereby mencoed to be graunted and confirmed, or in the Waie by Sea thither, or from thence, have full and Absolute Power and Authoritie to correct, punishe, pardon, governe, and rule all such the Subiects of Vs, our Heires and Successors, as shall from Tyme to Tyme adventure themselves in any Voyadge thither or from thence, or that shall at any Tyme hereafter, inhabite within the Precincts and Partes of Newe England aforasaid, according to the Orders, Lawes, Ordinnces, Instruccons, and Direccons aforesaid, not being repugnant to the

Defense

Lawes and Statutes of our Realme of England as aforesaid. AND WEE DOE further, for Vs, our Heires and Successors, give and graunte to the said Governor and Company and their Successors, by theis Presents, that it shall and maie be lawfull, to and for the Chiefe Comaunders, Governors, and officers of the said Company, for the Time being, who shalbe resident in the said Parte of Newe England in America, by theis Presents graunted, and others there inhabiting by their Appointment and Direccon, from Tyme to Tyme, and at all Tymes hereafter for their speciall Defence and Safety, to incounter, expulse, repell, and resist by Force of Armes, aswell by Sea as by Lande, and by all fitting Waies and Meanes whatsoever, all such Person and Persons, as shall at any Tyme hereafter, attempt or enterprise the Destruccon, Invasion, Detriment, or Annoyaunce to the said Plantation or Inhabitants, and to take and surprise by all Waies and Meanes whatsoever, all and every such Person and Persons, with their

THE CHARTER OF MASSACHUSETTS BAY

Shippes, Armour, Municōn, and other Goodes, as shall in hostile manner invade or attempt the defeating of the said Plantacon, or the Hurt of the said Company and Inhabitants: NEVERTHELES, our Will and Pleasure is, and Wee doe hereby declare to all Christian Kinges, Princes and States, that yf any Person or Persons which shall hereafter be of the said Company or Plantacōn, or any other by Lycense or Appointment of the said Governor and Company for the Tyme being, shall at any Tyme or Tymes hereafter, robb or spoyle, by Sea or by Land, or doe any Hurt, Violence, or vnlawful Hostilitie to any of the subjects of Vs, our Heires or Successors, or any of the Subjects of any Prince or State, being then in League and Amytie with Vs, our Heires and Successors, and that upon such injury don and vpon iust Complaint of such Prince or State or their Subjects, WEE, our Heires and Successors shall make open Proclamacōn within any of the Partes within our Realme of England, comōdious for that purpose, that the Person or Persons haveing comītted any such Roberie or Spoyle, shall within the Terme lymytted by such a Proclamacon, make full Restitucōn or Satisfaccōn of all such Iniureis don, soe as the said Princes or others so complayning, maie hould themselves fullie satisfied and contented; and that yf the said Person or Persons, haveing comītted such Robbery or Spoile, shall not make, or cause to be made Satisfaccōn accordinglie, within such Tyme soe to be lymytted, that then it shalbe lawfull for Vs, our Heires and Successors, to putt the said Person or Persons out of our Allegiance and Proteccōn, and that it shalbe lawfull and free for all Princes to prosecute with Hostilitie, the said Offendors, and every of them, their and every of their Procurers, Ayders, Abettors, and Comforters in that Behalf: PROVIDED also, and our expresse Will and Pleasure is, And Wee doe by theis Presents for Vs, our Heires and Successors ordeyne and appoint That theis Presents shall not in any manner envre, or be taken to abridge, barr, or hinder any of our loving subjects whatsoever, to vse and exercise the Trade of Fishing vpon that Coast of New England in America, by theis Presents mencōed to be graunted. But that they, and every, or any of them, shall have full and free Power and Liberty to continue and vse their said Trade of Fishing vpon the said Coast, in any the Seas therevnto adioyning, or any Armes of the Seas or Saltwater Rivers where they have byn wont to fishe, and to build and sett vp vpon the Landes by theis Presents graunted, such Wharfes, Stages, and Workehouses as shalbe necessarie for the salting, drying, keeping, and packing vp of their Fish, to be taken or gotten vpon that Coast; and to cutt down, and take such Trees and other Materialls there groweing, or being, or shalbe needefull for that Purpose, and for all other necessarie Easements, Helpes, and Advantage concerning their said Trade of Fishing there, in such Manner and Forme as they have byn heretofore at any tyme accustomed to doe, without making any wilfull Waste or Spoyle, any Thing in theis Presents conteyned to the contrarie notwithstanding. AND WEE DOE further, for Vs, our Heires and Successors, ordeyne and graunte to the said Governor and Company, and their Successors by theis Presents that theis our Letters-patents shalbe firme, good, effectuall, and availeable in all Things, and to all Intents and Construccōns of Lawe, according to our true Meaning herein before declared, and shalbe construed, reputed, and adiudged in all Cases most favourablie on the Behalf, and for the Benefitt

Unlawful acts by members of the company

Fishing trade

Construction of charter

and Behoofe of the saide Governor and Company and their Successors: ALTHOUH expresse mencõn of the true yearely Value or certenty of the Prem̃isses or any of them, or of any other Guiftes or Grauntes, by Vs, or any of our Progenitors or Predecessors to the foresaid Governor or Company before this tyme made, in theis Presents is not made; or any Statute, Acte, Ordiñnce, Provision, Proclamacõn, or Restrainte to the contrarie thereof, heretofore had, made, published, ordeyned, or provided, or any other Matter, Cause, or Thinge whatsoever to the contrarie thereof in any wise notwithstanding.

IN WITNES whereof, Wee have caused theis our Letters to be made Patents.

WITNES ourself, at Westminster, the fourth day of March, in the fourth Yeare of our Raigne.

Per Breve de Privato Sigillo,

WOLSELEY.

REFERENCES

Adams, James T. *The Founding of New England.* Boston: Little, Brown and Co., 1927.
Andrews, Charles M. *The Colonial Period of American History.* 3 vols. New Haven: Yale University Press, 1934. I, chaps. 17-20.
Channing, Edward. *A History of the United States.* 6 vols. New York: Macmillan Co., 1928. I, chap. 12.
Fiske, John. *The Beginnings of New England.* 11th ed. Boston: Houghton Mifflin Co., 1895.
Morison, Samuel E. *Builders of the Bay Colony.* Boston: Houghton Mifflin Co., 1930.
Newton, Arthur P. *The Colonising Activities of the English Puritans.* New Haven: Yale University Press, 1914.
Osgood, Herbert L. *The American Colonies in the Seventeenth Century.* 3 vols. New York: Macmillan Co., 1904-7. I, Part 2.
Tyler, Lyon G. *England in America, 1580-1652* (Vol. IV of *The American Nation: A History*). New York: Harper & Bros., 1904. Chaps. 11-13.

VIII. THE CHARTER OF MARYLAND
1632

This charter was one of the accomplishments of George Calvert, first Lord Baltimore. Born about 1580, Calvert rose to a high place in English government as a political leader, diplomat and court favorite. Before he devoted himself entirely to the problems of colonization he had been a member of Parliament, a member of the Privy Council, and Secretary of State. His activities in the colonial movement date back to 1609 when he became a member of the Virginia Company. He was also a member of the provisional council of Virginia, and in 1622 he was one of the eighteen councilors of the New England Company. In 1625 he became a member of the Roman Catholic Church and, at the same time, resigned his office as Secretary of State in order to devote all his efforts to the problems of colonization.

Origins

The charter is modeled upon the one granted to Baltimore in 1623 for Avalon, Newfoundland. That charter was, in turn, based upon the exceptionally high powers exercised by the Bishop of Durham over his palatinate.[1]

The Avalon charter, 1623

---

[1] See articles IV and V. During the Middle Ages the rank of count palatine was held by several Continental feudal lords who held border positions. Special powers were given these lords so that they might more readily and efficiently defend the borders in case of sudden invasion. William the Conqueror followed these examples, but his policy of consolidating the power of the central government made him seek to prevent the acquisition of excessive powers by the palatinates. The English palatinates included the earldom of Chester, the duchy of Lancaster, and the bishopric of Durham. When the Maryland Charter was granted, only the Durham palatinate survived. The Bishop of Durham had power to summon armed forces to resist invasion. He could appoint judges and other officers, pardon offenses, coin money, grant titles of honor, and create courts. In addition, all writs ran in his name instead of the king's. The county of Durham was not represented in the House of Commons, but the bishop was a member of the House of Lords as well as an officer of the church. He was required to pay taxes and had to submit to appeals to the Court of Exchequer. Baltimore was more independent of the king than was the bishop because he was not required to pay taxes. Instead, he delivered two arrows a year at Windsor Palace and promised a fifth part of the gold and silver mined. Clayton C. Hall, *The Lords Baltimore and the Maryland Palatinate* (Baltimore, 1902), 32-34; Lyon G. Tyler, *England in America, 1580-1652*, Vol. IV of *The American Nation: A History*, ed. A. B. Hart (28 vols.; New York, 1904-18), 123-25. Baltimore's power to erect manors constituted a prerogative denied in England even to the king. Matthew P. Andrews, *The Founding of Maryland* (Baltimore, 1933), 46.

When he visited Avalon, Baltimore was disappointed with the climate and the condition of the land. In 1629, therefore, he applied for a grant in Virginia with the same powers that had been given to him for Avalon. This application met with strong resistance from William Claiborne and other leaders in Virginia who disliked him because of his religion, his standing as a court favorite, and his desire to establish an independent state among the Virginia plantations. Baltimore finally overcame his opponents, but died before the charter could be issued to him. It was issued instead to his eldest son, Cecil Calvert, second Lord Baltimore. Leonard Calvert was appointed as the first governor, and he arrived at Point Comfort with the first colonists on February 27, 1634.

Effects The apparently autocratic powers conferred upon Lord Baltimore by article IV were offset in large measure by article VII which required that the laws should conform to those of England and which also created the third self-governing body in the colonies.[2] Because the charter expressly authorized the establishment of an assembly, the settlers were able immediately to assert powers which had been the product of slow and painful development at Jamestown.

Representative government It was Lord Baltimore's intention that he alone should have the right to initiate legislation and that the role of the assembly should be confined to approving or disapproving laws proposed by him.[3] This process, however, was actually reversed from the beginning. The first assembly, which was convened in February, 1635, rejected a body of laws which Baltimore had sent over from England. Instead of approving Baltimore's laws, it drew up its own laws and sent them to him for approval. Baltimore at first refused to recognize the right of the assembly to initiate legislation, but the colonists persisted and in 1638 the second assembly also drew up laws of its own making. Baltimore yielded to the desires of the colonists so that the colony would not continue indefinitely without laws adapted to its needs, and in 1639 he authorized Governor Leonard Calvert to assent to such laws as he should think fit. The respective powers of the proprietor and the assembly, however, continued to be a controversial subject for a number of years.[4]

[2] These "ambiguous and contradictory" clauses caused the proprietor's power to be circumscribed to such an extent that Maryland ultimately became more liberal than any other colony except Connecticut and Rhode Island. Edward Channing, *A History of the United States*, Vol. I: *The Planting of a Nation in the New World, 1000-1660* (New York, 1928), 245.

[3] See article VII; Andrews, *op. cit.*, 42, 75.

[4] See *ibid.*, 75-79; Tyler, *op. cit.*, 131-32.

THE CHARTER OF MARYLAND

It was not long before the assembly became a body of elected representatives instead of a convention of all the freemen of the colony. When he convened the assembly in 1639, Governor Leonard Calvert issued writs for the election of representatives from the different hundreds. That assembly enacted a law providing that seats in future assemblies should be limited to councilors, persons specially summoned by the proprietor and burgesses elected from the hundreds. Baltimore reverted to the old practice of summoning the entire body of freemen in 1642. The representative principle, however, was established permanently in 1650, and the assembly was divided into two chambers. The lower house consisted of the elected burgesses, and the upper house was composed of the councilors and those specially summoned by the governor.[5]

Although religious toleration was practiced by Lord Baltimore from the beginning, the charter itself contains no guarantee of religious freedom. The clauses of the charter bearing on religion are articles II, IV, and XXII. It has sometimes been asserted that these provisions merely permitted the establishment of the Church of England but did not prohibit the establishment of other churches, and that consequently a large measure of religious liberty was accorded by the charter. It seems more probable, however, that these provisions were inserted as a precaution against the establishment of the Catholic Church.[6] Regardless of the meaning of the charter, religious toleration was made a policy of Lord Baltimore as early as 1634. Religious toleration furnished a strong motive for many colonists who came to Maryland.[7]

Religious liberty

---

[5] *Ibid.*, 132.

[6] George Petrie, "Church and State in Early Maryland," *Johns Hopkins University Studies in Historical and Political Science* (10th series; Baltimore, 1892), 195-96. This interpretation is based primarily on the fact that the Avalon Charter, which was granted to Baltimore before he became a Catholic, does not contain the clause relating to the dedication of churches in accordance with the ecclesiastical laws of England. See article IV.

[7] In 1678 Charles Calvert, third Lord Baltimore, wrote: "My father, albeit he had an absolute liberty given to him and his heirs to carry thither any persons out of any the dominions that belonged to the Crown of England who should be willing to go thither, yet when he came to make use of this liberty he found very few who were inclined to go and seat themselves in those parts but such as for some reason or other, could not live with ease in other places and of these a great part were such as could not conform in all particulars to the several laws of England relating to religion. Many there were of this sort of people who declared their willingness to go and plant themselves in this province so as they might have a general toleration settled there by a law by which all of all sorts who professed Christianity in general might be at liberty to worship God in such manner as was most agreeable with their respective judgments and consciences, without being subject to any penalties whatever for their so doing, provided the civil peace were preserved. And that for the securing the civil peace, and preventing all heats and feuds which were generally observed to happen amongst such as differ in opinions upon occasion of reproachful nicknames, and reflecting upon each

Not only did Baltimore promise and practice religious toleration, but he also enforced tolerance in various ways. Before Leonard Calvert left England in 1634, Baltimore issued instructions that to preserve peace and unity among the passengers, the Catholics aboard ship should practice their religion as privately as possible; that they should not engage in religious discussions; and that they should treat the Protestants with as much favor as justice would permit. These instructions were to be observed after landing as well as during the voyage.[8] The governor and the councilors were required to take an oath to observe and promote toleration; attempts by the Jesuits to control testamentary and matrimonial matters were resisted; and legislation establishing the principles of toleration was proposed to the assembly.[9] In 1643 Baltimore offered the Puritans of New England liberty of religion and other liberties of the place if they would migrate to Maryland. The same offer was later made to the Puritans in Virginia. The only persons prosecuted for their religious beliefs were those who sought to impose conformity upon others.

Because the charter failed to guarantee religious freedom, this right was established by legislative enactment. This was done by the Act Concerning Religion of 1649, sometimes referred to as the Toleration Act. Although there has been some dispute about its over-all effect,[10] several of its provisions clearly enunciate broad concepts of religious liberty. It provided, among other things,

> that noe person or psons whatsoever within this Province, or the Islands, Ports, Harbors, Creekes, or havens thereunto belonging professing to beleive in Jesus Christ, shall from henceforth bee any waies troubled, Molested or discountenanced for or in respect of his or her religion nor in the free exercise thereof within this Province or the Islands thereunto belonging nor any way compelled to the beleife or exercise of any other Religion against his or her consent, soe as they be not unfaithfull to the Lord Proprietary, or molest or conspire against the civill Governemt established or to bee established in this Province vnder him or his heires.[11]

other's opinions, it might by the same law be made penal to give any offense in that kind. These were the conditions proposed by such as were willing to go and be the first planters of this province; and without the complying with these conditions, in all probability this province had never been planted...." Quoted in *ibid.*, 199-200.

[8] Andrews, *op. cit.*, 151.

[9] Petrie, *op. cit.*, 202-9.

[10] Andrews, *op. cit.*, 143; Hall, *op. cit.*, 66.

[11] William H. Browne (ed.), *Archives of Maryland: Proceedings and Acts of the General Assembly of Maryland, 1637-1664* (Baltimore, 1883), I, 246.

THE CHARTER OF MARYLAND

This act was based on a law proposed by Lord Baltimore, but it was probably not passed in exactly the form proposed by him.[12] In its final form the act undoubtedly represents a compromise of divergent views on the subject of toleration.[13]

Article X of the charter provided that the colonists should have the rights of Englishmen, and the efforts of the colonists to secure recognition of those rights constitutes one of the most important phases of the history of the colony. The struggle to secure those rights began at an early date, and the enactments of the early assemblies indicate that Magna Carta was considered to be their primary source. On March 6, 1639, the Act for the Liberties of the People was passed. It provided:

Rights of Englishmen

> Be it Enacted By the Lord Proprietarie of this Province of and with the advice and approbation of the ffreemen of the same that all the Inhabitants of this Province being Christians (Slaves excepted) Shall have and enjoy all such rights liberties immunities priviledges and free customs within this Province as any naturall born subject of England hath or ought to have or enjoy in the Realm of England by force or vertue of the common law or Statute Law of England (saveing in such Cases as the same are or may be altered or changed by the Laws and ordinances of this Province).
>
> And Shall not be imprisoned nor disseissed or dispossessed of their freehold goods or Chattels or be out Lawed Exiled or otherwise destroyed fore judged or punished then according to the Laws of this province saveing to the Lord proprietarie and his heirs all his rights and prerogatives by reason of his domination and Seigniory over this Province and the people of the same This Act to Continue till the end of the next Generall Assembly.[14]

On March 19, 1639, it was provided that "Holy Churches within this province shall have all her rights and liberties," and that "the Inhabitants of this Province shall have all their rights and liberties according to the great Charter of England."[15] After the English Revolution of 1688 an attempt by the Maryland Assembly to adopt Magna Carta was disallowed by the king because of the opinion of the Solicitor General that the liberties of Magna Carta might be inconsistent with the king's prerogative.[16]

---

[12] Hall, *op. cit.*, 66, 71-72, 79.

[13] It is doubtful that either the Protestants or the Catholics deserve most of the credit for the document. *Ibid.*, 78-79, 83. Although it seems probable that the Protestants were in the majority in the assembly, the influence and power of the Catholic minority were greater than their numerical proportion would indicate. Petrie, *op. cit.*, 217.

[14] Browne, *op. cit.*, I, 37, 41.

[15] *Ibid.*, 39, 83.

[16] Channing, *op. cit.*, II, 223n.

Later Significance

During most of the seventeenth century and the first two decades of the eighteenth, Maryland was the scene of a continuous struggle over the application of English laws in the colony. This struggle was, in general, waged between the colonists, on the one hand, and the proprietor, on the other. The efforts of the colonists to secure recognition of their rights as Englishmen were frustrated by the proprietor's control over legislation, a power which he often exercised.[17] This controversy concerned the applicability of the English statutes which secured the rights of the subject; the applicability of the general principles of the common law was not in doubt.

The common law of England came to be recognized at an early date as part of the law of Maryland, in so far as it was applicable and unmodified. As early as 1642 it had become established that the common law of England should be looked to by the courts in deciding cases, although they were apparently not bound to follow those principles in every detail.[18] More definite recognition of these principles was accorded in 1662.[19]

The applicability in Maryland of the English statutes declaring the liberties of the subject, however, led to more dispute. In 1674 a bill to determine

---

[17] St. George L. Sioussat, "The English Statutes in Maryland," *Johns Hopkins University Studies in Historical and Political Science* (21st series; Baltimore, 1903), 479.

[18] The Act for Rule of Judicature of 1642 provided: "Right & just in all civill Causes shall be determined according to the law or most Generall usage of the province since its plantacōn or former presidts, of the same or the like nature to be determined by the Judge And in defect of such Law usage or president then right & just shall be determined according to equity & good concience not neglecting (so far as the Judge or Judges shall be informed thereof & shall find no inconvenience in the applycation to this province) the rules by which right & just useth & ought to be determined in England in the same or the like cases And all crimes and offences shall be judged & determined according to the law of the Province or in defect of certain Law then they may be determined according to the best discretion of the Judge or Judges judging as neer as Conveniently may be to the laudable law or usage of England in the same or the like offences Provided that no person be adjudged of life member or freehold without Law certain of the Province This Act to endure till the end of the next Assembly." Browne, *op. cit.*, 147-48.

The power of the judges over the conduct of trials was much greater than in England. The judge could require either party to testify in civil cases, and he had extensive powers over verdicts. Paul S. Reinsch, "The English Common Law in the Early American Colonies," *Select Essays in Anglo-American Legal History* (Boston, 1907), I, 400-1.

[19] The Act Concerning Proceedings at Law of 1662 provided: "Whereas severall differences doe arise within this Province wherein there is noe Rule or Lawe prouided in the Province whereby to determine such differences And to leaue to much to discrecōn is to open a Gapp to Corrupcōn for the avoyding such Inconveniencys Be it Enacted by the Lord Proprietary by and with the Consent of the Vpper and Lower howse of this prsent Generall Assembly That in all cases where the Lawe of this Province is silent, Justice shall be administered according to the lawes and Statutes of England, if pleaded and produced And all Courts to Judge of the Right pleadeing and inconsistancy of the said Lawes with the good of this Province according to the best of their Judgemts Skill and Cunning This Acte to endure for three yeares or to the end of the next Generall Assembly." Browne, *op. cit.*, 448.

This statute has been described as "the first definite recognition in America of the power of the courts to apply the common law of England to colonial conditions and to reject provisions deemed unsuitable." Reinsch, *op. cit.*, I, 402.

what English statutes should be considered in force was defeated by the lower house of the assembly because of the opinion that all English statutes were applicable.[20] This position was maintained rather consistently by the popular party throughout the controversy. The struggle between the colonists and the proprietor saw its climax and conclusion in the decade 1722-32. The leading advocate of the position of the popular party was Daniel Dulany, the elder, Attorney General of the colony.

In 1722 the assembly declared that all English statutes extended to Maryland. This act was vetoed by the proprietor, who asserted that only those statutes which referred to the colony in express terms were applicable there.[21] Dulany attacked the proprietor's position in his pamphlet "The Right of the Inhabitants of Maryland, to the Benefit of the English Laws." Dulany's arguments were based on the leading legal treatises of the day including Puffendorf, Grotius, Coke, and Locke. He did not attempt to enumerate all of the statutes that had been made to establish and confirm the subject's rights, but he did claim the applicability of some that he considered of particular importance.[22] The first of these was Magna Carta, which he described as "A Declaration of the Common-Law."[23] He also cited two confirmations of Magna Carta,[24] the Petition of Right,[25] the Act Abolishing the Star Chamber,[26] the Habeas Corpus Act,[27] and the Bill of Rights.[28] In claiming these statutes for the colonists, Dulany pointed out that the Maryland Charter contained a grant to the people of all the rights, privileges, immunities, liberties, and franchises of English subjects. He did not rely solely on the charter, but also asserted that had the charter never been made the colonists would enjoy these rights because of their equality with other English subjects.[29]

In 1732 the right of the Maryland colonists to the benefits of the great

---

[20] Sioussat, *op. cit.*, 477.

[21] *Ibid.*, 496-97.

[22] Text of pamphlet in *ibid.*, 545-68. See particularly 555-58.

[23] "The 29th Chapter is not long, and ought to be read by every Body, and (in my humble Opinion,) taught to Children, with their first Rudiments." *Ibid.*, 555.

[24] 28 Edw. 3, c. 3, and 42 Edw. 3, c. 3. See pp. 6-7.

[25] See pp. 62-75.

[26] See pp. 125-42.

[27] See pp. 189-203.

[28] See pp. 222-50.

[29] Sioussat, *op. cit.*, 564-65.

English statutes of liberty was settled when the judges were directed by law to decide cases in accordance with the following oath:

> You shall do equal law and right to all the king's subjects, rich and poor, according to the laws, customs and directions of the Acts of Assembly of this province so far forth as they provide; and when they are silent, according to the laws, statutes and reasonable customs of England, as used and practised within this province.[30]

The claim made by the Maryland colonists to the benefits of the English statutes found expression elsewhere in America. The Declaration and Resolves of the First Continental Congress, 1774, for example, asserted that these statutes were the inheritance of the colonists.[31] The Maryland Constitution of 1776[32] showed that the adherence of the colonists to English precedents had survived the Revolution. Article III of that Constitution declared that the inhabitants of Maryland should be entitled to the benefits of English statutes found applicable to their circumstances. The question of what statutes were applicable to conditions in Maryland was not made definite, however, until 1809 when Chancellor William Kilty classified the English statutes from Magna Carta to 1773 into three categories: (a) those not applicable, (b) those applicable but not proper to be incorporated into the statute law of the State, and (c) those both applicable and proper to be incorporated. This work furnished a valuable guide in exploring what had previously been a very doubtful subject.[33]

---

[30] Quoted in *ibid.*, 503. Although this was a partial submission to the will of the proprietor, the colonists had accomplished the important purpose of securing the benefits of not only those statutes which had already been used and practiced in the colony, but also those which might be introduced in the future. John V. L. McMahon, *An Historical View of the Government of Maryland* (Baltimore, 1831), I, 127-28.

[31] Resolution 6. See p. 288.

[32] See pp. 341-51.

[33] Sioussat, *op. cit.*, 505.

THE CHARTER OF MARYLAND[34]

June 20, 1632

Charles, by the Grace of God, of England, Scotland, France, and Ireland, king, Defender of the Faith, &c. To all to whom these Presents come, Greeting.

II. Whereas our well beloved and right trusty Subject Caecilius Calvert, Baron of Baltimore, in our Kingdom of Ireland, Son and Heir of George Calvert, Knight, late Baron of Baltimore, in our said Kingdom of Ireland, treading in the steps of his Father, being animated with a laudable, and pious Zeal for extending the Christian Religion, and also the Territories of our Empire, hath humbly besought Leave of us, that he may transport, by his own Industry, and Expense, a numerous Colony of the English Nation, to a certain Region, herein after described, in a Country hitherto uncultivated, in the Parts of America, and partly occupied by Savages, having no knowledge of the Divine Being, and that all that Region, with some certain Privileges, and Jurisdiction, appertaining unto the wholesome Government, and State of his Colony and Region aforesaid, may by our Royal Highness be given, granted and confirmed unto him, and his Heirs. *Preamble*

III. Know Ye therefore, that We, encouraging with our Royal Favour, the pious and noble purpose of the aforesaid Barons of Baltimore, of our special Grace, certain knowledge, and mere Motion, have Given, Granted and Confirmed, and by this our present Charter, for Us our Heirs, and Successors, do Give, Grant and Confirm, unto the aforesaid Caecilius, now Baron of Baltimore, his Heirs, and Assigns, all that Part of the Peninsula, or Chersonese, lying in the Parts of America, between the Ocean on the East and the Bay of Chesapeake on the West, divided from the Residue thereof by a Right Line drawn from the Promontory, or Head-Land, called Watkin's Point, situate upon the Bay aforesaid, near the river Wigloo, on the West, unto the main Ocean on the East; and between that Boundary on the South, unto that Part of the Bay of Delaware on the North, which lieth under the Fortieth Degree of North Latitude from the Equinoctial, where New England is terminated; And all that Tract of Land within the Metes underwritten (that is to say) passing from the said Bay, called Delaware Bay, in a right Line, by the Degree aforesaid, unto the true meridian of the first Fountain of the River of Pattowmack, thence verging toward the South, *Description of territory granted*

---

[34] Francis N. Thorpe (ed.), *The Federal and State Constitutions, Colonial Charters, and Other Organic Laws* (Washington, 1909), III, 1677-86.

unto the further Bank of the said River, and following the same on the West and South, unto a certain Place, called Cinquack, situate near the mouth of the said River, where it disembogues into the aforesaid Bay of Chesapeake, and thence by the shortest Line unto the aforesaid Promontory or Place, called Watkin's Point; so that the whole tract of land, divided by the Line aforesaid, between the main Ocean and Watkin's Point, unto the Promontory called Cape Charles, and every the Appendages thereof, may entirely remain excepted for ever to Us, our Heirs and Successors.

Islands, inlets, harbors, bays, rivers and straits

IV. Also We do grant and likewise Confirm unto the said Baron of Baltimore, his Heirs, and Assigns, all Islands and Inlets within the Limits aforesaid, all and singular the Islands, and Islets, from the Eastern Shore of the aforesaid Region, towards the East, which had been, or shall be formed in the Sea, situate within Ten marine Leagues from the said shore; with all and singular the Ports, Harbours, Bays, Rivers, and Straits belonging to the Region or Islands aforesaid, and all the Soil, Plains, Woods, Marshes, Lakes, Rivers, Bays, and Straits, situate, or being within the Metes, Bounds, and Limits aforesaid, with the Fishings of every kind of Fish, as well of Whales, Sturgeons, and other royal Fish, as of other Fish, in the Sea, Bays, Straits, or Rivers, within the Premises, and the fish there taken; And moreover all Veins, Mines, and Quarries, as well opened as hidden, already found, or that shall be found within the Region, Islands, or Limits aforesaid, of Gold, Silver, Gems, and precious Stones, and any other whatsoever, whether they be of Stones, or Metals, or of any other Thing, or Matter whatsoever; And furthermore the Patronages, and Advowsons of all Churches which (with the increasing Worship and Religion of Christ) within the said Region, Islands, Islets, and Limits aforesaid, hereafter shall happen to be built, together with License and Faculty of erecting and founding Churches, Chapels, and Places of Worship, in convenient and suitable places, within the Premises, and of causing the same to be dedicated and consecrated according to the Ecclesiastical Laws of our Kingdom of England, with all, and singular such, and as ample Rights, Jurisdictions, Privileges, Prerogatives, Royalties, Liberties, Immunities, and royal Rights, and temporal Franchises whatsoever, as well by Sea as by Land, within the Region, Islands, Islets, and Limits aforesaid, to be had, exercised, used, and enjoyed, as any Bishop of Durham, within the Bishoprick or County Palatine of Durham, in our Kingdom of England, ever heretofore hath had, held, used, or enjoyed, or of right could, or ought to have, hold, use, or enjoy.

Fishing and mineral rights

Churches may be founded according to the ecclesiastical laws of England

Rights and privileges equal to those of the Bishop of Durham

Baltimore designated lord proprietor

V. And we do by these Presents, for us, our Heirs, and Successors, Make, Create, and Constitute Him, the now Baron of Baltimore, and his Heirs, the true and absolute Lords and Proprietaries of the Region aforesaid, and of all other Premises (except the before excepted) saving always the Faith and Allegiance and Sovereign Dominion due to Us, our Heirs, and Successors; to have, hold, possess, and enjoy the aforesaid Region, Islands, Islets, and other the Premises, unto the aforesaid now Baron of Baltimore, and to his Heirs and Assigns, to the sole and proper Behoof and Use of him,

Land to be held in common socage

the now Baron of Baltimore, his Heirs and Assigns, forever. To Hold of Us, our Heirs and Successors, Kings of England, as of our Castle of Windsor, in our County of Berks, in free and common Soccage, by Fealty only for all Services, and not in Capite, nor

THE CHARTER OF MARYLAND

by Knight's Service, yielding therefore unto Us, our Heirs and Successors Two Indian Arrows of these Parts, to be delivered at the said Castle of Windsor, every Year, on Tuesday in Easter Week: And also the fifth Part of all Gold and Silver Ore, which shall happen from Time to Time, to be found within the aforesaid Limits.

VI. Now, That the aforesaid Region, thus by us granted and described, may be eminently distinguished above all other Regions of that Territory, and decorated with more ample Titles, Know Ye, that We, of our more especial Grace, certain knowledge, and mere Motion, have thought fit that the said Region and Islands be erected into a Province, as out of the Plenitude of our royal Power and Prerogative, We do, for Us, our Heirs and Successors, erect and incorporate the same into a Province, and nominate the same Maryland, by which Name We will that it shall from henceforth be called. *Province to be called Maryland*

VII. And forasmuch as We have above made and ordained the aforesaid now Baron of Baltimore, the true Lord and Proprietary of the whole Province aforesaid, Know Ye therefore further, that We, for Us, our Heirs and Successors, do grant unto the said now Baron, (in whose Fidelity, Prudence, Justice, and provident Circumspection of Mind, We repose the greatest Confidence) and to his Heirs, for the good and happy Government of the said Province, free, full, and absolute Power, by the Tenor of these Presents, to Ordain, Make, and Enact Laws, of what Kind soever, according to their sound Discretions, whether relating to the Public State of the said Province, or the private Utility of Individuals, of and with the Advice, Assent, and Approbation of the Free-Men of the same Province, or the greater Part of them, or of their Delegates or Deputies, whom We will shall be called together for the framing of Laws, when, and as often as Need shall require, by the aforesaid now Baron of Baltimore, and his Heirs, and in the Form which shall seem best to him or them, and the same to publish under the Seal of the aforesaid now Baron of Baltimore, and his Heirs, and duly to execute the same upon all Persons, for the time being, within the aforesaid Province, and the Limits thereof, or under his or their Government and Power, in Sailing towards Maryland, or thence Returning, Outward-bound, either to England, or elsewhere, whether to any other Part of Our, or of any foreign Dominions, wheresoever established, by the Imposition of Fines, Imprisonment, and other Punishment whatsoever; even if it be necessary, and the Quality of the Offence require it, by Privation of Member, or Life, by him the aforesaid now Baron of Baltimore, and his Heirs, or by his or their Deputy, Lieutenant, Judges, Justices, Magistrates, Officers, and Ministers, to be constituted and appointed according to the Tenor and true Intent of these Presents, and to constitute and ordain Judges, Justices, Magistrates and Officers of what kind, for what Cause, and with what Power soever, within that Land, and the Sea of those Parts, and in such form as to the said now Baron of Baltimore, or his Heirs, shall seem most fitting; And also to Remit, Release, Pardon, and Abolish, all Crimes and Offences whatsoever against such Laws, whether before, or after Judgment passed; and to do all and singular other Things belonging to the Completion of Justice, and to Courts, Praetorian Judicatories, and Tribunals, Judicial Forms and Modes of Proceeding, although express Mention thereof in these

Power of the proprietor to make laws with the assent of the freemen or their delegates

Publication and execution of laws

Punishments

Power to appoint judges and officers

Pardons

Courts Presents be not made; and, by Judges by them delegated, to award Process, hold Pleas, and determine in those Courts, Praetorian Judicatories, and Tribunals, in all Actions, Suits, Causes, and Matters whatsoever, as well Criminal as Personal, Real and Mixed, and Praetorian: Which said Laws, so to be published as above-said, We will

Laws to be consonant to reason and agreeable to laws of England enjoin, charge, and command, to be most absolute and firm in Law, and to be Kept in those Parts by all the Subjects and Liege-Men of Us, our Heirs, and Successors, so far as they concern them, and to be inviolably observed under the Penalties therein expressed, or to be expressed. So, nevertheless, that the Laws aforesaid be consonant to Reason, and be not repugnant or contrary, but (so far as conveniently may be) agreeable to the Laws, Statutes, Customs, and Rights of this Our Kingdom of England.

Power of proprietor to make ordinances VIII. And forasmuch as, in the Government of so great a Province, sudden accidents may frequently happen, to which it will be necessary to apply a Remedy, before the Freeholders of the said Province, their Delegates, or Deputies, can be called together for the framing of Laws; neither will it be fit that so great a Number of People should immediately, on such emergent Occasion, be called together, We therefore, for the better Government of so great a Province, do Will and Ordain, and by these Presents, for Us, our Heirs and Successors, do grant unto the said now Baron of Baltimore, and to his Heirs, that the aforesaid now Baron of Baltimore, and his Heirs, by themselves, or by their Magistrates and Officers, thereunto duly to be constituted as aforesaid, may, and can make and constitute fit and Wholesome Ordinances from Time to Time, to be Kept and observed within the Province aforesaid, as well for the Conservation of the Peace, as for the better Government of the People inhabiting therein, and publicly to notify the same to all Persons whom the same in any wise do or may affect. Which Ordinances We will to be inviolably observed within the said Province, under the Pains to be expressed in the same. So that the said Ordinances be consonant to Reason and be not repugnant nor contrary, but (so far as conveniently may be done) agreeable to the Laws, Statutes, or Rights of our Kingdom of England: And so that the same Ordinances do not, in any Sort, extend to oblige, bind, charge, or take away the Right or Interest of any Person or Persons, of, or in Member, Life, Freehold, Goods or Chattels.

New settlers IX. Furthermore, that the New Colony may more happily increase by a Multitude of People resorting thither, and at the same Time may be more firmly secured from the Incursions of Savages, or of other Enemies, Pirates, and Ravagers: We therefore, for Us, our Heirs and Successors, do by these Presents give and grant Power, License and Liberty, to all the Liege-Men and Subjects, present and future, of Us, our Heirs and Successors, except such to whom it shall be expressly forbidden, to transport themselves and their Families to the said Province, with fitting Vessels, and suitable Provisions, and therein to settle, dwell and inhabit; and to build and fortify Castles, Forts, and other Places of Strength, at the Appointment of the aforesaid now Baron of Baltimore, and his Heirs, for the Public and their own Defence; the Statute of Fugitives, or any other whatsoever to the contrary of the Premises in any wise notwithstanding.

THE CHARTER OF MARYLAND

X. We will also, and of our more abundant Grace, for Us, our Heirs and Successors, do firmly charge, constitute, ordain, and command, that the said Province be of our Allegiance; and that all and singular the Subjects and Leige-Men of Us, our Heirs and Successors, transplanted, or hereafter to be transplanted into the Province aforesaid, and the Children of them, and of others their Descendants, whether already born there, or hereafter to be born, be and shall be Natives and Liege-Men of Us, our Heirs and Successors, of our Kingdom of England and Ireland; and in all Things shall be held, treated, reputed, and esteemed as the faithful Liege-Men of Us, and our Heirs and Successors, born within our Kingdom of England; also Lands, Tenements, Revenues, Services, and other Hereditaments whatsoever, within our Kingdom of England, and other our Dominions, to inherit, or otherwise purchase, receive, take, have, hold, buy, and possess, and the same to use and enjoy, and the same to give, sell, alien and bequeath; and likewise all Privileges, Franchises and Liberties of this our Kingdom of England, freely, quietly, and peaceably to have and possess, and the same may use and enjoy in the same manner as our Liege-Men born, or to be born within our said Kingdom of England, without Impediment, Molestation, Vexation, Impeachment, or Grievance of Us, or any of our Heirs or Successors; any Statute, Act, Ordinance, or Provision to the contrary thereof, notwithstanding. *Allegiance of settlers* *Liberties of settlers*

XI. Furthermore, That our Subjects may be incited to undertake this Expedition with a ready and cheerful mind: Know Ye, that We, of our especial Grace, certain Knowledge, and mere Motion, do, by the Tenor of these Presents, give and grant, as well as to the aforesaid Baron of Baltimore, and to his Heirs, as to all other Persons who shall from Time to Time repair to the said Province, either for the Sake of Inhabiting, or of Trading with the Inhabitants of the Province aforesaid, full License to Ship and Lade in any the Ports of Us, our Heirs and Successors, all and singular their Goods, as well movable, as immovable, Wares and Merchandizes, likewise Grain of what Sort soever, and other Things whatsoever necessary for Food and Clothing, by the Laws and Statutes of our Kingdoms and Dominions, not prohibited to be transported out of the said Kingdoms; and the same to transport, by themselves, or their Servants or Assigns, into the said Province, without the Impediment or Molestation of Us, our Heirs or Successors, or any Officers of Us, our Heirs or Successors, (Saving unto Us, our Heirs and Successors, the Impositions, Subsidies, Customs, and other Dues payable for the same Goods and Merchandizes) any Statute, Act, Ordinance, or other Thing whatsover to the contrary notwithstanding. *Trade and commerce*

XII. But because, that in so remote a Region, placed among so many barbarous Nations, the Incursions as well of the Barbarians themselves, as of other Enemies, Pirates and Ravagers, probably will be feared. Therefore We have Given, and for Us, our Heirs, and Sucessors, do Give by these Presents, as full and unrestrained Power, as any Captain-General of an Army ever hath had, unto the aforesaid now Baron of Baltimore, and to his Heirs and Assigns, by themselves, or by their Captains, or other Officers to summon to their Standards, and to array all men, of whatsoever Condition, or wheresoever born, for the Time being, in the said Province of Maryland, to wage *Defense*

War, and to pursue, even beyond the Limits of their Province, the Enemies and Ravagers aforesaid, infesting those Parts by Land and by Sea, and (if God shall grant it) to vanquish and captivate them, and the Captives to put to Death, or, according to their Discretion, to save, and to do all other and singular the Things which appertain, or have been accustomed to appertain unto the Authority and Office of a Captain-General of an Army.

Martial law

XIII. We also will, and by this our Charter, do give unto the aforesaid now Baron of Baltimore, and to his Heirs and Assigns, Power, Liberty, and Authority, that, in Case of Rebellion, sudden Tumult, or Sedition, if any (which God forbid) should happen to arise, whether upon Land within the Province aforesaid, or upon the High Sea in making a Voyage to the said Province of Maryland, or in returning thence, they may, by themselves, or by their Captains, or other Officers, thereunto deputed under their Seals (to whom We, for Us, our Heirs and Successors, by these Presents, do Give and Grant the fullest Power and Authority) exercise Martial Law as freely, and in as ample Manner and Form, as any Captain-General of an Army, by virtue of his Office may, or hath accustomed to use the same, against the seditious Authors of Innovations in those Parts, withdrawing themselves from the Government of him or them, refusing to serve in War, flying over to the Enemy, exceeding their Leave of Absence, Deserters, or otherwise howsoever offending against the Rule, Law, or Discipline of War.

Titles and honors

XIV. Moreover, left in so remote and far distant a Region, every Access to Honors and Dignities may seem to be precluded, and utterly barred, to Men well born, who are preparing to engage in the present Expedition, and desirous of deserving well, both in Peace and War, of Us, and our Kingdom; for this Cause, We, for Us, our Heirs and Successors, do give free and plenary Power to the aforesaid now Baron of Baltimore, and to his Heirs and Assigns, to confer Favors, Rewards and Honors, upon such Subjects, inhabiting within the Province aforesaid, as shall be well deserving, and to adorn them with whatsoever Titles and Dignities they shall appoint; (so that they

Founding of cities and towns

be not such as are now used in England) also to erect and incorporate Towns into Boroughs, and Boroughs into Cities, with suitable Privileges and Immunities, according to the Merits of the Inhabitants, and Convenience of the Places; and to do all and singular other Things in the Premises, which to him or them shall seem fitting and convenient; even although they shall be such as, in their own Nature, require a more special Commandment and Warrant than in these Presents may be expressed.

Imports and exports

XV. We will also, and by these Presents do, for Us, our Heirs and Successors, give and grant License by this our Charter, unto the aforesaid now Baron of Baltimore, his Heirs and Assigns, and to all Persons whatsoever, who are, or shall be Residents and Inhabitants of the Province aforesaid, freely to import and unlade, by themselves, their Servants, Factors or Assigns, all Wares and Merchandizes whatsoever, which shall be collected out of the Fruits and Commodities of the said Province, whether the Product of the Land or the Sea, into any the Ports whatsoever of Us, our Heirs and Successors, of England or Ireland, or otherwise to dispose of the same there; and, if Need be, within One Year, to be computed immediately from the

THE CHARTER OF MARYLAND

Time of unlading thereof, to lade the same Merchandizes again, in the same, or other Ships, and to export the same to any other Countries they shall think proper, whether belonging to Us, or any foreign Power which shall be in Amity with Us, our Heirs or Successors: Provided always, that they be bound to pay for the same to Us, our Heirs and Successors, such Customs and Impositions, Subsidies and Taxes, as our other Subjects of our Kingdom of England, for the Time being, shall be bound to pay, beyond which We will that the Inhabitants of the aforesaid Province of the said Land, called Maryland, shall not be burdened. *Customs*

XVI. And furthermore, of our more ample special Grace, and of our certain Knowledge, and mere Motion, We do, for Us, our Heirs and Successors, grant unto the aforesaid now Baron of Baltimore, his Heirs and Assigns, full and absolute Power and Authority to make, erect, and constitute, within the Province of Maryland, and the Islands and Islets aforesaid, such, and so many Sea-Ports, Harbors, Creeks, and other Places of Unlading and Discharge of Goods and Merchandizes out of Ships, Boats, and other Vessels, and of Lading in the same, and in so many, and such Places, and with such Rights, Jurisdictions, Liberties, and Privileges, unto such Parts respecting, as to him or them shall seem most expedient: And, that all and every the Ships, Boats, and other Vessels whatsoever, coming to, or going from the Province aforesaid, for the Sake of Merchandizing, shall be laden and unladen at such Ports only as shall be so erected and constituted by the said now Baron of Baltimore, his Heirs and Assigns, any Usage, Custom, or other Thing whatsoever to the contrary notwithstanding, Saving always to Us, our Heirs and Successors, and to all the Subjects of our Kingdoms of England and Ireland, of Us, our Heirs and Successors, the Liberty of Fishing for Sea-Fish, as well in the Sea, Bays, Straits, and navigable Rivers, as in the Harbors, Bays, and Creeks of the Province aforesaid; and the Privilege of Salting and Drying Fish on the Shores of the same Province; and, for that Cause, to cut down and take Hedging-Wood and Twigs there growing, and to build Huts and Cabins, necessary in this Behalf, in the same Manner, as heretofore they reasonably might, or have used to do. Which Liberties and Privileges, the said Subjects of Us, our Heirs and Successors, shall enjoy, without notable Damage or Injury in any wise to be done to the aforesaid now Baron of Baltimore, his Heirs or Assigns, or to the Residents and Inhabitants of the same Province in the Ports, Creeks, and Shores aforesaid, and especially in the Woods and Trees there growing. And if any Person shall do Damage or Injury of this Kind, he shall incur the Peril and Pain of the heavy Displeasure of Us, our Heirs and Successors, and of the due Chastisement of the Laws, besides making Satisfaction. *Ports* *Fishing rights*

XVII. Moreover, We will, appoint, and ordain, and by these Presents, for Us, our Heirs and Successors, do grant unto the aforesaid now Baron of Baltimore, his Heirs and Assigns, that the same Baron of Baltimore, his Heirs and Assigns, from Time to Time, forever, shall have, and enjoy the Taxes and Subsidies payable, or arising within the Ports, Harbors, and other Creeks and Places aforesaid, within the Province aforesaid, for Wares bought and sold, and Things there to be laden, or unladen, to be reasonably assessed by them, and the People there as aforesaid, on emergent Occasion; *Taxes* to whom We grant Power by these Presents, for Us, our Heirs and Successors, to assess and impose the said Taxes and Subsidies there, upon just Cause and in due Proportion.

Distribution of land

XVIII. And furthermore, of our special Grace, and certain Knowledge, and mere Motion, We have given, granted, and confirmed, and by these Presents, for Us, our Heirs and Successors, do give, grant and confirm, unto the said now Baron of Baltimore, his Heirs and Assigns, full and absolute License, Power, and Authority, that he, the aforesaid now Baron of Baltimore, his Heirs and Assigns, from Time to Time hereafter, forever, may and can, at his or their Will and Pleasure, assign, alien, grant, demise, or enfeoff so many, such, and proportionate Parts and Parcels of the Premises, to any Person or Persons willing to purchase the same, as they shall think convenient, to have and to hold to the same Person or Persons willing to take or purchase the same, and his and their Heirs and Assigns, in Fee-simple, or Fee-tail, or for Term of Life, Lives or Years; to hold of the aforesaid now Baron of Baltimore, his Heirs and Assigns, by so many, such, and so great Services, Customs and Rents of this Kind, as to the same now Baron of Baltimore, his Heirs, and Assigns, shall seem fit and agreeable, and not immediately of Us, our Heirs and Successors. And We do give,

Exception to rule against subinfeudation

and by these Presents, for Us, our Heirs and Successors, do grant to the same Person and Persons, and to each and every of them, License, Authority and Power, that such Person and Persons may take the Premises, or any Parcel thereof, of the aforesaid now Baron of Baltimore, his Heirs and Assigns, and hold the same to them and their Assigns, or Heirs, of the aforesaid Baron of Baltimore, his Heirs and Assigns, of what Estate of Inheritance soever, in Fee Simple or Fee-tail, or otherwise, as to them and the now Baron of Baltimore, his Heirs and Assigns, shall seem expedient; the Statute made in the Parliament of Lord Edward, Son of King Henry, late King of England, our Progenitor, commonly called the "Statute Quia Emptores Terrarum," heretofore published in our Kingdom of England, or any other Statute, Act, Ordinance, Usage, Law, or Custom, or any other Thing, Cause, or Matter, to the contrary thereof, heretofore had, done, published, ordained or provided to the contrary thereof notwithstanding.

Power to found manors and create manorial courts

XIX. We also, by these Presents, do give and grant License to the same Baron of Baltimore, and to his Heirs, to erect any Parcels of Land within the Province aforesaid, into Manors, and in every of those Manors, to have and to hold a Court-Baron, and all Things which to a Court Baron do belong; and to have and to Keep View of Frank-Pledge, for the Conservation of the Peace and better Government of those Parts, by themselves and their Stewards, or by the Lords, for the Time being to be deputed, of other of those Manors when they shall be constituted, and in the same to exercise all Things to the View of Frank Pledge belong.

Freedom from taxes and customs

XX. And further We will, and do, by these Presents, for Us, our Heirs and Successors, covenant and grant to, and with the aforesaid now Baron of Baltimore, His Heirs and Assigns, that We, our Heirs, and Successors, at no Time hereafter, will impose, or make or cause to be imposed, any Impositions, Customs, or other Taxations, Quotas, or Contributions whatsoever, in or upon the Residents or Inhabitants of the Province aforesaid for their Goods, Lands, or Tenements within the same Province, or upon any Tenements, Lands, Goods or Chattels within the Province aforesaid, or in or upon any Goods or Merchandizes within the Province aforesaid, or within the Ports or Harbors of the said Province, to be laden or unladen; And We will and do, for Us, our Heirs and Successors, enjoin and command that this our Declaration shall, from Time to Time, be received and allowed in all our Courts and Praetorian Judicatories, and before all the Judges whatsoever of Us, our Heirs and Successors, for a sufficient and lawful Discharge, Payment, and Acquittance thereof, charging all and singular the Officers and Ministers of Us, our Heirs and Successors, and enjoining them under our heavy Displeasure, that they do not at any Time presume to attempt any Thing to the contrary of the Premises, or that may in any wise contravene the same, but that they, at all Times, as is fitting, do aid and assist the aforesaid now Baron of Baltimore, and his Heirs, and the aforesaid Inhabitants and Merchants of the Province of Maryland aforesaid, and their Servants and Ministers, Factors and Assigns, in the fullest Use and Enjoyment of the Charter.

XXI. And furthermore We will, and by these Presents, for Us, our Heirs and Successors, do grant unto the aforesaid now Baron of Baltimore, his Heirs and Assigns, and to the Freeholders and Inhabitants of the said Province, both Present and to come, and to every of them, that the said Province, and the Freeholders or Inhabitants of the said Colony or Country, shall not henceforth be held or reputed a Member or Part of the Land of Virginia, or of any other Colony already transported, or hereafter to be transported, or be dependent on the same, or subordinate in any kind of Government, from which We do separate both the said Province, and Inhabitants thereof, and by these Presents do will to be distinct, and that they may be immediately subject to our Crown of England, and dependent on the same forever. *Maryland not to be part of Virginia nor subject to it*

XXII. And if, peradventure, hereafter it may happen, that any Doubts or Questions should arise concerning the true Sense and Meaning of any Word, Clause, or Sentence, contained in this our present Charter, We will charge and command, That Interpretation to be applied always, and in all Things, and in all Courts and Judicatories whatsoever, to obtain which shall be judged to be the more beneficial, profitable, and favorable to the aforesaid now Baron of Baltimore, his Heirs and Assigns: Provided always, that no Interpretation thereof be made, whereby God's holy and true Christian Religion, or the Allegiance due to Us, our Heirs and Successors, may in any wise suffer by Change, Prejudice, or Dimunution; although express Mention be not made in these Presents of the true yearly Value or Certainty of the Premises, or of any Part thereof; or of other Gifts and Grants made by Us, our Heirs and Successors, unto the said now Lord Baltimore, or any Statute, Act, Ordinance, Provision, Proclamation or Restraint, heretofore had, made, published, ordained or provided, or any other Thing, Cause, or Matter whatsoever, to the contrary thereof in any wise notwithstanding. *Construction of charter*

XXIII. In Witness Whereof We have caused these our Letters to be made Patent. Witness Ourself at Westminster, the Twentieth Day of June, in the Eighth Year of our Reign.

SOURCES OF OUR LIBERTIES

REFERENCES

Andrews, Matthew P. *The Founding of Maryland*. New York: D. Appleton-Century Co., 1933.
Channing, Edward. *A History of the United States*. 6 vols. New York: Macmillan Co., 1927-30. I, chap. 9.
Hall, Clayton C. *The Lords Baltimore and the Maryland Palatinate*. Baltimore: John Murphy Co., 1902.
McMahon, John V. L. *An Historical View of the Government of Maryland*. Baltimore: Lucas, Cushing and Sons, 1831.
Petrie, George. "Church and State in Early Maryland," *Johns Hopkins University Studies in Historical and Political Science*. Baltimore: Johns Hopkins Press, 1892. X, 193-238.
Reinsch, Paul S. "The English Common Law in the Early American Colonies," *Select Essays in Anglo-American Legal History*. 3 vols. Boston: Little, Brown and Co., 1907. I, 367-415.
Sioussat, St. George L. "The English Statutes in Maryland," *Johns Hopkins University Studies in Historical and Political Science*. Baltimore: Johns Hopkins Press, 1903. XXI, 465-568.
Tyler, Lyon G. *England in America, 1580-1652* (Vol. IV of *The American Nation: A History*). New York: Harper & Bros., 1904. Chaps. 7, 8.

IX. FUNDAMENTAL ORDERS OF CONNECTICUT
1639

James Bryce called the Fundamental Orders of Connecticut "the oldest truly political Constitution in America."[1] The document was certainly a landmark in the development of the written constitution. It should not be thought, however, that it represented a distinct break from the past; nor did it even embody much that was new. Its accomplishment was to transfer the corporate organization of the trading company to a document adopted by the peoples' representatives for the organization of political government.

The first settlers of the towns along the Connecticut River were led by the Rev. Thomas Hooker. They had come from Newton, Watertown, and Dorchester, Massachusetts, in 1635 and 1636, and their experiences with Massachusetts government influenced the policies of Connecticut. It has often been suggested that religious differences with the leaders in Massachusetts prompted the emigration, and it is entirely possible that this may have been one of the motives.[2] A more important motive, however, was disapproval of the wide discretionary powers of the magistrates who voted taxes and legislated as an autonomous body in Massachusetts.[3] The protest against such powers created a spirit of independence which pervaded the Connecticut movement.[4] In addition, many of those who followed Hooker

Origins

---

[1] *The American Commonwealth* (3d ed. rev.; New York, 1895), I, 429n.

[2] The later policy of the river towns would indicate that one motive of emigration was disapproval of the religious test. There is no contemporary evidence to support this, however. Herbert L. Osgood, *The American Colonies in the Seventeenth Century* (New York, 1904), I, 302.

[3] See pp. 77-79.

[4] John Cotton of Massachusetts had argued that democracy was "no fit government either for church or commonwealth." His view was supported by Winthrop, who wrote to Hooker that "the best part is always the least, and of that best part the wiser part is always the lesser." Hooker replied that "in matters which concern the common good a general council, chosen by all, to transact business which concerns all, I conceive most suitable to rule and most safe for the relief of the whole." Lyon G.

to Connecticut were influenced by reports of the richness and accessibility of the bottom lands.

Hooker and his followers acted under a commission issued by the Massachusetts General Court in May, 1635, which allowed them to settle outside of Massachusetts provided that they continued under the authority of the Massachusetts government.[5] Settlements were made in Hartford, Windsor, and Wethersfield along the Connecticut River. Commissioners were appointed with authority to conduct the government during the first year. They swore in constables for the towns, ordered the arming of the inhabitants and the keeping of a watch, and named the towns and fixed their boundaries. The first General Court of Connecticut was called at Hartford by the commissioners on May 1, 1637. It was modeled on the Massachusetts General Court and consisted of six magistrates and nine deputies elected by the towns. The authority of the commissioners and the establishment of a General Court

---

Tyler, *England in America, 1580-1652*, Vol. IV of *The American Nation: A History*, ed. A. B. Hart (28 vols.; New York, 1904-18), 243-44. In 1638 Hooker wrote to Winthrop objecting to the almost unlimited discretionary power of the magistrates in Massachusetts. He insisted that the judges must have some rule to judge by or government would degenerate into tyranny and confusion—a condition under which, he said, he would neither consent to live nor to leave to his posterity. Osgood, *op. cit.*, I, 303. Hooker's decision to emigrate thus paralleled the movement of the freemen of Massachusetts who promoted the enactment of the Body of Liberties in 1641. See pp. 143-61.

[5] The authorization of May, 1635, to the people of Roxbury provided: "The inhabitants of Rocksbury hath liberty graunted them to remove themselues to any place they shall thinke meete, not to piudice another plantacon, pvided they continue still vnder this goumt." The authorization to the inhabitants of Watertown and Dorchester was similar. Nathaniel B. Shurtleff (ed.), *Records of the Governor and Company of the Massachusetts Bay in New England* (Boston, 1853), I, 146, 148. In September, 1635, it was provided that the constables of the river towns should be sworn by Massachusetts magistrates. *Ibid.*, 160.

On March 3, 1636, a commission was issued to Roger Ludlow, William Pinchon, John Steele, William Swaine, Henry Smith, William Phelpes, William Westwood, and Andrew Ward to govern the people at Connecticut for the next year. Because "of the distance of place, this state and goumt cannot take notice of the same as to apply timely remedy, or to dispence equall iustice to them & their affaires, as may be desired." It was provided that the commissioners should have "full power & aucthoritie to hear & determine in a iudiciall way, by witnesses vpon oathe examine, wthin the said plantacon, all those differences wch may arise betweene ptie & ptie, as also, vpon misdemeanr, to inflicte corporall punishmt or imprisonmt, to ffine & levy the same if occacon soe require, to make & decree such orders, for the present, that may be for the peaceable & quiett ordering the affaires of the said plantacon; . . . provided, always, that this comission shall not extende any longer time then one whole yeare from the date thereof, & in the meane time it shalbe lawfull for this Court to recall the said psents if they see cause. . . ." *Ibid.*, 170-71.

In 1641 the Massachusetts General Court declared: "That the said comission was not granted upon any intent either to dismise the psons frō us, or to determine any thing about the limits of iurisdictions, the interest of the lands & or owne limits being as then unknowne; therefore it was granted onely for one yeare; & it may rather appeare, by or granting such a comission, & their accepting of it, as also that clause, viz, Till some other course were taken, by mutuall consent, etc., that wee intended to reserve an interest there upon the ryver, & that themselues also intended to stand to the condition of the first licence of departure given to the most of them, wch was, that they should remaine still of or body." *Ibid.*, 321.

thus gave the river towns a common government at an early date.⁶ This furthered the identity of interests among the three towns and led to the development of the central government which was later set forth in the Fundamental Orders.

The general character and content of the Fundamental Orders were influenced by a notable sermon preached by Hooker before the General Court on May 31, 1638. His ideals were that all public officials should be elected, that their powers should be defined, and that these things should be done by a body of freemen as numerous and inclusive as would consist with their acting "according to the blessed will and law of God."⁷ The credit for actually drafting the instrument, however, probably belongs to Roger Ludlow, one of the few members of the legal profession in the colonies at that time, and a lawyer of the highest attainments.⁸ The Fundamental Orders was adopted on January 14, 1639, by the General Court.⁹

General Significance

It is possible to overestimate the originality and importance of the Fundamental Orders unless the circumstances surrounding its creation are kept in mind. Its claim to fame as a document of constitutional significance rests solely upon the fact that its express purpose was to define the organs of political government rather than those of corporate government. It is this fact that entitles it to be called the first written constitution in America. This, however, did not give it the status of a true constitution. The Fundamental Orders was not considered to be a "higher law" in any sense. It was adopted by the General Court, and because it did not provide for its own amendment, it was amended by the General Court. Its provisions more explicitly defined the organs of government and their powers than did the Massachusetts

---

⁶ It has been said that the existence of the commission from Massachusetts and the establishment of a General Court upon the expiration of the term of the commissioners indicates that the towns were never truly independent. Osgood, *op. cit.*, I, 305-6.

⁷ *Ibid.*, 308.

⁸ Ludlow was one of three men in Connecticut who had been educated in the law. He was an Oxford graduate and a student in the Inner Temple in 1612. He had also been a member of the Massachusetts Court of Assistants. Charles Warren, *A History of the American Bar* (Boston, 1911), 128.

⁹ The document was probably not enacted by a body resembling a constitutional convention. The minutes of the General Court for December 1, 1645, refer to "the generall Orders formerly made by this Court." This statement undoubtedly refers to the Fundamental Orders. The accuracy of the conclusion that the document was adopted by the General Court is supported by the fact that at least eight of the members of the General Court in 1645, including the secretary, Thomas Welles, were probably also members in 1639. George M. Dutcher (ed.), *The Fundamental Orders of Connecticut* (New Haven, 1934), 2. Even assuming that the Fundamental Orders was adopted by a convention of all the free planters, the significance of the conclusion must be appraised in the light of the fact that such an assembly would not have differed materially from the Court of Election. Osgood, *op. cit.*, I, 311.

Charter of 1629, but there was still much vagueness in the instrument. To a large extent, many of the powers and functions of government were assumed by the document.

It was based upon the laws and practices of Plymouth and Massachusetts. The preamble was not a declaration of the colonists' independence from the king nor a statement of the right of the people to govern in their sovereign capacity. It was rather an agreement to abide by the government established in the colony, and was thus similar in purpose to the Mayflower Compact.[10] It expressed the Puritan principle of a church covenant designed to govern both the religious and the civil affairs of the people. The Fundamental Orders, however, went beyond the Mayflower Compact. The Connecticut document stated in some detail the government that was to be formed. The government established was not the invention of the Connecticut settlers but was based directly upon the actual governmental practices of Massachusetts and Plymouth with which the Connecticut settlers had close and frequent contacts.[11]

It was provided that the government should be under a governor, six magistrates, and deputies from the towns elected to the General Court; the Massachusetts government was under a governor, deputy governor, and a variable number of magistrates,[12] and deputies from the several plantations elected by the freemen to the General Court.[13] The governor and magistrates were given power, as in Massachusetts, to administer justice according to the laws of the colony and in the absence of applicable laws according to the word of God.[14] In both colonies the General Court had power to make laws, levy taxes, admit freemen, and dispose of lands.[15] In both, the deputies met before each General Court to prepare business to be submitted to the court.[16]

---

[10] See p. 60. The Mayflower Compact differed from the Fundamental Orders in that the former document expressly acknowledged allegiance to the king.

[11] Osgood, *op. cit.*, I, 309-13.

[12] The Massachusetts Charter provided for eighteen assistants, but during the early years there were always less than that number. The assent of six assistants was necessary for the transaction of business in the General Court. The Massachusetts assistants came to be called "magistrates" because of their duties as justices of the peace, and it is this term which is used in the Fundamental Orders. See pp. 78n, 88.

[13] The Massachusetts Charter contemplated the participation of all the freemen in the General Court. A representative system, however, was introduced by statute in 1634. See pp. 78-79.

[14] See pp. 145, 148.

[15] The powers given by the Massachusetts Charter were supplemented by the Act of 1634. Shurtleff, *op. cit.*, I, 117. See p. 79.

[16] In 1634 it was provided in Massachusetts that "when the deputyes of seuall townes are mett together before any Genall Court, it shalbe lawfull for them, or the maior pte of them, to heare &

FUNDAMENTAL ORDERS OF CONNECTICUT

The later history of the laws of Connecticut and Massachusetts also showed a close relationship and considerable borrowing between the colonies. In 1640 Massachusetts introduced a provision for the nomination of magistrates by the General Court similar to Article 3 of the Fundamental Orders.[17] Article 4 of the Fundamental Orders, which differed from the practice in Massachusetts by prohibiting the governor from serving more than one term, was repealed in 1660.[18] In 1645 a bicameral legislature was instituted as in Massachusetts.[19]

Conclusion

For the greater part, then, legal developments in Connecticut did not represent a significant deviation from the laws of Massachusetts and Plymouth. Instead, those developments represented a further working out of ideas already being applied in the other colonies. The Fundamental Orders was a step forward in the development of the written constitution, although not so large a step as is sometimes thought. Nevertheless, the document shows how the ideas and institutions which had been developed in the trading company charter were for the first time expressly applied in the organization of a political government.

---

determine any difference that may arise aboute the eleccon of any of their members, & to order things amongst themselues that may concerne the well ordering of their body." *Ibid.*, 142. This provision passed from use in Massachusetts at an early date. William E. Whitmore (ed.), *Colonial Laws of Massachusetts, 1672* (Boston, 1890), 4.

[17] Shurtleff, *op. cit.*, I, 293.

[18] Osgood, *op. cit.*, I, 310.

[19] See pp. 80-81. Before 1645 the deputies and the magistrates had voted together in the General Court. Tyler, *op. cit.*, 258. The two bodies in Massachusetts were formally separated in 1644. Shurtleff, *op. cit.*, II, 58.

FUNDAMENTAL ORDERS OF CONNECTICUT[20]

January 14, 1639

Preamble

FORASMUCH as it hath pleased the Allmighty God by the wise disposition of his diuyne pruidence so to Order and dispose of things that we the Inhabitants and Residents of Windsor, Harteford and Wethersfield are now cohabiting and dwelling in and vppon the River of Conectecotte and the Lands thereunto adioyneing; And well knowing where a people are gathered together the word of God requires that to mayntayne the peace and vnion of such a people there should be an orderly and decent Gouerment established according to God, to order and dispose of the affayres of the people at all seasons as occation shall require; doe therefore assotiate and conioyne our selues to be as one Publike State or Comonwelth; and doe, for our selues and our Successors and such as shall be adioyned to vs att any tyme hereafter, enter into Combination and Confederation togather, to mayntayne and prsearue the liberty and purity of the gospell of our Lord Jesus wch we now prfesse, as also the discipplyne of the Churches, wch according to the truth of the said gospell is now practised amongst vs; As also in or Ciuell Affaires to be guided and gouerned according to such Lawes, Rules, Orders and decrees as shall be made, ordered & decreed, as followeth:—

Court of Election and General Court

1. It is Ordered, sentenced and decreed, that there shall be yerely two generall Assemblies or Courts, the on the second thursday in Aprill, the other the second thursday in September, following; the first shall be called the Courte of Election, wherein shall be yerely Chosen frō tyme to tyme soe many Magestrats and other publike Officers as shall be found requisitte: Whereof one to be chosen Gouernour for the yeare ensueing and vntill another be chosen, and noe other Magestrate to be chosen for more then one yeare; pruided allwayes there be sixe chosen besids the Gouernour; wch being chosen and sworne according to an Oath recorded for that purpose shall haue power to administer iustice according to the Lawes here established, and for want thereof according to the rule of the word of God; wch choise shall be made by all that are admitted freemen and haue taken the Oath of Fidellity, and doe cohabitte wthin this Jurisdiction, (hauing beene admitted Inhabitants by the maior prt of the Towne wherein they liue,) or the mayor prte of such as shall be then prsent.

[20] Francis N. Thorpe (ed.), *The Federal and State Constitutions, Colonial Charters and Other Organic Laws* (Washington, 1909), I, 519-22. The date used here is determined in accordance with modern reckoning.

FUNDAMENTAL ORDERS OF CONNECTICUT

2. It is Ordered, sentensed and decreed, that the Election of the aforesaid Magestrats shall be on this manner: euery prson prsent and quallified for choyse shall bring in (to the prsons deputed to receaue thē) one single papr wth the name of him written in yt whom he desires to haue Gouernour, and he that hath the greatest nūber of papers shall be Gouernor for that yeare. And the rest of the Magestrats or publike Officers to be chosen in this manner: The Secretary for the tyme being shall first read the names of all that are to be put to choise and then shall seuerally nominate them distinctly, and euery one that would haue the prson nominated to be chosen shall bring in one single paper written vppon, and he that would not haue him chosen shall bring in a blanke: and euery one that hath more written papers than blanks shall be a Magistrat for that yeare; wch papers shall be receaued and told by one or more that shall be chosen by the court and sworne to be faythfull therein; but in case there should not be sixe chosen as aforesaid, besids the Gouernor, out of those wch are nominated, then he or they wch haue the most written paprs shall be a Magestrate or Magestrats for the ensueing yeare, to make vp the aforesaid nūber. *(Election of governor, magistrates, and other officers)*

3. It is Ordered, sentenced and decreed, that the Secretary shall not nominate any prson, nor shall any prson be chosen newly into the Magestracy wch was not prpownded in some Generall Courte before, to be nominated the next Election; and to that end yt shall be lawfull for ech of the Townes aforesaid by their deputyes to nominate any two whō they conceaue fitte to be put to election; and the Courte may ad so many more as they iudge requisitt. *(Nominations)*

4. It is Ordered, sentenced and decreed that noe prson be chosen Gouernor aboue once in two yeares, and that the Gouernor be always a mēber of some approved congregation, and formerly of the Magestracy wthin this Jurisdiction; and all the Magestrats Freemen of this Comōnwelth: and that no Magestrate or other publike officer shall execute any prte of his or their Office before they are seuerally sworne, wch shall be done in the face of the Courte if they be prsent, and in case of absence by some deputed for that purpose. *(Qualifications of governor and magistrates)*

5. It is Ordered, sentenced and decreed, that to the aforesaid Courte of Election the seurall Townes shall send their deputyes, and when the Elections are ended they may prceed in any publike searuice as at other Courts. Also the other Generall Courte in September shall be for makeing of lawes, and any other publike occasion, wch conserns the good of the Comōnwelth. *(Powers of Court of Election and General Court)*

6. It is Ordered, sentenced and decreed, that the Gournor shall, ether by himselfe or by the secretary, send out sumōns to the Constables of eur Towne for the cauleing of these two standing Courts, on month at lest before their seurall tymes: And also if the Gournor and the gretest prte of the Magestrats see cause vppon any spetiall occation to call a generall Courte, they may giue order to the secretary soe to doe wthin fowerteene dayes warneing; and if vrgent necessity so require, vppon a shorter notice, giueing sufficient grownds for yt to the deputyes when they meete, or els be questioned for the same; And if the Gournor and Mayor prte of Magestrats shall ether neglect ot refuse to call the two Generall standing Courts or ether of thē, as also at other tymes when the occasions of the Comōmwelth require, the Freemen thereof, or the *(Calling of Court of Election and General Court)*

Mayor prte of them, shall petition to them soe to doe: if then yt be ether denyed or neglected the said Freemen or the Mayor prte of them shall haue power to giue order to the Constables of the seuerall Townes to doe the same, and so may meete togather, and chuse to themselues a Moderator, and may prceed to do any Acte of power, wch any other Generall Courte may.

Election of deputies

7. It is Ordered, sentenced and decreed that after there are warrants giuen out for any of the said Generall Courts, the Constable or Constables of ech Towne shall forthwth give notice distinctly to the inhabitants of the same, in some Publike Assembly or by goeing or sending frō howse to howse, that at a place and tyme by him or them lymited and sett, they meet and assemble thē selues togather to elect and chuse certen deputyes to be att the Generall Courte then following to agitate the afayres of the comonwelth; wch said Deputyes shall be chosen by all that are admitted Inhabitants in the seurall Townes and haue taken the oath of fidellity; pruided that non be chosen a Deputy for any Generall Courte wch is not a Freeman of this Comonwelth.

Qualifications of deputies and electors

Procedure for elections

The a-foresaid deputyes shall be chosen in manner following: euery prson that is prsent and quallified as before exprssed, shall bring the names of such, written in seurrall papers, as they desire to haue chosen for that Imployment, and these 3 or 4, more or lesse, being the nūber agreed on to be chosen for that tyme, that haue greatest nūber of papers written for thē shall be deputyes for that Courte; whose names shall be endorsed on the backe side of the warrant and returned into the Courte, wth the Constable or Constables hand vnto the same.

Number of deputies

8. It is Ordered, sentenced and decreed, that Wyndsor, Hartford and Wethersfield shall haue power, ech Towne, to send fower of their freemen as deputyes to euery Generall Courte; And whatsoeuer other Townes shall be hereafter added to this Jurisdiction, they shall send so many deputyes as the Courte shall judge meete, as resonable prportion to the nūber of Freemen that are in the said Townes being to be attended therein; wch deputyes shall have the power of the whole Towne to giue their voats and alowance to all such lawes and orders as may be for the publike good, and unto wch the said Townes are to be bownd.

Caucus of deputies

9. It is ordered and decreed, that the deputyes thus chosen shall haue power and liberty to appoynt a tyme and a place of meeting togather before any Generall Courte to aduise and consult of all such things as may concerne the good of the publike, as also to examine their owne Elections, whether according to the order, and if they or the gretest prte of them find any election to be illegall they may seclud such for prsent frō their meeting, and returne the same and their resons to the Courte; and if yt proue true, the Courte may fyne the prty or prtyes so intruding and the Towne, if they see cause, and giue out a warrant to goe to a newe election in a legall way, either *in whole or* in prte. Also the said deputyes shall haue power to fyne any that shall be disorderly at their meetings, or for not coming in due tyme or place according to appoyntment; and they may returne the said fynes into the Courte if yt be refused to be paid, and the tresurer to take notice of yt, and to estreete or levy the same as he doth other fynes.

FUNDAMENTAL ORDERS OF CONNECTICUT

10. It is Ordered, sentenced and decreed, that euery Generall Courte, except such as through neglecte of the Gournor and the greatest prte of Magestrats the Freemen themselues doe call, shall consist of the Gouernor, or some one chosen to moderate the Court, and 4 other Magestrats at lest, wth the mayor prte of the deputyes of the seuerall Townes legally chosen; and in case the Freemen or mayor prte of thē through neglect or refusall of the Gouernor and mayor prte of the magestrats, shall call a Courte, that yt shall consist of the mayor prte of Freemen that are prsent or their deputyes, wth a Moderator chosen by thē: *In wch said Generall Courts shall consist the supreme power of the Comonwelth,* and they only shall haue power to make laws or repeale thē, to graunt leuyes, to admitt of Freemen, dispose of lands vndisposed of,, to seurall Townes or prsons, and also shall haue power to call ether Courte or Magestrate or any other prson whatsoeuer into question for any misdemeanour, and may for just causes displace or deale otherwise according to the nature of the offence; and also may deale in any other matter that concerns the good of this comon welth, excepte election of Magestrats, wch shall be done by the whole boddy of Freemen: In wch Courte the Gouernour or Moderator shall haue power to order the Courte to giue liberty of spech, and silence vnceasonable and disorderly speakeings, to put all things to voate, and in case the vote be equall to haue the casting voice. But non of these Courts shall be adiorned or dissolued wthout the consent of the maior prte of the Court.

Membership of General Court

Powers of General Court

Freedom of speech in General Court

11. It is ordered, sentenced and decreed, that when any Generall Courte vppon the occasions of the Comonwelth haue agreed vppon any sume or somes of mony to be leuyed vppon the seuerall Townes wthin this Jurisdiction, that a Comittee be chosen to sett out and appoynt wt shall be the prportion of euery Towne to pay of the said leuy, prvided the Comittees be made vp of an equall nūber out of each Towne.

Taxes

14th January, 1638, the 11 Orders abouesaid are voted.

THE OATH OF THE GOURNOR, FOR THE /PRSENT/

I N. W. being chosen to be Gournor wthin this Jurisdiction, for the yeare ensueing, and vntil a new be chosen, doe sweare by the greate and dreadfull name of the everliueing God, to prmote the publicke good and peace of the same, according to the best of my skill; as also will mayntayne all lawfull priuiledges of this Comonwealth; as also that all wholsome lawes that are or shall be made by lawfull authority here established, be duly executed; and will further the execution of Justice according to the rule of Gods word; so helpe me God, in the name of the Lo: Jesus Christ.

Oath of governor

THE OATH OF A MAGESTRATE, FOR THE PRSENT

I, N. W. being chosen a Magestrate wthin this Jurisdiction for the yeare ensueing, doe sweare by the great and dreadfull name of the euerliueing God, to prmote the

Oath of magistrates

publike good and peace of the same, according to the best of my skill, and that I will mayntayne all the lawfull priuiledges thereof according to my vnderstanding, as also assist in the execution of all such wholsome lawes as are made or shall be made by lawfull authority heare established, and will further the execution of Justice for the tyme aforesaid according to the righteous rule of Gods word; so helpe me God, etc.

REFERENCES

Andrews, Charles M. *The Colonial Period of American History.* 3 vols. New Haven: Yale University Press, 1936. II, chaps. 3, 4.

Channing, Edward. *A History of the United States.* 6 vols. New York: Macmillan Co., 1928. I, chap. 15.

Osgood, Herbert L. *The American Colonies in the Seventeenth Century.* 3 vols. New York: Macmillan Co., 1904-7. I, chap. 7.

Tyler, Lyon G. *England in America, 1580-1652* (Vol. IV of *The American Nation: A History*). New York: Harper & Bros., 1904. Chaps. 14, 15.

X. ABOLITION OF THE STAR CHAMBER
1641

By the abolition of the Court of Star Chamber the English Parliament, in dramatic fashion, reaffirmed the principle of due process of law as established by Magna Carta. Parliament did more than simply remove the principal instrumentality of oppression and persecution wielded by the Stuart kings; it established the ordinary courts of law as the rightful guardians of the liberties of the subject. Once the administration of justice had been taken from this powerful executive tribunal, the importance of the courts increased and the common law was strengthened and developed in the judicial system. The abolition of the Star Chamber also opened the way for the establishment of the privilege against self-incrimination.

Origins

The Court of Star Chamber was an offshoot of the King's Council. During the Middle Ages the Council exercised broad and undefined executive, legislative and judicial powers.[1] As governmental functions became better defined, there were split off from the Council several courts, each having a distinct jurisdiction. These were the courts of Exchequer, King's Bench, and Common Pleas.[2] The establishment of these courts, however, did not take all judicial business from the Council. Its judicial functions were largely

Origin of the Court of Star Chamber

---

[1] The Council developed from the Curia Regis of the Norman and Angevin kings. At first it was composed of a shifting group of bishops, barons and officers and it did not become a distinct body until the fourteenth century. At that time it consisted of the great officers of state, the officers of the household, a number of professional lawyers, occasionally some foreigners, some knights, and some of the lay and ecclesiastical nobility. Its functions thus constituted "government by royal favorites." The Council had a reviewing authority over the inferior courts and also had original jurisdiction in cases in which the king was especially interested. See Cora L. Scofield, *A Study of The Court of Star Chamber* (Chicago, 1900), xxiii-xxx; William S. Holdsworth, *A History of English Law* (4th ed.; Boston, 1931), I, 480-85.

[2] The judicial duties of the Exchequer developed as early as the twelfth century and were at first incidental to its executive functions as a financial board. See p. 111. The Common Pleas also split off from the Council in the twelfth century, and the King's Bench split off in the thirteenth. *Ibid.*, 477-80; Max Radin, *Handbook of Anglo-American Legal History* (St. Paul, 1936), 66.

unimpaired, and it continued to administer justice in its own fashion—a fashion which differed radically from the methods of the common law.[3]

Its powers and procedures aroused opposition as early as the fourteenth century. The common law courts were jealous of its judicial powers; Parliament looked upon it as an instrumentality of prerogative government; lawyers were suspicious of its encroachments upon their legal business; and laymen feared its arbitrary procedures and its mighty discretionary powers.[4] The fourteenth-century struggles against the Council helped establish Magna Carta as the principal document of the English constitution. Parliament passed a number of statutes which attempted to limit the Council's jurisdiction. These statutes were important not only because of their role in the immediate dispute, but also because they developed the principle of due process of law by building on Magna Carta.[5] Many of the ideas developed in

---

[3] Dicey's summary of the procedure of the Council is as follows: "The Council acted in one of two modes. The most summary was the proceeding *ore tenus*. On the reception of a charge by the Council —one grounded, it might be, on 'common report,' or on secret information, the accused person was privately arrested, and brought before the Council Board. There he was examined. If he confessed, or made admissions considered equivalent to a confession, he was condemned *ex ore suo*, and judgment was given against him. He knew neither his accuser nor the crime of which he was accused, and he was subjected to an examination which, as even Hudson admits, was conducted with scanty fairness to the prisoner. He might, indeed, refuse either to confess or to answer any questions. If so, he was not condemned, but remanded to prison, that the Council might adopt another course.

"This, the second mode of prosecution, was to proceed by bill. A bill of complaint was addressed to the Council, signed by a Councillor. When the bill was filed, or in some cases even before its filing, the accused was summoned by a writ of subpoena. On his appearance the defendant was bound to answer on oath the plaintiff's bill. If he refused to make a reply, he was committed to prison; and, after some delay, his crime was treated as acknowledged. If he put in an answer, his case was not much better; he was examined by the plaintiff on written interrogatories, a refusal to reply to any of which led to imprisonment of indefinite and sometimes life-long duration. After the plaintiff's examination, witnesses, whose character the accused was not allowed to shake, were privately examined. The cause was then ready for determination, and after, it might be, a long delay, sentence was given." *The Privy Council* (London, 1887), 102-3. See also Holdsworth, *op. cit.*, I, 496; Edward P. Cheyney, "The Court of Star Chamber," *American Historical Review*, XVIII (July, 1913), 737-42.

[4] Holdsworth, *op. cit.*, I, 486.

[5] See *ibid.*, 487-88; F. W. Maitland, *The Constitutional History of England* (Cambridge, 1909), 217. The statutes removed questions of freehold, treason, and felony from the Council. As a result, it came to be thought that the Council could never impose the sentence of death, a limitation which always applied to the Star Chamber. The more serious crimes were always tried in the courts. The principal fourteenth-century statutes intended to curb the Council provided:

"It is accorded and established, That it shall not be commanded by the great seal nor the little seal to disturb or delay common right; (2) and though such commandments do come, the justices shall not therefore leave to do right in any point." 2 Edw. 3, c. 8 (1328).

"That no man from henceforth shall be attached by any accusation, nor forejudged of life or limb, nor his lands, tenements, goods, nor chattels seised into the King's hands, against the form of the great charter, and the law of the land." 5 Edw. 3, c. 9. (1331).

"*Whereas it is contained in the great charter of the franchises of England, that none shall·be imprisoned nor put out of his freehold, nor of his franchises nor free custom, unless it be by the law of the land;* (2) it is accorded, assented, and stablished, That from henceforth none shall be taken by petition or suggestion made to our lord the King, or to his council, unless it be by indictment or presentment of good and lawful people of the same neighborhood where such deeds be done, in due manner, or by process made by writ original at the common law; (3) nor that none be out of his

ABOLITION OF THE STAR CHAMBER

the fourteenth century influenced the lawyers of the seventeenth century who abolished the Star Chamber. Thus, because Parliament had once exercised considerable control over the Council, it was not until the sixteenth and seventeenth centuries that the Council regained its former importance.

As early as the fourteenth century the name "Star Chamber" was used to designate the room in Westminster Palace where the Council sat as a judicial body.[6] The Star Chamber emerged as a separate court during the next century. At that time the judicial business of the Council came to be handled entirely by those of its members who stayed at Westminster and did not follow the king in his travels.[7] The increased importance of the Court of Star Chamber resulted from a general dissatisfaction with the common law courts. Those courts were dominated by the great magnates and had become corrupt during the years. In an effort to improve the administration of justice, wide powers were granted to the Court of Star Chamber. The principal statute affirming its powers was the Act of 1487, *Pro Camera*

Act of 1487

---

franchises, nor of his freeholds, unless he be duly brought into answer, and forejudged of the same by the course of the law; (4) and if any thing be done against the same, it shall be redressed and holden for none." 25 Edw. 3, stat. 5, c. 4 (1350).

"That no man of what estate or condition that he be, shall be put out of land or tenement, nor taken nor imprisoned, nor disinherited, nor put to death, without being brought in answer by due process of the law." 28 Edw. 3, c. 3 (1354).

"*Though that it be contained in the Great Charter, that no man be taken nor imprisoned, nor put out of his freehold, without process of the law; nevertheless divers people make false suggestion to the King himself, as well for malice as otherwise, whereof the King is often grieved, and divers of the realm put in damage, against the form of the same charter:* wherefore it is ordained, That all they that make such suggestion, be sent with the suggestions before the chancellor, treasurer and his council, and that they there find surety to pursue their suggestions, and incur the same pain that the other should have had if he were attainted, in case that his suggestion be found evil. And that then process of the law be made against them, without being taken or imprisoned against the form of the said charter and other statutes." 37 Edw. 3, c. 18 (1363).

"That no man be put to answer without presentment before justices, or matter of record, or by due process and writ original, according to the old law of the land: . . . and if any thing from henceforth be done to the contrary, it shall be void in the law, and holden for error." 42 Edw. 3, c. 3 (1368).

[6] A number of theories have been advanced as to the origin of the name. It has been said that it derives from the saxon word "*steoran*," "to steer or govern"; from the fact that the room in which the council sat was full of windows; that the roof of the room was decorated with gilded stars; that before the expulsion of the Jews, their contracts and obligations, called "Starra" or "Starrs," were kept in this room; and from the suggestion that as the king represented the sun, so did the judges represent the stars. See Scofield, *op. cit.*, 1n.; William Blackstone, *Commentaries on the Laws of England* (9th ed.; London, 1783), IV, 266n.; Holdsworth, *op. cit.*, I, 496.

[7] The separation between the Court of Star Chamber and the Council was not formally made until 1526, although it existed in fact before that date. The rest of the Council came to be called the Privy Council about the same time. Radin, *op. cit.*, 69-70. Although the Court of Star Chamber was a separate court with its own functions, a definite membership, its own functionaries, and a fixed location, it was always very closely connected with the Privy Council. The increase of business which led to the establishment of the court also resulted in the creation of a number of provincial councils with similar powers. The most important of these were the Council of Wales and the Marches and the Council of the North. The existence and legality of these councils was recognized in 1543 by 34 and 35 Henry 8, c. 26. Holdsworth, *op. cit.*, I, 499-502.

Stellata.[8] That statute came to play such an important role in its activities that during the Tudor and Stuart reigns many lawyers incorrectly believed that the act of 1487 had created the court. Its preamble listed the grievances against the common law courts. It recited the corruption of witnesses, the lawlessness of the nobility, and the lack of enforcement of the laws. It alleged the need for the summary proceedings of the Council; it affirmed certain parts of the Council's jurisdiction; and it provided for the selection of the members of the tribunal which was to hear and decide cases.[9] Because of the great latitude given to the court in the conduct of proceedings, it has even been asserted that the avowed purpose of the act was apparently to give the court power to convict and punish without due process of law.[10]

Court of Star Chamber during the Tudor period

During the reign of Elizabeth I the Star Chamber often acted as the champion of persons oppressed by overbearing and corrupt members of the nobility. For many years it was considered to be both a necessary and an efficient institution, and it heard a large number of cases both great and small. By the end of the sixteenth century its procedures had become well defined. In civil cases it acted much like the Court of Chancery. Two distinguished members of the court, Sir Edward Coke and Sir Francis Bacon, like other public figures, expressed highly laudatory opinions of its activities.

---

[8] 3 Hen. 7, c. 1. Later statutes supplemented that act. In 1495 the Chancellor, Treasurer, Chief Justices, and Master of the Rolls were given power to examine complaints as to perjuries committed by jurors and to punish offenders. 11 Hen. 7, c. 25. The Statute of Proclamations of 1539 established a tribunal of the most important officers of the state to deal with offenses against proclamations published in accordance with the act. 31 Hen. 8, c. 8, § 4.

[9] The preamble illustrates the extent to which corrupt influences had affected the administration of justice in the common law courts: "FIRST, *The King our said sovereign lord remembereth, how by unlawful maintenances, giving of liveries, signs and tokens, and retainders by indentures, promises, oaths, writings or otherwise embraceries of his subjects, untrue demeanings of sheriffs in making of panels, and other untrue returns, by taking of money, by juries, by great riots, and unlawful assemblies, the policy and good rule of this realm is almost subdued,, and for the not punishing of these inconveniences, and by occasion of the premisses, little or nothing may be found by inquiry, whereby the laws of this land in execution may take little effect, to the increase of murders, robberies, perjuries, and unsureties of all men living, and losses of their lands and goods, to the great displeasure of almighty God.*"
The members of the court were to be the Chancellor, the Treasurer, and the Keeper of the Privy Seal, or two of them; a bishop and a temporal lord of the Council; and the chief justices of the King's Bench and the Common Pleas, or, in their absence, two other justices. Although the statute thus provided for six or seven members of the court with jurisdiction over seven offenses, by the seventeenth century there were many more judges and the court's jurisdiction was much broader. Scofield, *op. cit.*, 11. The tribunal set up by the act was probably regarded as a special committee of the Council. The act did not detract from the ordinary jurisdiction of the Council, but instead affirmed its existing jurisdiction. Holdsworth, *op. cit.*, I, 494-95.

[10] Rodney L. Mott, *Due Process of Law* (Indianapolis, 1926), 6n. The act empowered the court "to examine, and such as they find therein defective, to punish them after their demerits, after the form and effect of statutes thereof made, in like manner and form as they should and ought to be punished, if they were thereof convict after the due order of the law."

"It is," said Coke, "the most honourable court, (our parliament excepted) that is in the Christian world, both in respect of the judges of the court, and of their honourable proceeding according to their just jurisdiction, and the ancient and just orders of the court."[11] Bacon called it "one of the sagest and noblest institutions of this kingdom."[12]

At the close of the sixteenth century, therefore, the Star Chamber was regarded as a separate court, but one closely connected with the Privy Council. Its members included some of the highest officers of the state. Its prestige and power were immense. It was not until the seventeenth century that even Parliament came to be regarded as a more important organ of government.[13] Its jurisdiction was vast. William Hudson said, "In a word, there is no offence punishable by any law, but if the court find it to grow in the Commonwealth, this court may lawfully punish it, except only where life is questioned."[14] The court had power to punish jurors for giving verdicts against the crown; it acted in cooperation with the Court of High Commission, a prerogative court established by Elizabeth I to punish religious offenders and particularly to persecute the Catholics and Puritans; it punished offenders against royal proclamations; and it dealt severely with individuals who criticized the king's taxation policies.[15]

Character of the court in 1600

The power of the court to issue and enforce proclamations gave it important legislative and executive functions in addition to its judicial duties. These functions were not much different from those exercised by the Privy Council.[16] During the reign of Henry VIII, this power was based on the Statute of Proclamations of 1539.[17] That act affirmed what had previously been a vague prerogative of the crown. In effect, it amounted to no less than an outright delegation to the crown of Parliament's right to legislate on any

Objections to the Court of Star Chamber during the seventeenth century

Proclamations

---

[11] *The Fourth Part of the Institutes of the Laws of England* (London, 1797), 65.

[12] "The History of the Reign of King Henry the Seventh," *The Essays of Lord Bacon* (Chandos Classics; New York, 1883), 418. Holdsworth said of the court during the Tudor period: "In fact, the powers wielded by the Council and Star Chamber guided England through the great changes of this century of Renaissance and Reformation, enforced a high standard of duty on all other courts and persons entrusted with governmental functions, and thus not only gave internal peace to the country, but fitted Englishmen to use wisely that large measure of liberty which they acquired in the following century." *Op. cit.*, I, 508.

[13] Charles H. McIlwain, *The High Court of Parliament and Its Supremacy* (New Haven, 1910), 37.

[14] William Hudson, "A Treatise on the Court of Star-Chamber," *Collectanea Juridica*, ed. Francis Hargrave (London, 1791), II, 117-18.

[15] See Scofield, *op. cit.*, 45-49.

[16] *Ibid.*, 49-55.

[17] 31 Hen. 8, c. 8.

subject.[18] The statute contained a few safeguards of the liberty of the subject. No proclamations were to be issued contrary to the common law, existing acts of Parliament, or in violation of property rights. In addition, the death penalty was forbidden. The Statute of Proclamations was repealed in the first year after the death of Henry VIII, however, and the power of the crown to issue proclamations relapsed into its former obscurity.[19]

During the reign of James I (1603-25), proclamations were issued much more frequently than during the Tudor period. They were enforced by the Court of Star Chamber. The proclamations covered a variety of topics. These included the regulation of trades and businesses and the conduct of municipal elections. Among the most important of its orders were those for the regulation of printing. A number of decrees were issued on this subject between 1566 and 1637 in order that "all persons using and professing the art, trade, or mystery of printing, or selling of books should from henceforth be ruled and directed therein by some certain or known rules or ordinances, which should be inviolably kept and observed, and the breakers and offenders of the same to be severely and sharply punished and corrected."[20]

In 1610 Parliament complained that proclamations had been issued creating new offenses unknown to the law; that penalties imposed were greater than authorized by law; and that persons were being tried by unauthorized tribunals. James submitted the question of proclamations to his judges. The reply of the judges, delivered by Coke, is considered a landmark in the history of individual liberties. He stated that the king could not create new crimes, and that the royal prerogative was subject to the law of the land.[21] The Stuart kings refused to be bound by these limitations. The Star Chamber

---

[18] "The King for the time being, with the advice of his council, or the most part of them, may set forth proclamations under such penalties and pains as to him and them shall seem necessary, which shall be observed as though they were made by act of parliament; but this shall not be prejudicial to any person's inheritance, offices, liberties, goods, chattels or life; and whosoever shall willingly offend any article contained in the said proclamations, shall pay such forfeitures, or be so long imprisoned, as shall be expressed in the said proclamations; and if any offending will depart the realm, to the intent he will not answer his said offence, he shall be adjudged a traitor."

[19] 1 Edw. 6, c. 12, § 4; Holdsworth, *op. cit.*, IV, 104.

[20] Quoted in Scofield, *op. cit.*, 52.

[21] "That the King by his proclamation cannot create any offence which was not an offence before, for then he may alter the law of the land by his proclamation in a high point, for if he may create an offence where none is, upon the ensues fine and imprisonment . . . That the King hath no prerogative but that which the law of the land allows him . . . But the King, for prevention of offences, may by proclamation admonish his subjects that they keep the laws and do not offend them, upon punishment to be inflicted by the law . . ." Quoted in J. R. Tanner, *English Constitutional Conflicts of the Seventeenth Century, 1603-1689* (Cambridge, 1928), 38.

continued to issue and enforce proclamations on any subject over which the king wished to exercise control.[22]

Several other factors also motivated the abolition of the court in 1641. A number of practices which had started to grow up during the reign of Queen Elizabeth became intolerable under Charles I.[23] The court's jurisdiction went beyond the act of 1487, and many people asserted that it was acting illegally. As we have seen, however, this was not the case because that act had merely affirmed part of the existing jurisdiction of the Council. The belief persisted, however, and the act of 1641 stated that the judges "have not kept themselves to the points limited by the said statute." Certainly, the court's powers were overbearing when abused. The famous cases it handled, such as the trials of John Lilburne, William Prynne, and Dr. Leighton,[24] helped bring the court into disrepute even though such cases constituted only a small part of its business. The sentences imposed were extremely cruel when judged by modern standards. These, however, were not much more severe than punishments which had been pronounced during the reign of Elizabeth,[25] but the abhorrence of torture was growing. It is possible that the total abolition of the court was the product of the religious prejudices of the times. The court had become dominated by church officials whom Parliament opposed, and a general attitude of condemnation developed which sought the complete abolition of the court.[26]

Other objections

---

[22] Holdsworth, *op. cit.*, VI, 27.

[23] See Henry E. I. Phillips, "The Last Years of the Court of Star Chamber, 1630-41," *Transactions of the Royal Historical Society* (4th ser.; London, 1939), XXI, 103-31.

[24] Leighton, a Scots divine, published an angry libel against the church. He was sentenced to be publicly whipped at Westminster and set in the pillory, to have one side of his nose slit, one ear cut off, and one side of his cheek branded with a hot iron. All this was to be repeated the next week at Cheapside, and he was then to suffer perpetual imprisonment in the Fleet. Lilburne, who had issued pamphlets against the bishops, was shipped from the Fleet to Westminster, where he was set in the pillory and treated with great cruelty. Prynne had published a book called *Histriomastix*, a denunciation of the immorality of the theater in the course of which he seemed to identify all female performers with the courtesans of the Roman stage. Six weeks after publication the queen appeared in a masque. Prynne, already obnoxious to the crown, was adjudged to stand twice in the pillory, to be branded on the forehead, to lose both his ears, to pay a fine of £5,000, and to suffer perpetual imprisonment. He later suffered further cruelties at the hands of the Star Chamber after he had used the leisure of the jail to write fresh libels against the hierarchy. Henry Hallam, *The Constitutional History of England* (5th ed.; London, 1847), 259.

[25] Only 19 of the 236 cases tried between 1630 and 1641 involved corporal punishment. Phillips, *op. cit.*, 118. The forms of corporal punishment used included the pillory, whipping, nailing or cutting of the ears, branding, slitting the nose, wearing papers describing the offense in public places, and riding a horse with face to the tail. Scofield, *op. cit.*, 76-77. Fines were very heavy during the Stuart period, but were often remitted and were considered *in terrorem populi*. *Ibid.*, 77-78; Cheyney, *op. cit.*, 744-45.

[26] Phillips, *op. cit.*, 130-31.

Effects
Due process of law

The main effect of the abolition of the Star Chamber was to establish in England a system of justice administered by the courts instead of by the administrative agencies of the executive branch of the government.[27] The statute thus constituted an important reaffirmation of the concept of due process of the law including the protection of trial by jury.

Habeas corpus

The Privy Council was deprived by this statute of all jurisdiction to hear and determine criminal cases, but it still had power to commit persons suspected of crime to prison pending trial.[28] Section VIII of the statute, however, stated that every person so committed should be entitled to a writ of habeas corpus so that the legality of his imprisonment could be determined. The statute was thus one of the principal enactments of the seventeenth century in which that right was strengthened.[29]

Privilege against self-incrimination

The abolition of the Court of Star Chamber and the Court of High Commission also opened the way for the establishment of the privilege against self-incrimination. One of the characteristic features of the procedure of those tribunals was the examination of the defendant upon his oath. This was called the oath *ex officio*. By that oath the defendant might be required to answer questions on any subject, however incriminating, about which the court wished to inquire.[30] The oath *ex officio* had been developed as part of the procedure of the ecclesiastical courts during the thirteenth century.[31] It was not until the seventeenth century, however, that strenuous objections to its use were raised. One of the earliest objections was made by the first Parliament of James I in 1604. It presented a petition to the king asking that "the oath *ex officio,* whereby men are forced to accuse themselves, be more sparingly used."[32] At first, opposition to the oath was based upon objections to the jurisdiction of the ecclesiastical courts. After Sir Edward Coke became Chief Justice of the Court of Common Pleas in 1606, he held in several cases that the ecclesiastical courts could not examine persons charged with crime by the oath *ex officio*. At that time the objection was apparently not that the accused should be allowed to remain silent, but that

---

[27] Holdsworth, *op. cit.*, I, 516; Albert V. Dicey, *Introduction to the Study of the Law of the Constitution* (8th ed.; London, 1915), 263-64.

[28] Maitland, *op. cit.*, 314.

[29] See pp. 191-93.

[30] William Blackstone, *op. cit.*, III, 100-1.

[31] John H. Wigmore, *A Treatise on the Anglo-American System of Evidence* (3d ed.; Boston, 1940), VIII, 281.

[32] Quoted in Tanner, *op. cit.*, 26.

the ecclesiastical courts should not exercise jurisdiction over criminal cases in addition to matrimonial and testamentary matters.[33] These decisions, of course, had no effect on the power of the Court of Star Chamber to examine defendants. Its authority to do so had been expressly conferred by the statute of 1487.[34]

Objections to the oath *ex officio* were linked with objections to other practices of the court. The objections became serious in the early seventeenth century as the result of the operations of the court under James I and Charles I. The most notable protest against the oath was made by John Lilburne during his trial in 1637 on a charge of printing or importing certain heretical and seditious books.[35] Although he was willing to answer questions concerning the charges made against him, Lilburne protested against questions designed to obtain information concerning other matters of an incriminating nature. After he had denied the charges made, he said:

> ... I am not willing to answer you to any more of these questions, because I see you go about this Examination to ensnare me: for seeing the things for which I am imprisoned cannot be proved against me, you will get other matter out of my examination: and therefore if you will not ask me about the thing laid to my charge, I shall answer no more....[36]

The oath *ex officio* disappeared in 1641 with the abolition of the Star Chamber and the High Commission. The act abolishing the High Commission expressly prohibited ecclesiastical courts from requiring persons to confess or accuse themselves of any crime or other matter whereby they might be exposed to criminal penalties.[37]

---

[33] Wigmore, *op. cit.*, VIII, 288-89.

[34] 3 Hen. 7, c. 1.

[35] *State Trials* (T. B. Howell, comp.), III, 1315.

[36] *Ibid.*, 1318.

[37] "That no archbishop, bishop nor vicar general, nor any chancellor, official nor commissary of any archbishop, bishop or vicar general, nor any ordinary whatsoever, nor any other spiritual or ecclesiastical judge, officer or minister of justice, nor any other person or persons whatsoever, exercising spiritual or ecclesiastical power, authority or jurisdiction, by any grant, licence or commission of the King's majesty, his heirs or successors, or by any power or authority derived from the King, his heirs or successors, or otherwise, shall from and after the first day of *August*, which shall be in the year of our Lord God one thousand six hundred forty and one, award, impose or inflict any pain, penalty, fine, amerciament, imprisonment or other corporal punishment upon any of the King's subjects, for any contempt, misdemeanor, crime, offence, matter or thing whatsoever, belonging to spiritual or ecclesiastical cognizance or jurisdiction, (2) or shall *ex officio*, or at the instance or promotion of any other person whatsoever, urge, enforce, tender, give or minister unto any churchwarden, side-man or other person whatsoever, any corporal oath, whereby he or she shall or may be charged or obliged to make any presentment of any crime or offence, or to confess or to accuse himself or herself of any crime, offence, delinquency or misdemeanor, or any neglect, matter or thing, whereby or by reason

The abolition of these tribunals did not establish the privilege against self-incrimination as the right of the subject in all cases. The procedures of the common law courts were unaffected by that action. Defendants were usually not examined upon oath by the common law courts, but they were questioned freely about criminal activities and pressed by the judges to answer.[38] Protests against such questioning were not raised until after the oath *ex officio* had been condemned because of its association with the prerogative courts. During the mid-seventeenth century, several cases recorded the growing opposition to the practice of the common law courts.[39] In addition, several proposals for legislative action on the subject were made to the Long Parliament. These proposals are significant because of the similarities and differences in language between them and American federal and state constitutions which secure the privilege.

Most of the agitation in favor of the privilege against self-incrimination came from the Levellers, a democratic faction in the government. They stated in the "Large Petition of the Levellers" of March, 1647, that no authority should compel persons to disclose incriminating evidence concerning themselves or their relatives, except in cases of private interest between one party and another.[40] Another Leveller petition presented to Sir Thomas Fairfax, head of the army, requested that no free commoner should be forced by any authority, including Parliament, to answer questions about himself in any criminal case concerning his life, liberty, or property.[41] The position of the Levellers was adopted by the army in "The Heads of the Proposals," August, 1647, but in somewhat different language. That document was pre-

whereof he or she shall or may be liable or exposed to any censure, pain, penalty or punishment whatsoever . . ." 16 Car. 1, c. 11, § 4.

[38] Wigmore, *op. cit.*, VIII, 294-95.

[39] *Ibid.*, 298.

[40] "As then the unjust power of the Star Chamber was exercised in compelling men and women to answer to interrogatories tending to accuse themselves and others, so is the same now frequently practised upon divers persons, even your cordial friends, that have been, and still are, punished for refusing to answer questions against themselves and nearest relations.

. . . .

"Thirdly, that you permit no authority whatsoever to compel any person or persons to answer any questions against themselves or nearest relations, except in cases of private interest between party and party in a legal way, and to release such as suffer by imprisonment or otherwise, for refusing to answer to such interrogatories." A. S. P. Woodhouse (ed.), *Puritanism and Liberty* (London, 1938), 318-19, 321.

[41] "That no free commoner of England be enforced, either by the High Court of Parliament or by any subordinate court . . . to make oath or to answer to any interrogatories concerning himself in any criminal case concerning his life, liberty, goods, or freehold. . . ." *Ibid.*, 336.

ABOLITION OF THE STAR CHAMBER

sented by Fairfax and the Council of the Army to the Commissioners of Parliament. It was a comprehensive plan for settling the differences between the king and the people by making the king's power subservient to that of Parliament, by making Parliament's power more amenable to the constituencies, and by restricting the powers of the state over the liberty of the subject. It provided:

> Next to the Proposals aforesaid for the present settling of a peace, we shall desire that no time may be lost by the Parliament for dispatch of other things tending to the welfare, ease, and just satisfaction of the kingdom, and in special manner:
>
> . . . .
>
> II. That . . . the common grievances of the people may be speedily considered of, and effectually redressed, and in particular:
>
> . . . .
>
> 8. Some provision to be made, that none may be compelled by penalties, or otherwise, to answer unto questions tending to the accusing of themselves or their nearest relations in criminal causes . . .[42]

In September, 1648, the Levellers expressed dissatisfaction with the failure of Parliament to enact the provision desired by their "Petition to the House of Commons."[43] The vital interest shown in the developing privilege against self-incrimination is indicated by the proceedings on "The Agreement of the People." This was a rough sketch for a written constitution presented to Parliament on behalf of the army on January 20, 1649. It was presented for discussion and amendment by Parliament and was to be tendered to the nation at a later and more convenient time.[44] No provision for the establishment of the privilege against self-incrimination was incorporated into that document because it was felt that this matter should not await the lengthy debates which were expected. According to Lilburne's *Foundations of Freedom*,

> These following particulars were offered to be inserted in the Agreement, but adjudged fit, as the most eminent grievances, to be redressed by the next Representative:
> 1. It shall not be in their power to punish or cause to be punished any person or persons for refusing to answer to questions against themselves in criminal cases. . . .[45]

[42] *Ibid.*, 424, 425.

[43] "The truth is (and we see we must either now speak [or] for ever be silent), we have long expected things of another nature from you, and such as, we are confident, would have given satisfaction to all serious people of all parties:

. . . .

"8. That you would have freed all men being examined against themselves, and from being questioned or punished for doing of that against which no law hath been provided." *Ibid.*, 338-39.

[44] Tanner, *op. cit.*, 156-57. [45] Woodhouse, *op. cit.*, 364.

Perhaps the most stirring defense of the privilege against self-incrimination during the seventeenth century was written by Lilburne in 1653 in his pamphlet "The Just Defence of John Lilburne." He said, in describing his conflicts with Charles I:

> Another fundamental right I then contended for, was, that no mans conscience ought to be racked by oaths imposed, to answer to questions concerning himself in matters criminal, or pretended to be so.
>
> The ancient known right and law of England being, that no man be put to his defence at law, upon any mans bare saying, or upon his own oath, but by presentment of lawful men, and by faithful witnesses brought for the same face to face; a law and known right, without which any that are in power may at pleasure rake into the brests of every man for matter to destroy life, liberty, or estate, when according to true law and due proceedings, there is nought against them; now it being my lot to be drawn out and required to take an oath, and to be required to answer to questions against my self and others whom I honoured, and whom I knew no evil by, though I might know such things by them as the oppossors and persecutors would have punished them for, in that I stood firm to our true English liberty, as resolvedly persisted therein, enduring a most cruel whipping, pilloring, gagging, and barbarous imprisonment, rather than betray the rights and liberties of every man . . .[46]

After the Restoration in 1660 the jurisdiction of the ecclesiastical courts was restored, except for the Court of High Commission. Power to administer the oath *ex officio* was not restored. Instead, it was stated that no officer or judge exercising ecclesiastical jurisdiction should

> tender or administer unto any person whatsoever, the oath usually called the oath *ex officio,* or any other oath whereby such person to whom the same is tendred or administred may be charged or compelled to confess or accuse, or to purge him or herself of any criminal matter or thing, whereby he or she may be liable to any censure or punishment; any thing in this statute, or any other law, custom or usage heretofore to the contrary hereof in any wise notwithstanding.[47]

This made it clear that no ecclesiastical court could require any person to testify to any matter whereby he might be incriminated. At the time of the Restoration, however, the extension of the privilege to the common law courts had not been completely settled. By the end of the reign of Charles II the privilege was probably recognized in all courts when claimed by a defendant or a witness. The old habit of questioning the accused did not completely die out, however, until the beginning of the eighteenth century.[48]

[46] William Haller and Godfrey Davies (eds.), *The Leveller Tracts, 1647-1653* (New York, 1944), 454-55.
[47] 13 Car. 2, c. 12, § 4.
[48] Wigmore, *op. cit.,* VIII, 298-300.

This extension of the privilege probably resulted from the similarity between the procedure of the oath *ex officio*, a characteristic feature of the hated Star Chamber and High Commission, and the questioning of persons as to criminal matters by the common law courts. As Jeremy Bentham put it:

> In a state of things like this, what could be more natural than that, by a people infants as yet in reason, giants in passion, every distinguishable feature of a system of procedure directed to such ends should be condemned in the lump, should be involved in one undistinguishing mass of odium and abhorrence; more especially any particular instrument or feature, from which the system was seen to operate with a particular degree of efficiency towards such abominable ends . . .[49]

Conclusion

The abolition of the Star Chamber is notable, therefore, not only for the advance which was made in the development of the principle of due process of law as administered by the ordinary courts of justice but also for the fact that, once that tribunal had been abolished, the way was open for the later establishment of the privilege against self-incrimination. That privilege is now embodied in the Constitution of the United States as part of the fifth amendment.[50]

[49] *The Works of Jeremy Bentham*, ed. John Bowring (Edinburgh, 1843), VII, 456.
[50] See p. 432.

ABOLITION OF THE STAR CHAMBER[51]
July 5, 1641

An act for the regulating of the privy council, and for taking away the court commonly called the star-chamber.

Recital of: Magna Carta	WHEREAS *by the great charter many times confirmed in parliament, it is enacted, That no freeman shall be taken or imprisoned, or disseised of his freehold or liberties, or free customs, or be outlawed or exiled or otherwise destroyed, and that the King will not pass upon him, or condemn him; but by lawful judgment of his peers, or by the*
5 Edw. 3, c. 9	*law of the land: (2) and by another statute made in the fifth year of the reign of King Edward the Third, it is enacted, That no man shall be attached by any accusation, nor forejudged of life or limb, nor his lands, tenements, goods nor chattels seized into the*
25 Edw. 3, stat. 5, c. 4	*King's hands, against the form of the great charter and the law of the land: (3) and by another statute made in the five and twentieth year of the reign of the same King Edward the Third, it is accorded, assented and established, That none shall be taken by petition or suggestion made to the King, or to his council, unless it be by indictment or presentment of good and lawful people of the same neighbourhood where such deeds be done, in due manner, or by process made by writ original at the common law, and that none be put out of his franchise or freehold, unless he be duly brought in to answer, and forejudged of the same by the course of the law, and if any thing*
28 Edw. 3, c. 3	*be done against the same, it shall be redressed and holden for none: (4) and by another statute made in the eight and twentieth year of the reign of the same King Edward the Third, it is amongst other things enacted, That no man of what estate or condition soever he be, shall be put out of his lands or tenements, nor taken, nor imprisoned, nor disinherited, without being brought in to answer by due process of*
42 Edw. 3, c. 3	*law: (5) and by another statute made in the two and fortieth year of the reign of the said King Edward the Third, it is enacted, That no man be put to answer, without presentment before justices, or matter of record, or by due process and writ original, according to the old law of the land, and if any thing be done to the contrary, it shall*
36 Edw. 3, stat. 1, c. 15	*be void in law, and holden for error: (6) and by another statute made in the six and thirtieth year of the same King Edward the Third, it is amongst other things enacted, That all pleas which shall be pleaded in any courts before any the King's justices, or in his other places, or before any of his other ministers, or in the courts and places of any*

[51] 16 Car. 1, c. 10. Danby Pickering (ed.), *Statutes at Large* (Cambridge, 1726-1807), VII, 338-42.

ABOLITION OF THE STAR CHAMBER

other lords within the realm, shall be entred and enrolled in latin: (7) and whereas by the statutes made in the third year of King Henry the Seventh, power is given to the chancellor, the lord treasurer of England for the time being, and the keeper of the King's privy seal, or two of them, calling unto them a bishop and a temporal lord of the King's most honourable council, and the two chief justices of the King's bench and common pleas for the time being, or other two justices in their absence, to proceed as in that act is expressed, for the punishment of some particular offences therein mentioned: (8) and by the statute made in the one and twentieth year of King Henry the Eighth, the president of the council is associated to join with the lord chancellor and other judges in the said statute of the Third of Henry the Seventh mentioned; (9) but the said judges have not kept themselves to the points limited by the said statute, but have undertaken to punish where no law doth warrant, and to make decrees for things having no such authority, and to inflict heavier punishments than by any law is warranted: *[3 Hen. 7, c. 1]* *[21 Hen. 8, c. 20]* *[Court has exceeded its jurisdiction and powers]*

II. And forasmuch as all matters examinable or determinable before the said judges, or in the court commonly called the star-chamber, may have their proper remedy and redress, and their due punishment and correction, by the common law of the land, and in the ordinary course of justice elsewhere; (2) and forasmuch as the reasons and motives inducing the erection and continuance of that court do now cease: (3) and the proceedings, censures and decrees of that court, have by experience been found to be an intolerable burthen to the subjects, and the means to introduce an arbitrary power and government; (4) and forasmuch as the council-table hath of late times assumed unto it self a power to intermeddle in civil causes and matters only of private interest between party and party, and have adventured to determine of the estates and liberties of the subject, contrary to the law of the land and the rights and privileges of the subject, by which great and manifold mischiefs and inconveniencies have arisen and happened, and much uncertainty by means of such proceedings hath been conceived concerning mens rights and estates; for settling whereof, and preventing the like in time to come, *[Reasons for abolishing the court]*

III. Be it ordained and enacted by the authority of this present parliament, That the said court commonly called the star-chamber, and all jurisdiction, power and authority belonging unto, or exercised in the same court, or by any the judges, officers, or ministers thereof, be from the first day of August in the year of our Lord God one thousand six hundred forty and one, clearly and absolutely dissolved, taken away and determined; (2) and that from the said first day of August neither the lord chancellor, or keeper of the great seal of England, the lord treasurer of England, the keeper of the King's privy seal, or president of the council, nor any bishop, temporal lord, privy counsellor or judge, or justice whatsoever, shall have any power or authority to hear, examine or determine any matter or thing whatsoever, in the said court commonly called the star-chamber, or to make, pronounce or deliver any judgment, sentence, order or decree, or to do any judicial or ministerial act in the said court: (3) and that all and every act and acts of parliament, and all and every article, clause and *[Abolition of the court]* sentence in them, and every of them, by which any jurisdiction, power or authority is given, limited or appointed unto the said court commonly called the star-chamber, or unto all or any the judges, officers or ministers thereof, or for any proceedings to be had or made in the said court, or for any matter or thing to be drawn into question, examined or determined there, shall for so much as concerneth the said court of star-chamber, and the power and authority thereby given unto it, be from the said first day of *August* repealed, and absolutely revoked and made void.

Abolition of other prerogative courts
IV. And be it likewise enacted, That the like jurisdiction now used and exercised in the court before the president and council in the marches of *Wales;* (2) and also in the court before the president and council established in the northern parts; (3) and also in the court commonly called the court of the duchy of *Lancaster,* held before the chancellor and council of that court; (4) and also in the court of exchequer of the county palatine of *Chester,* held before the chamberlain and council of that court; (5) the like jurisdiction being exercised there, shall from the said first day of *August* one thousand six hundred forty and one, be also repealed and absolutely revoked and made void; any law, prescription, custom or usage, or the said statute made in the third year of King *Henry* the Seventh, or the statute made the one and twentieth of *Henry* the Eighth, or any act or acts of parliament heretofore had or made, to the contrary thereof in any wise notwithstanding: (6) and that from henceforth no court, council or place of judicature, shall be erected, ordained, constituted or appointed within this realm of *England,* or dominion of *Wales,* which shall have, use or exercise the same or the like jurisdiction as is or hath been used, practised or exercised in the said court of star-chamber.

Jurisdiction of the ordinary courts
V. Be it likewise declared and enacted by authority of this present parliament, That neither his Majesty, nor his privy council, have or ought to have any jurisdiction, power or authority, by *English* bill, petition, articles, libel or any other arbitrary way whatsoever, to examine or draw into question, determine or dispose of the lands, tenements, hereditaments, goods or chattels of any the subjects of this kingdom, but that the same ought to be tried and determined in the ordinary courts of justice, and by the ordinary course of the law.

Penalty for violations
VI. And be it further provided and enacted, That if any lord chancellor, or keeper of the great seal of *England,* lord treasurer, keeper of the King's privy seal, president of the council, bishop, temporal lord, privy counsellor, judge or justice whatsoever, shall offend, or do any thing contrary to the purport, true intent and meaning of this law, then he or they shall for such offence forfeit the sum of five hundred pounds of lawful money of *England* unto any party grieved, his executors or administrators, who shall really prosecute for the same, and first obtain judgment thereupon, to be recorded in any court of record at *Westminster,* by action of debt, bill, plaint or information, wherein no essoin, protection, wager of law, aid prayer, privilege, injunction or order of restraint, shall be in any wise prayed, granted or allowed, nor any more than one imparlance: (2) and if any person against whom any such judgment or recovery shall be had as aforesaid, shall after such judgment or recovery offend again in the same, then he or they for such offence shall forfeit the sum of one thousand pounds of

ABOLITION OF THE STAR CHAMBER

lawful money of *England* unto any party grieved, his executors or administrators, who shall really prosecute for the same, and first obtain judgment thereupon, to be recorded in any court of record at *Westminster,* by action of debt, bill, plaint or information, in which no essoin, protection, wager of law, aid prayer, privilege, injunction or order of restraint shall be in any wise prayed, granted or allowed, nor any more than one imparlance: (3) and if any person against whom any such second judgment or recovery shall be had as aforesaid, shall after such judgment or recovery offend again in the same kind, and shall be therof duly convicted by indictment, information, or any other lawful way or means, that such person so convicted shall be from thenceforth disabled, and become by virtue of this act incapable *ipso facto,* to bear his and their said office and offices respectively; (4) and shall be likewise disabled to make any gift, grant, conveyance, or other disposition of any of his lands, tenements, hereditaments, goods or chattels, or to take any benefit of any gift, conveyance or legacy to his own use.

VII. And every person so offending shall likewise forfeit and lose unto the party grieved, by any thing done contrary to the true intent and meaning of this law, his treble damages which he shall sustain and be put into by means or occasion of any such act or thing done, the same to be recovered in any of his Majesty's courts of record at *Westminster,* by action of debt, bill, plaint or information, wherein no essoin, protection, wager of law, aid prayer, privilege, injunction or order of restraint, shall be in any wise prayed, granted or allowed, nor any more than one imparlance. *Recovery of penalties*

VIII. And be it also provided and enacted, That if any person shall hereafter be committed, restrained of his liberty, or suffer imprisonment, by the order or decree of any such court of star-chamber, or other court aforesaid, now or at any time hereafter, having or pretending to have the same or like jurisdiction, power or authority to commit or imprison as aforesaid, (2) or by the command or warrant of the King's majesty, his heirs or successors, in their own person, or by the command or warrant of the council-board, or of any of the lords or others of his Majesty's privy council; (3) that in every such case every person so committed, restrained of his liberty, or suffering imprisonment, upon demand or motion made by his counsel, or other employed by him for that purpose, unto the judges of the court of King's bench or common pleas, in open court, shall without delay, upon any pretence whatsoever, for the ordinary fees usually paid for the same, have forthwith granted unto him a writ of *habeas corpus,* to be directed generally unto all and every sheriffs, gaoler, minister, officer or other persons in whose custody the party committed or restrained shall be, (4) and the sheriffs, gaoler, minister, officer or other person in whose custody the party so committed or restrained shall be, shall at the return of the said writ, and according to the command thereof, upon due and convenient notice therof given unto him, at the charge of the party who requireth or procureth such writ, and upon security by his own bond given, to pay the charge of carrying back the prisoner, if he shall be remanded by the court to which he shall be brought, as in like cases hath been used, such charges of bringing up and carrying back the prisoner to be always ordered by the court, if an difference shall arise thereabout, bring on cause to be brought the body of the said *Writ of habeas corpus to be available to persons restrained of their liberty* party so committed or restrained unto and before the judges or justices of the said court from whence the same writ shall issue, in open court, (5) and shall then likewise certify the true cause of such his detainer or imprisonment, and thereupon the court, within three court-days after such return made and delivered in open court, shall proceed to examine and determine whether the cause of such commitment appearing upon the said return be just and legal, or not, and shall thereupon do what to justice shall appertain, either by delivering, bailing or remanding the prisoner: (6) and if any thing shall be otherwise wilfully done or omitted to be done by any judge, justice, officer or other person afore-mentioned, contrary to the direction and true meaning hereof, that then such person so offending shall forfeit to the party grieved his treble damages, to be recovered by such means, and in such manner as is formerly in this act limited and appointed for the like penalty to be sued for and recovered.

Applicability of statute

IX. Provided always, and be it enacted, That this act and the several clauses therein contained shall be taken and expounded to extend only to the court of star-chamber, (2) and to the said courts holden before the president and council in the marches of *Wales,* (3) and before the president and council in the northern parts, (4) and also to the court commonly called the court of the duchy of *Lancaster,* holden before the chancellor and council of that court, (5) and also in the court of exchequer of the county palatine of *Chester,* held before the chamberlain and council of that court, (6) and to all courts of like jurisdiction to be hereafter erected, ordained, constituted or appointed as aforesaid; and to the warrants and directions of the council-board, and to the commitments, restraints and imprisonments of any person or persons made, commanded or awarded by the King's majesty, his heirs or successors, in their own person, or by the lords and others of the privy council, and every one of them,

Limitation of actions

X. And lastly, provided, and be it enacted, That no person or persons shall be sued, impleaded, molested or troubled for any offence against this present act, unless the party supposed to have so offended shall be sued or impleaded for the same within two years at the most after such time wherein the said offence shall be committed.

REFERENCES

Cheyney, Edward P. "The Court of Star Chamber," *American Historical Review,* XVIII (July, 1913), 727-50.
Dicey, Albert V. *The Privy Council.* London: Macmillan and Co., 1887.
Hudson, William. "A Treatise on the Court of Star Chamber," *Collectanea Juridica,* ed. Francis Hargrave (London, 1791), 1-240.
Phillips, Henry E. I. "The Last Years of the Court of Star Chamber, 1630-41," *Transactions of the Royal Historical Society.* 4th ser. London: Royal Historical Society, 1939. XXI, 103-31.
Scofield, Cora L. *The Court of Star Chamber.* Chicago: University of Chicago Press, 1900.
Wigmore, John H. *A Treatise on the Anglo-American System of Evidence.* 10 vols. 3rd ed. Boston: Little, Brown and Co., 1940. VIII, § 2250.

XI. MASSACHUSETTS BODY OF LIBERTIES
1641

The Body of Liberties shows how American concepts of individual liberties were shaped during the early colonial period. Colonial lawmakers added to Magna Carta and the English common law the principles of Puritan theology and the results of their experiences with the circumstances in which they found themselves. The result was thus a combination of diverse elements and shows many distinctly American trends in constitutional thought. We find in the Body of Liberties the ideas that the fundamental law of the land should be embodied in a written instrument to which the people have assented; that this law should constitute a limitation upon the powers and discretion of administrators and judges; and that the liberties of the individual should be stated in the form of a bill of rights serving the same purpose as Magna Carta was thought to serve in England.

Although the Massachusetts Charter of 1629[1] had said that the freemen should make the laws, they allowed their powers to lie dormant for several years. During that time all laws were made and executed by the governor and the magistrates. This arrangement dissatisfied the colonists, and several results occurred. More freemen were admitted, and a representative system of government was established. Later a bicameral, or two-chamber, assembly was instituted.[2] Another result of the friction between the settlers and the officers of the colony was the enactment of the Body of Liberties.

On May 6, 1635, John Haynes, Richard Bellingham, John Winthrop, and Thomas Dudley were appointed by the General Court as a committee to prepare a draft of the laws of the colony. Winthrop described the purposes of the committee as follows:

Origins

[1] See pp. 76-96.   [2] See pp. 77-81.

The deputies having conceived great danger to our state, in regard that our magistrates, for want of positive laws, in many cases, might proceed according to their discretions, it was agreed that some men should be appointed to frame a body of grounds of laws, in resemblance to a Magna Charta, which, being allowed by some of the ministers, and the general court, should be received for fundamental laws.[3]

This committee did not produce the code which was desired and in May, 1636, another committee was appointed "to make a draught of laws agreeable to the word of God, which may be the Fundamentals of this Commonwealth, and to present the same to the next General Court."[4] John Cotton, a member of this committee, prepared a code which Winthrop described as "a model of Moses his judicials."[5] Cotton's draft consisted of ten chapters, and covered the government, laws, and practices of Massachusetts. His code was taken under consideration by the General Court, but was never approved. In 1638 the freemen were asked to assemble in the towns to propose "such necessary and fundamental laws" as might be suitable for adoption. These suggestions were to be submitted to the governor, the standing council, the elders, and certain named individuals whose task was to prepare the laws in the form of a code and submit it for final approval to the General Court. This complicated procedure never resulted in a code of laws. The next year John Cotton and Nathaniel Ward were designated to frame codes.[6] After these drafts had been altered, they were submitted to the towns to be considered first by the magistrates and elders and then to be published for the people. Every individual was given the right to present his ideas for alterations or additions. The code of Cotton was rejected and that of Ward was accepted after revision by the General Court. It has been said of this procedure that "a more careful process of legislation is perhaps nowhere recorded."[7]

General Significance The magistrates had fought the enactment of the Body of Liberties at every step. They knew that written laws would place a limitation on the wide discretionary powers which they had been exercising. To support their posi-

[3] James K. Hosmer (ed.), *Winthrop's Journal* (New York, 1908), I, 151.
[4] William H. Whitmore (ed.), *The Colonial Laws of Massachusetts, 1672* (Boston, 1890), 5.
[5] Hosmer, *op. cit.*, I, 196.
[6] The Rev. Nathaniel Ward of Ipswich, who drafted the Body of Liberties, had been a barrister of Lincoln's Inn in 1615. He entered the ministry in 1618, but had been suspended for his Puritan beliefs by Archbishop Laud. He was also the author of a curious book entitled *The Simple Cobbler of Agawam.* Charles Warren, *A History of the American Bar* (Boston, 1911), 63-64.
[7] Paul S. Reinsch, "The English Common Law in the Early American Colonies," *Select Essays in Anglo-American Legal History* (Boston, 1907), 1, 373.

tion they argued that the Massachusetts Charter had prohibited colonial laws which were repugnant to the laws of England.[8] They advanced the theory that laws developed by practice and custom would not violate that provision of the charter, but that written laws were different. They also pointed out that the lack of experience with the conditions of the country and the nature of the people made it advisable that the laws should be allowed to develop by custom, just as the common law of England had developed throughout the centuries.[9] It was also said that according to Puritan theology only God has the power to make laws, and that legislative enactments are no more than conventions among men, valid only when agreeable to the commands of God.[10] These arguments were persuasive, and several concessions were made to the magistrates in the Body of Liberties. It was provided that the document should not be enacted as binding law. The General Court, however, did "with one consent fullie Authorise, and earnestly intreate all that are and shall be in Authoritie to consider them as laws."[11] Another concession was that the magistrates were left free to decide according to the word of God in all cases not covered by the document.[12]

The language of sections 1 and 2 was based on chapters 39 and 40 of Magna Carta, modified in the light of colonial conditions and customs. The general reference of Magna Carta to "the law of the land" was replaced by references to the laws established by the General Court and the law derived from the word of God. Many other important liberties were secured by the document. Cattle and goods were not to be taken without reasonable compensation (section 8). Monopolies were forbidden, except in the case of inventions (section 9). The feudal incidents affecting rights to land were abolished (section 10). Freedom of speech in courts and public assemblies was protected (section 13). Judicial proceedings were not to be frustrated by a maze of legal technicalities (section 25). The right of trial by jury was secured and careful safeguards governing the jury system were

[8] See p. 89.

[9] Hosmer, *op. cit.*, I, 323-24.

[10] Because the divine law was considered to be the fundamental law, the common law was deemed to be controlling only in so far as it embodied divine law. Thus, although the Pilgrims regarded Magna Carta as the chief embodiment of the English common law, even that document would be subordinate to the Scriptures. Reinsch, *op. cit.*, I, 381. The marginal citations to the Bible with the capital laws lead to the conclusion that at least these provisions were considered as being directly based on divine law. See section 94.

[11] Section 96.

[12] Section 1.

provided (sections 29, 30, 31, 49, 50, and 76). No man could be placed in jeopardy more than once for the same crime or trespass (section 42). Cruel, inhuman, and barbarous punishments were forbidden (section 46). Confessions of crime elicited by torture could not be used to prove guilt (section 45). Toleration in religious worship was to be observed (section 95). Of special interest are the capital laws which give cross-references to the Bible (section 94). This adoption of literal biblical precepts shows the extent to which religious dogma was accepted as a guide to conduct.

Effects
The freemen were uneasy about the concessions which had been made to the magistrates. The magistrates were uneasy about having any written laws. For these reasons it was provided that the Body of Liberties should remain in force for three years. Its provisions would then be reviewed in the light of experience; amendments would be made if necessary, and it would then be established as a perpetual law.[13] This process of revision led to the Laws and Liberties of 1648 which, like the Body of Liberties, blended features of the Mosaic law, the customs and practices of the colony, and the common law of England.[14] As enacted legislation came to replace the previous vague reliance on the Scriptures, the common law of England, especially Magna Carta, came more and more to be considered as the main source of the liberties of the subject.[15]

[13] Section 98 does not provide that the amended version of the Body of Liberties should be perpetual. That intention, however, apparently existed. Hosmer, *op. cit.*, II, 49.

[14] In 1645 a new survey of laws was ordered, and a study was conducted by a new board of compilers. A revised code was presented to the General Court in 1647, but further study was thought necessary. As adopted, the Laws and Liberties was neither a code nor a digest, but was modeled on the *Abridgements of the Statutes* used by English lawyers. Charles M. Andrews, *The Colonial Period of American History* (New Haven, 1934), I, 456-58. In the course of revising the Body of Liberties certain lawbooks were ordered from England to assist the General Court in its task. These were: "Two of Sr Edwd Cooke upon Littleton; two of the Books of Entryes; two of Sr Edwd Cooke upon Magna Carta; two of the Newe Tearmes of the Lawe; two of Dalton's Justices of Peace; two of Sr Edwd Cooks Reports." Quoted in *ibid.*, I, 457.

[15] Reinsch, *op. cit.*, I, 380-84.
In 1646 a party led by Robert Child demanded the establishment of English law in the colony. They complained that no settled government had been established giving security to life, liberty and estate, and that discretionary judgments contravened the rule of law. In reply the General Court compared the provisions of the Body of Liberties with Magna Carta and the principles of the common law and concluded that liberty was as well protected in Massachusetts as it was in England. In the same year the General Court sent an address to the Long Parliament in which it set forth in parallel columns the laws of the colony and those of England. It asserted that the government of the colony was framed in accordance with the colonial charter and "the fundamental and common laws of England, and conceived according to the same—taking the words of eternal truth and righteousness along with them as that rule by which all kingdoms and jurisdictions must render account of every act and administration in the last day." Quoted in H. D. Hazeltine, "The Influence of Magna Carta on American Constitutional Development," *Magna Carta Commemoration Essays*, ed. Henry E. Malden (Cambridge, 1917), 193-94.

MASSACHUSETTS BODY OF LIBERTIES

The example set by Massachusetts was soon followed by other colonies. The Connecticut code of 1650 and the New Haven code of 1656, in particular, show the effects of the earlier Massachusetts codes. In both codes chapter 39 of Magna Carta was given an important position as a protection of individual liberties. The codes of the later colonial period such as the New York Charter of Liberties of 1683 and the act of 1712 and the act of 1715 in South and North Carolina included with Magna Carta such leading English statutes as the Petition of Right and the Habeas Corpus Act, and thus enlarged the protection of individual liberties beyond the scope of the earlier colonial codes such as the Body of Liberties.[16]

[16] *Ibid.*, 194-96. The New York Charter of Liberties was disallowed by the king as it was believed it would limit his prerogative.

MASSACHUSETTS BODY OF LIBERTIES
December 10, 1641

A COPPIE OF THE LIBERTIES OF THE MASSACHUSETS COLONIE
IN NEW ENGLAND.

Preamble   The free fruition of such liberties Immunities and priveledges as humanitie, Civilitie, and Christianitie call for as due to every man in his place and proportion without impeachment and Infringement hath ever bene and ever will be the tranquillitie and Stabilitie of Churches and Commonwealths. And the deniall or deprivall thereof, the disturbance if not the ruine of both.

We hould it therefore our dutie and safetie whilst we are about the further establishing of this Government to collect and expresse all such freedomes as for present we foresee may concerne us, and our posteritie after us, And to ratify them with our sollemne consent.

We doe therefore this day religiously and unanimously decree and confirme these following Rites, liberties and priveledges concerneing our Churches, and Civill State to be respectively impartiallie and inviolably enjoyed and observed throughout our Jurisdiction for ever.

Protection of life, liberty, and estate   1. No mans life shall be taken away, no mans honour or good name shall be stayned, no mans person shall be arested, restrayned, banished, dismembred, nor any wayes punished, no man shall be deprived of his wife or children, no mans goods or estaite shall be taken away from him, nor any way indammaged under coulor of law or Countenance of Authoritie, unlesse it be by vertue or equitie of some expresse law of the Country waranting the same, established by a generall Court and sufficiently published, or in case of the defect of a law in any parteculer case by the word of god. And in Capitall cases, or in cases concerning dismembring or banishment, according to that word to be judged by the Generall Court.

Equal protection of laws   2. Every person within this Jurisdiction, whether Inhabitant or forreiner shall enjoy the same justice and law, that is generall for the plantation, which we constitute and execute one towards another without partialitie or delay.

Oaths   3. No man shall be urged to take any oath or subscribe any articles, covenants or remonstrance, of a publique and Civill nature, but such as the Generall Court hath considered, allowed, and required.

[17] Whitmore, *op. cit.*, 33-61.

MASSACHUSETTS BODY OF LIBERTIES

4. No man shall be punished for not appearing at or before any Civill Assembly, Court, Councell, Magistrate, or Officer, nor for the omission of any office or service, if he shall be necessarily hindred by any apparent Act or providence of God, which he could neither foresee nor avoid. Provided that this law shall not prejudice any person of his just cost or damage, in any civill action. *Failure to appear before assemblies, etc.*

5. No man shall be compelled to any publique worke or service unlesse the presse be grounded upon some act of the generall Court, and have reasonable allowance therefore. *Compulsory service*

6. No man shall be pressed in person to any office, worke, warres or other publique service, that is necessarily and suffitiently exempted by any naturall or personall inpediment, as by want of yeares, greatnes of age, defect of minde, fayling of sences, or impotencie of Lymbes. *Same*

7. No man shall be compelled to goe out of the limits of this plantation upon any offensive warres which this Commonwealth or any of our freinds or confederats shall volentarily undertake. But onely upon such vindictive and defensive warres in our owne behalfe or the behalfe of our freinds and confederats as shall be enterprized by the Counsell and consent of a Court generall, or by Authority derived from the same. *Compulsory military service*

8. No mans Cattel or goods of what kinde soever shall be pressed or taken for any publique use or service, unlesse it be by warrant grounded upon some act of the generall Court, nor without such reasonable prices and hire as the ordinarie rates of the Countrie do afford. And if his Cattle or goods shall perish or suffer damage in such service, the owner shall be suffitiently recompenced. *Taking of goods for public use*

9. No monopolies shall be granted or allowed amongst us, but of such new Inventions that are profitable to the Countrie, and that for a short time. *Monopolies*

10. All our lands and heritages shall be free from all fines and licences upon Alienations, and from all hariotts,[18] wardships,[19] Liveries,[20] Primerseisins,[21] yeare day and wast,[22] Escheates,[23] and forfeitures, upon the deaths of parents or Ancestors, be they naturall, casuall or Juditiall. *Fines and forfeitures*

11. All persons which are of the age of 21 yeares, and of right understanding and meamories, whether excommunicate or condemned shall have full power and libertie to make there wills and testaments, and other lawfull alienations of theire lands and estates. *Wills and conveyances*

12. Every man whether Inhabitant or fforreiner, free or not free shall have libertie to come to any publique Court, Councel, or Towne meeting, and either by speech or writing to move any lawfull, seasonable, and materiall question, or to present any *Freedom to address courts and meetings*

---

[18] Payment of goods to the lord upon the death of the owner of land.

[19] The right of the lord to the custody of the body and lands of a minor heir.

[20] Payment by the ward to obtain the possession of land.

[21] Payment by the heir of a tenant of the king to obtain possession of land.

[22] The right of the king to use the lands of a person convicted of treason or felony for a year and a day.

[23] Forfeiture of lands to the crown.

necessary motion, complaint, petition, Bill or information, whereof that meeting hath proper cognizance, so it be done in convenient time, due order, and respective manner.

Foreign property

13. No man shall be rated[24] here for any estaite or revenue he hath in England, or in any forreine partes till it be transported hither.

Validation of conveyances

14. Any Conveyance or Alienation of land or other estaite what so ever, made by any woman that is married, any childe under age, Ideott or distracted person, shall be good if it be passed and ratified by the consent of a generall Court.

Fraudulent conveyances

15. All Covenous[25] or fraudulent Alienations or Conveyances of lands, tenements, or any hereditaments, shall be of no validitie to defeate any man from due debts or legacies, or from any just title, clame or possession, of that which is so fraudulently conveyed.

Fishing rights

16. Every Inhabitant that is an howse holder shall have free fishing and fowling in any great ponds and Bayes, Coves and Rivers, so farre as the sea ebbes and flowes within the presincts of the towne where they dwell, unlesse the free men of the same Towne or the Generall Court have otherwise appropriated them, provided that this shall not be extended to give leave to any man to come upon others proprietie without there leave.

Departure from the jurisdiction

17. Every man of or within this Jurisdiction shall have free libertie, notwithstanding any Civill power to remove both himselfe, and his familie at their pleasure out of the same, provided there be no legall impediment to the contrarie.

Judicial Proceedings

Rites Rules and Liberties concerning Juditiall proceedings.

Bail

18. No mans person shall be restrained or imprisoned by any Authority whatsoever, before the law hath sentenced him thereto, If he can put in sufficient securitie, bayle or mainprise, for his appearance, and good behaviour in the meane time, unlesse it be in Crimes Capital, and Contempts in open Court, and in such cases where some expresse act of Court doth allow it.

Discipline of assistants and deputies

19. If in a generall Court any miscariage shall be amongst the Assistants when they are by themselves that may deserve an Admonition or fine under 20 sh. it shall be examined and sentenced among themselves, If amongst the Deputies when they are by themselves, It shall be examined and sentenced amongst themselves, If it be when the whole Court is togeather, it shall be judged by the whole Court, and not severallie as before.

Censure of judges

20. If any which are to sit as Judges in any other Court shall demeane themselves offensively in the Court, the rest of the Judges present shall have power to censure him for it, if the cause be of a high nature it shall be presented to and censured at the next superior Court.

Summons

21. In all cases where the first summons are not served six dayes before the Court, and the cause breifly specified in the warrant, where appearance is to be made by

[24] Assessed.   [25] Convenient or well-appearing.

MASSACHUSETTS BODY OF LIBERTIES

the partie summoned, it shall be at his libertie whether he will appeare or no, except all cases that are to be handled in Courts suddainly called, upon extraordinary occasions, In all cases where there appears present and urgent cause Any Assistant or officer apointed shal have power to make out Attaichments for the first summons.

22. No man in any suit or action against an other shall falsely pretend great debts or damages to vex his Adversary, if it shall appeare any doth so, The Court shall have power to set a reasonable fine on his head. *False allegations of debts and damages*

23. No man shall be adjudged to pay for detaining any debt from any Crediter above eight pounds in the hundred for one yeare, And not above that rate proportionable for all somes what so ever, neither shall this be a coulour or countenance to allow any usurie amongst us contrarie to the law of god. *Usury*

24. In all Trespasses or damages done to any man or men, If it can be proved to be done by the meere default of him or them to whome the trespasse is done, It shall be judged no trespasse, nor any damage given for it. *Contributory negligence*

25. No Summons pleading Judgement, or any kinde of proceeding in Court or course of Justice shall be abated, arested or reversed upon any kinde of cercumstantiall errors or mistakes, If the person and cause be rightly understood and intended by the Court. *Harmless errors*

26. Every man that findeth himselfe unfit to plead his owne cause in any Court shall have Libertie to imploy any man against whom the Court doth not except, to helpe him, Provided he give him noe fee or reward for his paines. This shall not exempt the partie him selfe from Answering such Questions in person as the Court shall thinke meete to demand of him. *Employment of attorneys*

27. If any plantife shall give into any Court a declaration of his cause in writing, The defendant shall also have libertie and time to give in his answer in writing, And so in all further proceedings betwene partie and partie, So it doth not further hinder the dispach of Justice then the Court shall be willing unto. *Written pleadings*

28. The plantife in all Actions brought in any Court shall have libertie to withdraw his Action, or to be nonsuited before the Jurie hath given in their verdict, in which case he shall alwaies pay full cost and chardges to the defendant, and may afterwards renew his suite at an other Court if he please. *Nonsuits*

29. In all Actions at law it shall be the libertie of the plantife and defendant by mutual consent to choose whether they will be tryed by the Bench or by a Jurie, unlesse it be where the law upon just reason hath otherwise determined. The like libertie shall be granted to all persons in Criminall cases. *Election of trial by bench or jury*

30. It shall be in the libertie both of plantife and defendant, and likewise every delinquent (to be judged by a Jurie) to challenge any of the Jurors. And if his challenge be found just and reasonable by the Bench, or the rest of the Jurie, as the challenger shall choose it shall be allowed him, and tales de cercumstantibus impaneled in their room. *Challenge of jurors*

31. In all cases where evidence is so obscure or defective that the Jurie cannot clearly and safely give a positive verdict, whether it be a grand or petit Jurie, It *Special verdicts*

shall have libertie to give a non Liquit, or a spetiall verdict, in which last, that is in a spetiall verdict, the Judgement of the cause shall be left to the Court, and all Jurors shall have libertie in matters of fact if they cannot finde the maine issue, yet to finde and present in their verdict so much as they can, If the Bench and Jurors shall so differ at any time about their verdict that either of them cannot proceede with peace of conscience the case shall be referred to the Generall Court, who shall take the question from both and determine it.

Referral of cases by juries to General Court

32. Every man shall have libertie to replevy[26] his Cattell or goods impounded, distreined,[27] seised, or extended;[28] unlesse it be upon execution after Judgement, and in paiment of fines. Provided he puts in good securitie to prosecute his replevin, And to satisfie such demands as his Adversary shall recover against him in Law.

Recovery of goods

33. No mans person shall be Arrested, or imprisoned upon execution or judgment for any debt or fine, If the law can finde competent meanes of satisfaction otherwise from his estaite, and if not his person may be arrested and imprisoned where he shall be kept at his owne charge, not the plantife's till satisfaction be made: unlesse the Court that had cognizance of the cause or some superior Court shall otherwise provide.

Imprisonment for debt

34. If any man shall be proved and Judged a commen Barrator vexing others with unjust frequent and endlesse suites, It shall be in the power of Courts both to denie him the benefit of the law, and to punish him for his Barratry.

Barratry

35. No mans Corne nor hay that is in the feild or upon the Cart, nor his garden stuffe, nor any thing subject to present decay, shall be taken in any distresse,[29] unles he that takes it doth presently bestow it where it may not be imbesled nor suffer spoile or decay, or give securitie to satisfie the worth thereof if it comes to any harme.

Taking of goods for the satisfaction of debts

36. It shall be in the libertie of every man cast condemned or sentenced in any cause in any Inferior Court, to make their Appeale to the Court of Assistants, provided they tender their appeale and put in securitie to prosecute it before the Court be ended wherein they were condemned, And within six dayes next ensuing put in good securitie before some Assistant to satisfie what his Adversarie shall recover against him; And if the cause be of a Criminall nature, for his good behaviour, and appearance, And everie man shall have libertie to complaine to the Generall Court of any Injustice done him in any Court of Assistants or other.

Appeals

37. In all cases where it appears to the Court that the plantife hath wilingly and witingly done wronge to the defendant in commenceing and prosecuting any action or complaint against him, They shall have power to impose upon him a proportionable fine to the use of the defendant, or accused person, for his false complaint or clamor.

Improper prosecutions

38. Everie man shall have libertie to Record in the publique Rolles of any Court any Testimony given upon oath in the same Court, or before two Assistants, or any

Recording of evidence

---

[26] Recover by legal process.   [27] Held.   [28] Taken by a writ of execution.
[29] The taking of goods for the satisfaction of a wrong committed.

deede or evidence legally confirmed there to remaine in perpetuam rei memoriam, that is for perpetuall memoriall or evidence upon occasion.

39. In all actions both reall and personall betweene partie and partie, the Court shall have power to respite execution for a convenient time, when in their prudence they see just cause so to doe. *Stays of execution*

40. No Conveyance, Deede, or promise whatsoever shall be of validitie, If it be gotten by Illegal violence, imprisonment, threatenings, or any kinde of forcible compulsion called Dures. *Force and undue influence*

41. Everie man that is to Answere for any Criminall cause, whether he be in prison or under bayle, his cause shall be heard and determined at the next Court that hath proper Cognizance thereof, And may be done without prejudice of Justice. *Right to hearing*

42. No man shall be twise sentenced by Civill Justice for one and the same Crime, offence, or Trespasse. *Double jeopardy*

43. No man shall be beaten with above 40 stripes, nor shall any true gentleman, nor any man equall to a gentleman be punished with whipping, unles his crime be very shamefull, and his course of life vitious and profligate. *Excessive punishments*

44. No man condemned to dye shall be put to death within fower dayes next after his condemnation, unles the Court see spetiall cause to the contrary, or in case of martiall law, nor shall the body of any man so put to death be unburied 12 howers, unlesse it be in case of Anatomie. *Death sentence*

45. No man shall be forced by Torture to confesse any Crime against himselfe nor any other unlesse it be in some Capitall case where he is first fullie convicted by cleare and suffitient evidence to be guilty, After which if the cause be of that nature, That it is very apparent there be other conspiratours, or confederates with him, Then he may be tortured, yet not with such Tortures as be Barbarous and inhumane. *Self-incrimination*

46. For bodilie punishments we allow amongst us none that are inhumane Barbarous or cruel. *Inhuman punishment*

47. No man shall be put to death without the testimony of two or three witnesses or that which is equivalent thereunto. *Witnesses in capital cases*

48. Every Inhabitant of the Country shall have free libertie to search and veewe any Rooles, Records, or Regesters of any Court or office except the Councell, And to have a transcript or exemplification thereof written examined, and signed by the hand of the officer of the office paying the appointed fees therefore. *Public records*

49. No free man shall be compelled to serve upon Juries above two Courts in a yeare, except grand Jurie men, who shall hould two Courts together at the least. *Jury service*

50. All Jurors shall be chosen continuallie by the freemen of the Towne where they dwell. *Selection of jurors*

51. All Associates selected at any time to Assist the Assistants in Inferior Courts shall be nominated by the Townes belonging to that Court, by orderly agreement amonge themselves. *Court assistants*

52. Children, Idiots, Distracted persons, and all that are strangers, or new commers *Dispensations*

to our plantation, shall have such allowances and dispensations in any Cause whether Criminall or other as religion and reason require.

Age of discretion

53. The age of discretion for passing away of lands or such kinde of heredimints, or for giveing of votes, verdicts or Sentence in any Civill Courts or causes, shall be one and twentie yeares.

Duties of president or moderator

54. Whensoever anything is to be put to vote, any sentence to be pronounced, or any other matter to be proposed, or read in any Court or Assembly, If the president or moderator thereof shall refuse to performe it, the Major parte of the members of that Court or Assembly shall have power to appoint any other meete man of them to do it, And if there be just cause to punish him that should and would not.

Multiple claims

55. In all suites or Actions in any Court, the plaintife shall have libertie to make all the titles and claims to that he sues for he can. And the Defendant shall have libertie to plead all the pleas he can in answere to them, and the Court shall judge according to the entire evidence of all.

Behavior at town meetings

56. If any man shall behave himselfe offensively at any Towne meeting, the rest of the freemen then present, shall have power to sentence him for his offence. So be it the mulct or penaltie excede not twentie shilings.

Sudden death

57. Whensoever any person shall come to any very suddaine untimely and unnaturall death, Some assistant, or the Constables of that Towne shall forthwith sumon a Jury of twelve free men to inquire of the cause and manner of their death, and shall present a true verdict thereof to some neere Assistant, or the next Court to be helde for that Towne upon their oath.

Liberties of Freemen

Liberties more peculiarlie concerning the free men.

Civil authority over religion

58. Civill Authoritie hath power and libertie to see the peace, ordinances and Rules of Christ observed in every church according to his word. so it be done in a Civill and not in an Ecclesiastical way.

Same

59. Civill Authoritie hath power and libertie to deale with any Church member in a way of Civill Justice, notwithstanding any Church relation, office or interest.

Church censure

60. No church censure shall degrad or depose any man from any Civill dignitie, office, or Authoritie he shall have in the Commonwealth.

Secret knowledge of offenses

61. No Magestrate, Juror, Officer, or other man shall be bound to informe present or reveale any private crim or offence, wherein there is no perill or danger to this plantation or any member thereof, when any necessarie tye of conscience binds him to secresie grounded upon the word of god, unlesse it be in case of testimony lawfully required.

Selection of deputies

62. Any Shire or Towne shall have libertie to choose their Deputies whom and where they please for the Generall Court. So be it they be free men, and have taken there oath of fealtie, and Inhabiting in this Jurisdiction.

Expenses of officials

63. No Governor, Deputy Governor, Assistant, Associate, or grand Jury man at any Court, nor any Deputie for the Generall Court shall at any time beare his owne

chardges at any Court, but their necessary expences shall be defrayed either by the Towne or Shire on whose service they are, or by the Country in generall.

64. Everie Action betweene partie and partie, and proceedings against delinquents in Criminall causes shall be briefly and destinctly entered on the Rolles of every Court by the Recorder thereof. That such actions be not afterwards brought againe to the vexation of any man. *Record of proceedings*

65. No custome or prescription shall ever prevaile amongst us in any morall cause, our meaneing is maintaine anythinge that can be proved to bee morrallie sinfull by the word of god. *Custom*

66. The Freemen of every Towneship shall have power to make such by laws and constitutions as may concerne the wellfare of their Towne, provided they be not of a Criminall, but onely of a prudentiall nature, And that their penalties exceede not 20 sh. for one offence. And that they be not repugnant to the publique laws and orders of the Countrie. And if any Inhabitant shall neglect or refuse to observe them, they shall have power to levy the appointed penalties by distresse. *Bylaws of towns*

67. It is the constant libertie of the free men of this plantation to choose yearly at the Court of Election out of the freemen all the General officers of this Jurisdiction. If they please to dischardge them at the day of Election by way of vote. They may do it without shewing cause. But if at any other generall Court, we hould it due justice, that the reasons thereof be alleadged and proved. By Generall officers we meane, our Governor, Deputy Governor, Assistants, Treasurer, Generall of our warres. And our Admirall at Sea, and such as are or hereafter may be of the like genrall nature. *Election of officers*

68. It is the libertie of the freemen to choose such deputies for the Generall Court out of themselves, either in their owne Townes or elsewhere as they judge fitest. And because we cannot foresee what varietie and weight of occasions may fall into future consideration, And what counsells we may stand in neede of, we decree. That the Deputies (to attend the Generall Court in the behalfe of the Countrie) shall not any time be stated or inacted, but from Court to Court, or at the most but for one yeare, that the Countrie may have an Annuall libertie to do in that case what is most behoofefull for the best welfaire thereof. *Election of deputies*

69. No Generall Court shall be desolved or adjourned without the consent of the Major parte thereof. *Adjournment of Court*

70. All Freemen called to give any advise, vote, verdict, or sentence in any Court, Counsell, or Civill Assembly, shall have full freedome to doe it according to their true Judgements and Consciences, So it be done orderly and inoffensively for the manner. *Advice, votes, and verdicts*

71. The Governor shall have a casting voice whensoever an Equi vote shall fall out in the Court of Assistants, or generall assembly, So shall the presedent or moderator have in all Civill Courts or Assemblies. *Voting in case of ties*

72. The Governor and Deputy Governor Joyntly consenting or any three Assistants concurring in consent shall have power out of Court to reprive a condemned malefactour, till the next quarter or generall Court. The generall Court onely shall have power to pardon a condemned malefactor. *Reprieve*

Foreign service

73. The Generall Court hath libertie and Authoritie to send out any member of this Comanwealth of what qualitie, condition or office whatsoever into forreine parts about any publique message or Negotiation. Provided the partie sent be acquainted with the affaire he goeth about, and be willing to undertake the service.

Town officials

74. The freemen of every Towne or Towneship, shall have full power to choose yearly or for lesse time out of themselves a convenient number of fitt men to order the planting or prudentiall occasions of that Town, according to Instructions given them in writing, Provided nothing be done by them contrary to the publique laws and orders of the Countrie, provided also the number of such select persons be not above nine.

Minority opinions

75. It is and shall be the libertie of any member or members of any Court, Councell or Civill Assembly in cases of making or executing any order or law, that properlie concerne religion, or any cause capitall, or warres, or Subscription to any publique Articles or Remonstrance, in case they cannot in Judgement and conscience consent to that way the Major vote or suffrage goes, to make their contra Remonstrance or protestation in speech or writing, and upon request to have their dissent recorded in the Rolles of that Court. So it be done Christianlie and respectively for the manner. And their dissent onely be entered without the reasons thereof, for the avoiding of tediousness.

Advice for juries

76. Whensoever any Jurie of trialls or Jurours are not cleare in their Judgements or consciences conserneing any cause wherein they are to give their verdict, They shall have libertie in open Court to advise with any man they thinke fitt to resolve or direct them, before they give in their verdict.

Failure to vote

77. In all cases wherein any freeman is to give his vote, be it in point of Election, making constitutions and orders, or passing sentence in any case of Judicature or the like, if he cannot see reason to give it positively one way or an other, he shall have libertie to be silent, and not pressed to a determined vote.

Public money

78. The Generall or publique Treasure or any parte thereof shall never be exspended but by the appointment of a Generall Court, nor any Shire Treasure, but by the appointment of the freemen thereof, nor any Towne Treasurie but by the freemen of that Towneship.

Liberties of Women

Liberties of Woemen.

Rights of widows

79. If any man at his death shall not leave his wife a competent portion of his estaite, upon just complaint made to the Generall Court she shall be relieved.

Punishment of women

80. Everie marryed woeman shall be free from bodilie correction or stripes by her husband, unlesse it be in his owne defence upon her assalt. If there be any just cause of correction complaint shall be made to Authoritie assembled in some Court, from which onely she shall receive it.

MASSACHUSETTS BODY OF LIBERTIES

Liberties of Children.

81. When parents dye intestate, the Elder sonne shall have a doble portion of his whole estate reall and personall, unlesse the Generall Court upon just cause alleadged shall Judge otherwise.

82. When parents dye intestate haveing noe heires males of their bodies their Daughters shall inherit as copartners, unles the Generall Court upon just reason shall judge otherwise.

83. If any parents shall wilfullie and unreasonably deny any childe timely or convenient mariage, or shall exercise any unnaturall severitie towards them, such children shall have free libertie to complaine to Authoritie for redresse.

84. No Orphan dureing their minoritie which was not committed to tuition or service by the parents in their life time shall afterwards be absolutely disposed of by any kindred, freind, Executor, Towneship, or Church, nor by themselves without the consent of some Court, wherein two Assistants at least shall be present.

Liberties of Servants.

85. If any servants shall flee from the Tiranny and crueltie of their masters to the howse of any freeman of the same Towne, they shall be there protected and susteyned till due order be taken for their relife. Provided due notice thereof be speedily given to their maisters from whom they fled. And the next Assistant or Constable where the partie flying is harboured.

86. No servant shall be put of for above a yeare to any other neither in the life time of their maister nor after their death by their Executors or Administrators unlesse it be by consent of Authoritie assembled in some Court or two Assistants.

87. If any man smite out the eye or tooth of his man-servant, or maid servant, or otherwise mayme or much disfigure him, unlesse it be by meere casualtie, he shall let them goe free from his service. And shall have such further recompense as the Court shall allow him.

88. Servants that have served deligentlie and faithfully to the benefitt of their maisters seaven yeares, shall not be sent away emptie. And if any have bene unfaithfull, negligent or unprofitable in their service, notwithstanding the good usage of their maisters, they shall not be dismissed till they have made satisfaction according to the Judgement of Authoritie.

Liberties of Forreiners and Strangers.

89. If any people of other Nations professing the true Christian Religion shall flee to us from the Tiranny or oppression of their persecutors, or from famyne, warres, or

the like necessary and compulsarie cause, They shall be entertayned and succoured amongst us, according to that power and prudence god shall give us.

Shipwrecks 90. If any ships or other vessels, be it freind or enemy, shall suffer shipwrack upon our Coast, there shall be no violence or wrong offerred to their persons or goods. But their persons shall be harboured, and relieved, and their goods preserved in safety till Authoritie may be certified thereof, and shall take further order therein.

Slaves 91. There shall never be any bond slaverie, villinage or Captivitie amongst us unles it be lawfull Captives taken in just warres, and such strangers as willingly selle themselves or are sold to us. And these shall have all the liberties and Christian usages which the law of god established in Israell concerning such persons doeth morally require. This exempts none from servitude who shall be Judged thereto by Authoritie.

Animals

Off the Bruite Creature.

Cruel treatment 92. No Man shall exercise any Tirranny or Crueltie towards any bruite Creature which are usuallie kept for man's use.

Rest for animals 93. If any man shall have occasion to leade or drive Cattel from place to place that is far of, so that they be weary, or hungry, or fall sick, or lambe, It shall be lawful to rest or refresh them, for a competent time, in any open place that is not Corne, meadow, or inclosed for some peculiar use.

Capital Laws

94. Capitall Laws.

False gods	1. If any man after legall conviction shall have or worship any other god, but the lord god, he shall be put to death.	Dut. 13. 6, 10. Dut. 17. 2, 6. Ex. 22. 20.
Witches	2. If any man or woeman be a witch, (that is hath or consulteth with a familiar spirit,) They shall be put to death.	Ex. 22. 18. Lev. 20. 27. Dut. 18. 10.
Blasphemy	3. If any man shall Blaspheme the name of god, the father, Sonne or Holie ghost, with direct, expresse, presumptuous or high handed blasphemie, or shall curse god in the like manner, he shall be put to death.	Lev. 24. 15, 16.
Murder	4. If any person committ any wilfull murther, which is manslaughter, committed upon premeditated mallice, hatred, or Crueltie, not in a mans necessarie and just defence, nor by meere casualtie against his will, he shall be put to death.	Ex. 21. 12. Numb. 35. 13, 14, 30, 31.
Sudden anger	5. If any person slayeth an other suddaienly in his anger or Crueltie of passion, he shall be put to death.	Numb. 25. 20, 21. Lev. 24. 17.
Poisoning	6. If any person shall slay an other through guile, either	Ex. 21. 14.

	by poysoning or other such divelish practice, he shall be put to death.	
Lev. 20. 15, 16.	7. If any man or woeman shall lye with any beaste or bruite creature by Carnall Copulation, They shall surely be put to death. And the beast shall be slaine and buried and not eaten.	*Acts against nature*
Lev. 20. 13.	8. If any man lyeth with mankinde as he lyeth with a woeman, both of them have committed abhomination, they both shall surely be put to death.	*Same*
Lev. 20. 19, and 18, 20. Dut. 22. 23, 24.	9. If any person committeth Adultery with a maried or espoused wife, the Adulterer and Adulteresse shall surely be put to death.	*Adultery*
Ex. 21. 16.	10. If any man stealeth a man or mankinde, he shall surely be put to death.	*Larceny*
Deut. 19. 16, 18, 19.	11. If any man rise up by false witnes, wittingly and of purpose to take away any mans life, he shall be put to death.	*False witness*
	12. If any man shall conspire and attempt any invasion, insurrection, or publique rebellion against our commonwealth, or shall indeavour to surprize any Towne or Townes, fort or forts therein, or shall treacherously and perfediouslie attempt the alteration and subversion of our frame of politie or Government fundamentallie, he shall be put to death.	*Rebellion*

95. *A Declaration of the Liberties the Lord Jesus hath given to the Churches.* *Religion*

1. All the people of god within this Jurisdiction who are not in a church way, and be orthodox in Judgement, and not scandalous in life, shall have full libertie to gather themselves into a Church Estaite. Provided they doe it in a Christian way, with due observation of the rules of Christ revealed in his word. *Formation of churches*

2. Every Church hath full libertie to exercise all the ordinances of god, according to the rules of scripture. *Religious practices*

3. Every Church hath free libertie of Election and ordination of all their officers from time to time, provided they be able, pious and orthodox. *Election of officers*

4. Every Church hath free libertie of Admission, Recommendation, Dismission, and Expulsion, or deposall of their officers and members, upon due cause, with free exercise of the Discipline and Censures of Christ according to the rules of his word. *Officers, and members*

5. No Injunctions are to be put upon any Church, Church officers or member in point of Doctrine, worship or Discipline, whether for substance or cercumstance besides the Institutions of the lord. *Doctrine*

Religious days 6. Every Church of Christ hath freedome to celebrate dayes of fasting and prayer, and of thanksgiveing according to the word of god.

Meeting of elders 7. The Elders of Churches have free libertie to meete monthly, Quarterly, or otherwise, in convenient numbers and places, for conferences and consultations about Christian and Church questions and occasions.

Treatment of members 8. All Churches have libertie to deale with any of their members in a church way that are in the hand of Justice. So it be not to retard or hinder the course thereof.

Same 9. Every Church hath libertie to deale with any magestrate, Deputie of Court or other officer what soe ever that is a member in a church way in case of apparent and just offence given in their places, so it be done with due observance and respect.

Private meetings 10. Wee allowe private meetings for edification in religion amongst Christians of all sortes of people. So it be without just offence for number, time, place, and other cercumstances.

Conference of churches 11. For the preventing and removeing of errour and offence that may grow and spread in any of the Churches in this Jurisdiction, and for the preserveing of trueith and peace in the several churches within themselves, and for the maintenance and exercise of brotherly communion, amongst all the churches in the Countrie, It is allowed and ratified, by the Authoritie of this Generall Court as a lawfull libertie of the Churches of Christ. That once in every month of the yeare (when the season will beare it) It shall be lawfull for the minesters and Elders, of the Churches neere adjoyneing together, with any other of the breetheren with the consent of the churches to assemble by course in each severall Church one after an other. To the intent after the preaching of the word by such a minister as shall be requested thereto by the Elders of the church where the Assembly is held, The rest of the day may be spent in publique Christian Conference about the discussing and resolveing of any such doubts and cases of conscience concerning matter of doctrine or worship or government of the church as shall be propounded by any of the Breetheren of that church, with leave also to any other Brother to propound his objections or answeres for further satisfaction according to the word of god. Provided that the whole action be guided and moderated by the Elders of the Church where the Assemblie is helde, or by such others as they shall appoint. And that no thing be concluded and imposed by way of Authoritie from one or more Churches upon an other, but onely by way of Brotherly conference and consultations. That the trueth may be searched out to the satisfying of every mans conscience in the sight of god according his worde. And because such an Assembly and the worke theirof can not be duely attended to if other lectures be held in the same weeke. It is therefore agreed with the consent of the Churches. That in that weeke when such an Assembly is held, All the lectures in all the neighbouring Churches for that weeke shall be forborne. That so the publique service of Christ in this more solemne Assembly may be transacted with greater deligence and attention.

Enforcement of liberties 96. Howsoever these above specified rites, freedomes, Immunities, Authorities and priveledges, both Civill and Ecclesiastical are expressed onely under the name and title of Liberties, and not in the exact form of Laws or Statutes, yet we do with one

MASSACHUSETTS BODY OF LIBERTIES

consent fullie Authorise, and earnestly intreate all that are and shall be in Authoritie to consider them as laws, and not to faile to inflict condigne and proportionable punishments upon every man impartiallie, that shall infringe or violate any of them.

97. Wee likewise give full power and libertie to any person that shall at any time be denied or deprived of any of them, to commence and prosecute their suite, Complaint or action against any man that shall so doe in any Court that hath proper Cognizance or judicature thereof. *Same*

98. Lastly because our dutie and desire is to do nothing suddainlie which fundamentally concerne us, we decree that these rites and liberties, shall be Audably read and deliberately weighed at every Generall Court that shall be held, within three yeares next insueing. And such of them as shall not be altered or repealed they shall stand so ratified, That no man shall infringe them without due punishment. *Ratification of liberties*

And if any Generall Court within these next thre yeares shall faile or forget to reade and consider them as abovesaid. The Governor and Deputy Governor for the time being, and every Assistant present at such Courts shall forfeite 20sh. a man, and everie Deputie 10sh. a man for each neglect, which shall be paid out of their proper estate, and not by the Country or the Townes which choose them, and whensoever there shall arise any question in any Court amonge the Assistants and Associates thereof about the explanation of these Rites and liberties, The Generall Court onely shall have power to interprett them.

REFERENCES

See also references on p. 96.

Gray, F. C. "Remarks on the Early Laws of Massachusetts Bay; with the Code adopted in 1641, and called THE BODY OF LIBERTIES, now first printed," *Collections of the Massachusetts Historical Society.* 3d ser. Boston: Little, Brown & Co., 1838. VII, 191-237.

Haskins, George L. "The Capitall Lawes of New-England," *Harvard Law School Bulletin,* VII (February, 1956), 10.

Howe, Mark DeWolfe (ed.). *Readings in American History.* Cambridge: Harvard University Press, 1949. 181-86.

Reinsch, Paul S. "English Common Law in the Early American Colonies," *Select Essays in Anglo-American Legal History.* 3 vols. Boston: Little, Brown & Co., 1907. I, 367, 372-86.

XII. CHARTER OF RHODE ISLAND AND PROVIDENCE PLANTATIONS
1663

Although many liberties of the individual were brought to America from England, the establishment of religious liberty was a distinctly American achievement. Religious freedom first became a part of the fundamental colonial law of America in Rhode Island. The right was contained in the Rhode Island Charter granted in 1663 by Charles II.[1] The charter, however, recognized the right as it had already grown up in the colony.

Origins   The growth of toleration in Rhode Island can be traced in the life and works of one man—Roger Williams. Through his efforts a greater degree of religious freedom came to be practiced in Rhode Island than was known anywhere else in the world. It was not until many years later, however, that full religious liberty was established in all the colonies. Discriminations against Catholics were practiced in some up to the time of the Revolutionary War, and several states had established churches even at the time of adoption of the first amendment to the Constitution of the United States.

Roger Williams came to Massachusetts in 1631.[2] The development of

---

[1] Charles II had been attempting unsuccessfully to secure greater religious toleration in England. His Declaration of Breda, April 4, 1660, provided: "And because the passion and uncharitableness of the times have produced several opinions in religion, by which men are engaged in parties and animosities against each other (which, when they shall hereafter unite in a freedom of conversation, will be composed or better understood), we do declare a liberty to tender consciences, and that no man shall be disquieted or called in question for differences of opinion in matter of religion, which do not disturb the peace of the kingdom; and that we shall be ready to consent to such an Act of Parliament, as, upon mature deliberation, shall be offered to us, for the full granting that indulgence." Samuel R. Gardiner (ed.), *The Constitutional Documents of the Puritan Revolution, 1625-1660* (Oxford, 1906), 466.

[2] Little is known of Williams' earlier life. He was born in London in 1603 and belonged to the upper middle class. In his youth he was connected with Sir Edward Coke, whose patronage increased his opportunities. Louis M. Hacker, *The Shaping of the American Tradition* (New York, 1947), 107. He entered Charterhouse in 1621, and afterwards attended Pembroke College, Cambridge, from

his ideas of religious freedom grew from conflicts with his fellow Puritans in Massachusetts. He was a Separatist and held extreme views concerning religious practices. Differences of opinion became manifest shortly after his arrival in the colony. He was invited to become one of the ministers at Boston, but declined on the ground that the members of that church had never declared their complete separation from the Church of England. He also objected to the combined civil and religious authority exercised by the magistrates.[3] He soon went to Plymouth, where his views were more acceptable and where he formed friendships with the neighboring Indian tribes. Because not even the Pilgrims at Plymouth practiced the extreme form of Separatism which Williams demanded, he returned to Massachusetts in 1634, where he became minister of the Salem church.[4] Back in Massachusetts, his teachings continued to arouse the disfavor of the authorities. He even went so far as to challenge the legality of the Massachusetts Charter, claiming that the king could not by edict appropriate the lands of the natives and grant them to English colonists.[5] This contention was bound to arouse

Roger Williams in Massachusetts

which he received the degree of B.A. in 1627. He is described as having been temperamentally excitable, hasty in speech, and indiscreet in his attempts to promote his own opinions. Charles M. Andrews, *The Colonial Period of American History* (New Haven, 1934), I, 470-71.

[3] The Boston congregation refused to make a public declaration of repentance for having communion with the churches of England while they lived there. Williams also declared that the magistrates should not "punish the breach of the Sabbath, nor any other offence, as it was a breach of the first table." James K. Hosmer (ed.), *Winthrop's Journal* (New York, 1908), I, 61-62.
This difference of opinion was largely the result of the difference between the views of the Nonconformists and those of the Separatists. The founders of Massachusetts objected to certain features of the service, but nonetheless continued to attend the parish churches while in England. On sailing to America they had issued an address to their "brethren in and of the Church of England" and had referred to that church as "their dear mother." Williams, on the other hand, insisted on a clear renunciation of the Church of England on the ground that the established church was sinful. Edward Channing, *A History of the United States*, Vol. I: *The Planting of a Nation in the New World, 1000-1660* (New York, 1928), 363. Williams' objection was that the power of the magistrates should extend only to the bodies, goods, and outward state of men and not to the first four commandments of the decalogue. Andrews, *op. cit.*, I, 473.

[4] Bradford's account of Williams' stay in Plymouth is as follows: "Mr. Roger Williams (a man godly and zealous, having many precious parts, but very unsettled in judgmente) came over first to the Massachusetts, but upon some discontente left that place, and came hither, (wher he was friendly entertained, according to their poore abilitie,) and exercised his gifts amongst them, and after some. time was admitted a member of the church; and his teaching well approved, for the benefite whereof I still blese God, and am thankfull to him, even for his sharpest admonitions and reproufs, so farr as they agreed with truth. He this year begane to fall into some strang opinions, and from opinion to practise; which caused some controversie betweene the church and him, and in the end some discontente on his parte, by occasion whereof he left them some thing abruptly. Yet after wards sued for his dismission to the church of Salem, which was granted, with some caution to them concerning him, and what care they ought to have of him." *History of Plymouth Plantation* (Boston, 1917), II, 161-63.

[5] Williams had said that the colonists were "under a sin of usurpation of others' possessions." This was apparently a deduction he drew from theological premises rather than a conclusion based on legal principles. The law of England recognized the power of the crown to acquire title to land by discovery,

opposition because it was made at the same time that Sir Ferdinando Gorges and others in England were trying to have the charter recalled. Williams was thus promoting a movement which was actually dangerous to the colony. He was called before the General Court on July 8, 1635, to answer for his teachings [6] and was banished from the colony in September of the same year.[7] He departed to the wilderness in January, 1636.

Founding of Providence

Williams' congregation at Salem had yielded to the authorities. Only a few persons, mostly individuals who were out of favor in Massachusetts for various reasons, followed him and helped him found the settlement of Providence. Negotiations were conducted with the Indians for the purchase of land, and town lots were sold to persons desiring to become inhabitants. A town government was instituted in 1636, and it was clear from the first that religious freedom would be an essential feature of the administration. A written covenant drawn up in 1636 provided that the authority of civil government should not extend to religious matters;[8] it was thus in marked contrast to other plantation covenants of that time.[9] This principle was reaffirmed by the plantation agreement of 1640 which declared: "Wee agree, as formerly hath bin the liberties of the town, so still, to hould forth

and the presence of non-Christian natives did not affect that power under the law. In addition, the people at Plymouth and Massachusetts had taken care to compensate the original occupiers of the land. It is not likely, therefore, that Williams found many in support of his view. Channing, *op. cit.*, I, 364-65; Andrews, *op. cit.*, I, 472.

[6] The teachings objected to were: (1) that the magistrates ought not to punish the breach of the first table except in cases involving a breach of the peace; (2) that the oath of fidelity to the colony should not be administered to persons who were unregenerate, i.e., who had not renounced the Church of England; (3) that a man should not pray with an unregenerate person, even his wife or child; and (4) that a man should not give thanks after the sacrament or after meat. There was much debate as to what should be done about Williams, although all agreed that the opinions were erroneous, dangerous, and in contempt of authority. Williams and the Salem church were given until the next General Court to consider the matter, and it was made clear that he would be removed from the colony if he continued to be obstinate about his opinions. Hosmer, *op. cit.*, I, 154.

[7] The records of the General Court state: "Whereas Mr. Roger Williams, one of the elders of the church of Salem, hath broached & dyvulged dyvers newe & dangerous opinions, against the aucthoritie of magistrates, as also writt lres of defamacõn, both of the magistrates & churches here, & that before any conviccõn, & yet mainetaineth the same without retraccõn, it is therefore ordered, that the said Mr. Williams shall depte out of this jurisdiccõn within sixe weekes nowe nexte ensueing, wch if hee neglect to pforme, it shalbe lawfull for the Gounr & two of the magistrates to send him to some place out of this jurisdiccõn, not to returne any more without licence from the Court." Nathaniel B. Shurtleff (ed.), *Records of the Governor and Company of the Massachusetts Bay in New England* (Boston, 1853), I, 160-61.

[8] The inhabitants agreed to subject themselves "in active and passive obedience to all such orders and agreements as shall be made for public good of the body in an orderly way, by the major consent of the present inhabitants, masters of families incorporated together in a Towne fellowship, and others whom they shall admit unto them, *only in civil things.*" Emphasis added. Quoted in Herbert L. Osgood, *The American Colonies in the Seventeenth Century* (New York, 1904), I, 336.

[9] Cf. Mayflower Compact, pp. 55-61; Fundamental Orders of Connecticut, pp. 115-24.

CHARTER OF RHODE ISLAND

liberty of Conscience."[10] While Williams was building a government in Providence, other refugees from religious persecution in Massachusetts were beginning settlements at Newport and Portsmouth. They followed the example of Providence by recognizing the principles of religious freedom and democratic government at an early date.[11]

Charter of 1663

In 1643 Williams sailed from New Amsterdam to England for the purpose of obtaining a patent for Rhode Island from the Long Parliament. A patent was obtained from the Commission for Plantations on March 14, 1644. It made Providence, Newport, and Portsmouth a corporate body under the title of the Providence Plantations in Narragansett Bay in New England.[12] The colonists were given full power and authority to rule themselves "by such a Form of Civil Government, as by voluntary consent of all, or the greater Part of them, they shall find most suitable to their Estate and Condition." It was provided, however, that all laws made for the plantations should be conformable to the laws of England. The power of self-government given to the colonists was soon asserted. In 1647 they drew up a code to define the organization of the government. The code carefully observed the demarcation between the powers of the towns and those of the central government. The officers of the government were a president, four assistants, a recorder, a treasurer, and a sergeant, all of whom were to be chosen each year at a court of election. After 1650, when the General Court became a representative body instead of an assemblage of all the freemen, six deputies were sent from each town. Like the Massachusetts Body of Liberties,[13] the code was prefixed with an affirmation of chapter 39 of Magna Carta but, unlike the Massachusetts document, the word of God was not made a rule of judicature

---

[10] Francis N. Thorpe (ed.), *The Federal and State Constitutions, Colonial Charters, and Other Organic Laws* (Washington, 1909), VI, 3206.

[11] The union of Newport and Portsmouth in 1640 lasted for seven years. The union was governed according to an enactment of the General Court which provided, among other things: "It is ordered and unanimously agreed upon, that the Government which this Bodie Politick doth attend unto in this Island, and the Jurisdiction thereof, in favour of our Prince is a DEMOCRACIE, or Popular Government; that is to say, It is in the Powre of the Body of Freemen orderly assembled, or the major part of them, to make or constitute Just Lawes, by which they will be regulated, and to depute from among themselves such Ministers as shall see them faithfully executed between Man and Man.
"It was further ordered, by the authority of this present Courte, that none bee accounted a Delinquent for *Doctrine:* Provided, it be not directly repugnant to ye Government or Lawes established." *Ibid.*, VI, 3207-8.

[12] For text, see *ibid.*, VI, 3209-11. The patent did not mention any prior right of the crown to the soil. It is therefore possible that Williams may have been able to square his conscience with his previous objections to the Massachusetts Charter by regarding the patent as merely a confirmation of the purchases made by the colonists from the natives. Andrews, *op. cit.* (1936), II, 25.

[13] See pp. 143-61.

SOURCES OF OUR LIBERTIES

applicable in the absence of other laws. The code was based largely on English statutes, but the law of England was considered to be in force only in so far as it had been expressly adopted by the General Court.

After the restoration of the English monarchy in 1660, it became necessary to obtain a charter from the king to replace the patent from Parliament. The promptness with which Rhode Island had proclaimed Charles II and the desire of the crown to curb the claims of Massachusetts to additional territory caused the application for a charter to be regarded with favor. The charter was granted in 1663 largely through the efforts of John Clarke, who had acted as agent in England for Rhode Island on a number of occasions. The charter recognized and confirmed the forms of government already in effect in Rhode Island. Because it was liberal in recognizing the rights and institutions evolved by the colonists themselves, the charter was kept in force after the Revolutionary War and until as late as 1842. At that time it was replaced by a formal constitution.[14]

General Significance

The charter was not the first important colonial document containing a guarantee of religious liberty. It was preceded in time by the Maryland Toleration Act of 1649.[15] The Rhode Island Charter, however, had a significance not possessed by that act. It placed the provision for religious liberty not in an act of ordinary legislation but in the fundamental law of the colony, and the guarantee thus became a part of the same instrument which defined the basic framework of the government.

Other colonial charters

The provision for religious liberty was copied two years later in the Charter of Carolina granted by the king.[16] Several documents issued by colonial proprietors were also based on the wording of the Rhode Island Charter. The Concession of 1664 of New Jersey,[17] issued by Berkeley and Carteret, and the Concessions of the Proprietors of Carolina of 1665 [18] contain provisions copied almost verbatim from the Rhode Island Charter.

Other colonial documents expressed the principle of religious freedom in different language. The Fundamental Laws of West New Jersey of 1677 provided "That no men, nor number of men upon earth, hath power or authority to rule over men's consciences in religious matters." [19] The Carolina Charter

---

[14] The only other colony continuing under royal charter after the Revolution was Connecticut, whose charter of 1662 was, in most respects, similar to the Rhode Island Charter of 1663. The Connecticut Charter was in force until 1812. For text, see Thorpe, *op. cit.*, I, 529-36.

[15] See pp. 100-1.

[16] Thorpe, *op. cit.*, V, 2771.

[17] *Ibid.*, 2537.

[18] *Ibid.*, 2757.

[19] See p. 185. The charter for the Province of West Jersey of 1681 provided: "That liberty of conscience in matters of faith and worship towards God, shall be granted to all people within the Province

CHARTER OF RHODE ISLAND

of 1669 provided that "No person whatsoever shall disturb, molest, or persecute another for his speculative opinions in religion, or his way of worship."[20] The Pennsylvania Frame of Government of 1682[21] and Penn's Charter of Privileges of 1701[22] contained guarantees of religious freedom. The Fundamental Constitutions of East New Jersey of 1683[23] contained a provision almost identical with that of the earlier Pennsylvania document.

It should not be assumed that even these broad declarations of religious liberty established that right in the same manner, or to the same extent, as it exists under the first amendment to the Constitution of the United States. In several colonies religious liberty was extended to the various Protestant groups but not to Catholics. Even Rhode Island carried on its statute books from 1719 to 1783 a clause excluding Catholics from public office. It is doubtful, however, that this provision was ever actually enforced.[24] Discriminations against Catholics were, in general, eliminated following the American Revolution. The Commission to John Cutt of 1680[25] for the government of New Hampshire had extended liberty of conscience only to Protestants, but this was extended to all men by the constitution of 1784.[26] Likewise, the Charter of Georgia of 1732 provided "that all such persons, except papists, shall have a free exercise of their religion,"[27] but this was changed by the constitution of 1777[28] which extended the right to "all persons whatever." The same pattern likewise appeared in New York. Although the declaration of rights of 1691 provided liberty of conscience except for "any persons of the Romish Religion,"[29] the constitution of 1777 extended the right to "all mankind."[30]

Discrimination against Catholics

Another difference between some of the colonial documents and the first amendment to the Constitution of the United States was that some colonies required or authorized the establishment of one religious sect in preference to others. "By establishment of religion is meant the setting up or

Established churches

---

aforesaid; who shall live peaceably and quietly therein; and that none of the free people of the said Province, shall be rendered uncapable of office in respect of their faith and worship." *Ibid.*, 2567.

[20] *Ibid.*, 2785. This document was drafted by John Locke and Anthony Ashley Cooper, the Earl of Shaftesbury. It was only partially put into operation, and was abrogated by the proprietors in 1693.

[21] See pp. 207, 220.

[22] See pp. 251-52, 256, 259.

[23] Thorpe, *op. cit.*, V, 2579-80.

[24] Robert A. Rutland, *The Birth of the Bill of Rights, 1776-1791* (Chapel Hill, 1955), 17-18.

[25] Thorpe, *op. cit.*, IV, 2446. [28] See p. 310.

[26] See p. 382. [29] Rutland, *op. cit.*, 21.

[27] Thorpe, *op. cit.*, II, 773. [30] Thorpe, *op. cit.*, V, 2637.

recognition of a state church, or at least the conferring upon one church of special favors and advantages which are denied to others."[31] At the outbreak of the American Revolution, nine of the thirteen colonies had established churches in this sense. After the Revolution the breaking of ties with England resulted in the disestablishment of churches in four of the six colonies in which the Anglican religion held the favored position. Only Rhode Island, Pennsylvania, Delaware, and New Jersey have never had an established religion.[32] This movement against the establishment of religion produced the Virginia Statute of Religious Liberty of 1786,[33] drawn by Thomas Jefferson. This act condemned all religious establishments and all laws requiring persons to contribute money for the propagation of any religious opinions. It asserted that civil rights should have no dependence upon religious opinions and provided that no man should be required to frequent or support any religious worship, place, or ministry whatsoever. It was stated that no one should be "enforced, restrained, molested, or burthened" on account of his religious opinions. Freedom of speech on religious matters was guaranteed.

The first amendment to the Constitution of the United States[34] provides that Congress shall make no law respecting the establishment of religion. Of this provision, Jefferson made the following statement in a letter in 1802:

> Believing with you that religion is a matter which lies solely between man and his God, that he owes account to none other for his faith or his worship, that the legislative powers of government reach actions only, and not opinions, I contemplate with sovereign reverence that act of the whole American people which declared that their legislature should "make no law respecting an establishment of religion, or prohibiting the free exercise thereof," thus building a wall of separation between church and State.[35]

The first amendment's prohibition of interference by the government in religious matters thus constitutes a logical outgrowth of Roger Williams' protests of the 1630's against the religious powers exerted by the magistrates of Massachusetts.

---

[31] Thomas M. Cooley, *The General Principles of Constitutional Law in the United States of America* (Boston, 1880), 205.

[32] Some writers have found evidence of an Anglican establishment in New Jersey. Joseph H. Brady, *Confusion Twice Confounded* (South Orange, 1954), 5-6.

[33] Henry S. Commager (ed.), *Documents of American History* (3d ed.; New York, 1943), I, 125-26.

[34] See p. 432.

[35] Letter to Nehemiah Dodge, Ephraim Robbins, and Stephen S. Nelson, January 1, 1802. Text in Saul K. Padover (ed.), *The Complete Jefferson* (New York, 1943), 518-19.

CHARTER OF RHODE ISLAND AND PROVIDENCE PLANTATIONS

July 8, 1663

CHARLES THE SECOND, by the grace of *God*, King of England, Scotland, France and Ireland, Defender of the Faith, &c., to all to whome these presents shall come, greeting: *Whereas wee* have been informed, by the humble petition of our trustie and well beloved subject, John Clarke, on the behalf of Benjamine Arnold, William Brenton, William Codington, Nicholas Easton, William Boulston, John Porter, John Smith, Samuell Gorton, John Weeks, Roger Williams, Thomas Olnie, Gregorie Dexter, John Cogeshall, Joseph Clarke, Randall Holden, John Greene, John Roome, Samuell Wildbore, William Ffield, James Barker, Richard Tew, Thomas Harris, and William Dyre, and the rest of the purchasers and ffree inhabitants of our island, called *Rhode-Island,* and the rest of the colonie of Providence Plantations, in the Narragansett Bay, in New-England, in America, that they, pursueing, with peaceable and loyall mindes, their sober, serious and religious intentions, of godlie edifieing themselves, and one another, in the holie Christian ffaith and worshipp as they were perswaded; together with the gaineing over and conversione of the poore ignorant Indian natives, in those partes of America, to the sincere professione and obedienc of the same ffaith and worship, did, not onlie by the consent and good encouragement of our royall progenitors, transport themselves out of this kingdome of England into America, but alsoe, since their arrivall there, after their first settlement amongst other our subjects in those parts, ffor the avoideing of discorde, and those manie evills which were likely to ensue upon some of those oure subjects not beinge able to beare, in these remote parties, theire different apprehensiones in religious concernements, and in pursueance of the afforesayd ends, did once againe leave theire desireable stationes and habitationes, and with excessive labour and travell, hazard and charge, did transplant themselves into the middest of the Indian natives, who, as wee are infformed, are the most potent princes and people of all that country; where, by the good Providence of God, from whome the Plantationes have taken their name, upon theire labour and industrie, they have not onlie byn preserved to admiration, but have increased and prospered, and are seized and possessed, by purchase and consent of the said natives, to their ffull content, of such lands, islands, rivers, harbours and roades, as are verie convenient, both for

Preamble

---

[36] Thorpe, *op. cit.*, VI, 3211-22.

plantationes and alsoe for buildinge of shipps, suplye of pypestaves, and other merchandize; and which lyes verie commodious, in manie respects, for commerce, and to accommodate oure southern plantationes, and may much advance the trade of this oure realme, and greatlie enlarge the territories thereof; they haveinge by neare neighbourhoode to and friendlie societie with the greate bodie of the Narragansett Indians, given them encouragement, of theire owne accorde, to subject themselves, theire people and landes, unto us; whereby, as is hoped, there may, in due tyme, by the blessing of God upon theire endeavours, bee layd a sure ffoundation of happinesse to all America:

Religious liberty

And whereas, in theire humble addresse, they have ffreely declared, that it is much on their hearts (if they may be permitted), to hold forth a livlie experiment, that a most flourishing civill state may stand and best bee maintained, and that among our English subjects, with a full libertie in religious concernements; and that true pietye rightly grounded upon gospell principles, will give the best and greatest security to sovereignetye, and will lay in the hearts of men the strongest obligations to true loyaltye: *Now know yee,* that wee beinge willinge to encourage the hopefull undertakeinge of oure sayd loyall and loveinge subjects, and to secure them in the free exercise and enjoyment of all theire civill and religious rights, appertaining to them, as our loveing subjects; and to preserve unto them that libertye, in the true Christian ffaith and worshipp of God, which they have sought with soe much travaill, and with peaceable myndes, and loyall subjectione to our royall progenitors and ourselves, to enjoye; and because some of the people and inhabitants of the same colonie cannot, in theire private opinions, conforms to the publique exercise of religion, according to the litturgy, formes and ceremonyes of the Church of England, or take or subscribe the oaths and articles made and established in that behalfe; and for that the same, by reason of the remote distances of those places, will (as wee hope) bee noe breach of the unitie and unifformitie established in this nation: Have therefore thought ffit, and doe hereby publish, graunt, ordeyne and declare, That our royall will and pleasure is, that noe person within the sayd colonye, at any tyme hereafter, shall bee any wise molested, punished, disquieted, or called in question, for any differences in opinione in matters of religion, and doe not actually disturb the civill peace of our sayd colony; but that all and everye person and persons may, from tyme to tyme, and at all tymes hereafter, freelye and fullye hav and enjoye his and theire owne judgments and consciences, in matters of religious concernments, throughout the tract of lande hereafter mentioned; they behaving themselves peaceablie and quietlie, and not useing this libertie to lycentiousnesse and profanenesse, nor to the civill injurye or outward disturbeance of others; any lawe, statute, or clause, therein contayned, or to bee contayned, usage or custome of this realme, to the contrary hereof, in any wise, notwithstanding. And that they may bee in the better capacity to defend themselves, in theire just rights and libertyes against all the enemies of the Christian ffaith, and others, in all respects, wee have further thought fit, and at the humble petition of the persons aforesayd are gratiously pleased to declare, That they shall have and enjoye the benefitt of our late act of indempnity and ffree pardon, as the rest of our subjects in other our dominions

CHARTER OF RHODE ISLAND

and territoryes have; and to create and make them a bodye politique or corporate, with the powers and priviledges hereinafter mentioned.

And accordingely our will and pleasure is, and of our especiall grace, certaine knowledge, and meere motion, *wee have ordeyned*, constituted and declared, and by these presents, for us, our heires and successors, doe ordeyne, constitute and declare, That they, the sayd William Brenton, William Codington, Nicholas Easton, Benedict Arnold, William Boulston, John Porter, Samuell Gorton, John Smith, John Weekes, Roger Williams, Thomas Olneye, Gregorie Dexter, John Cogeshall, Joseph Clarke, Randall Holden, John Greene, John Roome, William Dyre, Samuell Wildbore, Richard Tew, William Ffeild, Thomas Harris, James Barker, ——— Rainsborrow, ——— Williams, and John Nickson, and all such others as now are, or hereafter shall bee admitted and made ffree of the company and societie of our collonie of Providence Plantations, in the Narragansett Bay, in New England, shall bee, from tyme to tyme, and forever hereafter, a bodie corporate and politike, in ffact and name, by the name of *The Governor and Company of the English Colony of Rhode-Island and Providence Plantations, in New-England, in America;* and that, by the same name, they and their successors shall and may have perpetuall succession, and shall and may bee persons able and capable, in the lawe, to sue and bee sued, to pleade and be impleaded, to answeare and bee answeared unto, to defend and to be defended, in all and singular suites, causes, quarrels, matters, actions and thinges, of what kind or nature soever; and alsoe to have, take, possesse, acquire and purchase lands, tenements or hereditaments, or any goods or chattels, and the same to lease, graunt, demise, aliene, bargaine, sell and dispose of, at their owne will and pleasure, as other our liege people of this our realme of England, or anie corporation or bodie politique within the same, may be lawfully doe: *And further*, that they the sayd Governor and Company, and theire successors, shall and may, forever hereafter, have a common seale, to serve and use for all matters, causes, thinges and affaires, whatsoever, of them and their successors; and the same seale to alter, change, breake, and make new, from tyme to tyme, at their will and pleasure, as they shall think ffitt.

Formation of the body politic

And further, wee will and ordeyne, and by these presents, for us, oure heires and successours, doe declare and apoynt that, for the better ordering and managing of the affaires and business of the sayd Company, and theire successours, there shall bee one Governour, one Deputie-Governour and ten Assistants, to bee from tyme to tyme, constituted, elected and chosen, out of the freemen of the sayd Company, for the tyme beinge, in such manner and fforme as is hereafter in these presents expressed; which sayd officers shall aplye themselves to take care for the best disposeinge and orderinge of the generall businesse and affaires of, and concerneinge the landes and hereditaments hereinafter mentioned, to be graunted, and the plantation thereof, and the government of the people there. *And* for the better execution of oure royall pleasure herein, wee doe, for us, oure heires and successours, assign, name, constitute and apoynt the aforesayd Benedict Arnold to bee the first and present Governor of the sayd Company, and the sayd William Brenton, to bee the Deputy-Governor, and the sayd William Boulston, John Porter, Roger Williams, Thomas Olnie, John Smith, John Greene, John

Officers: Governor, deputy governor, and assistants

Names of first officers

Cogeshall, James Barker, William Ffeild, and Joseph Clarke, to bee the tenn present Assistants of the sayd Companye, to continue in the sayd severall offices, respectively, untill the first Wednesday which shall bee in the month of May now next comeing. *And further,* wee will, and by these presents, for us, our heires and successessours, doe ordeyne and graunt, that the Governor of the sayd Company, for the tyme being, or, in his absence, by occasion of sicknesse, or otherwise, by his leave and permission, the Deputy-Governor, ffor the tyme being, shall and may, ffrom tyme to tyme, upon all occasions, give order ffor the assemblinge of the sayd Company and callinge them together, to consult and advise of the businesse and affaires of the sayd Company.

General Assembly
System of representation

And that forever hereafter, twice in every year, that is to say, on every first Wednesday in the month of May, and on every last Wednesday in October, or oftener, in case it shall bee requisite, the Assistants, and such of the ffreemen of the Company, not exceedinge six persons ffor Newport, ffoure persons ffor each of the respective townes of Providence, Portsmouth and Warwicke, and two persons for each other place, towne or city, whoe shall bee, from tyme to tyme, thereunto elected or deputed by the majour parte of the ffreemen of the respective townes or places ffor which they shall bee so elected or deputed, shall have a generall meetinge, or Assembly then and there to consult, advise and determine, in and about the affaires and businesse of the said Company and Plantations. *And further,* wee doe, of our especiall grace, certayne knowledge, and meere motion, give and graunt unto the sayd Governour and Company of the English Colonie of *Rhode-Island and Providence Plantations,* in New-England, in America, and theire successours, that the Governour, or, in his absence, or, by his permission, the Deputy-Governour of the sayd Company, for the tyme beinge, the Assistants, and such of the ffreemen of the sayd Company as shall bee soe as aforesayd elected or deputed, or soe many of them as shall bee present att such meetinge or assemblye, as afforesayde, shall bee called the Generall Assemblye; and that they, or the greatest parte of them present, whereof the Governour or Deputy-Governour, and sixe of the Assistants, at least to bee seven, shall have, and have hereby given and graunted unto them, ffull power authority, ffrom tyme tyme, and at all tymes hereafter, to apoynt, alter and change, such dayes, tymes and places of meetinge and Generall Assemblye, as theye shall thinke ffitt; and to choose, nominate, and apoynt, such and soe manye other persons as they shall thinke ffitt, and shall be willing to accept the same, to bee ffree of the sayd Company and body politique, and them into the same to admitt; and to elect and constitute such offices and officers, and to graunt such needfull commissions, as they shall thinke ffitt and requisite, ffor the ordering, managing and dispatching of the affaires of the sayd Governour and Company, and their successours; and from tyme to tyme, to make, ordeyne, constitute or repeal, such lawes, statutes, orders and ordinances, fformes and ceremonies of government and magistracye as to them shall seeme meete for the good nad wellfare of the sayd Company, and ffor the government and ordering of the landes and hereditaments, hereinafter mentioned to be graunted, and of the people that doe, or att any time hereafter shall, inhabitt or bee within the same; soe as such lawes, ordinances and constitutiones, soe made, bee not contrary and repugnant unto, butt, as neare as may bee, agreeable to the lawes of this our realme

Time and place of meeting

Admission of freemen

Lawmaking

Laws not to be repugnant

CHARTER OF RHODE ISLAND

of England, considering the nature and constitutione of the place and people there; and alsoe to apoynt, order and direct, erect and settle, such places and courts of jurisdiction, ffor the heareinge and determininge of all actions, cases, matters and things, happening within the sayd collonie and plantatione, and which shall be in dispute, and depending there, as they shall thinke ffit; and alsoe to distinguish and sett forth the severall names and titles, duties, powers and limitts, of each court, office and officer, superior and inferior; and alsoe to contrive and apoynt such formes of oaths and attestations, not repugnant, but, as neare as may bee, agreeable, as aforesayd, to the lawes and statutes of this oure realme, as are conveniente and requisite, with respect to the due administration of justice, and due execution and discharge of all offices and places of trust by the persons that shall bee therein concerned; and alsoe to regulate and order the waye and manner of all elections to offices and places of trust, and to prescribe, limitt and distinguish the numbers and boundes of all places, townes or cityes, within the limitts and bounds herein after mentioned, and not herein particularlie named, who have, and shall have, the power of electing and sending of ffreemen to the sayd Generall Assembly; and alsoe to order, direct and authorize the imposing of lawfull and reasonable ffynes, mulcts, imprisonments, and executing other punishments pecuniary and corporal, upon offenders and delinquents, according to the course of other corporations within this oure kingdom of England; and agayne to alter, revoke, annull or pardon, under their common seale or otherwyse, such ffynes, mulcts, imprisonments, sentences, judgments and condemnations, as shall bee thought ffitt; and to direct, rule, order and dispose of, all other matters and things, and particularly that which relates to the makinge of purchases of the native Indians, as to them shall seeme meete; whereby oure sayd people and inhabitants, in the sayd Plantationes, may be soe religiously, peaceably and civilly governed, as that, by theire good life and orderlie conversatione, they may win and invite the native Indians of the countrie to the knowledge and obedience of the onlie true God, and Saviour of mankinde; willing, commanding and requireing, and by these presents, for us, oure heires and successours, ordeyneing and apoynting, that all such lawes, statutes, orders and ordinances, instructions, impositions and directiones, as shall bee soe made by the Governour, deputye-Governour, Assistants and ffreemen, or such number of them as aforesayd, and published in writinge, under theire common seale, shall bee carefully and duely observed, kept, performed and putt in execution, according to the true intent and meaning of the same.

Courts
Titles
Oaths

Elections

Punishments

Pardons

Other matters

And these our letters patent, or the duplicate or exempliffication thereof, shall bee to all and everie such officer, superiour or inferiour, ffrom tyme to tyme, for the putting of the same orders, lawes, statutes, ordinances, instructions and directions, in due execution, against us, oure heires and successours, a sufficient warrant and discharge. And ffurther, our will and pleasure is, and wee doe hereby, for us, oure heires and successours, establish and ordeyne, that yearelie, once in the yeare, forever hereafter, namely, the aforesayd Wednesday in May, and at the towne of Newport, or elsewhere, if urgent occasion doe require, the Governour, Deputy-Governour and Assistants of the sayd Company, and other officers of the sayd Company, or such of them as the

Effect of charter

Elections

Generall Assemblye shall thinke ffitt, shall bee, in the sayd Generall Court or Assembly to bee held from that daye or tyme, newely chosen for the year ensueing, by such greater part of the sayd Company, for the tyme beinge, as shall bee then and there present; *and* if itt shall happen that the present Governour, Deputy-Governour and Assistants, by these presents apoynted, or any such as shall hereafter be newly chosen into their roomes, or any of them, or any other the officers of the sayd Company, shall die or bee removed ffrom his or their severall offices or places, before the sayd generall day of election, (whom wee doe hereby declare, for any misdemeanour or default, to be removeable by the Governour, Assistants and Company, or such greater parte of them, in any of the sayd publique courts, to bee assembled as aforesayd), that then, and in every such case, it shall and may bee lawfull to and ffor the sayd Governour, Deputy-Governour, Assistants and Company aforesayde, or such greater parte of them, soe to bee assembled as is aforesayde, in any theire assemblyes, to proceede to a new election of one or more of their Company, in the roome or place, roomes or places, of such officer or officers, soe dyeinge or removed, according to theire discretiones; and immediately upon and after such electione or elections made of such Governour, Deputy-Governour or Assistants, or any other officer of the sayd Company, in manner and forme aforesayde, the authoritie, office and power, before given to the fformer Governour, Deputy-Governour, and other officer and officers, soe removed, in whose steade and place new shall be chosen, shall, as to him and them, and every of them, respectively, cease and determine:

Oath of office   *Provided,* allwayes, and our will and pleasure is, that as well such as are by these presents apoynted to bee the present Governour, Deputy-Governour and Assistants, of the sayd Company, as those that shall succeede them, and all other officers to bee apoynted and chosen as aforesayde, shall, before the undertakeinge the execution of the sayd offices and places respectively, give theire solemn engagement, by oath, or otherwyse, for the due and faythfull performance of theire duties in their severall offices and places, before such person or persons as are by these presents hereafter apoynted to take and receive the same, that is to say: the sayd Benedict Arnold, whoe is hereinbefore nominated and apoynted the present Governour of the sayd Company, shall give the aforesayd engagement before William Brenton, or any two of the sayd Assistants of the sayd Company; unto whome, *wee doe* by these presentes give ffull power and authority to require and receive the same; and the sayd William Brenton, whoe is hereby before nominated and apoynted the present Deputy-Governour of the sayd Company, shall give the aforesayed engagement before the sayd Benedict Arnold, or any two of the Assistants of the sayd Company; unto whome *wee doe* by these presents give ffull power and authority to require and receive the same; and the sayd William Boulston, John Porter, Roger Williams, Thomas Olneye, John Smith, John Greene, John Cogeshall, James Barker, William Ffeild, and Joseph Clarke, whoe are hereinbefore nominated apoynted the present Assistants of the sayd Company, shall give the sayd engagement to theire offices and places respectively belongeing, before the sayd Benedict Arnold and William Brenton, or one of them; to whome, respectively *wee doe* hereby give ffull power and authority to require, administer or receive the

CHARTER OF RHODE ISLAND

same: *and ffurther,* our will and pleasure is, that all and every other future Governour or Deputy-Governour, to bee elected and chosen by vertue of these presents, shall give the sayd engagement before two or more of the sayd Assistants of the sayd Company ffor the tyme beinge; unto whome wee doe by these presents give ffull power and authority to require, administer or receive the same; and the sayd Assistants, and every of them, and all and every other officer or officers to bee hereafter elected and chosen by vertue of these presents, from tyme to tyme, shall give the like engagements, to their offices and places respectively belonging bofere the Governour or Deputy-Governour for the tyme being; unto which sayd Governour, or Deputy-Governour, *wee doe* by these presents give full power and authority to require, administer or receive the same accordingly.

And wee doe likewise, for vs, oure heires and successours, give and graunt vnto the sayd Governour and Company and theire successours by these presents, that, for the more peaceable and orderly government of the sayd Plantations, it shall and may bee lawfull ffor the Governour, Deputy-Governor, Assistants, and all other officers and ministers of the sayd Company, in the administration of justice, and exercise of government, in the sayd Plantations, to vse, exercise, and putt in execution, such methods, rules, orders and directions, not being contrary or repugnant to the laws and statutes of this oure realme, as have byn heretofore given, vsed and accustomed, in such cases respectively, to be putt in practice, untill att the next or some other Generall Assembly, special provision shall be made and ordeyned in the cases aforesayd. *And wee doe ffurther,* for vs, oure heires and successours, give and graunt vnto the sayd Governour and Company, and theire successours, by these presents, that itt shall and may bee lawfull to and for the sayd Governour, or in his absence, the Deputy-Governour, and majour parte of the sayd Assistants, for the tyme being, att any tyme when the sayd Generall Assembly is not sitting, to nominate, apoynt and constitute, such and soe many commanders, governours, and military officers, as to them shall seeme requisite, for the leading, conductinge and trayneing vpp the inhabitants of the sayd Plantations in martiall affaires, and for the defence and safeguard of the sayd Plantations; and that itt shall and may bee lawfull to and for all and every such commander, governour and military officer, that shall bee soe as aforesayd, or by the Governour, or, in his absence, the Deputy-Governour, and six of the sayd Assistants, and majour parte of the ffreemen of the sayd Company present att any Generall Assemblies, nominated, apoynted and constituted accordinge to the tenor of his and theire respective commissions and directions, to assemble, exercise in arms, martiall array, and putt in warlyke posture, the inhabitants of the sayd collonie, ffor theire speciall defence and safety; and to lead and conduct the sayd inhabitants, and to encounter, expulse, expell and resist, by force of armes, as well by sea as by lande; and alsoe to kill, slay and destroy, by all fitting wayes, enterprizes and meanes, whatsoever, all and every such person or persons as shall, att any tyme hereafter, attempt or enterprize the destruction, invasion, detriment or annoyance of the sayd inhabitants or Plantations; and to vse and exercise the lawe martiall in such cases only as occasion shall necessarily require; and to take or surprise, by all wayes and meanes whatsoever, all and every such person and persons,

Powers of officers

Rules and orders

Military affairs and defense

Martial law

Captures

with theire shipp or shipps, armor, ammunition or other goods of such persons, as shall, in hostile manner, invade or attempt the defeating of the sayd Plantations, or the hurt of the sayd Company and inhabitants; and vpon just causes, to invade and destroy the native Indians, or other enemyes of the sayd Collony. Neverthelesse, our will and pleasure is, and wee doe hereby declare to the rest of oure Collonies in New England, that itt shall not bee lawfull ffor this our sayd Collony of Rhode-Island and Providence Plantations, in America, in New-England, to invade the natives inhabiting within the boundes and limitts of theire sayd Collonies without the knowledge and consent of the sayd other Collonies. And itt is hereby declared, that itt shall not bee lawfull to or ffor the rest of the Collonies to invade or molest the native Indians, or any other inhabitants, inhabiting within the bounds and lymitts hereafter mentioned (they having subjected themselves vnto vs, and being by vs taken into our speciall protection), without the knowledge and consent of the Governour and Company of our Collony of Rhode-Island and Providence Plantations.

<small>*War against Indians*</small>

Alsoe our will and pleasure is, and wee doe hereby declare unto all Christian Kings, Princes and States, that if any person, which shall hereafter bee of the sayd Company or Plantations, or any other, by apoyntment of the sayd Governour and Company for the tyme beinge, shall at any tyme or tymes hereafter, rob or spoyle, by sea or land, or do any hurt, unlawfull hostillity to any of the subjects of vs, oure heires or successours, or any of the subjects of any Prince or State, beinge then in league with vs, oure heires, or successours, vpon complaint of such injury done to any such Prince or State, or theire subjects, wee, our heires and successours, will make open proclamation within any parts of oure realme of England, ffitt ffor that purpose, that the person or persons committing any such robbery or spoyle shall, within the tyme lymitted by such proclamation, make full restitution or satisfaction of all such injuries, done or committed, soe as the sayd Prince, or others soe complaineinge, may bee fully satisfyed and contented; and if the sayd person or persons whoe shall commit any such robbery or spoyle shall not make satysfaction, accordingly, within such tyme, soe to bee lymitted, that then wee, oure heires and successours, will putt such person or persons out of oure allegiance and protection; and that then itt shall and may bee lawfull and ffree ffor all Princes or others to prosecute, with hostillity, such offenders, and every of them, theire and every of theire procurers, ayders, abettors and counsellors, in that behalfe; *Provided* alsoe, and oure expresse will and pleasure is, *and wee doe,* by these presents, ffor vs, our heirs and successors, ordeyne and apoynt, that these presents shall not, in any manner, hinder any of oure lovinge subjects, whatsoever, ffrom vseing and exercising the trade of ffishing vpon the coast of New-England, in America; butt that they, and every or any of them, shall have ffull and ffree power and liberty to continue and vse the trade of ffishing vpon the sayd coast, in any of the seas thereunto adjoyninge, or any armes of the seas, or salt water, rivers and creeks, where they have been accustomed to ffish; and to build and to sett upon the waste land, belonginge to the sayd Collony and Plantations, such wharfes, stages and worke-houses as shall be necessary for the salting, drying and keepeing of theire ffish, to be taken or gotten upon that coast. *And ffurther,* for the encouragement of the inhabitants of our sayd Collony of Providence Plantations to sett vpon the businesse of takeing whales, itt shall bee lawefull ffor them, or any of them, having struck whale, dubertus, or other greate ffish, itt or them, to pursue vnto any parte of that coaste, and into any bay, river, cove, creeke or shoare, belonging thereto, and itt or them, vpon sayd coaste, or in the sayd bay, river, cove, creeke or shoare, belonging thereto, to kill and order for the best advantage, without molestation, they makeing noe wilfull waste or spoyle, any thinge in these presents conteyned, or any other matter or thing, to the contrary notwithstanding. And further alsoe, wee are gratiously pleased, and doe hereby declare, that if any of the inhabitants of oure sayd Collony doe sett upon the plantinge of vineyards (the soyle and clymate both seemeing naturally to concurr to the production of wynes), or bee industrious in the discovery of ffishing banks, in or about the sayd Collony, wee will, ffrom tyme to tyme, give and allow all due and fitting encouragement therein, as to others in cases of lyke nature. And further, of oure more ample grace, certayne knowledge, and meere *Emigrants* motion, wee have given and graunted, and by these presents, ffor vs, oure heires and successours, doe give and graunt vnto the sayd Governour and Company of the English Collony of Rhode-Island and Providence Plantations, in the Narragansett Bay, in New-England in America, and to every inhabitant there, and to every person and persons trading thither, and to every such person or persons as are or shall bee ffree of the sayd Collony, full power and authority, from tyme to tyme, and att all tymes hereafter, to take, shipp, transport and carry away, out of any of our realmes and dominions, for and towards the plantation and defence of the sayd Collony, such and soe many of oure loveing subjects and strangers as shall or will willingly accompany them in and to their sayd Collony and Plantation; except such person or persons as are or shall be therein restrained by vs, oure heires and successours, or any law or statute of this realme: and also to shipp and transport all and all manner of goods, chattels, merchandizes, and other things whatsoever, that are or shall bee vsefull or necessary ffor the sayd Plantations, and defence thereof, and vsually transported, and nott prohibited by any lawe or statute of this our realme; yielding and paying vnto vs, our heires and successours, such the duties, customes and subsidies, as are or ought to bee payd or payable for the same.

And ffurther, our will and pleasure is, and wee doe, ffor us, our heires and suc- *Liberties of* cessours, ordeyn, declare and graunt, vnto the sayd Governour and Company, and *inhabitants* their successours, that all and every the subjects of vs, our heires and successours, which are already planted and settled within our sayd Collony of Providence Plantations, or which shall hereafter goe to inhabit within the sayd Collony, and all and every of theire children, which have byn borne there, or which shall happen hereafter to bee borne there, or on the sea, goeing thither, or retourneing from thence, shall have and enjoye all libertyes and immunityes of ffree and naturall subjects within any the dominions of vs, our heires or successours, to all intents, constructions and purposes, whatsoever, as if they, and every of them, were borne within the realme of England. And ffurther, know ye, that wee, of our more abundant grace, certain knowledge and *Territory of* meere motion, have given, graunted and confirmed, and, by these presents, for vs, our *the province* heires and successours, doe give, graunt and confirme, vnto the sayd Governour and

Company, and theire successours, all that parte of our dominiones in New-England, in America, conteyneing the Nahantick and Nanhyganset Bay, and countryes and partes adjacent, bounded on the west, or westerly, to the middle or channel of a river there, commonly called and known by the name of Pawcatuck, alias Pawcawtuck river, and soe along the sayd river, as the greater or middle streame thereof reacheth or lyes vpp into the north countrye, northward, vnto the head thereoof, and from thence, by a streight lyne drawn due north, vntill itt meets with the south lyne of the Massachusetts Collonie; and on the north, or northerly, by the aforesayd south or southerly lyne of the Massachusettes Collony or Plantation, and extending towards the east, or eastwardly, three English miles to the east and north-east of the most eastern and north-eastern parts of the aforesayd Narragansett Bay, as the sayd bay lyeth or extendeth itself from the ocean on the south, or southwardly, vnto the mouth of the river which runneth towards the towne of Providence, and from thence along the eastwardly side or banke of the sayd river (higher called by the name of Seacunck river), vp to the ffalls called Patuckett ffalls, being the most westwardly lyne of Plymouth Collony, and soe from the sayd ffalls, in a streight lyne, due north, untill itt meete with the aforesayd line of the Massachusetts Collony; and bounded on the south by the ocean: and, in particular, the lands belonging to the townes of Providence, Pawtuxet, Warwicke, Misquammacok, alias Pawcatuck, and the rest vpon the maine land in the tract aforesayd, together with Rhode-Island, Blocke-Island, and all the rest of the islands and banks in the Narragansett Bay, and bordering vpon the coast of the tract aforesayd (Ffisher's Island only excepted), together with all firme lands, soyles, grounds, havens, ports, rivers, waters, ffishings, mines royall, and all other mynes, mineralls, precious stones, quarries, woods, wood-grounds, rocks, slates, and all and singular other commodities, jurisdictions, royalties, priviledges, franchises, preheminences and hereditaments, whatsoever, within the sayd tract, bounds, landes, and islands, aforesayd, or to them or any of them belonging, or in any wise appertaining: *to have and to hold the same,* vnto the sayd Governour and Company, and their successours, forever, vpon trust, for the vse and benefitt of themselves and their associates, ffreemen of the sayd Collony, their heires and assignes, to be holden of vs, our heires and successours, as of the Mannor of East-Greenwich, in our county of Kent, in free and comon soccage, and not in capite, nor by knight service; yeilding and paying therefor, to vs, our heires and successours, only the ffifth part of all the oare of gold and silver which, from tyme to tyme, and att all tymes hereafter, shall bee there gotten, had or obtained, in lieu and satisfaction of all services, duties, ffynes, forfeitures, made or to be made, claimes and demands, whatsoever, to bee to vs, our heires or successours, therefor or thereout rendered, made or paid; any graunt, or clause in a late graunt, to the Governour and Company of Connecticutt Colony, in America, to the contrary thereof in any wise notwithstanding; the aforesayd Pawcatuck river haveing byn yielded, after much debate, for the fixed and certain boundes betweene these our sayd Colonies, by the agents thereof; whoe have alsoe agreed, that the sayd Pawcatuck river shall bee alsoe called alias Norrogansett or Narrogansett river; and, to prevent future disputes, that otherwise might arise thereby, forever hereafter shall bee construed,

CHARTER OF RHODE ISLAND

deemed and taken to bee the Narragansett river in our late graunt to Connecticutt Colony mentioned as the easterly bounds of that Colony. *And further,* our will and pleasure is, that in all matters of publique controversy which may fall out betweene our Colony of Providence Plantations, and the rest of our Colonies in New-England, itt shall and may bee lawfull to and for the Governour and Company of the sayd Colony of Providence Plantations to make their appeales therein to vs, our heirs and successours, for redresse in such cases, within this our realme of England: and that itt shall bee lawfull to and for the inhabitants of the sayd Colony of Providence Plantations, without let or molestation, to passe and repasse with freedome, into and thorough the rest of the English Collonies, vpon their lawfull and civill occasions, and to converse, and hold commerce and trade, with such of the inhabitants of our other English Collonies as shall bee willing to admit them thereunto, they behaveing themselves peaceably among them; any act, clause or sentence, in any of the sayd Collonies provided, or that shall bee provided, to the contrary in anywise notwithstanding. *And lastly, wee doe,* for vs, our heires and successours, ordeyne and graunt vnto the sayd Governor and Company, and their successours, and by these presents, that these our letters patent shall be firme, good, effectuall and available in all things in the lawe, to all intents, constructions and purposes whatsoever, according to our true intent and meaning hereinbefore declared; and shall bee construed, reputed and adjudged in all cases most favorably on the behalfe, and for the benefitt and behoofe, of the sayd Governor and Company, and their successours; although *express mention* of the true yearly value or certainty of the premises, or any of them, or of any other gifts or graunts by vs, or by any of our progenitors or predecessors heretofore made to the sayd Governor and Company of the English Colony of Rhode-Island and Providence Plantations, in the Narragansett Bay, New-England, in America, in these presents is not made, or any statute, act, ordinance, provision, proclamation or restriction, heretofore had, made, enacted, ordeyned or provided, or any other matter, cause or thing whatsoever, to the contrary thereof in anywise notwithstanding. *In witnes* whereof, wee have caused these our letters to bee made patent. *Witnes* our Selfe att Westminster, the eighth day of July, in the ffifteenth yeare of our reigne.

Construction of charter

By the King:

HOWARD.

REFERENCES

Andrews, Charles M. *The Colonial Period of American History.* 3 vols. New Haven: Yale University Press, 1934-37. I, chap. 21; II, chaps. 1, 2.

Channing, Edward. *A History of the United States.* 6 vols. New York: Macmillan Co., 1927-30. I, chap. 13.

Osgood, Herbert L. *The American Colonies in the Seventeenth Century.* 3 vols. New York: Macmillan Co., 1904-7. I, chap. 8.

XIII. CONCESSIONS AND AGREEMENTS OF WEST NEW JERSEY
1677

Origins   On March 12, 1664, Charles II granted to his brother, James, Duke of York, the territory constituting New York and New Jersey.[1] In June of the same year the boundaries of New Jersey were established, and that tract of land was conveyed by the Duke of York to two prominent members of the court of Charles II, Lord John Berkeley and Sir George Carteret, "in as full and ample manner as the same is granted to the said Duke of York."[2]

Concession and Agreement of 1664   In an effort to attract colonists, Berkeley and Carteret issued the Concession and Agreement of February, 1664.[3] That document defined the framework of the government and was in effect until the province was divided between the proprietors in 1676. Land was offered on easy terms to the settlers and liberty of conscience was promised. The clause on religion was similar to that contained in the Rhode Island Charter of 1663.[4] A legislative assembly was

---

[1] New Jersey was not marked off in any way from the adjacent territories in this grant. The grant also included Long Island, certain lands in New England, and the mainland from the west bank of the Connecticut River to the east side of Delaware Bay. Edwin P. Tanner, *The Province of New Jersey, 1664-1738* (New York, 1908), 2.

[2] Francis N. Thorpe (ed.), *The Federal and State Constitutions, Colonial Charters, and Other Orgánic Laws* (Washington, 1909), V, 2534. The legal status of the documents issued by the New Jersey proprietors is questionable because there was no provision in the grant from the king to the Duke of York authorizing him to delegate his powers of government. The letter of 1672 from Charles II to Deputy Governor Berry probably did not constitute a legal acknowledgment of the proprietors' right to govern, and in any event the effect of the letter was destroyed by the Dutch occupation in 1673. The letter of June 13, 1674, to Carteret from Charles II, commanding all persons to comply with the laws that had been established, apparently implied that Carteret had a valid claim to govern all of New Jersey. That letter, however, was unofficial and was soon followed by the second grant to the Duke of York in June, 1674, in terms identical to the grant of 1664. Herbert L. Osgood, *The American Colonies in the Seventeenth Century* (New York, 1904), II, 169-71; Tanner, *op. cit.*, 7-8.

[3] Text in Thorpe, *op. cit.*, V, 2535-44.

[4] See pp. 169-79.

CONCESSIONS OF WEST NEW JERSEY

created with power to make all laws, acts, and constitutions as might be necessary for the government of the province, provided "that the same be consonant to reason, and as near as may be conveniently agreeable to the laws and customs of his majesty's kingdom of England."[5] It was also provided that no laws should be made contrary to the provision securing religious liberty. The assembly was given power to erect courts and prescribe their jurisdictions and to provide for the defense of the province. It was also declared that there should be no imposition of "any tax, custom, subsidy, tallage, assessment, or any other duty whatsoever upon any colour or pretence, upon the said Province and inhabitants thereof, other than what shall be imposed by the authority and consent of the General Assembly, and then only in manner as aforesaid."[6]

The liberality and democratic spirit of the Concession had much to do with the rapid settlement of New Jersey. As early as 1666 a number of Puritan settlers from New Haven, Connecticut, and elsewhere in New England received land in the northeastern part of the province. The first legislative assembly convened by the proprietors met in November, 1668, at Elizabethtown, and a number of laws were passed which showed the influence of the recent Puritan immigrants.[7]

Founding of West Jersey

Berkeley had little interest in America, and his only desire was to come out of the venture without showing a loss. In March, 1674, he sold his undivided share of New Jersey to two Quakers, John Fenwick and Edward Byllinge, for the sum of £1,000.[8] By the Quintipartite Deed of 1676[9] New Jersey was divided between Carteret and the Quakers. William Penn, a close associate of Byllinge, became the most influential of the Quaker proprietors. His co-proprietors were Byllinge, Gawen Lawrie, and Nicholas Lucas. The Quakers controlled West Jersey, and Carteret became sole proprietor of East Jersey.

Concessions of 1677

The Charter or Fundamental Laws of West New Jersey is found in Chapters XIII to XXIII of the Concessions and Agreements of the pro-

[5] Thorpe, *op. cit.*, V, 2538.

[6] *Ibid.*, 2540.

[7] Tanner, *op. cit.*, 83-84; Osgood, *op. cit.*, II, 177.

[8] The legal validity of this transfer was questionable inasmuch as the reconquest by the Dutch in July, 1673, had extinguished all English claims to the land. Tanner, *op. cit.*, 6. The rights of the Quaker proprietors were not finally settled until 1680 when the Duke of York surrendered his claims under his second grant from Charles II, 1674. *Ibid.*, 130-32.

[9] Thorpe, *op. cit.*, V, 2551-60. Inasmuch as the Quakers had no valid claim to New Jersey, this document was technically of no validity. Tanner, *op. cit.*, 11.

181

prietors, freeholders, and inhabitants of March 3, 1677. The Concessions and Agreements were, in all probability, drawn by William Penn,[10] and the document embodied many of the principles of civil government held by the Quakers. Of special interest is the clause which declared that the document should be considered as the fundamental law of the colony which the legislature might not change. In addition, freedom of conscience was secured, trial by jury was guaranteed, imprisonment for debt was abolished, and provisions were included to ensure that trials should be conducted fairly. The assembly was to consist of one hundred members elected annually by the proprietors, freeholders, and inhabitants, and a large measure of power was placed in that body. Members of the assembly were required to vote in accordance with the instructions from their constituents. The proprietors reserved almost no special powers for themselves.

Effects

The legal validity of the Charter or Fundamental Laws, as of all other documents issued by the New Jersey proprietors, is questionable.[11] The document was never fully put into effect because of the confusion caused by a dispute with Governor Edmund Andros of New York and an attempted usurpation of power by Edward Byllinge. During the first few years, the affairs of the colony were managed by commissioners named by the proprietors, and an assembly was not called until November, 1681.[12] One of the first enactments of the assembly was a set of "fundamentals" which were to be held inviolable in the colony.[13] That document showed the influence of the Charter or Fundamental Laws of 1677. It also contained several clauses guaranteeing rights which the Whig party in England was struggling at that time to secure for English subjects.[14] The "fundamentals" provided for the annual meeting of a general assembly consisting of representatives chosen by the people; the veto power over laws was denied to the governor; the governor and council were forbidden to make war or to maintain military forces without the consent of the general assembly; all laws had to receive the approval of the assembly; the assembly was not to be dissolved before a year after election without its consent; no taxes could be raised without the consent of the assembly; officers of state were to be nominated and elected by the assembly, and were accountable to that body; taxes and customs were limited in duration to one year; liberty of conscience was

Fundamental laws of 1681

[10] Tanner, *op. cit.*, 113.
[11] See notes 1, 8, and 9.
[14] See p. 223.
[12] Tanner, *op. cit.*, 115-16.
[13] Text in Thorpe, *op. cit.*, V, 2565-67.

granted to all people of the province; and no person could be disqualified from holding public office because of his religious convictions. West Jersey continued to be governed under the "fundamentals" until 1702, at which time the proprietary government was surrendered and East and West Jersey were united as a crown colony.[15]

Influence of Magna Carta

The general influence of Magna Carta upon colonial lawmakers has been noted elsewhere.[16] The effect of that document during the period following the Restoration in England was probably nowhere more apparent than in New Jersey. The Capital Laws of East Jersey of 1675 provided: "Concerning taking away of a man's life, it is enacted by this present General Assembly, that no man's life shall be taken away under any pretence but by virtue of some law established in this Province, and that it be proved by the mouth of two or three witnesses."[17] The Charter or Fundamental Laws of 1677 contained a provision based upon the same document.[18] The Fundamental Constitutions of East Jersey, 1683, provided: "That no person or persons within the said Province shall be taken and imprisoned, or be devised of his freehold, free custom or liberty, or be outlawed or exiled, or any other way destroyed; nor shall they be condemn'd or judgment pass'd upon them, but by lawful judgment of their peers: neither shall justice nor right be bought or sold, defered or delayed, to any person whatsoever . . ."[19] The laws of East Jersey of 1698 provided: "That no man of what condition or estate sover shall be put out of his lands, tenements, nor taken nor imprisoned, nor disinherited, nor banished, nor anyways destroyed or molested without being first brought to answer by due course of law. . . ."[20]

The Charter or Fundamental Laws of 1677 thus shows the influence of Quaker ideas of government. It also illustrates the fact that, even though the laws of England as a body were not in force in the colonies, those laws, particularly Magna Carta, were often looked to as the source of the protection of individual liberties.

[15] Joseph Story, *Commentaries on the Constitution of the United States* (4th ed.; Boston, 1873), I, 81.

[16] See pp. 9-10, 101, 145-47.

[17] Aaron Leaming and Jacob Spicer (eds.), *The Grants, Concessions, and Original Constitutions of the Province of New Jersey* (2d ed.; Somerville, N. J., 1881), 107.

[18] See pp. 184-88.

[19] Leaming and Spicer, *op. cit.*, 163.

[20] *Ibid.*, 371-72.

CONCESSIONS AND AGREEMENTS OF WEST NEW JERSEY[21]

March 13, 1677

THE CHARTER OR FUNDAMENTAL LAWS, OF WEST NEW JERSEY, AGREED UPON.

Chapter XIII

THAT THESE FOLLOWING CONCESSIONS ARE THE COMMON LAW, OR FUNDAMENTAL RIGHTS, OF THE PROVINCE OF WEST NEW JERSEY.

Fundamental rights and privileges not to be altered by legislature

THAT the common law or fundamental rights and privileges of West New Jersey, are individually agreed upon by the Proprietors and freeholders thereof, to be the foundation of the government, which is not to be altered by the Legislative authority, or free Assembly hereafter mentioned and constituted, but that the said Legislative authority is constituted according to these fundamentals, to make such laws as agree with, and maintain the said fundamentals, and to make no laws that in the least contradict, differ or vary from the said fundamentals, under what pretence or alligation soever.

Chapter XIV

Persons attempting to subvert fundamentals shall be deemed traitors

BUT if it so happen that any person or persons of the said General Assembly, shall therein designedly, willfully, and maliciously, move or excite any to move, any matter or thing whatsoever, that contradicts or any ways subverts, any fundamentals of the said laws in the Constitution of the government of this Province, it being proved by seven honest and and reputable persons, he or they shall be proceeded against as traitors to the said government.

[21] Leaming and Spicer, *op. cit.*, 393-98. The date used here is determined in accordance with modern reckoning.

Chapter XV

THAT these Concessions, law or great charter of fundamentals, be recorded in a fair table, in the Assembly House, and that they be read at the beginning and dissolving of every general free Assembly: And it is further agreed and ordained, that the said Concessions, common law, or great charter of fundamentals, be writ in fair tables, in every common hall of justice within this Province, and that they be read in solemn manner four times every year, in the presence of the people, by the chief magistrates of those places.

Concessions to be read and published

Chapter XVI

THAT no men, nor number of men upon earth, hath power or authority to rule over men's consciences in religious matters, therefore it is consented, agreed and ordained, that no person or persons whatsoever within the said Province, at any time or times hereafter, shall be any ways upon any pretence whatsoever, called in question, or in the least punished or hurt, either in person, estate, or priviledge, for the sake of his opinion, judgment, faith or worship towards God in matters of religion. But that all and every such person, and persons, may from time to time, and at all times, freely and fully have, and enjoy his and their judgements, and the exercises of their consciences in matters of religious worship throughout all the said Province.

Liberty of conscience

Chapter XVII

THAT no Proprietor, freeholder or inhabitant of the said Province of West New Jersey, shall be deprived or condemned of life, limb, liberty, estate, property or any ways hurt in his or their privileges, freedoms or franchises, upon any account whatsoever, without a due tryal, and judgment passed by twelve good and lawful men of his neighbourhood first had: And that in all causes to be tryed, and in all tryals, the person or persons, arraigned may except against any of the said neighbourhood, without any reason rendered, (not exceeding thirty five) and in case of any valid reason alleged, against every person nominated for that service.

Trial by jury

Chapter XVIII

AND that no Proprietor, freeholder, freedenison, or inhabitant in the said Province, shall be attached, arrested, or imprisoned, for or by reason of any debt, duty, or thing whatsoever (cases felonious, criminal and treasonable excepted) before he or she have personal summon or summons, left at his or her last dwelling place, if in the

Service of process.

said Province, by some legal authorized officer, constituted and appointed for that purpose, to appear in some court of judicature for the said Province, with a full and plain account of the cause or thing in demand, as also the name or names of the person or persons at whose suit, and the court where he is to appear, and that he hath at least fourteen days time to appear and answer the said suit, if he or she live or inhabit within forty miles English of the said court, and if at a further distance, to have for every twenty miles, two days time more, for his and their appearance, and so proportionably for a larger distance of place.

Arrest That upon the recording of the summons, and non-appearance of such person and persons, a writ or attachment shall or may be issued out to arrest, or attach the person or persons of such defaulters, to cause his or their appearance in such court, returnable at a day certain, to answer the penalty or penalties, in such suit or suits; and if he or they shall be condemned by legal tryal and judgment, the penalty or penalties shall be paid and satisfied out of his or their real or personal estate so condemned, or cause the person or persons so condemned, to lie in execution till satisfaction of the debt and damages be made. *Provided always,* if such person or persons so condemned, shall pay and deliver such estate, goods, and chattles which he or any other person hath for his or their use, and shall solemnly declare and aver, that he or they have not any further estate, goods or chattles wheresoever, to satisfy the person or persons, (at whose suit, he or they are condemned) their respective judgments, and shall also bring and produce three other persons as compurgators, who are well known and of honest reputation, and approved of by the commissioners of that division, where they dwell or inhabit, which shall in such open court, likewise solemnly declare and aver, that they believe in their consciences, such person and persons so condemned, have not werewith further to pay the said condemnation or condemnations, he or they shall be thence forthwith discharged from their said imprisonment, any law or custom to the contrary thereof, heretofore in the said Province, notwithstanding. And upon such summons and default of appearance, recorded as aforesaid, and such person and persons not appearing within forty days after, it shall and may be lawful for such court of judicature to proceed to tryal, of twelve lawful men to judgment, against such defaulters, and issue forth execution against his or their estate, real and personal, to satisfy such penalty or penalties, to such debt and damages so recorded, as far as it shall or may extend.

Chapter XIX

Justices to sit with jurors THAT there shall be in every court, three justices or commissioners, who shall sit with the twelve men of the neighbourhood, with them to hear all causes, and to assist the said twelve men of the neighbourhood in case of law; and that they the said justices shall pronounce such judgment as they shall receive from, and be directed by the said twelve men, in whom only the judgment resides, and not otherwise.

And in case of their neglect and refusal, that then one of the twelve, by consent of the rest, pronounce their own judgment as the justices should have done.

And if any judgment shall be past, in any case civil or criminal, by any other person or persons, or any other way, then according to this agreement and appointment, it shall be held null and void, and such person or persons so presuming to give judgment, shall be severely fin'd, and upon complaint made to the General Assembly, by them be declared incapable of any office or trust within this Province.

Chapter XX

THAT in all matters and causes, civil and criminal, proof is to be made by the solemn and plain averment, of at least two honest and reputable persons; and in case that any person or persons shall bear false witness, and bring in his or their evidence, contrary to the truth of the matter as shall be made plainly to appear, that then every such person or persons, shall in civil causes, suffer the penalty which would be due to the person or persons he or they bear witness against. And in case any witness or witnesses, on the behalf of any person or persons, indicted in a criminal cause, shall be found to have born false witness for fear, gain, malice or favour, and thereby hinder the due execution of the law, and deprive the suffering person or persons of their due satisfaction, that then and in all other cases of false evidence, such person or persons, shall be first severly fined, and next that he or they shall forever be disabled from being admitted in evidence, or into any publick office, employment, or service within this Province. *Testimony of two witnesses* *Perjury*

Chapter XXI

THAT all and every person and persons whatsoever, who shall prosecute or prefer any indictment or information against others for any personal injuries, or matter criminal, or shall prosecute for any other criminal cause, (treason, murther, and felony, only excepted) shall and may be master of his own process, and have full power to forgive and remit the person or persons offending against him or herself only, as well before as after judgment, and condemnation, and pardon and remit the sentence, fine and punishment of the person or persons offending, be it personal or other whatsoever. *Termination of prosecution and remission of sentence by person offended*

Chapter XXII

THAT the tryals of all causes, civil and criminal, shall be heard and decided by the virdict or judgment of twelve honest men of the neighbourhood, only to be summoned and presented by the sheriff of that division, or propriety where the fact or trespass is committed; and that no person or persons shall be compelled to fee any attorney *Summoning of juries*

Party may plead own cause

Fees

or councillor to plead his cause, but that all persons have free liberty to plead his own cause, if he please: And that no person nor persons imprisoned upon any account whatsoever within this Province, shall be obliged to pay any fees to the officer or officers of the said prison, either when committed or discharged.

Chapter XXIII

Courts to be open

THAT in all publick courts of justice for tryals of causes, civil or criminal, any person or persons, inhabitants of the said Province may freely come into, and attend the said courts, and hear and be present, at all or any such tryals as shall be there had or passed, that justice may not be done in a corner nor in any covert manner, being intended and resolved, by the help of the Lord, and by these our Concessions and Fundamentals, that all and every person and persons inhabiting the said Province, shall, as far as in us lies, be free from oppression and slavery.

REFERENCES

Andrews, Charles M. *The Colonial Period of American History.* 3 vols. New Haven: Yale University Press, 1934-37. III, chap. 4.

Mulford, Isaac S. *History of New Jersey.* Camden: Keen and Chandler, 1848.

Osgood, Herbert L. *The American Colonies in the Seventeenth Century.* 3 vols. New York: Macmillan Co., 1904-7. II, chap. 8.

Tanner, Edwin P. *The Province of New Jersey, 1664-1738.* New York: Columbia University Press, 1908.

XIV. HABEAS CORPUS ACT
1679

The writ of habeas corpus is a procedure for bringing prisoners before a court for the purpose of inquiring into the legality of their commitment. It is not, strictly speaking, one of the individual's primary liberties as a citizen. It is instead a mechanism for the protection of the basic right of personal liberty. The writ deserves its high status as part of the fundamental law embodied in the Constitution of the United States because of its distinguished history as an effective safeguard of that right. The history of the right of personal liberty, of course, began before the writ of habeas corpus was originated. The right was granted, at least to some English subjects, by chapter 39 of Magna Carta, which provided that no freeman should be arrested, imprisoned, or destroyed except by the judgment of his peers or by the law of the land.[1] Fourteenth-century statutes extended that right to all subjects and stated that no one could be deprived of his liberty without "due process of law."[2] It was not until the seventeenth century, however, that the writ of habeas corpus became fully established as an effective means for the protection of that right. In that century in England, as Lord Macaulay expressed it, "what was needed was not a new right, but a prompt and searching remedy."[3] The remedy was provided by strengthening the writ of habeas corpus. In 1628 John Selden called the writ "the highest remedy in law, for any man that is imprisoned,"[4] and in 1670 Chief Justice Vaughan called it "the most usual remedy by which a man is restored again to his liberty, if he

Habeas corpus and personal liberty

---

[1] See p. 17.
[2] See p. 6.
[3] Thomas Macaulay, *The History of England*, ed. Charles H. Firth (London, 1913-15), I, 237.
[4] *State Trials* (T. B. Howell, comp.), III, 95.

have been against law deprived of it."[5] A series of statutes in the seventeenth century made of this writ what has been called "the most efficient protection ever invented for the liberty of the subject."[6] The most important of these statutes was the Habeas Corpus Act of 1679.

In America the colonists claimed the writ as one of the "rights of Englishmen" to which they were entitled under their charters and by reason of the common law. As a result, the privilege of the writ of habeas corpus came to be incorporated into the constitutions adopted by the states at the time of the American Revolution, and it is also protected by the Constitution of the United States.

Origin of writ of habeas corpus

During the medieval period the courts developed several writs designed to secure the release of prisoners on bail in certain types of cases. For one reason or another, however, these had become ineffective and had fallen into disuse by the end of the sixteenth century.[7] When the liberty of the subject was being threatened by the despotism of the Stuart kings in the seventeenth century, the lawyers of that day turned to the writ of habeas corpus as the best device available for combating arbitrary imprisonment by the crown.

The writ of habeas corpus is of ancient origin, but in its earliest forms it was not intended to be a device for the protection of individual liberty. Instead, it was used for various procedural purposes in connection with the administration of civil as well as criminal justice. As early as the thirteenth century it was used, for example, as one of the intermediate steps in a judicial action for securing the appearance in court of the defendant. It was also used to summon juries.[8] Persons held unlawfully might appeal to the king's

---

[5] *Ibid.*, VI, 1002.

[6] William S. Holdsworth, *A History of English Law* (4th ed.; Boston, 1931), I, 227.

[7] The writ *de homine replegiando*, which dates from the first half of the thirteenth century, was directed to the sheriff or jailer for the purpose of obtaining the release of the prisoner on bail. If the prisoner had been taken to a distant county, the custodian was subject to summary imprisonment by a *capius in withernam*. The writ of *mainprize* could be directed to the sheriff or others with authority to bail the prisoner if they refused to do so. It directed the release of the prisoner in the custody of sureties responsible for his appearance. Both writs were of little importance in the controversies of the seventeenth century because they could not be used to release persons imprisoned at the command of the king. The writ *de odio et atia*, which chapter 36 of Magna Carta directed should be issued without charge, was used to secure the release on bail of persons imprisoned on appeals of felony where the charge had been preferred "of spite and hatred." This writ fell into disuse as the cumbersome procedure of the appeal became obsolete. *Ibid.*, IX, 105-8; Edward Jenks, "The Story of *Habeas Corpus*," *Select Essays in Anglo-American Legal History* (Boston, 1908), II, 533-35.

[8] Holdsworth, *op. cit.*, IX, 108-9. The early forms of the writ were *habeas corpus ad respondendum*, which was directed to the sheriff holding a prisoner under the process of an inferior court to secure the appearance of a defendant to a civil action in a higher court, and *habeas corpus ad subjiciendum et recipiendum*, which was directed to the person holding in custody a prisoner held on a criminal

courts for their release and sometimes obtain it, but there was no established machinery for this purpose.[9] It was not until the fifteenth and sixteenth centuries that the writ of habeas corpus came into prominence. This occurred because the common law courts, in their struggle for power over the rival central courts—the Chancery, the Star Chamber, the High Commission, and the Admiralty—used it for the purpose of obtaining jurisdiction over cases handled by the other courts and thus increasing their own importance.[10]

It was in the sixteenth century that the writ of habeas corpus began to attain its modern character. In that century the common law courts began to use the writ to release prisoners unlawfully held by the process of other courts. This practice was confirmed in 1592 by a pronouncement of the judges known as *The Resolution in Anderson*.[11] It can be said, therefore, that at the close of the sixteenth century the writ of habeas corpus had become established as a remedy available as of right for all prisoners for the purpose of bringing before the courts the question of the legality of their imprisonment.[12]

Although the writ was thus available to bring prisoners before the court, it did not yet afford complete protection against arbitrary imprisonment. The reason was that if the return to the writ showed that the prisoner was

The Petition of Right, 1628

---

charge wanted to appear as a defendant in pending proceedings. *Ibid.*, IX, 111. The *habeas corpus ad subjiciendum* in an immature form can be traced as early as the first year of the reign of King John (1199-1216). John C. Fox, "Process of Imprisonment at Common Law," *Law Quarterly Review*, XXXIX (January, 1923), 54, 58-59.

[9] Frederick Pollock and Frederic W. Maitland, *The History of English Law* (2d ed.; Cambridge, England, 1911), II, 586-87.

[10] At first the writ of habeas corpus was used as an accompaniment of the writ of *certiorari*, by which the actions of an inferior court might be brought before a higher court, and the writ of privilege, by which a person privileged to be sued only in a certain tribunal might have his case removed to that tribunal. It was not until the end of the sixteenth century that habeas corpus became independent of these writs. Holdsworth, *op. cit.*, IX, 109-11; Jenks, *op. cit.*, 538-44.

[11] The application of this resolution was extensively argued in the case of the *Five Knights*, see pp. 64-66. The version of the resolution approved by Coke during the debates in Parliament in 1628 stated: ". . . And where it pleased your lordships to will divers of us to set down in what cases a prisoner, sent to custody by her majesty, [or] her council, . . . are to be detained in prison, and not to be delivered by her majesty's courts or judges; we think that if any person be committed by her majesty's command, from her person, or by order from the council board; or if any one or two of her council commit one for high treason; such persons so in the case before committed, may not be delivered by any of her courts, without due trial by the law, and judgment of acquittal had; nevertheless the judges may award the queen's writs to bring the bodies of such prisoners before them; and if upon return thereof, the causes of their commitment be certified to the judges as it ought to be, then the judges in the cases before, ought not to deliver him, but to remand him to the place from whence he came, which cannot conveniently be done, unless notice of the cause in generality, or else specially be given to the keeper or gaoler that shall have the custody of such prisoner." Quoted in Holdsworth, *op. cit.*, VI, 32-33.

[12] *Ibid.*, 33; Jenks, *op. cit.*, 544.

being held for a cause for which he could not be bailed, the court had to return him to prison. The principal obstacle to the effective use of the writ in the seventeenth century was the rule that persons committed by the command of the king or his Council might be held without cause.[13] Thus, although the court might grant the writ and bring the prisoner into court, if the sheriff's return to the writ showed that the prisoner was being held at the command of the king he would be denied bail and returned to prison. This was the point established in 1627 by the *Five Knights' Case*.[14] This defect in the law was corrected by the Petition of Right, 1628.[15] The Petition declared that imprisonment by the command of the king without cause being shown for which the prisoner might make answer according to law was contrary to the principle of individual liberty guaranteed by Magna Carta. The Petition prohibited that practice of the Stuart kings.[16]

Abolition of the Star Chamber, 1641

The second great statute of the seventeenth century to strengthen the writ of habeas corpus was the act for the abolition of the Court of Star Chamber.[17] That statute abolished the Court of Star Chamber and other prerogative courts similarly constituted. It also eliminated the judicial functions of the Council. It did not, however, abolish the Council nor deprive it of its power to examine and commit accused persons before trial. This power to commit was made subject to an important limitation. It was provided in section VIII of the statute that the courts of King's Bench and

---

[13] The Statute of Westminster I, 1275, 3 Edw. 1, stat. 1, c. 15, was enacted to clear up uncertainties as to the power of sheriffs to admit prisoners to bail. Its provisions became the foundation of all later law on that subject. Among the offenders who could not be bailed were those arrested by command of the king. Holdsworth, *op. cit.*, IV, 526-27. During the conferences which led to the Petition of Right, Coke argued that the Statute of Westminster I applied only to proceedings in the sheriff's court, but other laws did not bear out this contention. Jenks, *op. cit.*, 545. The exception of persons imprisoned at the king's command was reaffirmed in *The Resolution in Anderson*, 1592. See p. 191, note 11.

[14] See pp. 64-66.

[15] See pp. 62-75.

[16] The connection made by the Petition of Right between Magna Carta and the writ of habeas corpus reflected Coke's thinking. He said, in his commentary on chapter 39 of Magna Carta: "Now it may be demanded, if a man be taken, or committed to prison *contra legem terrae*, against the law of the land, what remedy hath the party grieved? To this it is answered: . . . He may have an *habeas corpus* out of the kings bench or chancery, though there be no priviledge, &c. or in the court of common pleas, or eschequer, for any officer or priviledged person there; upon which writ the goaler must retourne, by whom he was committed, and the cause of his imprisonment, and if it appeareth that his imprisonment be just, and lawfull, he shall be remaunded to the former goaler, but if it shall appeare to the court, that he was imprisoned against the law of the land, they ought by force of this statute [Magna Carta] to deliver him: if it be doubtfull and under consideration, he may be bailed." *The Second Part of the Institutes of the Laws of England* (London, 1809), 54-55.

[17] See pp. 125-42.

Common Pleas must, upon the application of any person committed by the Council, issue a writ of habeas corpus, determine the legality of the commitment, and decide within three days whether to free, bail, or return the prisoner.

It was not until the Habeas Corpus Act of 1679 that the writ became fully established as an effective remedy in nearly all cases. The defects of the remedy which were disclosed after the Restoration in 1660 were possibly even more serious than those which had been corrected by the Petition of Right and the act for the abolition of the Court of Star Chamber.[18] Although there was considerable uncertainty as to the precise powers of the courts to issue the writ, a fact which showed that clarifying legislation was needed,[19] the real motive that led to the Habeas Corpus Act was furnished by the arbitrary imprisonment of political opponents ordered by Lord Clarendon, Charles II's chief minister. To avoid the service of writs of habeas corpus, he ordered the removal of prisoners from the kingdom, an act for which he was impeached in 1667.[20] A bill to prevent the refusal of habeas corpus was introduced in the House of Commons in 1668, and several other bills were taken under consideration during the next few years.[21] In 1679 the provisions of the bills designed to prevent removal of prisoners beyond the seas and the bills designed to improve the procedure on the writ were combined to form the Habeas Corpus Act. The House of Lords proposed certain amendments, and on the final day of the session agreement to the act was reached after conferences between the houses.

Habeas Corpus Act of 1679

The Habeas Corpus Act created no new right and introduced no new principle. Instead, it strengthened a right already existing by providing that the writ should be issued by the judges during vacations as well as in term time and that prisoners should be brought before the court promptly so that the legality of their imprisonment might be determined. In addition, imprisonment beyond the seas to avoid compliance with the writ was pro-

Effects

---

[18] Holdsworth, *op. cit.*, IX, 115.

[19] One of the principal areas of uncertainty was whether the writ could be issued in vacation as well as during term time. *Ibid.*, 115-16.

[20] The fourth article of the impeachment of Clarendon stated that he "advised and procured divers of his majesty's subjects to be imprisoned against law in remote islands, garrisons, and other places, thereby to prevent them from the benefit of the law, and to produce precedents for the imprisoning any other of his majesty's subjects in like manner." Quoted in Henry Hallam, *The Constitutional History of England* (5th ed.; New York, 1847), 406.

[21] Holdsworth, *op. cit.*, IX, 117.

hibited, and various procedural changes were made to make the writ a more effective safeguard. To assure compliance with the act severe penalties were provided for officials who refused to obey its terms.

Bill of Rights, 1689

The Habeas Corpus Act of 1679 provided the most effective safeguard of individual liberty that had been established up to that time. But one more step was yet to be taken in perfecting the writ of habeas corpus. James II resented the Habeas Corpus Act as an encroachment upon the authority of the crown and tried to have it repealed. In this he was unsuccessful, so his judges, who were subservient to his will, sought to evade it by requiring prisoners to provide bail in amounts they were unable to afford. This abuse led to the provision of the Bill of Rights of 1689 that excessive bail shall not be required.[22]

Habeas corpus in the American colonies

In the colonies the writ of habeas corpus was regarded as one of the rights of the individual guaranteed by the colonial charters and the English common law.[23] Writs were issued by the colonial courts much in the same manner as in England.[24] The Habeas Corpus Act of 1679, however, was not in effect in the colonies, and the writ was administered in accordance with the common law and the colonial bail laws.[25] Several attempts were made by the colonists, however, to secure the benefits of that act. The New York Charter of Liberties of 1683, later vetoed by the Privy Council, provided that the inhabitants of that colony should be governed according to the laws of England, a provision apparently intended to include the Habeas Corpus Act.[26] In 1692 Massachusetts passed a statute which was substantially the same as the Habeas Corpus Act.[27] Like the English act, that statute imposed heavy fines upon officials who failed to comply with its provisions. Unlike the Habeas Corpus Act, it provided that even in cases of treason and felony the prisoner should be released unless indicted at the next term of court. The statute was vetoed three years later by the Privy Council, but the writ of habeas corpus continued to be issued in Massachusetts as a common law

[22] See p. 247.

[23] For the effect of the colonial charters as guaranteeing the rights of Englishmen, see pp. 35-38.

[24] Rollin C. Hurd, *A Treatise on the Right of Personal Liberty and on the Writ of Habeas Corpus* (Albany, 1858), 116.

[25] English statutes enacted after the first settlement did not, in general, extend to the colonies unless the colonies were specifically mentioned therein or unless they were adopted by the colony. A. H. Carpenter, "Habeas Corpus in the Colonies," *American Historical Review*, VIII (October, 1902), 19-20.

[26] *Ibid.*, 21.

[27] *Acts and Resolves of the Province of Massachusetts Bay* (Boston, 1869), I, 95-99.

right of the individual. In 1692 South Carolina authorized the magistrates to put the Habeas Corpus Act into effect. That statute was disallowed by the proprietors, but it was apparently treated as in force in the colony. Another habeas corpus act was enacted in that colony in 1712, and it continued in force until the nineteenth century.[28] In 1710 the writ of habeas corpus was established as a right of the individual in Virginia by the instructions from Queen Anne to Governor Spotswood. The instructions embody much the same procedure as is found in the Habeas Corpus Act of 1679, but the only punishment for failure to carry out its provisions was the removal of the judges by the governor. Because no protection was provided against the possibility that an arbitrary governor might not enforce its provisions, the effectiveness of the right under the instructions was much less secure than under the English Habeas Corpus Act.

The establishment of the writ of habeas corpus in the Constitution of the United States came from a proposal made during the Federal Convention by Charles Pinckney of South Carolina. It stated:

> The privileges and benefit of the Writ of Habeas corpus shall be enjoyed in this Government in the most expeditious and ample manner; and shall not be suspended by the Legislature except upon the most urgent and pressing occasions, and for a limited time not exceeding _____ months.[29]

This and other proposals made by Pinckney were referred to the Committee of Detail without debate. Pinckney again pointed out the need of a constitutional safeguard of the writ, arguing "that it should not be suspended but on the most urgent occasions, & then only for a limited time not exceeding twelve months."[30] John Rutledge, also from South Carolina, spoke in favor of a declaration that the writ of habeas corpus should remain inviolable; he could not conceive that it could ever become necessary to suspend the writ. Gouverneur Morris of Pennsylvania summed up the discussion by moving the adoption of a clause which guarantees the right in almost the same words as were placed in the finished Constitution:

> The privilege of the writ of Habeas Corpus shall not be suspended, unless where in cases of Rebellion or invasion the public safety may require it.[31]

---

[28] Carpenter, *op. cit.*, 23.

[29] Max Farrand (ed.), *The Records of the Federal Convention of 1787* (New Haven, 1937), II, 341.

[30] *Ibid.*, 438.

[31] *Ibid.* See pp. 407, 412.

HABEAS CORPUS ACT[32]

May 27, 1679

Preamble

WHEREAS *great delays have been used by sheriffs, gaolers and other officers, to whose custody any of the King's subjects have been committed for criminal or supposed criminal matters, in making returns of writs of* habeas corpus *to them directed, by standing out an alias*[33] *and pluries*[34] habeas corpus, *and sometimes more, and by other shifts to avoid their yielding obedience to such writs, contrary to their duty and the known laws of the land, whereby many of the King's subjects have been and hereafter may be long detained in prison, in such cases where by law they are bailable, to their great charges and vexation:*

Prisoners to be brought before the court within three days after service of writ of habeas corpus

Exception of cases of felony and treason

II. For the prevention whereof, and the more speedy relief of all persons imprisoned for any such criminal or supposed criminal matters; (2) be it enacted by the King's most excellent majesty, by and with the advice and consent of the lords spiritual and temporal, and commons, in this present parliament assembled, and by the authority thereof, That whensoever any person or persons shall bring any *habeas corpus* directed unto any sheriff or sheriffs, gaoler, minister or other person whatsoever, for any person in his or their custody, and the said writ shall be served upon the said officer, or left at the gaol or prison with any of the under-officers, under-keepers or deputy of the said officers or keepers, that the said officer or officers, his or their under-officers, under-keepers or deputies, shall within three days after the service thereof as aforesaid (unless the commitment aforesaid were for treason or felony, plainly and specially expressed in the warrant of commitment) upon payment or tender of the charges of bringing the said prisoner, to be ascertained by the judge or court that awarded the same, and endorsed upon the said writ, not exceeding twelve pence *per* mile, and upon security given by his own bond to pay the charges of carrying back the prisoner, if he shall be remanded by the court or judge to which he shall be brought according to the true intent of this present act, and that he will not make any escape by the way, make return of such writ; (3) and bring or cause to be brought the body of the party so committed or restrained, unto or before the lord chancellor, or lord keeper of the great seal of *England* for the time being, or

---

[32] 31 Car. 2, c. 2. Danby Pickering (ed.), *Statutes at Large* (Cambridge, 1726-1807), VIII, 432-39.
[33] A second writ issued when the first was of no effect.
[34] A third writ issued when prior writs were of no effect.

the judges or barons of the said court from whence the said writ shall issue, or unto and before such other person or persons before whom the said writ is made returnable, according to the command thereof; (4) and shall then likewise certify the true causes of his detainer or imprisonment, unless the commitment of the said party be in any place beyond the distance of twenty miles from the place or places where such court or person is or shall be residing; and if beyond the distance of twenty miles, and not above one hundred miles, then within the space of ten days, and if beyond the distance of one hundred miles, then within the space of twenty days, after such delivery aforesaid, and not longer.

III. And to the intent that no sheriff, gaoler or other officer may pretend ignorance of the import of any such writ; (2) be it enacted by the authority aforesaid, That all such writs shall be marked in this manner, *Per statutum tricesimo primo Caroli secundi Regis,* and shall be signed by the person that awards the same; (3) and if any person or persons shall be or stand committed or detained as aforesaid, for any crime, unless for felony or treason plainly expressed in the warrant of commitment, in the vacation-time, and out of term, it shall and may be lawful to and for the person or persons so committed or detained (other than persons convict or in execution by legal process) or any one on his or their behalf, to appeal or complain to the lord chancellor or lord keeper, or any one of his Majesty's justices, either of the one bench or of the other, or the barons of the exchequer of the degree of the coif;[35] (4) and the said lord chancellor, lord keeper, justices or barons or any of them, upon view of the copy or copies of the warrant or warrants of commitment and detainer, or otherwise upon oath made that such copy or copies were denied to be given by such person or persons in whose custody the prisoner or prisoners is or are detained, are hereby authorized and required, upon request made in writing by such person or persons, or any on his, her or their behalf, attested and subscribed by two witnesses who were present at the delivery of the same, to award and grant an *habeas corpus* under the seal of such court whereof he shall then be one of the judges, (5) to be directed to the officer or officers in whose custody the party so committed or detained shall be, returnable *immediate* before the said lord chancellor or lord keeper, or such justice, baron or any other justice or baron of the degree of the coif of any of the said courts; (6) and upon service thereof as aforesaid, the officer or officers, his or their under-officer or under-officers, under-keeper or under-keepers, or their deputy, in whose custody the party is so committed or detained, shall within the times respectively before limited, bring such prisoner or prisoners before the said lord chancellor or lord keeper, or such justices, barons or one of them, before whom the said writ is made returnable, and in case of his absence before any other of them, with the return of such writ, and the true causes of the commitment and detainer; (7) and thereupon within two days after the party shall be brought before them, the said lord chancellor or lord keeper, or such justice or baron before whom the prisoner shall be brought as aforesaid, shall discharge the said prisoner from his imprisonment, taking his or their recognizance,

Identification of writ

Writ to be issued during vacation of court

[35] Of high standing.

with one or more surety or sureties, in any sum according to their discretions, having regard to the quality of the prisoner and nature of the offence, for his or their appearance in the court of King's bench the term following, or at the next assizes, sessions or general gaol-delivery of and for such county, city or place where the commitment was, or where the offence was committed, or in such other court where the said offence is properly cognizable, as the case shall require, and then shall certify the said writ with the return thereof, and the said recognizance or recognizances into the said court where such appearance is to be made; (8) unless it shall appear unto the said lord chancellor or lord keeper, or justice or justices, or baron or barons, that the party so committed is detained upon a legal process, order or warrant, out of some court that hath jurisdiction of criminal matters, or by some warrant signed and sealed with the hand and seal of any of the said justices or barons, or some justice or justices of the peace, for such matters or offences for the which by the law the prisoner is not bailable.

Excessive delay in applying for writ

IV. Provided always, and be it enacted, That if any person shall have wilfully neglected by the space of two whole terms after his imprisonment, to pray a *habeas corpus* for his enlargement, such person so wilfully neglecting shall not have any *habeas corpus* to be granted in vacation-time, in pursuance of this act.

Penalties for officials failing to comply with statute

V. And be it further enacted by the authority aforesaid, That if any officer or officers, his or their under-officer or under-officers, under-keeper or under-keepers, or deputy, shall neglect or refuse to make the returns aforesaid, or to bring the body or bodies of the prisoner or prisoners according to the command of the said writ, within the respective times aforesaid, or upon demand made by the prisoner or person in his behalf, shall refuse to deliver, or within the space of six hours after demand shall not deliver, to the person so demanding, a true copy of the warrant or warrants of commitment and detainer of such prisoner, which he and they are hereby required to deliver accordingly, all and every the head gaolers and keepers of such prisons, and such other person in whose custody the prisoner shall be detained, shall for the first offence forfeit to the prisoner or party grieved the sum of one hundred pounds; (2) and for the second offence the sum of two hundred pounds, and shall and is hereby made incapable to hold or execute his said office; (3) the said penalties to be recovered by the prisoner or party grieved, his executors or administrators, against such offender, his executors or administrators, by any action of debt, suit, bill, plaint or information, in any of the King's courts at *Westminster,* wherein no essoin,[36] protection, privilege, injunction, wager of law,[37] or stay of prosecution by *Non vult ulterius prosequi,* or otherwise, shall be admitted or allowed, or any more than one imparlance;[38] (4) and any recovery or judgment at the suit of any party grieved, shall be a sufficient conviction for the first offence; and any after recovery or judgment at the suit of a party grieved for any offence after the first judgment, shall be a sufficient conviction to bring the officers or person within the said penalty for the second offence.

[36] Excuse.
[37] The oath of the defendant supported by those of eleven neighbors, who were called "compurgators."
[38] A continuance or delay of the proceedings.

HABEAS CORPUS ACT

VI. And for the prevention of unjust vexation by reiterated commitments for the same offence; (2) be it enacted by the authority aforesaid, That no person or persons which shall be delivered or set at large upon any *habeas corpus,* shall at any time hereafter be again imprisoned or committed for the same offence by any person or persons whatsoever, other than by the legal order and process of such court wherein he or they shall be bound by recognizance to appear, or other court having jurisdiction of the cause; (3) and if any other person or persons shall knowingly contrary to this act recommit or imprison, or knowingly procure or cause to be recommitted or imprisoned, for the same offence or pretended offence, any person or persons delivered or set at large as aforesaid, or be knowingly aiding or assisting therein, then he or they shall forfeit to the prisoner or party grieved the sum of five hundred pounds; any colourable pretence or variation in the warrant or warrants of commitment notwithstanding, to be recovered as aforesaid.

Reimprisonment of persons released upon writ prohibited, except by order of court

VII. Provided always, and be it further enacted, That if any person or persons shall be committed for high treason or felony, plainly and specially expressed in the warrant of commitment, upon his prayer or petition in open court the first week of the term, or first day of the sessions of *oyer* and *terminer*[39] or general gaol-delivery,[40] to be brought to his trial, shall not be indicted some time in the next term, sessions of *oyer* and *terminer* or general gaol-delivery, after such commitment; it shall and may be lawful to and for the judges of the court of King's bench and justices of *oyer* and *terminer* or general gaol-deliverry, and they are hereby required, upon motion to them made in open court the last day of the term, sessions or gaol-delivery, either by the prisoner or any one in his behalf, to set at liberty the prisoner upon bail, unless it appear to the judges and justices upon oath made, that the witnesses for the King could not be produced the same term, sessions or general gaol-delivery; (2) and if any person or persons committed as aforesaid, upon his prayer or petition in open court the first week of the term or first day of the sessions of *oyer* and *terminer* and general gaol-delivery, to be brought to his trial, shall not be indicted and tried the second term, sessions of *oyer* and *terminer* or general gaol-delivery, after his commitment, or upon his trial shall be acquitted, he shall be discharged from his imprisonment.

Persons charged with treason or felony shall be indicted the next term or released on bail

Prisoners to be tried the second term or discharged

VIII. Provided always, That nothing in this act shall extend to discharge out of prison any person charged in debt, or other action, or with process in any civil cause, but that after he shall be discharged of his imprisonment for such his criminal offence, he shall be kept in custody according to the law, for such other suit.

Exception of civil cases

IX. Provided always, and be it enacted by the authority aforesaid, That if any person or persons, subjects of this realm, shall be committed to any prison or in custody of any officer or officers whatsoever, for any criminal or supposed criminal matter, that the said person shall not be removed from the said prison and custody into the custody of any other officer or officers; (2) unless it be by *habeas corpus* or some other legal writ; or where the prisoner is delivered to the constable or other

Restrictions upon removal of prisoners

---

[39] Trials of treason, felony, or misdemeanor.
[40] Trials of persons held in jails, or places of temporary confinement.

inferior officer to carry such prisoner to some common gaol; (3) or where any person is sent by order of any judge of assize [41] or justice of the peace, to any common workhouse or house of correction; (4) or where the prisoner is removed from one prison or place to another within the same county, in order to his or her trial or discharge in due course of law; (5) or in case of sudden fire or infection, or other necessity; (6) and if any person or persons shall after such commitment aforesaid make out and sign, or countersign any warrant or warrants for such removal aforesaid, contrary to this act; as well he that makes or signs, or countersigns such warrant or warrants, as the officer or officers that obey or execute the same, shall suffer and incur the pains and forfeitures in this act before mentioned, both for the first and second offence respectively, to be recovered in manner aforesaid by the party grieved.

Courts authorized to issue writs

X. Provided also, and be it further enacted by the authority aforesaid, That it shall and may be lawful to and for any prisoner and prisoners as aforesaid, to move and obtain his or their *habeas corpus* as well out of the high court of chancery or court of exchequer, as out of the courts of King's bench or common pleas, or either of them;

Penalty for judges failing to issue writ

(2) and if the said lord chancellor or lord keeper, or any judge or judges, baron or barons for the time being, of the degree of the coif, of any of the courts aforesaid, in the vacation time, upon view of the copy or copies of the warrant or warrants of commitment or detainer, or upon oath made that such copy or copies were denied as aforesaid, shall deny any writ of *habeas corpus* by this act required to be granted, being moved for as aforesaid, they shall severally forfeit to the prisoner or party grieved the sum of five hundred pounds, to be recovered in manner aforesaid.

Jurisdictions to which writ may be directed

XI. And be it declared and enacted by the authority aforesaid, That an *habeas corpus* according to the true intent and meaning of this act, may be directed and run into any county palatine,[42] the cinque-ports,[43] or other privileged places within the kingdom of *England,* dominion of *Wales,* or town of *Berwick* upon *Tweed,* and the islands of *Jersey* or *Guernsey;* any law or usage to the contrary notwithstanding.

Imprisonment beyond the seas prohibited

XII. And for preventing illegal imprisonments in prisons beyond the seas; (2) be it further enacted by the authority aforesaid, That no subject of this realm that now is, or hereafter shall be an inhabitant or resiant of this kingdom of *England,* dominion of *Wales,* or town of *Berwick* upon *Tweed,* shall or may be sent prisoner into *Scotland, Ireland, Jersey, Guernsey, Tangier,* or into parts, garrisons, islands or places beyond the seas, which are or at any time hereafter shall be within or without the dominions of his Majesty, his heirs or successors; (3) and that every such imprisonment is hereby enacted and adjudged to be illegal; (4) and that if any of the said subjects now is or hereafter shall be so imprisoned, every such person and persons so imprisoned, shall and may for every such imprisonment maintain by virtue of this act an action or actions of false imprisonment, in any of his Majesty's courts of record, against the person or

Remedies and penalties for failure to comply

---

[41] Courts presided over by judges on circuit under commission from the crown.

[42] Possessing royal privileges.

[43] Five ports on the southeast coast of England which possessed royal privileges.

persons by whom he or she shall be so committed, detained, imprisoned, sent prisoner or transported, contrary to the true meaning of this act, and against all or any person or persons that shall frame, contrive, write, seal or countersign any warrant or writing for such commitment, detainer, imprisonment or transportation, or shall be advising, aiding or assisting, in the same, or any of them; (5) and the plaintiff in every such action shall have judgment to recover his treble costs, besides damages, which damages so to be given, shall not be less than five hundred pounds; (6) in which action no delay stay or stop of proceeding by rule, order or command, nor no injunction, protection or privilege whatsoever, nor any more than one imparlance shall be allowed, excepting such rule of the court wherein the action shall depend, made in open court, as shall be thought in justice necessary, for special cause to be expressed in the said rule; (7) and the person or persons who shall knowingly frame, contrive, write, seal or countersign any warant for such commitment, detainer or transportation, or shall so commit, detain, imprison or transport any person or persons contrary to this act, or be any ways advising, aiding or assisting therein, being lawfully convicted thereof, shall be disabled from thenceforth to bear any office of trust or profit within the said realm of *England*, dominion of *Wales*, or town of *Berwick* upon *Tweed*, or any of the islands, territories or dominions thereunto belonging; (8) and shall incur and sustain the pains, penalties and forfeitures limited, ordained and provided in and by the statute of provision and praemunire[41] made in the sixteenth year of King *Richard* the Second; (9) and be incapable of any pardon from the King, his heirs or successors, of the said forfeitures, losses or disabilities, or any of them.

XIII. Provided always, That nothing in this act shall extend to give benefit to any person who shall by contract in writing agree with any merchant or owner of any plantation, or other person whatsoever, to be transported to any parts beyond the seas, and receive earnest upon such agreement, although that afterwards such person shall renounce such contract. *Exception of persons under contract*

XIV. Provided always, and be it enacted, That if any person or persons lawfully convicted of any felony, shall in open court pray to be transported beyond the seas, and the court shall think fit to leave him or them in prison for that purpose, such person or persons may be transported into any parts beyond the seas, this act or any thing therein contained to the contrary notwithstanding. *Exception of convicts desiring imprisonment beyond the seas*

XV. Provided also, and be it enacted, That nothing herein contained shall be deemed, construed or taken, to extend to the imprisonment of any person before the first day of *June* one thousand six hundred seventy and nine, or to any thing advised, procured, or otherwise done, relating to such imprisonment; any thing herein contained to the contrary notwithstanding. *Exception of imprisonments prior to June 1, 1679*

XVI. Provided also, That if any person or persons at any time resiant in this realm, shall have committed any capital offence in *Scotland* or *Ireland*, or any of the islands, or foreign plantations of the King, his heirs or successors, where he or she ought to be *Exception for trials of capital offenses committed in foreign lands*

[41] A statute imposing severe penalties for heinous offenses.

tried for such offence, such person or persons may be sent to such place, there to receive such trial, in such manner as the same might have been used before the making of this act; any thing herein contained to the contrary notwithstanding.

Limitation of actions

XVII. Provided also, and be it enacted, That no person or persons shall be sued, impleaded, molested, or troubled for any offence against this act, unless the party offending be sued or impleaded for the same within two years at the most after such time wherein the offence shall be committed, in case the party grieved shall not be then in prison; and if he shall be in prison, then within the space of two years after the decease of the person imprisoned, or his or her delivery out of prison, which shall first happen.

Return of writ to judges of assize after assizes proclaimed

XVIII. And to the intent no person may avoid his trial at the assizes or general gaol-delivery, by procuring his removal before the assizes, at such time as he cannot be brought back to receive his trial there; (2) be it enacted, That after the assizes proclaimed for that county where the prisoner is detained, no person shall be removed from the common gaol upon any *habeas corpus* granted in pursuance of this act, but upon any such *habeas corpus* shall be brought before the judge of assize in open court, who is thereupon to do what to justice shall appertain.

Termination of assizes

XIX. Provided nevertheless, That after the assizes are ended, any person or persons detained, may have his or her *habeas corpus* according to the direction and intention of this act.

Pleading in cases of alleged default

XX. And be it also enacted by the authority aforesaid, That if any information, suit or action shall be brought or exhibited against any person or persons for any offence committed or to be committed against the form of this law, it shall be lawful for such defendants to plead the general issue, that they are not guilty, or that they owe nothing, and to give such special matter in evidence to the jury that shall try the same, which matter being pleaded had been good and sufficient matter in law to have discharged the said defendant or defendants against the said information, suit or action, and the said matter shall be then as available to him or them, to all intents and purposes, as if he or they had sufficiently pleaded, set forth or alledged the same matter in bar or discharge of such information suit or action.

Exception of persons committed by justices of the peace in cases of petty treason or felony

XXI. *And because many times persons charged with petty treason or felony, or as accessaries thereunto, are committed upon suspicion only, whereupon they are bailable, or not, according as the circumstances making out that suspicion are more or less weighty, which are best known to the justices of peace that committed the persons, and have the examinations before them, or to other justices of the peace in the county;* (2) be it therefore enacted, That where any person shall appear to be committed by any judge or justice of the peace and charged as accessary before the fact, to any petty treason or felony, or upon suspicion thereof, or with suspicion of petty treason or felony, which petty treason or felony shall be plainly and specially expressed in the warrant of commitment, that such person shall not be removed or bailed by virtue of this act, or in any other manner than they might have been before the making of this act.

HABEAS CORPUS ACT

REFERENCES

Carpenter, A. H. "Habeas Corpus in the Colonies," *American Historical Review*, VIII (1903), 18-27.
Church, William S. *Writ of Habeas Corpus*. San Francisco: Bancroft-Whitney, 1893.
Fox, John C. "Process of Imprisonment at Common Law," *Law Quarterly Review*, XXXIX (1932), 54-59.
Hurd, Rollin C. *Writ of Habeas Corpus*. Albany: W. C. Little & Co., 1858.
Jenks, Edward. "The Story of the Habeas Corpus," *Select Essays in Anglo-American Legal History*. Boston, 1908. II, 531-48.
Relf, Francis H. *The Petition of Right*. Minneapolis: University of Minnesota, 1917.

XV. FRAME OF GOVERNMENT OF PENNSYLVANIA
1682

Origins   The frames of government of William Penn implanted on the American continent some of the Quaker ideas of government. They also helped make the colonists conscious of their English legal heritage during the period following the restoration in England of the Stuart dynasty. Penn had been impressed with the teachings of the Quakers during his youth in England. About 1668 he definitely announced his conversion to that faith. Like thousands of his fellow Quakers he was persecuted for his beliefs while in England. The manner in which he defended himself at the Old Bailey in 1670 provided a landmark in the development of individual liberties under the English constitution.[1]

Royal Charter of 1681   Penn's experiences in England led him to resolve to obtain land in the New World where he might conduct an experiment in society and govern-

---

[1] Following a meeting of the Friends at Gracechurch Street, William Penn and William Mead were indicted for a tumultuous assembly. Penn demanded to know on what law the indictment was founded. Upon being told that it was based upon the common law, the following dialogue occurred between him and the recorder:
"Penn: 'Where is that common-law?'
"Rec.: 'You must not think that I am able to run up so many years, and over so many adjudged cases, which we call common-law, to answer your curiosity.'
"Penn: 'This answer I am sure is very short of my question, for if it be common, it should not be so hard to produce.'" *Trials of Penn and Mead, State Trials* (T. B. Howell, comp.), VI, 951, 958 (1670).
Although Penn professed ignorance of the formality of the law, one of his answers showed a familiarity with the writings of Lord Coke: "Certainly, if the common law be so hard to be understood, it is far from being very common; but if the lord Coke in his Institutes be of any consideration, he tells us, That Common-Law is common right, and that Common Right is the Great Charter-Privileges: confirmed 9 Hen. 3, 29, 25 Edw. 1, 12 Ed. 3, 8 Coke Instit. 2 p. 56." *Ibid.*, 959. Although the jury found Penn not guilty, the mayor proposed to fine him for contempt of court. To this Penn replied: "I ask, if it be according to the fundamental laws of England, that any Englishman should be fined or amerced, but by the judgment of his peers or jury; since it expressly contradicts the 14th and 29th chapters of the Great Charter of England, which say, 'No freeman ought to be amerced but by the oath of good and lawful men of the vicinage.'" *Ibid.*, 968-69.

FRAME OF GOVERNMENT OF PENNSYLVANIA

ment in accordance with his ideas of religious and political freedom. He participated with other Quakers in the founding of West New Jersey,[2] but he soon desired even greater freedom to test his ideas of government. On March 4, 1681, he obtained a charter from Charles II which made him proprietor of the land north of Maryland and west of the Delaware River.[3] The land was given in consideration of a debt owed his father, Admiral William Penn, in memory of whom the province was named. The main features of the charter were similar to the Charter of Maryland of 1632 which had been granted to Lord Baltimore.[4] Penn had no difficulty in finding other Quakers in England to join his venture. His followers included even Quakers from Wales and Ireland and Mennonites and Pietists from Germany.

Penn formulated many plans for a frame of government before he produced a constitution with which he was satisfied. He called his first plan the "Fundamental Constitutions of Pennsylvania."[5] It consisted of twenty-four clauses embracing his general ideas of government. The Fundamental Constitutions was intended to establish "the frame of government that shall best preserve Magistracy in reverence with the people and best keep it from being hurtful to them." At the head of the document he placed the right of each person to worship according to his conscience. An important feature of the Fundamental Constitutions was the establishment of a colonial assembly with privileges like those of the English House of Commons. The assembly was to be elected yearly and it was to meet whether or not called by the governor. The province was to be divided into small districts, each sending two representatives to the assembly, which was to consist of up to three hundred eighty-four members. The representatives were to be bound by the instructions of their electors. The assembly was given power to select forty-eight councilmen from its own members. The council was to act as a permanent board and upper house of the legislature. It was also given coordinate powers of legislation with the assembly and was to have certain executive duties. The

Fundamental Constitutions of Pennsylvania

---

[2] See p. 181.

[3] Text in Francis N. Thorpe (ed.), *The Federal and State Constitutions, Colonial Charters, and Other Organic Laws* (Washington, 1909), V, 3035-44.

[4] See pp. 97-114. The principal differences between the Penn and Baltimore charters were that the rights and powers exercised by the Bishop of Durham were not conferred upon Penn; the right of the inhabitants to appeal to the king was expressly guaranteed; the proprietor was required to keep an agent resident in or near London; laws of the province had to be submitted to the Privy Council for approval within five years after their passage, and if they were not rejected within six months, they were to stand; and the legislative supremacy of Parliament was distinctly recognized.

[5] Isaac Sharpless, *A Quaker Experiment in Government* (Philadelphia, 1898), 58-61.

governor could veto laws within fourteen days after their presentation. The rights of individuals were recognized by provisions abolishing imprisonment for debt, abolishing capital punishment for felonies, substituting affirmations for oaths, and requiring that the law of habeas corpus should be observed. To conciliate prospective purchasers of land, Penn was forced to modify a number of these ideas, and the Frame of Government of 1682, which resulted from this revision, is thus somewhat less democratic in character than the Fundamental Constitutions.

Frame of Government of 1682

The Frame of Government of 1682 was drawn up as the fundamental law of the province by Penn himself, although probably the advice and opinions of others are also reflected by the document.[6] Its lengthy preface expresses many ideas of government shared by the Quakers. Penn believed that government is of divine origin and that its purpose is both to curb wrongdoers and protect those who do well. He stressed the latter of these two functions, and often dwelt upon the ameliorative rather than the compulsive features of government. Although he contended that frames of government are less important than the men who administer them, he was aware of the dangers of too much discretionary power in the hands of the rulers. His solution to this dilemma was to establish the rule of law and give the people a part of the lawmaking power.

As a result of his experiences in England, Penn had a keen awareness of the rights of Englishmen. Foremost among these he placed the existence of representative institutions, the protection of property, and the right of trial by jury.[7] He was responsible for the first publication in the colonies in 1687

---

[6] It is believed that Algernon Sidney was consulted by Penn in the preparation of the draft, although whether Sidney's advice was followed is unknown. The advice of some of the Friends who advanced money for the project probably led to some of the less democratic features of the document. Edward Channing, *A History of the United States*, Vol. II: *A Century of Colonial History, 1660-1760* (New York, 1927), 118.

[7] In 1675 Penn published "England's Present Interest" in which he expressed his opinions as to the best means of "composing, at least quieting, differences; for allaying the heat of contrary interests, and making them subservient to the interest of the government, and consistent with the prosperity of the kingdom." He placed first "an inviolable and impartial maintenance of English rights," and also emphasized the need for governors to balance diverse religious interests and the need for a sincere promotion of general and practical religion. *The Select Works of William Penn* (3d ed.; London, 1782), III, 202.

His interpretation of the fundamental rights of Englishmen relied for authority upon Lord Coke's commentaries on Magna Carta in the *Second Institute*. His conclusions as to these were: "Here are the three fundamentals comprehended, and expressed to have been the rights and privileges of Englishmen. I. *Ownership*, consisting of liberty and property. In that it supposes *Englishmen* to be *free*, there is liberty: next, that they have *freeholds*, there is property. II. That they have the *voting of their own laws*: for that was an ancient free custom, as I have already proved, and all of Magna Carta, Confirmatio Cartarum, the sentence of excommunication against breakers of the charters, and the statute *de Tallagio non Concedendo*.

The Frame of Government of 1682 is distinguished in the development of American constitutional law for several reasons. In the first place, it established a representative system designed to place important powers of government in the people. Two representative bodies were created, the Council and the General Assembly. The existence of an elective council represented a marked difference from the practice of many colonies. It was apparently intended that the Council should represent the more aristocratic elements of the province, but by making the Council an elective body it was made subject to the will of all the people. The power of the freemen was weakened by the provision that the General Assembly should be restricted to the task of approving or disapproving laws proposed to it and could not initiate legislation itself. The "Laws Agreed Upon in England" was in the nature of a bill of rights. Among its significant provisions are those providing for the admission of new freemen, prohibiting taxation by the executive, guaranteeing the right of trial by jury, granting humane conditions to prisoners, granting the right of bail, promoting education, and guaranteeing religious liberty. Of special importance is the fact that the Frame of Government was intended to be the fundamental law of the province. It was provided that the governor and six-sevenths of the freemen in the Council and General Assembly must approve all amendments to the document. Thus the document was not to be amended by the ordinary processes of legislation, but was to be given an especially high place among the laws of the province.

General Significance

Penn had sacrificed a number of his views in the Frame of Government of 1682 as it was finally executed, including the opinion, embodied in the earlier Fundamental Constitutions, that the General Assembly should be empowered to initiate legislation. The freemen also objected to the requirement of the frame that all legislation must be initiated by the governor and the Council. It is probable, therefore, that neither the proprietor nor the freemen had a strong motive for complying with its terms. When he arrived in America, Penn proceeded to organize the government without much regard to the provisions of the document. Although the frame called for a meeting of all the freemen the first year, it was ordered that the freemen should elect seven persons from the various parts of the province to serve as their representatives

Effects

such customs are expressly confirmed by this *great charter:* besides, the people helped to make it. III. An influence upon, and a real *share in, the judicatory power,* in the execution and application thereof." *Ibid.*, III, 218-19.

in the General Assembly. In 1683 a new frame was put into effect.[8] That document provided that the Council should consist of not less than eighteen members and the Assembly of not less than thirty-six. Security in the possession of lands was guaranteed to the holders upon payment of rents and services to the proprietor. Also the sole power of appointing officers of government was limited to the lifetime of the present proprietor. A third Frame of Government was issued in 1696 by Governor Markham with the approval of the legislature.[9] This was never approved by Penn, however, and cannot be considered as of binding force in the colony.

None of Penn's frames of government was ever submitted to the Privy Council as required by the royal charter of 1681, and the question as to their validity naturally arises. Since the charter required that the laws should be submitted for approval within five years after their enactment and did not expressly state that laws not submitted should be void, it is possible that the colonists were justified in treating them as binding and of full force and effect.[10] Certainly, they were considered to constitute the authoritative definition of the rights of the colonists in Pennsylvania. The ease with which these frames of government were replaced during the early years in Pennsylvania shows that Penn held rigid forms of government in low respect, that he was willing to yield to the views of others in the adoption of laws, and that the colonists themselves felt that they deserved more ample participation in the government than was originally given them. The last of Penn's famous laws was the Charter of Privileges of 1701[11] under which the province was governed until it was replaced by the Constitution of 1776.[12]

[8] Text in Thorpe, *op. cit.*, V, 3064-69.

[9] Text in *ibid.*, V, 3070-76.

[10] The charter provided: ". . . a transcript or Duplicate of all Lawes, which shall bee soe as aforesaid made and published within the said Province, shall within five yeares after the makeing thereof, be transmitted and delivered to the Privy Councell, for the time being, of us, our heires and successors: And if any of the said Lawes, within the space of six moneths after that they shall be soe transmitted and delivered, bee declared by us, Our heires or Successors, in Our or their Privy Councell, inconsistent with the Sovereigntey or lawful Prerogative of us, our heires or Successors, or contrary to the Faith and Allegiance due by the legall government of this Realme, from the said *William Penn*, or his heires, or of the Planters and Inhabitants of the said Province, and that thereupon any of the said Lawes shall bee adjudged and declared to bee void by us, our heires or Successors, under our or their Privy Seale, that then and from thenceforth, such Lawes, concerning which such Judgement and declaration shall bee made, shall become voyd: Otherwise the said Lawes so transmitted, shall remaine, and stand in full force, according to the true intent and meaneing thereof." *Ibid.*, V, 3039.

[11] See pp. 251-60.

[12] See pp. 323-31.

FRAME OF GOVERNMENT OF PENNSYLVANIA[13]

April 25, 1682

The frame of the government of the province of Pensilvania, in America: *together with certain* laws *agreed upon in England, by the Governor and divers freemen of the aforesaid province. To be further explained and confirmed there, by the first provincial Council, that shall be held, if they see meet.*

THE PREFACE

When the great and wise *God* had made the world, of all his creatures, it pleased *Preamble*
him to chuse man his Deputy to rule it: and to fit him for so great a charge and trust, he did not only qualify him with skill and power, but with integrity to use them justly. This native goodness was equally his honour and his happiness; and whilst he stood here, all went well; there was no need of coercive or compulsive means; the precept of divine love and truth, in his bosom, was the guide and keeper of his innocency. But lust prevailing against duty, made a lamentable breach upon it; and the law, that before had no power over him, took place upon him, and his disobedient posterity, that such as would not live comformable to the holy law within, should fall under the reproof and correction of the just law without, in a judicial administration.

This the Apostle teaches in divers of his epistles: "The law (says he) was added *Purpose*
because of transgression:" In another place, "Knowing that the law was not made for *of law*
the righteous man; but for the disobedient and ungodly, for sinners, for unholy and prophane, for murderers, for whoremongers, for them that defile themselves with mankind, and for man-stealers, for lyers, for perjured persons," &c., but this is not all, he opens and carries the matter of government a little further: "Let every soul be subject to the higher powers; for there is no power but of *God*. The powers that be are ordained of *God:* whosoever therefore resisteth the power, resisteth the ordinance of *God*. For rulers are not a terror to good works, but to evil: wilt thou then not be afraid of the power? do that which is good, and thou shalt have praise of the same." "He is the

---

[13] Thorpe, *op. cit.,* V, 3052-63. The "Laws Agreed Upon in England" were signed and sealed May 5, 1682.

minister of God to thee for good." "Wherefore ye must needs be subject, not only for wrath, but for conscience sake."

Theory of government

This settles the divine right of government beyond exception, and that for two ends: first, to terrify evil doers: secondly, to cherish those that do well; which gives government a life beyond corruption, and makes it as durable in the world, as good men shall be. So that government seems to me a part of religion itself, a thing sacred in its institution and end. For, if it does not directly remove the cause, it crushes the effects of evil, and is as such, (though a lower, yet) an emanation of the same Divine Power, that is both author and object of pure religion; the difference lying here, that the one is more free and mental, the other more corporal and compulsive in its operations: but that is only to evil doers; government itself being otherwise as capable of kindness, goodness and charity, as a more private society. They weakly err, that think there is no other use of government, than correction, which is the coarsest part of it: daily experience tells us, that the care and regulation of many other affairs, more soft, and daily necessary, make up much of the greatest part of government; and which must have followed the peopling of the world, had Adam never fell, and will continue among men, on earth, under the highest attainments they may arrive at, by the coming of the blessed *Second Adam*, the *Lord* from heaven. Thus much of government in general, as to its rise and end.

Purpose of frames of government

For particular *frames* and *models*, it will become me to say little; and comparatively I will say nothing. My reasons are:

First. That the age is too nice and difficult for it; there being nothing the wits of men are more busy and divided upon. It is true, they seem to agree to the end, to wit, happiness; but, in the means, they differ, as to divine, so to this human felicity; and the cause is much the same, not always want of light and knowledge, but want of using them rightly. Men side with their passions against their reason, and their sinister interests have so strong a bias upon their minds, that they lean to them against the good of the things they know.

Secondly. I do not find a model in the world, that time, place, and some singular emergences have not necessarily altered; nor is it easy to frame a civil government, that shall serve all places alike.

Thirdly. I know what is said by the several admirers of *monarchy, aristocracy* and *democracy*, which are the rule of one, a few, and many, and are the three common ideas of government, when men discourse on the subject. But I chuse to solve the controversy with this small distinction, and it belongs to all three: *Any government is free to the people under it* (whatever be the frame) *where the laws rule, and the people are a party to those laws,* and more than this is tyranny, oligarchy, or confusion.

Government depends on men

But, lastly, when all is said, there is hardly one frame of government in the world so ill designed by its first founders, that, in good hands, would not do well enough; and story tells us, the best, in ill ones, can do nothing that is great or good; witness the *Jewish* and *Roman* states. Governments, like clocks, go from the motion men give them; and as governments are made and moved by men, so by them they are ruined too. Wherefore governments rather depend upon men, than men upon governments.

FRAME OF GOVERNMENT OF PENNSYLVANIA

Let men be good, and the government cannot be bad; if it be ill, they will cure it. But, if men be bad, let the government be never so good, they will endeavor to warp and spoil it to their turn.

I know some say, let us have good laws, and no matter for the men that execute them: but let them consider, that though good laws do well, good men do better: for good laws may want good men, and be abolished or evaded [invaded in Franklin's print] by ill men; but good men will never want good laws, nor suffer ill ones. It is true, good laws have some awe upon ill ministers, but that is where they have not power to escape or abolish them, and the people are generally wise and good: but a loose and depraved people (which is the question) love laws and an administration like themselves. That, therefore, which makes a good constitution, must keep it, *viz:* men of wisdom and virtue, qualities, that because they descend not with worldly inheritances, must be carefully propagated by a virtuous education of youth; for which after ages will owe more to the care and prudence of founders, and the successive magistracy, than to their parents, for their private patrimonies. *[Good men more important than good laws]*

These considerations of the weight of government, and the nice and various opinions about it, made it uneasy to me to think of publishing the ensuing frame and conditional laws, forseeing both the censures, they will meet with, from men of differing humours and engagements, and the occasion they may give of discourse beyond my design.

But, next to the power of necessity, (which is a solicitor, that will take no denial) this induced me to a compliance, that we have (with reverence to God, and good conscience to men) to the best of our skill, contrived and composed the *frame* and *laws* of this government, to the great end of all government, viz: *To support power in reverence with the people, and to secure the people from the abuse of power;* that they may be free by their just obedience, and the magistrates honourable, for their just administration: for liberty without obedience is confusion, and obedience without liberty is slavery. To carry this evenness is partly owing to the constitution, and partly to the magistracy: where either of these fail, government will be subject to convulsions; but where both are wanting, it must be totally subverted; then where both meet, the government is like to endure. Which I humbly pray and hope *God* will please to make the lot of this of *Pensilvania*. Amen. *[Purpose of the Frame of Government]*

WILLIAM PENN.

THE FRAME, &C.—APRIL 25, 1682

To all Persons, to whom these presents may come. WHEREAS, king Charles the Second, by his letters patents, under the great seal of *England*, bearing date the fourth day of March in the Thirty and Third Year of the King, for divers considerations therein mentioned, hath been graciously pleased to give and grant unto me *William Penn*, by the name of *William Penn*, Esquire, son and heir of Sir *William Penn*, deceased, and to my heirs and assigns forever, all that tract of land, or Province, called *Pensylvania*, in *America*, with divers great powers, pre-eminences, royalties, jurisdic- *[Recital of Charter of 1681]* tions, and authorities, necessary for the well-being and government thereof: Now know ye, that for the well-being and government of the said province, and for the encouragement of all the freemen and planters that may be therein concerned, in pursuance of the powers aforementioned, I, the said *William Penn*, have declared, granted, and confirmed, and by these presents, for me, my heirs and assigns, do declare, grant, and confirm unto all the freemen, planters and adventurers of, in and to the said province, these liberties, franchises, and properties, to be held, enjoyed and kept by the freemen, planters, and inhabitants of the said province of *Pensilvania* for ever.

Liberties granted forever

Imprimis. That the government of this province shall, according to the powers of the patent, consist of the Governor and freemen of the said province, in form of a provincial Council and General Assembly, by whom all laws shall be made, officers chosen, and public affairs transacted, as is hereafter respectively declared, that is to say—

Governor, Council, and General Assembly

II. That the freemen of the said province shall, on the twentieth day of the twelfth month, which shall be in this present year one thousand six hundred eighty and two, meet and assemble in some fit place, of which timely notice shall be before hand given by the Governor or his Deputy; and then, and there, shall chuse out of themselves *seventy-two* persons of most note for their wisdom, virtue and ability, who shall meet, on the tenth day of the first month next ensuing, and always be called, and act as, the provincial Council of the said province.

Election of Council of seventy-two freemen

III. That, at the first choice of such provincial Council, one-third part of the said provincial Council shall be chosen to serve for three years, then next ensuing; one-third part, for two years then next ensuing; and one-third part, for one year then next ensuing such election, and no longer; and that the said third part shall go out accordingly: and on the twentieth day of the twelfth month, as aforesaid, yearly for ever afterwards, the freemen of the said province shall, in like manner, meet and assemble. together, and then chuse twenty-four persons, being one-third of the said number, to serve in provincial Council for three years: it being intended, that one-third part of the whole provincial Council (always consisting, and to consist, of seventy-two persons, as aforesaid) falling off yearly, it shall be yearly supplied by such new yearly elections, as aforesaid; and that no one person shall continue therein longer than three years: and, in case any member shall decease before the last election during his time, that then at the next election ensuing his decease, another shall be chosen to supply his place, for the remaining time, he was to have served, and no longer.

Term of office of councilors

IV. That, after the first seven years, every one of the said third parts, that goeth yearly off, shall be uncapable of being chosen again for one whole year following: that so all may be fitted for government, and have experience of the care and burden of it.

Successive terms prohibited

V. That the provincial Council, in all cases and matters of moment, as their arguing upon bills to be passed into laws, erecting courts of justice, giving judgment upon criminals impeached, and choice of officers, in such manner as is hereinafter mentioned, not less than two-thirds of the whole provincial Council shall make a *quorum,* and that the consent and approbation of two-thirds of such *quorum* shall be had in all

Quorums and voting

such cases and matters of moment. And moreover that, in all cases and matters of lesser moment, twenty-four Members of the said provincial Council shall make a *quorum*, the majority of which twenty-four shall, and may, always determine in such cases and causes of lesser moment.

VI. That, in this provincial Council, the Governor or his Deputy, shall or may, always preside, and have a treble voice; and the said provincial Council shall always continue, and sit upon its own adjournments and committees. *Governor to have three votes*

VII. That the Governor and provincial Council shall prepare and propose to the General Assembly, hereafter mentioned, all bills, which they shall, at any time, think fit to be passed into laws, within the said province; which bills shall be published and affixed to the most noted places, in the inhabited parts thereof, thirty days before the meeting of the General Assembly, in order to the passing them into laws or rejecting of them, as the General Assembly shall see meet. *Bills to be proposed to General Assembly by Governor and Council*

VIII. That the Governor and provincial Council shall take care, that all laws, statutes and ordinances, which shall at any time be made within the said province, be duly and diligently executed. *Execution of laws*

IX. That the Governor and provincial Council shall, at all times, have the care of the peace and safety of the province, and that nothing be by any person attempted to the subversion of this frame of government. *Maintenance of peace and safety*

X. That the Governor and provincial Council shall, at all times, settle and order the situation of all cities, ports, and market towns in every county, modelling therein all public buildings, streets, and market places, and shall appoint all necessary roads, and high-ways in the province. *Cities, buildings, markets, roads, etc.*

XI. That the Governor and provincial Council shall, at all times, have power to inspect the management of the public treasury, and punish those who shall convert any part thereof to any other use, than what hath been agreed upon by the Governor, provincial Council, and General Assembly. *Public treasury*

XII. That the Governor and provincial Council, shall erect and order all public schools, and encourage and reward the authors of useful sciences and laudable inventions in the said province. *Schools, sciences, and inventions*

XIII. That, for the better management of the powers and trust aforesaid, the provincial Council shall, from time to time, divide itself into four distinct and proper committees, for the more easy administration of the affairs of the Province, which divides the seventy-two into four eighteens, every one of which eighteens shall consist of six out of each of the three orders, or yearly elections, each of which shall have a distinct portion of business, as followeth: *First,* a committee of plantations, to situate and settle cities, ports, and market towns, and high-ways, and to hear and decide all suits and controversies relating to plantations. *Secondly,* a committee of justice and safety, to secure the peace of the Province, and punish the mal-administration of those who subvert justice to the prejudice of the public, or private, interest. *Thirdly,* a committee of trade and treasury, who shall regulate all trade and commerce, according to law, encourage manufacture and country growth, and defray the public charge of the Province. And, *Fourthly,* a committee of manners, education, and arts, that all wicked *Committees of the Council*

Committee of plantations

Committee of justice and safety

Committee of trade and treasury

and scandalous living may be prevented, and that youth may be successively trained up in virtue and useful knowledge and arts: the *quorum* of each of which committees being six, that is, two out of each of the three orders, or yearly elections, as aforesaid, make a constant and standing Council of *twenty-four,* which will have the power of the provincial Council, being the quorum of it, in all cases not excepted in the fifth article; and in the said committees, and standing Council of the Province, the Governor, or his Deputy, shall, or may preside, as aforesaid; and in the absence of the Governor, or his Deputy, if no one is by either of them appointed, the said committees or Council shall appoint a President for that time, and not otherwise; and what shall be resolved at such committees, shall be reported to the said Council of the province, and shall be by them resolved and confirmed before the same shall be put in execution; and that these respective committees shall not sit at one and the same time, except in cases of necessity.

Committee of manners
Standing Council

XIV. And, to the end that all laws prepared by the Governor and provincial Council aforesaid, may yet have the more full concurrence of the freemen of the province, it is declared, granted and confirmed, that, at the time and place or places, for the choice of a provincial Council, as aforesaid, the said freemen shall yearly chuse Members to serve in a General Assembly, as their representatives, not exceeding two hundred persons, who shall yearly meet on the twentieth day of the second month, which shall be in the year one thousand six hundred eighty and three following, in the capital town, or city, of the said province, where, during eight days, the several Members may freely confer with one another; and, if any of them see meet, with a committee of the provincial Council (consisting of three out of each of the four committees aforesaid, being twelve in all) which shall be, at that time, purposely appointed to receive from any of them proposals, for the alterations or amendment of any of the said proposed and promulgated bills: and on the ninth day from their so meeting, the said General Assembly, after reading over the proposed bills by the Clerk of the provincial Council, and the occasions and motives for them being opened by the Governor or his Deputy, shall give their affirmative or negative, which to them seemeth best, in such manner as hereinafter is expressed. But not less than two-thirds shall make a *quorum* in the passing of laws, and choice of such officers as are by them to be chosen.

General Assembly
Elections
Meetings
Approval of bills
Quorum

XV. That the laws so prepared and proposed, as aforesaid, that are assented to by the General Assembly, shall be enrolled as laws of the Province, with this stile: *By the Governor, with the assent and approbation of the freemen in provincial Council and General Assembly.*

Style of laws

XVI. That, for the establishment of the government and laws of this province, and to the end there may be an universal satisfaction in the laying of the fundamentals thereof: the General Assembly shall, or may, for the first year, consist of all the freemen of and in the said province; and ever after it shall be yearly chosen, as aforesaid; which number of two hundred shall be enlarged as the country shall increase in people, so as it do not exceed five hundred, at any time; the appointment and proportioning of

Membership of General Assembly

which, as also the laying and methodizing of the choice of the provincial Council and General Assembly, in future times, most equally to the divisions of the hundreds and counties, which the country shall hereafter be divided into, shall be in the power of the provincial Council to propose, and the General Assembly to resolve.

XVII. That the Governor and the provincial Council shall erect, from time to time, standing courts of justice, in such places and number as they shall judge convenient for the good government of the said province. And that the provincial Council shall, on the thirteenth day of the first month, yearly, elect and present to the Governor, or his Deputy, a double number of persons, to serve for Judges, Treasurers, Masters of Rolls, within the said province, for the year next ensuing; and the freemen of the said province, in the county courts, when they shall be erected, and till then, in the General Assembly, shall, on the three and twentieth day of the second month, yearly, elect and present to the Governor, or his Deputy, a double number of persons, to serve for Sheriffs, Justices of the Peace, and Coroners, for the year next ensuing; out of which respective elections and presentments, the Governor or his Deputy shall nominate and commissionate the proper number for each office, the third day after the said presentments, or else the first named in such presentment, for each office, shall stand and serve for that office the year ensuing. *Courts* *Selection of judges* *Selection of sheriffs, justices of the peace, and coroners*

XVIII. But forasmuch as the present condition of the province requires some immediate settlement, and admits not of so quick a revolution of officers; and to the end the said Province may, with all convenient speed, be well ordered and settled, I, *William Penn,* do therefore think fit to nominate and appoint such persons for Judges, Treasurers, Masters of the Rolls, Sheriffs, Justices of the Peace, and Coroners, as are most fitly qualified for those employments; to whom I shall make and grant commissions for the said offices, respectively, to hold to them, to whom the same shall be granted, for so long time as every such person shall well behave himself in the office, or place, to him respectively granted, and no longer. And upon the decease or displacing of any of the said officers, the succeeding officer, or officers, shall be chosen, as aforesaid. *Appointment of first officers*

XIX. That the General Assembly shall continue so long as may be needful to impeach criminals, fit to be there impeached, to pass bills into laws, that they shall think fit to pass into laws, and till such time as the Governor and provincial Council shall declare that they have nothing further to propose unto them, for their assent and approbation: and that declaration shall be a dismiss to the General Assembly for that time; which General Assembly shall be, notwithstanding, capable of assembling together upon the summons of the provincial Council, at any time during that year, if the said provincial Council shall see occasion for their so assembling. *Meetings of General Assembly*

XX. That all the elections of members, or representatives of the people, to serve in provincial Council and General Assembly, and all questions to be determined by both, or either of them, that relate to passing of bills into laws, to the choice of officers, to impeachments by the General Assembly, and judgment of criminals upon such impeachments by the provincial Council, and to all other cases by them respectively judged of importance, shall be resolved and determined by the ballot; and unless on *Ballot* sudden and indispensible occasions, no business in provincial Council, or its respective committees, shall be finally determined the same day that it is moved.

Minority of the governor

XXI. That at all times when, and so often as it shall happen that the Governor shall or may be an infant, under the age of one and twenty years, and no guardians or commissioners are appointed in writing, by the father of the said infant, or that such guardians or commissioners, shall be deceased; that during such minority, the provincial Council shall, from time to time, as they shall see meet, constitute and appoint guardians or commissioners, not exceeding three; one of which three shall preside as deputy and chief guardian, during such minority, and shall have and execute, with the consent of the other two, all the power of a Governor, in all the public affairs and concerns of the said province.

Lord's day

XXII. That, as often as any day of the month, mentioned in any article of this charter, shall fall upon the first day of the week, commonly called the *Lord's Day*, the business appointed for that day shall be deferred till the next day, unless in case of emergency.

Amendment of charter

XXIII. That no act, law, or ordinance whatsoever, shall at any time hereafter, be made or done by the Governor of this province, his heirs or assigns, or by the freemen in the provincial Council, or the General Assembly, to alter, change, or diminish the form, or effect, of this charter, or any part, or clause thereof, without the consent of the Governor, his heirs, or assigns, and six parts of seven of the said freemen in provincial Council and General Assembly.

Confirmation of liberties

XXIV. And lastly, that I, the said *William Penn*, for myself, my heirs and assigns, have solemnly declared, granted and confirmed, and do hereby solemnly declare, grant and confirm, that neither I, my heirs, nor assigns, shall procure or do any thing or things, whereby the liberties, in this charter contained and expressed, shall be infringed or broken; and if any thing be procured by any person or persons contrary to these premises, it shall be held of no force or effect. In witness whereof, I, the said *William Penn*, have unto this present character of liberties set my hand and broad seal, this five and twentieth day of the second month, vulgarly called April, in the year of our *Lord* one thousand six hundred and eighty-two.

WILLIAM PENN.

LAWS AGREED UPON IN ENGLAND, &C.

Charter of liberties approved and declared fundamental

I. That the charter of liberties, declared, granted and confirmed the five and twentieth day of the second month, called April, 1682, before divers witnesses, by *William Penn*, Governor and chief Proprietor of *Pensilvania*, to all the freemen and planters of the said province, is hereby declared and approved, and shall be for ever held for fundamental in the government thereof, according to the limitations mentioned in the said charter.

Freemen

II. That every inhabitant in the said province, that is or shall be, a purchaser of one hundred acres of land, or upwards, his heirs and assigns, and every person who shall have paid his passage, and taken up one hundred acres of land, at one penny an acre, and have cultivated ten acres thereof, and every person, that hath been a servant, or bonds-man, and is free by his service, that shall have taken up his fifty acres of land, and cultivated twenty thereof, and every inhabitant, artificer, or other resident in the said province, that pays scot and lot [14] to the government; shall be deemed and accounted a freeman of the said province: and every such person shall, and may, be capable of electing, or being elected, representatives of the people, in provincial Council, or General Assembly, in the said province.

III. That all elections of members, or representatives of the people and freemen of the province of *Pensilvania*, to serve in provincial Council, or General Assembly, to be held within the said province, shall be free and voluntary: and that the elector, that shall receive any reward or gift, in meat, drink, monies, or otherwise, shall forfeit his right to elect; and such person as shall directly or indirectly give, promise, or bestow any such reward as aforesaid, to be elected, shall forfeit his election, and be thereby incapable to serve as aforesaid: and the provincial Council and General Assembly shall be the sole judges of the regularity, or irregularity of the elections of their own respective Members. *Freedom of elections*

IV. That no money or goods shall be raised upon, or paid by, any of the people of this province by way of public tax, custom or contribution, but by a law, for that purpose made; and whoever shall levy, collect, or pay any money or goods contrary thereunto, shall be held a public enemy to the province and a betrayer of the liberties of the people thereof. *Taxes*

V. That all courts shall be open, and justice shall neither be sold, denied nor delayed. *Sale, denial, or delay of justice*

VI. That, in all courts all persons of all persuasions may freely appear in their own way, and according to their own manner, and there personally plead their own cause themselves; or, if unable, by their friends: and the first process shall be the exhibition of the complaint in court, fourteen days before the trial; and that the party, complained against, may be fitted for the same, he or she shall be summoned, no less than ten days before, and a copy of the complaint delivered him or her, at his or her dwelling house. But before the complaint of any person be received, he shall solemnly declare in court, that he believes, in his conscience, his cause is just. *Court appearances; process*

VII. That all pleadings, processes and records in courts, shall be short, and in *English*, and in an ordinary and plain character, that they may be understood, and justice speedily administered. *Court records*

VIII. That all trials shall be by twelve men, and as near as may be, peers or equals, and of the neighborhood, and men without just exception; in cases of life, there shall be first twenty-four returned by the sheriffs, for a grand inquest, of whom twelve, at least, shall find the complaint to be true; and then the twelve men, or peers, to be likewise returned by the sheriff, shall have the final judgment. But reasonable challenges shall be always admitted against the said twelve men, or any of them. *Trial by jury*

[14] A customary contribution paid by the subject according to his ability.

Fees   IX. That all fees in all cases shall be moderate, and settled by the provincial Council, and General Assembly, and be hung up in a table in every respective court; and whosoever shall be convicted of taking more, shall pay twofold, and be dismissed his employment; one moiety of which shall go to the party wronged.

Prisons   X. That all prisons shall be work-houses, for felons, vagrants, and loose and idle persons; whereof one shall be in every county.

Bail   XI. That all prisoners shall be bailable by sufficient sureties, unless for capital offences, where the proof is evident, or the presumption great.

Wrongful imprisonment   XII. That all persons wrongfully imprisoned, or prosecuted at law, shall have double damages against the informer, or prosecutor.

Prisons   XIII. That all prisons shall be free, as to fees, food and lodging.

Execution on land, etc.   XIV. That all lands and goods shall be liable to pay debts, except where there is legal issue, and then all the goods, and one-third of the land only.

Wills   XV. That all wills, in writing, attested by two witnesses, shall be of the same force as to lands, as other conveyances, being legally proved within forty days, either within or without the said province.

Adverse possession   XVI. That seven years quiet possession shall give an unquestionable right, except in cases of infants, lunatics, married women, or persons beyond the seas.

Bribery   XVII. That all briberies and extortion whatsoever shall be severely punished.

Fines   XVIII. That all fines shall be moderate, and saving men's contenements, merchandize, or wainage.

Marriage   XIX. That all marriages (not forbidden by the law of God, as to nearness of blood and affinity by marriage) shall be encouraged; but the parents, or guardians, shall be first consulted, and the marriage shall be published before it be solemnized; and it shall be solemnized by taking one another as husband and wife, before credible witnesses; and a certificate of the whole, under the hands of parties and witnesses, shall be brought to the proper register of that county, and shall be registered in his office.

Recording of charters, grants, etc.   XX. And, to prevent frauds and vexatious suits within the said province, that all charters, gifts, grants, and conveyances of and (except leases for a year or under) and all bills, bonds, and specialties above five pounds, and not under three months, made in the said province, shall be enrolled, or registered in the public enrolment office of the said province, within the space of two months next after the making thereof, else to be void in law, and all deeds, grants, and conveyances of land (except as aforesaid) within the said province, and made out of the said province, shall be enrolled or registered, as aforesaid, within six months next after the making thereof, and settling and constituting an enrolment office or registry within the said province, else to be void in law against all persons whatsoever.

Defacement of charters, grants, etc.   XXI. That all defacers or corrupters of charters, gifts, grants, bonds, bills, wills, contracts, and conveyances, or that shall deface or falsify any enrolment, registry or record, within this province, shall make double satisfaction for the same; half whereof shall go to the party wronged, and they shall be dismissed of all places of trust, and be publicly disgraced as false men.

XXII. That there shall be a register for births, marriages, burials, wills, and letters of administration, distinct from the other registry. *Register of births, marriages, servants, etc.*

XXIII. That there shall be a register for all servants, where their names, time, wages, and days of payment shall be registered.

XXIV. That all lands and goods of felons shall be liable, to make satisfaction to the party wronged twice the value; and for want of lands or goods, the felons shall be bondmen to work in the common prison, or work-house, or otherwise, till the party injured be satisfied. *Lands and goods of felons*

XXV. That the estates of capital offenders, as traitors and murderers, shall go, one-third to the next of kin to the sufferer, and the remainder to the next of kin to the criminal. *Estates of capital offenders*

XXVI. That all witnesses, coming, or called, to testify their knowledge in or to any matter or thing, in any court, or before any lawful authority, within the said province, shall there give or deliver in their evidence, or testimony, by solemnly promising to speak the truth, the whole truth, and nothing but the truth, to the matter, or thing in question. And in case any person so called to evidence, shall be convicted of wilful falsehood, such person shall suffer and undergo such damage or penalty, as the person, or persons, against whom he or she bore false witness, did, or should, undergo; and shall also make satisfaction to the party wronged, and be publicly exposed as a false witness, never to be credited in any court, or before any Magistrate, in the said province. *Witnesses* / *Perjury*

XXVII. And, to the end that all officers chosen to serve within this province, may, with more care and diligence, answer the trust reposed in them, it is agreed, that no such person shall enjoy more than one public office, at one time. *One office to be held at a time*

XXVIII. That all children, within this province, of the age of twelve years, shall be taught some useful trade or skill, to the end none may be idle, but the poor may work to live, and the rich, if they become poor, may not want. *Education*

XXIX. That servants be not kept longer than their time, and such as are careful, be both justly and kindly used in their service, and put in fitting equipage at the expiration thereof, according to custom. *Servants*

XXX. That all scandalous and malicious reporters, backbiters, defamers and spreaders of false news, whether against Magistrates, or private persons, shall be accordingly severely punished, as enemies to the peace and concord of this province. *Scandalous reports*

XXXI. That for the encouragement of the planters and traders in this province, who are incorporated into a society, the patent granted to them by *William Penn*, Governor of the said province, is hereby ratified and confirmed. *Confirmation of patent to planters and traders*

XXXII. * * *

XXXIII. That all factors or correspondents in the said province, wronging their employers, shall make satisfaction, and one-third over, to their said employers: and in case of the death of any such factor or correspondent, the committee of trade shall take care to secure so much of the deceased party's estate as belongs to his said respective employers. *Factors and agents*

Qualifications of officers   XXXIV. That all Treasurers, Judges, Masters of the Rolls, Sheriffs, Justices of the Peace, and other officers and persons whatsoever, relating to courts, or trials of causes, or any other service in the government; and all Members elected to serve in provincial Council and General Assembly, and all that have right to elect such Members, shall be such as possess faith in Jesus Christ, and that are not convicted of ill fame, or unsober and dishonest conversation, and that are of one and twenty years of age, at least; and that all such so qualified, shall be capable of the said several employments and privileges, as aforesaid.

Religious freedom   XXXV. That all persons living in this province, who confess and acknowledge the one Almighty and eternal God, to be the Creator, Upholder and Ruler of the world; and that hold themselves obliged in conscience to live peaceably and justly in civil society, shall, in no ways, be molested or prejudiced for their religious persuasion, or practice, in matters of faith and worship, nor shall they be compelled, at any time, to frequent or maintain any religious worship, place or ministry whatever.

Lord's day   XXXVI. That, according to the good example of the primitive Christians, and the case of the creation, every first day of the week, called the Lord's day, people shall abstain from their common daily labour, that they may the better dispose themselves to worship God according to their understandings.

Offenses against God   XXXVII. That as a careless and corrupt administration of justice draws the wrath of God upon magistrates, so the wildness and looseness of the people provoke the indignation of God against a country: therefore, that all such offences against God, as swearing, cursing, lying, prophane talking, drunkenness, drinking of healths, obscene words, incest, sodomy, rapes, whoredom, fornication, and other uncleanness (not to be repeated) all treasons, misprisions, murders, duels, felony, seditions, maims, forcible entries, and other violences, to the persons and estates of the inhabitants within this province; all prizes, stage-plays, cards, dice, May-games, gamesters, masques, revels, bull-baitings, cock-fightings, bear-baitings, and the like, which excite the people to rudeness, cruelty, looseness, and irreligion, shall be respectively discouraged, and severely punished, according to the appointment of the Governor and freemen in provincial Council and General Assembly; as also all proceedings contrary to these laws, that are not here made expressly penal.

Publication of laws   XXXVIII. That a copy of these laws shall be hung up in the provincial Council, and in public courts of justice: and that they shall be read yearly at the opening of every provincial Council and General Assembly, and court of justice; and their assent shall be testified, by their standing up after the reading thereof.

Amendment of laws   XXXIX. That there shall be, at no time, any alteration of any of these laws, without the consent of the Governor, his heirs, or assigns, and six parts of seven of the freemen, met in provincial Council and General Assembly.

Other matters   XL. That all other matters and things not herein provided for, which shall, and may, concern the public justice, peace or safety of the said province; and the raising and imposing taxes, customs, duties, or other charges whatsoever, shall be, and are, hereby referred to the order, prudence and determination of the Governor and freemen, in

FRAME OF GOVERNMENT OF PENNSYLVANIA

provincial Council and General Assembly, to be held, from time to time, in the said province.

Signed and sealed by the Governor and freemen aforesaid, the fifth day of the third month, called *May,* one thousand six hundred and eighty-two.

REFERENCES

Andrews, Charles M. *The Colonial Period of American History.* 3 vols. New Haven: Yale University Press, 1934-37. III, chap. 7.
Bolles, A. S. *Pennsylvania, Province and State, 1609-1790.* 2 vols. Philadelphia: T. Wanamaker, 1899. I, chaps. 1-8.
Channing, Edward. *A History of the United States.* 6 vols. New York: Macmillan Co., 1927. II, chaps. 4, 11.
Osgood, Herbert L. *The American Colonies in the Seventeenth Century.* 3 vols. New York: Macmillan Co., 1927-30. II, chap. 11.
Sharpless, Isaac. *A Quaker Experiment in Government.* Philadelphia: A. J. Ferris, 1898.

XVI. BILL OF RIGHTS
1689

The Revolution Settlement

The Declaration of Rights

The Bill of Rights, enacted December 16, 1689, established in statutory form the provisions of the Declaration of Rights. The Declaration had been agreed to by Parliament on February 12, 1689, and was presented to William and Mary the next day, when they were proclaimed king and queen of England.[1] On June 30 of the preceding year a group of Tories and Whigs had dispatched to William of Orange a request for assistance to aid in the restoration of English liberties and the delivery of the realm from the absolutism of James II (1685-89).[2] William landed in England on November 5, 1688, and marched unopposed to London. The royal army under James collapsed, and the king fled to the refuge of Louis XIV's court, never to return to England. In the absence of a king, a provisional government was organized with William at its head and letters were sent to the boroughs and counties requesting them to elect representatives to a convention. This

---

[1] Sections IV-XIII of the Bill of Rights do not appear in the Declaration. These additions imposed the test on the sovereign and provided that persons marrying papists should be disabled from ascending the throne. The most important change was section XII which relates to the dispensing power, a prerogative which the Lords had been unwilling absolutely to condemn. Although the Commons had at first asserted the complete illegality of the power, the Lords insisted on qualifying this by adding the words "as it hath been assumed and exercised of late." See clause 2 in the list of rights. When it came to drafting the Bill of Rights, the Commons desired to include a provision that no dispensation of any statute by *non obstante* should be allowed except as to be provided by a bill to be passed in the present session. This satisfied the Lords, and in the next Parliament they ordered the judges to prepare a bill for allowing the dispensing power where necessary and for repealing obsolete laws which had usually been dispensed with. The subject seems to have received no attention beyond this, and the dispensing power came to an end. Henry Hallam, *The Constitutional History of England* (5th ed.; London, 1847), 549; F. W. Maitland, *The Constitutional History of England* (Cambridge, 1909), 304-5.

[2] It has been said that "few documents have been so overrated as this letter of the 'immortal seven.' It is nothing more than a very cautiously worded statement of the assistance the Prince may expect to receive in England if he should come over." Lucile Pinkham, *William III and the Respectable Revolution* (Cambridge, Mass., 1954), 66.

BILL OF RIGHTS

assembly is called the Convention Parliament. It met on January 22, 1689, and shortly thereafter resolved that James II,

> having endeavored to subvert the constitution of the kingdom by breaking the original contract between king and people, and having, by the advice of Jesuits and other wicked persons, violated the fundamental laws and withdrawn himself out of the kingdom, has abdicated the government and the throne is hereby vacant.[3]

The first act of the new monarchy was to legalize the Convention Parliament, "notwithstanding any want of writ or writs of summons, or any other defect of form or default whatsoever."[4]

The Declaration of Rights was the principal document stating the Revolution Settlement.[5] Acceptance of the terms of the Declaration of Rights by the new king and queen was more than a condition upon which the crown was offered. The document's purpose was the correction of specific grievances which had arisen during the reigns of Charles II and James II. The declaration reflected the deep need of seventeenth-century England for a clarification of many points of law, and a logical time for such clarification had arrived.[6]

General significance of the Bill of Rights

The Bill of Rights and the other documents constituting the Revolution Settlement represented the triumph of the principles for which the recently formed Whig party had struggled against Charles II (1660-85) and James II. These documents asserted the supremacy of Parliament over the claimed divine right of kings. The royal prerogative was sharply curtailed, and even the possession of the crown became a statutory right, not a hereditary right.[7] Toleration for Protestant dissenters was assured, and a number of individual liberties, insisted upon as among the rights of the subject, were given formal recognition as part of the law of the land. The documentary counterparts of several of these rights appeared later in the Constitution of the United States and the first ten amendments thereof. The Bill of Rights of 1689, therefore, may be regarded as one of the sources of some of the most important individual liberties enjoyed by American citizens.

[3] Quoted in Goldwin Smith, *A Constitutional and Legal History of England* (New York, 1955), 366.
[4] 1 Will. & Mary, c. 1 § 2 (1689).
[5] For other documents comprising the Revolution Settlement see: Charles G. Robertson (ed.), *Select Statutes, Cases and Documents* (9th ed.; London, 1949), 105-57; Carl Stephenson and Frederick G. Marcham (eds.), *Sources of English Constitutional History* (New York, 1937), 599-612; George B. Adams and H. Morse Stephens (eds.), *Select Documents of English Constitutional History* (New York, 1935), 454-75.
[6] Pinkham, *op. cit.*, 234-35.
[7] Maitland, *op. cit.*, 281-83.

Origins and Effects

Dispensing with and suspension of laws

The reign of James II, and to a lesser extent that of Charles II, provided the historical background of the provisions of the Bill of Rights. One of the most serious grievances which the document sought to correct was the use of the royal prerogative for the purpose of suspending and dispensing with laws. In the past English kings had often exercised without question a rather vague dispensing power, that is, a power of making exceptions to the laws in particular cases. This power was closely related to the power of pardoning offenses against the laws.[8] The power of suspending the laws, in theory distinct from the dispensing power, was broader than the dispensing power. As that power was asserted by the Stuart kings, all persons might be authorized to treat particular laws as being nonexistent.[9] The Bill of Rights recognized that the dispensing power had once been legal, at least in some cases,[10] but probably there was no legal basis whatsoever for the claimed power of suspending laws.

Reign of Charles II

The achievement of Parliament in condemning the dispensing and the suspending powers was made at the expense of greater religious toleration. Charles II was sympathetic to the Catholic Church. He also wanted to strengthen the crown against the overwhelming power of the Anglican party in the Cavalier Parliament by gaining the support of the dissenting Protestant groups.[11] In March, 1672, he issued a Declaration of Indulgence in which he ordered that "the execution of all and all manner of penal laws in matters ecclesiastical, against whatsoever sort of non-comformists, or recusants, be immediately suspended, and they are hereby suspended."[12] Opposition to the declaration was widespread. Even the dissenting Protestant groups were among those who protested against it.[13] Some opponents of the government complained that the declaration suspended not less than forty statutes.[14] The House of Commons resolved "that penal Statutes, in Matters Ecclesiastical,

---

[8] *Ibid.*, 303.   [9] *Ibid.*, 302-3.   [10] See p. 222, note 1.

[11] George M. Trevelyan, *The English Revolution, 1688-1689* (London, 1938), 25-26.

[12] Robertson, *op. cit.*, 76. In December, 1662, Charles had issued a document, often called the first Declaration of Indulgence, announcing that he intended to ask Parliament to pass a measure to "enable him to exercise with a more universal satisfaction that power of dispensing which he conceived to be inherent in him." A bill to allow the king to dispense with the Act of Uniformity and all other laws relating to oaths, subscriptions, and religious conformity never reached the Commons from the Lords. Because of the strenuous opposition of Parliament, the matter was speedily dropped at that time. G. N. Clark, *The Later Stuarts, 1660-1714* (Oxford, 1934), 55-56; Smith, *op. cit.*, 353-54.

[13] The Anglicans disapproved the favor shown to both the Catholics and the Puritans. The Puritans felt little gratitude for a toleration which they were to share with Catholics. Thomas B. Macaulay, *The History of England*, ed. Charles H. Firth (London, 1913-15), I, 207.

[14] *Ibid.*

cannot be suspended, but by Act of Parliament."[15] The king withdrew the declaration, but Parliament was dissatisfied. In retaliation it passed the Test Act of 1673 which excluded from civil and military office all who refused to take the sacraments according to the rites of the Church of England.[16]

Charles II had shown great caution in promoting his policies of absolute government and religious toleration. His caution brought a certain measure of success. During the last years of his reign the penal laws against Catholics were not rigidly enforced, and a certain amount of religious toleration was observed in practice. His brother, James II, showed less political sense. Not content with toleration, James embarked upon a program aimed at the political ascendancy of his co-religionists.[17] The Commons refused to repeal the Test Act, so he dissolved Parliament. James got around Parliament's refusal by using the dispensing power to appoint Catholics to high offices in the government.

Reign of James II

His attempts to gain a semblance of legality for his conduct resulted in an attack upon the independence of the judges. The king discharged many of his judges in order to obtain a bench that would rule in favor of the dispensing power. One of the judges who was dismissed said to the king, "Your majesty may find twelve Judges of your mind, but hardly twelve lawyers."[18] James' wholesale use of the dispensing power was upheld in 1686, by a court composed of judges subservient to the king, in the case of Sir Edward Hales, a Catholic who had been appointed colonel in the royal army.[19] James proceeded to place Catholics into every branch of the government, both civil and military, until no Protestant felt safe in his office unless he was prepared to apostatize.[20]

James' next step was even more drastic. In 1687 and 1688 he issued Declarations of Indulgence which were more thoroughgoing than the one issued by Charles in 1672. Liberty of worship in public was granted to the Catholics and the Protestant dissenters, and the religious tests were suspended.[21] The first two rights listed by the Bill of Rights condemned the

---

[15] Robertson, *op. cit.*, 77.

[16] 25 Car. 2, c. 2. The test was extended to members of Parliament in 1678. 30 Car. 2, stat. 2, c. 1.

[17] Trevelyan, *op cit.*, 59-60.

[18] Quoted in Macaulay, *op. cit.*, II, 735.

[19] *State Trials* (T. B. Howell, comp.), XI, 1165.

[20] Trevelyan, *op. cit.*, 67.

[21] *Ibid.*, 73, 87; Clark, *op. cit.*, 119-20.

suspending power and the dispensing power as it had been exercised of late.

American constitutions condemning the suspension of laws

Several of the state constitutions adopted at the time of the American Revolution contained clauses condemning the suspension of laws. The Virginia Bill of Rights, for example, provided: "That all power of suspending laws, or the execution of laws, by any authority, without consent of the representatives of the people, is injurious to their rights, and ought not to be exercised."[22] Neither the Constitution of the United States nor the Bill of Rights contains a clause prohibiting the suspension of laws. At the time of the adoption of the Constitution, however, this restriction upon the government was declared to be an essential right of the people by the ratifying conventions of Virginia,[23] North Carolina,[24] and Rhode Island.[25]

Court of High Commission

The third clause in the list of rights contained in the Bill of Rights was intended to abolish the Court of High Commission. The High Commission had flourished under Charles I (1625-49) as a prerogative court the purpose of which was to persecute theological opponents and those who opposed his royalist theories of government. The court had been abolished in 1641[26] together with the Court of Star Chamber.[27] In 1661, after the restoration of the monarchy, ecclesiastical authorities were allowed to hold positions in the government and were restored to the ecclesiastical jurisdiction of which they had been deprived in 1641, but this partial repeal of the act of 1641 expressly excepted "what concerns the high commission-court, or the new erection of some such like court by commission."[28] In 1686 James II re-established the court without the slightest pretext of legality for the purpose of forcing the Catholic religion upon the national church. He appointed seven commissioners to the court, naming as chief commissioner Lord Jeffreys, who had gained the enmity of the nation for his conduct of the Bloody Assizes in 1685. James used the High Commission to place England's two great universities, Oxford and Cambridge—both strongholds of learning

---

[22] See p. 312.

[23] Charles C. Tansill (ed.), *Documents Illustrative of the Formation of the Union of the American States,* 69th Cong., 1st Sess., 1927, House Doc. 398, 1029.

[24] *Ibid.,* 1045.

[25] *Ibid.,* 1053.

[26] 16 Car. 1, c. 11. In addition, the Clerical Disabilities Act, 16 Car. 1, c. 27, had forbidden all persons in holy orders from sitting in Parliament, belonging to the Privy Council, holding any judicial office, or exercising any other temporal authority.

[27] See pp. 125-37.

[28] 13 Car. 2, stat. 1, c. 2; 13 Car. 2, stat. 1, c. 12.

of the Anglican Church—under the domination of the Catholic religion. Probably no other action of his reign did more to alienate the established church from the crown.[29] James finally abolished the High Commission in September, 1688, in one of his last attempts to appease the forces that were soon to drive him from the kingdom.[30] This clause of the Bill of Rights thus does no more than affirm the law as it had stood since 1641.

The fourth clause in the list of rights spoke the final word in the long contest between English kings and their subjects on the question of the power of the king to raise money without the consent of Parliament. King John's Charter, 1215, had required that the king receive the assent of an assembly of feudal lords in levying taxes.[31] Confirmatio Cartarum, 1297, and the statute *de Tallagio non Concedendo,* 1306, required that the "common assent of the realm" should be obtained in the levying of certain taxes.[32] These statutes did not, however, condemn all forms of prerogative taxation. The Petition of Right, 1628, made further restrictions by providing that no man should be compelled by the king to make any "gift, loan, benevolence, tax, or such-like charge," without the consent of Parliament.[33] Several statutes enacted by the Long Parliament, such as the Tonnage and Poundage Act,[34] the act declaring the illegality of ship money,[35] and the act prohibiting the exaction of knighthood fines[36] were designed to strike down particular forms of prerogative taxation. At the time of the Restoration, therefore, the proposition was probably firmly established as a matter of law that the crown might not levy money without the consent of Parliament. The clause of the Bill of Rights under consideration thus established no new principle. It was designed instead to condemn the relatively unimportant action of James II in continuing to exact for a period of two months between the time of his accession and the meeting of his first Parliament certain revenues which had expired on the death of Charles II.[37]

Prerogative taxation

The right of all subjects to present petitions to the king, established by the

[29] Trevelyan, *op. cit.,* 70-71.
[30] *Ibid.,* 106.
[31] See pp. 14, 24n
[32] 25 Edw. 1, c. 6; 34 Edw. 1, stat. 4, c. 1. See pp. 25-26, 31.
[33] 3 Car. 1, c. 1. See p. 75.
[34] 16 Car. 1, c. 8.
[35] 16 Car. 1, c. 14.
[36] 16 Car. 1, c. 20.
[37] Maitland, *op. cit.,* 309.

Right of petition fifth clause in the list of rights, was the outgrowth of the *Seven Bishops' Case*, 1688.[38] That trial has been called "the greatest historical drama that ever took place before an authorized English law court."[39] Lord Macaulay called the case "an event which stands by itself in our history."[40] When James issued his second Declaration of Indulgence in 1688, he ordered all bishops to have copies distributed throughout their dioceses, where it was to be read in the churches. Although obedience to the king had long been a doctrine of the Church of England, the widespread belief that the declaration was illegal induced Archbishop Sancroft to recommend universal disobedience of the king's order.[41] Sancroft and six bishops sent a petition to the king which stated: "Your petitioners therefore most humbly and earnestly beseech your majesty that you will be graciously pleased not to insist upon their distributing and reading your majesty's said declaration . . ."[42] Despite the respectful language of the petition, the bishops were tried on a charge of seditious libel before the Court of King's Bench. All the judges of that court had been specially chosen by the king because of the probability that they would render decisions favorable to the crown.[43] Two of the judges, however, instructed the jury in favor of the bishops—an act for which they were dismissed—and the jury returned a verdict of not guilty. The verdict met with widespread popular approval.

The Bill of Rights did not create the right to petition the crown, but merely affirmed what had been for hundreds of years a recognized right of the subject. Chapter 61 of King John's charter, 1215, provided:

> . . . if we or our justiciar, or our bailiffs, or any of our servants shall have done wrong in any way toward any one, or shall have transgressed any of the articles of peace or security; and the wrong shall have been shown to four barons of the aforesaid twenty-five barons, let those four barons come to us or to our justiciar, if we are out of the kingdom, laying before us the transgression, and let them ask that we cause that transgression to be corrected without delay.[44]

---

[38] *State Trials*, XII, 183.
[39] Trevelyan, *op. cit.*, 90.
[40] *Op. cit.*, II, 1035.
[41] Trevelyan, *op. cit.*, 87-88.
[42] Stephenson and Marcham, *op. cit.*, 584.
[43] The following account of the court is given by Macaulay: "Wright, who presided, had been raised to his high place over the heads of many abler and more learned men solely on account of his uncrupulous [sic] servility. Allibone was a Papist, and owed his situation to that dispensing power, the legality of which was now in question. Holloway had hitherto been a serviceable tool of the government. Even Powell, whose character for honesty stood high, had borne a part in some proceedings which it is impossible to defend. . . ." *Op. cit.*, II, 1020-21.
[44] See p. 21.

BILL OF RIGHTS

Petitions also played an important role from an early date in the process of legislation and in invoking the equity jurisdiction of the Lord Chancellor.[45] In 1661 an act against tumultuous petitioning was passed which provided that no more than twenty persons could sign any petition for the alteration of laws except by the order of three justices of the county, a majority of the grand jury, or by the mayor, aldermen, and council of London. Under that law petitions could not be presented to the king or Parliament by more than ten persons at a time.[46] Petitions continued to be subject to the restrictions imposed by this statute even after the enactment of the Bill of Rights.[47] In 1669 the House of Commons resolved:

> (1) That it is an inherent right of every commoner in England to prepare and present Petitions to the House of Commons in case of grievances, and the House of Commons to receive the same.
>
> (2) That it is an undoubted right and privilege of the Commons to judge and determine concerning the nature and matter of such petitions, how far they are fit or unfit to be received.[48]

In 1680 Charles issued a proclamation intended to discourage the petitions flooding in from all parts of the kingdom, which called for a new Parliament. He did not, however, go so far as to declare these petitions illegal.[49] Apparently neither the resolution of 1669 nor the Bill of Rights was intended to change the stringent laws of seditious libel, and persons presenting to Parliament petitions deemed seditious were prosecuted for contempt of that body despite those enactments.[50]

Right of petition in American constitutions

The right of petition was exercised by the American colonists as one of the chief means of making known their grievances to George III and Parliament. The fact that the king and Parliament ignored the petitions of the colonies became a grievance in itself.[51] The Declaration of Independence

---

[45] See Charles H. McIlwain, *The High Court of Parliament and Its Supremacy* (New Haven, 1910), 182-84, 198-216, 251-56; Max Radin, *Handbook of Anglo-American Legal History* (St. Paul, 1936), 425-26; K. Smellie, "Right of Petition," *Encyclopedia of Social Sciences* (New York, 1930-35), 98.

[46] 13 Car. 2, stat. 1, c. 5.

[47] Lord Chief Justice Mansfield said: "I speak the joint opinion of us all, that the act of Charles the second is in full force; there is not the colour for a doubt: the Bill of Rights does not mean to meddle with it at all . . . and consequently the attending a petition to the House of Commons by more than ten persons is criminal and illegal." *Rex v. Gordon* (1781), *State Trials*, XXI, 485, 646; William Blackstone, *Commentaries on the Laws of England* (9th ed.; London, 1783), I, 143.

[48] Robertson, *op. cit.*, 27.

[49] Hallam, *op. cit.*, 480.

[50] See Maitland, *op. cit.*, 323.

[51] See pp. 282-83.

stated: "Our repeated Petitions have been answered only by repeated injury."[52] The Declaration of Rights of Pennsylvania of 1776 stated that the people have a right to assemble together and to apply to the legislature for redress of grievances by address, petition, or remonstrance.[53] This right was also secured by other state constitutions, and appears in the first amendment to the Constitution of the United States.[54]

Standing armies   The provision that no standing army should be kept in time of peace without the consent of Parliament was intended to take the control of the military forces from the hands of the king and place it under the direction of Parliament. During the reign of Charles I (1625-49), the military forces had been under the sole command of the king.[55] In 1642 Parliament had asserted its authority to wield the "power of militia," but the power was returned to the king after the Restoration. In 1661 it was declared that *"the sole supream government, command and disposition of the militia, and of all forces by sea and land, and of all forts and places of strength, is, and by the laws of* England *ever was the undoubted right of his Majesty, and his royal predecessors, Kings and Queens of* England; ... *and that both, or either of the houses of parliament cannot, nor ought to pretend to the same ..."*[56] Parliament, however, soon reasserted its authority over the army. The impeachments of two of Charles II's chief advisers, Clarendon and Danby, in 1667 and 1679 were founded, in part, on the fact that both officials had helped raise standing armies not subject to the control of Parliament. One of James II's major objectives was the raising of a large standing army.[57] He had 20,000 troops in England—the largest force that an English king ever maintained during time of peace.[58] He staffed the army with Catholic officers, and quartered the troops at Hounslow Heath, near London, apparently for the purpose of keeping Parliament in awe.[59] The elimination of standing armies in time of peace without the approval of Parliament, unlike most clauses of the Bill of Rights, probably represented a change in the existing law instead of a declaration of an existing right of the people.[60]

Freedom from the oppression of standing armies was considered by the colonists to be one of their fundamental rights as Englishmen. The Declara-

[52] See p. 321.
[53] See p. 331.
[54] See p. 432.
[55] Maitland, *op. cit.*, 325-26.
[56] 13 Car. 2, stat. 1, c. 6.
[57] Maitland, *op. cit.*, 327-28.
[58] Macaulay, *op. cit.*, II, 664.
[59] Clark, *op. cit.*, 116-17.
[60] Hallam, *op. cit.*, 549.

tion and Resolves of the First Continental Congress, 1774, provided that "keeping a standing army in these colonies, in times of peace, without the consent of the legislature of that colony, in which such army is kept, is against law."[61] The Declaration of Independence listed as one of the offenses of the king that "he has kept among us, in times of peace, Standing Armies, without the Consent of our legislatures."[62] The Virginia Bill of Rights of 1776, which was followed in other colonies, provided that "standing armies, in time of peace, should be avoided, as dangerous to liberty."[63] The Constitution of the United States does not prohibit standing armies in time of peace. When it came to ratifying the Constitution, however, restrictions upon the authority to maintain standing armies in time of peace were proposed as amendments to the document by New Hampshire,[64] Virginia,[65] New York,[66] North Carolina,[67] and Rhode Island.[68] With the ultimate control of the military forces in Congress, the safeguards under the Constitution itself are as great as under the English Bill of Rights. Because control over standing armies was given to the people's representatives by the Constitution, the proposed amendment was not adopted.[69]

Standing armies in the American colonies

One of the policies of the Stuart kings following the Restoration was to bring the army under the control of the crown and to remove the influence of the Puritans who had dominated it during the Commonwealth. Shortly after Charles II had come to the throne, 50,000 troops were disbanded.[70] The discrimination against the right of Protestants to bear arms led to the seventh clause in the list of rights of the Bill of Rights.

Right of Protestants to bear arms

The American Revolution was opened by an attempt by the British redcoats to violate the colonists' right to bear arms. The Battle of Lexington, April 19, 1775, occurred while the British were marching to seize the arms

Right of the colonists to bear arms

---

[61] See p. 288.

[62] See p. 320.

[63] See p. 312.

[64] Tansill, *op. cit.*, 1026. Three fourths of each house of Congress might authorize a standing army.

[65] *Ibid.*, 1032. Two thirds of the members present in each house might authorize a standing army.

[66] *Ibid.*, 1040. Two thirds of the members present in each house might authorize a standing army.

[67] *Ibid.*, 1049. Two thirds of the members present in each house might authorize a standing army.

[68] *Ibid.*, 1058. Standing armies in time of peace were to be completely prohibited.

[69] Elbridge Gerry of Massachusetts had proposed in the Federal Convention that the number of troops to be kept should be limited. It was decided, however, that Congress could be trusted to prevent abuses. *Ibid.*, 567-68.

[70] Macaulay, *op. cit.*, I, 136.

and ammunition of the colonists at Concord.[71] The seizure of the colonists' arms by the British was cited as one of the causes of the war in the Declaration of the Causes and Necessity of Taking up Arms, July 6, 1775.[72] The right of the people to bear arms was secured by constitutions adopted in Virginia,[73] Pennsylvania,[74] North Carolina,[75] New York,[76] Vermont,[77] and Massachusetts.[78] The second amendment to the Constitution of the United States[79] was based directly on the earlier state documents.

Freedom of elections   Interference with the election of members of Parliament had been a common practice of English kings for more than a century before the Bill of Rights. The crown paid the salaries of representatives from the boroughs which elected representatives sympathetic to the crown. Henry VIII (1509-47) granted leaves of absence from Parliament to members of the opposition, but members who voted in favor of the king's measures were not excused from what was considered in that day to be an onerous duty. New boroughs were created by the crown where it was expected that a representative sympathetic to the crown could be returned. The Council sent instructions to sheriffs in an attempt to influence the conduct of elections; it also endorsed candidates. And members of the nobility, many of whom were in debt to the crown, were requested to exercise their influence in the elections.[80] By the Corporation Act of 1661 Charles II attempted to gain control of the election of representatives to Parliament by the indirect method of obtaining borough officials of proven loyalty.[81] Because of the great control over elections exercised by the local officials, this measure seemed well calculated to secure a loyal Parliament. As it turned out, however, the Corporation Act met with less success than had been hoped for.[82] As a result, Charles obtained the wholesale forfeiture of borough charters. He sought voluntary surrenders of the charters, and where voluntary compliance was not obtained

---

[71] See Henry S. Commager (ed.), *Documents of American History* (3d ed.; New York, 1943), I, 89-90.

[72] See p. 298.   [76] See pp. 309-10.
[73] See p. 312.   [77] See p. 366.
[74] See p. 330.   [78] See p. 376.
[75] See p. 356.   [79] See pp. 426-27, 432.

[80] William S. Holdsworth, *A History of English Law* (2d ed.; Boston, 1937), IV, 93-96.

[81] The Corporation Act of 1661, 13 Car. 2, stat. 2, c. 1, required all officials and employees of cities, corporations, boroughs, the Cinque Ports, and other port towns to take the oaths of allegiance and supremacy. They were also required to abjure the Solemn League and Covenant. Commissioners were appointed to enforce the act who had power to remove officials should they "deem it expedient for the publick safety."

[82] Holdsworth, *op. cit.*, VI, 210 and note.

quo warranto proceedings were brought to invalidate them by court action. New charters were granted in which control of the boroughs was given to royal partisans.[83] This and other techniques were later used with considerable effect by James II, and he might have obtained effective control of Parliament had not his religious policy aroused the opposition of the entire nation. The eighth clause of the list of rights was intended to prevent further abuses.

Interference by the king with the legislative processes, extending even to the outright suspension of colonial legislatures, constituted one of the chief grievances of the American colonists against George III (1760-1820). These grievances were set forth in detail by the Declaration and Resolves of the First Continental Congress[84] and the Declaration of Independence.[85] A provision of the Virginia Bill of Rights of 1776, followed in later state constitutions, provided: "That elections of members to serve as representatives of the people, in assembly, ought to be free . . ."[86] Article I, section 2, of the Constitution of the United States provides that electors of members of the House of Representatives shall have the qualifications requisite for electors of the most numerous branch of the state legislature.[87] There is no provision stating expressly that elections shall be free. Members of the Federal Convention, however, were aware that the state constitutions recognized a wide measure of freedom in elections. As Oliver Ellsworth of Connecticut expressed it, in answering a motion that a property qualification should be imposed upon electors:

Freedom of elections in American constitutions

> The right of suffrage [is] a tender point, and strongly guarded by most of the State Constitutions. The people will not readily subscribe to the Natl. Constitution if it should subject them to be disfranchised. The States are the best Judges of the circumstances & temper of their own people.[88]

The establishment of freedom of debate in Parliament ended a long-standing struggle between that body and the king over parliamentary privileges. During the Middle Ages the right of members of Parliament to debate freely was generally admitted.[89] The earliest statutory recognition of that

Freedom of debate in Parliament

---

[83] *Ibid.*, 210-11.
[84] See p. 287.
[85] See pp. 319-20.
[86] See p. 312.
[87] See p. 408.
[88] Tansill, *op. cit.*, 487.
[89] Maitland, *op. cit.*, 241.

right was Strode's Act, 1512. That act condemned all forms of punishment imposed upon members of Parliament for debating bills or other matters in Parliament.[90] Elizabeth I, however, consistently interfered with the deliberations of the Commons, and members who persisted in discussing forbidden topics were placed in the Tower.[91] In 1610 the House of Commons said in an address to James I: "We hold it an ancient, general, and undoubted right of parliament to debate freely all matters which do properly concern the subject and his right or state; which freedom of debate being once foreclosed, the essence of the liberty of parliament is withal dissolved."[92] James opposed this theory of parliamentary privilege, claiming that all the privileges of Parliament were derived "from the grace and permission of himself and his ancestors" and that "most of them grow from precedents, which shows rather a toleration than inheritance."[93] In 1621 the Commons issued a formal protestation against the king's denial of its right to discuss public issues.[94] In retaliation James dissolved Parliament, saying that certain "ill-tempered spirits have sowed tares among the corn" by taking the "inordinate liberty"

---

[90] 4 Hen. 8, c. 8: ". . . all suits, accusements, condemnations, executions, fines, amerciaments, punishments, corrections, grants, charges, and impositions, put or had, or hereafter to be put or had unto or upon the said *Richard,* and to every other of the person or persons afore specified, that now be of this present parliament, or that of any parliament hereafter shall be, for any bill, speaking, reasoning, or declaring of any matter or matters, concerning the parliament to be communed and treated of, be utterly void and of none effect." In the case of Eliot, Hollis, and Valentine, Charles I's judges held that this act applied only to proceedings in the Stannary Court. *State Trials,* III, 293. That decision was reversed after the Restoration by the House of Lords. See p. 235, note 98.

[91] In 1593 the Lord Keeper said to the Speaker of the House of Commons: "For libertie of speech, her majesty commaundeth me to tell you, that to saye yea or no to Bills, god forbid that any man should be restrained or afrayde to answear according to his best likinge, with some shorte declaracion of his reason therein, and therein to have a free voyce, which is the verye trew libertie of the house. Not as some suppose to speake there of All causes as him listeth, and to frame a form of Relligion, or a state of government as to their idle braynes shall seeme meetest, She sayth no king fitt for his state will suffer such absurdities." Quoted in Holdsworth, *op. cit.,* IV, 90.

[92] Stephenson and Marcham, *op. cit.,* 426.

[93] Quoted in Holdsworth, *op. cit.,* VI, 93.

[94] The protestation stated: "That the liberties, franchises, privileges, and jurisdictions of Parliament are the ancient and undoubted birthright and inheritance of the subjects of England; and that the arduous and urgent affairs concerning the king, state, and the defence of the realm, and of the church of England, and the maintenance and making of laws, and redress of mischiefs and grievances which daily happen within this realm, are proper subjects and matter of counsel and debate in Parliament: and that in the handling and proceeding of those businesses every member of the House of Parliament hath and of right ought to have freedom of speech, to propound, treat, reason, and bring to conclusion the same: that the Commons in Parliament have like liberty and freedom to treat of these matters in such order as in their judgments shall seem fittest: and that every member of the said House hath like freedom from all impeachment, imprisonment, and molestation (other than by censure of the House itself) for or concerning any speaking, reasoning, or declaring of any matter or matters touching the Parliament or Parliament business; and that if any of the said members be complained of, and questioned for anything done or said in Parliament, the same is to be showed to the king by the advice and assent of all the Commons assembled in Parliament before the king give credence to any private information." Quoted in *ibid.,* 94-95.

of discussing matters which were "no fit subjects to be treated of in parliament."[95]

In proceedings before the Court of King's Bench in 1629 against three members of the House of Commons, Eliot, Hollis and Valentine, it was decided that members of Parliament could be legally prosecuted for "contempts of the King and his government, and stirring up sedition."[96] The judgment violated the principle established by Strode's Act,[97] and the decision was declared illegal by resolution of Parliament in 1667.[98] The Bill of Rights confirmed the principles for which the Commons had been struggling by its declaration that speeches and debates in Parliament could not be brought into question outside that body.

Freedom of debate in Congress

In drafting the Constitution of the United States, the Federal Convention received proposals from the Committee of Detail which contained language very similar to that of the English Bill of Rights: "Freedom of speech and debate in the Legislature shall not be impeached or questioned in any Court or place out of the Legislature . . ."[99] This wording was later changed by the Committee of Style to the form in which the guarantee now appears in Article I, section 6, of the Constitution: ". . . for any speech or debate in either house, they shall not be questioned in any other place."[100]

Excessive bail

The clause of the Bill of Rights prohibiting excessive bail and cruel and unusual punishments was copied verbatim in the constitutions of many of the states at the time of the American Revolution, and it appears as the eighth amendment to the Constitution of the United States. The prohibition of excessive bail was designed to correct a defect of the Habeas Corpus Act of 1679. Although that statute did much to improve the effectiveness of the writ of habeas corpus in protecting personal liberty, the king's judges found a way to keep persons in prison for long periods of time without being brought to trial. They set bail in amounts greater than the prisoner could possibly

---

[95] Stephenson and Marcham, *op. cit.*, 430-31.

[96] *State Trials*, III, 293. In his opinion, Judge Whitlocke said: "In my opinion, the realm cannot consist without parliaments, but the behaviour of parliament-men ought to be parliamentary. No outrageous speeches were ever used against a great minister of state in parliament which have not been punished." *Ibid.*, 308.

[97] Holdsworth, *op. cit.*, VI, 98.

[98] *State Trials*, III, 314-19. The judgment was also brought before the Lords, acting in a judicial capacity, on a writ of error, and was reversed. *Ibid.*, 332-33.

[99] Max Farrand (ed.), *The Records of the Federal Convention of 1787* (New Haven, 1911), II, 180.

[100] *Ibid.*, 593.

Cruel and unusual punishments

hope to raise, and thereby frustrated the safeguards of the Habeas Corpus Act.[101] The Bill of Rights corrected this abuse.

The prohibition of cruel and unusual punishments was based on the long-standing principle of English law that the punishment should fit the crime. That is, the punishment should not be, by reason of its excessive length or severity, greatly disproportionate to the offense charged. This principle was set forth in a statute in 1553 which stated that the security of the kingdom depended more upon the love of the subject toward the king than upon the dread of laws imposing rigorous penalties and that laws made for the preservation of the commonwealth without great penalties were more often obeyed and kept than laws made with extreme punishments.[102] According to Blackstone, the provision of the Bill of Rights forbidding cruel and unusual punishments "had a retrospect to some unprecedented proceedings in the court of king's bench, in the reign of king James the Second." [103]

Even after the enactment of the Bill of Rights, punishments involving torture and mutilation continued to be legal in cases where such punishments were deemed proportionate to the crime. Blackstone's account of the punishments used in the middle of the eighteenth century is as follows:

> . . . the humanity of the English nation has authorized, by a tacit consent, an almost general mitigation of such part of these judgments as savour of torture or cruelty: a sledge or hurdle being usually allowed to such traitors as are condemned to be drawn; and there being very few instances (and those accidental or by negligence) of any person's being embowelled or burned, till previously deprived of sensation by strangling. Some punishments consist in exile or banishment, by abjuration of the realm, or transportation: others in loss of liberty, by perpetual or temporary imprisonment. Some extend

---

[101] See p. 194.

[102] 1 Mary, stat. 1, c. 1.

[103] *Op. cit.*, IV, 379. Following the unsuccessful rebellion of the Earl of Argyle and the Duke of Monmouth in 1685, Lord Jeffreys took the western circuit, where the Nonconformists were strong, to try persons who had participated in the rebellion or had aided the rebels. Among the trials which aroused the enmity of the nation were the following: Alice Lisle, widow of a high official of the Commonwealth, had sheltered two vanquished soldiers of the insurrection. Jeffreys illegally set the case for trial before the soldiers had been convicted, and intimidated the jury to obtain a verdict of guilty. He imposed the extreme sentence of burning, which was later commuted to beheading. Macaulay, *op. cit.*, II, 629-34. Tutchin, a young lad, was convicted of uttering seditious words and sentenced to imprisonment for seven years during which time he was to be flogged through every market town in Dorsetshire every year. Jeffreys refused to change the sentence even after it had been pointed out that the sentence amounted to a whipping once a fortnight for seven years. Tutchin petitioned for the death sentence instead. Jeffreys later remitted the sentence for a large bribe. *Ibid.*, 639. At the autumn sessions at the Old Bailey Elizabeth Gaunt was convicted of sheltering a fugitive, for which she was burned at the stake. *Ibid.*, 656-58. Two hundred ninety-two prisoners tried at the Bloody Assizes received the sentence of death. *Ibid.*, 634. In addition, Jeffreys directed that 841 prisoners should be bestowed upon court favorites on the condition that they be transported to the West Indies as slaves, not to be emancipated for at least ten years. *Ibid.*, 639-40.

to confiscation, by forfeiture of lands, or moveables, or both, or of the profits of lands for life: others induce a disability, of holding offices or employments, being heirs, executors, and the like. Some, though rarely, occasion a mutilation of dismembering, by cutting off the hand or ears; others fix a lasting stigma on the offender, by slitting the nostrils, or branding in the hand or cheek. Some are merely pecuniary, by stated or discretionary fines: and lastly there are others, that consist principally in their ignominy, though most of them are mixed with some degree of corporal pain; and these are inflicted chiefly for such crimes, as either arise from indigence, or render even opulence disgraceful. Such as whipping, hard labour in the house of correction or otherwise, the pillory, the stocks, and the ducking-stool.[104]

Punishments in American colonies

In the American colonies the punishments inflicted upon criminals during the eighteenth century were probably just as severe as those common in England. A Massachusetts law of 1711 provided that highway robbers should be burned on the forehead or hand, be imprisoned for six months, and render treble damages to the person robbed. A later statute inflicted the death penalty for the same offense. Thieves, particularly horse thieves, were severely dealt with. Flogging and branding were imposed for several offenses.[105]

Some question as to the kind of punishments condemned by the eighth amendment to the Constitution of the United States existed at the time of its adoption. When the Bill of Rights was being debated by Congress, one member objected:

> No cruel and unusual punishment is to be inflicted; it is sometimes necessary to hang a man, villains often deserve whipping, and perhaps having their ears cut off; but are we in future to be prevented from inflicting these punishments because they are cruel? If a more lenient mode of correcting vice and deterring others from the commission of it could be invented, it would be very prudent in the Legislature to adopt it; but until we have some security that this will be done, we ought not to be restrained from making necessary laws by any declaration of this kind.[106]

Reform of jury system

Following the restoration of the monarchy in 1660, the Stuart kings were confronted with a difficult problem in their efforts to control the administration of justice by the royal prerogative. Because the Court of Star Chamber had been abolished in 1641,[107] neither Charles II nor James II had an administrative court capable of asserting wide powers. As a result, they were unable to draw cases from the protection of trial by jury, although they

---

[104] *Op. cit.*, IV, 376.

[105] Edward Channing, *A History of the United States*, Vol. II: *A Century of Colonial History, 1660-1760* (New York, 1927), 392-94.

[106] *Annals of the Congress of the United States* (Washington, 1834), I, 754.

[107] See pp. 125-42.

might think that for reasons of state particular cases ought not to be judged by the rules of the common law. Abolition of the Star Chamber also meant a loss of the crown's power to punish juries for rendering verdicts against the weight of the evidence.[108] After the Restoration the crown could still control juries to some extent because the judges of the common law courts had authority to punish juries with whose verdicts they disagreed. This power was abolished, however, in 1670 in *Bushell's Case* in which Chief Justice Vaughan announced the rule that jurors could not be punished for their verdicts.[109] Thereafter the Stuart kings sought to control jury verdicts by influencing the manner in which jurors were selected. The device used for this purpose was similar to that which gave the king greater control over the election of members of Parliament.[110] The Corporation Act of 1661 [111] gave the crown wide authority over the appointment of the officials of cities and boroughs. These officials were relied upon to impanel juries who could be trusted to give verdicts favorable to the crown. It was this technique for the manipulation of juries which was condemned by the eleventh clause in the list of rights of the Bill of Rights. That clause provided that jurors ought to be duly impaneled and returned, and that jurors who passed upon men in trials for high treason ought to be freeholders.

Promises and grants of fines and forfeitures

The provision of the Bill of Rights that grants and promises of fines and forfeitures of particular persons before conviction shall be illegal was apparently intended to prevent the sale of pardons and exemptions from prosecution. That practice became widespread following Monmouth's unsuccessful rebellion in 1685.[112] Lord Jeffreys, in particular, was guilty of this form of graft in many instances. With the aid of disreputable companions who had the ability to drive hard bargains with the families of prisoners, he was able to accumulate a large fortune by plundering well-to-do Whigs.[113] The queen and members of the court also participated in what amounted to the worst kind of blackmail.[114] The twelfth clause in the list of rights was intended to correct these abuses.

---

[108] Holdsworth, *op. cit.*, I, 343-44.
[109] *State Trials*, VI, 999.
[110] Holdsworth, *op. cit.*, VI, 213-14; see pp. 232-33.
[111] 13 Car. 2, stat. 2, c. 1.
[112] Holdsworth, *op. cit.*, VI, 232n.
[113] Macaulay, *op. cit.*, II, 642.
[114] *Ibid.*, 642-45.

BILL OF RIGHTS

Frequency and duration of Parliaments

The vaguely worded promise that "parliaments ought to be held frequently" was intended to condemn Charles II's violation of the Triennial Act.[115] Throughout the last four years of his reign he had refused to summon a Parliament. The policy that Parliaments should be summoned frequently had been established since the time of Edward III (1327-77).[116] The Triennial Act of 1664 provided that there should be "a frequent calling, assembling, and holding of parliaments once in three years at the least." This provision of the Bill of Rights was made more precise by the Triennial Act of 1694[117] which provided that a Parliament should be held at least once in three years and which also limited the duration of Parliaments to three years. The policy which these enactments were intended to implement found its way into American constitutions, which provide for the election of members of the legislature at stated intervals.

Other Rights Established by the English Revolution

The main purpose of the Declaration of Rights had been to recite those existing rights of Parliament and the people which Charles II and James II had flagrantly violated and which William was required to observe. A number of other matters of greater complexity also confronted the nation. The settlement of these matters was not taken under consideration until a legal Parliament had been summoned for the purpose of discussing and passing appropriate legislation.[118] These statutes had an important bearing on the development of the liberties of the individual in Anglo-American constitutional law, and it is appropriate briefly to mention their general effect at this point.

The Mutiny Act of 1689

The Mutiny Act,[119] passed in April, 1689, authorized the king to maintain discipline among his soldiers. It was in force for seven months and was thereafter renewed by Parliament from year to year. The authority granted was provided by a temporary statute to assure that Parliaments would be summoned frequently and to make certain that the discipline and control of the army would always rest upon parliamentary enactment. Although the act authorized the king to maintain a standing army, it carefully stated that

---

[115] 16 Car. 2, c. 1. Cf. 16 Car. 1, c. 1.

[116] In 1362 it was provided that "for maintenance of the said articles and statutes, and redress of divers mischiefs and grievances which daily happen, a parliament shall be holden every year, as another time was ordained by statute." 36 Edw. 3, stat. 1, c. 10. The statute referred to was apparently 5 Edw. 3, c. 14.

[117] 6 & 7 Will. & Mary, c. 2.

[118] Trevelyan, *op. cit.*, 151.

[119] 1 Will. & Mary, c. 5.

standing armies not authorized by Parliament were illegal. The act is also important because it restated the principle established by the Petition of Right that civilians may not be tried by courts-martial.[120] The Mutiny Act also provided that no man may be forejudged of life or limb in any other manner than by the judgment of his peers and according to the known and established laws of the realm. This statement is of interest because it illustrates the belief which had become orthodox by that time that the judgment of peers guaranteed by Magna Carta was the same as trial by jury.[121]

The Toleration Act of 1689

The Toleration Act,[122] passed in May, 1689, was intended to grant the right of free public worship to Protestant dissenters. This right had long been advocated by the Whig party. The main body of Nonconformists had opposed James II's Declaration of Indulgence of 1687 despite that document's promise of toleration. They withheld their support because the Tory leaders and the high bishops of the established church had promised that they would join the Whigs in supporting a bill to relieve Protestants from persecution as soon as a free Parliament should meet.[123] The Toleration Act put an end to the persecutions that had been common since the Restoration. Ministers were no longer confined in prison for years; religious services no longer had to be held in secret; congregations were not imprisoned; the schools of the Nonconformists were opened; and ruinous fines were no longer exacted. A large measure of religious freedom was thus secured by the Toleration Act. Many civil disabilities remained, however, the principal one being that the Nonconformists could not hold public office. No relief whatsoever was accorded Unitarians and Catholics.[124] Thus, although the Toleration Act was a step forward, it fell far short of the concepts of religious freedom which had already developed in some of the American colonies.[125]

Trial of Treasons Act of 1696

The Trial of Treasons Act of 1696 was intended to provide procedural safeguards against miscarriages of justice such as had occurred during the reigns of Charles II and James II. Until this statute the law of treason had been governed principally by the famous statute of Edward III, 1351. That statute provided, among other things, that it should be treason "if a man do

---

[120] See pp. 74-75.
[121] Maitland, *op. cit.*, 329. See pp. 7-9.
[122] 1 Will. & Mary, c. 18.
[123] Trevelyan, *op. cit.*, 152-53.
[124] *Ibid.*, 151-58; Holdsworth, *op. cit.*, VI, 200-2.
[125] See pp. 162-79.

levy war against our lord the King in his realm, or be adhereent to the King's enemies in his realm, giving to them aid and comfort in the realm, or elsewhere, and thereof be provably attainted of open deed by the people of their condition." [126] By two statutes in 1547 and 1552 it was established that in prosecutions for treason there must be two witnesses against the defendant and that they should give their testimony before his was given.[127] The rule that there should be two witnesses to prove treason was confirmed after the Restoration by the Treason Act of 1661.[128] The act of 1696 provided that there should be "two lawful-witnesses, either both of them to the same overt act, or one of them to one, and the other of them to another overt act of the same treason." [129]

In addition, the accused was allowed to have a copy of the indictment and had the right to be represented by counsel and to produce witnesses. The statute marked an important advance in the development of the right to counsel. Before 1696 persons charged with felony, including treason or misprision of treason, had no right to be assisted by counsel. The Trial of Treasons Act thus made an important exception to the general rule. This exception was probably made because charges of treason were frequently the concomitants of political careers during the seventeenth century. In passing this bill, Parliament provided safeguards for what its members considered to be acceptable political behavior.[130]

The law of treason under the Constitution of the United States is stricter in its requirements than the English statutes. That document provides:

> Treason against the United States, shall consist only in levying war against them, or in adhering to their enemies, giving them aid and comfort. No person shall be convicted of treason unless on the testimony of two witnesses to the same overt act, or on confession in open court.[131]

Act of Settlement of 1701

The Act of Settlement of 1701 [132] completed the Revolution Settlement. It prescribed additional limitations on the prerogatives of the crown, defined the conditions on which the crown should be held, and determined the order

---

[126] 25 Edw. 3, stat. 5, c. 2.
[127] 1 Edw. 6, c. 12; 5 and 6 Edw. 6, c. 11.
[128] 13 Car. 2, c. 1.
[129] 7 & 8 Will. 3, c. 3.
[130] William M. Beaney, *The Right to Counsel in American Courts* (Ann Arbor, 1955), 9.
[131] See p. 415.
[132] 12 & 13 Will. 3, c. 2.

SOURCES OF OUR LIBERTIES

of succession to the throne. The most important provision of this document to find its way into American constitutional law is the clause making the courts independent. Throughout the reigns of the Stuart kings judges had been the servile creatures of the king, subject to dismissal if they withstood him. They held their offices only during the king's good pleasure. The Act of Settlement provided that judges should hold office during good behavior, that they should receive ascertained and established salaries, and that they could be dismissed only upon the address of both houses of Parliament.

The Declaration of Independence charged that George III had interfered with the independence of judges.[133] This safeguard was secured by the Delaware Declaration of Rights of 1776[134] and by later state constitutions. The principle of the Act of Settlement appears in the Constitution of the United States in the following language: "The Judges, both of the supreme and inferior Courts, shall hold their Offices during good Behaviour, and shall, at stated Times, receive for their Services, a compensation, which shall not be diminished during their Continuance in Office."[135]

Licensing of the press

Following the invention of printing in the fifteenth century the publication of books was regarded as a business, subject to regulation by the appropriate crafts or by the government like other businesses. During the Elizabethan period the business of printing was regulated under detailed rules to protect the state against nonconforming religious and political opinions and to prevent destructive trade practices. In 1586 an ordinance issued by the Star Chamber provided that no printing was to take place in any place except London, Oxford, or Cambridge; the Archbishop of Canterbury and the Bishop of London were to decide the number of presses needed; all books were to be licensed by appropriate officials; and no books contrary to any statute or royal order were to be printed.[136] An even stricter licensing ordinance was issued by the Star Chamber in 1637. This provided an elaborate scheme of licensing designed to prevent the appearance of unlicensed books; all books were to bear the names of the printer and author; the number of master printers was limited to twenty; no one was allowed to erect a new press or cast type without notifying the Stationers' Company; wide powers of search to find violations of the ordinance were given to that company; and restrictions were placed upon the importation of books.[137]

[133] See p. 320.
[134] See p. 340.
[135] See p. 414.
[136] Holdsworth, *op. cit.*, VI, 367-68.
[137] *Ibid.*, 368-69.

When the Star Chamber was abolished in 1641, the question of control of the press arose. Representatives of the printing industry pointed out that an unlicensed press was dangerous to religion and to the state. They also argued that the abolition of licensing would destroy copyrights, a form of property which had become inseparably connected with licensing. This result, they said, would impoverish members of the industry and ruin orphans and widows whose estates consisted of income derived from copyrights. John Milton spoke out in favor of unlicensed printing and set forth his views in the famous *Areopagitica,* addressed to Parliament in 1644. The revolutionary government, being sensitive to criticism, decided to continue licensing under an ordinance similar to the one promulgated by the Star Chamber in 1637.[138] Milton himself realized that his own views were "a strain of too high a mood."

After the Restoration the provisions of the Star Chamber ordinance were substantially re-enacted by the Licensing Act of 1662,[139] which was entitled *"an act for preventing abuses in printing seditious, treasonable, and unlicensed books and pamphlets, and for regulating of printing and printing-presses."* This act was temporary, but it was renewed from time to time. After William and Mary ascended the throne, opposition to the Licensing Act grew because it gave large powers to the crown. Finally, the Licensing Act was allowed to expire in 1695. This happened partly because Milton's arguments in *Areopagitica* received greater consideration and partly because Parliament felt that many of the restrictions imposed by the Licensing Act were both illogical and inconvenient. The expiration of the Licensing Act thus constituted one of the landmarks in the establishment of the freedom of the press.

The general significance of the English Declaration and Bill of Rights was summed up by Lord Macaulay as follows: **Conclusion**

> The Declaration of Right, though it made nothing law which had not been law before, contained the germ of the law which gave religious freedom to the Dissenter, of the law which secured the independence of the Judges, of the law which limited the duration of Parliaments, of the law which placed the liberty of the press under the protection of juries, of the law which prohibited the slave trade, of the law which abolished the sacramental test, of the law which relieved the Roman Catholics from civil disabilities, of the law which reformed the representative system, of every good law

[138] *Ibid.,* 371.
[139] 13 & 14 Car. 2, c. 33.

which has been passed during more than a century and a half, of every good law which may hereafter, in the course of ages, be found necessary to promote the public weal, and to satisfy the demands of public opinion.[140]

The Bill of Rights of 1689 was the direct ancestor of the bills of rights adopted by the states at the time of the American Revolution and of the first ten amendments to the Constitution of the United States. Many of its provisions directly affected the form and content of specific provisions found in those documents under which the liberties of the citizen of the United States are protected even today.

[140] *Op. cit.*, III, 1311.

BILL OF RIGHTS[141]
December 16, 1689

An act for declaring the rights and liberties of the subject, and settling the succession of the crown.

WHEREAS *the lords spiritual and temporal, and commons assembled at Westminster, lawfully, fully, and freely representing all the estates of the people of this realm, did upon the thirteenth day of* February, *in the year of our Lord one thousand six hundred eighty eight, present unto their Majesties, then called and known by the names and stile of* William *and* Mary, *prince and princess of* Orange, *being present in their proper persons, a certain declaration in writing, made by the said lords and commons, in the words following; viz.* — Preamble

WHEREAS *the late King* James *the Second, by the assistance of divers evil counsellors, judges, and ministers employed by him, did endeavour to subvert and extirpate the protestant religion, and the laws and liberties of this kingdom.* — Grievances

1. *By assuming and exercising a power of dispensing with and suspending of laws, and the execution of laws, without consent of parliament.* — Suspension of laws

2. *By committing and prosecuting divers worthy prelates, for humbly petitioning to be excused from concurring to the said assumed power.* — Prosecution of bishops

3. *By issuing and causing to be executed a commission under the great seal for erecting a court called,* The court of commissioners for ecclesiastical causes. — Court of High Commission

4. *By levying money for and to the use of the crown, by pretence of prerogative, for other time, and in other manner, than the same was granted by parliament.* — Prerogative taxation

5. *By raising and keeping a standing army within this kingdom in time of peace, without consent of parliament, and quartering soldiers contrary to law.* — Standing army

6. *By causing several good subjects, being protestants, to be disarmed, at the same time when papists were both armed and employed, contrary to law.* — Disarming of Protestants

7. *By violating the freedom of election of members to serve in parliament.* — Free elections

8. *By prosecutions in the court of King's bench, for matters and causes cognizable only in parliament; and by divers other arbitrary and illegal courses.* — Illegal prosecutions

9. *And whereas of late years, partial, corrupt, and unqualified persons have been returned and served on juries in trials, and particularly divers jurors in trials for high treason, which were not freeholders.* — Juries

---

[141] 1 Will. and Mary, sess. 2, c. 2. Danby Pickering (ed.), *Statutes at Large* (Cambridge, 1726-1807), IX, 67-73.

Bail	10. And excessive bail hath been required of persons committed in criminal cases, to elude the benefit of the laws made for the liberty of the subjects.
Fines and punishments	11. And excessive fines have been imposed; and illegal and cruel punishments inflicted.
Grants and promises of fines and forfeitures	12. And several grants and promises made of fines and forfeitures, before any conviction or judgment against the persons, upon whom the same same were to be levied.

All which are utterly and directly contrary to the known laws and statutes, and freedom of this realm.

Throne declared vacant

And whereas the said late King James *the Second having abdicated the government, and the throne being thereby vacant, his highness the prince of* Orange (*whom it hath pleased Almighty God to make the glorious instrument of delivering this kingdom from popery and arbitrary power*) *did* (*by the advice of the lords spiritual and temporal, and divers principal persons of the commons*) *cause letters to be written to the lords spiritual and temporal, being protestants; and other letters to the several counties, cities, universities, boroughs, and cinque-ports, for the choosing of such persons to represent them, as were of right to be sent to parliament, to meet and sit at* Westminster *upon the two and twentieth day of* January, *in this year one thousand six hundred eighty and eight, in order to such an establishment, as that their religion, laws, and liberties might not again be in danger of being subverted: upon which letters, elections have been accordingly made,*

Rights of the People

And thereupon the said lords spiritual and temporal, and commons, pursuant to their respective letters and elections, being now assembled in a full and free representative of this nation, taking into their most serious consideration the best means for attaining the ends aforesaid; do in the first place (*as their ancestors in like case have usually done*) *for the vindicating and asserting their ancient rights and liberties, declare;*

Suspension of laws

1. *That the pretended power of suspending of laws, or the execution of laws, by regal authority, without consent of parliament, is illegal.*

Dispensing with laws

2. *That the pretended power of dispensing with laws, or the execution of laws, by regal authority, as it hath been assumed and exercised of late, is illegal.*

Court of High Commission

3. *That the commission for erecting the late court of commissioners for ecclesiastical causes, and all other commissions and courts of like nature are illegal and pernicious.*

Prerogative taxation

4. *That levying money for or to the use of the crown, by pretence of prerogative, without grant of parliament, for longer time, or in other manner than the same is or shall be granted, is illegal.*

Petitions

5. *That it is the right of the subjects to petition the King, and all committments and prosecutions for such petitioning are illegal.*

Standing armies

6. *That the raising or keeping a standing army within the kingdom in time of peace, unless it be with consent of parliament, is against law.*

Protestants may bear arms

7. *That the subjects which are protestants, may have arms for their defence suitable to their conditions, and as allowed by law.*

Free elections

8. *That election of members of parliament ought to be free.*

BILL OF RIGHTS

9. That the freedom of speech, and debates or proceedings in parliament, ought not to be impeached or questioned in any court or place out of parliament. *— Free speech in Parliament*

10. That excessive bail ought not to be required, nor excessive fines imposed; nor cruel and unusual punishments inflicted. *— Bail, fines, and punishments*

11. That jurors ought to be duly impanelled and returned, and jurors which pass upon men in trials for high treason ought to be freeholders. *— Juries*

12. That all grants and promises of fines and forfeitures of particular persons before conviction, are illegal and void. *— Fines and forfeitures*

13. And that for redress of all grievances, and for the amending, strengthening, and preserving of the laws, parliaments ought to be held frequently. *— Frequent Parliaments*

And they do claim, demand, and insist upon all and singular the premisses, as their undoubted rights and liberties; and that no declarations, judgments, doings or proceedings, to the prejudice of the people in any of the said premisses, ought in any wise to be drawn hereafter into consequence or example.

To which demand of their rights they are particularly encouraged by the declaration of his highness the prince of Orange, as being the only means for obtaining a full redress and remedy therein.

Having therefore an entire confidence, That his said highness the prince of Orange will perfect the deliverance so far advanced by him, and will still preserve them from the violation of their rights, which they have here asserted, and from all other attempts upon their religion, rights, and liberties. *— William and Mary declared king and queen*

II. The said lords spiritual and temporal, and commons, assembled at Westminster, do resolve, That William and Mary prince and princess of Orange be, and be declared, King and Queen of England, France and Ireland, and the dominions thereunto belonging, to hold the crown and royal dignity of the said kingdoms and dominions to them the said prince and princess during their lives, and the life of the survivor of them; and that the sole and full exercise of the regal power be only in, and executed by the said prince of Orange, in the names of the said prince and princess, during their joint lives; and after their deceases, the said crown and royal dignity of the said kingdoms and dominions to be to the heirs of the body of the said princess; and for default of such issue to the princess Anne of Denmark, and the heirs of her body; and for default of such issue to the heirs of the body of the said prince of Orange. And the lords spiritual and temporal, and commons, do pray the said prince and princess to accept the same accordingly. *— Regal power to be exercised by William*

III. And that the oaths hereafter mentioned be taken by all persons of whom the oaths of allegiance and supremacy might be required by law, instead of them; and that the said oaths of allegiance and supremacy be abrogated. *— Oaths of allegiance and supremacy*

I A. B. do sincerely promise and swear, That I will be faithful, and bear true allegiance, to their Majesties King William and Queen Mary:
                                                              So help me God.

I A. B. do swear, That I do from my heart abhor, detest, and abjure as impious and heretical, that damnable doctrine and position, That princes excommunicated or deprived by the pope, or any authority of the see of *Rome*, may be deposed or murdered by their subjects, or any other whatsoever. *And I do declare, That no foreign prince, person, prelate, state, or potentate hath, or ought to have any jurisdiction, power, superiority, pre-eminence, or authority ecclesiastical or spiritual, within this realm:*

So help me God.

Acceptance of the crown

IV. *Upon which their said Majesties did accept the crown and royal dignity of the kingdoms of* England, France, *and* Ireland, *and the dominions thereunto belonging, according to the resolution and desire of the said lords and commons contained in the said declaration.*

Parliament to continue to sit

V. *And thereupon their Majesties were pleased, That the said lords spiritual and temporal, and commons, being the two houses of parliament, should continue to sit, and with their Majesties royal concurrence make effectual provision for the settlement of the religion, laws and liberties of this kingdom, so that the same for the future might not be in danger again of being subverted; to which the said lords spiritual and temporal, and commons, did agree and proceed to act accordingly.*

Confirmation of liberties

VI. Now in pursuance of the premisses, the said lords spiritual and temporal, and commons, in parliament assembled, for the ratifying, confirming and establishing the said declaration, and the articles, clauses, matters, and things therein contained, by the force of a law made in due form by authority of parliament, do pray that it may be declared and enacted, That all and singular the rights and liberties asserted and claimed in the said declaration, are the true, ancient, and indubitable rights and liberties of the people of this kingdom, and so shall be esteemed, allowed, adjudged, deemed, and taken to be, and that all and every the particulars aforesaid shall be firmly and strictly holden and observed, as they are expressed in the said declaration; and all officers and ministers whatsoever shall serve their Majesties and their successors according to the same in all times to come.

William and Mary declared sovereign liege lord and lady

VII. And the said lords spiritual and temporal, and commons, seriously considering how it hath pleased Almighty God, in his marvellous providence, and merciful goodness to this nation, to provide and preserve their said Majesties royal persons most happily to reign over us upon the throne of their ancestors, for which they render unto him from the bottom of their hearts their humblest thanks and praises, do truly, firmly, assuredly, and in the sincerity of their hearts think, and do hereby recognize, acknowledge and declare, That King *James* the Second having abdicated the government, and their Majesties having accepted the crown and royal dignity as aforesaid, their said Majesties did become, were, are, and of right ought to be, by the laws of this realm, our sovereign liege lord and lady, King and Queen of *England, France,* and *Ireland,* and the dominions thereunto belonging, in and to whose princely persons the royal state, crown, and dignity of the said realms, with all honours, stiles, titles, regalities, prerogatives, powers, jurisdictions and authorities to the same belonging and appertaining, are most fully, rightfully, and intirely invested and incorporated, united and annexed.

VIII. And for preventing all questions and divisions in this realm, by reason of any pretended titles to the crown, and for preserving a certainty in the succession thereof, in and upon which the unity, peace, tranquillity, and safety of this nation doth, under God, wholly consist and depend, The said lords spiritual and temporal, and commons, do beseech their Majesties that it may be enacted, established and declared, That the crown and regal government of the said kingdoms and dominions, with all and singular the premisses thereunto belonging and appertaining, shall be and continue to their said Majesties, and the survivor of them, during their lives, and the life of the survivor of them: And that the intire, perfect, and full exercise of the regal power and government be only in, and executed by his Majesty, in the names of both their Majesties during their joint lives; and after their deceases the said crown and premisses shall be and remain to the heirs of the body of her Majesty; and for default of such issue, to her royal highness the princess *Anne* of *Denmark,* and the heirs of her body; and for default of such issue, to the heirs of the body of his said Majesty: And thereunto the said lords spiritual and temporal, and commons, do, in the name of all the people aforesaid, most humbly and faithfully submit themselves, their heirs and posterities for ever; and do faithfully promise, That they will stand to, maintain, and defend their said Majesties, and also the limitation and succession of the crown herein specified and contained, to the utmost of their powers, with their lives and estates, against all persons whatsoever, that shall attempt any thing to the contrary. *(Succession to the throne)*

IX. *And whereas it hath been found by experience, that it is inconsistent with the safety and welfare of this protestant kingdom, to be governed by a popish prince, or by any King or Queen marrying a papist;* the said lords spiritual and temporal, and commons, do further pray that it may be enacted, That all and every person and persons that is, are or shall be reconciled to, or shall hold communion with, the see or church of *Rome,* or shall profess the popish religion, or shall marry a papist, shall be excluded, and be for ever incapable to inherit, possess, or enjoy the crown and government of this realm, and *Ireland,* and the dominions thereunto belonging, or any part of the same, or to have, use, or exercise any regal power, authority, or jurisdiction within the same; and in all and every such case or cases the people of these realms shall be, and are hereby absolved of their allegiance; and the said crown and government shall from time to time descend to, and be enjoyed by such person or persons, being protestants, as should have inherited and enjoyed the same, in case the said person or persons so reconciled, holding communion, or professing, or marrying as aforesaid, were naturally dead. *(Catholics and persons marrying Catholics barred from inheriting the throne)*

X. And that every King and Queen of this realm, who at any time hereafter shall come to and succeed in the imperial crown of this kingdom, shall on the first day of the meeting of the first parliament, next after his or her coming to the crown, sitting in his or her throne in the house of peers, in the presence of the lords and commons therein assembled, or at his or her coronation, before such person or persons who shall administer the coronation oath to him or her, at the time of his or her taking the said oath *(King and queen required to take the test oath)* (which shall first happen) make, subscribe, and audibly repeat the declaration mentioned in the statute made in the thirtieth year of the reign of King *Charles* the Second, intituled, *An act for the more effectual preserving the King's person and government, by disabling papists from sitting in either house of parliament*. But if it shall happen, that such King or Queen, upon his or her succession to the crown of this realm, shall be under the age of twelve years, then every such King or Queen shall make, subscribe, and audibly repeat the said declaration at his or her coronation, or the first day of the meeting of the first parliament as aforesaid, what shall first happen after such King or Queen shall have attained the said age of twelve years.

Foregoing provisions to be the law of the realm forever

XI. All which their Majesties are contented and pleased shall be declared, enacted, and established by authority of this present parliament, and shall stand, remain, and be the law of this realm for ever; and the same are by their said Majesties, by and with the advice and consent of the lords spiritual and temporal, and commons, in parliament assembled, and by the authority of the same, declared, enacted, and established accordingly.

Power of dispensation to be settled during the present session

XII. And be it further declared and enacted by the authority aforesaid, That from and after this present session of parliament, no dispensation by *non obstante* of or to any statute, or any part thereof, shall be allowed, but that the same shall be held void and of no effect, except a dispensation be allowed of in such statute, and except in such cases as shall be specially provided for by one or more bill or bills to be passed during this present session of parliament.

Validity of charters, etc., before October 23, 1689

XIII. Provided that no charter, or grant, or pardon, granted before the three and twentieth day of *October*, in the year of our Lord one thousand six hundred eighty nine shall be any ways impeached or invalidated by this act, but that the same shall be and remain of the same force and effect in law, and no other then as if this act had never been made.

REFERENCES

Clark, G. N. *The Later Stuarts, 1660-1714* (*The Oxford History of England*). Oxford: Clarendon Press, 1934.
Pinkham, Lucile. *William III and the Respectable Revolution*. Cambridge, Mass.: Harvard University Press, 1954.
Plum, Harry G. *Restoration Puritanism*. Chapel Hill: University of North Carolina Press, 1943.
Robertson, Charles G. (ed.). *Select Statutes, Cases, and Documents*. London: Methuen & Co., 1949.
Trevelyan, George M. *The English Revolution, 1688-1689*. London: Thornton Butterworth, Ltd., 1938.
Yonge, Charles D. *History of the English Revolution of 1688*. London: Henry S. King & Co., 1874.

XVII. PENNSYLVANIA CHARTER OF PRIVILEGES[1]

1701

Penn made his second voyage to the province in 1700. At that time the Frame of Government issued in 1696 by Governor Markham was being treated as in force. The question of the organization of the government, always uppermost in the minds of the colonists, was again raised. Penn refused to be bound by the Markham charter because he had never assented to it. He probably would have preferred to see the government continue under the Charter of 1681 and the Frame of Government of 1683, but his customary conciliatory attitude toward the wishes of the colonists overcame his own preferences. "Friends," he said, "if in the Constitution by charter there be anything that jars, alter it." In addition, Penn had received information that Parliament was considering a bill to abolish all proprietary governments including his own. He desired, therefore, that agreement be reached as soon as possible so that he could return to England to protect his interests. The council resolved to read both the Markham frame and the Frame of Government of 1683 "and keep what's good in either, to lay aside what's inconvenient and burdensome, and to add to both what may best suit the common good." The result was to be presented to Penn for approval. The subject was debated at intervals for several months, and the Frame of Government of 1683 was abolished by a six-sevenths vote of the General Assembly. The Charter of Privileges of 1701 was issued in its place.

Origins

This document has been described as "the most famous of all colonial constitutions."[2] A guarantee of liberty of conscience was placed at the head

General Significance

---

[1] See pp. 204-21.
[2] Edward Channing, *A History of the United States*, Vol. II: *A Century of Colonial History, 1660-1760* (New York, 1927), 322.

of the articles of government. The independence of the assembly was fully recognized. It functioned as a unicameral body, and was given the right to initiate legislation. Persons accused of crime were given the right to have witnesses in their defense. The concept of due process of law was preserved by the provision that in matters relating to property the "ordinary course of justice" should be followed. The charter was established as the fundamental law of the province by the provision that amendments and contrary laws should require a six-sevenths vote of the assembly. The provision for religious liberty, however, was to be kept inviolable forever.

Right to counsel A marked advance over English law was made by article V, which provided that criminals should have the same right to counsel as their prosecutors. It was not until 1836 that English law gave defendants an absolute right to be assisted by counsel in all cases.[3]

During the reign of Queen Elizabeth I (1558-1603), the rights of persons accused of crime were restricted by several rules designed to enable the state successfully to prosecute traitors and other lawbreakers. The prisoner was often confined in secret until trial and had no opportunity to prepare his defense; no notice was given of the evidence or witnesses against him; there was no right to confront the accusers; there were no established rules of evidence; and the accused was not allowed to summon witnesses in his favor or have the advice of counsel.[4]

Persons charged with misdemeanors were allowed counsel. The right was denied, however, in capital cases. It was said that the judge should be counsel for the prisoner. The judge's duty to assure the fairness of the trial, however, could not justify the distinction made between cases involving petty offenses and those involving more serious charges. An important exception to this strict rule was made in 1696 by the Trial of Treasons Act.[5] That statute recognized that in treason cases political influences might often prevent the judges from acting impartially toward the prisoner.[6] At that time, of course, the judges were appointed by the crown and served at the monarch's pleasure.[7] Not only did the Trial of Treasons Act give prisoners the right to counsel, but it also required the court to assign counsel to the defendant.

[3] William M. Beaney, *The Right to Counsel in American Courts* (Ann Arbor, 1955), 9.
[4] James F. Stephen, *A History of the Criminal Law of England* (London, 1883), I, 350.
[5] See pp. 240-41.
[6] William Blackstone, *Commentaries on the Laws of England* (9th ed.; London, 1783), IV, 355-56.
[7] See pp. 241-42.

PENNSYLVANIA CHARTER OF PRIVILEGES

Colonial documents such as the Massachusetts Body of Liberties of 1641[8] and the Pennsylvania Frame of Government of 1682[9] gave defendants the right to be represented by individuals serving without pay or by their friends. A Rhode Island statute of 1660 gave defendants the right to employ counsel for the limited purpose of arguing questions of law.[10] By the middle of the eighteenth century the English common law had progressed no further than this.[11]

By giving defendants the right to employ counsel for every purpose in making a defense against a charge of crime, the Pennsylvania Charter of Privileges of 1701 was thus considerably in advance of the English common law courts. After the American Revolution the right to retain counsel was secured by the Pennsylvania Declaration of Rights of 1776[12] and by the constitutions of several other states. That right now appears as part of the sixth amendment to the Constitution of the United States.[13]

Article V of the Pennsylvania Charter of Privileges also gave defendants the same right as their prosecutors to summon witnesses. During the medieval period, witnesses did not play a prominent part in the administration of justice. The reason for this was that members of the jury were men of the neighborhood who decided the case on the basis of their personal knowledge. Proof of the facts by witnesses was thus generally unnecessary.

Right to summon witnesses

It was not until the sixteenth century that the jury began to try the facts of the case on the basis of evidence presented to it.[14] This fundamental change in the jury system required greater reliance on the testimony of witnesses. Persons accused of crime, however, were denied the right to call witnesses in their defense. The reason given for this rule was that it was up to the prosecutor to prove his case; and once he had proved it, it could only be an invitation to perjury if the defendant were allowed to rebut his evidence. This reasoning concealed the real motive for the rule, which was to strengthen the position of the crown in criminal prosecutions. In the latter half of the seventeenth century defendants were allowed to have witnesses, but they were not examined under oath.[15]

Exceptions to the strict rule against witnesses were made by Mary

[8] See p. 151.
[9] See p. 217.
[10] Beaney, *op. cit.*, 17-18.
[11] Blackstone, *op. cit.*, IV, 355.
[12] See p. 330.
[13] See p. 432.
[14] William S. Holdsworth, *A History of English Law* (4th ed.; Boston, 1938), IX, 131.
[15] *Ibid.*, I, 336; Stephen, *op. cit.*, I, 350-55.

(1553-58) and Elizabeth I; and Sir Edward Coke protested vigorously against this injustice to defendants.[16] The right of the defendant to call witnesses was established in treason cases by the Trial of Treasons Act of 1696.[17] The right was extended to all defendants in England in 1702.[18] The sixth amendment to the Constitution of the United States gives defendants the right to have compulsory process to secure witnesses for their defense.

The Pennsylvania Charter of Privileges thus paralleled the development in England of the right of defendants in capital cases to have witnesses for their defense. It was far ahead of English law, however, in so far as the right to counsel was concerned.

[16] Blackstone, *op. cit.*, IV, 359-60.

[17] See pp. 240-41.

[18] Witnesses for the prisoner were required to "take an oath to depose the truth, the whole truth, and nothing but the truth, in such manner, as the witnesses for the Queen are by law obliged to do; and if convicted of any wilful perjury in such evidence, shall suffer all the punishments, penalties, forfeitures, and disabilities, which by any of the laws and statutes of this realm are and may be inflicted upon persons convicted of wilful perjury." 1 Anne stat. 2, c. 9, § 3.

PENNSYLVANIA CHARTER OF PRIVILEGES[19]

October 28, 1701

WILLIAM PENN, Proprietary and Governor of the Province of *Pensilvania* and Territories thereunto belonging, To all to whom these Presents shall come, sendeth Greeting. WHEREAS King CHARLES *the Second,* by His Letters Patents, under the Great Seal of *England,* bearing Date the *Fourth* Day of *March,* in the Year *One Thousand Six Hundred and Eighty-one,* was graciously pleased to give and grant unto me, and my Heirs and Assigns for ever, this Province of *Pensilvania,* with divers great Powers and Jurisdictions for the well Government thereof. *Recital of Charter of 1681*

AND WHEREAS the King's dearest Brother, JAMES *Duke of* YORK *and* ALBANY, &c. by his Deeds of Feoffment, under his Hand and Seal duly perfected, bearing Date the *Twenty-Fourth* Day of *August,* One Thousand Six Hundred Eighty and Two, did grant unto me, my Heirs and Assigns, all that Tract of Land, now called the Territories of *Pensilvania,* together with Powers and Jurisdictions for the good Government thereof. *Recital of deed from the Duke of York, 1682*

AND WHEREAS for the Encouragement of all the Freemen and Planters, that might be concerned in the said Province and Territories, and for the good Government thereof, I the said WILLIAM PENN, in the Year *One Thousand Six Hundred Eighty and Three,* for me, my Heirs and Assigns, did grant and confirm unto all the Freemen, Planters and Adventurers therein, divers Liberties, Franchises and Properties, as by the said Grant, entituled, *The* FRAME *of the Government of the Province of* Pensilvania, *and Territories thereunto belonging, in* America, may appear; which Charter or Frame being found in some Parts of it, not so suitable to the present Circumstances of the Inhabitants, was in the *Third* Month, in the Year *One Thousand Seven Hundred,* delivered up to me, by *Six* Parts of *Seven* of the Freemen of this Province and Territories, in General Assembly met, Provision being made in the said Charter, for that End and Purpose. *Recital of Frame of Government of 1683*

AND WHEREAS I was then pleased to promise, That I would restore the said Charter to them again, with necessary Alterations, or in lieu thereof, give them

---

[19] Francis N. Thorpe (ed.), *The Federal and State Constitutions, Colonial Charters, and Other Organic Laws* (Washington, 1909), V, 3076-81. The document's full title is: "Charter of Privileges Granted by William Penn, Esq. to the Inhabitants of Pennsylvania and Territories."

another, better adapted to answer the present Circumstances and Conditions of the said Inhabitants; which they have now, by their Representatives in General Assembly met at *Philadelphia,* requested me to grant.

Liberties of inhabitants to be held forever

KNOW YE THEREFORE, That for the further Well-being and good Government of the said Province, and Territories; and in Pursuance of the Rights and Powers before-mentioned, I the said *William Penn* do declare, grant and confirm, unto all the Freemen, Planters and Adventurers, and other Inhabitants of this Province and Territories, these following Liberties, Franchises and Privileges, so far as in me lieth, to be held, enjoyed and kept, by the Freemen, Planters and Adventurers, and other Inhabitants of and in the said Province and Territories thereunto annexed, for ever.

FIRST

Liberty of conscience

BECAUSE no People can be truly happy, though under the greatest Enjoyment of Civil Liberties, if abridged of the Freedom of their Consciences, as to their Religious Profession and Worship: And Almighty God being the only Lord of Conscience, Father of Lights and Spirits; and the Author as well as Object of all divine Knowledge, Faith and Worship, who only doth enlighten the Minds, and persuade and convince the Understandings of People, I do hereby grant and declare, That no Person or Persons, inhabiting in this Province or Territories, who shall confess and acknowledge *One* almighty God, the Creator, Upholder and Ruler of the World; and profess him or themselves obliged to live quietly under the Civil Government, shall be in any Case molested or prejudiced, in his or their Person or Estate, because of his or their conscientious Persuasion or Practice, nor be compelled to frequent or maintain any religious Worship, Place or Ministry, contrary to his or their Mind, or to do or suffer any other Act or Thing, contrary to their religious Persuasion.

Qualifications of officers

AND that all Persons who also profess to believe in *Jesus Christ,* the Saviour of the World, shall be capable (notwithstanding their other Persuasions and Practices in Point of Conscience and Religion) to serve this Government in any Capacity, both legislatively and executively, he or they solemnly promising, when lawfully required, Allegiance to the King as Sovereign, and Fidelity to the Proprietary and Governor, and taking the Attests as now established by the Law made at *New-Castle,* in the Year One Thousand and Seven Hundred, entitled, *An Act directing the Attests of several Officers and Ministers,* as now amended and confirmed this present Assembly.

II

Assembly
Selection of members

FOR the well governing of this Province and Territories, there shall be an Assembly yearly chosen, by the Freemen thereof, to consist of *Four* Persons out of each County, of most Note for Virtue, Wisdom and Ability, (or of a greater number at any Time, as

PENNSYLVANIA CHARTER OF PRIVILEGES

the Governor and Assembly shall agree) upon the *First* Day of *October* for ever; and shall sit on the *Fourteenth* Day of the same Month, at *Philadelphia,* unless the Governor and Council for the Time being, shall see Cause to appoint another Place within the said Province or Territories: Which Assembly shall have Power to chuse a Speaker and other their Officers; and shall be Judges of the Qualifications and Elections of their own Members; sit upon their own Adjournment; appoint Committees; prepare Bills in order to pass into Laws; impeach Criminals, and redress Grievances; and shall have all other Powers and Privileges of an Assembly, according to the Rights of the free-born Subjects of *England,* and as is usual in any of the King's Plantations in *America.* *Meetings* *Officers* *Adjournment* *Committees; laws; impeachment; grievances; other powers*

AND if any County or Counites, shall refuse or neglect to chuse their respective Representatives as aforesaid, or if chosen, do not meet to serve in Assembly, those who are so chosen and met, shall have the full Power of an Assembly, in as ample Manner as if all the Representatives had been chosen and met, provided they are not less than *Two Thirds* of the whole Number that ought to meet. *Quorum*

AND that the Qualifications of Electors and Elected, and all other Matters and Things relating to Elections of Representatives to serve in Assemblies, though not herein particularly expressed, shall be and remain as by a Law of this Government, made at *New-Castle* in the Year *One Thousand Seven Hundred,* entitled, *An Act to ascertain the Number of Members of Assembly, and to regulate the Elections.* *Qualifications of electors and representatives*

III

THAT the Freemen in each respective County, at the Time and Place of Meeting for Electing their Representatives to serve in Assembly, may as often as there shall be Occasion, chuse a double Number of Persons to present to the Governor for Sheriffs and Coroners to serve for *Three* Years, if so long they behave themselves well; out of which respective Elections and Presentments, the Governor shall nominate and commissionate one for each of the said Offices, the *Third* Day after such Presentment, or else the *First* named in such Presentment, for each Office as aforesaid, shall stand and serve in that Office for the Time before respectively limited; and in Case of Death or Default, such Vacancies shall be supplied by the Governor, to serve to the End of the said Term. *Election of sheriffs and coroners*

PROVIDED ALWAYS, That if the said Freemen shall at any Time neglect or decline to chuse a Person or Persons for either or both the aforesaid Offices, then and in such Case, the Persons that are or shall be in the respective Offices of Sheriffs or Coroners, at the Time of Election, shall remain therein, until they shall be removed by another Election as aforesaid. *In absence of an election*

AND that the Justices of the respective Counties shall or may nominate and present to the Governor *Three* Persons, to serve for Clerk of the Peace for the said County, when there is a Vacancy, one of which the Governor shall commissionate within *Ten* *Clerk of the peace*

Days after such Presentment, or else the *First* nominated shall serve in the said Office during good Behavior.

IV

Records of laws

THAT the Laws of this Government shall be in this Stile, viz. *By the Governor, with the Consent and Approbation of the Freemen in General Assembly met;* and shall be, after Confirmation by the Governor, forthwith recorded in the Rolls Office, and kept at *Philadelphia,* unless the Governor and Assembly shall agree to appoint another Place.

V

Witnesses and counsel

THAT all Criminals shall have the same Privileges of Witnesses and Council as their Prosecutors.

VI

Complaints before the governor and council

THAT no Person or Persons shall or may, at any Time hereafter, be obliged to answer any Complaint, Matter or Thing whatsoever, relating to Property, before the Governor and Council, or in any other Place, but in ordinary Course of Justice, unless Appeals thereunto shall be hereafter by Law appointed.

VII

Licensing of taverns

THAT no Person within this Government, shall be licensed by the Governor to keep an Ordinary, Tavern or House of Publick Entertainment, but such who are first recommended to him, under the Hands of the Justices of the respective Counties, signed in open Court; which Justices are and shall be hereby impowered, to suppress and forbid any Person, keeping such Publick-House as aforesaid, upon their Misbehaviour, on such Penalties as the Law doth or shall direct; and to recommend others from time to time, as they shall see Occasion.

VIII

No forfeiture in cases of suicide

IF any person, through Temptation or Melancholy, shall destroy himself; his Estate, real and personal, shall notwithstanding descend to his Wife and Children, or Relations, as if he had died a natural Death; and if any Person shall be destroyed or killed by Casualty or Accident, there shall be no Forfeiture to the Governor by reason thereof.

PENNSYLVANIA CHARTER OF PRIVILEGES

AND no Act, Law or Ordinance whatsoever, shall at any Time hereafter, be made or done, to alter, change or diminish the Form or Effect of this Charter, or of any Part or Clause therein, contrary to the true Intent and Meaning thereof, without the Consent of the Governor for the Time being, and *Six* Parts of *Seven* of the Assembly met. *Amendment of charter*

BUT because the Happiness of Mankind depends so much upon the Enjoying of Liberty of their Consciences as aforesaid, I do hereby solemnly declare, promise and grant, for me, my Heirs and Assigns, That the *First* Article of this Charter relating to Liberty of Conscience, and every Part and Clause therein, according to the true Intent and Meaning thereof, shall be kept and remain, without any Alteration, inviolably for ever. *Liberty of conscience*

AND LASTLY, I the said *William Penn,* Proprietary and Governor of the Province of *Pensilvania,* and Territories thereunto belonging, for myself, my Heirs and Assigns, have solemnly declared, granted and confirmed, and do hereby solemnly declare, grant and confirm, That neither I, my Heirs or Assigns, shall procure or do any Thing or Things whereby the Liberties in this Charter contained and expressed, nor any Part thereof, shall be infringed or broken: And if any thing shall be procured or done, by any Person or Persons, contrary to these Presents, it shall be held of no Force or Effect. *Actions against the charter to be of no force and effect*

IN WITNESS whereof, I the said *William Penn,* at *Philadelphia* in *Pensilvania,* have unto this present Charter of Liberties, set my Hand and broad Seal, this *Twenty-Eighth* Day of *October,* in the Year of Our Lord *One Thousand Seven Hundred and One,* being the *Thirteenth* Year of the Reign of King WILLIAM *the Third,* over *England, Scotland, France* and *Ireland,* &c. and the *Twenty-First* Year of my Government. *Sealed by William Penn, October 28, 1701*

AND NOTWITHSTANDING the Closure and Test of this present Charter as aforesaid, I think fit to add this following Proviso thereunto, as Part of the same, *That is to say,* That notwithstanding any Clause or Clauses in the above-mentioned Charter, obliging the Province and Territories to join together in Legislation, I am content, and do hereby declare, that if the Representatives of the Province and Territories shall not hereafter agree to join together in Legislation, and that the same shall be signified unto me, or my Deputy, in open Assembly, or otherwise from under the Hands and Seals of the Representatives, for the Time being, of the Province and Territories, or the major Part of either of them, at any Time within *Three* Years from the Date hereof, that in such Case, the Inhabitants of each of the *Three* Counties of this Province, shall not have less than *Eight* Persons to represent them in Assembly, for the Province; and the Inhabitants of the Town of *Philadelphia* (when the said Town is incorporated) *Two* Persons to represent them in Assembly; and the Inhabitants of each County in the Territories, shall have as many Persons to represent them in a distinct Assembly for the Territories, as shall be by them requested as aforesaid. *Separate assembly for the territories*

NOTWITHSTANDING which Separation of the Province and Territories, in Respect of Legislation, I do hereby promise, grant and declare, That the Inhabitants *Liberties confirmed* of both Province and Territories, shall separately enjoy all other Liberties, Privileges and Benefits, granted jointly to them in this Charter, any Law, Usage or Custom of this Government heretofore made and practised, or any Law made and passed by this General Assembly, to the Contrary hereof, notwithstanding.

WILLIAM PENN.

Approved by Assembly — THIS CHARTER OF PRIVILEGES *being distinctly read in Assembly; and the whole and every Part thereof, being approved of and agreed to, by us, we do thankfully receive the same from our Proprietary and Governor, at* Philadelphia, *this* Twenty-Eighth *Day of* October, One Thousand Seven Hundred and One. *Signed on Behalf, and by Order of the Assembly,*

per JOSEPH GROWDON, Speaker.

EDWARD SHIPPEN,	GRIFFITH OWEN,
PHINEAS PEMBERTON,	CALEB PUSEY,
SAMUEL CARPENTER,	THOMAS STORY,

Proprietary and Governor's Council.

REFERENCES

See references on p. 221.

XVIII. RESOLUTIONS OF THE STAMP ACT CONGRESS
1765

The movement toward independence from England began long before independence was finally declared in 1776. Even before the crisis precipitated by the Stamp Act, the American colonists had asserted an independent spirit. As the colonial assemblies had grown in power and influence during the first half of the eighteenth century, they were able to solve many of the colonists' problems at the local level. The indifference of England to American affairs made the colonists indifferent to the problems of preserving the British Empire. The average colonist was keenly aware of his rights as a subject of the British crown, but was unconcerned with the duties attached to that status.

Origins
Colonial administration

The French and Indian War (1754-63) exposed serious weaknesses in British imperial administration. No shame was felt in the colonies that it had been English redcoats who had won the war and not the provincial troops.[1] Outside of New England there were few evidences of loyalty. Georgia was too poor to provide for the protection of her own frontiers; South Carolina did little more than ward off attacks on her own border; North Carolina was rent by party factions and suffered from financial problems; Virginia supplied only a few troops, and these were described by Washington as "loose idle persons"; the assemblies of Pennsylvania and Maryland did little more than argue constitutional issues with their proprietors; and the

---

[1] Claude H. Van Tyne, *The Causes of the War of Independence* (Boston, 1922), 77. In 1766 Benjamin Franklin stated that the colonies had raised and supported 25,000 troops. This was fairly accurate for the years 1758 and 1759, but during the other six years of the war the number of troops supplied fell far short of that figure. George L. Beer, *British Colonial Policy, 1754-1765* (New York, 1907), 27 on.

SOURCES OF OUR LIBERTIES

New York Assembly placed burdensome restrictions upon expenditures.[2]

Treaty of Paris, 1763

The Treaty of Paris of 1763 ended the war.[3] Britain's new status as a world power imposed responsibilities that taxed its financial resources. The Treaty of Paris recognized Britain's claim to half of the American continent, giving it a vast territory to defend. In addition, the British debt had doubled since the beginning of the war. British statesmen reasoned that since the American colonies had been the chief beneficiaries of the expulsion of the French, they should bear the financial responsibility for the government and defense of the American continent.

Proposal for a stamp tax

In February, 1763, Charles Townshend became First Lord of Trade, and he soon announced that the acts of trade and navigation would be enforced vigorously. Furthermore, a program of parliamentary taxation would replace the requisitions by the king. The salaries of the colonial governors and judges and the expenses of a large standing army were to be paid by the crown from the revenues raised by the new taxes.

Existing sources of colonial revenue were insufficient for the purpose. When George Grenville became Chancellor of the Exchequer in April, 1763, he discovered that the colonial customs were producing less than £2,000 annually at a cost of collection of more than £8,000.[4] In March, 1764, Grenville introduced in Parliament a series of twenty-one resolutions which outlined the terms of the Sugar Act.[5] The resolutions also stated that "certain stamp duties" would be levied.[6] Because the scheme was novel, Grenville was willing to give the American assemblies a chance to suggest more agreeable methods of raising the funds needed.

The colonists protested against the proposed stamp duties. The only suggestion offered in place of the duties, however, was to return to the old plan of requisitions. The colonies could not agree what amount each should raise by the requisitions. Grenville, therefore, gave up hope of finding an alternative solution, and plans went ahead in England for the stamp tax.

The Stamp Act

The Stamp Act was passed March 22, 1765. It was to go into effect in November of that year. It placed stamp duties on all legal documents, news-

[2] Van Tyne, *op. cit.*, 78-81.
[3] Text in William MacDonald (ed.), *Select Charters and Other Documents Illustrative of American History, 1606-1775* (New York, 1899), 261-66.
[4] Edward Channing, *A History of the United States*, Vol. III: *The American Revolution, 1761-1789* (New York, 1927), 36.
[5] 4 Geo. 3, c. 15.
[6] Van Tyne, *op. cit.*, 140.

papers, pamphlets, college degrees, almanacs, liquor licenses, playing cards, and dice. Certain papers were specifically exempted. Schoolbooks, religious works, records of the assemblies, and unsealed commercial paper were not taxed. Jurisdiction to enforce the act was given to the courts of Admiralty. These courts operated without a jury. They were apparently given jurisdiction for the express purpose of avoiding the jury system because juries were often sympathetic toward persons who operated the vast smuggling business of the eighteenth century.[7] The stamp duties were much lighter than the comparable duties in England, and the Stamp Act contained several exemptions not found in the English law.[8]

British statesmen did not anticipate that the act would arouse widespread hostility in the colonies. There was little debate on the measure in Parliament, and it passed by a wide margin. King George III (1760-1820) referred to the measure as "the wise regulations which had been established to augment the public revenues, to unite the interests of the most distant possessions of the crown, and to encourage and secure their commerce with Great Britain."[9] American patriots had opposed the measure, but such men as Benjamin Franklin, Richard Henry Lee, and Jared Ingersoll assumed that the act would eventually be accepted without protest.[10] Even these well-informed observers had misjudged the temper of the colonists. The act aroused immediate and vigorous opposition. *Protests against the Stamp Act*

Behind the cry "no taxation without representation" lay social and economic conditions which furnished a strong motive for the protests. The Stamp Act, being a direct tax payable in specie, came at a time when there was an actual shortage of money in the colonies. Strict enforcement of the acts of trade and navigation had cut off the principal means by which the colonies could acquire gold and silver specie with which to purchase British manufactures.[11] In addition, much of the economic activity of the colonies consisted of barter, a situation which tended to keep the amount of money available for the payment of direct taxes at a low level. *Reasons for the protests*

---

[7] Edmund S. Morgan and Helen M. Morgan, *The Stamp Act Crisis* (Chapel Hill, 1953), 24. Cf. Channing, *op. cit.*, III, 50.

[8] *Ibid.*, 49 and note.

[9] Quoted in Richard Frothingham, *The Rise of the Republic of the United States* (5th ed.; Boston, 1890), 164.

[10] Van Tyne, *op. cit.*, 142.

[11] See Guy S. Callender (ed.), *Selections from the Economic History of the United States, 1765-1860* (Boston, 1909), 125-37.

The Stamp Act was unsuited to conditions in the colonies for several other reasons. The colonial population lived on farms and plantations and had little contact and intercourse with the rest of the world. Men who did not directly experience the benefits of government felt little responsibility for supporting it financially.[12] The duties imposed by the Stamp Act upon deeds and legal papers filed in court were probably especially objectionable because of the litigious character of the colonists and because of the large number of land transfers which were made in the course of the settlement of the frontier.

The Stamp Act had the further disadvantage of being a novel method of raising revenue. John Dickinson stated that he had examined every English statute relating to the colonies since the first settlement and that prior to the Stamp Act all taxing measures had been incidental to the regulation of trade.[13]

Organized opposition

The earliest organized opposition to the proposed Stamp Act was taken at the annual meeting of the town of Boston on May 24, 1764. In a set of instructions prepared by Samuel Adams, the town instructed its representatives in the Massachusetts General Court to endeavor to have the colony's agent in London protest the measure. The instructions called the act an annihilation of the right to govern and tax conferred on the colony by its charter, and a blow at the privileges which the colonists held in common with all British subjects.[14] Pursuant to these instructions, James Otis, one of the Boston representatives, prepared a memorial to the London agent on the proposed Stamp Act and the Sugar Act in which he contended that the authority of Parliament was circumscribed by certain bounds; that acts which went beyond these bounds were wrongful, and consequently void; and that, as British subjects, the colonists had the right to make local laws and tax themselves.[15] Otis soon followed this with his famous pamphlet "The Rights of the British Colonies Asserted and Proved," in which he argued that Parliament had no absolute powers of taxation and that acts of Parliament contrary to the law of nature were void.[16]

[12] See *ibid.*, 137-40.

[13] Samuel E. Morison (ed.), *Sources and Documents Illustrating the American Revolution, 1764-1788* (Oxford, 1923), 39. Stamp duties had been collected temporarily in Massachusetts, however, by the laws of that province. Channing, *op. cit.*, III, 48.

[14] Frothingham, *op. cit.*, 167-68.   [15] *Ibid.*, 168-69.

[16] "To say the Parliament is absolute and arbitrary is a contradiction. The Parliament cannot make 2 and 2, 5: Omnipotency cannot do it. The supreme power in a state is *ius dicere* only:—*ius dare*,

RESOLUTIONS OF THE STAMP ACT CONGRESS

In May, 1765, the Virginia House of Burgesses took into consideration seven resolutions on the Stamp Act which had been introduced by Patrick Henry.[17] These declared: (1) That the first settlers of Virginia brought with them all the liberties, privileges, franchises, and immunities of British subjects; (2) that this principle was declared by two of the charters for Virginia issued by James I; (3) that under the British constitution taxes could be levied only by the people or their representatives; (4) that the right of the people to be governed by laws "respecting their internal polity and taxation" made by themselves and approved by the king had never been surrendered; (5) that the General Assembly, therefore, had the "sole and exclusive" right to levy taxes; (6) that the colonists were not bound to yield obedience to any law imposing a tax except for laws approved by the General Assembly; and (7) that any person who should assert that anyone other than the General Assembly had power to levy taxes should be deemed an enemy of the people. It was in connection with these resolutions that Henry, a new member of the legislature, established his reputation as a great orator with his famous "Caesar had his Brutus" speech.[18]

Virginia Stamp Act Resolutions

The last three of Henry's resolutions were not approved by the House of Burgesses. All seven resolutions, however, were published in the newspapers, and the impression was given that they had all been passed by the House of Burgesses. Rhode Island soon followed Virginia and passed, with minor modifications, the first, second, fourth, fifth, and sixth resolutions, thus taking a more extreme position than Virginia had actually done. Rhode Island was thus the only colony to approve outright resistance to the Stamp Act. Several other colonies adopted less extreme resolutions against the stamp duties.[19]

In June, 1765, the House of Representatives of Massachusetts sent a circular letter to the other colonies. The letter proposed the appointment of committees from each colony to meet at New York in October. The purpose

Stamp Act Congress

---

strictly speaking, belongs alone to God. Parliaments are in all cases to declare what is for the good of the whole; but it is not the declaration of Parliament that makes it so: There must be in every instance a higher authority, viz. God. Should an Act of Parliament be against any of His natural laws, which are immutably true, their declaration would be contrary to eternal truth, equity, and justice, and consequently void: and so it would be adjudged by the Parliament itself, when convinced of their mistake...." Morison, *op. cit.*, 7.

[17] Text in Henry S. Commager (ed.), *Documents of American History* (3d ed.; New York, 1943), I, 55-56.

[18] For variant accounts of this speech see Morison, *op. cit.*, 14-17.

[19] The history of Henry's resolutions is analyzed by Morgan and Morgan, *op. cit.*, 88-98.

of the meeting was "to consult together on the present circumstances of the colonies, and the difficulties to which they are and must be reduced by the operation of the acts of parliament for levying duties and taxes on the colonies, and to consider of a general and united, dutiful, loyal, and humble representation of their condition to his majesty and to the parliament, and to implore relief."[20] Nine colonies responded to the invitation. New Hampshire declined, but formally approved the proceedings after the meeting of the Stamp Act Congress. Virginia, North Carolina, and Georgia were prevented from participating; their governors refused to convene the assemblies to elect delegates.[21] General Gage described the members of the Congress as follows: "They are of various Characters and opinions, but it's to be feared in general, that the Spirit of Democracy, is strong amongst them."[22]

Timothy Ruggles of Massachusetts was chosen chairman of the meeting. Probably John Dickinson of Pennsylvania prepared the first draft of the Stamp Act Resolutions. It took the Congress about two weeks to debate and draft them. Only a few changes in Dickinson's draft were made.

General Significance   There was little difference of opinion as to the fundamental questions involved. The resolutions carefully stated that the colonies acknowledged allegiance to the crown and "all due subordination" to Parliament. Resolutions 2 to 8 expressed the constitutional theory of the colonists that all taxation, whether internal or external, without the consent of the people's representatives was illegal.[23] Resolutions 9 to 12 expressed the economic objections to the Stamp Act and the acts of trade. The last resolution asserted the right of the colonists to petition both the crown and Parliament for a redress of grievances. The resolutions were agreed to October 19. Before the Stamp Act Congress adjourned on October 25, petitions were prepared for submission to the king and Parliament calling for repeal of the act.

The legal question which the resolutions answered was whether Englishmen in the colonies could be taxed by Parliament, a body in which they were

---

[20] Quoted in Frothingham, *op. cit.*, 178n.

[21] Morgan and Morgan, *op. cit.*, 103.

[22] Quoted in *ibid.*, 105.

[23] It has sometimes been asserted that the effect of the resolutions was to confine the constitutional objections of the Congress to internal taxes such as the Stamp Act, and that external taxes, such as customs duties, were not included. The petition and memorial to Parliament, however, linked the two kinds of taxes. In addition, both William Samuel Johnson and John Dickinson apparently believed that the resolutions were intended to condemn both internal and external taxes. *Ibid.*, 114-15. Both internal and external taxes were specifically condemned by the Declaration and Resolves of the First Continental Congress. See pp. 287-88.

not represented. The right of the people to participate in the levying of taxes had long been established as a fundamental part of the English constitution.[24] As one British writer said, "No nation ought to be taxed against its own consent. England has passed through many a year of civil war in defence of the proposition."[25] Whether this right extended to the colonies was another question.

Taxation without representation

British spokesmen argued that many English communities were taxed although they did not send representatives to Parliament. In addition, persons in England not owning land were taxed although they could not vote for representatives. It was said that these communities and individuals were "virtually" represented in Parliament. There was, it was argued, a community of interest between those subjects who could vote and those who could not. Daniel Dulany, in a masterful pamphlet called "Considerations on the Propriety of Imposing Taxes in the British Colonies," answered the argument of "virtual representation":

> There is not that intimate and inseparable relation between the electors of Great Britain and the inhabitants of the colonies which must inevitably involve both in the same taxation; on the contrary, not a single actual elector in England might be immediately affected by a taxation in America . . . Moreover, even Acts oppressive and injurious to the colonies in an extreme degree might become popular in England, from the promise or expectation that the very measures which depressed the colonies, would give ease to the inhabitants of Great Britain.[26]

One of the principal objections to the Stamp Act was the extension of the jurisdiction of the courts of Admiralty to enforce the act. This removed a substantial area of the criminal law from the protection of the jury system. In the words of John Adams:

Trial by jury

> But the most grievous innovation of all, is the alarming extension of the power of courts of admiralty. In these courts, one judge presides alone! No juries have any concern there! The law and the fact are both to be decided by the same single judge, whose commission is only during pleasure, and with whom, as we are told, the most mischievous of all customs has become established, that of taking commissions on all condemnations; so that he is under a pecuniary temptation always against the subject. . . . We have all along thought the acts of trade in this respect a grievance; but the Stamp Act has opened a vast number of sources of new crimes, which may be committed by any man, and cannot but be committed by multitudes, and prodigious penalties are annexed, and all these are to be tried by such a judge of such a court! . . .

[24] See p. 227.
[25] Viscount Burg, M.P., quoted in Frothingham, *op. cit.*, 299n.
[26] Morison, *op. cit.*, 27.

> We cannot help asserting, therefore, that this part of the act will make an essential change in the constitution of juries, and it is directly repugnant to the Great Charter itself...[27]

Effects   Hostility to the Stamp Act was so strong that enforcement proved to be completely impossible. Americans had begun to encourage home manufactures and cut down on imports in 1764 after passage of the Sugar Act. The Stamp Act aroused more drastic action. Hundreds of merchants in New York, Boston, Philadelphia, and other ports signed agreements to import nothing from Great Britain until the Stamp Act had been repealed. This action damaged British exports of manufactured goods to such an extent that Parliament received numerous petitions urging repeal of the act from merchants throughout the kingdom.[28]

Repeal of the Stamp Act   The Stamp Act posed a dilemma for Parliament. Enforcement was impossible, but an important principle would be sacrificed by repealing it. The fall of the Grenville ministry and the establishment of a new one under the Marquis of Rockingham made it easier to effect a change of policy. William Pitt, a powerful opponent of Rockingham, sided with the colonists and glorified the riots that had occurred in America against the act. He urged:

> ... that the Stamp Act be repealed absolutely, totally, and immediately. That the reason for the repeal be assigned, because it was founded on an erroneous principle. At the same time, let the sovereign authority of this country over the colonies, be asserted in as strong terms as can be devised, and be made to extend to every point of legislation whatsoever. That we may bind their trade, confine their manufactures, and exercise every power whatsoever, except that of taking their money out of their pockets without their consent.[29]

The Declaratory Act   The Stamp Act was repealed March 18, 1766. It had been in effect only four months and was never enforced. The repeal was accompanied by the Declaratory Act.[30] Parliament made it clear that it would not accept the constitutional principles argued by the colonists. The act stated:

---

[27] "Instructions of the Town of Braintree, Massachusetts on the Stamp Act," October 14, 1765. Commager, *op. cit.* (6th ed., 1958), I, 56-57.

[28] See the "Petition of London Merchants Against the Stamp Act," January 17, 1766, in *ibid.*, 59-60.

[29] Quoted in Morgan and Morgan, *op. cit.*, 267.

[30] 6 Geo. 3, c. 12. The Declaratory Act was intended to repudiate Pitt's proposal which denied that taxation was part of sovereign power. This statute was apparently modeled upon the Irish Declaratory Act of 1719, 6 Geo. 1, c. 5. Daniel Dulany later argued that the American Declaratory Act did not affirm the right of Parliament to tax the colonies because it had always been admitted that the Irish Declaratory Act did not give Parliament the right to tax Ireland. Morgan and Morgan, *op. cit.*, 286.

RESOLUTIONS OF THE STAMP ACT CONGRESS

... That the said Colonies and plantations in *America* have been, are, and of right ought to be, subordinate unto, and dependent upon the imperial crown and parliament of *Great Britain;* and that the King's majesty, by and with the advice and consent of the lords spiritual and temporal, and commons of *Great Britain,* in parliament assembled, had, hath, and of right ought to have, full power and authority to make laws and statutes of sufficient force and validity to bind the colonies and people of *America,* subjects of the crown of *Great Britain,* in all cases whatsoever.

. . . .

... That all resolutions, votes, orders, and proceedings, in any of the said colonies or plantations, whereby the power and authority of the parliament of Great Britain, to make laws and statutes as aforesaid, is denied, or drawn into question, are, and are hereby declared to be, utterly null and void to all intents and purposes whatsoever.

Repeal of the Stamp Act was greeted in America with the greatest popular acclaim. The colonists were not alarmed by the ambiguous Declaratory Act, which avoided the word "taxation." Rockingham was soon replaced by Pitt, whose opposition to the Stamp Act had made his reputation that of a firm friend of the colonies. The Stamp Act, however, had marked the beginning of the active movement toward independence. A few observers realized this. James Scott wrote in the London newspapers: "The Americans imbibe notions of independance and liberty with their very milk, and will some time or other shake off all subjection. If we yield to them in this particular, by repealing the Stamp-Act, it is all over; they will from that moment assert their freedom."[31]

Repeal of the act had merely terminated the immediate controversy. Understanding between the colonies and England had been impaired and the disposition of both sides to compromise had been weakened. More serious problems were soon to place even greater strains upon the relationships of England and America.

[31] Quoted in *ibid.,* 290.

RESOLUTIONS OF THE STAMP ACT CONGRESS[32]

October 19, 1765

DECLARATION OF RIGHTS.

Preamble — The members of this congress, sincerely devoted, with the warmest sentiments of affection and duty to his majesty's person and government, inviolably attached to the present happy establishment of the protestant succession, and with minds deeply impressed by a sense of the present and impending misfortunes of the British colonies on this continent; having considered as maturely as time would permit, the circumstances of said colonies, esteem it our indispensable duty to make the following declarations, of our humble opinions, respecting the most essential rights and liberties of the colonists, and of the grievances under which they labor, by reason of several late acts of parliament.

Declaration of allegiance — 1st. That his majesty's subjects in these colonies, owe the same allegiance to the crown of Great Britain, that is owing from his subjects born within the realm, and all due subordination to that august body, the parliament of Great Britain.

Rights of Englishmen — 2d. That his majesty's liege subjects in these colonies are entitled to all the inherent rights and privileges of his natural born subjects within the kingdom of Great Britain,

Imposition of taxes — 3d. That it is inseparably essential to the freedom of a people, and the undoubted rights of Englishmen, that no taxes should be imposed on them, but with their own consent, given personally, or by their representatives.

Colonists not represented — 4th. That the people of these colonies are not, and from their local circumstances, cannot be represented in the house of commons in Great Britain.

Taxation by colonial legislatures — 5th. That the only representatives of the people of these colonies, are persons chosen therein by themselves; and that no taxes ever have been, or can be constitutionally imposed on them, but by their respective legislatures.

Unconstitutionality of taxation — 6th. That all supplies to the crown, being free gifts of the people, it is unreasonable and inconsistent with the principles and spirit of the British constitution, for the people of Great Britain to grant to his majesty the property of the colonists.

Trial by jury — 7th. That trial by jury is the inherent and invaluable right of every British subject in these colonies.

[32] *Journal of the First Congress of the American Colonies, in Opposition to the Tyrannical Acts of the British Parliament* (New York, 1845), 27-29.

RESOLUTIONS OF THE STAMP ACT CONGRESS

8th. That the late act of parliament entitled, an act for granting and applying certain stamp duties, and other duties in the British colonies and plantations in America, &c., by imposing taxes on the inhabitants of these colonies, and the said act, and several other acts, by extending the jurisdiction of the courts of admiralty beyond its ancient limits, have a manifest tendency to subvert the rights and liberties of the colonists. *Stamp Act declared subversive of colonial rights and liberties*

9th. That the duties imposed by several late acts of parliament, from the peculiar circumstances of these colonies, will be extremely buthensome and grievous, and from the scarcity of specie, the payment of them absolutely impracticable. *Impracticability of taxes*

10th. That as the profits of the trade of these colonies ultimately centre in Great Britain, to pay for the manufactures which they are obliged to take from thence, they eventually contribute very largely to all supplies granted there to the crown. *Payments for manufactures*

11th. That the restrictions imposed by several late acts of parliament, on the trade of these colonies, will render them unable to purchase the manufactures of Great Britain. *Effect of trade restrictions*

12th. That the increase, prosperity, and happiness of these colonies, depend on the full and free enjoyment of their rights and liberties, and an intercourse, with Great Britain, mutually affectionate and advantageous. *Advantages of free trade*

13th. That it is the right of the British subjects in these colonies, to petition the king or either house of parliament. *Right of petition*

Lastly, That it is the indispensable duty of these colonies to the best of sovereigns, to the mother country, and to themselves, to endeavor, by a loyal and dutiful address to his majesty, and humble application to both houses of parliament, to procure the repeal of the act for granting and applying certain stamp duties, of all clauses of any other acts of parliament, whereby the jurisdiction of the admiralty is extended as aforesaid, and of the other late acts for the restriction of the American commerce. *Need for repeal of Stamp Act*

REFERENCES

Bancroft, George. *History of the United States of America.* 6 vols. Last rev.; New York: Appleton & Co., 1893. III, chaps. 1-17.

Beer, George L. *British Colonial Policy, 1754-1765.* New York: Macmillan Co., 1907. Chaps. 10-14.

Channing, Edward. *A History of the United States.* 3 vols. New York: Macmillan Co., 1927-30. III, chaps. 1-3.

Ericson, Fred J. "The Contemporary British Opposition to the Stamp Act, 1764-65," *Papers of the Michigan Academy of Science, Arts, and Letters,* XXIX (1944), 489-505.

Frothingham, Richard. *The Rise of the Republic of the United States.* 7th ed. Boston: Little, Brown & Co., 1899. Chap. 5.

Morgan, Edmund S., and Morgan, Helen M. *The Stamp Act Crisis.* Chapel Hill: University of North Carolina Press, 1953.

Schlesinger, Arthur M. "The Colonial Newspapers and the Stamp Act," *New England Quarterly,* VIII (March, 1935), 63-83.

Van Tyne, Claude H. *The Causes of the War of Independence.* Boston: Houghton Mifflin Co., 1922. Chaps. 5-7.

XIX. DECLARATION AND RESOLVES OF THE FIRST CONTINENTAL CONGRESS
1774

Origins   Repeal of the Stamp Act in 1766[1] brought only temporary relief to the colonies from taxation by the English Parliament. The Declaratory Act had made it clear that England expected to assert full powers of sovereignty in colonial matters. These powers, however, were exercised in the most inept fashion, and the colonies, instead of becoming integrated members of the British Empire, were driven further and further from the mother country.

Oppressive measures were resisted by the colonists. Acts of colonial resistance were met by acts of retaliation. These conflicts, during almost a decade before the Declaration and Resolves of 1774, did much to shape colonial ideas of individual liberties. The Declaration and Resolves of the First Continental Congress of 1774 was perhaps the most significant statement of those liberties before the final break with England.

First Continental Congress   By the spring of 1774 it had become clear that the problems of individual colonies were really the problems of all. United action by the colonies was necessary. One writer in the *Boston Evening Post* said: "It is now time for the colonies to have a Grand Congress to complete the system for the American Independent Commonwealth, as it is so evident that no other plan will secure the rights of this people from rapacious and plotting tyrants."[2] One of the first bodies to propose the calling of a continental congress was a town meeting in Providence, Rhode Island, on May 17, 1774. Virginia was the first colony to make such a proposal.[3]

---

[1] See pp. 268-69.

[2] Quoted in Richard Frothingham, *The Rise of the Republic of the United States* (Boston, 1890), 314n.

[3] *Ibid.*, 332n.; Claude H. Van Tyne, *The Causes of the War of Independence* (Boston, 1922), 428-29; Arthur M. Schlesinger, *The Colonial Merchants and the American Revolution, 1763-1776* (New York, 1917), 360-63.

RESOLVES OF THE FIRST CONTINENTAL CONGRESS

On June 17 the Massachusetts House of Representatives authorized the appointment of five delegates to a meeting of the colonies to consider measures to be taken for the recovery and establishment of their just rights and liberties and for the restoration of union and harmony between Great Britain and the colonies.[4] Massachusetts suggested that the delegates meet at Philadelphia on September 1. By August 25 colonial legislatures, provincial conventions, and other bodies in each colony except Georgia had selected delegates to the Continental Congress.[5] The delegates of the colonies met in Philadelphia on September 5, except the delegates from North Carolina; representatives from that colony arrived September 14.

Peyton Randolph, speaker of the Virginia House of Burgesses, was chosen chairman of the meeting, and it was decided that the official title of the body should be "The Congress" and that of the presiding officer, "The President."[6] The first step toward the framing of the Declaration and Resolves was the appointment on September 7 of two committees. The larger and more important of these was given the task of stating the rights of the colonies, the instances in which those rights had been violated or infringed, and the means most proper for restoring them.[7] The function of the smaller committee was to examine and report the statutes which affected the trade and manufactures of the colonies.[8] The work of the large committee was divided between two subcommittees, one to prepare a "bill of rights" and the other to prepare a list of infringements of those rights. Both the organization and the content of the Declaration and Resolves reflect the work of these committees.

Committees of Congress

The report of the committee on statutes was made on September 17 and was referred to the committee on rights and grievances. The large committee made two reports, one on colonial rights and one on the infringement of those rights. The scope of the report on infringements was limited by a resolution of September 24 which provided: "That the Congress do confine themselves, at present, to the consideration of such rights, as have been infringed by acts of the British parliament since the year 1763, postponing the further consideration of the general state of American rights to a future day."[9] The decision to confine the report to the grievances which had arisen since what may be called "The Stamp Act Administration" had come to power

---

[4] Frothingham, *op. cit.*, 333n.; Edmund C. Burnett, *The Continental Congress* (New York, 1941), 20.
[5] See Burnett, *op. cit.*, 20-21.
[6] *Ibid.*, 34.
[7] *Journals of the American Congress, 1774-1788* (Washington, 1823), I, 7-8.
[8] *Ibid.*
[9] *Ibid.*, 15.

Suffolk Resolves

was attributable to a desire to avoid the possibility of an irreconcilable difference of opinion on abstract principles.[10]

Two documents received by the Congress had an important bearing on its deliberations. The first of these was the Suffolk Resolves.[11] The delegates of Suffolk County, Massachusetts, had declared that the allegiance of the colonies to George III was founded upon compact; that the colonists had a duty to preserve by all lawful means those liberties for which their fathers had fought, bled, and died; that the repressive measures taken against Massachusetts violated the laws of nature, the British constitution, and the colony's charter; that no allegiance was owed to those acts; that royal judges and officers could not command the obedience of the colonists because they had not been chosen for office in accordance with the charter; and that until the colonists' rights were restored, commercial intercourse with Great Britain and the consumption of British goods should be suspended. The resolves added: "That this county, confiding in the wisdom and integrity of the continental Congress, now sitting at Philadelphia, pay all due respect and submission to such measures as may be recommended by them to the colonies, for the restoration and establishment of their just rights, civil and religious, and for renewing that harmony and union between Great-Britain and the colonies, so earnestly wished for by all good men." The Suffolk Resolves undoubtedly helped stir Congress to action and focused its attention upon the grievances of Massachusetts. Congress resolved:

> That this assembly deeply feels the suffering of their countrymen in the Massachusetts-Bay, under the operation of the late unjust, cruel, and oppressive acts of the British parliament—that they most thoroughly approve the wisdom and fortitude, with which opposition to these wicked ministerial measures has hitherto been conducted, and they earnestly recommend to their brethren, a perseverance in the same firm and temperate conduct as expressed in the resolutions determined upon . . .[12]

Galloway's Plan of Union

The second document presented to the Congress was the Plan of Union framed by Joseph Galloway of Pennsylvania.[13] This plan was based upon the principle that the best way to secure colonial rights was by a system of union with Great Britain in which a British and American legislature would regu-

---

[10] Charles F. Adams (ed.), *The Works of John Adams* (Boston, 1850), II, 376n.

[11] Text in *Journals*, I, 9-13.

[12] *Ibid.*, I, 14.

[13] Text in Henry S. Commager (ed.), *Documents of American History* (3d ed.; New York, 1943), I, 81-82.

RESOLVES OF THE FIRST CONTINENTAL CONGRESS

late the general affairs of America and the colonial charters would be retained for the regulation of internal affairs. The Plan of Union appealed to the more conservative members of Congress. It failed of adoption by only one vote, however, and was later stricken from the *Journal* of Congress.

The Resolutions of the Stamp Act Congress [14] had been founded upon the principles of the British constitution; no reference was made to the law of nature. That document, while acknowledging "all due subordination" to Parliament, had denied the authority of that body to levy taxes in the colonies or to infringe the right of trial by jury.

General Significance

1. Law of nature and powers of Parliament

The source of colonial rights and the just powers of Parliament was also considered by the First Continental Congress. Writing in 1802, John Adams said:

> The two points which labored the most were: 1. Whether we should recur to the law of nature, as well as to the British constitution, and our American charters and grants. . . . 2. The other great question was, what authority we should concede to Parliament; whether we should deny the authority of Parliament in all cases; whether we should allow any authority to it in our internal affairs; or whether we should allow it to regulate the trade of the empire with or without any restrictions.[15]

It was decided that the law of nature should be recognized as one of the foundations of the rights of the colonists. The law of nature, thus adopted by Congress in 1774 as a basis of individual liberties, later exerted an important influence in the drafting of such documents as the Declaration of Independence.[16]

The question of Parliament's power was finally settled by the fourth resolution of the Declaration and Resolves, which provided that the provincial legislatures were entitled to a free and exclusive power of legislation "in all cases of taxation and internal polity," subject to veto by the king.

The theory of Congress as to the power of Parliament to levy taxes was stated in the fourth resolution of the Declaration and Resolves. Many other grievances, however, arose indirectly from Parliament's taxation policy and are reflected by other provisions of the document.

2. Taxation

Taxation of the colonies by Parliament was the cornerstone of British colonial administration. In 1766 Charles Townshend succeeded William Pitt as leader of the House of Commons, and announced his objective of subjecting the colonies to the sovereign power of Parliament:

The Townshend Acts

---

[14] See pp. 261-71. [15] Adams, *op. cit.*, II, 374. [16] See pp. 314-22.

It has long been my opinion that America should be regulated and deprived of its militating and contradictory charters, and its royal governors, judges, and attorneys be rendered independent of the people. I therefore expect that the present administration will, in the recess of parliament, take all necessary previous steps for compassing so desirable an event.[17]

These political objectives depended upon obtaining an adequate revenue from the colonies to meet the expenses of colonial administration and defense.

Steps to achieve these objectives were taken by Townshend in 1767 after he had become Chancellor of the Exchequer. The Townshend Acts, adopted in that year, were intended to provide the needed revenue. The first of these acts reorganized the customs service by replacing the commissioners of customs in England with a board of commissioners resident in the colonies.[18] This provided a more efficient method for the collection of revenues under all customs laws. Additional revenues were called for by the Townshend Revenue Act.[19] That act imposed duties on the importation into the colonies of glass, red and white lead, painters' colors, tea, and paper.

Writs of assistance

To facilitate enforcement of the act, it was provided that writs of assistance might be issued by the superior or supreme court of justice having jurisdiction within each colony.[20] The writs of assistance empowered customs officers to enter any house, warehouse, shop, cellar, or other place to search for and seize illegal goods.

Opposition to the Townshend Acts

John Dickinson, as much as any individual, spearheaded opposition to the Townshend Acts by his series of essays entitled "Letters from a Farmer." The "Letters" were widely circulated in the newspapers and also appeared in pamphlet form.[21] The united action of all colonies was stimulated by the "Massachusetts Circular Letter" approved by the General Court February 11, 1768.[22] The constitutional theory it advocated was stated as follows:

---

[17] Quoted in Frothingham, *op. cit.*, 203.

[18] 7 Geo. 3, c. 41.

[19] 7 Geo. 3, c. 46. The preamble of the act set forth its purposes: "WHEREAS *it is expedient that a revenue should be raised, in your Majesty's dominions in* America, *for making a more certain and adequate provision for defraying the charge of the administration of justice, and the support of civil government, in such provinces where it shall be found necessary; and towards further defraying the expences of defending, protecting, and securing, the said dominions; we, your Majesty's most dutiful and loyal subjects, the commons of* Great Britain, *in parliament assembled, have therefore resolved to give and grant unto your Majesty the several rates and duties herein after mentioned.*"

[20] Section 10.

[21] The first appeared in the *Pennsylvania Chronicle and Universal Advertiser* in Philadelphia on December 2, 1767. Altogether, there were twelve letters. Frothingham, *op. cit.*, 208n.

[22] Text in Commager, *op. cit.*, I, 66-67; William MacDonald (ed.), *Select Charters and Other Documents Illustrative of American History, 1606-1775* (New York, 1899), 330-34.

RESOLVES OF THE FIRST CONTINENTAL CONGRESS

That in all free States the Constitution is fixed; & as the supreme Legislative derives its Power & Authority from the Constitution, it cannot overleap the Bounds of it, without destroying its own foundation; That the constitution ascertains & limits both Sovereignty and allegiance, &, therefore, his Majesty's American Subjects, who acknowledge themselves bound by the Ties of Allegiance, have an equitable Claim to the full enjoyment of the fundamental Rules of the British Constitution: That it is an essential, unalterable Right, in nature, ungrafted into the British Constitution, as a fundamental Law, & ever held sacred & irrevocable by the Subjects within the Realm, that what a man has honestly acquired is absolutely his own, which he may freely give, but cannot be taken from him without his consent: That the American Subjects may, therefore, exclusive of any Consideration of Charter Rights, with a decent firmness, adapted to the Character of free men & subjects assert this natural and constitutional Right.

The "Circular Letter" achieved its purpose, and a number of colonies passed resolutions supporting its objectives.

Collective action against the Townshend Acts took the form of nonimportation agreements. These were similar to those used to obtain repeal of the Stamp Act.[23] The nonimportation agreements exerted sufficient pressure on the ministry of Lord North to cause the repeal in 1770 of the Townshend Revenue Act.[24] The duty on tea, however, was not repealed. That duty was retained to make it clear that Parliament had not surrendered its claimed right to tax the colonies.[25]

The Boston Tea Party

The Tea Acts of 1767 and 1773 [26] permitted the East India Company to export tea directly to the American colonies free from all duties except the tax imposed by the Townshend Revenue Act. This was done to allow the East India Company's tea to compete successfully with smuggled tea.

Because of opposition to the tea tax and because of the threatened monopoly of the East India Company, the importation of tea was strongly resisted in the colonies. The New York Sons of Liberty resolved in November, 1773: "That whoever shall aid, or abet, or in any manner assist in the introduction of tea, from any place whatsoever, into this colony, while it is subject, by a British act to [sic] parliament, to the payment of a duty, for the purpose of raising a revenue in America, he shall be deemed an enemy to the liberties of America." [27] The attempt to land tea in Boston led to the Boston Tea Party of December 16, 1773. Tea shipped to New York and Philadelphia was not

[23] See p. 268.
[24] 10 Geo. 3, c. 17.
[25] Van Tyne, op. cit., 307-8.
[26] 7 Geo. 3, c. 56 and 13 Geo. 3, c. 44.
[27] Commager, op. cit., I, 70.

landed. In Charleston the tea was landed, but was placed in government warehouses.

The Intolerable Acts

In retaliation against the Boston Tea Party, Parliament passed a series of statutes known as the Intolerable Acts. The most oppressive of these was the Boston Port Act, March 31, 1774,[28] which closed the port of Boston to all shipping until reparations had been made to the East India Company.

Taxation and the Declaration and Resolves

The fourth resolution of the Declaration and Resolves stated that all taxes, whether internal or external, levied by Parliament for the purpose of raising a revenue violated the free and exclusive power of the provincial legislatures. The Sugar Act and the Townshend Acts were cited among the statutes which infringed colonial rights. The Intolerable Acts, which were passed as a result of the dispute over the tea tax and the threatened monopoly of the East India Company, also were cited as infringements of those rights.

3. Standing armies and the quartering of soldiers

The ninth resolution of the Declaration and Resolves stated that it was illegal to maintain standing armies without the consent of the colonial legislatures. In addition, the Quartering Act of 1774,[29] one of the Intolerable Acts, was cited as an infringement of colonial rights.

One of the most serious grievances of the colonists was the existence of a standing army of redcoats quartered in the colonies. An important feature of British colonial policy at the time of the Stamp Act had been to place the financial burden for the defense of the colonies upon the colonists themselves.[30] It was intended that a force of 10,000 troops should be maintained in the colonies.[31] The Quartering Act of 1765 provided for their accommodation.[32] The Quartering Act of 1774, cited as an infringement of colonial rights, was passed at the request of Lord North's ministry because the city fathers of Boston had insisted that Colonel Dalrymple lodge his troops in barracks on an island in Boston Harbor, where they would have been useless to quell riots within the city. The act of 1774 gave the British commander and the governor of the province authority to quarter troops wherever their presence might be necessary.

No specific objection was made in the Declaration and Resolves to the Quartering Act of 1765. That statute had not violated the rule established

[28] 14 Geo. 3, c. 19.
[29] 14 Geo. 3, c. 54.
[30] See pp. 262-63.
[31] Van Tyne, *op. cit.*, 145.
[32] 5 Geo. 3, c. 33, quoted on p.72. This statute was supplemented by 6 Geo. 3, c. 18.

by the Petition of Right that troops should not be quartered in private dwelling houses.[33] The Quartering Act of 1774, which was intended to facilitate the operation of the act of 1765, however, was listed as one of the statutes infringing colonial rights. The maintenance of a standing army in the colonies without the consent of the colonial legislatures was also specifically condemned. The ninth resolution of the Declaration and Resolves was thus primarily a demand that the protection of the English Bill of Rights[34] be applied to the colonial situation.

New York was subjected to heavy expenses in complying with the Quartering Act of 1765. The burden of the act fell with particular severity upon that colony because of General Gage's decision that strategic considerations required a heavier concentration of troops there than elsewhere.[35] New York complied with all the requirements of the act except its obligation to provide salt, vinegar, beer, and cider for the troops. As a result, in June, 1767, all acts of the New York legislature were declared by Parliament to be null and void until compliance was made.[36] New York eventually complied and its legislative powers were restored, but the threat against the principles of representative government did not go unnoticed. One of the first to call attention to that threat was John Dickinson of Pennsylvania. In November, 1767, he said in the "Farmer's Letters": "With a good deal of surprize I have observed that little notice has been taken of an Act of Parliament, as injurious in its principle to the liberties of these colonies, as the Stamp Act was: I mean the act for suspending the legislation of New York."[37] On December 17, 1767, the legislature sent to Parliament a resolution calling the act of suspension "destructive of the very end of representation."[38]

The dissolution of colonial assemblies was also used as a retaliatory measure against colonial resistance to British oppression. The "Massachusetts Circular Letter" of February, 1768, brought a threat from Lord Hillsborough, in the name of the king, that unless that "rash and hasty proceeding" were promptly rescinded, the Massachusetts Assembly would be dissolved. By a vote of 92 to 17 the assembly refused to rescind the letter, and Governor

4. Interferences with representative government

Suspension of New York legislation by Parliament

Dissolution of assemblies by royal governors

[33] See pp. 74-75.
[34] See pp. 230-31.
[35] Van Tyne, *op. cit.*, 276-77.
[36] 7 Geo. 3, c. 59.
[37] Samuel E. Morison (ed.), *Sources and Documents Illustrating the American Revolution, 1764-1788* (Oxford, 1923), 35.
[38] Van Tyne, *op. cit.*, 279.

Bernard dissolved the assembly by proclamation on July 1.[39] The other colonies were warned by royal order not to support the "Circular Letter," but most of them openly endorsed it with a remarkable unity of spirit. As a result, the royal governors dissolved the legislatures of several colonies.[40]

The power of dissolution of the legislature was also used against the Virginia House of Burgesses in 1769. Governor Botetourt acted because the Burgesses had refused to rescind its resolutions of May 16, 1769.[41] Those resolutions had declared that the House of Burgesses had the sole right to impose taxes upon the inhabitants of Virginia; that it was the undoubted right of the colonists to petition the king for a redress of grievances and to procure the concurrence of other colonies in preparing addresses to the king; and that trials for treason and other crimes should be by a jury of the vicinage and that defendants should be allowed to summon witnesses for their defense.

Other threats to representative government

The Massachusetts Government Act of 1774,[42] one of the Intolerable Acts, was intended to make certain reforms, long urged by Governor Bernard, in the constitution of that colony. Governor Bernard and Lord North wanted to secure better enforcement of the orders of the governor and to limit the power of the town meetings.[43] North announced that the purpose of the Massachusetts Government Act was "to take the executive power from the hands of the democratic part of the government."[44] The act provided that councilors should be appointed by the king with the advice and consent of the Privy Council,[45] instead of by the General Court as provided by the charter.[46] Town meetings were forbidden without the consent of the governor.[47] As a result, the act was considered by the colonists to be one of the greatest threats of that period against representative institutions. The tenth resolution of the Declaration and Resolves was apparently intended to condemn the Massachusetts Government Act.

---

[39] *Ibid.*, 297-99; Frothingham, *op. cit.*, 216-20. Authority to prorogue and dissolve the legislature was conferred upon the governor by the Charter of Massachusetts Bay of 1691 and the Explanatory Charter of 1725. Texts in Francis N. Thorpe (ed.), *The Federal and State Constitutions, Colonial Charters, and Other Organic Laws* (Washington, 1909), III, 1870-88.

[40] Frothingham, *op. cit.*, 222-28.

[41] Text in *ibid.*, 236n.

[42] 14 Geo. 3, c. 45.

[43] Van Tyne, *op. cit.*, 396-97.

[44] Quoted in *ibid.*

[45] Section 1.

[46] Thorpe, *op. cit.*, III, 1879.

[47] Section 7.

RESOLVES OF THE FIRST CONTINENTAL CONGRESS

The assertion in the fifth resolution that the colonists were entitled to the benefit of the common law, particularly the right of trial by jury, was probably motivated by several acts of Parliament which made changes in the jury system.

5. Trial by jury

The threat to the right of trial by jury created by conferring jurisdiction to enforce the Stamp Act and the Sugar Act upon the courts of Admiralty has been noted elsewhere.[48] Other threatened invasions of that right occurred after the Stamp Act had been repealed. One of the most serious of these was the resolution passed by Parliament which stated that alleged traitors, such as the instigators of the "Massachusetts Circular Letter" of 1768, should be brought to England to be tried for treason.[49] The resolutions of Parliament rested for authority upon a statute of 1543, enacted during the reign of Henry VIII.[50] At the time that statute was passed, England had no colonies. The statute was completely inapplicable to the colonial situation.[51] It would seriously have infringed the right of the colonists to a trial by a jury composed of men of the vicinity where the alleged crime occurred. A trial beyond the seas would have made it difficult for defendants effectively to exercise their right to challenge jurors, and would have made it virtually impossible for defendants to call witnesses in their defense, a right which had been conferred in cases of treason by the Trial of Treasons Act of 1696.[52]

The act of 1772 for the protection of his Majesty's dockyards infringed the right of trial by jury in the same way as had the act of Henry VIII.[53] It provided the death sentence for persons convicted of burning or otherwise destroying his Majesty's ships in any dockyard or any arsenal, magazine, timber, or stores. It was stated that persons committing these offenses outside the realm might be tried either within the realm or where the offense was committed.

---

[48] See pp. 267-68.

[49] Van Tyne, *op. cit.*, 300-5; Frothingham, *op. cit.*, 231-32.

[50] 35 Hen. 8, c. 2.

[51] The Treason Act of 1351, 25 Edw. 3, stat. 5, c. 2, by condemning as treason the aiding and comforting of the king's enemies "in the realm, or elsewhere," recognized that treason might be committed outside the realm. The act of 1543 was intended to clarify the rules of venue for such cases. According to the preamble of the act: "*Some doubts and questions have been moved, That certain kinds of treasons, misprisions, and concealments of treasons, done, perpetrated, or committed out of the King's majesty's realm of England, and other his Grace's dominions, cannot ne may by the common laws of this realm be enquired of, heard and determined within this his said realm of England.*"

[52] 7 Will. 3, c. 3, § 7. See pp. 240-41.

[53] 12 Geo. 3, c. 24.

Another measure which was considered by the colonists to constitute an infringement of the right of trial by jury was contained in the Massachusetts Government Act.[54] The act provided that jurors should be selected by the county sheriffs instead of by the town meetings, as had previously been the practice.[55] Because the royal governor was given power to appoint and remove sheriffs,[56] the Massachusetts Government Act indirectly gave control over the jury system to the crown. This method of controlling the jury system was similar to that which Charles II had imposed in England by the Corporation Act of 1661.[57]

A relatively unimportant change in the jury system was made by the Massachusetts Administration of Justice Act of 1774,[58] another of the Intolerable Acts. The act provided that persons indicted for murder or other capital offenses in Massachusetts for acts committed in the course of their duty as magistrates, in the suppression of riots, or in the execution of the revenue laws might obtain a trial in another colony or in Great Britain if it appeared to the governor that a fair trial could not be obtained in Massachusetts. The act was passed so that government officers and loyal subjects aiding them would not be discouraged in the execution of the laws for fear that they might receive an unfair trial at the hands of a colonial jury. This act was apparently motivated by the trials of the British soldiers following the Boston Massacre, although there had been no indication that they had not received a fair trial.[59] The act was cited by the Declaration and Resolves as one of the grievances of the colonists. It was sometimes referred to as the "murder act." The Declaration of Causes and Necessity of Taking up Arms and the Declaration of Independence also cited the exemption from punishment of the "murderers" of the colonists as one of the grievances against Parliament and the king.[60]

6. Right of petition

The wording of the eighth resolution was apparently based on language found in the English Bill of Rights, which provided: "That it is the right of the subjects to petition the King, and all committments and prosecutions for

---

[54] 14 Geo. 3, c. 45.
[55] Section 8.
[56] Section 5.
[57] See pp. 237-38.
[58] 14 Geo. 3, c. 39.
[59] Van Tyne, *op. cit.*, 288-89, 398-99.
[60] See pp. 296, 320.

such petitioning are illegal."[61] The Resolutions of the Stamp Act Congress had declared the right of the colonists to present petitions to the king and Parliament.[62] The Declaration and Resolves connected that right with the right of the people to assemble and consider their grievances. This resolution was probably motivated by the threats and prohibitory proclamations issued to combat the numerous petitions, memorials, and addresses protesting the Townshend Acts. Of these, the most important had been the "Massachusetts Circular Letter" of 1768 and the address to the king which accompanied it.[63]

Probably the least dangerous of the Intolerable Acts was the Quebec Act of 1774.[64] The act had extended the boundaries of the Province of Quebec to the area south of the Great Lakes as far as the Ohio Valley and west of Pennsylvania to the Mississippi. To the colonists, the most objectionable feature of the act was the provision "that his Majesty's subjects, professing the religion of the church of *Rome* of and in the said province of *Quebec*, may have, hold, and enjoy, the free exercise of the religion of the church of *Rome*, subject to the King's supremacy."[65] Catholics were not required to take the oath of supremacy, but they were required to swear allegiance to the king. Although the effect of the act was merely to grant religious toleration to Catholics in Quebec, many colonists entertained the view, expressed in the Declaration and Resolves, that its purpose was to "establish" the Catholic religion in that province.[66] A more substantial objection to the act was that it threatened the claims of several colonies to the lands north of the Ohio.[67]

7. The Quebec Act and the establishment of religion

Congress took up the report on the rights and grievances of the colonies on October 12, and the Declaration and Resolves was approved in final form on the 14th. Congress then resumed consideration of methods for obtaining recognition of colonial rights. On October 20 a nonimportation, nonexportation, and nonconsumption agreement, called the Association, was adopted.[68] The Association promised that no British goods would be imported, including

Effects

The Association

---

[61] See p. 246.

[62] See p. 271.

[63] See Edward Channing, *A History of the United States*, Vol. III: *The American Revolution, 1761-1789* (New York, 1927), 97-99; Van Tyne, *op. cit.*, 296-97; Frothingham, *op. cit.*, 211-22.

[64] 14 Geo. 3, c. 83.

[65] Section 5.

[66] Van Tyne, *op. cit.*, 402-4.

[67] Channing, *op. cit.*, III, 142.

[68] Text in *Journals*, I, 23-26; Commager, *op. cit.*, I, 84-87; MacDonald, *op. cit.*, 362-67.

the tea of the East India Company and the products of British plantations of the West Indies. The slave trade was to be wholly discontinued. The promise not to import British goods was backed up by a promise not to consume such goods. This promise, in turn, was supported by an agreement to encourage frugality, economy, and industry and to discourage extravagance and dissipation. Merchants were asked to freeze prices at the level prevailing during the preceding twelve months. Responsibility for enforcement of the Association was given to committees chosen in every county, city, and town. These committees were to publicize all violations of the document.

Once the Association had been finished, Congress devoted its efforts to the completion of petitions, addresses, and memorials to the king, Parliament, the people of Great Britain, the colonial agents in London, and their own constituents. It was resolved that unless the desired redress of grievances had been obtained before May 10, 1775, another congress of the colonies should be convened in Philadelphia.

Address to the inhabitants of Quebec

Of the addresses prepared by Congress, none more clearly demonstrates the opinions of its members regarding the essential rights of the colonists than the one approved October 26 to the inhabitants of Quebec. The address was phrased in plain language. It was designed to convince the French settlers in Canada of the advantages of supporting the American cause. It stated in part:

Representative government

... the first grand right, is that of the people having a share in their own government, by their representatives chosen by themselves, and in consequence of being ruled by laws which they themselves approve, not by edicts of men, over whom they have no controul. This is a bulwark surrounding and defending their property, so that no portions of it can legally be taken from them, but with their own full and free consent, when they in their judgment deem it just and necessary to give them for public services, and precisely direct the easiest, cheapest, and most equal methods in which they shall be collected.

Taxation

The influence of this right extends still farther. If money is wanted by rulers, who have in any manner oppressed the people, they may retain it, until their grievances are redressed; and thus peaceably procure relief, without trusting to despised petitions, or disturbing the public tranquillity.

Trial by jury

The next great right is that of trial by jury. This provides, that neither life, liberty, nor property, can be taken from the possessor, until twelve of his unexceptionable countrymen and peers of his vicinage, who from that neighbourhood may reasonably be supposed to be acquainted with his character, and the characters of the witnesses, upon a fair trial, and full enquiry, face to face, in open court, before as many of the people as chuse to attend, shall pass their sentence upon oath against him; a sentence that cannot injure him, without injuring their own reputation, and probably their interest also; as the question may turn on points, that, in some degree, concern the general welfare; and, if it does not, their verdict may form a precedent, that, on a similar trial of their own, may militate against themselves.

Another right relates merely to the liberty of the person. If a subject is seized and imprisoned, though by order of government, he may, by virtue of this right, immediately obtain a writ, termed a *habeas corpus,* from a judge, whose sworn duty it is to grant it, and thereupon, procure any illegal restraint to be quickly enquired into, and redressed. *Writ of habeas corpus*

A fourth right, is that of holding lands by the tenure of easy rents, and not by rigorous and oppressive services, frequently forcing the possessors from their families, and their business, to perform what ought to be done, in all well regulated states, by men hired for the purpose. *Easy rents*

The last right we shall mention, regards the freedom of the press. The importance of this consists, besides the advancement of truth, science, morality, and arts in general, in its diffusion of liberal sentiments on the administration of government, its ready communication of thoughts between subjects, and its consequential promotion of union among them, whereby oppressive officers are shamed or intimidated, into more honourable and just modes of conducting affairs.[69] *Freedom of the press*

The Declaration and Resolves of the First Continental Congress was one of the most important forerunners of the Declaration of Independence and the declarations of rights found in the first state constitutions. Unlike the Resolutions of the Stamp Act Congress, it based the rights of the colonists not only on the principles of the English constitution and the colonial charters but also upon the law of nature. It carried forward the principles expressed in the earlier document that there should be no taxation of the colonists without adequate representation in Parliament, that the right of trial by jury should be preserved intact, and that the colonists should be allowed freely to petition the king and Parliament for redress of grievances. Its condemnation of standing armies, found among the principles of the English Bill of Rights and later appearing in the constitutions of the several states, was an addition to the list of rights contained in the Stamp Act Resolutions. Although the privilege of the writ of habeas corpus and freedom of the press were not mentioned by the Declaration and Resolves, the "Address to the Inhabitants of Quebec," illustrates the importance attached to those rights by the members of Congress. **Conclusion**

[69] *Journals,* I, 41-42.

DECLARATION AND RESOLVES OF THE FIRST CONTINENTAL CONGRESS[70]

October 14, 1774

<table>
<tr><td>Recital of Grievances

Taxation

Commissioners; Courts of Admiralty

Dependence of judges

Standing armies

Trials beyond the seas

Boston Port Act

Massachusetts Government Act

Administration of Justice Act

Quebec Act</td><td>Whereas, since the close of the last war, the British parliament, claiming a power, of right, to bind the people of America by statutes in all cases whatsoever, hath, in some acts, expressly imposed taxes on them, and in others, under various pretences, but in fact for the purpose of raising a revenue, hath imposed rates and duties payable in these colonies, established a board of commissioners, with unconstitutional powers, and extended the jurisdiction of courts of admiralty, not only for collecting the said duties, but for the trial of causes merely arising within the body of a county.

And whereas, in consequence of other statutes, judges, who before held only estates at will in their offices, have been made dependant on the crown alone for their salaries, and standing armies kept in times of peace: And whereas it has lately been resolved in parliament, that by force of a statute, made in the thirty-fifth year of the reign of King Henry the Eighth, colonists may be transported to England, and tried there upon accusations for treasons and misprisions, or concealments of treasons committed in the colonies, and by a late statute, such trials have been directed in cases therein mentioned:

And whereas, in the last session of parliament, three statutes were made; one entitled, "An act to discontinue, in such manner and for such time as are therein mentioned, the landing and discharging, lading, or shipping of goods, wares and merchandise, at the town, and within the harbour of Boston, in the province of Massachusetts-Bay in North-America;" another entitled, "An act for the better regulating the government of the province of Massachusetts-Bay in New England;" and another entitled, "An act for the impartial administration of justice, in the cases of persons questioned for any act done by them in the execution of the law, or for the suppression of riots and tumults, in the province of the Massachusetts-Bay in New Eigland;" and another statute was then made, "for making more effectual provision for the government of the province of Quebec, etc." All which statutes are impolitic, unjust, and cruel, as well as unconstitutional, and most dangerous and destructive of American rights:</td></tr>
</table>

[70] Charles C. Tansill (ed.), *Documents Illustrative of the Formation of the Union of the American States*, 69th Cong., 1st Sess., 1927, House Doc. 398, 1-5.

RESOLVES OF THE FIRST CONTINENTAL CONGRESS

And whereas, assemblies have been frequently dissolved, contrary to the rights of the people, when they attempted to deliberate on grievances; and their dutiful, humble, loyal, and reasonable petitions to the crown for redress, have been repeatedly treated with contempt, by his Majesty's ministers of state: *（Dissolution of assemblies / Petitions）*

The good people of the several colonies of New-Hampshire, Massachusetts-Bay, Rhode-Island and Providence Plantations, Connecticut, New-York, New-Jersey, Pennsylvania, Newcastle, Kent, and Sussex on Delaware, Maryland, Virginia, North-Carolina, and South-Carolina, justly alarmed at these arbitrary proceedings of parliament and administration, have severally elected, constituted, and appointed deputies to meet, and sit in general Congress, in the city of Philadelphia, in order to obtain such establishment, as that their religion, laws, and liberties, may not be subverted: Whereupon the deputies so appointed being now assembled, in a full and free representation of these colonies, taking into their most serious consideration, the best means of attaining the ends aforesaid, do, in the first place, as Englishmen, their ancestors in like cases have usually done, for asserting and vindicating their rights and liberties, DECLARE, *（Purposes of Continental Congress）*

That the inhabitants of the English colonies in North-America, by the immutable laws of nature, the principles of the English constitution, and the several charters or compacts, have the following RIGHTS: *（Declaration of Rights）*

Resolved, N. C. D. 1. That they are entitled to life, liberty and property: and they have never ceded to any foreign power whatever, a right to dispose of either without their consent. *（Life, liberty, and property）*

Resolved, N. C. D. 2. That our ancestors, who first settled these colonies, were at the time of their emigration from the mother country, entitled to all the rights, liberties, and immunities of free and natural-born subjects, within the realm of England. *（Rights of Englishmen）*

Resolved, N. C. D. 3. That by such emigration they by no means forfeited, surrendered, or lost any of those rights, but that they were, and their descendants now are, entitled to the exercise and enjoyment of all such of them, as their local and other circumstances enable them to exercise and enjoy. *（Rights not lost by emigration）*

Resolved, 4. That the foundation of English liberty, and of all free government, is a right in the people to participate in their legislative council: and as the English colonists are not represented, and from their local and other circumstances, cannot properly be represented in the British parliament, they are entitled to a free and exclusive power of legislation in their several provincial legislatures, where their right of representation can alone be preserved, in all cases of taxation and internal polity, subject only to the negative of their sovereign, in such manner as has been heretofore used and accustomed: But, from the necessity of the case, and a regard to the mutual interest of both countries, we cheerfully consent to the operation of such acts of the British parliament, as are bona fide, restrained to the regulation of our external commerce, for the purpose of securing the commercial advantages of the whole empire to the mother country, and the commercial benefits of its respective members; excluding *（Representative government / Acts of Parliament for the regulation of commerce）* every idea of taxation internal or external, for raising a revenue on the subjects, in America, without their consent.

Common law
Trial by jury
Resolved, N. C. D. 5. That the respective colonies are entitled to the common law of England, and more especially to the great and inestimable privilege of being tried by their peers of the vicinage, according to the course of that law.

English statutes
Resolved, 6. That they are entitled to the benefit of such of the English statutes, as existed at the time of their colonization; and which they have, by experience, respectively found to be applicable to their several local and other circumstances.

Charters and other laws
Resolved, N. C. D. 7. That these, his majesty's colonies, are likewise entitled to all the immunities and privileges granted and confirmed to them by royal charters, or secured by their several codes of provincial laws.

Rights of assembly and petition
Resolved, N. C. D. 8. That they have a right peaceably to assemble, consider of their grievances, and petition the king; and that all prosecutions, prohibitory proclamations, and commitments for the same, are illegal.

Standing armies
Resolved, N. C. D. 9. That the keeping a standing army in these colonies, in times of peace, without the consent of the legislature of that colony, in which such army is kept, is against law.

Separation of powers
Resolved, N. C. D. 10. It is indispensably necessary to good government, and rendered essential by the English constitution, that the constituent branches of the legislature be independent of each other; that, therefore, the exercise of legislative power in several colonies, by a council appointed, during pleasure, by the crown, is unconstitutional, dangerous and destructive to the freedom of American legislation.

Rights cannot be altered
All and each of which the aforesaid deputies, in behalf of themselves, and their constituents, do claim, demand, and insist on, as their indubitable rights and liberties; which cannot be legally taken from them, altered or abridged by any power whatever, without their own consent, by their representatives in their several provincial legislatures.

Infringements of Rights
In the course of our inquiry, we find many infringements and violations of the foregoing rights, which, from an ardent desire, that harmony and mutual intercourse of affection and interest may be restored, we pass over for the present, and proceed to state such acts and measures as have been adopted since the last war, which demonstrate a system formed to enslave America.

Resolved, N. C. D. That the following acts of parliament are infringements and violations of the rights of the colonists; and that the repeal of them is essentially necessary, in order to restore harmony between Great-Britain and the American colonies, viz.

Revenue acts
The several acts of 4 Geo. III. ch. 15, and ch. 34.—5 Geo. III. ch. 25.—6 Geo. III. ch. 52.—7 Geo. III. ch. 41. and ch. 46.—8 Geo. III. ch. 22. which impose duties for the purpose of raising a revenue in America, extend the power of the admiralty courts beyond their ancient limits, deprive the American subject of trial by jury, authorise the judges certificate to indemnify the prosecutor from damages, that he might otherwise be liable to, requiring oppressive security from a claimant of ships and goods seized,

RESOLVES OF THE FIRST CONTINENTAL CONGRESS

before he shall be allowed to defend his property, and are subversive of American rights.

Also 12 Geo. III. ch. 24. intituled, "An act for the better securing his majesty's dockyards, magazines, ships, ammunition, and stores," which declares a new offence in America, and deprives the American subject of a constitutional trial by jury of the vicinage, by authorising the trial of any person, charged with the committing any offence described in the said act, out of the realm, to be indicted and tried for the same in any shire or county within the realm. *Trials beyond the seas*

Also the three acts passed in the last session of parliament, for stopping the port and blocking up the harbour of Boston, for altering the charter and government of Massachusetts-Bay, and that which is entitled, "An act for the better administration of justice, etc." *Boston Port Act; other acts*

Also the act passed in the same session for establishing the Roman Catholic religion, in the province of Quebec, abolishing the equitable system of English laws, and erecting a tyranny there, to the great danger (from so total a dissimilarity of religion, law and government) of the neighbouring British colonies, by the assistance of whose blood and treasure the said country was conquered from France. *Quebec Act*

Also the act passed in the same session, for the better providing suitable quarters for officers and soldiers in his majesty's service, in North-America. *Quartering Act of 1774*

Also, that the keeping a standing army in several of these colonies, in time of peace, without the consent of the legislature of that colony, in which such army is kept, is against law. *Standing armies*

To these grievous acts and measures, Americans cannot submit, but in hopes their fellow subjects in Great-Britain will, on a revision of them, restore us to that state, in which both countries found happiness and prosperity, we have for the present, only resolved to pursue the following peaceable measures: 1. To enter into a non-importation, non-consumption, and non-exportation agreement or association. 2. To prepare an address to the people of Great-Britain, and a memorial to the inhabitants of British America: and 3. To prepare a loyal address to his majesty, agreeable to resolutions already entered into. **Action to Be Taken by Colonists**

REFERENCES

Beer, George L. *British Colonial Policy, 1754-1765*. New York: Macmillan Co., 1907.
Burnett, Edmund C. *The Continental Congress*. New York: Macmillan Co., 1941. Chaps. 1-3.
Channing, Edward. *A History of the United States*. 6 vols. New York: Macmillan Co., 1927. III, chaps. 4, 5.
Frothingham, Richard. *The Rise of the Republic of the United States*. 7th ed. Boston: Little, Brown & Co., 1899. Chaps. 8, 9.
Schlesinger, Arthur M. *The Colonial Merchants and the American Revolution, 1763-1776*. New York: Columbia University Press, 1917.
Van Tyne, Claude H. *The Causes of the War of Independence*. Boston: Houghton Mifflin Co., 1922. Chaps. 8-12.

XX. DECLARATION OF THE CAUSES AND NECESSITY OF TAKING UP ARMS
1775

Origins   Even after hostilities had broken out at Lexington on April 19, 1775, most of the colonists desired reconciliation with Great Britain and dreaded the prospect of a complete break from the empire. The Declaration of the Causes and Necessity of Taking up Arms held out hope of reconciliation, but at the same time approved the use of force to obtain recognition by Britain of colonial rights.

The Declaration of Causes stood midway in time and principle between the Declaration and Resolves of the First Continental Congress[1] and the Declaration of Independence.[2] All three documents were concerned with obtaining recognition of the rights of the people. The Declaration and Resolves sought to obtain recognition of those rights by means of the trade restrictions of the Association.[3] The Declaration of Causes went a step further by approving the use of armed resistance to secure those rights. The Declaration of Independence took the final step. It recognized that the people's rights could be secured only by a government completely independent of Great Britain, formed by the people themselves, and founded solely upon their consent.

Second Continental Congress   Pursuant to the resolution of the First Congress,[4] delegates from the colonies met at Philadelphia on May 10, 1775. As had been true of the First Congress, many delegates were chosen by extra-legal assemblies.[5] For this reason the membership of Congress, in general, was representative of the

---
[1] See pp. 272-89.
[2] See pp. 314-22.
[3] See pp. 283-84.
[4] See p. 284.
[5] Edmund C. Burnett, *The Continental Congress* (New York, 1941), 61-62.

more radical elements of the colonies.[6] Most of the members of the First Congress were also chosen for the Second. A few noteworthy additions to the body were made, however. These included John Hancock of Massachusetts, Benjamin Franklin and James Wilson of Pennsylvania, and Thomas Jefferson of Virginia. Some of the delegates were already on their way to Philadelphia when hostilities broke out at Lexington on April 19. The battles of the Revolution thus furnished the background of Congress' deliberations.

Once Congress had assembled, the credentials of the delegates were presented. In general, the delegates were authorized to consent and agree to all measures which Congress might deem necessary for obtaining a redress of grievances and restoring harmony with Great Britain. In other words, the Second Continental Congress was to carry forward the objectives of the First. The credentials of the Massachusetts delegates, for example, provided: *Objectives of Congress*

> That the proceedings of the American Continental Congress, held at Philadelphia, on the 5th day of September last, and reported by the honorable delegates from this colony, have, with the deliberation due to their high importance, been considered by us; and the American bill of rights, therein contained, appears to be formed with the greatest ability and judgment, to be founded on the immutable laws of nature and reason, the principles of the English constitution, and respective charters and constitutions of the colonies, and to be worthy of their most vigorous support, as essentially necessary to liberty; likewise the ruinous and iniquitous measures, which, in violation of these rights, at present convulse and threaten destruction to America, appear to be clearly pointed out, and judicious plans adopted for defeating them.[7]

The purpose of Congress was to seek reconciliation, not independence. The Massachusetts delegates were instructed to agree upon "such further measures, as shall to them appear to be best calculated for the recovery and establishment of American rights and liberties, and for restoring harmony between Great-Britain and the colonies."[8]

On June 23 Congress appointed a committee of five to draw a declaration to be proclaimed by General Washington upon his arrival at camp near Boston. The members of the committee were John Rutledge of South Carolina, William Livingston of New Jersey, Benjamin Franklin, John Jay of New York, and Thomas Johnson of Maryland.[9] The committee's draft was *Drafting the Declaration*

[6] Edward Channing, *A History of the United States,* Vol. III: *The American Revolution, 1761-1789* (New York, 1927), 161-62.
[7] *Journals of the American Congress, 1774-1788* (Washington, 1823), I, 50-51.
[8] *Ibid.,* 51.
[9] *Ibid.,* 88.

presented to Congress the next day. It was read and debated. On June 26, after further consideration, Congress sent back the declaration for revision. It was clear that Congress was dissatisfied with the committee's efforts. John Dickinson of Pennsylvania and Thomas Jefferson were added to the committee, apparently in the belief that they could be trusted to express the sentiments of Congress in appropriate language. At the request of the committee, Jefferson prepared a draft. Dickinson thought that some of Jefferson's language was too strong. At Jefferson's request, Dickinson prepared an entirely new statement, preserving, however, the last four and one-half paragraphs of Jefferson's draft.[10] This draft was approved without change by Congress July 6.

Effects   The declaration expressly disavowed all thoughts of independence. Congress promised to lay down arms when the freedoms the colonists claimed as their birthright had been secured and hostilities had ceased.

Efforts to effect reconciliation   Hope for a peaceful solution died slowly. The Association, adopted by the First Continental Congress, forced England to take the first steps. The nonimportation agreement embodied in the Association caused a reduction of 90 per cent of imports from England. As a result, the merchants of London petitioned the House of Commons in January, 1775:

> ... the minds of his Majesty's subjects in the British colonies have been greatly disquieted, a total stop is now put to the export trade with the greatest and most important part of North America, the public revenue is threatened with a large and fatal diminution, the petitioners with grievous distress, and thousands of industrious artificers and manufacturers with utter ruin; under these alarming circumstances, the petitioners receive no small comfort, from a persuasion that the representatives of the people, newly delegated to the most important of all trusts, will take the whole of these weighty matters into their most serious consideration; and therefore praying the House, that they will enter into a full and immediate examination of that system of commercial policy, which was formerly adopted, and uniformly maintained, to the happiness and advantage of both countries, and will apply such healing remedies as can alone restore and establish the commerce between Great Britain and her colonies on a permanent foundation ...[11]

Lord North's conciliatory resolution   On February 20 Lord North unexpectedly presented to the House of Commons a conciliatory resolution.[12] North was willing to agree that if any colony should bear its share of the cost of defense, civil government, and administration of justice, Great Britain would not impose upon that colony

---

[10] Burnett, *op. cit.*, 85-86.

[11] Henry S. Commager (ed.), *Documents of American History* (6th ed.; New York, 1958), I, 88-89.

[12] Text in William MacDonald (ed.), *Select Charters and Other Documents Illustrative of American History, 1606-1775* (New York, 1899), 367-68.

CAUSES AND NECESSITY OF TAKING UP ARMS

any duty, tax, or assessment, "except only such Duties as it may be expedient to continue to levy or to impose for the regulation of commerce; the nett produce of the Duties last mentioned to be carried to the account of such Province or Colony respectively."

In May the New Jersey House of Assembly formally transmitted Lord North's plan to Congress, stating that all proper means of effecting a reconciliation should be explored. In June the Virginia House of Burgesses, in a report drawn by Thomas Jefferson, rejected the plan.[13] Immediately after completing this report, Jefferson went to take his seat in Congress. Lord North's plan was not taken under consideration by Congress until July 22. On that date Franklin, Jefferson, John Adams of Massachusetts, and Richard Henry Lee of Virginia were appointed as a committee to consider the plan.[14] Because Virginia's report rejecting the plan was favored by Congress, Jefferson was called on to prepare the report of the committee.[15]

The committee's report was agreed to by Congress July 31. It stated, among other things:

> We are of opinion that the proposition contained in this resolution is unreasonable and insidious: Unreasonable, because, if we declare we accede to it, we declare, without reservation, we will purchase the favour of parliament, not knowing at the same time at what price they will please to estimate their favour; it is insidious, because, individual colonies, having bid and bidden again, till they find the avidity of the seller too great for all their powers to satisfy; are then to return into opposition, divided from their sister colonies whom the minister will have previously detached by a grant of easier terms, or by an artful procrastination of a definitive answer.[16]

Congress desired reconciliation, but on its own terms. Its most important effort to achieve that objective was the preparation of a petition to the king, known as the "Olive Branch" petition. That petition was agreed to July 5.[17] It was drafted by Dickinson, leader of the party of conciliation. Couched in the most respectful language, it professed alarm at the "new system of statutes and regulations adopted for the administration of the colonies, that filled their minds with the most painful fears and jealousies." No blame for the plight of the colonists was ascribed to George III. It was, instead, "the irksome variety of artifices, practised by many of your majesty's ministers"

Congress' "Olive Branch" petition

---
[13] Burnett, *op. cit.*, 95.
[14] *Journals*, I, 121.
[15] Burnett, *op. cit.*, 95.
[16] *Journals*, I, 132.
[17] Text in MacDonald, *op. cit.*, 381-85.

that were responsible for colonial problems. The petition, together with other addresses adopted by Congress, was given to Richard Penn to be carried to England and presented to the king. On August 23, the day Penn was to have presented the petition to Lord Dartmouth, King George issued a proclamation of rebellion.[18] He declared that the colonists had renounced their allegiance and had become traitors to the crown. The colonial representatives in England later requested an audience with the king. Their request was refused, and they were informed that no answer to the petition would be given.

Hope of reconciliation ended. It could no longer be expected that the force of arms would secure a recognition of the people's rights while the colonies remained within the British Empire. Complete independence from Britain remained the only means of securing those rights.

[18] Text in *ibid.*, 389-91.

DECLARATION OF THE CAUSES AND NECESSITY OF TAKING UP ARMS[19]

July 6, 1775

A DECLARATION BY THE REPRESENTATIVES OF THE UNITED COLONIES OF NORTH-AMERICA, NOW MET IN CONGRESS AT PHILADELPHIA, SETTING FORTH THE CAUSES AND NECESSITY OF THEIR TAKING UP ARMS

If it was possible for men, who exercise their reason to believe, that the divine Author of our existence intended a part of the human race to hold an absolute property in, and an unbounded power over others, marked out by his infinite goodness and wisdom, as the objects of a legal domination never rightfully resistible, however severe and oppressive, the inhabitants of these colonies might at least require from the parliament of Great-Britain some evidence, that this dreadful authority over them, has been granted to that body. But a reverence for our great Creator, principles of humanity, and the dictates of common sense, must convince all those who reflect upon the subject, that government was instituted to promote the welfare of mankind, and ought to be administered for the attainment of that end. The legislature of Great-Britain, however, stimulated by an inordinate passion for a power not only unjustifiable, but which they know to be peculiarly reprobated by the very constitution of that kingdom, and desparate of success in any mode of contest, where regard should be had to truth, law, or right, have at length, deserting those, attempted to effect their cruel and impolitic purpose of enslaving these colonies by violence, and have thereby rendered it necessary for us to close with their last appeal from reason to arms.—Yet, however blinded that assembly may be, by their intemperate rage for unlimited domination, so to slight justice and the opinion of mankind, we esteem ourselves bound by obligations of respect to the rest of the world, to make known the justice of our cause.

Purpose of government is to promote the welfare of mankind

Violence of Parliament has resulted in recourse to arms

Our forefathers, inhabitants of the island of Great-Britain, left their native land, to seek on these shores a residence for civil and religious freedom. At the expense of their blood, at the hazard of their fortunes, without the least charge to the country from which they removed, by unceasing labour, and an unconquerable spirit, they effected settlements in the distant and inhospitable wilds of America, then filled with numerous

First settlers

---

[19] Charles C. Tansill (ed.), *Documents Illustrative of the Formation of the Union of the American States*, 69th Cong., 1st Sess., 1927, House Doc. 398, 10-17.

Colonial assemblies

and warlike nations of barbarians.—Societies or governments, vested with perfect legislatures, were formed under charters from the crown, and an harmonious intercourse was established between the colonies and the kingdom from which they derived their origin. The mutual benefits of this union became in a short time so extraordinary, as to excite astonishment. It is universally confessed, that the amazing increase of the wealth, strength, and navigation of the realm, arose from this source; and the minister, who so wisely and successfully directed the measures of Great-Britain in the late war, publicly declared, that these colonies enabled her to triumph over her enemies.— Towards the conclusion of that war, it pleased our sovereign to make a change in his counsels.—From that fatal moment, the affairs of the British empire began to fall into confusion, and gradually sliding from the summit of glorious prosperity, to which they had been advanced by the virtues and abilities of one man, are at length distracted by the convulsions, that now shake it to its deepest foundations.—The new ministry finding the brave foes of Britain, though frequently defeated, yet still contending, took up the unfortunate idea of granting them a hasty peace, and of then subduing her faithful friends.

French and Indian War

New British ministry

British colonial policy

These devoted colonies were judged to be in such a state, as to present victories without bloodshed, and all the easy emoluments of statuteable plunder.—The uninterrupted tenor of their peaceable and respectful behaviour from the beginning of colonization, their dutiful, zealous, and useful services during the war, though so recently and amply acknowledged in the most honourable manner by his majesty, by the late king, and by parliament, could not save them from the meditated innovations.— Parliament was influenced to adopt the pernicious project, and assuming a new power over them, have in the course of eleven years, given such decisive specimens of the spirit and consequences attending this power, as to leave no doubt concerning the effects of acquiescence under it. They have undertaken to give and grant our money without our consent, though we have ever exercised an exclusive right to dispose of our own property; statutes have been passed for extending the jurisdiction of courts of admiralty and vice-admiralty beyond their ancient limits; for depriving us of the accustomed and inestimable privilege of trial by jury, in cases affecting both life and property; for suspending the legislature of one of the colonies; for interdicting all commerce to the capital of another; and for altering fundamentally the form of government established by charter, and secured by acts of its own legislature solemnly confirmed by the crown; for exempting the "murderers" of colonists from legal trial, and in effect, from punishment; for erecting in a neighbouring province, acquired by the joint arms of Great-Britain and America, a despotism dangerous to our very existence; and for quartering soldiers upon the colonists in time of profound peace. It has also been resolved in parliament, that colonists charged with committing certain offences, shall be transported to England to be tried.

Specific grievances

Declaratory Act

But why should we enumerate our injuries in detail? By one statute it is declared, that parliament can "of right make laws to bind us in all cases whatsoever." What is to defend us against so enormous, so unlimited a power? Not a single man of those who assume it, is chosen by us; or is subject to our controul or influence; but, on the contrary, they are all of them exempt from the operation of such laws, and an American revenue, if not diverted from the ostensible purposes for which it is raised, would actually lighten their own burdens in proportion, as they increase ours. We saw the misery to which such despotism would reduce us. We for ten years incessantly and ineffectually besieged the throne as supplicants; we reasoned, we remonstrated with parliament, in the most mild and decent language.

Administration sensible that we should regard these oppressive measures as freemen ought to do, sent over fleets and armies to enforce them. The indignation of the Americans was roused, it is true; but it was the indignation of a virtuous, loyal, and affectionate people. A Congress of delegates from the United Colonies was assembled at Philadelphia, on the fifth day of last September. We resolved again to offer an humble and dutiful petition to the King, and also addressed our fellow-subjects of Great-Britain. We have pursued every temperate, every respectful measure: we have even proceeded to break off our commercial intercourse with our fellow-subjects, as the last peaceable admonition, that our attachment to no nation upon earth should supplant our attachment to liberty.—This, we flattered ourselves, was the ultimate step of the controversy: but subsequent events have shewn, how vain was this hope of finding moderation in our enemies. *[Actions of colonists toward oppressive measures]*

Several threatening expressions against the colonies were inserted in his majesty's speech; our petition, tho' we were told it was a decent one, and that his majesty had been pleased to receive it graciously, and to promise laying it before his parliament, was huddled into both houses among a bundle of American papers, and there neglected. The lords and commons in their address, in the month of February, said, that "a rebellion at that time actually existed within the province of Massachusetts-Bay; and that those concerned in it, had been countenanced and encouraged by unlawful combinations and engagements, entered into by his majesty's subjects in several of the other colonies; and therefore they besought his majesty, that he would take the most effectual measures to inforce due obedience to the laws and authority of the supreme legislature." *[Actions of British] [Declaration of rebellion]*

—Soon after, the commercial intercourse of whole colonies, with foreign countries, and with each other, was cut off by an act of parliament; by another several of them were intirely prohibited from the fisheries in the seas near their co[a]sts, on which they always depended for their sustenance; and large reinforcements of ships and troops were immediately sent over to general Gage. *[Commerce halted; fishing rights infringed; troops sent]*

Fruitless were all the entreaties, arguments, and eloquence of an illustrious band of the most distinguished peers, and commoners, who nobly and stren[u]ously asserted the justice of our cause, to stay, or even to mitigate the heedless fury with which these accumulated and unexampled outrages were hurried on.—Equally fruitless was the interference of the city of London, of Bristol, and many other respectable towns in our favour. Parliament adopted an insidious manoeuvre calculated to divide us, to establish a perpetual auction of taxations where colony should bid against colony, all of them uninformed what ransom would redeem their lives; and thus to extort from *[British policy]* us, at the point of the bayonet, the unknown sums that should be sufficient to gratify, if possible to gratify, ministerial rapacity, with the miserable indulgence left to us of raising, in our own mode, the prescribed tribute. What terms more rigid and humiliating could have been dictated by remorseless victors to conquered enemies? in our circumstances to accept them, would be to deserve them.

Battles of Lexington and Concord

Soon after the intelligence of these proceedings arrived on this continent, general Gage, who in the course of the last year had taken possession of the town of Boston, in the province of Massachusetts-Bay, and still occupied it is [*as*] a garrison, on the 19th day of April, sent out from that place a large detachment of his army, who made an unprovoked assault on the inhabitants of the said province, at the town of Lexington, as appears by the affidavits of a great number of persons, some of whom were officers and soldiers of that detachment, murdered eight of the inhabitants, and wounded many others. From thence the troops proceeded in warlike array to the town of Concord, where they set upon another party of the inhabitants of the same province, killing several and wounding more, until compelled to retreat by the country people suddenly assembled to repel this cruel aggression. Hostilities, thus commenced by the British troops, have been since prosecuted by them without regard to faith or reputation.

Confinement of inhabitants of Boston

Seizure of arms

—The inhabitants of Boston being confined within that town by the general their governor, and having, in order to procure their dismission, entered into a treaty with him, it was stipulated that the said inhabitants having deposited their arms with their own magistrates, should have liberty to depart, taking with them their other effects. They accordingly delivered up their arms, but in open violation of honour, in defiance of the obligation of treaties, which even savage nations esteemed sacred, the governor ordered the arms deposited as aforesaid, that they might be preserved for their owners, to be seized by a body of soldiers; detained the greatest part of the inhabitants in the town, and compelled the few who were permitted to retire, to leave their most valuable effects behind.

Hardships to colonists

By this perfidy wives are separated from their husbands, children from their parents, the aged and the sick from their relations and friends, who wish to attend and comfort them; and those who have been used to live in plenty and even elegance, are reduced to deplorable distress.

Declaration of rebellion

The general, further emulating his ministerial masters, by a proclamation bearing date on the 12th day of June, after venting the grossest falsehoods and calumnies against the good people of these colonies, proceeds to "declare them all, either by name or description, to be rebels and traitors, to supersede the course of the common law, and instead thereof to publish and order the use and exercise of the law martial."

Depredations of troops

—His troops have butchered our countrymen, have wantonly burnt Charlestown, besides a considerable number of houses in other places; our ships and vessels are seized; the necessary supplies of provisions are intercepted, and he is exerting his utmost power to spread destruction and devastation around him.

Hostility of Canadians

We have received certain intelligence, that general Carelton [*Carleton*], the governor of Canada, is instigating the people of that province and the Indians to fall upon us; and we have but too much reason to apprehend, that schemes have been formed to excite domestic enemies against us. In brief, a part of these colonies now feel, and all of them are sure of feeling, as far as the vengeance of administration can inflict them, the complicated calamities of fire, sword, and famine. We [20] are reduced to the alternative of chusing an unconditional submission to the tyranny of irritated ministers, or resistance by force.—The latter is our choice.—We have counted the cost of this contest, and find nothing so dreadful as voluntary slavery.—Honour, justice, and humanity, forbid us tamely to surrender that freedom which we received from our gallant ancestors, and which our innocent posterity have a right to receive from us. We cannot endure the infamy and guilt of resigning succeeding generations to that wretchedness which inevitably awaits them, if we basely entail hereditary bondage upon them.

Resistance preferable to slavery

Our cause is just. Our union is perfect. Our internal resources are great, and, if necessary, foreign assistance is undoubtedly attainable.—We gratefully acknowledge, as signal instances of the Divine favour towards us, that his Providence would not permit us to be called into this severe controversy, until we were grown up to our present strength, had been previously exercised in warlike operation, and possessed of the means of defending ourselves. With hearts fortified with these animating reflections, we most solemnly, before God and the world, *declare,* that, exerting the utmost energy of those powers, which our beneficent Creator hath graciously bestowed upon us, the arms we have been compelled by our enemies to assume, we will, in defiance of every hazard, with unabating firmness and perseverence, employ for the preservation of our liberties; being with one mind resolved to die freemen rather than to live slaves.

Recourse to arms for the preservation of liberties

Lest this declaration should disquiet the minds of our friends and fellow-subjects in any part of the empire, we assure them that we mean not to dissolve that union which has so long and so happily subsisted between us, and which we sincerely wish to see restored.—Necessity has not yet driven us into that desperate measure, or induced us to excite any other nation to war against them.—We have not raised armies with ambitious designs of separating from Great-Britain, and establishing independent states. We fight not for glory or for conquest. We exhibit to mankind the remarkable spectacle of a people attacked by unprovoked enemies, without any imputation or even suspicion of offence. They boast of their privileges and civilization, and yet proffer no milder conditions than servitude or death.

Union not dissolved

In our own native land, in defence of the freedom that is our birthright, and which we ever enjoyed till the late violation of it—for the protection of our property, acquired solely by the honest industry of our fore-fathers and ourselves, against violence actually offered, we have taken up arms. We shall lay them down when hostilities shall cease on the part of the aggressors, and all danger of their being renewed shall be removed, and not before.

Arms to be laid down when hostilities cease

[20] From this point the declaration follows Jefferson's draft.

Divine protection asked   With an humble confidence in the mercies of the supreme and impartial Judge and Ruler of the Universe, we most devoutly implore his divine goodness to protect us happily through this great conflict, to dispose our adversaries to reconciliation on reasonable terms, and thereby to relieve the empire from the calamities of civil war.

REFERENCES

See references on p. 289.

XXI. CONSTITUTION OF VIRGINIA
1776

In May, 1774, the Virginia House of Burgesses expressed its approval of the circular letter sent by Massachusetts asking the aid of the colonies in the crisis brought about by the Boston Port Bill. On May 26 Governor Dunmore dissolved the House for this action, but the burgesses did not go home. Instead, they convened at a nearby tavern and proceeded to adopt an association calling for a boycott on all trade with England. In addition, they directed the counties to elect members to a convention to meet August 1.[1]

Origins

Once the convention had assembled, it supervised enforcement in Virginia of the Continental Association,[2] directed the activities of local committees of safety and correspondence, and carried on the general legislative and executive affairs of the colony.[3] The membership of the body did not differ greatly from that of the House of Burgesses. Conventions were assembled from time to time in Virginia to deal with the affairs of the colony.

The Virginia Convention

It was the convention, technically an extra-legal body, that adopted the Bill of Rights of 1776. The body that adopted the Virginia declaration thus resembled in several respects the English Convention Parliament of 1689 which adopted the English Declaration of Rights.[4] Both bodies were extra-legal and had come into existence after the regular legislature had been dissolved.

---

[1] Claude H. Van Tyne, *The War of Independence: American Phase* (New York, 1929), 195.

[2] See pp. 283-84.

[3] The General Assembly was convened briefly by Governor Dunmore, June 1, 1775, following his seizure of the colony's supply of gunpowder. Because of the hostility which its members showed toward him on that occasion, Dunmore took refuge aboard the "Fowey." The assembly finally voted that Dunmore had abdicated his office. The body voted its own dissolution on June 24 and reassumed the character of a convention. Kate M. Rowland, *The Life of George Mason, 1725-1792* (New York, 1892), I, 197-98.

[4] See pp. 222-23.

George Mason and the Bill of Rights

The Bill of Rights was drafted by George Mason, a well-to-do planter of Fairfax County, Virginia. In July, 1775, Mason came from retirement to fill a vacancy in the Virginia Convention caused by George Washington's appointment as commander in chief of the Continental Army. There were a number of close contests for seats in the last convention, which met at Williamsburg in May, 1776, and it was with some difficulty that Mason secured a seat as representative of Fairfax County. He took his seat on May 17.

Two days before Mason arrived, the convention passed two important resolutions drafted by President Edmund Pendleton and others.[5] The first of these instructed the Virginia delegates in the Continental Congress to propose the adoption by that body of a declaration of independence.[6] The second resolution called for the appointment of a committee "to prepare a Declaration of Rights, and such a plan of Government as will be most likely to maintain peace and order in this Colony, and secure substantial and equal liberty to the people."

A committee of twenty-eight delegates was appointed to draft the declaration and constitution. It was headed by Archibald Cary, and included Patrick Henry, Edmund Randolph, James Madison, and Mason. Mason assumed the leadership in drafting the documents. It is probable that he deserves credit for drafting all sections of the declaration except the tenth and fourteenth.[7] According to his own account, those clauses, together with minor amendments of the draft reported by the select committee, were added by the convention.[8]

The Bill of Rights was presented to the convention on May 27. It was discussed at intervals until June 11 by the committee of the whole, and was passed unanimously the next day. The convention then proceeded to the consideration of a constitution setting up the framework of government. The constitution was prepared by Mason as a member of the same committee that had prepared the Bill of Rights. The constitution was adopted by the

---

[5] Text in Charles C. Tansill (ed.), *Documents Illustrative of the Formation of the Union of the American States*, 69th Cong., 1st Sess., 1927, House Doc. 398, 19-20.

[6] See pp. 316-17.

[7] Writing about thirty years after the event, Edmund Randolph ascribed the fifteenth and sixteenth sections to Patrick Henry. The evidence in support of Henry's authorship of those clauses, however, is weak. Rowland, *op. cit.*, I, 235-39.

[8] Mason described the tenth and fourteenth sections as "not of fundamental nature," and said that some of the alterations and additions made by the Convention were "not for the better." *Ibid.*, I, 436.

convention on June 29.[9] The body of the constitution was prefaced by a lengthy preamble, prepared by Thomas Jefferson, which set forth the grievances of the colonists against George III.[10]

The Bill of Rights contained statements of general political philosophy and clauses establishing specific rights of the individual. Several of its provisions are similar to clauses found in the English Bill of Rights.[11] That document had prohibited the suspension of laws, the maintenance of standing armies without the consent of Parliament, and the imposition of excessive bail, excessive fines, and cruel and unusual punishments. It had also provided that elections of members of the legislature should be free and that the jury system should be preserved. In addition, the English document declared illegal James II's Court of High Commission, the practices of which were antithetical to the common law procedures required by Section 8 of the Virginia declaration. It had also given Protestants the right to bear arms for their defense. *General Significance* *Compared with the English Bill of Rights, 1689*

The Declaration and Resolves of the First Continental Congress[12] was a closer ancestor of the Virginia document than the English Declaration of Rights. Perhaps the chief point of similarity was the adoption by both documents of the law of nature as a source of the rights of the individual. Mason's statement of this principle was, however, much more eloquent than the reference to it found in the Declaration and Resolves. Both documents declared that taxes should be levied only by the legislature. Both stated that the right of trial by jury should be preserved, and both condemned the maintenance of standing armies without the consent of the people or their representatives. *Compared with the Declaration and Resolves of the First Continental Congress, 1774*

Important differences between the Virginia Bill of Rights and the Declaration and Resolves, however, existed. The Declaration and Resolves claimed for the colonists the benefit of the English common law and English statutes in existence at the time of colonization which had been applicable to the situation in the colonies. It also claimed the benefit of the colonial charters

---

[9] Text in Francis N. Thorpe (ed.), *The Federal and State Constitutions, Colonial Charters, and Other Organic Laws* (Washington, 1909), VII, 3814-19.

[10] This list of charges against the king is similar to the one found in the Declaration of Independence, pp. 319-21, but it is not so lengthy. There also exists a similarity between the preamble of the Virginia Constitution and the list of grievances against Parliament set forth in the Declaration of the Causes and Necessity of Taking up Arms, 1775, which was drafted in part by Jefferson, 296. See Julian Boyd, *The Declaration of Independence* (Princeton, 1945), 12-15.

[11] See pp. 222-50.

[12] See pp. 272-89.

and the provincial statutes. The Virginia declaration omitted all reference to the English common law, the colonial charters, and the statutes. Some of its provisions, of course, show the influence of those sources.

Searches and seizures

Section 10, which condemned general warrants, was a notable advance in the protection of personal security. As a general rule, the common law of England prohibited search warrants and warrants of arrest which did not describe in detail the places to be searched and the things or persons to be seized.[13] The reasons for this rule were given by Blackstone:

> A *general* warrant to apprehend all persons suspected, without naming or particularly describing any person in special, is illegal and void for it's certainty; for it is the duty of the magistrate, and ought not to be left to the officer, to judge of the ground of suspicion. And a warrant to apprehend all persons, guilty of a crime therein specified, is no legal warrant: for the point, upon which it's authority rests, is a fact to be decided on a subsequent trial; namely, whether the person apprehended thereupon be really guilty or not.[14]

Parliament, however, might authorize exceptions to this general rule.[15] It had done so in two situations each of which had an important bearing on the development of American rights.

Writs of assistance

One exception was the general search warrant, called a writ of assistance, which was used in the enforcement of the acts of trade.[16] The writs of assistance were more effective than ordinary search warrants in dealing with the practices of smugglers. They enabled royal officers to search any house or ship, to break down doors, open trunks and boxes, and seize goods at will.

James Otis' argument against writs of assistance

By law, the writs of assistance which had been issued by the Superior Court of Massachusetts were to expire six months after the death of George II (1727-60). The renewal of the writs furnished the occasion for the famous argument in 1761 of James Otis.[17] He argued that the writ was against the

---

[13] William S. Holdsworth, *A History of English Law* (4th ed.; Boston, 1938), X, 667-68.

[14] *Commentaries on the Laws of England* (9th ed.; London, 1783), IV, 291.

[15] *Leach v. Money* (1765), *State Trials* (T. B. Howell, comp.), XIX, 1026-27.

[16] In 1662 it was enacted that customs officers might go aboard any vessel and seize prohibited goods. It was also provided that any person authorized by a writ of assistance under the seal of the Court of Exchequer might "take a constable, head-borough or other publick officer inhabiting near unto the place, and in the day time to enter, and go into any house, shop, cellar, warehouse or room, or other place, and in case of resistance, to break open doors, chests, trunks and other package, there to seize, and from thence to bring, any kind of goods or merchandize whatsoever, prohibited and uncustomed, and to put and secure the same in his majesty's storehouse, in the port next to the place where such seizure shall be made." 13 & 14 Car. 2, c. 11, §§ 4, 5. These powers were conferred upon the officials of plantation trade in 1696. 7 & 8 Will. 3, c. 22, § 6.

[17] John Adams' account of that argument is given in Charles F. Adams (ed.), *The Works of John Adams* (Boston, 1850), II, 521-25.

fundamental principles of law and that it violated the maxim that each man's house is his castle. A special warrant to search particular houses, he said, was valid when it was sworn that there was good ground for suspicion. General warrants, on the other hand, were subject to abuses at the hands of incompetent or overbearing officials. He said he had found only one such writ in the lawbooks, and that had been issued during the reign of Charles I (1625-49) when the powers of the Star Chamber had been pushed to extremes. Otis went so far as to deny the power of Parliament to sanction a practice so contrary to the fundamental law of the land.[18] The court suspended judgment in order to consider Otis' arguments, but eventually the writs were reissued.

The issuance of writs of assistance was later expressly authorized by the Townshend Revenue Act of 1767.[19] The Declaration and Resolves of the First Continental Congress[20] cited that act as one of the violations of the rights of the colonists, and condemned the establishment of "a board of commissioners, with unconstitutional powers."

The Townshend Revenue Act

The second kind of general warrant which infringed colonial rights was the warrant for the search and seizure of libelous publications and the arrest of offenders against the sedition laws. The Licensing Act of 1662 had authorized royal officials, acting under a warrant issued by the Secretary of State or an official of the Stationers' Company, to search all houses and shops where they suspected "upon some probable reason" that unlicensed publications were kept.[21] Offenders were to be brought before justices of the peace, and were to be committed to prison, "there to remain until they shall be tried and acquitted, or convicted and punished for the said offenses."

General warrants to search for and seize libelous publications

With the expiration in 1695 of the Licensing Act,[22] the authority to issue these warrants lapsed. Royal officials, however, continued to issue such warrants and even broadened their scope so as to permit seizure of all the papers and effects of suspected persons. Objections to this practice were raised as early as 1733,[23] but it was not until 1765 that the English courts finally ruled that the warrants were illegal.[24] In the course of his opinion, Lord Camden said:

---

[18] See p. 28.
[19] 7 Geo. 3, c. 46, § 10; see pp. 275-77.
[20] See pp. 288-89.
[21] 13 & 14 Car. 2, c. 33, § 15.
[22] See pp. 242-43.
[23] Holdsworth, *op. cit.*, X, 668.
[24] *Entick v. Carrington* (1765), *State Trials*, XIX, 1029.

> The messenger, under this warrant, is commanded to seize the person described, and to bring him with his papers to be examined before the secretary of state. In consequence of this, the house must be searched; the lock and doors of every room, box, or trunk must be broken open; all the papers and books without exception, if the warrant be executed according to its tenor, must be seized and carried away; for it is observable, that nothing is left either to the discretion or to the humanity of the officer.
>
> . . . .
>
> Such is the power, and therefore one should naturally expect that the law to warrant it should be clear in proportion as the power is exorbitant.
>
> If it is law, it will be found in our books. If it is not to be found there, it is not law.[25]

It has been said that the law of sedition in the colonies was exactly like that of England,[26] and there appear to have been instances of general warrants issued in America for the seizure of seditious publications.[27] By condemning general warrants the Virginia Bill of Rights thus greatly strengthened the freedom of the press, a right referred to in Section 12 of the document.

Freedom of the press

Section 12 of the Virginia Bill of Rights, establishing the freedom of the press, was the earliest declaration of that right in a document of constitutional significance. That clause, however, probably did not mean that all restrictions on the press were to be abolished. The relaxation of restrictions on the press was a slow process marked by several distinct steps. Some of the restrictions remained until the end of the eighteenth century.

The law of seditious libel

The contribution of the seventeenth century to the freedom of the press was the abolition of the licensing system which had been originated by the Star Chamber and carried on by Parliament until 1695.[28] In the eighteenth century the press was free from the restraints of licensing. Persons writing and publishing books, pamphlets, and newspapers, however, were still subject to the stringent law of seditious libel, and juries had no authority to determine whether or not the language used constituted sedition. As Blackstone put it:

> The liberty of the press is indeed essential to the nature of a free state: but this consists in laying no *previous* restraints upon publications, and not in freedom from censure for criminal matter when published. . . . To punish (as the law does at present) any dangerous or offensive writings, which, when published, shall on a fair and impartial trial be adjudged of a pernicious tendency, is necessary for the preservation of peace and good order, of government and religion, the only solid foundations of civil liberty.[29]

---

[25] *Ibid.*, 1063, 1066.

[26] Zechariah Chafee, *Free Speech in the United States* (Cambridge, Mass., 1942), 21.

[27] Joseph Story, *Commentaries on the Constitution of the United States* (4th ed.; Boston, 1873), II, 622.

[28] See pp. 130, 242-43.

[29] *Op. cit.*, IV, 151-52.

CONSTITUTION OF VIRGINIA

The contributions of the eighteenth century to freedom of the press were as important as those of the seventeenth. The development of freedom of discussion in that century paralleled the growth of democratic institutions. One of the landmarks in the development of this right was the address to the people of Quebec prepared by the First Continental Congress.[30] Freedom of the press was also greatly strengthened by the prohibition of general warrants by Section 10 of the Virginia Bill of Rights and by the declarations of rights enacted by other states.

None of these events, however, changed the stringent law of seditious libel. Even though several states adopted constitutions containing general guarantees of freedom of speech and the press, American courts continued to punish persons who criticized the government. One of the greatest events in the achievement of full freedom of discussion, therefore, was the eighteenth-century reform of the law of seditious libel. This process involved three steps: (1) Juries were given authority to determine whether the statement in question was really seditious; (2) the truth of statements said to constitute sedition was admitted as a complete defense to the charge; and (3) the area of permissible criticism of government officials was broadened.

Trial of John Peter Zenger

The most famous landmark in the development of freedom of the press during the colonial period was the trial in 1735 of John Peter Zenger. Zenger, a newspaper publisher, had printed articles relating to a political dispute critical of the New York administration. He was arrested and brought to trial on a charge of seditious libel. He secured for his defense the services of Andrew Hamilton, a Philadelphia lawyer of the highest standing in his profession.

The court refused Hamilton's offer to prove the truth of the matter published. Hamilton then turned to the jury and urged them to render their verdict according to the truth of the publication as they knew it of their own knowledge. He argued further that it was for the jury to determine the nature and effect of the language used—whether or not it was of a seditious character. Hamilton's argument, considered a classic of American law, won Zenger a verdict of not guilty.

The points of the English common law at dispute in Zenger's trial were not changed by Hamilton's success with the jury. The truth of a statement remained no defense to a charge of seditious libel. In fact, it was sometimes said, "The greater the truth, the greater the libel." The reason for this rule

[30] Quoted on pp. 284-85.

was stated by Blackstone, writing in the middle of the eighteenth century: "Every libel has a tendency to break the peace, or provoke others to break it; which offence is the same whether the matter contained be true or false; and therefore the defendant, on an indictment for publishing a libel, is not allowed to allege the truth of it by way of justification." [31]

Hamilton's second point—the authority of the jury to determine whether the words used actually amounted to "sedition"—was likewise on weak ground in so far as the strict rules of the common law were concerned. The jury's function in such cases was to determine solely whether the statement in question had in fact been written or published by the defendant. The more important question of whether the words were "seditious" was considered to be a matter of law for the judges to decide.[32]

The two points contended for by Hamilton were not definitively established until after the adoption in 1791 of the first amendment to the Constitution of the United States. An English statute of 1792 called Fox's Libel Act placed the determination of whether or not the language used amounted to a "sedition" in the hands of the jury. It stated:

> That, on every such trial, the jury sworn to try the issue may give a general verdict of guilty or not guilty upon the whole matter put in issue upon such indictment or information; and shall not be required or directed, by the court or judge before whom such indictment or information shall be tried, to find the defendant or defendants guilty, merely on the proof of the publication by such defendant or defendants of the paper charged to be a libel...[33]

The same rule was established in the United States, and the truth of the matter was allowed as a defense by the Sedition Act of 1798. It provided:

> That if any person shall be prosecuted under this act, for the writing or publishing any libel aforesaid, it shall be lawful for the defendant, upon the trial of the cause, to give in evidence in his defence, the truth of the matter contained in the publication charged as a libel. And the jury who shall try the cause, shall have a right to determine the law and the fact, under the direction of the court, as in other cases.[34]

One of the clearest statements of the principle that truth should be admitted as a complete defense was given by Alexander Hamilton in 1804. Freedom of the press, he said, consists of "the right to publish, with impunity,

---

[31] *Op. cit.* (7th ed.; 1775), III, 125-26.
[32] Chafee, *op. cit.*, 500.
[33] 32 Geo. 3, c. 60.
[34] 1 U.S. *Statutes at Large* 597.

truth, with good motives, for justifiable ends, though reflecting on government, magistracy, or individuals."[35]

The Virginia Bill of Rights was one of the most important forerunners of the first ten amendments to the Constitution of the United States.[36] It exerted an even more direct influence upon the first bills of rights adopted by six of the other states and by Vermont, which claimed the powers of a state. The bills of rights adopted by Delaware[37] and Pennsylvania[38] most closely followed the Virginia model.

Effects

Four states framed constitutions, but did not preface them with a bill of rights. Those documents, however, did not overlook the principle, represented by the Virginia Bill of Rights, that the liberties of the citizen should be embodied in the fundamental law of the land.

Liberties in states which did not adopt a bill of rights

The New Jersey Constitution of 1776[39] provided that criminals should have the same privileges of witnesses and counsel as their prosecutors; that no person should be denied the privilege of worshiping God according to the dictates of his own conscience nor should be required to attend or support any church against his will; that no religious sect should be established in preference to others; that the common and statutory law of England, as practiced in the colony, should remain in force until altered by the legislature; and that the right of trial by jury should remain forever, without repeal.

New Jersey

The New York Constitution of 1777[40] was prefaced by a recital of the Declaration of Independence. It also provided that on impeachment or indictment for crimes or misdemeanors the defendant should have the right to counsel; that the English common and statutory law and colonial enactments in force on April 19, 1775, should continue in effect, subject to alteration by the legislature; that the Church of England should be disestablished; that liberty of conscience should be allowed without discrimination or preference; that church officials should be disqualified from holding civil or military positions in the government; that trial by jury, in cases where it had been used, should remain inviolate forever; that no acts of attainder

New York

---

[35] *People* v. *Croswell* (1804), 3 Johns. R. 337, 359.
[36] See pp. 418-33.
[37] See pp. 332-40.
[38] See pp. 323-31.
[39] Text in Thorpe, *op. cit.*, V, 2594-98.
[40] Text in *ibid.*, 2623-38.

should be passed except for crimes committed before the termination of the present war, and that such acts should not work corruption of the blood; and that the legislature should not erect new courts whose procedures would be contrary to the course of the common law. A militia was to be kept in readiness for service in time of peace, as well as in war. Quakers, however, were excused from service.

South Carolina   The Constitution of South Carolina of 1776[41] was prefaced by a recital of infringements against colonial rights. It established a representative form of government, and provided that the resolutions of the Continental Congress, then in force in the state, should continue in effect. The Constitution of 1778[42] provided a certain measure of religious toleration for persons not adhering to the established church; it provided that punishments in some cases should be less sanguinary and more proportionate to the crime; it stated that no freeman should be "taken or imprisoned, or disseized of his freehold, liberties, or privileges, or outlawed, exiled, or in any manner destroyed or deprived of his life, liberty, or property, but by the judgment of his peers or by the law of the land"; it subordinated military power to civil authority; and it stated that the liberty of the press should be inviolably preserved.

Georgia   The Constitution of Georgia of 1777[43] provided that the legislative, executive, and judicial branches of the government should be separate and distinct; it contained a number of provisions for the regulation of jury trials and provided for grand juries; it granted persons the right of religious freedom and stated that they should not be required to support religious teachings. It also prohibited excessive bail and fines, adopted the principles of the writ of habeas corpus, prohibited clergymen from sitting in the legislature, and provided that freedom of the press and trial by jury should remain inviolate forever.

Connecticut and Rhode Island   Two states, Connecticut and Rhode Island, did not adopt constitutions, but instead continued the form of government provided by their liberal colonial charters. Connecticut adopted a short declaration of rights as a kind of preamble to the old charter.[44]

[41] Text in *ibid.*, VI, 3241-48.
[42] Text in *ibid.*, 3248-57.
[43] Text in *ibid.*, II, 777-85.
[44] Benjamin F. Wright, *American Interpretations of Natural Law* (Cambridge, Mass., 1931), 115n.

CONSTITUTION OF VIRGINIA[45]

June 12, 1776

BILL OF RIGHTS

A declaration of rights made by the representatives of the good people of Virginia, assembled in full and free convention; which rights do pertain to them and their posterity, as the basis and foundation of government. — *Preamble*

SECTION 1. That all men are by nature equally free and independent, and have certain inherent rights, of which, when they enter into a state of society, they cannot, by any compact, deprive or divest their posterity; namely, the enjoyment of life and liberty, with the means of acquiring and possessing property, and pursuing and obtaining happiness and safety. — *Rights cannot be surrendered by compact*

SEC. 2. That all power is vested in, and consequently derived from, the people; that magistrates are their trustees and servants, and at all times amenable to them. — *Source of power*

SEC. 3. That government is, or ought to be, instituted for the common benefit, protection, and security of the people, nation, or community; of all the various modes and forms of government, that is best which is capable of producing the greatest degree of happiness and safety, and is most effectually secured against the danger of maladministration; and that, when any government shall be found inadequate or contrary to these purposes, a majority of the community hath an indubitable, inalienable, and indefeasible right to reform, alter, or abolish it, in such manner as shall be judged most conducive to the public weal. — *Government may be altered or abolished by a majority of the people*

SEC. 4. That no man, or set of men, are entitled to exclusive or separate emoluments or privileges from the community, but in consideration of public services; which, not being descendible, neither ought the offices of magistrate, legislator, or judge to be hereditary. — *Offices should not be hereditary*

SEC. 5. That the legislative and executive powers of the State should be separate and distinct from the judiciary; and that the members of the two first may be restrained from oppression, by feeling and participating the burdens of the people, they should, at fixed periods, be reduced to a private station, return into that body from which they were originally taken, and the vacancies be supplied by frequent, certain, and — *Separation of powers / Frequent elections*

---

[45] Thorpe, *op. cit.*, VII, 3812-14. The second half of the document, which is not reproduced here, is entitled the "Constitution or Form of Government." *Ibid.*, 3814-19.

regular elections, in which all, or any part of the former members, to be again eligible, or ineligible, as the laws shall direct.

Free elections
Representative government
SEC. 6. That elections of members to serve as representatives of the people, in assembly, ought to be free; and that all men, having sufficient evidence of permanent common interest with, and attachment to, the community, have the right of suffrage, and cannot be taxed or deprived of their property for public uses, without their own consent, or that of their representatives so elected, nor bound by any law to which they have not, in like manner, assembled, for the public good.

Suspension of laws
SEC. 7. That all power of suspending laws, or the execution of laws, by any authority, without consent of the representatives of the people, is injurious to their rights, and ought not to be exercised.

Individual rights in criminal proceedings
SEC. 8. That in all capital or criminal prosecutions a man hath a right to demand the cause and nature of his accusation, to be confronted with the accusers and witnesses, to call for evidence in his favor, and to a speedy trial by an impartial jury of twelve men of his vicinage, without whose unanimous consent he cannot be found guilty; nor can he be compelled to give evidence against himself; that no man be deprived of his liberty, except by the law of the land or the judgment of his peers.

Bail and punishments
SEC. 9. That excessive bail ought not to be required, nor excessive fines imposed, nor cruel and unusual punishments inflicted.

General warrants and seizures
SEC. 10. That general warrants, whereby an officer or messenger may be commanded to search suspected places without evidence of a fact committed, or to seize any person or persons not named, or whose offence is not particularly described and supported by evidence, are grievous and oppressive, and ought not to be granted.

Juries in civil cases
SEC. 11. That in controversies respecting property, and in suits between man and man, the ancient trial by jury is preferable to any other, and ought to be held sacred.

Freedom of press
SEC. 12. That the freedom of the press is one of the great bulwarks of liberty, and can never be restrained but by despotic governments.

Militia and standing armies
SEC. 13. That a well-regulated militia, composed of the body of the people, trained to arms, is the proper, natural, and safe defence of a free State; that standing armies, in time of peace, should be avoided, as dangerous to liberty; and that in all cases the military should be under strict subordination to, and governed by, the civil power.

Uniform government
SEC. 14. That the people have a right to uniform government; and, therefore, that no government separate from, or independent of the government of Virginia, ought to be erected or established within the limits thereof.

Recurrence to fundamentals
SEC. 15. That no free government, or the blessings of liberty, can be preserved to any people, but by a firm adherence to justice, moderation, temperance, frugality, and virtue, and by frequent recurrence to fundamental principles.

Freedom of conscience
SEC. 16. That religion, or the duty which we owe to our Creator, and the manner of discharging it, can be directed only by reason and conviction, not by force or violence; and therefore all men are equally entitled to the free exercise of religion, according to the dictates of conscience; and that it is the mutual duty of all to practise Christian forbearance, love, and charity towards each other.

CONSTITUTION OF VIRGINIA

REFERENCES

Eckenrode, Hamilton J. *The Revolution in Virginia.* Boston: Houghton Mifflin Co., 1916. Chap. 6.
Grigsby, Hugh B. *The Virginia Convention of 1776.* Richmond: J. W. Randolph, 1855.
Rowland, Kate M. *The Life of George Mason, 1725-1792.* 2 vols. New York: G. P. Putnam's Sons, 1892. I, chap. 7.
Rutland, Robert A. *The Birth of the Bill of Rights, 1776-1791.* Chapel Hill: University of North Carolina Press, 1955. Chap. 3.
Wright, Benjamin F. *American Interpretations of Natural Law.* Cambridge, Mass.: Harvard University Press, 1931. Chap. 5.

XXII. DECLARATION OF INDEPENDENCE
1776

Origins
The Mecklenburg Resolves, May 31, 1775

One of the earliest steps in the direction of independence was taken by the people of Mecklenburg County, North Carolina. On May 31, 1775, a committee of that county resolved: "We conceive that all Laws and Commissions confirmed by, or derived from the Authority of the King or Parliament, are annulled and vacated, and the former civil Constitution of these Colonies for the present wholly suspended."[1] The resolves declared that all legislative and executive powers were vested in the provincial congress of each colony "under the Direction of the Great Continental Congress." A provisional government for Mecklenburg County was provided for. That government was to continue in effect "until Instructions from the General Congress of this Province, regulating the Jurisprudence of this Province, shall provide otherwise, or the legislative Body of *Great-Britain* resign its unjust and arbitrary Pretentions with Respect to *America*." The Mecklenburg Resolves thus did not declare complete independence from Great Britain.[2] By declaring British authority to be suspended, however, the document represented a more advanced step in the direction of independence than any other organized body had taken.[3]

The outbreak of hostilities at Lexington on April 19, 1775, gave impetus

---

[1] Charles C. Tansill (ed.), *Documents Illustrative of the Formation of the Union of the American States*, 69th Cong., 1st Sess., 1927, House Doc. 398, 6.

[2] The so-called "Mecklenburg Declaration of Independence" was a spurious document dated May 20, 1775, published in the *Raleigh Register* and *North-Carolina Gazette* April 30, 1819. Because it incorporated various phrases apparently taken from the Declaration of Independence, it was erroneously considered to be a predecessor of that document. The resolves of May 20 were written from memory by John McKnitt Alexander in 1800, after the records of the event in his possession had been destroyed. The resolves of May 31 have been found in the *South-Carolina Gazette; and Country Journal* of June 13, 1775. The history of the controversy over these documents is given in William H. Hoyt, *The Mecklenburg Declaration of Independence* (New York, 1907).

[3] *Ibid.*, 29.

to the movement toward independence. At the same time, hope for reconciliation with Great Britain began to fade. The crystallization of opinion in favor of independence, however, was a process requiring many months. In 1775 Congress was able to justify the use of armed resistance in defense of colonial liberties. Its Declaration of the Causes and Necessity of Taking up Arms,[4] however, repudiated the idea of independence. It stated, "we mean not to dissolve that union which has so long and so happily subsisted" between Great Britain and the colonies. Congress adjourned August 1, 1775, and did not again convene until September 5. At that time sentiment against independence was strong. During the winter of 1775-76, and as late as January, 1776, some of the delegates, including those from Pennsylvania, New York, New Jersey, and Maryland, received instructions from their constituents to vote against independence.[5]

The movement toward independence

Trade restrictions imposed by Parliament engendered ever-increasing hostility. In October, 1775, Congress recommended to New York, Delaware, North Carolina, and Georgia that they ought not to seek commercial advantages by reason of their exemption from the acts of March and April, 1775, restraining the trade of the other colonies.[6] Congress' admonition was not needed for long, however; on December 22, 1775, Parliament suspended trade with all the colonies.[7] It was this action which convinced many minds that independence was the only course open to the colonies.[8]

One of the most important influences that directed colonial sentiment toward the goal of independence was the publication on January 8, 1776, of "Common Sense" by Thomas Paine. This pamphlet was a direct attack upon the kingship itself. Paine called George III "the royal brute of Britain." "In America," he said, "the law is king."[9] Independence was openly advocated:

"Common Sense"

> To talk of friendship with those in whom our reason forbids us to have faith, and our affections, wounded through a thousand pores, instruct us to detest, is madness and folly. Every day wears out the little remains of kindred between us and them; and can

---

[4] See pp. 290-300.

[5] Edward Channing, *A History of the United States,* Vol. III: *The American Revolution, 1761-1789* (New York, 1927), 187, 196.

[6] *Journals of the American Congress, 1774-1788* (Washington, 1823), I, 160. The New England Restraining Act, March 30, 1775, 15 Geo. 3, c. 10, restricted the trade of Massachusetts, New Hampshire, Connecticut, and Rhode Island and Providence Plantations. In April New Jersey, Pennsylvania, Maryland, Virginia, and South Carolina were brought within the scope of that act. 15 Geo. 3, c. 18.

[7] 16 Geo. 3, c. 5.

[8] Channing, *op. cit.,* III, 188.

[9] Thomas Paine, "Common Sense" (Baltimore, n.d.), 37.

there be any reason to hope, that, as the relationship expires, the affection will increase, or that we shall agree better when we have ten times more and greater concerns to quarrel over than ever? . . . The last cord now is broken . . .[10]

Probably no other individual did more to crystallize sentiment in favor of independence.[11]

When Congress learned of the king's proclamation of rebellion of August 23,[12] it recommended that New Hampshire and South Carolina, which were being governed by provincial congresses and committees of safety, form more permanent forms of government for the duration of hostilities.[13] On May 10, 1776, Congress urged all the colonies to form separate governments for the exercise of all authority. It resolved: "That it be recommended to the respective assemblies and conventions of the United Colonies, where no government sufficient to the exigencies of their affairs hath been hitherto established, to adopt such government as shall, in the opinion of the representatives of the people, best conduce to the happiness and safety of their constituents in particular, and America in general."[14]

The Resolution of Independence

The first official proposal of a declaration of independence came from the Virginia Convention at Williamsburg. It instructed its delegates in Congress "to propose to that respectable body to declare the United Colonies free and independent States, absolved from all allegiance to, or dependance upon, the Crown or Parliament of *Great Britain* . . ."[15] Pursuant to this instruction, Richard Henry Lee of Virginia introduced in Congress on June 7 three formal resolutions.[16] He proposed that Congress declare the colonies to be independent, that steps be taken to form foreign alliances, and that a plan of confederation be prepared and transmitted to the colonies for consideration. At the insistence of moderates in Congress like John Dickinson, consideration of the resolutions was deferred until July 1. Because their eventual

---

[10] *Ibid.*, 38

[11] See Edmund C. Burnett, *The Continental Congress* (New York, 1941), 131-38.

[12] See pp. 293-94.

[13] "*Resolved,* That it be recommended to the provincial convention of New-Hampshire, to call a full and free representation of the people, and that the representatives, if they think it necessary, establish such a form of government, as, in their judgment, will best produce the happiness of the people, and most effectually secure peace and good order in the province, during the continuance of the present dispute between Great-Britain and the colonies." *Journals,* I, 162. Congress' recommendation to South Carolina was similar. *Ibid.*, I, 165-66.

[14] *Ibid.*, 339. A preamble to the resolution, drawn up by John Adams, Edward Rutledge, and Richard Henry Lee, was approved May 15. *Ibid.*, 345.

[15] Tansill, *op. cit.*, 20.

[16] Text in *ibid.*, 21.

DECLARATION OF INDEPENDENCE

passage was a foregone conclusion, a committee was appointed June 11 to prepare a declaration for announcing to the world the expected action. The colonies became legally independent of Great Britain on July 2 with the passage of Lee's first resolution: "That these United Colonies are, and, of right, ought to be, Free and Independent States; that they are absolved from all allegiance to the British crown, and that all political connexion between them, and the state of Great-Britain, is, and ought to be, totally dissolved."[17]

The Declaration of Independence

The committee appointed June 11 consisted of Thomas Jefferson of Virginia, John Adams of Massachusetts, Benjamin Franklin of Pennsylvania, Roger Sherman of Connecticut, and Robert R. Livingston of New York. The committee probably discussed the form the document was to take,[18] but the task of drawing it was Jefferson's. A few minor changes in his draft were made by Franklin and Adams. Other changes were later made by Congress. The most important of these eliminated Jefferson's condemnation of the slave trade[19] and his censure of the people of Great Britain. The final paragraph was amended to include the language of the resolution of July 2.

General Significance

The list of colonial rights that had been invaded by England is similar to the statements of rights found in the Declaration and Resolves of the First Continental Congress, 1774,[20] and the Declaration of the Causes and Necessity of Taking up Arms, 1775.[21] It was the king, however, not Parliament, who was named as the instigator of the oppressive measures against the colonists. Omission of the word "Parliament" from the Declaration was deliberate. By 1776 it had become the accepted theory of the colonists that Parliament had no power whatsoever over them and that they were bound to the British empire only by their allegiance to the king. It was this tie with Britain which the Declaration stated was severed.

---

[17] *Journals*, I, 392.

[18] Julian P. Boyd, *The Declaration of Independence* (Princeton, 1945), 12.

[19] The draft presented to Congress stated: "he has waged cruel war against human nature itself, violating its most sacred rights of life & liberty in the persons of a distant people who never offended him, captivating & carrying them into slavery in another hemisphere, or to incur miserable death in their transportation thither. this piratical warfare, the opprobrium of *infidel* powers, is the warfare of the *Christian* king of Great Britain. *determined to keep open a market where MEN should be bought & sold*, he has prostituted his negative for suppressing every legislative attempt to prohibit or to restrain this execrable commerce and that this assemblage of horrors might want no fact of distinguished die, he is now exciting those very people to rise in arms among us, and to purchase that liberty. of which *he* has deprived them, by murdering the people upon whom *he* also obtruded them; thus paying off former crimes committed against the *liberties* of one people, with crimes which he urges them to commit against the *lives* of another." Quoted in Carl Becker, *The Declaration of Independence* (New York, 1942), 166-67.

[20] See pp. 270-71.   [21] See pp. 296-97.

The first paragraph of the Declaration states its purpose. The document was intended as a justification of the decision of independence which had already been reached; the Declaration was prompted by "a decent respect to the opinions of mankind." The second paragraph succinctly sets forth the political philosophy of the Declaration. There was nothing in that philosophy that was new. It was not Jefferson's task to create a new system of politics or government but rather to apply accepted principles to the situation at hand. There follows a recital of the colonists' grievances against George III. Jefferson's indictment of the king was similar to the one he had recently prepared for the Constitution of Virginia.[22] The actions of that monarch were declared to be in violation of the inalienable rights of man; they had as their object the establishment of an absolute tyranny over the states. No mention was made, however, of the rights of Englishmen. Because the Declaration denied that any tie with the British constitution existed, reference to English rights would have been superfluous. The long dispute over the right of the colonists to enjoy the benefit of the principles of English liberty, however, certainly furnished the background of much of the document.

It was not long before the states exercised their newly won independence by forming governments based on the will of the people. Within a few years all the states except Connecticut and Rhode Island had adopted constitutions. Those two states continued to be governed according to their colonial charters after those documents had been amended slightly to reflect the independent status of their governments.

[22] See pp. 301-13.

DECLARATION OF INDEPENDENCE[23]

July 4, 1776

THE UNANIMOUS DECLARATION OF THE THIRTEEN UNITED STATES OF AMERICA.

WHEN, in the course of human events, it becomes necessary for one people to dissolve the political bands which have connected them with another, and to assume, among the powers of the earth, the separate ánd equal station to which the laws of nature and of nature's God entitle them, a decent respect to the opinions of mankind requires that they should declare the causes which impel them to the separation. *[Political Theory of the Declaration]*

We hold these truths to be self-evident: that all men are created equal; that they are endowed, by their Creator, with certain unalienable rights; that among these are life, liberty, and the pursuit of happiness. That to secure these rights, governments are instituted among men, deriving their just powers from the consent of the governed; that whenever any form of government becomes destructive of these ends, it is the right of the people to alter or to abolish it, and to institute a new government, laying its foundation on such principles, and organizing its powers in such form, as to them shall seem most likely to effect their safety and happiness. Prudence, indeed, will dictate, that governments long established, should not be changed for light and transient causes; and accordingly all experience hath shown, that mankind are more disposed to suffer, while evils are sufferable, than to right themselves by abolishing the forms to which they are accustomed. But when a long train of abuses and usurpations, pursuing invariably the same object, evinces a design to reduce them under absolute despotism, it is their right, it is their duty, to throw off such government, and to provide new guards for their future security. Such has been the patient sufferance of these colonies; and such is now the necessity which constrains them to alter their former systems of government. The history of the present King of Great Britain is a history of repeated injuries and usurpations, all having in direct object the establishment of an absolute tyranny over these states. To prove this, let facts be submitted to a candid world. *[Grievances Against George III]*

He has refused his assent to laws the most wholesome and necessary for the public good. *[Interference with the legislative process]*

He has forbidden his governors to pass laws of immediate and pressing importance,

---

[23] 1 U.S. *Statutes at Large* 1.

unless suspended in their operation till his assent should be obtained; and when so suspended, he has utterly neglected to attend to them.

He has refused to pass other laws for the accommodation of large districts of people, unless those people would relinquish the right of representation in the legislature; a right inestimable to them, and formidable to tyrants only. He has called together legislative bodies at places unusual, uncomfortable, and distant from the depository of their public records, for the sole purpose of fatiguing them into compliance with his measures.

He has dissolved representative houses repeatedly, for opposing, with manly firmness, his invasions on the rights of the people.

He has refused for a long time, after such dissolutions, to cause others to be elected; whereby the legislative powers, incapable of annihilation, have returned to the people at large for their exercise; the state remaining, in the mean time, exposed to all the dangers of invasions from without, and convulsions within.

Emigration He has endeavored to prevent the population of these States; for that purpose obstructing the laws for naturalization of foreigners; refusing to pass others to encourage their migrations hither, and raising the conditions of new appropriations of lands.

Administration of justice; dependence of judges He has obstructed the administration of justice, by refusing his assent to laws for establishing judiciary powers.

He has made judges dependent on his will alone, for the tenure of their offices, and the amount and payment of their salaries.

New offices He has erected a multitude of new offices, and sent hither swarms of officers, to harass our people, and eat out their substance.

Standing armies He has kept among us, in times of peace, standing armies, without the consent of our legislatures.

Military authority He has affected to render the military independent of, and superior to the civil power.

Foreign jurisdiction He has combined with others to subject us to a jurisdiction foreign to our constitution, and unacknowledged by our laws; giving his assent to their acts of pretended legislation:

Quartering of troops For quartering large bodies of armed troops among us;

For protecting them, by a mock trial, from punishment for any murders which they should commit on the inhabitants of these States;

Trade and taxes For cutting off our trade with all parts of the world;

For imposing taxes on us without our consent;

Trials For depriving us, in many cases, of the benefits of trial by jury;

For transporting us beyond seas to be tried for pretended offences;

Abolition of laws For abolishing the free system of English laws in a neighbouring province, establishing therein an arbitrary government, and enlarging its boundaries, so as to render it at once an example and fit instrument for introducing the same absolute rule into these colonies;

Abolition of charters For taking away our charters, abolishing our most valuable laws, and altering fundamentally the forms of our governments;

DECLARATION OF INDEPENDENCE

For suspending our own legislatures, and declaring themselves invested with power to legislate for us in all cases whatsoever. *Suspension of legislatures*

He has abdicated government here, by declaring us out of his protection, and waging war against us. *Waging war*

He has plundered our seas, ravaged our coasts, burnt our towns, and destroyed the lives of our people. *Acts against the people*

He is at this time transporting large armies of foreign mercenaries to complete the works of death, desolation, and tyranny, already begun with circumstances of cruelty and perfidy, scarcely paralleled in the most barbarous ages, and totally unworthy the head of a civilized nation. *Mercenaries*

He has constrained our fellow-citizens, taken captive on the high seas, to bear arms against their country, to become the executioners of their friends and brethren, or to fall themselves by their hands. *Impressment of seamen*

He has excited domestic insurrections amongst us, and has endeavoured to bring on the inhabitants of our frontiers the merciless Indian savages, whose known rule of warfare is an undistinguished destruction of all ages, sexes, and conditions. *Domestic insurrections*

In every stage of these oppressions we have petitioned for redress in the most humble terms. Our repeated petitions have been answered only by repeated injury. A prince, whose character is thus marked by every act which may define a tyrant, is unfit to be the ruler of a free people. *Petitions*

Nor have we been wanting in attentions to our British brethren. We have warned them, from time to time, of attempts by their legislature to extend an unwarrantable jurisdiction over us. We have reminded them of the circumstances of our emigration and settlement here. We have appealed to their native justice and magnanimity, and we have conjured them by the ties of our common kindred to disavow these usurpations, which would inevitably interrupt our connexions and correspondence. They too have been deaf to the voice of justice and of consanguinity. We must, therefore, acquiesce in the necessity which denounces our separation, and hold them, as we hold the rest of mankind, enemies in war, in peace friends.

We, therefore, the representatives of the UNITED STATES OF AMERICA, in General Congress assembled, appealing to the Supreme Judge of the world for the rectitude of our intentions, do, in the name, and by authority of the good people of these colonies, solemnly publish and declare, That these United Colonies are, and of right ought to be, FREE and INDEPENDENT STATES; that they are absolved from all allegiance, to the British crown, and that all political connexion between them and the state of Great Britain is, and ought to be, totally dissolved; and that, as FREE and INDEPENDENT STATES, they have full power to levy war, conclude peace, contract alliances, establish commerce, and to do all other acts and things which INDEPENDENT STATES may of right do. And for the support of this Declaration, with a firm reliance on the protection of DIVINE PROVIDENCE, we mutually pledge to each other our lives, our fortunes, and our sacred honour. *Declaration of Independence*

JOHN HANCOCK.

Names of Signers

New Hampshire.—Josiah Bartlett, William Whipple, Matthew Thornton.

Massachusetts Bay.—Samuel Adams, John Adams, Robert Treat Paine, Elbridge Gerry.

Rhode Island, &c.—Stephen Hopkins, William Ellery.

Connecticut.—Roger Sherman, Samuel Huntington, William Williams, Oliver Wolcott.

New York.—William Floyd, Philip Livingston, Francis Lewis, Lewis Morris.

New Jersey.—Richard Stockton, John Witherspoon, Francis Hopkinson, John Hart, Abraham Clark.

Pennsylvania.—Robert Morris, Benjamin Rush, Benjamin Franklin, John Morton, George Clymer, James Smith, George Taylor, James Wilson, George Ross.

Delaware.—Caesar Rodney, George Read, Thomas M'Kean.

Maryland.—Samuel Chase, William Paca, Thomas Stone, Charles Carroll of Carrollton.

Virginia.—George Wythe, Richard Henry Lee, Thomas Jefferson, Benjamin Harrison, Thomas Nelson, Jun., Francis Lightfoot Lee, Carter Braxton.

North Carolina.—William Hooper, Joseph Hewes, John Penn.

South Carolina.—Edward Rutledge, Thomas Hayward, Jun., Thomas Lynch, Jun., Arthur Middleton.

Georgia.—Button Gwinnett, Lyman Hall, George Walton.

REFERENCES

Becker, Carl. *The Declaration of Independence.* New York: Alfred A. Knopf, Inc., 1942.
Boyd, Julian. *The Declaration of Independence.* Princeton: Princeton University Press, 1945.
Burnett, Edmund C. *The Continental Congress.* New York: Macmillan Co., 1941. Chaps. 8, 9.
Channing, Edward. *A History of the United States.* 6 vols. New York: Macmillan Co., 1927-30. III, chap. 7.
Chinard, Gilbert. *Thomas Jefferson, The Apostle of Americanism.* 2d ed., rev. Boston: Little, Brown & Co., 1946. Bk. 2, chap 1.
Dumbauld, Edward. *The Declaration of Independence and What It Means Today.* Norman: University of Oklahoma Press, 1950.
Frothingham, Richard. *The Rise of the Republic of the United States.* 7th ed. Boston: Little, Brown & Co., 1899. Chap. 11.
Hazelton, John H. *The Declaration of Independence: Its History.* New York: Dodd, Mead & Co., 1906.
Hoyt, William H. *The Mecklenburg Declaration of Independence.* New York: G. P. Putnam's Sons, 1907.
Van Tyne, Claude H. *The War of Independence: American Phase.* Boston: Houghton Mifflin Co., 1929. Chaps. 16, 17.
Wright, Benjamin F. *American Interpretations of Natural Law.* Cambridge, Mass.: Harvard University Press, 1931. Chap. 4.

XXIII. CONSTITUTION OF PENNSYLVANIA
1776

The Pennsylvania Constitution of 1776 reflected the political ideals of the extremists of that state. The gradual weakening of constituted authority and the growing ascendancy of the radicals between 1774 and 1776 furnish the background of the first Pennsylvania Constitution. *Origins*

One of the first reactions against the constituted authority occurred in 1774. In that year Governor John Penn refused to convene the assembly to consider measures against the Intolerable Acts. As a result, a popular convention was assembled without the governor's approval to deal with that matter. It issued a declaration calling for a congress of all the colonies. When the assembly was later convened by the governor, it approved the convention's recommendation and appointed delegates to the Continental Congress. *Convention of 1774*

The conservatives in the assembly lagged behind public opinion when it came to putting into effect the Association.[1] That document, approved by Congress, had called for the nonimportation of English goods. The conservatives, led by Joseph Galloway, lost control of the assembly to the moderates, like John Dickinson and James Wilson, who were able to secure approval of the Association. *End of conservative power*

Although the moderates were able to control the assembly in 1775, that body still continued to lag behind public opinion as the movement toward independence swept on. The membership of the committees of correspondence did not depend upon the restricted franchise, and they were often dominated by the radicals. Through those committees the radicals became influential in formulating public opinion and in undermining the authority of the assembly. In 1776 that body made several concessions to the radical party, *End of the assembly*

[1] See pp. 283-84.

but it was not willing to go fast enough toward independence. Dissatisfied, the radicals withdrew from the assembly, and the assembly passed from existence for want of a quorum.

Provincial Conference of 1776

The county committees elected deputies to a provincial conference, dominated by the radicals, which met at Philadelphia on June 18. Thomas McKean was elected president. One of the first actions of the body was to resolve that, because the present government of the province was not sufficient to deal with the exigencies of government, a provincial convention should be called to form a new government, based on the authority of the people. The election of members to the convention was to be held July 8. In order to strengthen the power of the radicals in the convention, no property qualifications were imposed upon electors and the right of suffrage was extended to every associator over twenty-one who had resided in the province for a year and had been assessed for any provincial or county tax. The conference also provided that members of the convention should be required to take an oath declaring their belief in God, Christ, and the Scriptures.

Constitutional Convention of 1776

The convention met a week after the election, and its membership showed that the radicals were in control of the situation. Experienced statesmen like Dickinson, Wilson, and Robert Morris were not present. Instead, the body was composed of extremists like Timothy Matlack, James Cannon, George Bryan, Thomas Young, and Thomas Paine. One of the best-qualified members, Benjamin Franklin, was chosen president. The convention did not confine its activities to the drafting of a constitution. It also assumed general powers of government, and appointed a council of safety to discharge its executive functions.

Declaration of Rights

On July 18 a committee was appointed to prepare a declaration of rights. The convention made a number of changes in the committee's draft before approving it August 16. The constitution itself was adopted later, after further debate.

General Significance

Compared with Virginia Bill of Rights

The Pennsylvania Declaration of Rights is very similar to the declaration adopted by Virginia June 12.[2] Both documents declared that men are born equally free and independent and have certain natural, inherent, and inalienable rights; that all power is derived from the people; that elections should be free; that defendants should have certain rights including the right to know the cause and nature of the accusation, the right to confront accusers, the right to call for evidence for the defense, the right to a speedy, public

[2] See pp. 301-13.

CONSTITUTION OF PENNSYLVANIA

trial by jury, the privilege not to be compelled to give evidence against oneself, and the right not to be deprived of liberty except by the law of the land or the judgment of peers. Both documents also provided that general warrants should not be issued; that trial by jury should be observed in civil cases; that standing armies should not be maintained in time of peace; and that there should be a frequent recurrence to fundamental principles. The Pennsylvania Declaration of Rights did not prohibit excessive fines and bail or condemn cruel and unusual punishments. The body of the constitution, however, contained provisions corresponding to these rights, found in the Virginia Bill of Rights.[3]

Like the Virginia Bill of Rights, the Pennsylvania document guaranteed liberty of conscience. Pennsylvania went further than Virginia, however, by providing that no man should be compelled to attend any religious worship or support any place of worship or ministry and that no man acknowledging the being of a God could be deprived of any civil right. Unlike the Virginia document, the Pennsylvania Declaration provided that the people of that state had the sole, exclusive, and inherent right of governing and regulating matters of internal police. It also declared that defendants should have the right to be represented by counsel, a right which had been established in Pennsylvania since 1701.[4] The Pennsylvania document stated that the people should enjoy the right of freedom of speech and, as in Virginia, provided that the freedom of the press should be preserved. Two other rights were added by the Pennsylvania Declaration. The prohibition against erecting new governments, found in the Virginia document, was repudiated, and it was provided instead that the people should have the right to emigrate from one state to another and to form new states. Another new feature was the right given to the people to assemble, instruct their representatives, and petition their representatives for a redress of grievances. *Provisions added by Pennsylvania*

Although the Pennsylvania Declaration admitted that the people have the right to reform, alter, or abolish the government, it did not follow Virginia in stating that this might be done by "a majority of the community." The prohibition of hereditary offices found in the Virginia Bill of Rights was likewise omitted in Pennsylvania. Virginia's provision that "the legisla- *Provisions omitted by Pennsylvania*

---

[3] Excessive bail was not to be exacted for bailable offenses, and fines were to be moderate. The penal laws were to be reviewed, and punishments were to be made less sanguinary in some cases, and more proportionate to the crime. Francis N. Thorpe (ed.), *The Federal and State Constitutions, Colonial Charters, and Other Organic Laws* (Washington, 1909), V, 3089.

[4] See p. 258.

tive and executive powers of the State should be separate and distinct from the judiciary" also was omitted. Finally, no prohibition of the power of suspending laws without the consent of the legislature was provided in Pennsylvania.

Individual liberties in the Pennsylvania Frame of Government

The Frame of Government contained several provisions bearing on the liberties of the individual. It was provided that the legislative power should be vested in a House of Representatives elected by the freemen. Property qualifications for electors were abolished. Representatives were obliged to swear that they would do nothing to abridge the rights and privileges declared by the constitution. The religious test for legislators was eased by the requirement that they should swear only that they believed in one God and acknowledged the Scriptures of the Old and New Testaments. Bills were to be printed for the consideration of the people before being passed into law, except on occasions of sudden necessity. Judges were to have fixed salaries and terms of office. Trials were to be by jury "as heretofore." It was provided that "the printing presses shall be free to every person who undertakes to examine the proceedings of the legislature, or any part of government." No tax was to be imposed except by law, and "the purpose for which any tax is to be raised ought to appear clearly to the legislature to be of more service to the community than the money would be, if not collected." It was also stated: "The declaration of rights is hereby declared to be a part of the constitution of this commonwealth, and ought never to be violated on any pretence whatever."

Effects Amendment of the Constitution of 1776

The constitution provided for the election every seven years of a Council of Censors "whose duty it shall be to enquire whether the constitution has been preserved inviolate in every part." The censors were to review laws passed by the legislature, study the performance of all legislative and executive duties, and inquire whether taxes had been justly laid and collected. That body was also given power to call a constitutional convention for the amendment of any article of the constitution or the addition of new articles.

Constitution of 1790

Opposition to the Constitution of 1776 was intense. The moderate and conservative elements of the state attempted to overthrow the radical document in 1777, 1778, 1783, and 1789. The last effort was successful, largely because it was believed that various changes would have to be made in the state constitution to remove inconsistencies with the recently framed United States Constitution. The Constitution of 1790[5] was prepared by an able

[5] Text in Thorpe, *op. cit.*, V, 3092-3103.

CONSTITUTION OF PENNSYLVANIA

convention. Among the important changes found in the new frame of government was the establishment of a bicameral legislature. Executive authority was given to a governor with the power to veto laws, subject to being overridden by a two-thirds vote of each house. Judges were to hold office during good behavior and were to have fixed salaries.

Many provisions of the Declaration of Rights which accompanied the Constitution of 1790 were based on the Declaration of 1776. There were a few additions to that list, however. Among these, it was stated:

Declaration of Rights of 1790

> The free communication of thoughts and opinions is one of the invaluable rights of man; and every citizen may freely speak, write, and print on any subject, being responsible for the abuse of that liberty. In prosecutions for the publication of papers investigating the official conduct of officers or men in a public capacity, or where the matter published is proper for public information, the truth thereof may be given in evidence; and in all indictments for libels the jury shall have a right to determine the law and the facts, under the direction of the court, as in other cases.[6]

It was also provided that "no person shall, for the same offence, be twice put in jeopardy of life or limb." The power of suspending laws without the consent of the legislature was condemned. It was stated that "the writ of *habeas corpus* shall not be suspended, unless when, in cases of rebellion or invasion, the public safety may require it." Ex post facto laws and laws impairing contracts were forbidden. Bills of attainder for treason or felony were prohibited, and no attainder was to work corruption of the blood or forfeiture of estate, except during the life of the offender. The quartering of soldiers in any house during time of peace without the consent of the owner was prohibited, and no soldiers were to be quartered during time of war but in a manner to be prescribed by law. Finally, titles of nobility and hereditary distinctions were forbidden. The Declaration of Rights of 1790 thus shows the influence of certain provisions found in the recently framed Constitution of the United States and also provisions which appeared in various state constitutions adopted after the first constitution makers of Pennsylvania had finished their work.

[6] *Ibid.*, V, 3100.

CONSTITUTION OF PENNSYLVANIA
August 16, 1776

Preamble WHEREAS all government ought to be instituted and supported for the security and protection of the community as such, and to enable the individuals who compose it to enjoy their natural rights, and the other blessings which the Author of existence has bestowed upon man; and whenever these great ends of government are not obtained, the people have a right, by common consent to change it, and take such measures as to them may appear necessary to promote their safety and happiness. AND WHEREAS the inhabitants of this commonwealth have in consideration of protection only, heretofore acknowledged allegiance to the king of Great Britain; and the said king has not only withdrawn that protection, but commenced, and still continues to carry on, with unabated vengeance, a most cruel and unjust war against them, employing therein, not only the troops of Great Britain, but foreign mercenaries, savages and slaves, for the avowed purpose of reducing them to a total and abject submission to the despotic domination of the British parliament, with many other acts of tyranny, (more fully set forth in the declaration of Congress) whereby all allegiance and fealty to the said king and his successors, are dissolved and at an end, and all power and authority derived from him ceased in these colonies. AND WHEREAS it is absolutely necessary for the welfare and safety of the inhabitants of said colonies, that they be henceforth free and independent States, and that just, permanent, and proper forms of government exist in every part of them, derived from and founded on the authority of the people only, agreeable to the directions of the honourable American Congress. We, the representatives of the freemen of Pennsylvania, in general convention met, for the express purpose of framing such a government, confessing the goodness of the great Governor of the universe (who alone knows to what degree of earthly happiness mankind may attain, by perfecting the arts of government) in permitting the people of this State, by common consent, and without violence, deliberately to form for themselves such just rules as they shall think best, for governing their future society; and being fully convinced, that it is our indispensable duty to establish such original principles of government, as will best promote the general happiness of the people of this State, and their posterity, and provide for future improvements, without partiality for, or prejudice against any particular class, sect, or denomination of men whatever,

---

[7] *Ibid.*, V, 3081-84. The second half of the document, which is not reproduced here, is entitled the "Plan or Frame of Government." *Ibid.*, 3084-92.

CONSTITUTION OF PENNSYLVANIA

do, by virtue of the authority vested in use by our constituents, ordain, declare, and establish, the following *Declaration of Rights* and *Frame of Government*, to be the CONSTITUTION of this commonwealth, and to remain in force therein for ever, unaltered, except in such articles as shall hereafter on experience be found to require improvement, and which shall by the same authority of the people, fairly delegated as this frame of government directs, be amended or improved for the more effectual obtaining and securing the great end and design of all government, herein before mentioned.

A DECLARATION OF THE RIGHTS OF THE INHABITANTS OF THE COMMONWEALTH, OR STATE OF PENNSYLVANIA

I. That all men are born equally free and independent, and have certain natural, inherent and inalienable rights, amongst which are, the enjoying and defending life and liberty, acquiring, possessing and protecting property, and pursuing and obtaining happiness and safety. *Natural rights of men*

II. That all men have a natural and unalienable right to worship Almighty God according to the dictates of their own consciences and understanding: And that no man ought or of right can be compelled to attend any religious worship, or erect or support any place of worship, or maintain any ministry, contrary to, or against, his own free will and consent: Nor can any man, who acknowledges the being of a God, be justly deprived or abridged of any civil right as a citizen, on account of his religious sentiments or peculiar mode of religious worship: And that no authority can or ought to be vested in, or assumed by any power whatever, that shall in any case interfere with, or in any manner controul, the right of conscience in the free exercise of religious worship. *Freedom of conscience*

III. That the people of this State have the sole, exclusive and inherent right of governing and regulating the internal police of the same. *People's right to govern*

IV. That all power being originally inherent in, and consequently derived from, the people; therefore all officers of government, whether legislative or executive, are their trustees and servants, and at all times accountable to them. *Power derived from people*

V. That government is, or ought to be, instituted for the common benefit, protection and security of the people, nation or community; and not for the particular emolument or advantage of any single man, family, or sett of men, who are a part only of that community; And that the community hath an indubitable, unalienable and indefeasible right to reform, alter, or abolish government in such manner as shall be by that community judged most conducive to the public weal. *Government may be altered or abolished by the community*

VI. That those who are employed in the legislative and executive business of the State, may be restrained from oppression, the people have a right, at such periods as they may think proper, to reduce their public officers to a private station, and supply the vacancies by certain and regular elections. *Certain and regular elections*

Free elections

VII. That all elections ought to be free; and that all free men having a sufficient evident common interest with, and attachment to the community, have a right to elect officers, or to be elected into office.

Property may not be taken without consent

VIII. That every member of society hath a right to be protected in the enjoyment of life, liberty and property, and therefore is bound to contribute his proportion towards the expence of that protection, and yield his personal service when necessary, or an equivalent thereto: But no part of a man's property can be justly taken from him, or applied to public uses, without his own consent, or that of his legal representatives:

Conscientious objectors

Nor can any man who is conscientiously scrupulous of bearing arms, be justly compelled thereto, if he will pay such equivalent, nor are the people bound by any laws, but such as they have in like manner assented to, for their common good.

Criminal procedure

Trial by jury

Self-incrimination; personal liberty

IX. That in all prosecutions for criminal offences, a man hath a right to be heard by himself and his council, to demand the cause and nature of his accusation, to be confronted with the witnesses, to call for evidence in his favour, and a speedy public trial, by an impartial jury of the country, without the unanimous consent of which jury he cannot be found guilty; nor can he be compelled to give evidence against himself; nor can any man be justly deprived of his liberty except by the laws of the land, or the judgment of his peers.

Search and seizure

X. That the people have a right to hold themselves, their houses, papers, and possessions free from search and seizure, and therefore warrants without oaths or affirmations first made, affording a sufficient foundation for them, and whereby any officer or messenger may be commanded or required to search suspected places, or to seize any person or persons, his or their property, not particularly described, are contrary to that right, and ought not to be granted.

Juries in civil cases

XI. That in controversies respecting property, and in suits between man and man, the parties have a right to trial by jury, which ought to be held sacred.

Speech and press

XII. That the people have a right to freedom of speech, and of writing, and publishing their sentiments; therefore the freedom of the press ought not to be restrained.

Right to bear arms; standing armies

XIII. That the people have a right to bear arms for the defence of themselves and the state; and as standing armies in the time of peace are dangerous to liberty, they ought not to be kept up; And that the military should be kept under strict subordination to, and governed by, the civil power.

Recurrence to fundamentals

XIV. That a frequent recurrence to fundamental principles, and a firm adherence to justice, moderation, temperance, industry, and frugality are absolutely necessary to preserve the blessings of liberty, and keep a government free: The people ought therefore to pay particular attention to these points in the choice of officers and representatives, and have a right to exact a due and constant regard to them, from their legislatures and magistrates, in the making and executing such laws as are necessary for the good government of the state.

Right to emigrate

XV. That all men have a natural inherent right to emigrate from one state to another that will receive them, or to form a new state in vacant countries, or in such countries as they can purchase, whenever they think that thereby they may promote their own happiness.

CONSTITUTION OF PENNSYLVANIA

XVI. That the people have a right to assemble together, to consult for their common good, to instruct their representatives, and to apply to the legislature for redress of grievances, by address, petition, or remonstrance. *Assembly and petition*

REFERENCES

Bolles, Albert S. *Pennsylvania: Province and State, 1609-1790.* 2 vols. Philadelphia: John Wanamaker, 1899. I, chap. 7.
Brunhouse, Robert L. *The Counter-Revolution in Pennsylvania, 1776-1790.* Philadelphia: University of Pennsylvania Press, 1942.
Selsam, J. Paul. *The Pennsylvania Constitution of 1776.* Philadelphia: University of Pennsylvania Press, 1936.
Selsam, J. Paul, and Rayback, Joseph G. "French Comment on the Pennsylvania Constitution of 1776," *Pennsylvania Magazine of History and Biography*, LXXVI, 311-25. Philadelphia: Historical Society of Pennsylvania, 1952.

XXIV. DELAWARE DECLARATION OF RIGHTS
1776

Origins In accordance with Congress' recommendation of May 10-15, 1776,[1] that the colonies should take action to meet the exigencies of government, the Delaware Assembly on July 27 called on the counties to elect delegates to a constitutional convention.

The convention met at New Castle August 27. Its members took an oath to support and maintain the independence of the state and to endeavor to form a system of government for the people to promote happiness and secure to them the enjoyment of their "national, civil and religious rights and privileges." The Declaration of Rights was prepared by a committee under the chairmanship of George Read and was adopted by the convention on September 11. The constitution itself was adopted September 20.

General Significance Most of the principles found in the Virginia Bill of Rights[2] and the Pennsylvania Declaration of Rights[3] were repeated in the Delaware document. One significant exception was the omission by Delaware of the statement that all men are created equally free and independent. In addition, Delaware restricted the guarantee of civil rights to Christians instead of extending it to all citizens who acknowledged the being of a God.

Ex post facto laws According to George Read, the Declaration of Rights was derived largely from the Declaration of Rights adopted by Pennsylvania August 16 and the draft of the Maryland Declaration of Rights reported by committee on August 10.[4] The Pennsylvania Declaration did not contain a prohibition of ex post facto laws, but the Maryland Declaration, as finally adopted, did. It

---
[1] See p. 316.
[2] See pp. 301–313.
[3] See pp. 323–331.
[4] See p. 341.

seems very possible, therefore, that the prohibition in Section 11 of the Delaware Declaration of ex post facto laws was actually derived from the Maryland document. Because the Delaware Declaration was officially adopted before that of Maryland, however, Delaware is entitled to the distinction of having furnished the first document of constitutional significance to prohibit the enactment of ex post facto laws.

An ex post facto law is defined comprehensively as one which changes the legal consequences of an act performed before its passage. An ex post facto law is thus simply retroactive legislation. Such laws are unfair because they attach illegality to activities of persons who, when they acted, had no notice of the illegality. The condemnation of ex post facto laws thus affirms one of the basic features of Anglo-American institutions, described by Professor Dicey as "the rule of law": "that no man is punishable or can be lawfully made to suffer in body or goods except for a distinct breach of law established in the ordinary legal manner before the ordinary Courts of the land." [5] *Definition of ex post facto laws*

The abstract principle stated by Dicey has been applied to concrete situations by means of certain legal rules. Probably the most important of these is the long-standing rule that no person may be deprived of life, liberty, or property without due process of law. The principle that no person should be punished or deprived of his goods except in accordance with laws "established by a generall Court and sufficiently published" was recognized by the Massachusetts Body of Liberties, 1641.[6] This clause of the Body of Liberties was apparently derived from chapter 39 of Magna Carta. The Body of Liberties thus implied that no one should be punished by laws which he had no opportunity to know, and created a standard of fairness similar to that announced by the prohibition in the Delaware Declaration of Rights of ex post facto laws. *Ex post facto legislation and due process of law*

In England the doctrine of parliamentary sovereignty makes impossible the imposition of restrictions upon the character of legislative enactments. During the seventeenth century when proposals for a written constitution were being considered, however, several suggestions were made to prohibit the enactment of ex post facto laws. These proposals came from the Leveller party, which urged that such laws were contrary to the principle of due process of law. In the course of the struggles between Parliament and Charles I (1625-49), William Walwyn, one of the leaders of the Levellers, wrote in his pamphlet *Protests of the Levellers*

[5] A. V. Dicey, *Introduction to the Study of the Law of the Constitution* (8th ed.; London, 1915), 183-84.

[6] See p. 148.

"The Bloody Project": "That Parliaments should have no power to punish any person for doing that which is not against a known declared Law, or to take away general property, or to force men to answer to questions against themselves, or to order tryals, or proceed by any other ways then by twelve sworn men . . ."[7]

John Lilburne, another of the Levellers, made a similar contention when his activities were called into question by the Council of State. His pamphlet "The Picture of the Councel of State," 1649, described how he defended himself before that body: "A crime it cannot be, unless it be a Transgression of a Law in being, before it was committed, acted, or done; For where there is no Law, there is no Transgression. And if it be a Transgression of a Law, that Law provides a punishment for it, and by the Rules and method of that Law am I to be tryed, and by no other whatsoever, made *ex post facto*."[8]

The Levellers, by their "Petition to the House of Commons," September 11, 1648, formally urged Parliament to grant relief from ex post facto laws.[9] The Levellers again urged Parliament to establish relief from ex post facto laws as one of the rights of the subject in the second "Agreement of the People," 1648: "That the Representatives intermeddle not with the execution of laws, or give judgment upon any man's person or estate, where no law hath been before provided, save only in calling to an accompt, and punishing public officers for abusing or failing their trust."[10]

Blackstone's view

The lawyers of the eighteenth century also recognized the injustice of retroactive legislation. Blackstone said:

> . . . a bare resolution, confined in the breast of the legislator, without manifesting itself by some external sign, can never be properly a law. It is requisite that this resolution be notified to the people who are to obey it. . . . It is incumbent on the promulgators to do it in the most public and perspicuous manner; not like Caligula, who (according to Dio Cassius) wrote his laws in a very small character, and hung them up upon high pillars, the more effectually to ensnare the people. There is still a more unreasonable method than this, which is called making of laws *ex post facto:* when after an action (indifferent in itself) is committed, the legislator then for the first time declares it to have been a crime, and inflicts a punishment upon the person who has committed it. Here it is impossible that the party could foresee that an action, innocent when it was done, should be afterwards converted to guilt by a subsequent law; he had therefore

---

[7] William Haller and Godfrey Davies (eds.), *The Leveller Tracts, 1647-1653* (New York, 1944), 144.

[8] *Ibid.*, 198.

[9] Quoted on p. 135n.

[10] A. S. P. Woodhouse (ed.), *Puritanism and Liberty* (London, 1938), 363.

no cause to abstain from it; . . . All laws should be therefore made to commence *in futuro*, and be notified before their commencement . . .[11]

Although Delaware was the first state to adopt a prohibition of ex post facto laws, such a provision had been considered and rejected by the convention which framed the Virginia Bill of Rights, 1776.[12] According to a document in the handwriting of George Mason and Thomas L. Lee, two ex post facto clauses were considered by the committee which framed the Bill of Rights: (1) "That laws having a retrospect to crimes, and punishing offences committed before the existence of such laws, are generally dangerous, and ought to be avoided"; and (2) "That all laws having a retrospect to crimes and punishing offences committed before the existence of such laws are dangerous, and ought to be avoided, except in cases of great and evident necessity, when the safety of the State absolutely requires them."[13] The provision was opposed by Patrick Henry, who drew "a terrifying picture of some towering public offender, against whom ordinary laws would be impotent."[14] Henry's opposition probably had much to do with the eventual defeat of the proposal. No state copied the Delaware provision verbatim; various forms of language were used.

Rejection of ex post facto clause in Virginia

In addition to the provision of the Maryland Declaration of Rights, 1776,[15] prohibitions against ex post facto laws appeared in the bills of rights adopted in North Carolina, 1776;[16] Massachusetts, 1780;[17] New Hampshire, 1784;[18] Pennsylvania, 1790;[19] and South Carolina, 1790.[20]

Effects State bills of rights

According to James Madison's notes of the Federal Convention of 1787 the prohibition by the Constitution of ex post facto laws came from a motion made August 22 by Elbridge Gerry of Massachusetts and James McHenry of Maryland: "The Legislature shall pass no bill of attainder nor any ex post

The Federal Convention, 1787

---

[11] *Commentaries on the Laws of England* (London, 1783), I, 45-46.
[12] See pp. 301-13.
[13] Quoted in Kate M. Rowland, *The Life of George Mason, 1725-1792* (New York, 1892), I, 438.
[14] Quoted in Robert A. Rutland, *The Birth of the Bill of Rights, 1776-1791* (Chapel Hill, 1955), 38.
[15] See pp. 341-51.
[16] See pp. 352-57.
[17] See p. 377.
[18] See p. 385.
[19] "That no *ex post facto* law, nor any law impairing contracts, shall be made." Francis N. Thorpe (ed.), *The Federal and State Constitutions, Colonial Charters, and Other Organic Laws* (Washington, 1909), V, 3101.
[20] ". . . nor shall any bill of attainder, *ex post facto* law, or law impairing the obligation of contracts, ever be passed by the legislature of this State." *Ibid.*, VI, 3264.

facto law."[21] Although the motion met no resistance in so far as bills of attainder were concerned, it met strong opposition for its proposal to prohibit ex post facto laws. Such influential men as Gouverneur Morris and James Wilson of Pennsylvania spoke against the prohibition. The phrase, they said, was unnecessary; if inserted, the Convention would thereby proclaim its ignorance of the first principles of government or would at least admit that it was forming a government ignorant of those principles. Oliver Ellsworth of Connecticut said that there was no lawyer who would deny that such laws were void of themselves. The motion passed by a divided vote.

Later two more objections were made in the Convention to the wording of the ex post facto clause. On August 29 John Dickinson of Pennsylvania said that he had found, on examining Blackstone's *Commentaries*, that the term "ex post facto" related only to criminal cases and that a further provision was needed to restrain the states from enacting retroactive laws in civil cases.[22] The second objection was made on September 14 by George Mason.[23] His interpretation of the term "ex post facto" was just the opposite of Dickinson's. He feared that the term was not confined to criminal matters, and that Congress should not be prevented from adopting retroactive laws in civil matters. Mason's motion to strike the clause met with no success. Gerry, who had originally proposed the ex post facto clause, favored expanding the clause so as expressly to cover civil cases. His views, likewise, were not accepted by the Convention.

It was also agreed that the states, as well as the federal government, should be prevented from enacting ex post facto laws. They were also prohibited from passing laws impairing the obligation of contracts. Gerry's motion to prohibit Congress from impairing the obligation of contracts was not seconded.[24]

Interpretations of the ex post facto clause

The debates of the Convention illustrate the fact that at the time of the adoption of the Constitution there was a difference of opinion as to whether the term "ex post facto law" meant any law of retroactive application, or whether the term was confined to laws dealing with criminal matters.[25]

---

[21] Charles C. Tansill (ed.), *Documents Illustrative of the Formation of the Union of the American States*, 69th Cong., 1st Sess., 1927, House Doc. 398, 596.

[22] *Ibid.*, 633. This statement by Dickinson, of course, misstated Blackstone's views. See pp. 334-35.

[23] *Ibid.*, 726.

[24] *Ibid.*, 728.

[25] See Joseph Story, *Commentaries on the Constitution of the United States* (4th ed.; Boston, 1873), II, 212-14.

DELAWARE DECLARATION OF RIGHTS

During the period of the Confederation, several states had passed "paper-money" acts which retroactively affected debts payable in gold and silver, and these were often denounced as "ex post facto." The uncertainty continued during the struggle for ratification of the Constitution.[26] In 1798 the Supreme Court ruled on this question. It stated that an ex post facto law is one making acts criminal which were innocent when done, aggravating a crime or increasing the punishment for it after the act, or adversely changing the rules of evidence after the act for which the defendant is tried.[27]

[26] The colonial precedents and the interpretations following the adoption of the Constitution are analyzed by William W. Crosskey, *Politics and the Constitution in the History of the United States* (Chicago, 1953), I, 324-51.

[27] *Calder* v. *Bull*, 3 Dall. 386 (1798).

DELAWARE DECLARATION OF RIGHTS[28]

September 11, 1776

A Declaration of Rights and Fundamental Rules of the Delaware State, formerly stiled, The Government of the counties of New-Castle, Kent and Sussex, upon Delaware.

Origin of government

SECTION 1. That all government of right originates from the people, is founded in compact only, and instituted solely for the good of the whole.

Liberty of conscience

SECT. 2. That all men have a natural and unalienable right to worship Almighty God according to the dictates of their own consciences and understandings; and that no man ought or of right can be compelled to attend any religious worship or maintain any ministry contrary to or against his own free will and consent, and that no authority can or ought to be vested in, or assumed by any power whatever that shall in any case interfere with, or in any manner controul the right of conscience in the free exercise of religious worship.

Christians to enjoy equal rights

SECT. 3. That all persons professing the Christian religion ought forever to enjoy equal rights and privileges in this state, unless, under colour of religion, any man disturb the peace, the happiness or safety of society.

People's right to govern

SECT. 4. That people of this state have the sole exclusive and inherent right of governing and regulating the internal police of the same.

Officials are trustees and servants of people

SECT. 5. That persons intrusted with the Legislative and Executive Powers are the Trustees and Servants of the public, and as such accountable for their conduct; wherefore whenever the ends of government are perverted, and public liberty manifestly endangered by the Legislative singly, or a treacherous combination of both, the people may, and of right ought to establish a new, or reform the old government.

Elections to be free and frequent; suffrage

SECT. 6. That the right in the people to participate in the Legislature, is the foundation of liberty and of all free government, and for this end all elections ought to be free and frequent, and every freeman, having sufficient evidence of a permanent common interest with, and attachment to the community, hath a right of suffrage.

Suspension of laws

SECT. 7. That no power of suspending laws, or the execution of laws, ought to be exercised unless by the Legislature.

---

[28] *Laws of the State of Delaware, 1700-1797* (New Castle, 1797), I, Appendix, 79-81.

DELAWARE DECLARATION OF RIGHTS

SECT. 8. That for redress of grievances, and for amending and strengthening of the laws, the Legislature ought to be frequently convened. *Meetings of legislature*

SECT. 9. That every man hath a right to petition the Legislature for the redress of grievances in a peaceable and orderly manner. *Right of petition*

SECT. 10. That every member of society hath a right to be protected in the enjoyment of life, liberty and property, and therefore is bound to contribute his proportion towards the expense of that protection, and yield his personal service when necessary, or an equivalent thereto; but no part of a man's property can be justly taken from him or applied to public uses without his own consent or that of his legal Representatives: Nor can any man that is conscientiously scrupulous of bearing arms in any case be justly compelled thereto if he will pay such equivalent. *Protection of life, liberty, and property* *Conscientious objectors*

SECT. 11. That retrospective laws, punishing offences committed before the existence of such laws, are oppressive and unjust, and ought not to be made. *Retroactive laws*

SECT. 12. That every freeman for every injury done him in his goods, lands or person, by any other person, ought to have remedy by the course of the law of the land, and ought to have justice and right for the injury done to him freely without sale, fully without any denial, and speedily without delay, according to the law of the land. *Justice not to be sold, denied, or delayed*

SECT. 13. That trial by jury of facts where they arise is one of the greatest securities of the lives, liberties and estates of the people. *Trial by jury*

SECT. 14. That in all prosecutions for criminal offences, every man hath a right to be informed of the accusation against him, to be allowed counsel, to be confronted with the accusers or witnesses, to examine evidence on oath in his favour, and to a speedy trial by an impartial jury, without whose unanimous consent he ought not to be found guilty. *Procedure in criminal cases*

SECT. 15. That no man in the Courts of Common Law ought to be compelled to give evidence against himself. *Self-incrimination*

SECT. 16. That excessive bail ought not to be required, nor excessive fines imposed, nor cruel or unusual punishments inflicted. *Bail, fines, and punishment*

SECT. 17. That all warrants without oath to search suspected places, or to seize any person or his property, are grievous and oppressive; and all general warrants to search suspected places, or to apprehend all persons suspected, without naming or describing the place or any person in special, are illegal and ought not to be granted. *Searches and seizures*

SECT. 18. That a well regulated militia is the proper, natural and safe defence of a free government. *Militia*

SECT. 19. That standing armies are dangerous to liberty, and ought not to be raised or kept up without the consent of the Legislature. *Standing armies*

SECT. 20. That in all cases and at all times the military ought to be under strict subordination to and governed by the civil power. *Subordination of military*

SECT. 21. That no soldier ought to be quartered in any house in time of peace without the consent of the owner; and in time of war in such manner only as the Legislature shall direct. *Quartering of soldiers*

Independence of judges   SECT. 22. That the independency and uprightness of judges are essential to the impartial administration of justice, and a great security to the rights and liberties of the people.

Freedom of press   SECT. 23. That the liberty of the press ought to be inviolably preserved.

REFERENCES

Conrad, Henry C. *History of the State of Delaware.* 3 vols. Wilmington: Henry C. Conrad, 1908. I, 150-56.

Powell, Walter A. *A History of Delaware.* Boston: Christopher Publishing House, 1928. Chaps. 30-32.

XXV. CONSTITUTION OF MARYLAND
1776

The Maryland Declaration of Rights of 1776 was framed by a convention composed of delegates chosen by each county. The convention had formally assumed control of the government in July, 1775, and it proceeded to exercise general authority over the conduct of the war. Executive responsibilities were given to a committee of safety elected by the convention. Although the convention assumed autocratic powers, it referred important questions to the people. Its democratic character was further assured by the fact that its members were elected annually.

Origins
Maryland Convention of 1776

The delegates who framed the Declaration of Rights of 1776 were elected August 1 of that year, and they convened at Annapolis on the 14th. Matthew Tilghman was elected president of the convention. One of the first items of business was the election of a committee by ballot to prepare and report a declaration of rights and a plan of government. The members chosen were Tilghman, Charles Carroll of Annapolis, William Paca, Charles Carroll of Carrollton, George Plater, Samuel Chase, and Robert Goldsborough. Six of these men were prominent lawyers, and three had been signers of the Declaration of Independence.

The committee reported a draft of the Declaration of Rights and the constitution on August 10. On the 17th it was ordered that copies of this report should be printed and distributed throughout the counties so that the delegates might learn the sentiments of their constituents. Urgent military and governmental problems forced postponement of consideration of the committee's report until October. Once those problems had been settled, the convention took up the draft and discussed it from day to day. Many amendments were made. The Declaration of Rights was adopted in final form on November 3; the constitution was adopted November 8.

General Significance

Many of the liberties found in the Maryland Declaration of Rights had appeared earlier in the declarations of rights adopted by Virginia,[1] Pennsylvania,[2] and Delaware.[3] There were a few additions, alterations, and omissions, however. The statement that men are born equally free and independent was omitted by Maryland, as in Delaware. In addition, Maryland made no reference to the natural rights of men. Instead, the English common law and the English statutes as used and practiced in Maryland constituted the primary basis for the rights of the citizen.

English common law and statutes

The influence of English precedents is nowhere more apparent in America than in Maryland. Reliance on those sources showed the effects of the old struggle by the Maryland colonists to secure recognition of their rights as Englishmen.[4] Some of the declaration's provisions, like the declarations of other states, had specific counterparts in English statutes. Magna Carta,[5] for example, contains provisions similar to articles XVII and XXI of the Maryland document. The English Petition of Right[6] contains counterparts of articles XXVIII and XXIX. The English Bill of Rights[7] contains counterparts of articles V, VII, VIII, X, XI, XIV, XXII, and XXVI. Several other articles of the Maryland Declaration were based either on English statutes or on principles of the English common law.

New provisions

The abolition of poll taxes and the exemption of paupers from taxation were new provisions. The Maryland Declaration was the first state constitution which called for a rotation of office in the executive departments, prohibited persons from holding more than one public office at a time, incorporated the principles of the mortmain statutes, prohibited monopolies, and prohibited the granting of titles of nobility. The legislature was expressly forbidden to alter or abolish the Declaration of Rights.

Bills of attainder

The most significant addition made by Maryland to the individual's liberties is found in article XVI, which prohibited the enactment of bills of attainder. A bill of attainder is defined as an act of the legislature which declared a person or persons guilty of felony or treason, condemned him or them to death, and imposed the penalties of attainder. The consequences of

---

[1] See pp. 301-13.
[2] See pp. 323-31.
[3] See pp. 332-40.
[4] See pp. 102-4.
[5] See pp. 1-22.
[6] See pp. 62-75.
[7] See pp. 222-50.

attainder were deprivation of all civil rights, the forfeiture of estate, and the corruption of blood, an ancient doctrine which disabled the individual from receiving or granting property. A "bill of pains and penalties" was similar to the bill of attainder, except that it declared the person guilty of lesser crimes and imposed lesser penalties. By modern interpretation and usage the term "bill of attainder" includes bills of pains and penalties.

The objectionable feature of the bill of attainder was not its consequences, but its procedure. It involved the imposition of penalties by means which ignored the safeguards of a judicial trial. The validity of a bill of attainder rested solely upon the sovereignty of the legislature. Safeguards like the right to confront one's accusers, the right to be heard, the right to be represented by counsel, the admission of relevant evidence, trial by jury, and a decision by an impartial authority were all unnecessary to assure the legality of the procedure.

Bills of attainder and due process of law

For many years lawyers and judges had been aware of the fact that the bill of attainder was unfair. Although Sir Edward Coke did not doubt the authority of Parliament to enact such bills by virtue of its sovereign power, that great seventeenth-century expositor of Magna Carta pointed out that such bills violated the spirit of due process of law. In discussing the right to be heard of individuals whom Parliament threatened to attaint, Coke said:

> I had it of Sir Thomas Gawdye knight, a grave and reverend judge of the kings bench, who lived at that time, that king H. 8. commanded him to attend the chiefe justices, and to know whether a man that was forth-coming might be attainted of high treason by parliament, and never called to his answer. The judges answered, that it was a dangerous question, and that the high court of parliament ought to give examples to inferior courts for proceeding according to justice, and no inferior court could do the like; and they thought that the high court of parliament would never do it. But being by the expresse commandement of the king, and pressed by the said earle to give a direct answer: they said, that if he be attainted by parliament, it could not come in question afterwards, whether he were called or not called to answer. And albeit their opinion was according to law, yet might they have made a better answer, for by the statutes of Mag. Cart. ca. 29. 5 E. 3. cap. 9. & 28 E. 3. cap. [3]. No man ought to be condemned without answer...[8]

Bills of attainder first appeared in England during the fifteenth century.[9] Their original purpose was a meliorative one. They were used in place of the

History of attainder

---

[8] *The Fourth Part of the Institutes of the Laws of England* (London, 1797), 37-38. For the statutes cited by Coke, see pp. 5-7, 17, 126n.

[9] James F. Stephen, *A History of the Criminal Law of England* (London, 1883), I, 161.

older and more cumbersome procedure of the impeachment[10] for the purpose of checking the illegal activities of royal officials and others who were too powerful to be dealt with by the courts.[11] The bill of attainder thus promoted the purposes of the law by means which were flagrantly inconsistent with regular legal procedures.

The bill of attainder became a powerful weapon against political opponents in the hands of Henry VIII (1509-47) and a subservient parliament. In addition, the bill of attainder, as well as the impeachment, was often used during the constitutional conflicts of the seventeenth century. Among the most famous attainders of that century were those of the Earl of Strafford in 1640, Archbishop Laud in 1645, the regicides in 1660, and Sir John Fenwick in 1696.

Attainder of Strafford   The unfairness of the bill of attainder is nowhere better illustrated than by the attainder in 1640 of the Earl of Strafford, the chief adviser of Charles I. Strafford was called back from Ireland by the king, who promised him safety in "person, honour, and fortune." John Pym, leader of the House of Commons, procured an impeachment on a charge of treason, and Strafford was arrested. Upon trial before the Lords, no probative evidence was produced to support the charge, and the impeachment failed. Although Strafford was thus exonerated, the Commons brought a bill of attainder. No proof, of course, was necessary to support the bill. The king's threatened use of force against Parliament and the fear of mob violence were probably responsible for the passage of the bill by the Lords. The pusillanimous king signed the bill, evoking Strafford's sardonic comment, "Put not your trust in princes."

Fenwick's attainder in 1696 was the last bill of attainder in England to inflict the death penalty, but lesser penalties were inflicted by the same means after that time.[12] The bill of attainder passed from use in England during the eighteenth century. It is possible to suggest several factors which contributed to this result. The absence of great political upheavals during that century made recourse to the perfunctory procedures of the bill unnecessary.

[10] The impeachment was brought by the House of Commons, acting as the grand jury of the whole nation. The case was tried by the Lords, who acted in a judicial capacity. The trial before the Lords was a formal procedure which gave greater protection to the accused than the bill of attainder. The Pennsylvania Charter of Privileges of 1701 and the Pennsylvania Constitution of 1776 gave the assembly power to impeach criminals. Page 257 and Francis N. Thorpe (ed.), *The Federal and State Constitutions, Colonial Charters, and Other Organic Laws* (Washington, 1909), V, 3085. The essential character of the English procedure on impeachments is preserved by Article I, sections 2 and 3 of the Constitution of the United States, although the penalty is limited. See p. 409.

[11] William S. Holdsworth, *A History of English Law* (4th ed.; Boston, 1931), I, 380-81.

[12] F. W. Maitland, *The Constitutional History of England* (Cambridge, England, 1909), 319-20.

CONSTITUTION OF MARYLAND

Adequate enforcement of the laws by the common law courts was made possible when the position of those courts was strengthened by the abolition of the Star Chamber [13] and the establishment of an independent judiciary.[14] It is also possible that all judicial functions exercised by the legislature became suspect by the acceptance in the seventeenth century of the theory that Parliament should be a lawmaking, rather than a law-declaring, body and by the acceptance in the eighteenth century of the theory of the separation of judicial powers from legislative and executive powers. Certainly the refinements in the concept of due process of law which occurred during the seventeenth century contributed to an attitude which condemned all procedures which violated acceptable standards of fair conduct.

Many bills of attainder were passed in the colonies at the time of the Revolutionary War. These usually took the form of statutes confiscating the property of Tories. The New York Constitution of 1777 expressly sanctioned this practice, although it forbade such bills in the future. New York also provided that no attainder should work corruption of the blood. In a few instances notorious bandits and outlaws and their adherents were condemned by bills of attainder.

The Massachusetts Constitution of 1780 [15] and the Vermont Constitution of 1786 [16] included prohibitions of bills of attainder similar to that found in the Maryland document. At the Federal Convention of 1787, sentiment against bills of attainder was so strong that a motion to prevent both state and federal governments from enacting them met with no opposition.[17] Both the federal government and the states are now prohibited from enacting bills of attainder. These provisions are contained in Article I, sections 9 and 10, of the Constitution of the United States.[18]

Effects

[13] See pp. 125-42.
[14] See pp. 241-42.
[15] See p. 377.
[16] Thorpe, *op. cit.*, VI, 3757.
[17] See pp. 335-36.
[18] See p. 412.

345

CONSTITUTION OF MARYLAND[19]

November 3, 1776

A Declaration of Rights, and the Constitution and Form of Government agreed to by the Delegates of Maryland, in free and full Convention assembled.

A DECLARATION OF RIGHTS, &C.

Preamble THE parliament of Great Britain, by a declaratory act, having assumed a right to make laws to bind the Colonies in all cases whatsoever, and, in pursuance of such claim, endeavoured, by force of arms, to subjugate the United Colonies to an unconditional submission to their will and power, and having at length constrained them to declare themselves independent States, and to assume government under the authority of the people;—Therefore we, the Delegates of Maryland, in free and full Convention assembled, taking into our most serious consideration the best means of establishing a good Constitution in this State, for the sure foundation and more permanent security thereof, declare,

Origin of government I. That all government of right originates from the people, is founded in compact only, and instituted solely for the good of the whole.

People's right to govern II. That the people of this State ought to have the sole and exclusive right of regulating the internal government and police thereof.

Common law; trial by jury; English statutes III. That the inhabitants of Maryland are entitled to the common law of England, and the trial by jury, according to the course of that law, and to the benefit of such of the English statutes, as existed at the time of their first emigration, and which, by experience, have been found applicable to their local and other circumstances, and of such others as have been since made in England, or Great Britain, and have been introduced, used and practised by the courts of law or equity; and also to acts of Assembly, in force on the first of June seventeen hundred and seventy-four, except such as may have since expired, or have been or may be altered by acts of Convention, or this Declaration of Rights—subject, nevertheless, to the revision of, and amendment or repeal by, the Legislature of this State: and the inhabitants of Maryland

---

[19] Thorpe, *op. cit.*, III, 1686-91. The second half of the document, which is not reproduced here, is entitled the "Constitution, or Form of Government." *Ibid.*, 1691-1701.

CONSTITUTION OF MARYLAND

are also entitled to all property, derived to them, from or under the Charter, granted by his Majesty Charles I. to Caecilius Calvert, Baron of Baltimore.

IV. That all persons invested with the legislative or executive powers of government are the trustees of the public, and, as such, accountable for their conduct; wherefore, whenever the ends of government are perverted, and public liberty manifestly endangered, and all other means of redress are ineffectual, the people may, and of right ought, to reform the old or establish a new government. The doctrine of non-resistance, against arbitrary power and oppression, is absurd, slavish, and destructive of the good and happiness of mankind. *Government may be reformed, or a new one established, by the people*

V. That the right in the people to participate in the Legislature is the best security of liberty, and the foundation of all free government; for this purpose, elections ought to be free and frequent, and every man, having property in, a common interest with, and an attachment to the community, ought to have a right of suffrage. *Free elections*

VI. That the legislative, executive and judicial powers of government, ought to be forever separate and distinct from each other. *Separation of powers*

VII. That no power of suspending laws, or the execution of laws, unless by or derived from the Legislature, ought to be exercised or allowed. *Suspension of laws*

VIII. That freedom of speech and debates, or proceedings in the Legislature, ought not to be impeached in any other court to judicature. *Freedom of speech*

IX. That a place for the meeting of the Legislature ought to be fixed, the most convenient to the members thereof, and to the depository of public records; and the Legislature ought not to be convened or held at any other place, but from evident necessity. *Meetings of legislature*

X. That, for redress of grievances, and for amending, strengthening and preserving the laws, the Legislature ought to be frequently convened. *Frequent meetings*

XI. That every man hath a right to petition the Legislature, for the redress of grievances, in a peaceable and orderly manner. *Petition*

XII. That no aid, charge, tax, fee, or fees, ought to be set, rated, or levied, under any pretence, without consent of the Legislature. *Taxation by legislature*

XIII. That the levying taxes by the poll is grievous and oppressive, and ought to be abolished; that paupers ought not to be assessed for the support of government; but every other person in the State ought to contribute his proportion of public taxes, for the support of government, according to his actual worth, in real or personal property, within the State; yet fines, duties, or taxes, may properly and justly be imposed or laid, with a political view, for the good government and benefit of the community. *Taxation*

XIV. That sanguinary laws ought to be avoided, as far as is consistent with the safety of the State: and no law, to inflict cruel and unusual pains and penalties, ought to be made in any case, or at any time hereafter. *Cruel and unusual pains and penalties*

XV. That retrospective laws, punishing facts committed before the existence of such laws, and by them only declared criminal, are oppressive, unjust, and incompatible with liberty; wherefore no *ex post facto* law ought to be made. *Ex post facto laws*

Bills of attainder XVI. That no law, to attaint particular persons of treason or felony, ought to be made in any case, or at any time hereafter.

Sale, denial, or delay of justice XVII. That every freeman, for any injury done him in his person or property, ought to have remedy, by the course of the law of the land, and ought to have justice and right freely without sale, fully without any denial, and speedily without delay, according to the law of the land.

Place of trial XVIII. That the trial of facts where they arise, is one of the greasest securities of the lives, liberties and estates of the people.

Criminal procedure
Counsel; confrontation
Trial by jury XIX. That, in all criminal prosecutions, every man hath a right to be informed of the accusation against him; to have a copy of the indictment or charge in due time (if required) to prepare for his defence; to be allowed counsel; to be confronted with the witnesses against him; to have process for his witnesses; to examine the witnesses, for and against him, on oath; and to a speedy trial by an impartial jury, without whose unanimous consent he ought not to be found guilty.

Self-incrimination XX. That no man ought to be compelled to give evidence against himself, in a common court of law, or in any other court, but in such cases as have been usually practised in this State, or may hereafter be directed by the Legislature.

Protection of life, liberty, and property XXI. That no freeman ought to be taken, or imprisoned, or disseized of his freehold, liberties, or privileges, or outlawed, or exiled, or in any manner destroyed, or deprived of his life, liberty, or property, but by the judgment of his peers, or by the law of the land.

Bail, fines, and punishments XXII. That excessive bail ought not to be required, nor excessive fines imposed, nor cruel or unusual punishments inflicted, by the courts of law.

Searches and seizures XXIII. That all warrants, without oath or affirmation, to search suspected places, or to seize any person or property, are grievous and oppressive; and all general warrants—to search suspected places, or to apprehend suspected persons, without naming or describing the place, or the person in special—are illegal, and ought not to be granted.

Forfeitures XXIV. That there ought to be no forfeiture of any part of the estate of any person, for any crime except murder, or treason against the State, and then only on conviction and attainder.

Militia XXV. That a well-regulated militia is the proper and natural defence of a free government.

Standing armies XXVI. That standing armies are dangerous to liberty, and ought not to be raised or kept up, without consent of the Legislature.

Subordination of military XXVII. That in all cases, and at all times, the military ought to be under strict subordination to and control of the civil power.

Quartering of soldiers XXVIII. That no soldier ought to be quartered in any house, in time of peace, without the consent of the owner; and in time of war, in such manner only, as the Legislature shall direct.

Martial law XXIX. That no person, except regular soldiers, mariners, and marines in the service of this State, or militia when in actual service, ought in any case to be subject to or punishable by martial law.

CONSTITUTION OF MARYLAND

XXX. That the independency and uprightness of Judges are essential to the impartial administration of justice, and a great security to the rights and liberties of the people; wherefore the Chancellor and Judges ought to hold commissions during good behaviour; and the said Chancellor and Judges shall be removed for misbehaviour, on conviction in a court of law, and may be removed by the Governor, upon the address of the General Assembly; *Provided,* That two-thirds of all the members of each House concur in such address. That salaries, liberal, but not profuse, ought to be secured to the Chancellor and the Judges, during the continuance of their commissions, in such manner, and at such times, as the Legislature shall hereafter direct, upon consideration of the circumstances of this State. No Chancellor or Judge ought to hold any other office, civil or military, or receive fees or perquisites of any kind. *— Independence of judges*

XXXI. That a long continuance, in the first executive departments of power or trust, is dangerous to liberty; a rotation, therefore, in those departments, is one of the best securities of permanent freedom. *— Rotation in executive departments*

XXXII. That no person ought to hold, at the same time, more than one office of profit, nor ought any person, in public trust, to receive any present from any foreign prince or state, or from the United States, or any of them, without the approbation of this State. *— Holding of public office*

XXXIII. That, as it is the duty of every man to worship God in such manner as he thinks most acceptable to him; all persons, professing the Christian religion, are equally entitled to protection in their religious liberty; wherefore no person ought by any law to be molested in his person or estate on account of his religious persuasion or profession, or for his religious practice; unless, under colour of religion, any man shall disturb the good order, peace or safety of the State, or shall infringe the laws of morality, or injure others, in their natural, civil, or religious rights; nor ought any person to be compelled to frequent or maintain, or contribute, unless on contract, to maintain any particular place of worship, or any particular ministry; yet the Legislature may, in their discretion, lay a general and equal tax, for the support of the Christian religion; leaving to each individual the power of appointing the payment over of the money, collected from him, to the support of any particular place of worship or minister, or for the benefit of the poor of his own denomination, or the poor in general of any particular county: but the churches, chapels, glebes, and all other property now belonging to the church of England, ought to remain to the church of England forever. And all acts of Assembly, lately passed, for collecting monies for building or repairing particular churches or chapels of ease, shall continue in force, and be executed, unless the Legislature shall, by act, supersede or repeal the same: but no county court shall assess any quantity of tobacco, or sum of money, hereafter, on the application of any vestrymen or church-wardens; and every encumbent of the church of England, who hath remained in his parish, and performed his duty, shall be entitled to receive the provision and support established by the act, entitled "An act for the support of the clergy of the church of England, in this Province," till the November court of this present year, to be held for the county in which his parish *— Freedom of conscience / Support of religious practices* shall lie, or partly lie, or for such time as he hath remained in his parish, and performed his duty.

Certain gifts, sales, and devises of land to the church declared void

XXXIV. That every gift, sale, or devise of lands, to any minister, public teacher, or preacher of the gospel, as such, or to any religious sect, order or denomination, or to or for the support, use or benefit of, or in trust for, any minister, public teacher, or preacher of the gospel, as such, or any religious sect, order or denomination—and every gift or sale of goods, or chattels, to go in succession, or to take place after the death of the seller or donor, or to or for such support, use or benefit—and also every devise of goods or chattels to or for the support, use or benefit of any minister, public teacher, or preacher of the gospel, as such, or any religious sect, order, or denomination, without the leave of the Legislature, shall be void; except always any sale, gift, lease or devise of any quantity of land, not exceeding two acres, for a church, meeting, or other house of worship, and for a burying-ground, which shall be improved, enjoyed or used only for such purpose—or such sale, gift, lease, or devise, shall be void.

Oath of office

XXXV. That no other test or qualification ought to be required, on admission to any office of trust or profit, than such oath of support and fidelity to this State, and such oath of office, as shall be directed by this Convention, or the Legislature of this State, and a declaration of a belief in the Christian religion.

Administration of oaths

XXXVI. That the manner of administering an oath to any person, ought to be such, as those of the religious persuasion, profession, or denomination, of which such person is one, generally esteem the most effectual confirmation, by the attestation of the Divine Being. And that the people called Quakers, those called Dunkers, and those called Menonists, holding it unlawful to take an oath on any occasion, ought to be allowed to make their solemn affirmation, in the manner that Quakers have been heretofore allowed to affirm; and to be of the same avail as an oath, in all such cases, as the affirmation of Quakers hath been allowed and accepted within this State, instead of an oath. And further, on such affirmation, warrants to search for stolen goods, or for the apprehension or commitment of offenders, ought to be granted, or security for the peace awarded, and Quakers, Dunkers or Menonists ought also, on their solemn affirmation as aforesaid, to be admitted as witnesses, in all criminal cases not capital.

Charter of Annapolis

XXXVII. That the city of Annapolis ought to have all its rights, privileges and benefits, agreeable to its Charter, and the acts of Assembly confirming and regulating the same, subject nevertheless to such alteration as may be made by this Convention, or any future Legislature.

Press

XXXVIII. That the liberty of the press ought to be inviolably preserved.

Monopolies

XXXIX. That monopolies are odious, contrary to the spirit of a free government, and the principles of commerce; and ought not to be suffered.

Titles of nobility

XL. That no title of nobility, or hereditary honours, ought to be granted in this State.

Resolves to continue in force

XLI. That the subsisting resolves of this and the several Conventions held for this Colony, ought to be in force as laws, unless altered by this Convention, or the Legislature of this State.

CONSTITUTION OF MARYLAND

XLII. That this Declaration of Rights, or the Form of Government, to be established by this Convention, or any part or either of them, ought not to be altered, changed or abolished, by the Legislature of this State, but in such manner as this Convention shall prescribe and direct. *Amendment*

This Declaration of Rights was assented to, and passed, in Convention of the Delegates of the freemen of Maryland, begun and held at Annapolis, the 14th day of August, A. D. 1776.

By order of the Convention.

MAT. TILGHMAN, President.

REFERENCES

Andrews, Matthew P. *History of Maryland.* New York: Doubleday, Doran & Co., 1929. Chaps. 6, 7.
McSherry, James. *History of Maryland.* Baltimore: John Murphy, 1869. Chap. 10.
Scharf, J. Thomas. *History of Maryland.* 3 vols. Baltimore: John B. Piet, 1879. II, chaps. 21, 22.

XXVI. CONSTITUTION OF NORTH CAROLINA
1776

Origins The North Carolina Assembly was dissolved by Governor Martin on March 30, 1774, and from that time the affairs of the colony were governed, as in Virginia, by a provincial congress of deputies elected by the people. The first assemblage of North Carolina representatives independent of royal authority met at New Bern on August 25, 1774.

The Provincial Congress Steps toward the framing of the Constitution of 1776 were taken on April 4, 1776, when the Provincial Congress met at Halifax. The congress appointed a committee of nineteen to prepare a temporary civil government. Differences in opinion as to the formation of the new government hampered the committee's work. Some of its members favored the establishment of a pure democracy. They wanted all officers and judges to be chosen by the people, and every freeman given the right to vote regardless of the ownership of property. Conservatives like Samuel Johnston and Thomas Jones urged the establishment of a representative republic with annual elections for members of the legislature. They wanted to establish a stable and independent judiciary and allow the assembly to appoint the chief officers of government. Many members of the committee held opinions between the two extremes.

The committee was finally able to agree on several points for a plan of government. Under its plan the government would consist of a house of representatives elected annually by all free householders of one year's standing, a legislative council consisting of one deputy from each county elected annually, and a president and executive council of six members, also to be elected annually. The committee apparently reached no agreement on the judicial system. These proposals were debated by the congress, but differences of opinion in that body prevented agreement on a plan. Consideration of a

CONSTITUTION OF NORTH CAROLINA

permanent constitution, therefore, was postponed until November, and a council of safety was appointed meanwhile to conduct the affairs of the colony.

In August the Council of Safety prepared an address to the people recommending that each county choose five delegates to a congress which would make laws and frame a permanent constitution. Elections were held in October and the congress met November 12 at Halifax. Richard Caswell was elected president of the body, and one of its first actions was the selection of a committee to frame a constitution. The membership of the committee was about evenly divided between the conservatives and the extreme democrats. The constitution, as reported by the committee, was presented to the Congress December 6 and the Declaration of Rights was presented December 12. The committee's reports probably represented the joint efforts of most or all of its members. A number of amendments were made after debate by the congress. The Declaration of Rights was adopted December 14 and the constitution December 17.

Constitution of 1776

Except for matters of organization and phrasing, the North Carolina Declaration of Rights did not depart significantly from the statements of individual liberties found in the declarations of rights of Virginia,[1] Pennsylvania,[2] Delaware,[3] and Maryland.[4] The committee that framed the North Carolina Declaration had before it not only those models, but also the colonial charters of Rhode Island and Connecticut and the recently enacted constitutions of South Carolina and New Jersey.

General Significance

In addition to the principles contained in the Declaration of Rights, the body of the constitution[5] contained a number of clauses bearing on the protection of individual liberties. Although a property qualification was imposed upon electors of senators, residents for one year who were over twenty-one could vote for members of the House of Commons.[6] Judges were to hold office during good behavior and were guaranteed adequate salaries.[7] Persons denying the being of God, the truth of the Protestant religion, or the divine

The Constitution

---

[1] See pp. 301-13.
[2] See pp. 323-31.
[3] See pp. 332-40.
[4] See pp. 341-51.
[5] Text in Francis N. Thorpe (ed.), *The Federal and State Constitutions, Colonial Charters, and Other Organic Laws* (Washington, 1909), V, 2789-94.
[6] Sections VII, VIII.
[7] Sections XIII, XXI.

authority of the Old and New Testaments were declared incapable of holding public office.[8] Freedom of worship, however, was guaranteed, and the establishment of one religious denomination in preference to any other was prohibited.[9] Imprisonment for debt was condemned, and all prisoners were to be admitted to bail, "unless for capital offences, when the proof is evident, or the presumption great."[10] It was also declared that the Declaration of Rights should be considered a part of the constitution and that it "ought never to be violated, on any pretence whatsoever."[11]

[8] Section XXXII.
[9] Section XXXIV.
[10] Section XXXIX.
[11] Section XLIV.

CONSTITUTION OF NORTH CAROLINA[12]

December 14, 1776

A DECLARATION OF RIGHTS, &C.

I. That all political power is vested in and derived from the people only. — *Origin of political power*

II. That the people of this State ought to have the sole and exclusive right of regulating the internal government and police thereof.

III. That no man or set of men are entitled to exclusive or separate emoluments or privileges from the community, but in consideration of public services. — *Emoluments and privileges*

IV. That the legislative, executive, and supreme judicial powers of government, ought to be forever separate and distinct from each other. — *Separation of powers*

V. That all powers of suspending laws, or the execution of laws, by any authority, without consent of the Representatives of the people, is injurious to their rights, and ought not to be exercised. — *Suspension of laws*

VI. That elections of members, to serve as Representatives in General Assembly, ought to be free. — *Free elections*

VII. That, in all criminal prosecutions, every man has a right to be informed of the accusation against him, and to confront the accusers and witnesses with other testimony, and shall not be compelled to give evidence against himself. — *Criminal procedure*

VIII. That no freeman shall be put to answer any criminal charge, but by indictment, presentment, or impeachment. — *Criminal charges*

IX. That no freeman shall be convicted of any crime, but by the unanimous verdict of a jury of good and lawful men, in open court, as heretofore used. — *Trial by jury*

X. That excessive bail should not be required, nor excessive fines imposed, nor cruel or unusual punishments inflicted. — *Bail, fines, and punishments*

XI. That general warrants—whereby an officer or messenger may be commanded to search suspected places, without evidence of the fact committed, or to seize any person or persons, not named, whose offences are not particularly described, and supported by evidence—are dangerous to liberty, and ought not to be granted. — *General warrants*

XII. That no freeman ought to be taken, imprisoned, or disseized of his freehold, liberties or privileges, or outlawed, or exiled, or in any manner destroyed, or deprived of his life, liberty, or property, but by the law of the land. — *Taking of life, liberty, and property*

---

[12] Thorpe, *op. cit.*, V, 2787-89. The second half of the document, which is not reproduced here, is entitled "The Constitution, or Form of Government." *Ibid.*, 2789-94.

Availability of remedies XIII. That every freeman, restrained of his liberty, is entitled to a remedy, to inquire into the lawfulness thereof, and to remove the same, if unlawful; and that such remedy ought not to be denied or delayed.

Juries in civil cases XIV. That in all controversies at law, respecting property, the ancient mode of trial, by jury, is one of the best securities of the rights of the people, and ought to remain sacred and inviolable.

Freedom of press XV. That the freedom of the press is one of the great bulwarks of liberty, and therefore ought never to be restrained.

Taxation by the General Assembly XVI. That the people of this State ought not to be taxed, or made subject to the payment of any impost or duty, without the consent of themselves, or their Representatives in General Assembly, freely given.

Right to bear arms XVII. That the people have a right to bear arms, for the defence of the State; and, as standing armies, in time of peace, are dangerous to liberty, they ought not to be kept up; and that the military should be kept under strict subordination to, and governed by, the civil power.

Assembly XVIII. That the people have a right to assemble together, to consult for their common good, to instruct their Representatives, and to apply to the Legislature, for redress of grievances.

Liberty of conscience XIX. That all men have a natural and unalienable right to worship Almighty God according to the dictates of their own consciences.

Frequent elections XX. That, for redress of grievances, and for amending and strengthening the laws, elections ought to be often held.

Recurrence to fundamentals XXI. That a frequent recurrence to fundamental principles is absolutely necessary, to preserve the blessings of liberty.

Hereditary privileges XXII. That no hereditary emoluments, privileges or honors ought to be granted or conferred in this State.

Monopolies XXIII. That perpetuities and monopolies are contrary to the genius of a free State, and ought not to be allowed.

Ex post facto laws XXIV. That retrospective laws, punishing facts committed before the existence of such laws, and by them only declared criminal, are oppressive, unjust, and incompatible with liberty; wherefore no *ex post facto* law ought to be made.

Boundaries of the state XXV. The property of the soil, in a free government, being one of the essential rights of the collective body of the people, it is necessary, in order to avoid future disputes, that the limits of the State should be ascertained with precision; and as the former temporary line between North and South Carolina, was confirmed, and extended by Commissioners, appointed by the Legislatures of the two States, agreeable to the order of the late King George the Second, in Council, that line, and that only, should be esteemed the southern boundary of this State as follows: that is to say, beginning on the sea side, at a cedar stake, at or near the mouth of Little River (being the southern extremity of Brunswick county,) and running from thence a northwest course, through the boundary house, which stands in thirty-three degrees fifty-six minutes, to thirty-five degrees north latitude; and from thence a west course so far as is mentioned in the Charter of King Charles the Second, to the late Proprietors of Carolina. Therefore all the territories, seas, waters, and harbours, with their appurtenances, lying between the line above described, and the southern line of the State of Virginia, which begins on the sea shore, in thirty-six degrees thirty minutes, north latitude, and from thence runs west, agreeable to the said Charter of King Charles, are the right and property of the people of this State, to be held by them in sovereignty; any partial line, without the consent of the Legislature of this State, at any time thereafter directed, or laid out, in anywise notwithstanding:—*Provided always,* That this Declaration of Rights shall not prejudice any nation or nations of Indians, from enjoying such hunting-grounds as may have been, or hereafter shall be, secured to them by any former or future Legislature of this State:—*And provided also,* That it shall not be construed so as to prevent the establishment of one or more governments westward of this State, by consent of the Legislature:—*And provided further,* That nothing herein contained shall affect the titles or possessions of individuals holding or claiming under the laws heretofore in force, or grants heretofore made by the late King George the Second, or his predecessors, or the late lords proprietors, or any of them.

REFERENCES

Ashe, Samuel A. *History of North Carolina.* 2 vols. Greensboro: Charles L. Van Noppen, 1908. I, chaps. 29-32.
Connor, R. D. W. *History of North Carolina.* 6 vols. Chicago: Lewis Publishing Co., 1919. I, chaps. 1-23.
Moore, John W. *History of North Carolina.* 2 vols. Raleigh, n.p. 1880.
Wheeler, John H. *Historical Sketches of North Carolina, 1584-1851.* 2 vols. Philadelphia: Lippincott, Grambo & Co., 1851. I, ser. 2, chap. 1.

XXVII. CONSTITUTION OF VERMONT
1777

Origins   The status of the Vermont Constitution and Declaration of Rights of 1777 in the history of constitutional government is somewhat different from that of the constitutions adopted at the time of the American Revolution by other states. Vermont had never been a crown colony, and it had never been recognized as a separate governmental entity by any state. Indeed, it was not until 1791 that it was admitted by Congress to membership in the Union. By 1777, however, Vermont had claimed the position of an independent state and had assumed the prerogatives of sovereignty. Vermont's first constitution and declaration of rights are thus further evidence of the principles of individual liberties being applied in America.

Territorial disputes   For many years ownership of the Green Mountain territory was disputed by New York and New Hampshire. Following the French and Indian War (1754-63), Governor Wentworth of New Hampshire granted charters to many towns west of the Connecticut River. As a result, that territory came to be called the "New Hampshire Grants." New York made no grants and denied the validity of the ones made by its rival. On July 20, 1764, the king recognized New York's claim and declared the west bank of the Connecticut River to be the boundary between that colony and New Hampshire.

Spirit of independence in Vermont   The people of the New Hampshire Grants were far from the capitals of New Hampshire and New York and were able to establish without interference an autonomous government based on the town meeting system practiced by Massachusetts and Connecticut, from which most of them had come. The Vermonters feared the prospect of being ruled by New York, not only because they wanted to preserve their independent status but also because New York threatened to invalidate the titles of the farms which the settlers had defended during the French and Indian War.

CONSTITUTION OF VERMONT

Delegates of the towns, meeting at Westminster April 11, 1775, declared that the inhabitants were in great danger of having their property "unjustly, cruelly, and unconstitutionally" taken from them by the "arbitrary and designing" administration of New York. They decided to renounce and resist that government until security for their lives and property was provided or until they could lay their grievances before the king. *Conflicts with New York*

A convention of delegates was called to meet January 16, 1776, at the inn of Cephas Kent in Dorset. Captain Heman Allen was delegated to present to the Continental Congress a petition requesting that no action be taken by that body concerning the dispute with New York until the end of the war. The petition was withdrawn, however, when it appeared that Congress was prepared to recommend that the New Hampshire Grants submit temporarily to the government of New York. An important step in the direction of independence was taken by the convention at an adjourned session on September 25, when it was resolved not to submit even temporarily to the authority of New York, to reject a proposed plan of union with New Hampshire, and give full support to the American nation.

Meeting at Westminster January 15, 1777, the convention adopted a resolution which cited the recommendation of May 10-15, 1776, from Congress that the colonies should take steps to meet the exigencies of government.[1] It stated: *Declaration of independence by Vermont*

> Your committee, having duly deliberated on the continued conduct of the authority of New York, before recited, and on the equitableness on which the aforesaid resolution of Congress was founded, and considering that a just right exists in the people to adopt measures for their own security, not only to enable them to secure their rights against the usurpations of Great Britain, but also against that of New York, and the several other governments claiming jurisdiction of this territory, do offer the following declaration, viz.:
>
> This convention whose members are duly chosen by the free voice of their constituents in the several towns, on the New Hampshire Grants, in public meeting assembled, in our own names, and in behalf of our constituents, do hereby proclaim and publicly declare that the district of territory comprehending and usually known by the name and description of the New Hampshire Grants, of right ought to be, and is hereby declared forever hereafter to be considered a separate, free and independent jurisdiction or State; by the name, and to be forever hereafter called, and known and distinguished by the name of New Connecticut...[2]

---

[1] See p. 316.
[2] Quoted in Walter H. Crockett, *Vermont, The Green Mountain State* (New York, 1921), II, 197-98.

SOURCES OF OUR LIBERTIES

A formal declaration of independence was prepared. It stated that the people were without law or government and were, therefore, in a state of nature and that the people had the right to form a government best suited to secure their property, well-being, and happiness.

Constitution of 1777

Formation of the first Constitution of Vermont was greatly influenced by Dr. Thomas Young of Philadelphia, a friend of Ethan Allen and one of the framers of the Pennsylvania Constitution of 1776.[3] On April 11, 1777, he addressed a letter to "the inhabitants of Vermont," encouraging them to form an independent government and promising to assist them in obtaining recognition from Congress as a state. It was probably Young who was responsible for the adoption by the new state of the name "Vermont."[4]

A convention met at Windsor July 2, 1777, to frame a constitution and to deal with other matters. Following the recommendation of Dr. Young, the convention not only adopted the name "Vermont" but also based the first constitution of the state on the extremely democratic Pennsylvania document. The proposed constitution was read and discussed until July 8. On that day news came of the evacuation of Ticonderoga by General St. Clair. Many members favored immediate adjournment so that they could defend their families. A heavy thunderstorm, however, made travel impossible, and during the interlude the constitution and Declaration of Rights were passed.

General Significance

Compared with Pennsylvania Constitution of 1776

The document is prefaced with a recital of the quarrel with New York. The Declaration of Rights and the constitution were apparently directly inspired by the Pennsylvania Constitution of 1776. In many instances the exact language of the latter document was used by Vermont. Several differences between the two declarations are worthy of attention. The Vermont Declaration, after stating that all men are born equally free and independent, expressly forbade the importation of slaves. The provision on religious freedom was weakened in Vermont by the clause which granted only to Protestants freedom from civil disability. In addition to the provisions of the Pennsylvania document, Vermont added a clause restraining the use of writs of attachment and provided that no person should be transported out of the state to be tried for any offense committed within the state.

The body of the constitution[5] also contained several provisions bearing on

[3] See pp. 323-31.
[4] See Hiland Hall, *The History of Vermont* (Albany, 1868), 497-500.
[5] Text in Francis N. Thorpe (ed.), *The Federal and State Constitutions, Colonial Charters, and Other Organic Laws* (Washington, 1909), VI, 3742-49.

the liberties of the individual. The Pennsylvania Constitution had allowed all taxpayers to vote regardless of property ownership, but Vermont was even more liberal. Its constitution extended the franchise to every man over twenty-one who had resided in the state for a year and who took an oath to vote to further the good of the state without fear or favor of any man. The requirement that electors pay taxes was dropped.[6] As in Pennsylvania, it was provided that excessive bail should not be exacted for bailable offenses and that all fines should be moderate.[7] The constitution also stated that houses of correction should be provided "to make sanguinary punishments less necessary."[8] Finally, it was provided that the Declaration of Rights should be a part of the constitution, and ought never to be violated on any pretense whatsoever.[9]

Constitution of 1786

When the first Council of Censors met in 1785 and 1786 to review the operation of the constitution, there was much criticism of the executive and legislative departments. The council recommended that a convention be summoned to pass on proposed amendments to the constitution. One delegate from each town was selected for this purpose. They met at Manchester June 29, 1786, and the revised constitution was certified July 4.[10] A few changes in the Declaration of Rights resulted from this process. It was declared that no man could be deprived of any civil right on account of his religious sentiments. Justice was not to be sold, denied, or delayed. Speeches and debates in the legislature were not to be questioned outside that body. The suspension of laws without the consent of the legislature was prohibited. No person was to be subjected to pains or penalties by martial law except those in the army or militia.

[6] Section VI.
[7] Section XXVI.
[8] Section XXXV.
[9] Section XLIII.
[10] Text in Thorpe, *op. cit.*, VI, 3749-61.

CONSTITUTION OF VERMONT[11]
July 8, 1777

Preamble
Purpose of government

WHEREAS, all government ought to be instituted and supported, for the security and protection of the community, as such, and to enable the individuals who compose it, to enjoy their natural rights, and the other blessings which the Author of existence has bestowed upon man; and whenever those great ends of government are not obtained, the people have a right, by common consent, to change it, and take such measures as to them may appear necessary to promote their safety and happiness.

Termination of royal authority

And whereas, the inhabitants of this State have (in consideration of protection only) heretofore acknowledged allegiance to the King of Great Britain, and the said King has not only withdrawn that protection, but commenced, and still continues to carry on, with unabated vengeance, a most cruel and unjust war against them; employing therein, not only the troops of Great Britain, but foreign mercenaries, savages and slaves, for the avowed purpose of reducing them to a total and abject submission to the despotic domination of the British parliament, with many other acts of tyranny, (more fully set forth in the declaration of Congress) whereby all allegiance and fealty to the said King and his successors, are dissolved and at an end; and all power and authority derived from him, ceased in the American Colonies.

New Hampshire grants

And whereas, the territory which now comprehends the State of *Vermont*, did antecedently, of right, belong to the government of *New-Hampshire;* and the former Governor thereof, viz. his Excellency *Benning Wentworth*, Esq., granted many charters of lands and corporations, within this State, to the present inhabitants and others. And whereas, the late Lieutenant Governor *Colden*, of *New York*, with others, did, in violation of the tenth command, covet those very lands; and by a false representation made to the court of Great Britain, (in the year 1764, that for the convenience of trade and administration of justice, the inhabitants were desirous of being annexed to that government,) obtained jurisdiction of those very identical lands *ex-parte;* which ever was, and is, disagreeable to the inhabitants. And whereas, the legislautre of *New-York*, ever have, and still continue to disown the good people of this State, in their landed property, which will appear in the complaints hereafter inserted, and in the 36th section of their present constitution, in which is established the grants of land made by that government.

[11] *Ibid.*, VI, 3737-42. The second half of the document, which is not reproduced here, is entitled the "Plan or Frame of Government." *Ibid.*, 3742-49.

CONSTITUTION OF VERMONT

They have refused to make regrants of our lands to the original proprietors and occupants, unless at the exorbitant rate of 2300 dollars fees for each township; and did enhance the quit-rent, three fold, and demanded an immediate delivery of the title derived before, from *New-Hampshire*. — *Terms of prospective New York grants*

The judges of their supreme court have made a solemn declaration, that the charters, conveyances, &c. of the lands included in the before described premises, were utterly null and void, on which said title was founded: in consequence of which declaration, writs of possession have been by them issued, and the sheriff of the county of Albany sent, at the head of six or seven hundred men, to enforce the execution thereof. — *Invalidation of New Hampshire grants by New York*

They have passed an act, annexing a penalty thereto, of thirty pounds fine and six months imprisonment, on any person who should refuse assisting the sheriff, after being requested, for the purpose of executing writs of possession. — *Enforcement of writs of possession*

The Governors, *Dunmore, Tryon* and *Colden*, have made re-grants of several tracts of land, included in the premises, to certain favorite land jobbers in the government of *New-York*, in direct violation of his Britannic majesty's express prohibition, in the year 1767. — *Regrants of land*

They have issued proclamations, wherein they have offered large sums of money, for the purpose of apprehending those very persons who have dared boldly, and publicly, to appear in defence of their just rights. — *New York proclamations*

They did pass twelve acts of outlawry, on the 9th day of March, A. D. 1774, impowering the respective judges of their supreme court, to award execution of death against those inhabitants in said district, that they should judge to be offenders, without trial. — *Acts of outlawry*

They have, and still continue, an unjust claim to those lands, which greatly retards emigration into, and the settlement of, this State. — *Emigration*

They have hired foreign troops, emigrants from *Scotland*, at two different times, and armed them, to drive us out of possession. — *Foreign troops*

They have sent the savages on our frontiers, to distress us. — *Indians*

They have proceeded to erect the counties of Cumberland and Glocester, and establish courts of justice there, after they were discountenanced by the authority of Great Britain. — *New counties*

The free convention of the State of *New-York*, at *Harlem*, in the year 1776, unanimously voted, "That all quit-rents, formerly due to the King of Great Britain, are now due and owing to this Convention, or such future government as shall be hereafter established in this State." — *Quitrents*

In the several stages of the aforesaid oppressions, we have petitioned his Britannic majesty, in the most humble manner, for redress, and have, at very great expense, received several reports in our favor; and, in other instances, wherein we have petitioned the late legislative authority of *New-York*, those petitions have been treated with neglect. — *Petitions*

And whereas, the local situation of this State, from *New-York*, at the extreme part, — *Distance*

Independence

is upward of four hundred and fifty miles from the seat of that government, which renders it extreme difficult to continue under the jurisdiction of said State.

Therefore, it is absolutely necessary, for the welfare and safety of the inhabitants of this State, that it should be, henceforth, a free and independent State; and that a just, permanent, and proper form of government, should exist in it, derived from, and founded on, the authority of the people only, agreeable to the direction of the honorable American Congress.

Declaration of Rights and Constitution

We the representatives of the freemen of *Vermont,* in General Convention met, for the express purpose of forming such a government,—confessing the goodness of the Great Governor of the universe, (who alone, knows to what degree of earthly happiness, mankind may attain, by perfecting the arts of government,) in permitting the people of this State, by common consent, and without violence, deliberately to form for themselves, such just rules as they shall think best for governing their future society; and being fully convinced that it is our indispensable duty, to establish such original principles of government, as will best promote the general happiness of the people of this State, and their posterity, and provide for future improvements, without partiality for, or prejudice against, any particular class, sect, or denomination of men whatever,—do, by virtue of authority vested in us, by our constituents ordain, declare, and establish, the following declaration of rights, and frame of government, to be the CONSTITUTION of this COMMONWEALTH, and to remain in force therein, forever, unaltered, except in such articles, as shall, hereafter, on experience, be found to require improvement, and which shall, by the same authority of the people, fairly delegated, as this frame of government directs, be amended or improved, for the more effectual obtaining and securing the great end and design of all government, herein before mentioned.

CHAPTER I

Declaration of Rights

A DECLARATION OF THE RIGHTS OF THE INHABITANTS OF THE STATE OF VERMONT

Natural rights of men

I. THAT all men are born equally free and independent, and have certain natural, inherent and unalienable rights, amongst which are the enjoying and defending life and liberty; acquiring, possessing and protecting property, and pursuing and obtaining happiness and safety. Therefore, no male person, born in this country, or brought from over sea, ought to be holden by law, to serve any person, as a servant, slave or apprentice, after he arrives to the age of twenty-one years, nor female, in like manner, after she arrives to the age of eighteen years, unless they are bound by their own consent, after they arrive to such age, or bound by law, for the payment of debts, damages, fines, costs, or the like.

II. That private property ought to be subservient to public uses, when necessity requires it; nevertheless, whenever any particular man's property is taken for the use of the public, the owner ought to receive an equivalent in money. *Compensation for property*

III. That all men have a natural and unalienable right to worship ALMIGHTY GOD, according to the dictates of their own consciences and understanding, regulated by the word of GOD; and that no man ought, or of right can be compelled to attend any religious worship, or erect, or support any place of worship, or maintain any minister, contrary to the dictates of his conscience; nor can any man who professes the protestant religion, be justly deprived or abridged of any civil right, as a citizen, on account of his religious sentiment, or peculiar mode of religious worship, and that no authority can, or ought to be vested in, or assumed by, any power whatsoever, that shall, in any case, interfere with, or in any manner controul, the rights of conscience, in the free exercise of religious worship: nevertheless, every sect or denomination of people ought to observe the Sabbath, or the Lord's day, and keep up, and support, some sort of religious worship, which to them shall seem most agreeable to the revealed will of GOD. *Liberty of conscience*

IV. That the people of this State have the sole, exclusive and inherent right of governing and regulating the internal police of the same. *Internal police matters*

V. That all power being originally inherent in, and consequently, derived from, the people; therefore, all officers of government, whether legislative or executive, are their trustees and servants, and at all times accountable to them. *Accountability of officials*

VI. That government is, or ought to be, instituted for the common benefit, protection, and security of the people, nation or community; and not for the particular emolument or advantage of any single man, family or set of men, who are a part only of that community; and that the community hath an indubitable, unalienable and indefeasible right to reform, alter, or abolish, government, in such manner as shall be, by that community, judged most conducive to the public weal. *Government may be altered or abolished by the people*

VII. That those who are employed in the legislative and executive business of the State, may be restrained from oppression, the people have a right, at such periods as they may think proper, to reduce their public officers to a private station, and supply the vacancies by certain and regular elections. *Regular elections*

VIII. That all elections ought to be free; and that all freemen, having a sufficient, evident, common interest with, and attachment to, the community, have a right to elect officers, or be elected into office. *Free elections*

IX. That every member of society hath a right to be protected in the enjoyment of life, liberty and property, and therefore, is bound to contribute his proportion towards the expense of that protection, and yield his personal service, when necessary, or an equivalent thereto; but no part of a man's property can be justly taken from him, or applied to public uses, without his own consent, or that of his legal representatives; nor can any man who is conscientiously scrupulous of bearing arms, be justly compelled thereto, if he will pay such equivalent; nor are the people bound by any law, but such as they have, in like manner, assented to, for their common good. *Property not to be taken without the consent of the individual or his representative*

Criminal procedure
Counsel; witnesses; trial by jury; self-incrimination

X. That, in all prosecutions for criminal offences, a man hath a right to be heard, by himself and his counsel—to demand the cause and nature of his accusation—to be confronted with the witnesses—to call for evidence in his favor, and a speedy public trial, by an impartial jury of the country; without the unanimous consent of which jury, he cannot be found guilty; nor can he be compelled to give evidence against himself; nor can any man be justly deprived of his liberty, except by the laws of the land or the judgment of his peers.

Searches and seizures

XI. That the people have a right to hold themselves, their houses, papers and possessions free from search or seizure; and therefore warrants, without oaths or affirmations first made, affording a sufficient foundation for them, and whereby any officer or messenger may be commanded or required to search suspected places, or to seize any person or persons, his, her or their property, nor particularly described, are contrary to that right, and ought not to be granted.

Writs of attachment

XII. That no warrant or writ to attach the person or estate, of any freeholder within this State, shall be issued in civil action, without the person or persons, who may request such warrant or attachment, first make oath, or affirm, before the authority who may be requested to issue the same, that he, or they, are in danger of losing his, her or their debts.

Juries in civil cases

XIII. That, in controversies respecting property, and in suits between man and man, the parties have a right to a trial by jury; which ought to be held sacred.

Speech and press

XIV. That the people have a right to freedom of speech, and of writing and publishing their sentiments; therefore, the freedom of the press ought not be restrained.

Right to bear arms; standing armies

XV. That the people have a right to bear arms for the defence of themselves and the State; and, as standing armies, in the time of peace, are dangerous to liberty, they ought not to be kept up; and that the military should be kept under strict subordination to, and governed by, the civil power.

Recurrence to fundamentals

XVI. That frequent recurrence to fundamental principles, and a firm adherence to justice, moderation, temperance, industry and frugality, are absolutely necessary to preserve the blessings of liberty, and keep government free. The people ought, therefore, to pay particular attention to these points, in the choice of officers and representatives, and have a right to exact a due and constant regard to them, from their legislators and magistrates, in the making and executing such laws as are necessary for the good government of the State.

Right to emigrate and form states

XVII. That all people have a natural and inherent right to emigrate from one State to another, that will receive them; or to form a new State in vacant countries, or in such countries as they can purchase, whenever they think that thereby they can promote their own happiness.

Assembly

XVIII. That the people have a right to assemble together, to consult for their common good—to instruct their representatives, and to apply to the legislature for redress of grievances, by address, petition or remonstrance.

Trials out of state

XIX. That no person shall be liable to be transported out of this State for trial, for any offence committed within this State.

CONSTITUTION OF VERMONT

REFERENCES

Crockett, Walter H. *Vermont, The Green Mountain State*. 5 vols. New York: Century History Co., 1921-23. II, chaps. 20-27.
Hall, Hiland. *The History of Vermont*. Albany: Joel Munsell, 1868.
Newton, Earle W. *The Vermont Story*. Montpelier: Vermont Historical Society, 1949.
Stackpole, Everett S. *History of New Hampshire*. 4 vols. New York: American Historical Society, 1916. II, chap. 7.
Thompson, Charles M. *Independent Vermont*. Boston: Houghton Mifflin Co., 1942.

XXVIII. CONSTITUTION OF MASSACHUSETTS
1780

Origins   The Massachusetts Constitution of 1780 is important not only for its enumeration of individual liberties but also for the method by which it was drawn up and adopted. That method was based on the principle that the fundamental law of the land should be founded upon the will of the people. Massachusetts, to a greater extent than any other state, developed the theory and practice of the constitutional convention, a body of delegates selected by the people for the sole purpose of framing the basic structure of government. Once the document had been framed, it was then ratified by the people. The method employed in framing and adopting the Massachusetts Constitution thus closely paralleled that which led to the Constitution of the United States seven years later.

Revival of the Charter of 1691   The General Court of Massachusetts was dissolved by the last royal governor of that colony in September, 1774. Thereafter members of the General Court formed a provincial congress to direct the movement of resistance against British oppression. After General Gage was deposed in May, 1775, the Provincial Congress ordered the election of a regular General Court, as had been done under the royal charter of 1691. From that time the governmental affairs of the colony were carried on by a regularly elected General Court without a governor.

The Pittsfield proposal   The movement toward framing a permanent constitution began May 29, 1776, when the town of Pittsfield questioned the authority of the General Court to govern. Because the charter of 1691 was a compact, it said, it was dissolved when George III violated it; and the General Court had no right to assume that it was still in effect. Pittsfield suggested that the General Court frame a constitution to be referred for the people's approval.

CONSTITUTION OF MASSACHUSETTS

In the spirit of the Pittsfield proposal, the General Court in September, 1776, requested the people to authorize it to draft a constitution. It made no offer to convene a special body for that purpose; the legislature itself would formulate the fundamental law of the state. Three towns—Middleborough, Concord, and Acton—objected to this procedure and demanded the calling of a special convention. The Concord resolutions of October 22, 1776, stated the reasons for the objections:

Proposals for a constitutional convention

> That the Supreme Legislative, either in their proper capacity or in joint committee, are by no means a body proper to form and establish a constitution or form of government; for reasons following. First, because we conceive that a Constitution in its proper idea intends a system of principles established to secure the subject in the possession and enjoyment of their rights and priviliges, against any encroachments of the governing part. Second, because the same body that forms a constitution have of consequence a power to alter it. Third, because a Constitution alterable by the Supreme Legislative is no security at all to the subject against any encroachment of the governing part on any, or on all of their rights and priviliges.[1]

The General Court ignored the good advice of the three towns. A constitution was drawn up by a committee of twelve. Its members included Robert Treat Paine, James Warren, James Prescott, and Thomas Cushing. The work proceeded slowly, and it was not until February, 1778, that the finished constitution was approved by the legislature. The instrument met with widespread disapproval when it was submitted to the people for ratification. It was defeated by a 5-to-1 vote of the freemen.

The General Court's constitution of 1778

Following the defeat of the General Court's constitution, an important paper known as the "Essex Result" was published. It listed the reasons for the conservatives' opposition. It cited the absence of a bill of rights and called for a separation of the branches of government, exclusion of the governor from the legislature, a fairer apportionment of representation, and a better method of electing senators.[2] The emphasis placed by the paper on property rights was not in accord with the constitutional ideals of the ultra-democratic faction. The "Essex Result" demonstrated, however, that both conservatives and radicals were agreed on the need for a bill of rights in the new constitution.

The "Essex Result"

In February, 1779, the General Court asked the people to decide in their town meetings whether they wished to have a constitutional convention sum-

Convention of 1779

---

[1] Samuel E. Morison (ed.), *Sources and Documents Illustrating the American Revolution, 1764-1788* (Oxford, 1923), 177.

[2] Allan Nevins, *The American States During and After the Revolution, 1775-1789* (New York, 1924), 177-78.

moned. The proposal was approved and delegates to the convention were elected. The property qualification customary for electors of members of the House of Representatives was ignored, and all freemen over twenty-one were allowed to vote. Each town was given as many delegates to the convention as it had representatives in the General Court. The first session of the convention was attended by 293 members and met at Cambridge in September, 1779. James Bowdoin was elected president of the convention, and a committee of thirty was appointed to prepare a draft. The drafting committee delegated its functions to John Adams, who was considered to be the most capable member for the task.

The convention held two sessions during which Adams' draft was discussed and amended. The second of these lasted from January, 1780, to March 2. On the latter date the convention adjourned to June 7, and copies of the constitution were distributed to the towns for consideration. The towns were instructed to vote on the document article by article, and a majority of two-thirds was necessary for adoption. More than two hundred towns made returns to the convention. The most serious objections to the Declaration of Rights made by the towns were directed at Article III, which had not been drafted by Adams. That article was intended to place the Congregational Church in a favored position. The final meeting of the convention, acting by authority of a fresh popular mandate, began at Boston, June 7. The returns made by the towns were examined, and the Declaration of Rights and the constitution were formally ratified by the convention June 15. The document went into effect October 25, 1780.

General Significance The framers of the first state constitutions generally accepted the idea that government is based on a "social contract." According to the social contract theory, the people as a whole agree with each individual, and each individual agrees with the people as a whole, that all shall be governed by certain laws for the common good. This theory of government rests upon the fundamental principle that all powers of government are based on the consent of the governed.

Constitutional convention The practical application of the social contract theory is clearly illustrated by the method used for adopting the Massachusetts Constitution of 1780. A constitutional convention which derived its authority directly from the people formulated the document, and the instrument, as prepared by the convention, was subsequently ratified by the people.

These ideas, however, were not new when the Massachusetts Constitution was framed. The New England Puritans of the seventeenth century were familiar with church covenants by which men voluntarily associated for purposes of civil, as well as religious, government. The Mayflower Compact of 1620[3] was an early evidence of this kind of organization. The theory of popular ratification of the fundamental law was given practical application in 1641 with the adoption of the Massachusetts Body of Liberties.[4]

One of the earliest suggestions for a constitutional convention to frame the fundamental law is found in the documents recording the seventeenth-century struggles to obtain a written constitution in England. In describing the Levellers' attempts in 1648 to agree with the more conservative elements of Parliament upon a constitution, John Lilburne said in his pamphlet "Legal Fundamental Liberties":

> That in our conceptions the only way of settlement is:
> 1. That some persons be chosen by the Army to represent the whole body and that the well-affected in every county (if it may be) choose some persons to represent them, and those to meet at the headquarters.
> 2. That those persons ought not to exercise any legislative power, but only to draw up the foundations of a just government, and to propound them to the well-affected people in every county, to be agreed to. Which agreement ought to be above law, and therefore the bounds, limits, and extent of the people's legislative deputies in parliament, contained in the Agreement, [ought] to be drawn up into a formal contract to be mutually signed by the well-affected people and their said deputies upon the days of their election respectively.[5]

The similarity between Lilburne's statement and the Concord resolutions of October 22, 1776, is worthy of notice.

Most of the principles of individual liberty found in the Massachusetts Declaration of Rights had already appeared in the earlier declarations of other states. Framed by the people, the document states clearly the rights for which the people fought the Revolutionary War. Article XXX, declaring the separation of governmental powers "to the end it may be a government of laws and not of men," is perhaps the most explicit statement of that theory to be found. The body of the constitution provided that all laws which had been adopted, used, and approved in Massachusetts should remain in full force until altered or repealed by the legislature, except such parts as were repugnant to the rights and liberties contained in the constitution. It was also

Rights of the individual

Separation of powers

Habeas corpus

---

[3] See pp. 55-61.
[4] See pp. 143-61.
[5] A. S. P. Woodhouse (ed.), *Puritanism and Liberty* (London, 1938), 343-44.

provided: "The privilege and benefit of the writ of *habeas corpus* shall be enjoyed in this commonwealth, in the most free, easy, cheap, expeditious, and ample manner; and shall not be suspended by the legislature, except upon the most urgent and pressing occasions, and for a limited time, not exceeding twelve months." The provision on habeas corpus contained in Article I, section 8, of the Constitution of the United States came from the proposal of Charles Pinckney of South Carolina. The clause proposed by him was in the language of the Massachusetts Constitution of 1780.[6]

[6] See p. 195

CONSTITUTION OF MASSACHUSETTS[7]

October 25, 1780

PREAMBLE

The end of the institution, maintenance, and administration of government, is to secure the existence of the body politic, to protect it, and to furnish the individuals who compose it with the power of enjoying in safety and tranquillity their natural rights, and the blessings of life: and whenever these great objects are not obtained, the people have a right to alter the government, and to take measures necessary for their safety, prosperity, and happiness.

The body politic is formed by a voluntary association of individuals: it is a social compact, by which the whole people covenants with each citizen, and each citizen with the whole people, that all shall be governed by certain laws for the common good. It is the duty of the people, therefore, in framing a constitution of government, to provide for an equitable mode of making laws, as well as for an impartial interpretation and a faithful execution of them; that every man may, at all times, find his security in them.

We, therefore, the people of Massachusetts, acknowledging, with grateful hearts, the goodness of the great Legislator of the universe, in affording us, in the course of His providence, an opportunity, deliberately and peaceably, without fraud, violence, or surprise, of entering into an original, explicit, and solemn compact with each other; and of forming a new constitution of civil government, for ourselves and posterity; and devoutly imploring His direction in so interesting a design, do agree upon, ordain, and establish, the following *Declaration of Rights, and Frame of Government*, as the CONSTITUTION OF THE COMMONWEALTH OF MASSACHUSETTS.

---

[7] Francis N. Thorpe (ed.), *The Federal and State Constitutions, Colonial Charters, and Other Organic Laws* (Washington, 1909), III, 1888-93. The document's full title is "Constitution or Form of Government for the Commonwealth of Massachusetts." The second half of the document, which is not reproduced here, is entitled the "Frame of Government." *Ibid.*, 1893-1922.

PART THE FIRST

A DECLARATION OF THE RIGHTS OF THE INHABITANTS OF THE COMMONWEALTH OF MASSACHUSETTS

Natural rights of men

ARTICLE I. All men are born free and equal, and have certain natural, essential, and unalienable rights; among which may be reckoned the right of enjoying and defending their lives and liberties; that of acquiring, possessing, and protecting property; in fine, that of seeking and obtaining their safety and happiness.

Freedom of conscience

II. It is the right as well as the duty of all men in society, publicly, and at stated seasons, to worship the SUPREME BEING, the great Creator and Preserver of the universe. And no subject shall be hurt, molested, or restrained, in his person, liberty, or estate, for worshipping GOD in the manner and season most agreeable to the dictates of his own conscience; or for his religious profession of sentiments; provided he doth not disturb the public peace, or obstruct others in their religious worship.

Support of public worship

III. As the happiness of a people, and the good order and preservation of civil government, essentially depend upon piety, religion, and morality; and as these cannot be generally diffused through a community but by the institution of the public worship of GOD, and of public instructions in piety, religion, and morality: Therefore, to promote their happiness, and to secure the good order and preservation of their government, the people of this commonwealth have a right to invest their legislature with power to authorize and require, and the legislature shall, from time to time, authorize and require, the several towns, parishes, precincts, and other bodies politic, or religious societies, to make suitable provision, at their own expense, for the institution of the public worship of GOD, and for the support and maintenance of public Protestant teachers of piety, religion, and morality, in all cases where such provision shall not be made voluntarily.

Attendance at religious instructions

And the people of this commonwealth have also a right to, and do, invest their legislature with authority to enjoin upon all the subjects an attendance upon the instructions of the public teachers aforesaid, at stated times and seasons, if there be any on whose instructions they can conscientiously and conveniently attend.

Elections and support of public teachers

Provided, notwithstanding, that the several towns, parishes, precincts, and other bodies politic, or religious societies, shall, at all times, have the exclusive right of electing their public teachers, and of contracting with them for their support and maintenance.

Application of moneys paid for support of religion

And all moneys paid by the subject to the support of public worship, and of the public teachers aforesaid, shall, if he require it, be uniformly applied to the support of the public teacher or teachers of his own religious sect or denomination, provided there be any on whose instructions he attends; otherwise it may be paid towards the support of the teacher or teachers of the parish or precinct in which the said moneys are raised.

And every denomination of Christians, demeaning themselves peaceably, and as good subjects of the commonwealth, shall be equally under the protection of the law: and no subordination of any one sect or denomination to another shall ever be established by law. *— Equal status for all denominations*

IV. The people of this commonwealth have the sole and exclusive right of governing themselves, as a free, sovereign, and independent state; and do, and forever hereafter shall, exercise and enjoy every power, jurisdiction, and right, which is not, or may not hereafter be, by them expressly delegated to the United States of America, in Congress assembled. *— Reservation of powers not delegated*

V. All power residing originally in the people, and being derived from them, the several magistrates and officers of government, vested with authority, whether legislative, executive, or judicial, are their substitutes and agents, and are at all times accountable to them. *— All power derived from the people*

VI. No man, nor corporation, or association of men, have any other title to obtain advantages, or particular and exclusive privileges, distinct from those of the community, than what arises from the consideration of services rendered to the public; and this title being in nature neither hereditary, nor transmissible to children, or descendants, or relations by blood, the idea of a man born a magistrate, lawgiver, or judge, is absurd and unnatural. *— Offices should not be hereditary*

VII. Government is instituted for the common good; for the protection, safety, prosperity, and happiness of the people; and not for the profit, honor, or private interest of any one man, family, or class of men: Therefore the people alone have an incontestible unalienable, and indefeasible right to institute government; and to reform, alter, or totally change the same, when their protection, safety, prosperity, and happiness require it. *— Government may be altered or totally changed by the people*

VIII. In order to prevent those who are vested with authority from becoming oppressors, the people have a right, at such periods and in such manner as they shall establish by their frame of government, to cause their public officers to return to private life; and to fill up vacant places by certain and regular elections and appointments. *— Regular elections*

IX. All elections ought to be free; and all the inhabitants of this commonwealth, having such qualifications as they shall establish by their frame of government, have an equal right to elect officers, and to be elected, for public employments. *— Free elections*

X. Each individual of the society has a right to be protected by it in the enjoyment of his life, liberty, and property, according to standing laws. He is obliged, consequently, to contribute his share to the expense of this protection; to give his personal service, or an equivalent, when necessary: but no part of the property of any individual can, with justice, be taken from him, or applied to public uses, without his own consent, or that of the representative body of the people. In fine, the people of this commonwealth are not controllable by any other laws than those to which their constitutional representative body have given their consent. And whenever the public exigencies *— Taxation with the consent of representative body* require that the property of any individual should be appropriated to public uses, he shall receive a reasonable compensation therefor.

Remedies

Justice shall not be denied or delayed

XI. Every subject of the commonwealth ought to find a certain remedy, by having recourse to the laws, for all injuries or wrongs which he may receive in his person, property, or character. He ought to obtain right and justice freely, and without being obliged to purchase it; completely, and without any denial; promptly, and without delay; conformably to the laws.

Criminal procedure; self-incrimination; witnesses and counsel

XII. No subject shall be held to answer for any crimes or offence, until the same is fully and plainly, substantially, and formally, described to him; or be compelled to accuse, or furnish evidence against himself. And every subject shall have a right to produce all proofs that may be favorable to him; to meet the witnesses against him face to face, and to be fully heard in his defence by himself, or his counsel, at his election. And no subject shall be arrested, imprisoned, despoiled, or deprived of his property, immunities, or privileges, put out of the protection of the law, exiled, or deprived of his life, liberty, or estate, but by the judgment of his peers, or the law of the land.

Trial by jury

And the legislature shall not make any law that shall subject any person to a capital or infamous punishment, excepting for the government of the army and navy, without trial by jury.

Verification of facts in the vicinity

XIII. In criminal prosecutions, the verification of facts, in the vicinity where they happen, is one of the greatest securities of the life, liberty, and property of the citizen.

Searches and seizures

Warrants

XIV. Every subject has a right to be secure from all unreasonable searches, and seizures, of his person, his houses, his papers, and all his possessions. All warrants, therefore, are contrary to this right, if the cause or foundation of them be not previously supported by oath or affirmation, and if the order in the warrant to a civil officer, to make search in suspected places, or to arrest one or more suspected persons, or to seize their property, be not accompanied with a special designation of the persons or objects of search, arrest, or seizure; and no warrant ought to be issued but in cases, and with the formalities prescribed by the laws.

Juries in civil cases

XV. In all controversies concerning property, and in all suits between two or more persons, except in cases in which it has heretofore been otherways used and practised, the parties have a right to a trial by jury; and this method of procedure shall be held sacred, unless, in causes arising on the high seas, and such as relate to mariners' wages, the legislature shall hereafter find it necessary to alter it.

Liberty of the press

XVI. The liberty of the press is essential to the security of freedom in a state it ought not, therefore, to be restricted in this conmonwealth.

Right to bear arms; standing armies

XVII. The people have a right to keep and to bear arms for the common defence. And as, in time of peace, armies are dangerous to liberty, they ought not to be maintained without the consent of the legislature; and the military power shall always be held in an exact subordination to the civil authority, and be governed by it.

Recurrence to fundamentals

XVIII. A frequent recurrence to the fundamental principles of the constitution, and a constant adherence to those of piety, justice, moderation, temperance, industry, and frugality, are absolutely necessary to preserve the advantages of liberty, and to maintain

CONSTITUTION OF MASSACHUSETTS

a free government. The people ought, consequently, to have a particular attention to all those principles, in the choice of their officers and representatives: and they have a right to require of their lawgivers and magistrates an exact and constant observance of them, in the formation and execution of the laws necessary for the good administration of the commonwealth.

XIX. The people have a right, in an orderly and peaceable manner, to assemble to consult upon the common good; give instructions to their representatives, and to request of the legislative body, by the way of addresses, petitions, or remonstrances, redress of the wrongs done them, and of the grievances they suffer. *Assembly; instruction of representatives*

XX. The power of suspending the laws, or the execution of the laws, ought never to be exercised but by the legislature, or by authority derived from it, to be exercised in such particular cases only as the legislature shall expressly provide for. *Suspension of laws*

XXI. The freedom of deliberation, speech, and debate, in either house of the legislature, is so essential to the rights of the people, that it cannot be the foundation of any accusation or prosecution, action or complaint, in any other court or place whatsoever. *Freedom of speech in legislature*

XXII. The legislature ought frequently to assemble for the redress of grievances, for correcting, strengthening, and confirming the laws, and for making new laws, as the common good may require. *Legislature to meet frequently*

XXIII. No subsidy, charge, tax, impost, or duties ought to be established, fixed, laid, or levied, under any pretext whatsoever, without the consent of the people or their representatives in the legislature. *Taxation by consent of legislature*

XXIV. Laws made to punish for actions done before the existence of such laws, and which have not been declared crimes by preceding laws, are unjust, oppressive, and inconsistent with the fundamental principles of a free government. *Ex post facto laws*

XXV. No subject ought, in any case, or in any time, to be declared guilty of treason or felony by the legislature. *Bills of attainder*

XXVI. No magistrate or court of law shall demand excessive bail or sureties, impose excessive fines, or inflict cruel or unusual punishments. *Bail, fines, and punishments*

XXVII. In time of peace, no soldier ought to be quartered in any house without the consent of the owner; and in time of war, such quarters ought not to be made but by the civil magistrate, in a manner ordained by the legislature. *Quartering of soldiers*

XXVIII. No person can in any case be subject to law-martial, or to any penalties or pains, by virtue of that law, except those employed in the army or navy, and except the militia in actual service, but by authority of the legislature. *Martial law*

XXIX. It is essential to the preservation of the rights of every individual, his life, liberty, property, and character, that there be an impartial interpretation of the laws, and administration of justice. It is the right of every citizen to be tried by judges as free, impartial, and independent as the lot of humanity will admit. It is, therefore, not only the best policy, but for the security of the rights of the people, and of every citizen, that the judges of the supreme judicial court should hold their offices as long as they behave themselves well; and that they should have honorable salaries ascertained and established by standing laws. *Administration of justice* *Independence of judges*

Separation of powers   XXX. In the government of this commonwealth, the legislative department shall never exercise the executive and judicial powers, or either of them: the executive shall never exercise the legislative and judicial powers, or either of them: the judicial shall never exercise the legislative and executive powers, or either of them: to the end it may be a government of laws and not of men.

REFERENCES

McLaughlin, Andrew C. *The Foundations of American Constitutionalism.* New York: New York University Press, 1932. Chap. 4.

Morison, Samuel E. "The Formation of the Massachusetts Constitution," *Massachusetts Law Quarterly,* XL, No. 4 (December, 1955), 1-17.

———. "The Struggle Over the Adoption of the Constitution of Massachusetts, 1780," *Massachusetts Historical Society, Proceedings,* L, 353-411. Boston: Massachusetts Historical Society, 1917.

XXIX. CONSTITUTION OF NEW HAMPSHIRE
1784

Between July, 1774, when the New Hampshire Assembly was dissolved by Governor Wentworth, and December, 1775, the colony was governed by a series of provincial congresses. These congresses regulated governmental affairs and sent delegates to the Continental Congress. In October, 1775, New Hampshire's delegates petitioned Congress for permission to frame a government to preserve order. In the lingering hope of reconciliation with Great Britain, Congress delayed its answer until November 3, at which time both New Hampshire and South Carolina were advised to form independent governments.[1] *Origins*

Acting through town meetings, the people selected delegates to the Provincial Congress. In January, 1776, that body adopted the first American constitution of the revolutionary period.[2] The Constitution of 1776, designed "to continue during the present unhappy and unnatural contest with Great Britain," set up an uncomplicated system of government. It was provided that the Provincial Congress should become the first assembly under the constitution. The assembly was given power to elect an upper house, or Council, of twelve members. No provision was made for the appointment of a governor. No judiciary was established and the document contained no bill of rights. During adjournments of the legislature the affairs of government were carried on by a committee of safety. Although dissatisfaction with the Constitution of 1776 was expressed at an early date, the document served as the fundamental law of the state for eight years. *Constitution of 1776*

[1] See p. 316.
[2] Text in Francis N. Thorpe (ed.), *The Federal and State Constitutions, Colonial Charters, and Other Organic Laws* (Washington, 1909), IV, 2451-53.

Constitutional Convention of 1778

Delegates from some of the western towns, meeting in Hanover in June, 1777, resolved that any permanent constitution should be framed by a convention held for that express purpose. The Council and House of Representatives, meeting in joint session, voted in February, 1778, to call a constitutional convention. Delegates from about ninety towns assembled at Concord in June, 1778, to frame the constitution. The first New Hampshire Constitutional Convention thus preceded the convention that framed the Massachusetts Constitution of 1780.[3] The instrument was prepared by a committee headed by Meshech Weare, who was also president of the convention. The committee completed its work in June, 1779, and copies of the constitution, prefaced by a brief declaration of rights, were sent to the towns. It was rejected.

Constitutional Convention of 1781

Another convention met at Concord in June, 1781. A committee headed by General Nathaniel Peabody was appointed to draw up the constitution. The committee's draft closely followed the Massachusetts Declaration of Rights and Constitution of 1780. As in Massachusetts, a two-thirds vote was required for adoption, and the towns were instructed to vote on the instrument article by article. This constitution was rejected by the towns in January, 1782. Changes were made by the convention, and a second draft was submitted. In December this draft also was rejected. A third draft received the necessary number of votes, and on October 31, 1783, the convention declared that the constitution had been adopted. June 2, 1784, was set as the date for the new government to go into effect.

Few changes in the Declaration of Rights were made in these redrafts of the constitution. The major objections to the constitution had been directed at the system of representation in the lower house of the legislature, the term of office of the president and his power to veto laws, and property qualifications for electors and officeholders.

New Hampshire Constitution compared with Massachusetts Constitution of 1780

Perhaps the most important difference between the New Hampshire and Massachusetts bills of rights is found in the articles on religion. In Massachusetts the legislature was given power to authorize or require the towns to support Protestant ministers and to compel the people to attend religious instruction. Taxes collected for the support of churches might be used by a denomination to which the individual did not belong, provided there were no ministers of his denomination in the community.

[3] See pp. 369-70.

CONSTITUTION OF NEW HAMPSHIRE

In New Hampshire the legislature might authorize the towns to make provision for the support of ministers, but could not require it. Persons could not be required to attend religious services, and no one could be compelled to contribute to a denomination to which he did not belong.

Ex post facto laws and bills of attainder

Another important difference between the two documents was that New Hampshire proscribed retroactive laws in both civil and criminal matters, whereas the Massachusetts Declaration proscribed retroactive criminal laws. New Hampshire omitted the prohibition of bills of attainder found in the Massachusetts document. It was the first state bill of rights, however, which expressly adopted the common law rule that no person should be tried for a crime of which he had been formerly acquitted. Freedom from double jeopardy had long been considered one of the rights of Englishmen embodied in the common law. "It is contrary to the genius and spirit of the law of England," said Blackstone, "to suffer any man to be tried twice for the same offense in a criminal way, especially if acquitted upon the first trial." [4] As in Massachusetts, the body of the constitution [5] preserved the writ of habeas corpus and the legislature was prohibited from suspending the writ for more than three months.

Double jeopardy

Habeas corpus

[4] William Blackstone, *Commentaries on the Laws of England* (9th ed.; London, 1783), IV, 259.
[5] Text in Thorpe, *op. cit.*, IV, 2458-70.

CONSTITUTION OF NEW HAMPSHIRE[6]

June 2, 1784

PART I.—THE BILL OF RIGHTS

ARTICLE I

Origin of government
All men are born equally free and independent; therefore, all government of right originates from the people, is founded in consent, and instituted for the general good.

Natural rights of men
II. All men have certain natural, essential, and inherent rights; among which are— the enjoying and defending life and liberty—acquiring, possessing and protecting property—and in a word, of seeking and obtaining happiness.

Surrender of natural rights
III. When men enter into a state of society, they surrender up some of their natural rights to that society, in order in insure the protection of others; and, without such an equivalent, the surrender is void.

Liberty of conscience
IV. Among the natural rights, some are in their very nature unalienable, because no equivalent can be given or received for them. Of this kind are the RIGHTS OF CONSCIENCE.

Same
V. Every individual has a natural and unalienable right to worship GOD according to the dictates of his own conscience, and reason; and no subject shall be hurt, molested, or restrained in his person, liberty or estate for worshipping GOD, in the manner and season most agreeable to the dictates of his own conscience, or for his religious profession, sentiments or persuasion; provided he doth not disturb the public peace, or disturb others, in their religious worship.

Public worship and instruction
VI. As morality and piety, rightly grounded on evangelical principles, will give the best and greatest security to government, and will lay in the hearts of men the strongest obligations to due subjection; and as the knowledge of these, is most likely to be propagated through a society by the institution of the public worship of the DEITY, and of public instruction in morality and religion; therefore, to promote those important purposes, the people of this state have a right to impower, and do hereby fully impower the legislature to authorize from time to time, the several towns, parishes, bodies-corporate, or religious societies within this state, to make adequate provision at their

---

[6] Thorpe, *op. cit.*, IV, 2453-57. The second half of the document, which is not reproduced here, is entitled the "Form of Government." *Ibid.*, 2458-70.

CONSTITUTION OF NEW HAMPSHIRE

own expence, for the support and maintenance of public protestant teachers of piety, religion and morality:

Provided notwithstanding, That the several towns, parishes, bodies-corporate, or religious societies, shall at all times have the exclusive right of electing their own public teachers, and of contracting with them for their support and maintenance. And no portion of any one particular religious sect or denomination, shall ever be compelled to pay towards the support of the teacher or teachers of another persuasion, sect or denomination. — *Support of public teachers*

And every denomination of christians demeaning themselves quietly, and as good subjects of the state, shall be equally under the protection of the law: and no subordination of any one sect or denomination to another, shall ever be established by law. — *No establishment of one sect*

And nothing herein shall be understood to affect any former contracts made for the support of the ministry; but all such contracts shall remain, and be in the same state as if this constitution had not been made. — *Contracts for support of the ministry*

VII. The people of this state, have the sole and exclusive right of governing themselves as a free, sovereign, and independent state, and do, and forever hereafter shall, exercise and enjoy every power, jurisdiction and right pertaining thereto, which is not, or may not hereafter be by them expressly delegated to the United States of America in Congress assembled. — *Reservation of powers not delegated*

VIII. All power residing originally in, and being derived from the people, all the magistrates and officers of government, are their substitutes and agents, and at all times accountable to them. — *All power is derived from the people*

IX. No office or place whatsoever in government, shall be hereditary—the abilities and integrity requisite in all, not being transmissible to posterity or relations. — *No hereditary offices*

X. Government being instituted for the common benefit, protection, and security of the whole community, and not for the private interest or emolument of any one man, family or class of men; therefore, whenever the ends of government are perverted, and public liberty manifestly endangered, and all other means of redress are ineffectual, the people may, and of right ought, to reform the old, or establish a new government. The doctrine of non-resistance against arbitrary power, and oppression, is absurd, slavish, and destructive of the good and happiness of mankind. — *Government may be reformed and new governments established by the people*

XI. All elections ought to be free, and every inhabitant of the state having the proper qualifications, has equal right to elect, and be elected into office. — *Free elections*

XII. Every member of the community has a right to be protected by it in the enjoyment of his life, liberty and property; he is therefore bound to contribute his share in the expence of such protection, and to yield his personal service when necessary, or an equivalent. But no part of a man's property shall be taken from him, or applied to public uses, without his own consent, or that of the representative body of the people. Nor are the inhabitants of this state controllable by any other laws than those to which they or their representative body have given their consent. — *Property not to be taken without the consent of the individual or his representatives*

XIII. No person who is conscientiously scrupulous about the lawfulness of bearing arms, shall be compelled thereto, provided he will pay an equivalent. — *Conscientious objectors*

Justice not to be denied or delayed

XIV. Every subject of this state is entitled to a certain remedy, by having recourse to the laws, for all injuries he may receive in his person, property or character, to obtain right and justice freely, without being obliged to purchase it; completely, and without any denial; promptly, and without delay, conformably to the laws.

Criminal procedure; self-incrimination; proof and counsel

XV. No subject shall be held to answer for any crime, or offence, until the same is fully and plainly, substantially and formally, described to him; or be compelled to accuse or furnish evidence against himself. And every subject shall have a right to produce all proofs that may be favorable to himself; to meet the witnesses against him face to face, and to be fully heard in his defence by himself, and counsel. And no subject shall be arrested, imprisoned, despoiled, or deprived of his property, immunities, or privileges, put out of the protection of the law, exiled or deprived of his life, liberty, or estate, but by the judgment of his peers or the law of the land.

Double jeopardy
Trial by jury

XVI. No subject shall be liable to be tried, after an acquittal, for the same crime or offence.—Nor shall the legislature make any law that shall subject any person to a capital punishment, excepting for the government of the army and navy, and the militia in actual service, without trial by jury.

Facts to be ascertained in the vicinity

XVII. In criminal prosecutions, the trial of facts in the vicinity where they happen, is so essential to the security of the life, liberty and estate of the citizen, that no crime or offence ought to be tried in any other county than that in which it is committed; except in cases of general insurrection in any particular county, when it shall appear to the Judges of the Superior Court, that an impartial trial cannot be had in the county where the offence may be committed, and upon their report, the assembly shall think proper to direct the trial in the nearest county in which an impartial trial can be obtained.

Punishment

XVIII. All penalties ought to be proportioned to the nature of the offence. No wise legislature will affix the same punishment to the crimes of theft, forgery and the like, which they do to those of murder and treason; where the same undistinguishing severity is exerted against all offences; the people are led to forget the real distinction in the crimes themselves, and to commit the most flagrant with as little compunction as they do those of the lightest dye: For the same reason a multitude of sanguinary laws is both impolitic and unjust. The true design of all punishments being to reform, not to exterminate, mankind.

Searches and seizures

XIX. Every subject hath a right to be secure from all unreasonable searches and seizures of his person, his houses, his papers, and all his possessions. All warrants, therefore, are contrary to this right, if the cause or foundation of them be not previously supported by oath, or affirmation; and if the order in the warrant to a civil officer, to make search in suspected places, or to arrest one or more suspected persons, or to seize their property, be not accompanied with a special designation of the persons or objects of search, arrest, or seizure; and no warrant ought to be issued but in cases, and with the formalities prescribed by the laws.

Juries in civil cases

XX. In all controversies concerning property, and in all suits between two or more persons, except in cases in which it has been heretofore otherwise used and practiced, the parties have a right to a trial by jury; and this method of procedure shall be held

CONSTITUTION OF NEW HAMPSHIRE

sacred, unless in causes arising on the high seas, and such as relate to mariners wages, the legislature shall think it necessary hereafter to alter it.

XXI. In order to reap the fullest advantage of the inestimable privilege of the trial by jury, great care ought to be taken that none but qualified persons should be appointed to serve; and such ought to be fully compensated for their travel, time and attendance. *Jurors*

XXII. The Liberty of the Press is essential to the security of freedom in a state; it ought, therefore, to be inviolably preserved. *Liberty of the press*

XXIII. Retrospective laws are highly injurious, oppressive and unjust. No such laws, therefore, should be made, either for the decision of civil causes, or the punishment of offences. *Retroactive laws*

XXIV. A well regulated militia is the proper, natural, and sure defence of a state. *Militia*

XXV. Standing armies are dangerous to liberty, and ought not to be raised or kept up without the consent of the legislature. *Standing armies and subordination of military*

XXVI. In all cases, and at all times, the military ought to be under strict subordination to, and governed by the civil power.

XXVII. No soldier in time of peace, shall be quartered in any house without the consent of the owner; and in time of war, such quarters ought not to be made but by the civil magistrate, in a manner ordained by the legislature. *Quartering of soldiers*

XXVIII. No subsidy, charge, tax, impost or duty shall be established, fixed, laid, or levied, under any pretext whatsoever, without the consent of the people or their representatives in the legislature, or authority derived from that body. *Taxation by the legislature*

XXIX. The power of suspending the laws, or the execution of them, ought never to be exercised but by the legislature, or by authority derived therefrom, to be exercised in such particular cases only as the legislature shall expressly provide for. *Suspension of laws*

XXX. The freedom of deliberation, speech, and debate, in either house of the legislature, is so essential to the rights of the people, that it cannot be the foundation of any action, complaint, or prosecution, in any other court or place whatsoever. *Freedom of speech in the legislature*

XXXI. The legislature ought frequently to assemble for the redress of grievances, for correcting, strengthening and confirming the laws, and for making new ones, as the common good may require. *Legislature to assemble frequently*

XXXII. The people have a right in an orderly and peaceable manner, to assemble and consult upon the common good, give instructions to their representatives; and to request of the legislative body, by way of petition or remonstrance, redress of the wrongs done them, and of the grievances they suffer. *Assembly and petition*

XXXIII. No magistrate or court of law shall demand excessive bail or sureties, impose excessive fines, or inflict cruel or unusual punishments. *Bail, fines, and punishments*

XXXIV. No person can in any case be subjected to law martial, or to any pains, or penalties, by virtue of that law, except those employed in the army or navy, and except the militia in actual service, but by authority of the legislature. *Martial law*

XXXV. It is essential to the preservation of the rights of every individual, his life, liberty, property and character, that there be an impartial interpretation of the laws, and administration of justice. It is the right of every citizen to be tried by judges as *Administration of justice*

Independence of judges — impartial as the lot of humanity will admit. It is therefore not only the best policy, but for the security of the rights of the people, that the judges of the supreme (or superior) judicial court should hold their offices so long as they behave well; and that they should have honorable salaries, ascertained and established by standing laws.

Pensions — XXXVI. Economy being a most essential virtue in all states, especially in a young one; no pension shall be granted, but in consideration of actual services, and such pensions ought to be granted with great caution, by the legislature, and never for more than one year at a time.

Separation of powers — XXXVII. In the government of this state, the three essential powers thereof, to wit, the legislative, executive and judicial, ought to be kept as separate from and independent of each other, as the nature of a free government will admit, or as is consistent with that chain of connection that binds the whole fabric of the constitution in one indissoluble bond of union and amity.

Recurrence to fundamentals — XXXVIII. A frequent recurrence to the fundamental principles of the Constitution, and a constant adherence to justice, moderation, temperance, industry, frugality, and all the social virtues, are indispensably necessary to preserve the blessings of liberty and good government; the people ought, therefore, to have a particular regard to all those principles in the choice of their officers and representatives: and they have a right to require of their law-givers and magistrates, an exact and constant observance of them in the formation and execution of the laws necessary for the good administration of government.

REFERENCES

McClintock, John N. *History of New Hampshire*. Boston: B. B. Russell, 1888. Chaps. 11, 12.

Pillsbury, Hobart. *New Hampshire*. 5 vols. New York: Lewis Historical Publishing Co., 1927-28. I, chaps. 21, 22.

Stackpole, Everett S. *History of New Hampshire*. 4 vols. New York: American Historical Society, 1916. II, chap. 8.

Upton, Richard F. *Revolutionary New Hampshire*. Hanover: Dartmouth College Publications, 1936.

XXX. NORTHWEST ORDINANCE
1787

The Northwest Ordinance contains the first bill of rights enacted by the federal government of the United States. More important, it established as part of the colonial policy of the United States the principle that the settlers of uninhabited territories should enjoy the same personal liberties as the citizens of the parent country. In this respect the Northwest Ordinance is comparable to the Virginia Charter of 1606[1] which had announced that principle as one feature of English colonial administration. *Origins*

The general statement in the Virginia Charter that the colonists should enjoy the liberties, franchises, and immunities of natural-born subjects was the counterpart of the detailed list of rights found in the Northwest Ordinance. During the one hundred eighty years which separated the two documents, the practice of listing the essential liberties of the individual in a bill of rights had become a familiar feature of Anglo-American law. In addition, a number of new rights had become established as part of the law during that time.

The disposition of the vast territory west of the Appalachians had been a subject of dispute even before the American Revolution. The charters of several colonies gave rise to conflicting claims over those lands. Following the Treaty of Paris in 1763, the king issued a proclamation which cast doubt on the validity of all claims made by the colonies. During the Revolution, the controversy was resumed by the states. *Territorial disputes*

Seven states—New York, Massachusetts, Connecticut, Virginia, North Carolina, South Carolina, and Georgia—laid claim to the western lands. The other six states contended that the territory should be used for the

[1] See pp. 32-46.

387

benefit of all the states under the direction of Congress. Of the states having no western claims, Maryland took the most determined position. It refused to agree to the Articles of Confederation until all claims to western lands had been given up. An additional incentive for the states to surrender their claims was furnished by Congress' resolution of October, 1780. Congress promised that all ceded lands would be settled and formed into distinct republican states which would become members of the Union with the same rights of sovereignty, freedom, and independence as the other states. Expenses incurred by the states in defending the western territory during the war were to be reimbursed by Congress when the lands were ceded.

Cessions by the states

In 1780 New York agreed to give up its claims. Virginia, whose claims were based not only upon its charter but also on the achievements of George Rogers Clark, agreed in 1781 to make a cession. Virginia's first offer was coupled with conditions which were unacceptable to Congress, but it later surrendered its title unconditionally. The other states, in turn, agreed to yield their lands. Connecticut, however, refused to relinquish its claim to the Western Reserve until 1800.

The ordinances of 1784 and 1785

In March, 1784, shortly after the Virginia cession, Thomas Jefferson introduced in Congress an ordinance for the government of the lands "ceded or to be ceded." The ordinance provided for the establishment of a temporary government and contemplated the eventual admission of new states into the Union on terms of equality with the older members. Ultimate control of the government was to be vested in Congress, but the settlers were, from the first, to be given a large measure of self-government. Jefferson's plan contained several important principles: (1) The new states should forever remain a part of the United States; (2) they should be subject to Congress and the Articles of Confederation; (3) they should pay their share of the revolutionary debts; (4) their governments should be republican in form; and (5) after 1800 slavery should be abolished.[2] Only six states supported Jefferson's proposal to abolish slavery, and so it was defeated.

The ordinance of 1784, as amended, was passed by Congress but it never went into effect. Another ordinance, enacted the next year, embodied a surveying system for the division of the territory into new states.

The ordinance of 1787

Although the ordinance of 1787 was based on the work of many years, it was drafted and passed by Congress during a burst of activity in July, 1787. The immediate motive for the document was furnished by officers of

[2] Frederic L. Paxson, *History of the American Frontier, 1763-1893* (Boston, 1924), 62.

the Ohio Company, which had been organized in 1786 for the purpose of purchasing land and promoting the settlement of the west. Dr. Manasseh Cutler, one of the company's directors, came to Congress prepared to buy millions of acres of land. The attractive prospect of an immediate revenue induced Congress to take action, and the ordinance was approved on July 13, soon after Cutler's offer had been received.

The Northwest Ordinance set forth the method by which the government of the territory was transferred from the hands of Congress to sovereign states organized on a republican basis by the settlers of the territory. At first, all governmental functions were to be under the direction of a governor, secretary, and three judges appointed by Congress. *General Significance* *Republican form of government*

The settlers were given the right to participate in the affairs of government as soon as there were five thousand free male inhabitants of full age. At that time a legislative assembly, which was to include representatives elected by the people, was to be formed with power to make laws "not repugnant to the principles and articles in this ordinance established and declared." The representatives were also given power to nominate members of the council. The territory was not represented in Congress, but it was allowed to send a delegate who was given the right to speak in that body.

Finally, new states were to be admitted to the Union "on an equal footing with the original States" whenever there were sixty thousand inhabitants. The new states were authorized to frame their own constitutions, subject only to the restriction that "the constitution and government, so to be formed, shall be republican, and in conformity to the principles contained in these articles."

Unlike the Constitution of the United States, which was then being framed by the Federal Convention, the Northwest Ordinance contained a bill of rights as part of the "articles of compact between the original States and the people" of the territory. The ordinances of 1784 and 1785 had not contained bills of rights. These provisions were probably included in the ordinance of 1787 as an inducement to prospective settlers. *Other liberties of the people*

The specific rights listed by the ordinance had already appeared in many state constitutions and declarations of rights enacted by the original states. By carrying these concepts of liberty from the earlier state documents to the territories, the Northwest Ordinance was a source of the liberties established by the constitutions of the states which were later admitted to the Union.

The delegates in the Federal Convention, meeting at Philadelphia to frame *Effects*

New states   the Constitution, were, of course, aware of the enactment by Congress of the Northwest Ordinance. On August 18, 1787, James Madison of Virginia proposed the following additions to the powers of Congress as set forth in the report of the Committee of Detail: "To dispose of the unappropriated lands of the U. States. To institute temporary Governments for New States arising therein."[3] This language was expanded by a motion made on August 30 by Gouverneur Morris of Pennsylvania. By Morris' motion the disposition and government of territories was placed under the control of Congress. This power now appears in Article IV, section 3, of the Constitution.

The contracts clause   The Northwest Ordinance also had an influence on the development of the clause found in Article I, section 10, of the Constitution, which provides that the states shall pass no law impairing the obligation of contracts. On August 28 Rufus King of Massachusetts made a motion that the states should be prohibited from interfering with private contracts "in the words used in the Ordinance of Congs. establishing new States."[4] Gouverneur Morris objected that the proposal went too far, and that there were a thousand laws, such as those relating to bringing actions, which affected contracts. James Wilson of Pennsylvania and Madison favored King's proposal.

A substitute clause proposed by John Rutledge of South Carolina was adopted. That clause declared that the states should not "pass bills of attainder [or] retrospective laws."[5] The report of the Committee of Style, presented September 12, changed this to prevent the states from enacting "any bill of attainder, [or] ex post facto laws, [or] laws altering or impairing the obligation of contracts."[6] An amendment made September 14 changed this to read "any bill of attainder, ex post facto law, or law impairing the obligation of contracts."[7] The next day George Mason moved to strike out the ex post facto clause and prohibit the states from "impairing the obligation of previous contracts."[8] Mason's proposal was refused, and the contracts clause now appears in the form established on September 14.

[3] Charles C. Tansill (ed.), *Documents Illustrative of the Formation of the Union of the American States*, 69th Cong., 1st Sess., 1927, House Doc. 398, 563.
[4] *Ibid.*, 628.
[5] *Ibid.*, 629.
[6] *Ibid.*, 707.
[7] *Ibid.*, 728.
[8] Max Farrand (ed.), *The Records of the Federal Convention of 1787* (New Haven, 1937), IV, 59.

NORTHWEST ORDINANCE

Probably the most famous clause in the Northwest Ordinance is Article VI, which prohibited slavery in the territory. This clause, of course, was in accordance with Jefferson's ideals. No comparable provision appeared in either the Constitution or the Bill of Rights. Slavery was abolished throughout the United States, however, in 1865 by the thirteenth amendment.[9] The language of that amendment is similar to this provision of the Northwest Ordinance.

Prohibition of slavery

[9] See p. 436.

NORTHWEST ORDINANCE[10]

July 13, 1787

AN ORDINANCE FOR THE GOVERNMENT OF THE TERRITORY OF THE UNITED STATES NORTHWEST OF THE RIVER OHIO

Territory temporarily to be one district

Section 1. *Be it ordained by the United States in Congress assembled,* That the said Territory, for the purpose of temporary government, be one district, subject, however, to be divided into two districts, as future circumstances may, in the opinion of Congress, make it expedient.

Descent and distribution of estates

Sec. 2. *Be it ordained by the authority aforesaid,* That the estates both of resident and non-resident proprietors in the said territory, dying intestate, shall descend to, and be distributed among, their children and the descendants of a deceased child in equal parts, the descendants of a deceased child or grandchild to take the share of their deceased parent in equal parts among them; and where there shall be no children or descendants, then in equal parts to the next of kin, in equal degree; and among collaterals, the children of a deceased brother or sister of the intestate shall have, in equal parts among them, their deceased parent's share; and there shall, in no case, be a distinction between kindred of the whole and half blood; saving in all cases to the widow of the intestate, her third part of the real estate for life, and one-third part of the personal estate; and this law relative to descents and dower, shall remain in full force until altered by the legislature of the district. And until the governor and judges shall adopt laws as hereinafter mentioned, estates in the said territory may be devised or bequeathed by wills in writing, signed and sealed by him or her in whom the estate may be, (being of full age,) and attested by three witnesses; and real estates may be conveyed by lease and release, or bargain and sale, signed, sealed, and delivered by the person, being of full age, in whom the estate may be, and attested by two witnesses, provided such wills be duly proved, and such conveyances be acknowledged, or the execution thereof duly proved, and be recorded within one year after proper magistrates, courts, and registers, shall be appointed for that purpose; and personal property may be transferred by delivery, saving, however, to the French and Canadian inhabitants, and other settlers of the Kaskaskies, Saint Vincents, and the neighboring villages, who have heretofore professed themselves citizens of Virginia, their laws and customs now in force among them, relative to the descent and conveyance of property.

[10] Tansill, *op. cit.,* 47-54.

NORTHWEST ORDINANCE

Sec. 3. *Be it ordained by the authority aforesaid,* That there shall be appointed, from time to time, by Congress, a governor, whose commission shall continue in force for the term of three years, unless sooner revoked by Congress; he shall reside in the district, and have a freehold estate therein, in one thousand acres of land, while in the exercise of his office. *— Governor*

Sec. 4. There shall be appointed from time to time, by Congress, a secretary, whose commission shall continue in force for four years, unless sooner revoked; he shall reside in the district, and have a freehold estate therein, in five hundred acres of land, while in the exercise of his office. It shall be his duty to keep and preserve the acts and laws passed by the legislature, and the public records of the district, and the proceedings of the governor in his executive department, and transmit authentic copies of such acts and proceedings every six months to the Secretary of Congress. There shall also be appointed a court, to consist of three judges, any two of whom to form a court, who shall have a common-law jurisdiction and reside in the district, and have each therein a freehold estate, in five hundred acres of land, while in the exercise of their offices; and their commissions shall continue in force during good behavior. *— Secretary / Court*

Sec. 5. The governor and judges, or a majority of them, shall adopt and publish in the district such laws of the original States, criminal and civil, as may be necessary, and best suited to the circumstances of the district, and report them to Congress from time to time, which laws shall be in force in the district until the organization of the general assembly therein, unless disapproved of by Congress; but afterwards the legislature shall have authority to alter them as they shall think fit. *— Temporary provision for laws*

Sec. 6. The governor, for the time being, shall be commander-in-chief of the militia, appoint and commission all officers in the same below the rank of general officers; all general officers shall be appointed and commissioned by Congress. *— Militia*

Sec. 7. Previous to the organization of the general assembly the governor shall appoint such magistrates, and other civil officers, in each county or township, as he shall find necessary for the preservation of the peace and good order in the same. After the general assembly shall be organized the powers and duties of magistrates and other civil officers shall be regulated and defined by the said assembly; but all magistrates and other civil officers, not herein otherwise directed, shall, during the continuance of this temporary government, be appointed by the governor. *— Magistrates and other officers*

Sec. 8. For the preveniton of crimes, and injuries, the laws to be adopted or made shall have force in all parts of the district, and for the execution of process, criminal and civil, the governor shall make proper divisions thereof; and he shall proceed, from time to time, as circumstances may require, to lay out the parts of the district in which the Indian titles shall have been extinguished, into counties and townships, subject, however, to such alterations as may thereafter be made by the legislature. *— Applicability of laws / Counties and townships*

Sec. 9. So soon as there shall be five thousand free male inhabitants, of full age, in the district, upon giving proof thereof to the governor, they shall receive authority, with time and place, to elect representatives from their counties or townships, to *— Representation in the assembly*

Number of representatives represent them in the general assembly: *Provided,* That for every five hundred free male inhabitants there shall be one representative, and so on, progressively, with the number of free male inhabitants, shall the right of representation increase, until the number of representatives shall amount to twenty-five; after which the number and proportion of representatives shall be regulated by the legislature: *Provided,*

Qualifications of representatives That no person be eligible or qualified to act as a representative, unless he shall have been a citizen of one of the United States three years, and be a resident in the district, or unless he shall have resided in the district three years; and, in either case, shall likewise hold in his own right, in fee-simple, two hundred acres of land within the same: *Provided also,* That a freehold in fifty acres of land in the district, having been a citizen of one of the States, and being resident in the district, or the like freehold and two years' residence in the district, shall be necessary to qualify a man as an elector of a representative.

Term of office of representatives Sec. 10. The representatives thus elected shall serve for the term of two years; and in case of the death of a representative, or removal from office, the governor shall issue a writ to the county or township, for which he was a member, to elect another in his stead, to serve for the residue of the term.

General Assembly
Legislative Council Sec. 11. The general assembly, or legislature, shall consist of the governor, legislative council, and a house of representatives. The legislative council shall consist of five members, to continue in office five years, unless sooner removed by Congress; any three of whom to be a quorum; and the members of the council shall be nominated and appointed in the following manner, to wit: As soon as representatives shall be elected the governor shall appoint a time and place for them to meet together, and when met they shall nominate ten persons, resident in the district, and each possessed of a freehold in five hundred acres of land, and return their names to Congress, five of whom Congress shall appoint and commission to serve as aforesaid; and whenever a vacancy shall happen in the Council, by death or removal from office, the house of representatives shall nominate two persons, qualified as aforesaid, for each vacancy, and return their names to Congress, one of whom Congress shall appoint and commission for the residue of the term; and every five years, four months at least before the expiration of the time of service of the members of the council, the said house shall nominate ten persons, qualified as aforesaid, and return their names to Congress, five of whom Congress shall appoint and commission to serve as members of the council five years,

Powers unless sooner removed. And the governor, legislative council, and house of representatives shall have authority to make laws in all cases for the good government of the district, not repugnant to the principles and articles in this ordinance established and

Assent to bills by governor declared. And all bills, having passed by a majority in the house, and by a majority in the council, shall be referred to the governor for his assent; but no bill, or legislative act whatever, shall be of any force without his assent. The governor shall have power to convene, prorogue, and dissolve the general assembly when, in his opinion, it shall be expedient.

Sec. 12. The governor, judges, legislative council, secretary, and such other officers as Congress shall appoint in the district, shall take an oath or affirmation of fidelity, and of office; the governor before the President of Congress, and all other officers before the governor. As soon as a legislature shall be formed in the district, the council and house assembled, in one room, shall have authority, by joint ballot, to elect a delegate to Congress, who shall have a seat in Congress, with a right of debating, but not of voting, during this temporary government. *Oath of office*

Delegate to Congress

Sec. 13. And for extending the fundamental principles of civil and religious liberty, which form the basis whereon these republics, their laws and constitutions, are erected; to fix and establish those principles as the basis of all laws, constitutions, and governments, which forever hereafter shall be formed in the said territory; to provide, also, for the establishment of States, and permanent government therein, and for their admission to a share in the Federal councils on an equal footing with the original States, at as early periods as may be consistent with the general interest: *Preamble to articles of compact*

Sec. 14. It is hereby ordained and declared, by the authority aforesaid, that the following articles shall be considered as articles of compact, between the original States and the people and States in the said territory, and forever remain unalterable, unless by common consent, to wit: **Articles of Compact**

ARTICLE I

No person, demeaning himself in a peaceable and orderly manner, shall ever be molested on account of his mode of worship, or religious sentiments, in the said territory. *Religious liberty*

ARTICLE II

The inhabitants of the said territory shall always be entitled to the benefits of the writs of *habeas corpus,* and of the trial by jury; of a proportionate representation of the people in the legislature, and of judicial proceedings according to the course of the common law. All persons shall be bailable, unless for capital offences, where the proof shall be evident, or the presumption great All fines shall be moderate; and no cruel or unusual punishment shall be inflicted. No man shall be deprived of his liberty or property, but by the judgment of his peers, or the law of the land, and should the public exigencies make it necessary, for the common preservation, to take any person's property, or to demand his particular services, full compensation shall be made for the same. And, in the just preservation of rights and property, it is understood and declared, that no law ought ever to be made or have force in the said territory, that shall, in any manner whatever, interfere with or affect private contracts, or engagements, *bona fide,* and without fraud previously formed. *Habeas corpus; trial by jury; proportionate representation; common law; bail; fines; punishments; judgment of peers; taking of property; contracts*

ARTICLE III

Education

Indian affairs

Religion, morality, and knowledge being necessary to good government and the happiness of mankind, schools and the means of education shall forever be encouraged. The utmost good faith shall always be observed towards the Indians; their lands and property shall never be taken from them without their consent; and in their property, rights, and liberty they never shall be invaded or disturbed unless in just and lawful wars authorized by Congress; but laws founded in justice and humanity shall, from time to time, be made, for preventing wrongs being done to them, and for preserving peace and friendship with them.

ARTICLE IV

Applicability of Articles of Confederation and other laws

Debts and expenses of government

Taxes

Title to land

Navigable waters

The said territory, and the States which may be formed therein, shall forever remain a part of this confederacy of the United States of America, subject to the articles of Confederation, and to such alterations therein as shall be constitutionally made; and to all the acts and ordinances of the United States in Congress assembled, conformable thereto. The inhabitants and settlers in the said territory shall be subject to pay a part of the Federal debts, contracted, or to be contracted, and a proportional part of the expenses of government to be apportioned on them by Congress, according to the same common rule and measure by which apportionments thereof shall be made on the other States, and the taxes for paying their proportion shall be laid and levied by the authority and direction of the legislatures of the district, or districts, or new States, as in the original States, within the time agreed upon by the United States in Congress assembled. The legislatures of those districts, or new States, shall never interfere with the primary disposal of the soil by the United States in Congress assembled, nor with any regulations Congress may find necessary for securing the title in such soil to the *bona-fide* purchasers. No tax shall be imposed on lands the property of the United States; and in no case shall non-resident proprietors be taxed higher than residents. The navigable waters leading into the Mississippi and Saint Lawrence, and the carrying places between the same, shall be common highways, and forever free, as well to the inhabitants of the said territory as to the citizens of the United States, and those of any other States that may be admitted into the confederacy, without any tax, impost, or duty therefor.

ARTICLE V

Creation of new states

There shall be formed in the said territory not less than three nor more than five States; and the boundaries of the States, as soon as Virginia shall alter her act of cession and consent to the same, shall become fixed and established as follows, to wit:

NORTHWEST ORDINANCE

The western State, in the said territory, shall be bounded by the Mississippi, the Ohio, and the Wabash Rivers; a direct line drawn from the Wabash and Post Vincents, due north, to the territorial line between the United States and Canada; and by the said territorial line to the Lake of the Woods and Mississippi. The middle State shall be bounded by the said direct line, the Wabash from Post Vincents to the Ohio, by the Ohio, by a direct line drawn due north from the mouth of the Great Miami to the said territorial line, and by the said territorial line. The eastern State shall be bounded by the last-mentioned direct line, the Ohio, Pennsylvania, and the said territorial line: *Provided, however,* And it is further understood and declared, that the boundaries of these three States shall be subject so far to be altered, that, if Congress shall hereafter find it expedient, they shall have authority to form one or two States in that part of the said territory which lies north of an east and west line drawn through the southerly bend or extreme of Lake Michigan. And whenever any of the said States shall have sixty thousand free inhabitants therein, such State shall be admitted by its delegates, into the Congress of the United States, on an equal footing with the original States, in all respects whatever; and shall be at liberty to form a permanent constitution and State government: *Provided,* The constitution and government, so to be formed, shall be republican, and in conformity to the principles contained in these articles, and, so far as it can be consistent with the general interest of the confederacy, such admission shall be allowed at an earlier period, and when there may be a less number of free inhabitants in the State than sixty thousand. *[Alteration of boundaries of states]* *[Republican government]*

ARTICLE VI

There shall be neither slavery nor involuntary servitude in the said territory, otherwise than in the punishment of crimes, whereof the party shall have been duly convicted: *Provided always,* That any person escaping into the same, from whom labor or service is lawfully claimed in any one of the original States, such fugitive may be lawfully reclaimed, and conveyed to the person claiming his or her labor or service as aforesaid. *[Slavery prohibited]*

Be it ordained by the authority aforesaid, That the resolutions of the 23d of April, 1784, relative to the subject of this ordinance, be, and the same are hereby, repealed, and declared null and void. *[Resolutions of April 23, 1784]*

Done by the United States, in Congress assembled, the 13th day of July, in the year of our Lord 1787, and of their sovereignty and independence the twelfth.

SOURCES OF OUR LIBERTIES

REFERENCES

Hinsdale, B. A. *The Old Northwest*. Rev. ed. New York: Silver, Burdett & Co., 1899.
Hulbert, Archer B. *The Records of the Original Proceedings of the Ohio Company*. Marietta: Marietta Historical Commission, 1917.
McLaughlin, Andrew C. *The Confederation and the Constitution, 1783-1789*. (Vol. X of *The American Nation: A History*.) New York: Harper & Bros., 1905. Chap. 7.
Merriam, John M. "The Legislative History of the Ordinance of 1787," *Proceedings of the American Antiquarian Society*, V, 303-42. New ser.; Worcester: American Antiquarian Society, 1889.
Paxson, Frederic L. *History of the American Frontier, 1763-1893*. Boston: Houghton Mifflin Co., 1924. Chaps. 5-7.

XXXI. THE CONSTITUTION OF THE UNITED STATES
1787

The first major step in forming a permanent union of all the states was taken by the Continental Congress. On June 11, 1776, the same day that the committee was appointed to frame the Declaration of Independence, Congress also decided to appoint a committee to "prepare and digest the form of a confederation to be entered into between these colonies."[1] The plan presented by the committee was debated by Congress from time to time for more than a year. The Articles of Confederation,[2] which resulted from this discussion, was agreed to by Congress in November, 1777. Although the Articles of Confederation was not approved by all the states until March 1, 1781, Congress used it as a guide before that time.

Origins

The Articles of Confederation

By the Articles of Confederation the states entered "a firm league of friendship with each other, for their common defence, the security of their Liberties, and their mutual and general welfare." The document contained only a few provisions designed to protect individual liberties. One of these provided that "the free inhabitants of each of these states, paupers, vagabonds and fugitives from justice excepted, shall be entitled to all privileges and immunities of free citizens in the several states; and the people of each state shall have free ingress and regress to and from any other state, and shall enjoy therein all the privileges of trade and commerce . . . as the inhabitants thereof . . ." Each state was required to give full faith and credit to the records, acts, and judicial proceedings of the courts of the other states. In addition, it was provided that members of Congress should have freedom of

---

[1] *Journals of the American Congress, 1774-1788* (Washington, 1823), I, 370.
[2] Text in Charles C. Tansill (ed.), *Documents Illustrative of the Formation of the Union of the American States*, 69th Cong., 1st Sess., 1927, House Doc. 398, 27-37.

speech and debate in that body and that they should be free from arrest while going to or from Congress, except for treason, felony, or breach of the peace.

Deficiencies of the Articles

The Articles of Confederation contemplated that the states should assume the primary responsibility for the protection of the liberties of their citizens. Only a few powers were given to the central government. That government was so weak that special restrictions upon its powers in favor of individual liberties were probably unnecessary. State powers, however, were largely unimpaired. It was provided: "Each state retains its sovereignty, freedom, and independence, and every Power, Jurisdiction and right, which is not by this confederation expressly delegated to the United States, in Congress assembled." State sovereignty was also protected by the provision that each state should have one vote in Congress. Important questions were to be determined by a two-thirds vote and proposed amendments to the Articles had to be determined by the unanimous consent of all the states.

The kind of government provided by the Articles of Confederation was too weak to survive for long. Except for special committees established by Congress, there was no executive department. The central government also had no permanent judicial branch. Congress had to rely for funds upon the good will of the states, and there was no power to regulate commerce and prevent discriminatory trade practices by the states.

Annapolis Convention

Problems of trade prompted the movement to create "a more perfect Union." In January, 1786, the Virginia House of Burgesses proposed a meeting of commissioners from the states "to take into consideration the trade of the United States; to examine the relative situations and trade of the said States; to consider how far a uniform system in their commercial regulations may be necessary to their common interest and their permanent harmony...."[3]

Despite widespread interest in the proposal, only five states—New York, New Jersey, Pennsylvania, Delaware, and Virginia—were represented at the trade convention. Delegates of those states met at Annapolis in September, 1786. Of the twelve delegates who attended the Annapolis Convention, seven were later members of the Federal Convention. These were Edmund Randolph and James Madison of Virginia, Alexander Hamilton of New York, John Dickinson, George Read, and Richard Bassett of Delaware, and William Houston of New Jersey.

[3] *Ibid.*, 38.

THE CONSTITUTION OF THE UNITED STATES

The Annapolis Convention remained in session for only a few days and did little to solve the trade problems. Before it dissolved, however, it made a proposal which led directly to the Federal Convention of 1787. It proposed:

> the appointment of Commissioners, to meet at Philadelphia on the second Monday in May next, to take into consideration the situation of the United States, to devise such further provisions as shall appear to them necessary to render the constitution of the Foederal Government adequate to the exigencies of the Union; and to report such an Act for that purpose to the United States in Congress assembled, as when agreed to, by them, and afterwards confirmed by the Legislatures of every State, will effectually provide for the same.[4]

Copies of this resolution were sent to the states and to Congress.

The Federal Convention of 1787

Congress followed the recommendation of the Annapolis Convention. In February, 1787, it recommended that the states appoint delegates to meet at Philadelphia on the second Monday in May. The Convention was to meet, however, "for the sole and express purpose of revising the Articles of Confederation and reporting to Congress and the several legislatures such alterations and provisions therein as shall when agreed to in Congress and confirmed by the states render the federal constitution adequate to the exigencies of Government & the preservation of the Union."[5]

Six states—Delaware, Georgia, New Jersey, North Carolina, Pennsylvania, and Virginia—appointed delegates to the Convention even before Congress had acted. By June, 1787, Maryland, Connecticut, Massachusetts, New Hampshire, New York, and South Carolina also had appointed delegates. Rhode Island alone was not represented.

The credentials of the delegates from Massachusetts and New York followed the language used by Congress, and expressly restricted the objectives to be sought to the revision of the Articles of Confederation. The delegates from Delaware were instructed to agree to nothing which would deprive each state of an equal vote in Congress. The other states authorized their delegates to discuss and decide upon the best means of remedying the defects of the Union and making it adequate to meet the exigencies of government. Altogether, fifty-five delegates attended the Convention. Thirty-nine of these signed the finished Constitution.

On May 14, 1787, the day set for the first meeting of the Convention, not enough delegates for a quorum had arrived in Philadelphia. By the 25th seven states were represented, and the Convention was organized. George

[4] *Ibid.,* 43.   [5] *Ibid.,* 46.

Washington's name was placed in nomination to preside over the body, and he was unanimously elected President.

Plans presented to the Convention

The first major step taken in the framing of the Constitution was the introduction on May 29 of the Virginia Plan,[6] a series of fifteen resolutions presented on behalf of the Virginia delegation by Edmund Randolph, governor of that state. The Virginia Plan was expanded and developed step by step. It was from these resolutions that the Constitution grew.

In opposition to the Virginia Plan was the New Jersey Plan, proposed on June 15 by William Paterson.[7] The New Jersey Plan was designed to protect the interests of the small states. It proposed to do no more than revise the Articles of Confederation, and it did not embody the principle of proportional representation in the legislature, the feature of the Virginia Plan which aroused the strongest opposition of the small states. Various ideas about what form the federal government should take were also presented by individuals. The two most notable individual contributions were the plans of government proposed by Charles Pinckney of South Carolina[8] and Alexander Hamilton.[9]

Committees of the Convention

Some of the most important work of the Convention was performed by committees to which were assigned specific tasks. On July 24 a Committee of Detail was appointed to prepare a draft of the Constitution based on the resolutions which had been adopted by the Convention. The members of this important committee were Oliver Ellsworth of Connecticut, Nathaniel Gorham of Massachusetts, Edmund Randolph of Virginia, John Rutledge of South Carolina, and James Wilson of Pennsylvania. The Committee of Detail reported its draft of the Constitution on August 6. This document served as the basis for the further deliberations of the Convention.

On August 31 one delegate from each state was appointed to a Committee on the Unfinished Parts of the Constitution. The function of that committee was to make recommendations on matters which had been postponed or had not been taken up by the Convention.

Once agreement on all essential points had been reached by the Convention, a Committee of Style and Arrangement was appointed for the purpose of preparing the final draft of the Constitution. The Committee of Style and Arrangement was given the task of drafting the document in appropriate

---

[6] Variant texts in *ibid.*, 116-19, 953-63; Max Farrand (ed.), *The Records of the Federal Convention of 1787* (New Haven, 1937), I, 20-23.

[7] Variant texts in Tansill, *op. cit.*, 204-7, 967-78; Farrand, *op. cit.*, I, 242-45, and III, 611-16.

[8] Variant texts in Tansill, *op. cit.*, 964-66; Farrand, *op. cit.*, III, 595-609.

[9] Variant texts in Tansill, *op. cit*, 979-88; Farrand, *op. cit.*, III, 617-30.

language and organizing it properly; it had no authority to make changes in the substance of the Constitution. The members of that committee were William Samuel Johnson of Connecticut, Alexander Hamilton of New York, Rufus King of Massachusetts, James Madison of Virginia, and Gouverneur Morris of Pennsylvania. The Committee of Style and Arrangement made its report on September 12. The Constitution was agreed to on the 15th. It was signed on the 17th, and the Convention adjourned.

Proposals for a bill of rights came late in the Convention. The members of the Convention did not doubt that the citizen was entitled to certain liberties such as those which appeared in the state declarations of rights. These liberties were not controversial; there was, therefore, no reason to raise the subject at an early stage of the proceedings. More controversial matters occupied the attention of the delegates.

Proposals for a bill of rights

It is possible that the delegates were at first unaware of all the implications of the great change that was being made in the character of the federal government. The central government provided by the Articles of Confederation was weak and often powerless. Under that government the state bills of rights were perfectly capable of adequately protecting individual liberties. The Federal Convention, however, did much more than merely amend the Articles of Confederation. It replaced the Articles by a document conferring much greater powers on the central government. Luther Martin of Maryland wrote in the *Maryland Journal* in March, 1788: "The more the system advanced the more I was impressed with the necessity of not merely attempting to secure a few rights, but of digesting and forming a complete Bill of Rights including those of States and individuals."[10]

None of the plans presented to the Convention offered a bill of rights.[11] The resolutions of the Convention which were submitted to the Committee of Detail on July 26 likewise did not contain a bill of rights. The first individual liberty to be embodied in the Constitution appeared in the report of the Committee of Detail, presented August 6: "The trial of all criminal offences (except in cases of impeachments) shall be in the State where they shall be committed; and shall be by Jury."[12]

---

[10] Quoted in Charles Warren, *The Making of the Constitution* (Boston, 1929), 508n.

[11] A reconstructed version of the plan presented May 29 by Charles Pinckney provides for the privilege of the writ of habeas corpus and contains guarantees of trial by jury in both criminal and civil cases, freedom of the press, and a prohibition of religious tests as qualifications for offices of trust or emolument. It is questionable, however, whether these provisions, included in Pinckney's proposals of August 20, also appeared in his original plan. Farrand, *op. cit.*, III, 609 and note.

[12] Tansill, *op. cit.*, 479.

The first attempt to secure a comprehensive statement of the liberties of the citizen was made by Charles Pinckney. On August 20 he submitted a series of thirteen propositions for the consideration of the Convention. The following rights were included:

> The privileges and benefit of the Writ of Habeas corpus shall be enjoyed in this Government in the most expeditious and ample manner; and shall not be suspended by the Legislature except upon the most urgent and pressing occasions, and for a limited time not exceeding   months.
>
> The liberty of the Press shall be inviolably preserved
>
> No troops shall be kept up in time of peace, but by consent of the Legislature
>
> The military shall always be subordinate to the Civil power, and no grants of money shall be made by the Legislature for supporting military Land forces, for more than one year at a time
>
> No soldier shall be quartered in any House in time of peace without consent of the owner.
>
> . . . .
>
> No religious test or qualification shall ever be annexed to any oath of office under the authority of the U.S.[13]

Pinckney's proposals were referred to the Committee of Detail without debate, and that committee made no report on them.

So far it might be said that the Convention had merely ignored or postponed consideration of a bill of rights. Many members of the Convention, however, actually did not want a bill of rights. They believed that provisions to safeguard individual liberties were originally created to protect the subject from rulers claiming absolute powers and that such provisions had no place in a constitution founded upon the will of the people themselves.

Toward the close of the Convention the question was squarely presented. The statements of the delegates at that time showed the same division of opinion which was to become so prominent during the struggle for ratification of the Constitution.

On September 12 Hugh Williamson of North Carolina recommended a guarantee of the right of trial by jury in civil cases. He was supported by Elbridge Gerry, who argued that the jury system was necessary to protect the people from corrupt judges. Nathaniel Gorham opposed the idea, saying that it would be impossible to prepare a provision which would differentiate accurately between equity proceedings, in which juries were not used, and other

---

[13] *Ibid.*, 572.

kinds of civil proceedings. He stated that the legislature could be trusted to provide a suitable law on the subject. George Mason, framer of the Virginia Declaration of Rights of 1776, said that he appreciated the difficulty mentioned by Gorham but that he believed that a general provision on the subject could be framed.

Mason also said that the Constitution should be prefaced by a bill of rights and that he would gladly second a motion for that purpose. It was Mason's opinion that a bill of rights could be prepared in a few hours with the aid of the state declarations. Gerry moved that a committee be appointed to frame a bill of rights, and Mason seconded the motion.

Roger Sherman of Connecticut spoke against the motion. He argued that the state declarations of rights were not to be repealed by the Constitution and that they were sufficient to protect the liberties of the citizen. Mason pointed out, however, that the laws of the United States, being the supreme law of the land, might override the state constitutions. When Gerry's motion was put to a vote, all the states opposed it except Massachusetts, which was recorded as absent.[14]

A final attempt was later made to obtain approval of three of the principles found in the state bills of rights. Although he was not willing absolutely to condemn standing armies, Mason moved that a clause be added to the provision authorizing Congress to organize, arm, and discipline the militia: "And that the liberties of the people may be better secured against the danger of standing armies in time of peace."[15] Pinckney and Gerry proposed provisions to secure the liberty of the press and the right of trial by jury in civil cases. All three proposals failed.

Although the movement to frame a formal bill of rights to accompany the Constitution was unsuccessful, the document nevertheless contains many provisions recognizing important liberties of the citizen. In this respect, the Constitution was similar to several earlier state constitutions which were not accompanied by formal bills of rights. The bodies of those constitutions also recognized specific rights of the individual.[16]

Historical Origins of the Individual Liberties Secured by the Constitution

Foremost among the liberties secured by the Constitution is the right of representative government. The right of the people to participate in law-making and the levying of taxes had been established in England as early as

Representative government

[14] *Ibid.*, 716.
[15] *Ibid.*, 725.
[16] See pp. 309-10.

the thirteenth century.[17] That right was brought to America in 1618 by the farsighted leaders of the London Company.[18] The right of the people to participate in the decisions of government was recognized by a number of documents framed by the colonists themselves, such as the Mayflower Compact[19] and the Fundamental Orders of Connecticut.[20] The right of the people to participate in the legislative process and choose the officers of government was also recognized by many royal charters. During the seventeenth and eighteenth centuries the legislative assembly, elected by the people, became the characteristic feature of American government.

Interferences by Great Britain with colonial lawmaking processes and denial of the right of the colonists to participate in the levying of taxes furnished one of the strongest motives for the American Revolution.[21] At the time of the Revolution the new states formed governments based upon the principles of republican government and founded upon the will of the people.

Under the Constitution of the United States ultimate power rests with the people. Members of Congress were to be chosen by the state legislatures and by the people themselves.[22] The President and the Vice-President were elected by special electors chosen in accordance with the directions of the state legislatures.

Trial by jury   Article III of the Constitution secured the right of trial by jury. The origins of that right antedate Magna Carta.[23] Trial by jury was one of the "rights of Englishmen" brought to America by the earliest colonists, and the jury system became a fundamental feature of the administration of American justice. Infringements of that right by Great Britain furnished another motive for the American Revolution,[24] and it was safeguarded by the bills of rights adopted by the states prior to the Constitution.

Treason   The restrictive definition of the crime of treason found in Article III of the Constitution is an important safeguard of the rights of persons whose

[17] See pp. 24-25.
[18] See pp. 46-54.
[19] See pp. 55-61.
[20] See pp. 115-24.
[21] See pp. 275-78.
[22] Direct election of senators was established in 1913 by the seventeenth amendment. See pp. 437-38.
[23] See pp. 7-9.
[24] See pp. 267-68, 281-82.

political conduct does not conform with the ideals of the majority for the time being. English statutes since the fourteenth century have furnished the documentary antecedents of the provision. The Constitution, however, is more zealous of the rights of the individual than were its English antecedents.[25]

The Constitution also protected the privilege of the writ of habeas corpus. That writ has been called the most effective safeguard of the right of personal liberty ever devised. The writ of habeas corpus was established in England as a right of the individual near the end of the sixteenth century. A series of English statutes during the seventeenth century strengthened the writ and made it more efficient.[26] In the American colonies the writ was one of the common law rights of the individual. It was protected by several of the state constitutions enacted prior to the Constitution of the United States.

Writ of habeas corpus

The prohibition in Article I of bills of attainder and ex post facto laws recognized rights of the individual which did not become definitely established in Anglo-American law until the eighteenth century.[27] These restrictions on legislative power, however, were considered by the Federal Convention to be so important that the prohibitions were imposed upon the state governments as well as on the federal government.

Bills of attainder and ex post facto laws

[25] See pp. 240-41.
[26] See pp. 189-95.
[27] See pp. 332-37.

THE CONSTITUTION OF THE UNITED STATES[28]

September 17, 1787[29]

Preamble

WE, the people of the United States, in order to form a more perfect Union, establish justice, insure domestic tranquillity, provide for the common defence, promote the general welfare, and secure the blessings of liberty to ourselves and our posterity, do ordain and establish this Constitution for the United States of America.

Legislature

ARTICLE I. § 1. All legislative powers herein granted, shall be vested in a Congress of the United States, which shall consist of a Senate and House of Representatives.

House of Representatives

§ 2. The House of Representatives shall be composed of members chosen every second year by the people of the several States; and the electors in each State shall have the qualifications requisite for electors of the most numerous branch of the State Legislature.

Qualifications of representatives

No person shall be a representative who shall not have attained to the age of twenty-five years, and been seven years a citizen of the United States, and who shall not, when elected, be an inhabitant of that State in which he shall be chosen.[30]

Apportionment

Representatives and direct taxes shall be apportioned among the several States which may be included within this Union, according to their respective numbers, which shall be determined by adding to the whole number of free persons, including those bound to service for a term of years, and excluding Indians not taxed, three fifths of all other persons.[31] The actual enumeration shall be made within three years after the first meeting of the Congress of the United States, and within every subsequent term of ten years, in such manner as they shall by law direct. The number of representatives shall not exceed one for every thirty thousand, but each State shall have at least one representative, and until such enumeration shall be made, the state of New Hampshire shall be entitled to choose three, Massachusetts eight, Rhode Island and

---

[28] 1 U.S. *Statutes at Large* 10.

[29] The Constitution was approved by the Federal Convention on September 17, 1787. Pursuant to Article VII, it became binding on the states that had ratified on June 21, 1788, when New Hampshire, the ninth state, ratified. Tansill, *op. cit.*, 1024. The Constitution was ordered by Congress to be put into operation on September 13, 1788. Edward S. Corwin (ed.), *The Constitution of the United States of America: Analysis and Interpretation*, 82d Cong., 2d Sess., 1953, Senate Doc. 170, 15.

[30] See Amendment XIV, section 3.

[31] See Amendment XIV, section 2.

THE CONSTITUTION OF THE UNITED STATES

Providence Plantations one, Connecticut five, New York six, New Jersey four, Pennsylvania eight, Delaware one, Maryland six, Virginia ten, North Carolina five, South Carolina five, and Georgia three.

When vacancies happen in the representation from any State, the Executive authority thereof shall issue writs of election to fill such vacancies. *Vacancies*

The House of Representatives shall choose their speaker and other officers; and shall have the sole power of impeachment. *Officers; impeachment*

§ 3. The Senate of the United States shall be composed of two Senators from each State, chosen by the Legislature thereof, for six years; and each Senator shall have one vote.[32] *Senate*

Immediately after they shall be assembled, in consequence of the first election, they shall be divided as equally as may be into three classes. The seats of the Senators of the first class shall be vacated at the expiration of the second year, of the second class at the expiration of the fourth year, and of the third class at the expiration of the sixth year, so that one third may be chosen every second year; and if vacancies happen by resignation, or otherwise, during the recess of the Legislature of any State, the Executive thereof may make temporary appointments until the next meeting of the Legislature, which shall then fill such vacancies.[33] *Terms of senators*

No person shall be a Senator who shall not have attained to the age of thirty years, and been nine years a citizen of the United States, and who shall not, when elected, be an inhabitant of that State for which he shall be chosen.[34] *Qualifications of senators*

The Vice President of the United States shall be president of the Senate, but shall have no vote, unless they be equally divided. *Vice-president*

The Senate shall choose their other officers, and also a president *pro tempore,* in the absence of the Vice President, or when he shall exercise the office of President of the United States. *Other officers*

The Senate shall have the sole power to try all impeachments. When sitting for that purpose, they shall be on oath or affirmation. When the President of the United States is tried, the Chief Justice shall preside; and no person shall be convicted without the concurrence of two thirds of the members present. *Impeachments*

Judgment in cases of impeachment shall not extend further than to removal from office, and disqualification to hold and enjoy any office of honour, trust or profit, under the United States; but the party convicted shall nevertheless be liable and subject to indictment, trial, judgment, and punishment according to law.

§ 4. The times, places and manner of holding elections for Senators and Representatives, shall be prescribed in each State by the Legislature thereof; but the Congress may at any time by law make or alter such regulations, except as to the places of choosing Senators. *Time and place of elections*

The Congress shall assemble at least once in every year, and such meeting shall be *Sessions*

---
[32] See Amendment XVII.
[33] See Amendment XVII.
[34] See Amendment XIV, section 3.

on the first Monday in December, unless they shall by law appoint a different day.[35]

Proceedings of Congress

§ 5. Each House shall be the judge of the elections, returns, and qualifications of its own members, and a majority of each shall constitute a quorum to do business; but a smaller number may adjourn from day to day, and may be authorized to compel the attendance of absent members, in such manner, and under such penalties, as each House may provide.

Each House may determine the rules of its proceedings, punish its members for disorderly behaviour, and, with the concurrence of two thirds, expel a member.

Each House shall keep a journal of its proceedings, and from time to time publish the same, excepting such parts as may, in their judgment, require secrecy; and the yeas and nays of the members of either House on any question, shall, at the desire of one fifth of those present, be entered on the journal.

Neither House, during the session of Congress, shall, without the consent of the other, adjourn for more than three days, nor to any other place than that in which the two Houses shall be sitting.

Compensation and privileges of members

§ 6. The Senators and Representatives shall receive a compensation for their services, to be ascertained by law, and paid out of the Treasury of the United States. They shall, in all cases, except treason, felony, and breach of the peace, be privileged from arrest during their attendance at the session of their respective Houses, and in going to, and returning from, the same; and for any speech or debate in either House, they shall not be questioned in any other place.

No Senator or Representative shall, during the time for which he was elected, be appointed to any civil office under the authority of the United States, which shall have been created, or the emoluments whereof shall have been increased during such time; and no person holding any office under the United States, shall be a member of either House during his continuance in office.

Money bills

§ 7. All bills for raising revenue shall originate in the House of Representatives; but the Senate may propose or concur with amendments as on other bills.

Veto of bills by the President

Every bill which shall have passed the House of Representatives and the Senate, shall, before it become a law, be presented to the President of the United States; if he approve he shall sign it, but if not he shall return it, with his objections, to that House in which it shall have originated, who shall enter the objections at large on their journal, and proceed to reconsider it. If after such reconsideration two thirds of that House shall agree to pass the bill, it shall be sent, together with the objections, to the other House, by which it shall likewise be reconsidered, and if approved by two thirds of that House, it shall become a law. But in all such cases the votes of both Houses shall be determined by yeas and nays, and the names of the persons voting for and against the bill shall be entered on the journal of each House respectively. If any bill shall not be returned by the President within ten days, (Sundays excepted,) after it shall have been presented to him, the same shall be a law, in like manner as if he had signed it, unless the Congress by their adjournment prevent its return, in which case it shall not be a law.

[35] See Amendment XX, section 2.

THE CONSTITUTION OF THE UNITED STATES

Every order, resolution, or vote, to which the concurrence of the Senate and House of Representatives may be necessary, (except on a question of adjournment,) shall be presented to the President of the United States; and before the same shall take effect, shall be approved by him, or being disapproved by him, shall be re-passed by two thirds of the Senate and House of Representatives, according to the rules and limitations prescribed in the case of a bill.

§ 8. The Congress shall have power *Powers of Congress*

To lay and collect taxes, duties, imposts and excises, to pay the debts, and provide for the common defence and general welfare of the United States; but all duties, imposts, and excises shall be uniform throughout the United States:[36]

To borrow money on the credit of the United States:

To regulate commerce with foreign nations, and among the several States, and with the Indian tribes:

To establish an uniform rule of naturalization, and uniform laws on the subject of bankruptcies throughout the United States:

To coin money, regulate the value thereof, and of foreign coin, and fix the standard of weights and measures:

To provide for the punishment of counterfeiting the securities and current coin of the United States:

To establish post-offices and post-roads:

To promote the progress of science and useful arts, by securing, for limited times, to authors and inventors, the exclusive right to their respective writings and discoveries:

To constitute tribunals inferior to the Supreme Court:

To define and punish piracies and felonies committed on the high seas, and offences against the law of nations:

To declare war, grant letters of marque and reprisal, and make rules concerning captures on land and water:

To raise and support armies: but no appropriation of money to that use shall be for a longer term than two years:

To provide and maintain a navy:

To make rules for the government and regulation of the land and naval forces:

To provide for calling forth the militia to execute the laws of the Union, suppress insurrections and repel invasions:

To provide for organizing, arming, and disciplining the militia, and for governing such part of them as may be employed in the service of the United States, reserving to the States respectively, the appointment of the officers, and the authority of training the militia according to the discipline prescribed by Congress.

To exercise exclusive legislation, in all cases whatsoever, over such district (not exceeding ten miles square) as may by cession of particular States, and the acceptance of Congress, become the seat of the government of the United States, and to exercise like authority over all places purchased by the consent of the legislature of the State

---

[36] See Amendment XVI.

in which the same shall be, for the erection of forts, magazines, arsenals, dock-yards, and other needful buildings. And,

To make all laws which shall be necessary and proper for carrying into execution the foregoing powers, and all other powers vested by this Constitution in the government of the United States, or in any department or officer thereof.

Powers denied to Congress

§ 9. The migration or importation of such persons as any of the States now existing shall think proper to admit, shall not be prohibited by the Congress prior to the year one thousand eight hundred and eight; but a tax or duty may be imposed on such importation, not exceeding ten dollars for each person.

The privilege of the writ of *habeas corpus* shall not be suspended, unless when in cases of rebellion or invasion the public safety may require it.

No bill of attainder or *ex post facto* law shall be passed.

No capitation, or other direct tax, shall be laid, unless in proportion to the *census* or enumeration herein before directed to be taken.

No tax or duty shall be laid on articles exported from any State. No preference shall be given by any regulation of commerce or revenue to the ports of one State over those of another; nor shall vessels bound to, or from, one State be obliged to enter, clear, or pay duties in another.

No money shall be drawn from the treasury, but in consequence of appropriations made by law; and a regular statement and account of the receipts and expenditures of all public money shall be published from time to time.

No title of nobility shall be granted by the United States; and no person holding any office of profit or trust under them, shall, without the consent of the Congress, accept of any present, emolument, office, or title of any kind whatever, from any king, prince, or foreign state.

Powers denied to the states

§ 10. No State shall enter into any treaty, alliance, or confederation; grant letters of marque and reprisal; coin money; emit bills of credit; make any thing but gold and silver coin a tender in payment of debts; pass any bill of attainder, *ex post facto* law, or law impairing the obligation of contracts, or grant any title of nobility.

No State shall, without the consent of the Congress, lay any imposts or duties on imports or exports, except what may be absolutely necessary for executing its inspection laws; and the net produce of all duties and imposts, laid by any State on imports or exports, shall be for the use of the treasury of the United States; and all such laws shall be subject to the revision and control of the Congress. No State shall, without the consent of Congress, lay any duty of tonnage, keep troops, or ships of war, in time of peace, enter into any agreement or compact with another State, or with a foreign power, or engage in war, unless actually invaded, or in such imminent danger as will not admit of delay.

Executive

President

ART. II. § 1. The executive power shall be vested in a President of the United States of America. He shall hold his office during the term of four years, and together with the Vice President, chosen for the same term, be elected as follows: [37]

[37] See Amendment XXII.

THE CONSTITUTION OF THE UNITED STATES

Each State shall appoint, in such manner as the legislature thereof may direct, a number of electors equal to the whole number of Senators and Representatives to which the State may be entitled in the Congress; but no Senator or Representative, or person holding an office of trust or profit under the United States, shall be appointed an elector. *Election of President*

The electors shall meet in their respective States, and vote by ballot for two persons, of whom one at least shall not be an inhabitant of the same State with themselves. And they shall make a list of all the persons voted for, and of the number of votes for each; which list they shall sign and certify, and transmit sealed to the seat of the government of the United States, directed to the President of the Senate. The President of the Senate shall, in the presence of the Senate and House of Representatives, open all the certificates, and the votes shall then be counted. The person having the greatest number of votes shall be the President, if such number be a majority of the whole number of electors appointed; and if there be more than one who have such majority, and have an equal number of votes, then the House of Representatives shall immediately choose by ballot one of them for President; and if no person have a majority, then from the five highest on the list the said House shall in like manner choose the President. But in choosing the President, the votes shall be taken by States, the representation from each State having one vote; a quorum for this purpose shall consist of a member or members from two thirds of the States, and a majority of all the States shall be necessary to a choice. In every case, after the choice of the President, the person having the greatest number of votes of the electors shall be the Vice President. But if there should remain two or more who have equal votes, the Senate shall choose from them by ballot the Vice President.[38]

The Congress may determine the time of choosing the electors, and the day on which they shall give their votes; which day shall be the same throughout the United States.

No person except a natural born citizen, or a citizen of the United States, at the time of the adoption of this Constitution, shall be eligible to the office of President; neither shall any person be eligible to that office who shall not have attained to the age of thirty-five years, and been fourteen years a resident within the United States. *Qualifications of President*

In case of the removal of the President from office, or of his death, resignation, or inability to discharge the powers and duties of the said office, the same shall devolve on the Vice President, and the Congress may by law provide for the case of removal, death, resignation, or inability, both of the President and Vice President, declaring what officer shall then act as President, and such officer shall act accordingly until the disability be removed, or a President shall be elected.[39] *Succession to the presidency*

The President shall at stated times, receive for his services, a compensation, which shall neither be increased nor diminished during the period for which he shall have been elected, and he shall not receive within that period any other emolument from the United States or any of them. *Compensation*

[38] See Amendment XII.   [39] See Amendment XX, section 3.

Oath — Before he enter on the execution of his office, he shall take the following oath or affirmation:

"I do solemnly swear, (or affirm,) that I will faithfully execute the office of President of the United States, and will, to the best of my ability, preserve, protect, and defend the Constitution of the United States."

Commander in chief — § 2. The President shall be commander-in-chief of the army and navy of the United States, and of the militia of the several States, when called into the actual service of the United States; he may require the opinion, in writing, of the principal officer in each of the executive departments, upon any subject relating to the duties of their respective offices, and he shall have power to grant reprieves and pardons for offences against the United States, except in cases of impeachment.

Treaties — He shall have power, by and with the advice and consent of the Senate, to make treaties, provided two thirds of the Senators present concur; and he shall nominate, and by and with the advice and consent of the Senate, shall appoint ambassadors, other public ministers and consuls, judges of the Supreme Court, and all other officers of the United States, whose appointments are not herein otherwise provided for, and which shall be established by law. But the Congress may by law vest the appointment of such inferior officers, as they think proper, in the President alone, in the courts of law, or in the heads of departments.

Vacancies — The President shall have power to fill up all vacancies that may happen during the recess of the Senate, by granting commissions which shall expire at the end of their session.

Various powers and duties — § 3. He shall, from time to time, give to the Congress information of the state of the Union, and recommend to their consideration such measures as he shall judge necessary and expedient. He may on extraordinary occasions, convene both Houses, or either of them; and in case of disagreement between them, with respect to the time of adjournment, he may adjourn them to such time as he shall think proper. He shall receive ambassadors and other public ministers. He shall take care that the laws be faithfully executed; and shall commission all the officers of the United States.

Impeachment — § 4. The President, Vice President, and all civil officers of the United States, shall be removed from office on impeachment for, and conviction of, treason, bribery, or other high crimes and misdemeanors.

Judiciary
Courts
Independence of judges — ART. III. § 1. The judicial power of the United States shall be vested in one Supreme Court, and in such inferior courts as the Congress may, from time to time, ordain and establish. The judges, both of the Supreme and inferior courts, shall hold their offices during good behaviour; and shall, at stated times, receive for their services, a compensation, which shall not be diminished during their continuance in office.

Jurisdiction — § 2. The judicial power shall extend to all cases, in law and equity, arising under this Constitution, the laws of the United States, and treaties made, or which shall be made, under their authority; to all cases affecting ambassadors, other public ministers, and consuls; to all cases of admiralty and maritime jurisdiction; to controversies to which the United States shall be a party; to controversies between two or more States, between a State and citizens of another State,[40] between citizens of different States, between citizens of the same State claiming lands under grants of different States, and between a State, or the citizens thereof, and foreign States, citizens or subjects.

In all cases affecting ambassadors, other public ministers and consuls, and those in which a State shall be party, the Supreme Court shall have original jurisdiction. In all the other cases before mentioned, the Supreme Court shall have appellate jurisdiction, both as to law and fact, with such exceptions, and under such regulations, as the Congress shall make.

The trial of all crimes, except in cases of impeachment, shall be by jury; and such trial shall be held in the State where the said crimes shall have been committed; but when not committed within any State, the trial shall be at such place or places as the Congress may by law have directed. *Trial by jury*

§ 3. Treason against the United States, shall consist only in levying war against them, or in adhering to their enemies, giving them aid and comfort. No person shall be convicted of treason unless on the testimony of two witnesses to the same overt act, or on confession in open court. *Treason*

The Congress shall have power to declare the punishment of treason, but no attainder of treason shall work corruption of blood, or forfeiture, except during the life of the person attainted.

ART. IV. § 1. Full faith and credit shall be given in each State to the public acts, records, and judicial proceedings of every other State. And the Congress may by general laws prescribe the manner in which such acts, records, and proceedings shall be proved, and the effect thereof. *The Federal System* / *Full faith and credit*

§ 2. The citizens of each State shall be entitled to all privileges and immunities of citizens in the several States.[41] *Privileges and immunities*

A person charged in any State with treason, felony, or other crime, who shall flee from justice, and be found in another State, shall, on demand of the executive authority of the State from which he fled, be delivered up, to be removed to the State having jurisdiction of the crime. *Fugitives*

No person held to service or labour in one State, under the laws thereof, escaping into another, shall, in consequence of any law or regulation therein, be discharged from such service or labour, but shall be delivered up on claim of the party to whom such service or labour may be due.[42]

§ 3. New States may be admitted by the Congress into this Union; but no new State shall be formed or erected within the jurisdiction of any other State; nor any State be formed by the junction of two or more States, or parts of States, without the consent of the legislatures of the States concerned, as well as of the Congress. *New states*

The Congress shall have power to dispose of and make all needful rules and regulations respecting the territory or other property belonging to the United States; *Territories*

---

[40] See Amendment XI.
[41] See Amendment XIV, section 1.
[42] See Amendment XIII.

Republican form of government
and nothing in this Constitution shall be so construed as to prejudice any claims of the United States, or of any particular State.

§ 4. The United States shall guarantee to every State in this Union a republican form of government, and shall protect each of them against invasion; and on application of the legislature, or of the executive, (when the legislature cannot be convened) against domestic violence.

Amendments
ART. V. The Congress, whenever two thirds of both Houses shall deem it necessary, shall propose amendments to this Constitution, or, on the application of the legislatures of two thirds of the several States, shall call a convention for proposing amendments, which, in either case, shall be valid to all intents and purposes, as part of this Constitution, when ratified by the legislatures of three fourths of the several States, or by conventions in three fourths thereof, as the one or the other mode of ratification may be proposed by the Congress; provided, that no amendment, which may be made prior to the year one thousand eight hundred and eight, shall in any manner affect the first and fourth clauses in the ninth section of the first article; and that no State, without its consent, shall be deprived of its equal suffrage in the Senate.

Other Matters
Debts
ART. VI. All debts contracted, and engagements entered into, before the adoption of this Constitution, shall be as valid against the United States, under this Constitution, as under the confederation.

Supreme law of the land
This Constitution, and the laws of the United States which shall be made in pursuance thereof, and all treaties made, or which shall be made, under the authority of the United States, shall be the supreme law of the land: and the judges, in every State, shall be bound thereby, any thing in the Constitution or laws of any State to the contrary notwithstanding.

Oaths
The Senators and Representatives before mentioned, and the members of the several State legislatures, and all executive and judicial officers, both of the United States and of the several States, shall be bound, by oath or affirmation, to support this Constitution; but no religious test shall ever be required as a qualification to any office or public trust under the United States.

Religious tests prohibited

Ratification
ART. VII. The ratification of the conventions of nine States, shall be sufficient for the establishment of this Constitution between the States so ratifying the same.

Done in Convention, by the unanimous consent of the States present, the seventeenth day of September, in the year of our Lord one thousand seven hundred and eighty-seven, and of the independence of the United States of America the twelfth. In witness whereof we have hereunto subscribed our names.

GEORGE WASHINGTON, PRESIDENT, and Deputy from Virginia.

New Hampshire.—John Langdon, Nicholas Gilman.
Massachusetts.—Nathaniel Gorham, Rufus King.
Connecticut.—William Samuel Johnson, Roger Sherman.

THE CONSTITUTION OF THE UNITED STATES

New York.—Alexander Hamilton.

New Jersey.—William Livingston, David Brearley, William Paterson, Jonathan Dayton.

Pennsylvania.—Benjamin Franklin, Thomas Mifflin, Robert Morris, George Clymer, Thomas Fitzsimons, Jared Ingersoll, James Wilson, Gouverneur Morris.

Delaware.—George Read, Gunning Bedford, Jun., John Dickinson, Richard Bassett, Jacob Broom.

Maryland.—James M'Henry, Daniel of St. Thomas Jenifer, Daniel Carroll.

Virginia.—John Blair, James Madison, Jun.

North Carolina.—William Blount, Richard Dobbs Spaight, Hugh Williamson.

South Carolina.—John Rutledge, Charles Cotesworth Pinckney, Charles Pinckney, Pierce Butler.

Georgia.—William Few, Abraham Baldwin

Attest: WILLIAM JACKSON, *Secretary.*

REFERENCES

Bancroft, George. *History of the Formation of the Constitution of the United States of America.* 2 vols. 2d ed. New York: D. Appleton & Co., 1882.

Channing, Edward. *A History of the United States.* 6 vols. New York: Macmillan Co., 1927. III, chaps. 15, 16.

Farrand, Max. *The Framing of the Constitution of the United States.* New Haven: Yale University Press, 1913.

Fiske, John. *The Critical Period of American History, 1783-1789.* Boston: Houghton Mifflin Co., 1888. Chaps. 6, 7.

Frothingham, Richard. *The Rise of the Republic of the United States.* 7th ed. Boston: Little, Brown & Co., 1899. Chap. 12.

McLaughlin, Andrew C. *The Confederation and the Constitution, 1783-1789.* (Vol. X of *The American Nation: A History.*) New York: Harper & Bros., 1905.

Rutland, Robert A. *The Birth of the Bill of Rights, 1776-1791.* Chapel Hill: University of North Carolina Press, 1955.

Story, Joseph. *Commentaries on the Constitution of the United States.* 2 vols. 4th ed. Boston: Little, Brown & Co., 1873.

Warren, Charles. *The Making of the Constitution.* Boston: Little, Brown & Co., 1929.

Wright, Benjamin F. *American Interpretations of Natural Law.* Cambridge, Mass.: Harvard University Press, 1931. Chap. 6.

XXXII. THE FIRST TEN AMENDMENTS TO THE CONSTITUTION

1791

Origins

Ratification of the Constitution without a bill of rights

The first ten amendments to the Constitution were a product of the intense struggle over the ratification of the Constitution. The Constitution was submitted by the Federal Convention to Congress on September 17, 1787. It contained many compromises. Few delegates at the Convention considered it perfect, but most of them felt that it provided the best government that could be obtained under the circumstances.

The attitude of the Convention is illustrated by the letter transmitting the Constitution. The letter, signed by George Washington by order of the Convention, stated in part:

> It is obviously impracticable in the federal government of these states, to secure all rights of independent sovereignty to each, and yet provide for the interest and safety of all: Individuals entering into society, must give up a share of liberty to preserve the rest. The magnitude of the sacrifice must depend as well on situation and circumstance, as on the object to the obtained. It is at all times difficult to draw with precision the line between those rights which must be surrendered, and those which may be reserved; and on the present occasion this difficulty was encreased by a difference among the several states as to their situation, extent, habits, and particular interests.
>
> In all our deliberations on this subject we kept steadily in our view, that which appears to us the greatest interest of every true American, the consolidation of our Union, in which is involved our prosperity, felicity, safety, perhaps our national existence. This important consideration, seriously and deeply impressed on our minds, led each state in the Convention to be less rigid on points of inferior magnitude, than might have been otherwise expected; and thus the Constitution, which we now present, is the result of a spirit of amity, and of that mutual deference and concession which the peculiarity of our political situation rendered indispensible.[1]

[1] Charles C. Tansill (ed.), *Documents Illustrative of the Formation of the Union of the American States,* 69th Cong., 1st Sess., 1927, House Doc. 398, 1003-4.

FIRST TEN AMENDMENTS TO THE CONSTITUTION

On September 28 Congress sent the Constitution to the states. In accordance with the recommendation of the Convention, a special convention chosen by the people was to meet in each state to decide whether or not to ratify. Congress recommended neither ratification nor rejection; that was a question for the states alone to decide.

On December 7, 1787, Delaware became the first state to ratify the Constitution. Delaware was soon followed by Pennsylvania, New Jersey, Georgia, and Connecticut.

The ratifying conventions

The Massachusetts ratifying convention was the first one to propose amendments to the Constitution. By a close vote, that state ratified the document unconditionally. It enjoined its representatives in Congress, however, to use all reasonable means to secure approval of nine amendments which "would remove the fears & quiet the apprehensions of many of the good people of this Commonwealth & more effectually guard against an undue administration of the Federal Government."[2] Massachusetts proposed a declaration that all powers not expressly delegated by the Constitution were reserved by the states; Congress should be forbidden to establish commercial monopolies; persons tried for crimes involving infamous punishments or the loss of life should be indicted by a grand jury; and the right of trial by jury in civil cases should be protected.

Maryland was next to ratify, and no amendments were proposed. South Carolina was next; it proposed two amendments. The necessary nine states had ratified the Constitution by June 21, 1788, when New Hampshire gave its approval. The vote in that convention was very close, and twelve amendments were proposed. New Hampshire added to the amendments proposed by Massachusetts a prohibition of standing armies in time of peace except with the consent of three fourths of each branch of Congress, a provision that Congress should make no laws touching religion or infringing the rights of conscience, and a provision that Congress should never disarm any citizen except during a rebellion.

The votes of the ratifying conventions of Virginia, New York, and Rhode Island also were very close. Each convention ratified the Constitution, but all three passed declarations of rights and proposed a large number of amendments to the body of the Constitution. New York, which proposed thirty-three amendments, stated that until a convention should be called for the purpose of proposing amendments to the Constitution it would not

[2] *Ibid.*, 1018.

permit its militia to leave the state for more than six weeks without the consent of the legislature. The declarations of rights proposed by these conventions were largely based on the declarations found in the state constitutions.

In August, 1788, the North Carolina convention resolved that the state would not ratify the Constitution until a declaration of rights together with amendments to the "most ambiguous and exceptionable parts" of the Constitution had been presented to Congress or to whatever convention might be called to consider amendments. A declaration of twenty rights together with twenty-six proposed amendments to the Constitution accompanied the resolution. North Carolina reversed this action on November 21 and ratified the Constitution unconditionally.

The last state to ratify the Constitution was Rhode Island, which gave its approval in May, 1790. Vermont ratified the document in January, 1791, a month before it was formally admitted to the Union.

Demands for a bill of rights

The absence of a bill of rights in the Constitution evoked some of the strongest protests of the opponents of the proposed government. It was not, however, the only objection of the Antifederalists to the document.[3] They also protested against the threat of a consolidated federal government which would weaken or abolish the states. Fearing that the Constitution put too much power in the hands of the executive, they maintained that the President should not be eligible for re-election. They did not approve the powers given to the Senate and also claimed that Congress had been given inordinate power in the regulation of commerce.

Although the ratification struggle produced much discussion of the question of whether a bill of rights was desirable or undesirable, the decision of that question would not determine the immediate issue which was whether the Constitution should be ratified without a bill of rights. As a practical matter it would have been easier for the proponents of a bill of rights to obtain one after the Constitution had been put into effect, instead of before. A second Federal Convention would have involved unnecessary delay and inconvenience. As Alexander Hamilton put it: "I should esteem it the extreme of imprudence to prolong the precarious state of our national affairs, and to expose the Union to the jeopardy of successive experiments, in the chimerical pursuit of a perfect plan."[4]

[3] See Charles Warren, *The Making of the Constitution* (Boston, 1929), 759-77.
[4] *The Federalist*, No. 85 (New York, 1937), 570.

FIRST TEN AMENDMENTS TO THE CONSTITUTION

The Antifederalists sought the complete defeat of the plan of government proposed by the Federal Convention, and they would not have been satisfied unless another convention were called for the purpose of drastically reforming that plan. The absence of a bill of rights was only one of the grounds on which they urged the unqualified rejection of the Constitution; they would probably have taken the same position if a bill of rights had been included.

The Federalists, on the other hand, were not sufficiently convinced of the undesirability of a bill of rights as to prefer the defeat of the Constitution to the ratification of the document accompanied by a bill of rights. If the Federal Convention made a great tactical error by not framing a bill of rights, the Antifederalists made one nearly as great by focusing so much attention upon a subject to which the Federalists were not fundamentally opposed. By agreeing to support a bill of rights when the First Congress had been assembled, the Federalists deprived their opponents of an important argument and thereby made ratification of the Constitution easier. In fact, the Federalists themselves sought to focus attention upon the absence of a bill of rights. James Madison of Virginia, a strong supporter of the Constitution, also took the lead in introducing and supporting the Bill of Rights in the First Congress. He said:

> There have been objections of various kinds made against the Constitution. Some were levelled against its structure because the President was without a council; because the Senate, which is a legislative body, had judicial powers in trials on impeachments; and because the powers of that body were compounded in other respects, in a manner that did not correspond with a particular theory; because it grants more power than is supposed to be necessary for every good purpose, and controls the ordinary powers of the State Governments. I know some respectable characters who opposed this Government on these grounds; but I believe that the great mass of the people who opposed it, disliked it because it did not contain effectual provisions against the encroachments on particular rights, and those safeguards which they have been long accustomed to have interposed between them and the magistrate who exercises the sovereign power; nor ought we to consider them safe, while a great number of our fellow-citizens [sic] think these securities necessary.[5]

Madison's proposed amendments

Madison, a member of the House of Representatives, introduced his long-awaited amendments on June 8, 1789. He wanted to avoid consideration of the sweeping amendments which had been proposed by some of the state ratifying conventions. He said at a later period of the debates: "I venture

[5] Joseph Gales (comp.), *The Debates and Proceedings in the Congress of the United States* (Washington, 1834), I, 433.

to say, that if we confine ourselves to an enumeration of simple, acknowledged principles, the ratification will meet with but little difficulty."⁶

Madison's proposals were based largely on the declarations of rights in the state constitutions, particularly that of Virginia. He moved that the following paragraphs be prefixed to the Constitution:

Powers of the people

That all power is originally vested in, and consequently derived from, the people.

That Government is instituted and ought to be exercised for the benefit of the people; which consists in the enjoyment of life and liberty, with the right of acquiring and using property, and generally of pursuing and obtaining happiness and safety.

That the people have an indubitable, unalienable, and indefeasible right to reform or change their Government, whenever it be found adverse or inadequate to the purposes of its institution.⁷

Madison's next amendment would have given Congress authority to regulate the number of members of the House of Representatives after that body had reached a certain size. Next, Madison proposed to add at the end of the first clause of Article I, section 6: "But no law varying the compensation last ascertained shall operate before the next ensuing election of Representatives."⁸ Between the third and fourth paragraphs of Article I, section 9, he proposed to add the following provisions:

Freedom of religion

The civil rights of none shall be abridged on account of religious belief or worship, nor shall any national religion be established, nor shall the full and equal rights of conscience be in any manner, or on any pretext, infringed.

Freedom of speech and of the press

The people shall not be deprived or abridged of their right to speak, to write, or to publish their sentiments; and the freedom of the press, as one of the great bulwarks of liberty, shall be inviolable.

Assembly and petition

The people shall not be restrained from peaceably assembling and consulting for their common good; nor from applying to the Legislature by petitions, or remonstrances, for redress of their grievances.

Right to bear arms

The right of the people to keep and bear arms shall not be infringed; a well armed and well regulated militia being the best security of a free country: but no person religiously scrupulous of bearing arms shall be compelled to render military service in person.

Quartering of soldiers

No soldier shall in time of peace be quartered in any house without the consent of the owner; nor at any time, but in a manner warranted by law.

Double jeopardy; self-incrimination; due process

No person shall be subject, except in cases of impeachment, to more than one punishment or one trial for the same offence; nor shall be compelled to be a witness against himself; nor be deprived of life, liberty, or property, without due process of law; nor be

⁶ *Ibid.*, 738.   ⁷ *Ibid.*, 433-34.   ⁸ *Ibid.*, 434.

obliged to relinquish his property, where it may be necessary for public use, without a just compensation. *Compensation for property*

Excessive bail shall not be required, nor excessive fines imposed, nor cruel and unusual punishments inflicted. *Bail, fines, and punishments*

The rights of the people to be secured in their persons, their houses, their papers, and their other property, from all unreasonable searches and seizures, shall not be violated by warrants issued without probable cause, supported by oath or affirmation, or not particularly describing the places to be searched, or the persons or things to be seized. *Searches and seizures*

In all criminal prosecutions, the accused shall enjoy the right to a speedy and public trial, to be informed of the cause and nature of the accusation, to be confronted with his accusers, and the witnesses against him; to have a compulsory process for obtaining witnesses in his favor; and to have the assistance of counsel for his defence. *Trial by jury; accusation; witnesses; counsel*

The exceptions here or elsewhere in the Constitution, made in favor of particular rights, shall not be so construed as to diminish the just importance of other rights retained by the people, or as to enlarge the powers delegated by the Constitution; but either as actual limitations of such powers, or as inserted merely for greater caution.[9] *Construction of rights*

Madison proposed adding between the first and second paragraphs of Article I, section 10, a provision prohibiting the states from violating the equal rights of conscience, the freedom of the press, or the right of trial by jury in criminal cases. *Liberties protected from state action*

He proposed an amendment to Article III, section 2, which would limit appeals to the Supreme Court to cases which involve a certain minimum amount of money and which would have added to that section: "nor shall any fact triable by jury, according to the course of common law, be otherwise re-examinable than may consist with the principles of common law."[10] He proposed replacing the third paragraph of the same section with the following provision: *Appeals to Supreme Court*

The trial of all crimes (except in cases of impeachments, and cases arising in the land or naval forces, or the militia when on actual service, in time of war or public danger) shall be by an impartial jury of freeholders of the vicinage, with the requisite of unanimity for conviction, of the right of challenge, and other accustomed requisites; and in all crimes punishable with loss of life or member, presentment or indictment by a grand jury shall be an essential preliminary, provided that in cases of crimes committed within any county which may be in possession of an enemy, or in which a general insurrection may prevail, the trial may by law be authorized in some other county of the same State, as near as may be to the seat of the offence. *Trial by jury*

In cases of crimes committed not within any county, the trial may by law be in such county as the laws shall have prescribed. In suits at common law, between man and

[9] Ibid., 434-35. [10] Ibid., 435.

man, the trial by jury, as one of the best securities to the rights of the people, ought to remain inviolate.[11]

Finally, Madison proposed to add the following provisions as a separate article following Article VI:

Separation of powers

> The powers delegated by this Constitution are appropriated to the departments to which they are respectively distributed: so that the Legislature Department shall never exercise the powers vested in the Executive or Judicial, nor the Executive exercise the powers vested in the Legislative or Judicial, nor the Judicial exercise the powers vested in the Legislative or Executive Departments.

Reserved powers

> The powers not delegated by this Constitution, nor prohibited by it to the States, are reserved to the States respectively.[12]

Amendments proposed by the House of Representatives

These proposals were referred to the committee of the whole, but they were not discussed very much. On July 21 it was decided to appoint a select committee to consider Madison's proposals together with the amendments which had been proposed by the state ratifying conventions. The report of that committee was presented on July 28 and was discussed from time to time until August 24. On that date seventeen amendments were approved and sent to the Senate. In accordance with a motion made by Roger Sherman, the amendments were in the form of a supplement to the Constitution instead of being incorporated into the body of the document.

As approved by the House of Representatives, the amendments closely followed Madison's proposals. There were, however, a few changes. Madison's three paragraphs to be prefixed to the Constitution were omitted. The clauses on freedom of religion, speech, press, assembly, and petition were expressed in the following language:

> Congress shall make no law establishing religion or prohibiting the free exercise thereof, nor shall the rights of conscience be infringed.
>
> The freedom of speech, and of the press, and the right of the people peaceably to assemble and consult for their common good, and to apply to the government for redress of grievances, shall not be infringed.[13]

The clause governing the construction of the amendments was phrased as follows: "The enumeration in this Constitution of certain rights, shall not be construed to deny or disparage others retained by the people."[14]

---

[11] *Ibid.*

[12] *Ibid.*, 435-36.

[13] *Journal of the House of Representatives of the United States* (New York, 1789), 107.

[14] *Ibid.*, 108.

FIRST TEN AMENDMENTS TO THE CONSTITUTION

The Senate proposed a number of amendments to the document as it came from the House of Representatives, and a conference was called to settle the differences. Final agreement was reached September 25. Congress sent twelve amendments to the states, but only the last ten were ratified. The two amendments which did not receive the states' approval would have regulated the number of members of the House of Representatives and prevented members of Congress from changing their compensation until an election of representatives had intervened.

Amendments proposed by Congress

The first amendment states several of the citizen's essential liberties. Freedom of religion was a right for which many men had struggled unsuccessfully in England. America offered the persecuted minorities of many countries an opportunity to worship unmolested according to the dictates of their consciences. Religious motives caused people to come to this country, and it was in America that the principles of toleration were first practiced. The earliest major documentary evidence of the right of freedom of religion was the Charter of Rhode Island of 1663.[15]

Historical Origins of the First Ten Amendments

Freedom of religion

Freedom of speech and of the press are essential rights in a government based upon the will of the people. The development of these rights paralleled the growth of the people's political power during the seventeenth and eighteenth centuries. The first major step in that development was the expiration of licensing of the English press in 1695.[16]

Freedom of speech and of the press

In America the press became a powerful force in rallying colonial opposition against British oppression. In 1774 the First Continental Congress listed freedom of the press as one of the essential rights of the colonists.[17] The Virginia Bill of Rights of 1776[18] was the first state bill of rights expressly to safeguard this freedom. The Virginia document was soon followed by the Pennsylvania Declaration of Rights,[19] which included freedom of speech.

There was little discussion of freedom of speech and of the press when Congress was considering amendments to the Constitution. Many people, however, believed that these rights were intended to change the English common law by permitting free discussion of public issues. In 1800 James Madison said in his "Report on the Virginia Resolutions":

---

[15] See pp. 162-79.
[16] See pp. 242-43.
[17] See p. 285.
[18] See pp. 301-13.
[19] See pp. 323-31.

425

In the British government, the danger of encroachments on the rights of the people is understood to be confined to the executive magistrate. The representatives of the people in the legislature are not only exempt themselves from distrust, but are considered as sufficient guardians of the rights of their constituents against the danger from the executive. Hence it is a principle, that the Parliament is unlimited in its power; or, in their own language, is omnipotent. Hence, too, all the ramparts for protecting the rights of the people,—such as their Magna Charta, their bill of rights, &c.,—are not reared against the Parliament, but against the royal prerogative. They are merely legislative precautions against executive usurpation. Under such a government as this, an exemption of the press from previous restraint by licensers appointed by the king, is all the freedom that can be secured to it.

In the United States, the case is altogether different. The people, not the government, possess the absolute sovereignty. The legislature, no less than the executive, is under limitations of power. Encroachments are regarded as possible from the one as well as from the other. Hence, in the United States, the great and essential rights of the people are secured against legislative as well as executive ambition. They are secured, not by laws paramount to prerogative, but by constitutions paramount to laws. This security of the freedom of the press requires that it should be exempt, not only from previous restraint of the executive, as in Great Britain, but from legislative restraint also; and this exemption, to be effectual, must be an exemption, not only from the previous inspection of licensers, but from the subsequent penalty of laws.[20]

Rights to assembly and petition

The rights of the people to assemble and petition the government for a redress of grievances are, of course, closely related to the right of free discussion. For centuries petitions of the people had been used to present grievances to the king. Flagrant violations of this customary privilege by James II (1685-89) led to one of the provisions of the English Bill of Rights of 1689.[21]

Petitions were often used by the American colonists to make known their grievances to the king and Parliament. This right was claimed in 1765 by the Resolutions of the Stamp Act Congress[22] and the Declaration and Resolves of the First Continental Congress.[23] The Pennsylvania Declaration of Rights of 1776[24] was the first state constitution expressly to declare this right.

Right to bear arms

Infringements by the Stuart kings of the right of the people to bear arms led to one of the provisions of the English Bill of Rights.[25] Interferences

---

[20] Jonathan Elliot (ed.), *The Debates in the Several State Conventions* (Philadelphia, 1866), IV, 569-70.

[21] See pp. 227-30.

[22] See p. 271.

[23] See pp. 282-83, 288.

[24] See p. 331.

[25] See pp. 245, 246.

with colonial militias had been one of the grievances of the colonists against English officials.[26] The second amendment to the Constitution relates the right to bear arms to the maintenance of the militia for the security of a free state.

Quartering of soldiers

The quartering of soldiers in private homes led to one of the rights established by the English Petition of Right of 1628.[27] In the American colonies troops were sometimes quartered in homes during the French and Indian War (1754-63), but that practice was not authorized by the Quartering Act of 1765.[28] The Quartering Act, however, imposed heavy financial burdens on the colonists, and the quartering of soldiers became a major grievance.[29]

Objections to the presence of redcoats in the colonies were also based on the provision of the English Bill of Rights that no standing armies should be maintained in time of peace without the consent of Parliament.[30] The colonists argued that because they were entitled to the same rights as Englishmen no standing armies should be maintained without the consent of the colonial assemblies.[31]

Under the Constitution the maintenance of standing armies must be authorized by the legislature in peace, as well as in war. The third amendment continues the safeguards against the quartering of soldiers established by the Petition of Right.

Searches and seizures

The fourth amendment grew out of the use by British officials of general warrants to enforce the acts of trade and to search for seditious publications. Virginia was the first state to prohibit the use of such warrants.[32]

Proceedings against individuals

The fifth amendment states several rules, long established in the English common law, governing proceedings against the life, liberty, or property of individuals. All these rules may be summed up by the expression "due process of law." The use of grand juries to bring criminal charges against individuals began before Magna Carta.[33]

1. Grand jury

2. Double jeopardy

The second clause of the fifth amendment requires that no person shall be accused and put to his defense twice for the same offense. The Massachusetts Body of Liberties of 1641 [34] allowed a defendant to plead a previous conviction and sentence to defeat a second charge. By the common law a

---

[26] See pp. 231-32.
[27] See pp. 65-72.
[28] See p. 72.
[29] See pp. 278-79.
[30] See pp. 230-31.
[31] See pp. 278-79.
[32] See pp. 304-6.
[33] See pp. 7-8.
[34] See pp. 143-61.

previous acquittal might also be pleaded to defeat a second accusation.[35] This clause incorporates both rules.

3. Self-incrimination

The third clause of the fifth amendment provides that no individual shall be required to accuse himself in a criminal case nor be deprived of life, liberty, or property without due process of law. The privilege against self-incrimination developed from protests against the oath *ex officio,* a procedure which first appeared in the ecclesiastical courts. By that procedure individuals were required to give evidence against themselves concerning criminal matters.[36] The oath *ex officio,* together with the use of torture to elicit confessions, were among the regular procedures of the Court of Star Chamber, as well as of the ecclesiastical courts. The common law courts also questioned defendants, sometimes trying to trap them into an admission. This was not done under oath, however.

Seventeenth-century protests against the oath *ex officio* were based on the principle that the accusation should be brought by the regular procedures of the common law, that is, by indictment or presentment of a grand jury, and not by evidence forced from the defendant himself.

In 1641 the use of torture to obtain evidence on which to base a conviction was abolished by the Massachusetts Body of Liberties.[37] The oath *ex officio* disappeared in England in the same year as the abolition of the Court of Star Chamber and the criminal jurisdiction of the ecclesiastical courts. By an association of ideas, the practice of questioning defendants in the common law courts had also disappeared by the end of the seventeenth century.

The Virginia Bill of Rights of 1776[38] was the first state constitution to recognize this privilege, and the privilege was embodied in every declaration of rights enacted by the other states prior to the Constitution of the United States.

4. Due process of law

The origins of the principle that no person shall be deprived of life, liberty, or property without due process of law are older than Magna Carta. Chapter 39 of that document was apparently intended to announce this rule.[39] What is equally important, many other individual liberties owe their origin to the strength of this principle.

The principle of due process of law furnished the legal basis for such

---

[35] William Blackstone, *Commentaries on the Laws of England* (9th ed.; London, 1783), IV, 335-36.
[36] See pp. 132-37.
[37] See p. 153.
[38] See p. 312.
[39] See pp. 5-7, 17.

FIRST TEN AMENDMENTS TO THE CONSTITUTION

famous English documents as the Petition of Right of 1628[40] and the Act for the Abolition of the Star Chamber in 1641.[41] Probably no other principle of individual liberty was more frequently embodied in the colonial charters and statutes. Like the privilege against self-incrimination, the due process clause, in one form of language or another, is found in all the state declarations of rights adopted prior to the Constitution of the United States.

The power of the government to take the property of its citizens for public purposes is one of the attributes of sovereignty. A long-standing rule of law, however, required that just compensation be made for the property so taken. King John's Charter of 1215, for example, provided: "No constable or other bailiff of ours shall take anyone's grain or other chattels, without immediately paying for them in money, unless he is able to obtain a postponement at the good will of the seller."[42] The last clause of the fifth amendment affirms this ancient rule. *5. Compensation for private property*

The sixth amendment relates to the procedural rights of the individual once he has been charged with a crime. The first of these rights is trial by jury. The origins of that right antedate Magna Carta.[43] Infringements of the right of trial by jury led the American colonists to claim it as one of their most cherished liberties.[44] It appeared in the Virginia Bill of Rights of 1776[45] and later declarations enacted by the other states. *Criminal procedures* *1. Trial by jury*

For many years persons accused of felony or treason were not entitled to the privileges of witnesses and counsel. This rule was one of the most unfair doctrines of the English common law. Although certain exceptions were made to this rule from time to time, it was the Pennsylvania Charter of Privileges of 1701[46] that first established these rights in the fullest sense. The Virginia Bill of Rights of 1776[47] gave defendants the right to call for evidence in their favor and the Pennsylvania Declaration of Rights of 1776[48] added the right to be assisted by counsel. *2. Witnesses and counsel*

The seventh amendment answered a question which had been hotly debated by the delegates in the Federal Convention of 1787. Hugh Williamson of North Carolina and Elbridge Gerry of Massachusetts had urged the adoption in the Constitution of a general provision to safeguard the jury *Juries in civil cases*

[40] See pp. 62-75.
[41] See pp. 125-42.
[42] See p. 16.
[43] See pp. 7-9.
[44] See pp. 267-68, 281-82.
[45] See p. 312.
[46] See pp. 252-54.
[47] See p. 312.
[48] See pp. 325, 330.

429

system in civil cases.⁴⁹ The proposal was defeated, not because the delegates opposed the use of juries in such cases but because they felt that differing practices of the states made it impossible to frame a general rule.

Bail, fines, and punishments

The eighth amendment closely follows the wording of one of the provisions of the English Bill of Rights.⁵⁰ The provision also appeared in the state declarations of rights adopted at the time of the American Revolution.

Rights not enumerated

The ninth amendment provides a rule of construction governing all the preceding amendments. The framers of the Bill of Rights did not intend to enumerate all the rights of the citizen. The ninth amendment requires that the Bill of Rights shall not be interpreted to mean that the citizen has no rights except those specifically mentioned.

This amendment was thought necessary to avoid a suggestion made during the ratification struggle. It was argued by members of the Federalist party, notably James Wilson and Alexander Hamilton, that a bill of rights was not only unnecessary in the Constitution but even dangerous. The enumeration of certain rights, they argued, might raise implications against rights not specifically mentioned. Hamilton went even further and argued that implications would also be raised against the rights which were mentioned:

> I go further, and affirm that bills of rights, in the sense and to the extent in which they are contended for, are not only unnecessary in the proposed Constitution, but would even be dangerous. They would contain various exceptions to powers not granted; and, on this very account, would afford a colorable pretext to claim more than were granted. For why declare that things shall not be done which there is no power to do? Why, for instance, should it be said that the liberty of the press shall not be restrained, when no power is given by which restrictions may be imposed? I will not contend that such a provision would confer a regulating power; but it is evident that it would furnish, to men disposed to usurp, a plausible pretence for claiming that power. They might urge with a semblance of reason, that the Constitution ought not to be charged with the absurdity of providing against the abuse of an authority which was not given, and that the provisions against restraining the liberty of the press afforded a clear implication, that a power to prescribe proper regulations concerning it was intended to be vested in the national government. This may serve as a specimen of the numerous handles which would be given to the doctrine of constructive powers, by the indulgence of an injudicious zeal for bills of rights.⁵¹

Reserved powers

The tenth amendment is a more or less direct successor of the second provision of the Articles of Confederation of 1781. The Articles stated: "Each

---

⁴⁹ See pp. 404-5.
⁵⁰ See pp. 235-36, 247.
⁵¹ *The Federalist*, No. 84, 559.

state retains its sovereignty, freedom, and independence, and every Power, Jurisdiction and right, which is not by this confederation expressly delegated to the United States, in Congress assembled."[52] During the First Congress several attempts to insert the word "expressly" before the word "delegated" were defeated.

[52] Tansill, *op. cit.*, 27. The history of this provision of the Articles of Confederation is discussed by William W. Crosskey, *Politics and the Constitution in the History of the United States* (Chicago, 1953), I, chap. 22.

THE FIRST TEN AMENDMENTS TO THE CONSTITUTION[53]

December 15, 1791

Religion, speech, press, assembly, and petition

ART. I. Congress shall make no law respecting an establishment of religion, or prohibiting the free exercise thereof; or abridging the freedom of speech, or of the press; or the right of the people peaceably to assemble, and to petition the government for a redress of grievances.

Right to bear arms

ART. II. A well regulated militia being necessary to the security of a free State, the right of the people to keep and bear arms shall not be infringed.

Quartering of soldiers

ART. III. No soldier shall, in time of peace, be quartered in any house without the consent of the owner; nor in time of war, but in a manner to be prescribed by law.

Searches and seizures
Warrants

ART. IV. The right of the people to be secure in their persons, houses, papers, and effects, against unreasonable searches and seizures, shall not be violated; and no warrants shall issue, but upon probable cause, supported by oath or affirmation, and particularly describing the place to be searched, and the persons or things to be seized.

Grand jury

ART. V. No person shall be held to answer for a capital or otherwise infamous crime, unless on a presentment or indictment of a grand jury, except in cases arising in the land or naval forces, or in the militia, when in actual service, in time of war

Double jeopardy; self-incrimination; due process; compensation for property

or public danger; nor shall any person be subject for the same offence to be twice put in jeopardy of life or limb; nor shall be compelled, in any criminal case, to be witness against himself; nor be deprived of life, liberty, or property, without due process of law; nor shall private property be taken for public use without just compensation.

Trial by jury

ART. VI. In all criminal prosecutions the accused shall enjoy the right to a speedy and public trial, by an impartial jury of the State and district wherein the crime shall have been committed, which district shall have been previously ascertained by

Accusation; witnesses; counsel

law, and to be informed of the nature and cause of the accusation; to be confronted with the witnesses against him; to have compulsory process for obtaining witnesses in his favour; and to have the assistance of counsel for his defence.

[53] 1 U.S. *Statutes at Large* 21.

FIRST TEN AMENDMENTS TO THE CONSTITUTION

ART. VII. In suits at common law, where the value in controversy shall exceed twenty dollars, the right of trial by jury shall be preserved; and no fact tried by a jury shall be otherwise re-examined in any court of the United States than according to the rules of the common law. *Juries in civil cases*

ART. VIII. Excessive bail shall not be required, nor excessive fines imposed, nor cruel and unusual punishments inflicted. *Bail, fines, and punishments*

ART. IX. The enumeration in the Constitution of certain rights, shall not be construed to deny or disparage others retained by the people. *Reservation of other rights and powers*

ART. X. The powers not delegated to the United States by the Constitution, nor prohibited by it to the States, are reserved to the States respectively or to the people.

REFERENCES

See references on p. 417.

APPENDIX
LATER AMENDMENTS TO THE CONSTITUTION

ARTICLE XI[1]

The Judicial power of the United States shall not be construed to extend to any suit in law or equity, commenced or prosecuted against one of the United States by Citizens of another State, or by Citizens or Subjects of any Foreign State.

ARTICLE XII[2]

The electors shall meet in their respective States, and vote by ballot for President and Vice President, one of whom, at least, shall not be an inhabitant of the same State with themselves; they shall name in their ballots the person voted for as President, and in distinct ballots the person voted for as Vice President; and they shall make distinct lists of all persons voted for as President, and of all persons voted for as Vice President, and of the number of votes for each, which list they shall sign and certify, and transmit sealed to the seat of the government of the United States, directed to the President of the Senate; the President of the Senate shall, in the presence of the Senate and House of Representatives, open all the certificates, and the votes shall then be counted: the person having the greatest number of votes for President shall be the President, if such number be a majority of the whole number of electors appointed; and if no person have such majority, then from the persons having the highest numbers, not exceeding three, on the list of those voted for as President, the House of Representatives shall choose immediately by ballot the President. But in choosing the President, the vote shall be taken by States, the representation from each State having one vote; a quorum for this purpose shall consist of a member or members from two thirds of the States, and a majority of all the States shall be necessary to a choice. And if the House of Representatives shall not choose a President whenever the right

---

[1] 1 U.S. *Statutes at Large* 402 (1798).
[2] 2 U.S. *Statutes at Large* 306 (1804).

of choice shall devolve upon them, before the fourth day of March next following, then the Vice President shall act as President, as in the case of the death or other constitutional disability of the President.

The person having the greatest number of votes as Vice President shall be the Vice President, if such number be a majority of the whole number of electors appointed; and if no person have a majority, then from the two highest numbers on the list the Senate shall choose the Vice President: a quorum for that purpose shall consist of two thirds of the whole number of Senators, and a majority of the whole number shall be necessary to a choice.

But no person constitutionally ineligible to the office of President shall be eligible to that of Vice President of the United States.

ARTICLE XIII[3]

SEC. 1. Neither slavery nor involuntary servitude, except as a punishment for crime whereof the party shall have been duly convicted, shall exist within the United States, or any place subject to their jurisdiction.

SEC. 2. Congress shall have power to enforce this article by appropriate legislation.

ARTICLE XIV[4]

SEC. 1. All persons born or naturalized in the United States, and subject to the jurisdiction thereof, are citizens of the United States and of the State wherein they reside. No State shall make or enforce any law which shall abridge the privileges or immunities of citizens of the United States; nor shall any State deprive any person of life, liberty, or property, without due process of law, nor deny to any person within its jurisdiction the equal protection of the laws.

SEC. 2. Representatives shall be apportioned among the several States according to their respective numbers, counting the whole number of persons in each State, excluding Indians not taxed. But when the right to vote at any election for the choice of electors for President and Vice-President of the United States, representatives in Congress, the executive and judicial officers of a State, or the members of the legislature thereof, is denied to any of the male inhabitants of such State, being twenty-one years of age, and citizens of the United States, or in any way abridged, except for participation in rebellion or other crime, the basis of representation therein shall be reduced in the proportion which the number of such male citizens shall bear to the whole number of male citizens twenty-one years of age in such State.

SEC. 3. No person shall be a senator or representative in Congress, or elector of President and Vice-President, or hold any office, civil or military, under the United

---

[3] 13 U.S. *Statutes at Large* 567 (1865).
[4] 14 U.S. *Statutes at Large* 358 (1868).

LATER AMENDMENTS TO THE CONSTITUTION

States, or under any State, who having previously taken an oath, as a member of Congress, or as an officer of the United States, or as a member of any State legislature, or as an executive or judicial officer of any State, to support the Constitution of the United States, shall have engaged in insurrection or rebellion against the same, or given aid or comfort to the enemies thereof. But Congress may by a vote of two-thirds of each house remove such disability.

SEC. 4. The validity of the public debt of the United States, authorized by law, including debts incurred for payment of pensions and bounties for services in suppressing insurrection or rebellion, shall not be questioned. But neither the United States nor any State shall assume or pay any debt or obligation incurred in aid of insurrection or rebellion against the United States, or any claim for the loss or emancipation of any slave; but all such debts, obligations, and claims shall be held illegal and void.

SEC. 5. The Congress shall have power to enforce, by appropriate legislation, the provisions of this article.

ARTICLE XV[5]

SEC. 1. The right of citizens of the United States to vote shall not be denied or abridged by the United States or by any State on account of race, color, or previous condition of servitude.

SEC. 2. The Congress shall have power to enforce this article by appropriate legislation.

ARTICLE XVI[6]

The Congress shall have power to lay and collect taxes on incomes, from whatever source derived, without apportionment among the several States, and without regard to any census or enumeration.

ARTICLE XVII[7]

The Senate of the United States shall be composed of two Senators from each State, elected by the people thereof, for six years; and each Senator shall have one vote. The electors in each State shall have the qualifications requisite for electors of the most numerous branch of the State legislatures.

When vacancies happen in the representation of any State in the Senate, the executive authority of such State shall issue writs of election to fill such vacancies:

[5] 15 U.S. *Statutes at Large* 346 (1870).
[6] 36 U.S. *Statutes at Large* 184 (1913).
[7] 37 U.S. *Statutes at Large* 646 (1913).

Provided, That the legislature of any State may empower the executive thereof to make temporary appointments until the people fill the vacancies by election as the legislature may direct.

This amendment shall not be so construed as to affect the election or term of any Senator chosen before it becomes valid as part of the Constitution.

ARTICLE XVIII [8]

SEC. 1. After one year from the ratification of this article the manufacture, sale, or transportation of intoxicating liquors within, the importation thereof into, or the exportation thereof from the United States and all territory subject to the jurisdiction thereof for beverage purposes is hereby prohibited.

SEC. 2. The Congress and the several States shall have concurrent power to enforce this article by appropriate legislation.

SEC. 3. This article shall be inoperative unless it shall have been ratified as an amendment to the Constitution by the legislatures of the several States, as provided in the Constitution, within seven years from the date of the submission hereof to the States by the Congress.

ARTICLE XIX [9]

The right of citizens of the United States to vote shall not be denied or abridged by the United States or by any State on account of sex.

Congress shall have power to enforce this article by appropriate legislation.

ARTICLE XX [10]

SEC. 1. The terms of the President and Vice President shall end at noon on the 20th day of January, and the terms of Senators and Representatives at noon on the 3d day of January, of the years in which such terms would have ended if this article had not been ratified; and the terms of their successors shall then begin.

SEC. 2. The Congress shall assemble at least once in every year, and such meeting shall begin at noon on the 3d day of January, unless they shall by law appoint a different day.

SEC. 3. If, at the time fixed for the beginning of the term of the President, the President elect shall have died, the Vice President elect shall become President. If a

---

[8] 40 U.S. *Statutes at Large* 1050 (1919).

[9] 41 U.S. *Statutes at Large* 362 (1920).

[10] 47 U.S. *Statutes at Large* 745 (1933).

LATER AMENDMENTS TO THE CONSTITUTION

President shall not have been chosen before the time fixed for the beginning of his term, or if the President elect shall have failed to qualify, then the Vice President elect shall act as President until a President shall have qualified; and the Congress may by law provide for the case wherein neither a President elect nor a Vice President elect shall have qualified, declaring who shall then act as President, or the manner in which one who is to act shall be selected, and such person shall act accordingly until a President or Vice President shall have qualified.

SEC. 4. The Congress may by law provide for the case of the death of any of the persons from whom the House of Representatives may choose a President whenever the right of choice shall have devolved upon them, and for the case of the death of any of the persons from whom the Senate may choose a Vice President whenever the right of choice shall have devolved upon them.

SEC. 5. Sections 1 and 2 shall take effect on the 15th day of October following the ratification of this article.

SEC. 6. This article shall be inoperative unless it shall have been ratified as an amendment to the Constitution by the legislatures of three-fourths of the several States within seven years from the date of its submission.

ARTICLE XXI [11]

SEC. 1. The eighteenth article of amendment to the Constitution of the United States is hereby repealed.

SEC. 2. The transportation or importation into any State, Territory, or possession of the United States for delivery or use therein of intoxicating liquors, in violation of the laws thereof, is hereby prohibited.

SEC. 3. This article shall be inoperative unless it shall have been ratified as an amendment to the Constitution by conventions in the several States, as provided in the Constitution, within seven years from the date of the submission hereof to the States by the Congress.

ARTICLE XXII [12]

SEC. 1. No person shall be elected to the office of the President more than twice, and no person who has held the office of President, or acted as President, for more than two years of a term to which some other person was elected President shall be elected to the office of the President more than once. But this Article shall not apply to any person holding the office of President when this Article was proposed by the Congress, and shall not prevent any person who may be holding the office of President,

---

[11] 47 U.S. *Statutes at Large* 1625 (1933).
[12] 61 U.S. *Statutes at Large* 959 (1951).

or acting as President, during the term within which this Article becomes operative from holding the office of President or acting as President during the remainder of such term.

SEC. 2. This Article shall be inoperative unless it shall have been ratified as an amendment to the Constitution by the legislatures of three-fourths of the several States within seven years from the date of its submission to the States by the Congress.

ARTICLE XXIII[13]

SEC. 1. The District constituting the seat of Government of the United States shall appoint in such manner as the Congress may direct:

A number of electors of President and Vice President equal to the whole number of Senators and Representatives in Congress to which the District would be entitled if it were a State, but in no event more than the least populous State; they shall be in addition to those appointed by the States, but they shall be considered, for the purposes of the election of President and Vice President, to be electors appointed by a State; and they shall meet in the District and perform such duties as provided by the twelfth article of amendment.

SEC. 2. The Congress shall have power to enforce this article by appropriate legislation.

ARTICLE XXIV[14]

SEC. 1. The right of citizens of the United States to vote in any primary or other election for President or Vice President, for electors for President or Vice President, or for Senator or Representative in Congress, shall not be denied or abridged by the United States or any State by reason of failure to pay any poll tax or other tax.

SEC. 2. The Congress shall have power to enforce this article by appropriate legislation.

ARTICLE XXV[15]

SEC. 1. In case of the removal of the President from office or of his death or resignation, the Vice President shall become President.

---

[13] 75 U.S. *Statutes at Large* 847 (1961).
[14] 78 U.S. *Statutes at Large* 1117 (1964).
[15] 81 U.S. *Statutes at Large* 983 (1967).

SEC. 2. Whenever there is a vacancy in the office of the Vice President, the President shall nominate a Vice President who shall take office upon confirmation by a majority vote of both Houses of Congress.

SEC. 3. Whenever the President transmits to the President pro tempore of the Senate and the Speaker of the House of Representatives his written declaration that he is unable to discharge the powers and duties of his office, and until he transmits to them a written declaration to the contrary, such powers and duties shall be discharged by the Vice President as Acting President.

SEC. 4. Whenever the Vice President and a majority of either the principal officers of the executive departments or of such other body as Congress may by law provide, transmit to the President pro tempore of the Senate and the Speaker of the House of Representatives their written declaration that the President is unable to discharge the powers and duties of his office, the Vice President shall immediately assume the powers and duties of the office as Acting President.

Thereafter, when the President transmits to the President pro tempore of the Senate and the Speaker of the House of Representatives his written declaration that no inability exists, he shall resume the powers and duties of his office unless the Vice President and a majority of either the principal officers of the executive department or of such other body as Congress may by law provide, transmit within four days to the President pro tempore of the Senate and the Speaker of the House of Representatives their written declaration that the President is unable to discharge the powers and duties of his office. Thereupon Congress shall decide the issue, assembling within forty-eight hours for that purpose if not in session. If the Congress, within twenty-one days after receipt of the latter written declaration, or, if Congress is not in session, within twenty-one days after Congress is required to assemble, determines by two-thirds vote of both Houses that the President is unable to discharge the powers and duties of his office, the Vice President shall continue to discharge the same as Acting President; otherwise, the President shall resume the powers and duties of his office.

ARTICLE XXVI[16]

SEC. 1. The right of citizens of the United States, who are eighteen years of age or older, to vote shall not be denied or abridged by the United States or by any State on account of age.

SEC. 2. The Congress shall have power to enforce this article by appropriate legislation.

[16] 84 U.S. *Statutes at Large* 314 (1970).

SELECTED BIBLIOGRAPHY

I. *Books*

Adams, James T. *The Founding of New England.* 3 vols. Boston: Little, Brown & Co., 1927.
———. *New England in the Republic, 1776-1850.* Boston: Little, Brown & Co., 1926.
———. *Revolutionary New England, 1691-1776.* Boston: The Atlantic Press, 1923.
Andrews, Charles M. *The Colonial Period of American History.* 3 vols. New Haven: Yale University Press, 1934-37.
Andrews, Matthew P. *The Founding of Maryland.* New York: D. Appleton-Century Co., 1933.
Bancroft, George. *History of the Formation of the Constitution of the United States of America.* 2 vols. 2d ed. New York: D. Appleton & Co., 1882.
Barrington, Boyd C. *The Magna Charta and Other Great Charters of England.* Philadelphia: William J. Campbell, 1900.
Beaney, William M. *The Right to Counsel in American Courts.* Ann Arbor: University of Michigan Press, 1955.
Beard, Charles A. *An Economic Interpretation of the Constitution of the United States.* New York: Macmillan Co., 1929.
———. *The Republic; Conversations on Fundamentals.* New York: Viking Press, 1943.
Becker, Carl. *The Declaration of Independence.* New York: Harcourt, Brace & Co., 1922.
Beer, George L. *British Colonial Policy, 1754-1765.* New York: Macmillan Co., 1907.
Boyd, Julian. *The Declaration of Independence.* Princeton: Princeton University Press, 1945.
Brown, Alexander. *The First Republic in America.* Boston: Houghton Mifflin Co., 1898.
Bryce, James. *The American Commonwealth.* 2 vols. 2d ed. rev. New York: Macmillan Co., 1891.
Burnett, Edmund C. *The Continental Congress.* New York: Macmillan Co., 1941.
Chafee, Zechariah. *Free Speech in the United States.* Cambridge: Harvard University Press, 1948.
Channing, Edward. *A History of the United States.* 6 vols. New York: Macmillan Co., 1927-30.
Cheyney, Edward P. *European Background of American History, 1300-1600.* (Vol. I of *The American Nation: A History.*) New York: Harper & Bros., 1904.
Chinard, Gilbert. *Thomas Jefferson, The Apostle of Americanism.* Boston: Little, Brown & Co., 1939.
Churchill, Winston S. *A History of the English-Speaking Peoples.* 4 vols. New York: Dodd, Mead & Co., 1956-58.
Clark, G. N. *The Later Stuarts, 1660-1714.* (The Oxford History of England.) Oxford: Clarendon Press, 1934.
———. *The Seventeenth Century.* 2d ed. Oxford: Clarendon Press, 1947.
Cooley, Thomas M. *Constitutional Limitations.* 2d ed. Boston: Little, Brown & Co., 1871.
Craven, Wesley F. *Dissolution of the Virginia Company.* New York: Oxford University Press, 1932.
DeHaas, Elsa. *Antiquities of Bail.* New York: Columbia University Press, 1940.
Dicey, Albert V. *Introduction to the Study of the Law of the Constitution.* 8th ed. London: Macmillan & Co., 1915.
———. *The Privy Council.* London: Macmillan & Co., 1887.
Eckenrode, Hamilton J. *The Revolution in Virginia.* Boston: Houghton Mifflin Co., 1916.

SOURCES OF OUR LIBERTIES

Farrand, Max. *The Framing of the Constitution of the United States.* New Haven: Yale University Press, 1913.
Figgis, John N. *The Divine Right of Kings.* 2d ed. Cambridge, England: University Press, 1914.
Fiske, John. *The Beginnings of New England.* 11th ed. Boston: Houghton Mifflin Co., 1895.
———. *The Critical Period of American History, 1783-1789.* Boston: Houghton Mifflin Co., 1888.
Frothingham, Richard. *The Rise of the Republic of the United States.* 7th ed. Boston: Little, Brown & Co., 1899.
Griswold, Erwin N. *The Fifth Amendment Today.* Cambridge, Mass.: Harvard University Press, 1955.
Hall, Clayton C. *The Lords Baltimore and the Maryland Palatinate.* Baltimore: John Murphy Co., 1902.
Heller, Francis H. *The Sixth Amendment to the Constitution of the United States.* Lawrence: University of Kansas Press, 1951.
Holdsworth, William S. *A History of English Law.* 12 vols. 4th ed. Boston: Little, Brown & Co., 1927.
Hoyt, William H. *The Mecklenburg Declaration of Independence.* New York: G. P. Putnam's Sons, 1907.
Jenks, Edward. *A Short History of English Law.* 4th ed. London: Methuen & Co., 1928.
———. *Law and Politics in the Middle Ages.* New York: Henry Holt & Co., 1912.
Jensen, Merrill. *The Articles of Confederation.* Madison: University of Wisconsin Press, 1940.
———. *The New Nation: A History of the United States During the Confederation, 1781-1789.* New York: Alfred A. Knopf, 1950.
Jordan, W. K. *The Development of Religious Toleration in England.* Cambridge, Mass.: Harvard University Press, 1940.
Keir, David L. *The Constitutional History of Modern Britain, 1485-1937.* 3d ed. London: Adam & Charles Black, 1946.
Kelly, Alfred H. *Foundations of Freedom.* New York: Harper & Bros., 1958.
Latourette, Kenneth S. *A History of Christianity.* New York: Harper & Bros., 1953.
McIlwain, Charles H. *Constitutionalism, Ancient and Modern.* Ithaca: Cornell University Press, 1940.
———. *The High Court of Parliament and Its Supremacy.* New Haven: Yale University Press, 1910.
McKechnie, William S. *Magna Carta.* 2d ed. rev. Glasgow: J. Maclehose & Sons, 1914.
McLaughlin, Andrew C. *A Constitutional History of the United States.* New York: D. Appleton-Century Co., 1935.
———. *The Confederation and the Constitution, 1783-1789.* (Vol. X of *The American Nation: A History.*) New York: Harper & Bros., 1905.
———. *The Foundations of American Constitutionalism.* New York: New York University Press, 1932.
McMaster, John B. *A History of the People of the United States from the Revolution to the Civil War.* 8 vols. New York: Appleton & Co., 1883-1913.
Macaulay, Thomas B. *History of England,* ed. Charles H. Firth. 6 vols. London: Macmillan & Co., 1913-15.
Maitland, Frederic W. *The Constitutional History of England.* Cambridge, England: University Press, 1909.
Malden, Henry E. (ed.). *Magna Carta Commemoration Essays.* Aberdeen: University Press, 1917.
Morison, Samuel E. *Builders of the Bay Colony.* Boston: Houghton Mifflin Co., 1930.
Mott, Rodney L. *Due Process of Law.* Indianapolis: Bobbs-Merrill Co., 1926.
Mullett, Charles F. *Fundamental Law and the American Revolution, 1760-1776.* New York: Columbia University Press, 1933.
Nevins, Allan. *The American States During and After the Revolution, 1775-1789.* New York: Macmillan Co., 1924.
Newton, Arthur P. *The Colonising Activities of the English Puritans.* New Haven: Yale University Press, 1914.
Osgood, Herbert L. *The American Colonies in the Seventeenth Century.* 3 vols. New York: Macmillan Co., 1904-7.
Painter, Sidney. *The Reign of King John.* Baltimore: Johns Hopkins Press, 1949.
Pargellis, Stanley M. *Lord Loudoun in North America.* New Haven: Yale University Press, 1933.

SELECTED BIBLIOGRAPHY

Paterson, James. *The Liberty of the Press, Speech, and Public Worship.* London: Macmillan & Co., 1880.
Patterson, Giles J. *Free Speech and a Free Press.* Boston: Little, Brown & Co., 1939.
Pinkham, Lucile. *William III and the Respectable Revolution.* Cambridge, Mass.: Harvard University Press, 1954.
Pollock, Frederick, and Maitland, Frederic W. *The History of English Law.* 2 vols. 2d ed. Cambridge, England: University Press, 1911.
Radin, Max. *Handbook of Anglo-American Legal History.* St. Paul: West Publishing Co., 1936.
Relf, Frances H. *The Petition of Right.* Minneapolis: University of Minnesota Press, 1917.
Rutland, Robert A. *The Birth of the Bill of Rights, 1776-1791.* Chapel Hill: University of North Carolina Press, 1955.
Schlesinger, Arthur M. *The Colonial Merchants and the American Revolution, 1763-1776.* New York: Columbia University Press, 1917.
Scofield, Cora L. *A Study of the Court of Star Chamber.* Chicago: University of Chicago Press, 1900.
Scott, Arthur P. *Criminal Law in Colonial Virginia.* Chicago: University of Chicago Press, 1930.
Scott, James Brown. *The United States of America: A Study in International Organization.* New York: Oxford University Press, 1920.
Sharpless, Isaac. *A Quaker Experiment in Government.* Philadelphia: Alfred J. Ferris, 1898.
Stephen, James F. *A General View of the Criminal Law of England.* London: Macmillan & Co., 1863.
———. *A History of the Criminal Law of England.* 3 vols. London: Macmillan & Co., 1883.
Story, Joseph. *Commentaries on the Constitution of the United States,* ed. Thomas M. Cooley. 2 vols. 4th ed. Boston: Little, Brown & Co., 1873.
———. *A Familiar Exposition of the Constitution of the United States.* New York: Harper & Bros., 1840.
Stubbs, William. *The Constitutional History of England in Its Origin and Development.* 3 vols. Oxford: Clarendon Press, 1896-97.
———. *Lectures on Early English History.* London: Longmans, Green & Co., 1906.
Sweet, William W. *Religion in Colonial America.* New York: C. Scribner's Sons, 1942.
———. *The Story of Religion in America.* New York: Harper & Bros., 1939.
Swisher, Carl B. *American Constitutional Development.* Boston: Houghton Mifflin Co., 1943.
Tanner, J. R. *English Constitutional Conflicts of the Seventeenth Century, 1603-1689.* Cambridge, England: University Press, 1928.
Thompson, Faith. *Magna Carta.* Minneapolis: University of Minnesota Press, 1948.
Trevelyan, George M. *The English Revolution, 1688-1689.* London: Thornton Butterworth, Ltd., 1938.
Trevelyan, George O. *The American Revolution.* 4 vols. New ed.; London: Longmans, Green & Co., 1905-29.
Tyler, Lyon G. *England in America, 1580-1652.* (Vol. IV of *The American Nation: A History.*) New York: Harper & Bros., 1904.
Van Tyne, Claude H. *The Causes of the War of Independence.* Boston: Houghton Mifflin Co., 1922.
———. *The War of Independence: American Phase.* Boston: Houghton Mifflin Co., 1929.
Warren, Charles. *A History of the American Bar.* Boston: Little, Brown & Co., 1911.
———. *The Making of the Constitution.* Boston: Little, Brown & Co., 1929.
Willison, George F. *Saints and Strangers.* New York: Reynal and Hitchcock, 1945.
Wormuth, Francis D. *The Origins of Modern Constitutionalism.* New York: Harper & Bros., 1949.
Wright, Benjamin F. *American Interpretations of Natural Law.* Cambridge, Mass.: Harvard University Press, 1931.
———. *Consensus and Continuity, 1776-1787.* Boston: Boston University Press, 1958.
Yonge, Charles D. *History of the English Revolution of 1688.* London: Henry S. King & Co., 1874.

II. Articles

Adair, E. R. "The Petition of Right," *History,* V (new series; July, 1920), 99-103.
Baldwin, Simeon E. "Constitutional Law, 1701-1901," *Two Centuries' Growth of American Law, 1701-1901.* New York: C. Scribner's Sons, 1901.
Cheyney, Edward P. "The Court of Star Chamber," *American Historical Review,* XVIII (July, 1913), 727-50.

Collins, Arthur J. "The Documents of the Great Charter of 1215," *Proceedings of the British Academy* (1948), 233-79.

Corwin, Edward S. "The 'Higher Law' Background of American Constitutional Law," *Harvard Law Review*, XLII (December, 1928, and January, 1929), 149-85, 365-409.

Dumbauld, Edward. "State Precedents for the Bill of Rights," *Journal of Public Law*, VII (Fall, 1958), 323-44.

Edwards, J. G. "Confirmatio Cartarum and Baronial Grievances in 1297," *English Historical Review*, LVIII (1943), 147-71, 273-300.

Ericson, Fred J. "The Contemporary British Opposition to the Stamp Act, 1764-65," *Papers of the Michigan Academy of Science, Arts, and Letters*, XXIX (1944), 489-505.

Jameson, J. Franklin. "An Introduction to the Study of the Constitutional and Political History of the Individual States," *Johns Hopkins University Studies in Historical and Political Science*. Baltimore: Johns Hopkins Press, 1886. IV, 185-209.

Jenks, Edward. "The Story of the Habeas Corpus," *Select Essays in Anglo-American Legal History*. Boston: Little, Brown & Co., 1908. II, 531-48.

McIlwain, Charles H. "Due Process of Law in Magna Carta," *Columbia Law Review*, XIV (January, 1914), 27-51.

Morey, William C. "The First State Constitutions," *Annals of the American Academy of Political and Social Science*, IV (1893), 201-32.

Morison, Samuel E. "Struggle Over the Adoption of the Constitution of Massachusetts," *Massachusetts Historical Society Proceedings*, L (1917), 353-411.

Petrie, George. "Church and State in Early Maryland," *Johns Hopkins University Studies in Historical and Political Science*. Baltimore: Johns Hopkins Press, 1892. X, 193-238.

Radin, Max. "The Myth of Magna Carta," *Harvard Law Review*, LX (September, 1947), 1060-91.

Reinsch, Paul S. "The English Common Law in the Early American Colonies," *Select Essays in Anglo-American Legal History*. Boston: Little, Brown & Co., 1907. I, 367-415.

Rothwell, Harry. "The Confirmation of the Charters, 1297," *English Historical Review*. LX (1945), 16-35, 177-91, 300-15.

Schlesinger, Arthur M. "The Colonial Newspapers and the Stamp Act," *New England Quarterly*, VIII (1935). 63-83.

Sioussat, St. George L. "The English Statutes in Maryland," *Johns Hopkins University Studies in Historical and Political Science*. Baltimore: Johns Hopkins Press, 1903. XXI, 465-568.

Smellie, K. "Right of Petition," *Encyclopedia of the Social Sciences*. New York: Macmillan Co., 1933-35. XII, 98-101.

Webster, William C. "Comparative Study of the State Constitutions of the American Revolution," *Annals of the American Academy of Political and Social Science*, IX (1897), 380-420.

Woodburn, James A. "Causes of the American Revolution," *Johns Hopkins University Studies in Historical and Political Science*. Baltimore: Johns Hopkins Press, 1892. X, 557-609.

III. *Sources*

Adams, George B., and Stephens, H. Morse (eds.). *Select Documents of English Constitutional History*. New York: Macmillan Co., 1901.

Brown, Alexander. *The Genesis of the United States*. 2 vols. Boston: Houghton Mifflin Co., 1891.

Callender, Guy S. *Selections from the Economic History of the United States, 1765-1860*. Boston: Ginn & Co., 1909.

Chafee, Zechariah (ed.). *Documents on Fundamental Human Rights*. 3 vols. Cambridge, Mass.: Harvard University Press, 1951-52.

Commager, Henry S. (ed.). *Documents of American History*. 6th ed. New York: Appleton-Century-Crofts, Inc., 1958.

Dykes, David O. (ed.). *Source Book of Constitutional History from 1660*. London: Longmans, Green & Co., 1930.

Elliot, Jonathan (ed.). *The Debates in the State Conventions on the Adoption of the Federal Constitution*. 5 vols. 2d ed. Philadelphia: J. B. Lippincott & Co., 1866.

Gardiner, Samuel R. (ed.). *The Constitutional Documents of the Puritan Revolution, 1625-1660*. 3d ed. rev. Oxford: Clarendon Press, 1906.

SELECTED BIBLIOGRAPHY

Gee, Henry, and Hardy, William J. (eds.). *Documents Illustrative of English Church History.* London: Macmillan & Co., 1896.

Gooch, Robert K. *Source Book on the Government of England.* New York: D. Van Nostrand Co., 1939.

Hacker, Louis M. (ed.). *The Shaping of the American Tradition.* New York: Columbia University Press, 1947.

Lodge, Eleanor C., and Thornton, Gladys A. *English Constitutional Documents, 1307-1485.* Cambridge, England: University Press, 1935.

MacDonald, William (ed.). *Documentary Source Book of American History, 1606-1913.* New York: Macmillan Co., 1916.

——. *Select Charters and Other Documents Illustrative of American History, 1606-1775.* New York: Macmillan Co., 1899.

Morison, Samuel E. (ed.). *Sources and Documents Illustrating the American Revolution, 1764-1788.* Oxford: Clarendon Press, 1923.

Niles, H. *Principles and Acts of the Revolution in America.* Baltimore: W. O. Niles, 1822.

Prothero, George W. (ed.). *Select Statutes and Other Constitutional Documents Illustrative of the Reigns of Elizabeth and James I.* 3d ed. Oxford: Clarendon Press, 1906.

Stephenson, Carl, and Marcham, Frederick G. (eds.). *Sources of English Constitutional History.* New York: Harper & Bros., 1937.

Stubbs, William (ed.). *Select Charters and Other Illustrations of English Constitutional History.* 8th ed. Oxford: Clarendon Press, 1900.

Tansill, Charles C. (ed.). *Documents Illustrative of the Formation of the Union of the American States,* 69th Cong., 1st Sess., 1927, House Doc. 398.

Thorpe, Francis N. (ed.). *The Federal and State Constitutions, Colonial Charters, and other Organic Laws.* 7 vols. Washington: Government Printing Office, 1909.

Woodhouse, A. S. P. (ed.). *Puritanism and Liberty.* London: J. M. Dent & Sons, 1938.

POSTSCRIPT 1978: BIBLIOGRAPHICAL NOTE
by Stanley N. Katz

In the two decades since the original publication of *Sources of Our Liberties*, two "birthday" celebrations—the 750th anniversary of Magna Carta in 1965 and the 200th anniversary of United States independence in 1976—have stimulated a steady flow of scholarship in the well-established field of British constitutional history and a veritable explosion in the newly emergent field of American legal history. It is foreseeable that the bicentennial of the United States Constitution, in 1987, will be even more stimulating, inasmuch as the 1787 Constitution is widely recognized as being perhaps the most important document in the legal tradition of the Western world. Under the name Project 87, the American Historical Association and the American Political Science Association have already begun an ambitious program to coordinate the scholarly contribution to the constitutional bicentennial. The republication of *Sources of Our Liberties* thus comes as a welcome forerunner to what promises to be a decade of intense scholarly activity in American legal and constitutional history.

In the field of British constitutional history, Magna Carta studies have predominated since 1959. The leading work is J. C. Holt's *Magna Charta*, published in the anniversary year.[1] Anne Pallister's shorter and more recent volume, *Magna Charta: The Heritage of Liberty*,[2] surveys the scholarship to date. Together, Holt and Pallister consider the creation and use of the Great Charter in the context of modern refinements in the social, political, and legal history of the Middle Ages. These works can be supplemented with

---

[1] Cambridge: At the University Press, 1965.
[2] London: Clarendon Press, 1971.

two books that provide an overview of the role of law in early English society: Doris Mary Stenton's *English Justice Between the Norman Conquest and the Great Charter, 1066–1215*[3] and Helen Cam's *Law-Finders and Law-Makers in Medieval England*.[4] In *Magna Charta in the Historiography of the Sixteenth and Seventeenth Centuries*, Herbert Butterfield considers the Great Charter in the context of the seventeenth-century constitutional crisis,[5] thus illuminating the relationship between the charter and the Petition of Right, the Habeas Corpus Act, and the Bill of Rights. In *The Road from Runnymeade: Magna Charta and American Constitutionalism*, A. E. Dick Howard considers the document in a long-term American context.[6] The most recent edition of a classic text is A. V. Dicey's *Introduction to the Study of the Law of the Constitution*.[7] Attention should also be drawn to the admirable series of essays on the Magna Carta which was published in the 1960s by the University Press of Virginia.[8]

Through many recent works by historians focusing on seventeenth-century English history, our understanding of the constitutional problems of the English civil war era has deepened considerably. These new books, too numerous to list here, may be represented by Christopher Hill's *The Century of Revolution, 1603–1714*.[9] The two critical works from a legal point of view are J. W. Gough's *Fundamental Law in English Constitutional History*[10] and J. G. A. Pocock's *The Ancient Constitution and the Feudal Law*.[11] Pocock, in particular, demonstrates the manner in which seventeenth-century radicals manipulated a newly constructed version of the English constitutional past in order to serve their political needs in the revolutionary era. Certain aspects of this theme have been carried forward by Caroline

---

[3] Philadelphia: American Philosophical Society, 1964.

[4] London: Merlin Press, 1962.

[5] Reading: University of Reading, 1969.

[6] Charlottesville: University Press of Virginia, 1968.

[7] 10th ed.; London: Macmillan, 1959.

[8] These include Maurice Percey Ashley, *Magna Carta in the Seventeenth Century* (Charlottesville: University Press of Virginia, 1965); John E. Bebout, *An Ancient Partnership: Local Government, Magna Carta, and the National Interest* (1966); Gottfried Dietze, *Magna Carta and Property* (1965); Arthur L. Goodhart, *Law of the Land* (1966); Daniel John Meador, *Habeas Corpus and Magna Carta: Dualism of Power and Liberty* (1966); and Doris M. Stenton, *After Runnymeade: Magna Carta in the Middle Ages* (1965).

[9] London: Thomas Nelson & Sons, 1961.

[10] Oxford: Clarendon Press, 1961.

[11] Cambridge: At the University Press, 1957.

POSTSCRIPT 1978

Robbins in *The Eighteenth-Century Commonwealthman*.[12] An excellent sourcebook for the period is John Phillips Kenyon, ed., *The Stuart Constitution, 1603–1688: Documents and Commentary*.[13] For an intensely American view of the English experience, by an American lawyer, see Bernard Schwartz, *The Roots of Freedom: A Constitutional History of England*.[14]

The following works also should be consulted by the reader who is curious to explore the larger dimensions of the English background to American constitutional and legal history: J. H. Baker, *An Introduction to English Legal History*;[15] Arthur R. Hogue, *The Origins of the Common Law*;[16] and S. F. C. Milsom, *Historical Foundations of the Common Law*.[17] Two casebooks in United States legal history explore the connection between the English experience and American institutions: Joseph H. Smith, *Cases and Materials on the Development of Legal Institutions*,[18] and Spencer L. Kimball, *Historical Introduction to the Legal System*.[19]

Although from a scholarly point of view it was disappointing, the bicentennial of the American Revolution produced two excellent law review symposia on our constitutional tradition: Constitutional Government—Strengths, Weaknesses, Future, in the *William and Mary Law Review*,[20] and Law and the American Revolution, in the *University of Pennsylvania Law Review*.[21] The most notable volume of American legal history produced for the bicentennial was John Phillip Reid, *In a Defiant Stance: The Conditions of Law in Massachusetts Bay, the Irish Comparison, and the Coming of the Ameri-*

---

[12] Cambridge, Mass.: Harvard University Press, 1959.
[13] Cambridge: At the University Press, 1966.
[14] New York: Hill & Wang, 1967.
[15] London: Butterworth & Co., 1971.
[16] Bloomington: Indiana University Press, 1966.
[17] London: Butterworth & Co., 1969.
[18] St. Paul, Minn.: West Publishing Co., 1965.
[19] St. Paul, Minn.: West Publishing Co., 1966.

[20] Vol. 17 (Spring 1976), pp. 417–541. Notable in the *William and Mary* symposium are O. Hood Phillips, "The British Constitution: From Revolution to Devolution" (pp. 423–71); David Ammerman, "The British Constitution and the American Revolution: A Failure of Precedent" (pp. 473–501); and William F. Swindler, "Seedtime of an American Judiciary: From Independence to the Constitution" (pp. 503–26).

[21] Vol. 124 (May 1976), pp. 1083–1292. The *Pennsylvania* symposium includes William F. Swindler, "'Rights of Englishmen' Since 1776: Some Anglo-American Notes" (pp. 1083–1103); Joseph H. Smith, "An Independent Judiciary: The Colonial Background" (pp. 1104–56); Barbara A. Black, "The Constitution of Empire: The Case for the Colonists" (pp. 1157–1211); G. Edward White, "The Path of American Jurisprudence" (pp. 1212–59); and Herbert Alan Johnson, "John Jay: Lawyer in a Time of Transition, 1764–1775" (pp. 1260–92).

can Revolution.[22] Readers who are interested in the legal and constitutional history of the original states will also benefit from two ambitious bicentennial series: A History of the American Colonies Series, being published by Charles Scribner's Sons;[23] and The States and the Nation Series, by W. W. Norton and Company.[24]

In the last ten years, our knowledge of the colonial and revolutionary origins of the American constitutional tradition has been immeasurably enriched, principally through the efforts of Harvard historian Bernard Bailyn and his students. Professor Bailyn began his reassessment of the intellectual roots of the Revolution with the first volume of *Pamphlets of the American Revolution, 1750–1776,*[25] and carried it through in *The Origins of American Politics*[26] and *The Ideological Origins of the American Revolution.*[27] In relating the history of eighteenth-century English radicalism to the political development of the American colonies, Bailyn suggested an entirely new view of the relationship between constitutionalism and the Revolution. This relationship has been elaborated with great elegance and detail by Gordon S. Wood in *The Creation of the American Republic, 1776–1787,* the single most important volume for understanding how our modern constitutional tradition emerged.[28] Other aspects of revolutionary political and constitutional thought are treated in Pauline Maier, *From Resistance to Revolution: Colonial Radicals and the Development of American Opposition to Britain, 1765–1776;*[29] and Richard Buel, *Securing the Revolution: Ideology in American Politics, 1789–1815.*[30] Stanley N. Katz surveys much of this

---

[22] University Park: Pennsylvania State University Press, 1977.

[23] This series includes thus far John E. Pomfret, *Colonial New Jersey: A History* (New York: Charles Scribner's Sons, 1973); Hugh T. Lefler and William S. Powell, *Colonial North Carolina: A History* (1973); Michael G. Kammen, *Colonial New York: A History* (1975); Sydney V. James, *Colonial Rhode Island: A History* (1975); Joseph E. Illick, *Colonial Pennsylvania: A History* (1976); and Kenneth Coleman, *Colonial Georgia: A History* (1976).

[24] This series includes Louis B. Wright, *South Carolina: A Bicentennial History* (New York: W. W. Norton & Co., 1976); Thomas J. Fleming, *New Jersey: A Bicentennial History* (1977); Carol E. Hoffecker, *Delaware: A Bicentennial History* (1977); Harold H. Martin, *Georgia: A Bicentennial History* (1977); Elizabeth Forbes Morison, *New Hampshire: A Bicentennial History* (1977); William Stevens Powell, *North Carolina: A Bicentennial History* (1977); and Louis D. Rubin, *Virginia: A Bicentennial History* (1977).

[25] Cambridge, Mass.: Harvard University Press, Belknap Press, 1965.

[26] New York: Alfred A. Knopf, Inc., 1968.

[27] Cambridge, Mass.: Harvard University Press, Belknap Press, 1967.

[28] Chapel Hill: University of North Carolina Press, 1969.

[29] New York: Alfred A. Knopf, Inc., 1972.

[30] Ithaca, N.Y.: Cornell University Press, 1972.

POSTSCRIPT 1978

literature in "The Origins of American Constitutional Thought."[31] The leading text is George Dargo's *Roots of the Republic: A New Perspective on Early American Constitutionalism*.[32]

Although Merril Jensen's work on the era of the Confederacy[33] has yet to be superseded, Jackson Turner Main has greatly enriched our understanding of the performance of the newly independent states in *The Sovereign States, 1775–1783*.[34] Perhaps more important for an understanding of the alternatives to the system of 1787 are the two leading works on the Antifederalists: Jackson Turner Main, *The Antifederalists: Critics of the Constitution*;[35] and Cecilia M. Kenyon, ed., *The Antifederalists*.[36] Note also Kenyon's "Men of Little Faith: Anti-Federalists on the Nature of Representative Government."[37] New light on judicial development during the Confederation period is provided in Henry J. Bourguignon, *The First Federal Court: The Federal Appellate Prize Court of the American Revolution, 1776–1787*.[38]

The drafting of the federal Constitution has been the subject of a number of scholarly articles. These include John P. Roche, "The Founding Fathers: A Reform Caucus in Action";[39] Howard A. Ohline, "Republicanism and Slavery: Origins of the Three-Fifths Clause in the U.S. Constitution";[40] and M. A. Banks, "Drafting the American Constitution—Attitudes in the Philadelphia Convention Towards the British System of Government."[41] Two important studies have challenged Charles Beard's allegation that the framers were motivated by economic self-interest:[42] Robert E. Brown, *Charles Beard and the Constitution*;[43] and Forrest McDonald, *We the Peo-

---

[31] *Perspectives in American History* 3 (1969): 474–90.
[32] New York: Praeger Publishers, 1974.
[33] *The New Nation* (New York: Alfred A. Knopf, Inc., 1950).
[34] New York: New Viewpoints, 1973.
[35] Chapel Hill: University of North Carolina Press, 1961.
[36] Indianapolis, Ind.: Bobbs-Merrill Co., 1966.
[37] *William and Mary Quarterly* (3d ser.) 12 (1955): 3–43.
[38] Philadelphia: American Philosophical Society, 1977.
[39] *American Political Science Review* 55 (1961): 799–816.
[40] *William and Mary Quarterly* (3d ser.) 28 (1971): 563–84.
[41] *American Journal of Legal History* 10 (1966): 15–33.
[42] *An Economic Interpretation of the Constitution of the United States* (New York: Macmillan Co., 1913).
[43] Princeton, N.J.: Princeton University Press, 1956.

ple: The Economic Origins of the Constitution.[44] Probably the most original and controversial account of the movement for the Constitution is Staughton Lynd's *Class Conflict, Slavery, and the United States Constitution.*[45] The Philadelphia Convention of 1787 has recently been the subject of general accounts by Catherine Drinker Bowen, *Miracle at Philadelphia: Story of the Constitutional Convention,*[46] and Clinton Lawrence Rossiter, *1787: The Grand Convention.*[47]

The history of the ratification of the Constitution has become a scholarly field unto itself. The major work, here, is the Merril Jensen edition of *The Documentary History of the Ratification of the Constitution*, a multivolume collection of original sources relating to ratification in all of the new states.[48] Linda Grant De Pauw has studied the ratification struggle in *The Eleventh Pillar: New York State and the Federal Constitution.*[49] Even more intensively studied has been the intellectual contest over the new constitutional structure—in particular, the significance of the *Federalist Papers.*[50] See especially Martin Diamond, "Democracy and the Federalist: A Reconsideration of the Framers' Intent"[51] and "The Federalist on Federalism: Neither a National nor a Federal Constitution, but a Composition of Both";[52] Gottfried Dietze, "Jay's Federalist—Treatise for Free Government,"[53] "Hamilton's Federalist—Treatise for Free Government,"[54] and "Madison's Federalist —a Treatise for Free Government";[55] William Jeffrey, "Letters of 'Brutus'— a Neglected Element in the Ratification Campaign of 1787–88";[56] and Judith N. Shklar, "Publius and the Science of the Past."[57]

---

[44] Chicago: University of Chicago Press, 1958.

[45] Indianapolis, Ind.: Bobbs-Merrill Co., 1967.

[46] Boston: Little, Brown & Co., 1966.

[47] New York: Macmillan Co., 1966.

[48] Madison: State Historical Society of Wisconsin, 1976–.

[49] Ithaca, N.Y.: Cornell University Press, 1966.

[50] The Benjamin Fletcher Wright edition (Cambridge, Mass.: Harvard University Press, Belknap . Press, 1961) is perhaps the most convenient.

[51] *American Political Science Review* 53 (1959): 52–68.

[52] *Yale Law Journal* 86 (1977): 1273–85.

[53] *Maryland Law Review* 17 (1957): 217–30.

[54] *Cornell Law Quarterly* 42 (1957): 307–28.

[55] *Georgetown Law Journal* 46 (1957): 21–51.

[56] *University of Cincinnati Law Review* 40 (1971): 643–777.

[57] *Yale Law Journal* 86 (1977): 1286–96.

POSTSCRIPT 1978

The Bill of Rights remains a flourishing field of scholarship. Several general accounts have been written of the creation, enactment, and intent of the first ten Amendments: Irving Brant, *The Bill of Rights: Its Origin and Meaning*;[58] Learned Hand, *The Bill of Rights*;[59] Bernard Schwartz, *The Bill of Rights: A Documentary History*[60] and *The Great Rights of Mankind: A History of the American Bill of Rights*.[61] Leonard W. Levy, who has undertaken the ambitious task of investigating the history of each of the rights enshrined in the Constitution in 1971, has thus far published *Legacy of Suppression: Freedom of Speech and Press in Early American History*[62] and *Origins of the Fifth Amendment: The Right Against Self-Incrimination*.[63] Levy has also written "Liberty and the First Amendment, 1790–1800,"[64] which may be compared with Thomas I. Emerson, "Colonial Intentions and Current Realities of the First Amendment."[65] Other articles of interest include Roy G. Weatherup, "Standing Armies and Armed Citizens: An Historical Analysis of the Second Amendment";[66] René de Visme Williamson, "Political Process of Judicial Process: The Bill of Rights and the Framers of the Constitution";[67] Charles W. Wolfram, "Constitutional History of the Seventh Amendment";[68] and Edith Guild Henderson, "The Background of the Seventh Amendment."[69]

Julius Goebel, Jr., has provided us with a magisterial overview of the antecedents of the modern American constitutional system in *Antecedents and Beginnings to 1801*, the first volume of his Oliver Wendell Holmes Devise History of the United States Supreme Court.[70] *Sources of Our Liberties* is intended to bring the reader only to the very beginning of the constitutional era; the standard accounts of our constitutional history remain Alfred H.

---

[58] Indianapolis, Ind.: Bobbs-Merrill Co., 1965.
[59] Cambridge, Mass.: Harvard University Press, 1958.
[60] New York: Chelsea House Publishers, 1971.
[61] New York: Oxford University Press, 1977.
[62] Cambridge, Mass.: Harvard University Press, 1960.
[63] New York: Oxford University Press, 1968.
[64] *American Historical Review* 68 (1962): 22–37.
[65] *University of Pennsylvania Law Review* 125 (1977): 737–760.
[66] *Hastings Constitutional Law Quarterly* 2 (1975): 961–1001.
[67] *Journal of Politics* 23 (1971): 199–211.
[68] *Minnesota Law Review* 57 (1973): 639–747.
[69] *Harvard Law Review* 80 (1966): 289–337.
[70] New York: Macmillan Co., 1971.

Kelly and Winfred A. Harbison, *The American Constitution: Its Origins and Development*;[71] Charles Herman Pritchett, *The American Constitution*;[72] and Arthur E. Sutherland, *Constitutionalism in America: Origin and Evolution of Its Fundamental Ideas*.[73] Finally, one must mention the brilliant, cranky, and essential work omitted from the original bibliography: William W. Crosskey, *Politics and the Constitution in the History of the United States*.[74]

The books and articles that have been mentioned here constitute only a fraction of the relevant commentaries on American constitutionalism which have been published since the original printing of *Sources* in 1959. They should, however, provide the reader with an adequate starting point for an exploration of the subject. It is possible that the writing of the next two decades will be even more interesting, for the character of the period is likely to be quite different. In the 1970s, the mood of the nation is clearly less optimistic than it has been for many years; and American constitutional studies have always been an intriguing barometer of national self-confidence. The republication of *Sources of Our Liberties* finds Americans somewhat less sure of their role as a "nation among nations" and correspondingly less sure of the uniqueness and vitality of the constitutional structure that is at the core of our history. Serious reflection upon our traditional constitutional values cannot fail to be a vital step in regaining our traditional faith in the future of human progress in a democratic republic.

[71] 5th ed.; New York: W. W. Norton & Co., 1976.
[72] 3d ed.; New York: McGraw-Hill Book Co., 1977.
[73] New York: Blaisdell Publishing Co., 1965.
[74] Chicago: University of Chicago Press, 1953.

INDEX

References to editorial matter are in roman type; references to documents are in *italics*.

Act of Settlement, 241-42
Act of Supremacy, 55n
Act of Uniformity, 55n, 224n
Adams, John, 10, 267-68, 275, 293, 304n, 316n, 317, 322, 370
Adams, Samuel, 28, 264, *322*
Address to the Inhabitants of Quebec, 284-85, *307*
Admiralty, Court of, 191, 263, 267, *271*, 281, *286, 288, 296*
"Agreement of the People, the": *see* Levellers
Allen, Ethan, 360
Allen, Heman, 359
American Revolution: *see* Declaration and Resolves of the First Continental Congress; Declaration of the Causes and Necessity of Taking up Arms; Declaration of Independence
Andros, Edmund, 182
Annapolis Convention, 400-401
Anne, Queen, 195
Areopagitica, 243
Argall, Captain Samuel, 47-48, 49
Arms, right to bear
  in colonies, 231-32, *310, 312, 330, 356, 366, 376*
  in England, 231, *245, 246*
  in United States Constitution, 232, 419, *422, 426-27, 432*
Articles of Confederation, 388, 396, 399-400, 401, 402, 403, 430-31
Articles of the Barons, 3n, 6n, 12n
Assemblies, colonial
  bicameral form, 80-81, 99, 119, 143, 207, 327, 379
  development of, 47, 48-51, *53,* 58, 77-78, *88-90,* 98-99, 116-17, *120-23,* 165, *172,* 180-81, *182-83,* 205-6, 207, *212-15,* 252, 256-57, *259,* 261, *347,* 377, 379, *385, 393-94,* 406
  dissolution by king, 279-80, *287*

Assemblies, colonial (Cont.)
  relationship to Parliament, 79-80, 205n, 262, 264-69, 270, 274-75, 278-80, 317
Assembly, right of, 288, *325, 331, 356, 366, 377, 385*
  in United States Constitution, 422, 424, 426, *432*
Assistance, writ of, 276, 304-5; *see also* Searches and seizures
Association of the First Continental Congress, the, 283-84, *289,* 290, 292, 301, 323
Avalon Charter (1623), 97-98, 99n

Bacon, Sir Francis, 37n, 128-29
Bail, right to
  colonial development of, *150,* 207, *218,* 235, *310, 312,* 354, *395*
  in England, 62, 64n, 67n, 68n, 192n, 194, *246, 247*
  prohibition of excessive, 235-36, *247,* 310, *312, 325, 339, 348, 355,* 361, *377, 385, 433*
  in United States Constitution, 235, *423,* 430, *433*
Bank of Columbia v. Okely (1819), 10
Bassett, Richard, 400, *417*
Bates' Case (1607), 63
Bellingham, Richard, 143
Bentham, Jeremy, 137
Berkeley, Lord John, 166, 180-81
Bill of Rights, English (1689), 103, 194, 222-44, 285, 426
  as source of colonial rights, 279, 282-83, 305, 342, 427, 430
  text of, *245-50*
Bill of Rights, United States (1791): *see* First Ten Amendments to the Constitution
Bills of attainder
  Coke on, 343

457

INDEX

Bills of attainder (Cont.)
 in colonies, 309-10, 327, 343, 345, *348*, 377, 381
 defined, 342-43
 in England, 71, 343-45
 in United States Constitution, 335-36, 345, 390, 407, *412*, *415*
Bill of rights, 273, 369, 389, 420
 American documents as, 80, 143, 207, 244, 309, 387
 English documents as, 9, 62, 143, 244
 proposals for in Federal Convention, 403-5
 see also Bill of Rights, English (1689); First Ten Amendments to the Constitution (1791)
Blackstone, William, 236-37, 304, 306, 307-8, 334-35, 336, 381
Bloody Assizes (1685), 226, 236n
Bodin, Jean, 69
Bonham's Case (1610): *see* Sir Edward Coke; higher law
Boniface VIII, Pope, 25
Boston Massacre, 282
Boston Port Act, 278, *286*, *289*, *296*, 301; *see also* Intolerable Acts
Boston Tea Party, 277-78
Bowdoin, James, 370
Bradford, William, 57, 58n, *60*, 163n
Brownists: *see* Separatists
Bryan, George, 324
Bryce, James, 115
Buckingham, Duke of, 64, 70
Bushell's Case (1670), 238
Byllinge, Edward, 181, 182

Calder v. *Bull* (1798), 337
Calvert, Cecil, Second Lord Baltimore, 98, 100, *105*, 205
Calvert, Charles, Third Lord Baltimore, 99n
Calvert, George, First Lord Baltimore, 97-98, *105*
Calvert, Governor Leonard, 98-99, 100
Cambridge Agreement, 77
Cannon, James, 324
Carolina
 "Great Deed of Grant," 10
 Charter of 1663, 35
 Charter of 1665, 166
 Charter of 1669, 166-67
 Concessions of the Proprietors of, 166
Carroll, Charles, of Annapolis, 341
Carroll, Charles, of Carrollton, *322*, 341
Carteret, Sir George, 166, 180, 181
Carver, John, 56, 57n, *60*
Cary, Archibald, 302
Caswell, Richard, 353
Cavalier Parliament, 224
Cecil, Sir Robert, 37n
Certiorari, writ of, 191n
Chancery, Court of, 128, 191, *200*
Charles I, 65, 69-70, 76, 82, *105*, 133, 136, 226, 230, 234n, 305, 344

Charles I (Cont.)
 parliamentary grievances against, 62, 65-70, 131, 333-34
Charles II, 136, 162, 166, *169*, 180, 181n, 205, *211*, 223, 229, 232, 237, 240, *250*, *255*, 282
 parliamentary grievances against, 224-25, 230-31, 239, 240-41
Charter of Stephen (1136), 12n
Charter of the Forest (1217), 4n, 18n, 25, 27, *30*
Chase, Samuel, *322*, 341
Child, Robert, 146n
Church of England, 99, 163n, 228
Claiborne, William, 98
Clarendon, Lord, 193, 230
Clark, George Rogers, 388
Clarke, John, 166
Clerical Disabilities Act, 226n
Clericis laicos, bull (1296), 25n
Coke, Sir Edward, 33, 128-29, 130, 132, 162n, 204n, 254, 343
 and *Bonham's Case*, 27, 28
 and colonial legal development, 103, 146n, 206n
 commentary on Magna Carta, 4n, 5, 7, 192n, 206n
 and Petition of Right, 65-69, 191n, 192n
Common law
 English development of, 26n, 30, 67n, 125-26, 238, 304, 427-28
 in colonies, 36, 102, .143, 145n, 146, 190, 194, 281, *288*, 303-4, 307-8, 309, 342, *346*, 381, *395*, 407, 423, 425, 427, *433*
Common Pleas, Court of, *15*, 125, *139*, *141*, 192-93, *200*
"Common Sense": *see* Thomas Paine
Compact, social, 57-58, 274, *311*, *319*, 338, *346*, 368, 370-71, *373*, *382*, 389; *see also* Mayflower Compact; Puritans
Concord Resolutions (1776), 369, 371
Confirmatio Cartarum, 23-29, 207
 text of, *30-31*
Connecticut
 Charter of 1662, 35, 77n, 166n, 310, 353
 Code of 1650, 147
 Fundamental Orders of 1639, 115-19, 406
 text of, *120-24*
Conscientious objectors, 310, *330*, 339, *365*, *383*, 422
Constitution, United States, 231, 233, 235, 241, 242, 326, 327, 345, 368, 372, 389, 390, 391, 399-407
 compared with English documents, 10, 23, 223
 ratification of, 418-21, 430
 text of, *408-17*
 see also Federal Convention; First Ten Amendments to the Constitution; various subject matter headings
Constitutional Convention of 1787: *see* Federal Convention
Constitutions of Clarendon (1164), 12n
Continental Congress
 First, 290-91, 292, 297, 307, 323, 425

INDEX

Continental Congress (Cont.)
  Second, 290-94, 359, 379, 399
    see also Declaration and Resolves of the First Continental Congress
Contracts, impairment of the obligation of, 327, 335n, 336-37, 390, *395, 412*; see also Ex post facto laws
Convention Parliament, 222-23, 301
Cooper, Anthony Ashley, 167n
Corporation Act (1661), 232, 238, 282
Cotton, John, 115n, 144
Council of the Army, 135
Council of the North, 127n, *140, 142*
Council of Wales and the Marches, 127n, *140, 142*
Counsel, right to
  colonial development of, *151*, 252-54, *258*, 309, *325, 330, 339, 348, 366, 376, 384*
  in England, 241, 252, 254
  in United States Constitution, 253, 423, 429, *432*
Courts
  common law, 6, 125, 126, 127-28, 134, 136, 137, *140*, 191, 238, 253, 428
  ecclesiastical, 132-33, 136, 226, 428
  manorial, 1n, 17n
  see also Chancery; Common Pleas; Exchequer; High Commission; King's Bench; Star Chamber
Cradock, Matthew, 77
Cruel and unusual punishments: see Punishments
Curia Regis, 125n
Cushing, Thomas, 369
Cushman, Robert, 56
Cutler, Manasseh, 389
Cutt, John, 167

Dale, Sir Thomas, 36n, 47, 49
Danby, Lord, 230
Darnel's Case: see *Five Knights' Case*
Dartmouth, Lord, 294
Debtors, *13-14, 16*, 152, 182, 206, 354, *366*
Declaration and Resolves of the First Continental Congress, 72, 104, 230-31, 233, 266n, 273-85, 290, 303, 305, 317, 426
  text of, *286-89*
Declaration of Breda, 162n
Declaration of Independence, 285, 290, 302, 303, 309, 314-18, 341, 399
  grievances underlying, 72, 229-30, 231, 233, 242, 282, *319-21*
  natural law basis of, 275
  text of, *319-22*
Declaration of Indulgence
  of 1662, 224n
  of 1672, 224-25
  of 1687, 225, 240
  of 1688, 225, 228

Declaration of Rights, English (1689), **222-23**, 243, 301, 303; see also Bill of Rights, English (1689)
Declaration of the Causes and Necessity of Taking up Arms, 232, 282, 290-94, 303n, 315, 317
  text of, *295-300*
Declaratory Act (1766), 268-69, 272, *296-97*
Delaware Declaration of Rights (1776), 242, 309, 332-37, 342, 353
  text of, *338-40*
Delaware, Lord, 36
De Tallagio non Concedendo, statute (1306), 26, 68n, 73, 207, 227
Dicey, Albert V., 126n, 333
Dickinson, John, 264, 266, 292, 293, 316, 323, 324, 336, 400, *417*
  and the "Farmer's Letters," 276, 279
Dispensation, power of, 224, 225-26, *245, 246, 250*
Divine right of kings, 5, 223
Dodderidge, Sir John, 33
Domesday Book, 8
Double jeopardy, 146, *153*, 327, 381, *384*
  Blackstone on, 381
  in United States Constitution, 422, 427-28, *432*
Dudley, Thomas, 77, 143
Due process of law
  in colonies, *148*, 252, *330, 333, 348, 355, 366*
  in England, 64n, 65-66, 71, 125, 126, 132, 137, *138*, 189, 240, 343, 345, 428-29
  genesis of concept, 2n, 5, 7
  in United States Constitution, 6, 422, 427-28, *432, 436*
Dulany, Daniel, the elder, 103
Dulany, Daniel, the younger, 267, 268n
Durham, Bishop of, 97, *106*, 205n

East India Company, 33, 277-78, 284
East New Jersey
  Capital Laws of 1675, 183
  Fundamental Constitutions of 1683, 167, 183
  see also New Jersey; West New Jersey
Education, 211, 214, 219, 396
Edward I, 17n, 23n, 24-25, 73
Edward III, 23n, 62, 73, 74, *138*, 239, 240
Edward the Confessor, 1n, 3n
Egerton, Sir Thomas, 33
Elections
  freedom of
    in colonies, 217, *233, 257, 312, 324, 330, 338, 347, 355, 365, 375, 383*
    in England, 232-33, *245, 246*
    in United States Constitution, 233, *409, 413, 435-36*
  frequency of, 89-90, 93, 155, 239, 311, *338, 347, 356*
  regularity of, 329, 365, 375
  see also Colonial assemblies; Suffrage
Eliot, Hollis and Valentine, case of (1629), 234n, 235

INDEX

Eliot, John, 64n
Elizabeth I, 32, 55n, 62-63, 128, 129, 131, 234, 252, 254
Ellsworth, Oliver, 233, 336, 402
Eminent domain, *16*, 145, *149*, *330*, *365*, *395*, *422-23*, *429*, *432*
Entick v. Carrington (1765), 305-6
Equal protection of the law, *148*, *436*
"Essex Result," 369
Established church
   in colonies, 99, 162, 167-68, 283, 309, *338*, *349*, *354*, *365*, *370*, *375*, *383*
   in England, 55, 62, 226-27
   in United States Constitution, 424, 432
   see also Church of England
Exchequer, Court of, 1n, 63, 97n, 125, 200, 304n
Ex officio, oath, 132-34, 136-37, 428; *see also* self-incrimination
Ex post facto laws
   Blackstone on, 334-35, 336
   defined, 333, 337
   in colonies, 327, 332-33, 335-37, *339*, *347*, *356*, *377*, *381*, *385*
   in England, 333-34
   in United States Constitution, 335-36, 390, 407, *412*
Extradition, *415*

Fairfax, Sir Thomas, 134-35
Federal Convention (1787), 195, 233, 235, 335-36, 345, 389, 401-5, 418, 429
   Committee of Detail, 195, 235, 390, 402-4
   Committee of Style and Arrangement, 235, 390, 402
   Committee on Unfinished Parts, 402
   see also Constitution, United States
Fenwick, John, 181, 344
Fines, *15*, *19-20*, *149*, *218*, *238*, *246*, *247*
   excessive prohibited
      in colonies, 310, *312*, 325, *339*, *348*, *355*, *361*, *377*, *385*, *395*, *430*
      in United States Constitution, 423, 430, *433*
First Ten Amendments to the Constitution, 237, 244, 309, 391, 418-31
   1st Amendment, 162, 167-68, 230, 308, 425-26
   2d Amendment, 232, 426-27
   3rd Amendment, 427
   4th Amendment, 427
   5th Amendment, 6, 137, 427-29
   6th Amendment, 253, 254, 429
   7th Amendment, 429-30
   8th Amendment, 237, 430
   9th Amendment, 430
   10th Amendment, 430-31
   text of, *432-33*
   see also subject matter headings
Fitz-Walter, Robert, 3
Five Knights' Case, 64-65, 66, 76, 191n, 192
"Foundations of Freedom," 135-36
Fox's Libel Act (1792), 308

Franklin, Benjamin, 261n, 263, 291, 293, 317, 322, 324, *417*
French and Indian War, 261-62, *296*, 358, 427
Full faith and credit, 399, *415*
Fundamental law
   colonial documents as, 27-28, 143, 166, 182, *184*, 205-6, 207, 252, *259*, 326, 342, 354, 361, *364*, 368, 369, 379
   enforcement of, 23, 27-29, 369, *416*
   English documents as, 23, 26-27, 62
   relation to divine law, 145n
   United States Constitution as, 23, 27, 28-29, 405, *416*, 426

Gage, General, 72, 266, 279, 297-98, 368
Galloway, Joseph, 274-75, 323
Gates, Sir Thomas, 36n
Gaunt, Elizabeth, 236n
George II, 304, *357*
George III, 10, 263, 274, 293, 294, 315, 368
   grievances of colonists against, 72, 229, 233, 242, 303, 317, 318, *319-21*
Georgia
   Charter of 1732, 35, 167
   Constitution of 1777, 167, 310
Gerry, Elbridge, 231n, 322, 335, 336, 404-5, 429
Gilbert, Sir Humphrey, 32, 33n
Goldsborough, Robert, 341
Gorges, Sir Ferdinando, 164
Gorham, Nathaniel, 402, 404-5, *416*
Grand jury
   in colonies, 310, 355
   in England, 7, *17*, 126n, 428
   in United States Constitution, 419, 423, 427, *432*
Great Contract, the, 63n
Grenville, George, 262, 268
Grotius, Hugo, 103

Habeas Corpus Act (1679), 70-71, 103, 147, 189-95, 235
   text of, *196-203*
Habeas corpus, writ of
   defined, 189
   in American colonies, 190, 194-95, 206, 285, 310, 327, *372*, *381*, *395*
   English development of, 5, 9, 64n, 66, 68n, 69n, 70-71, 74, 132, *141-42*, 189-94, 235
   in United States Constitution, 190, 195, 403n, 404, 407, *412*
   see also Habeas Corpus Act (1679)
Hales, Sir Edward, 225
Hamilton, Alexander, 308-9, 400, 402, 403, *417*, 420, 430
Hamilton, Andrew, 307-8
Hampden's Case (1637), 26n, 70n
Hancock, John, 291, *321*
Haynes, John, 143
"Heads of the Proposals, the": *see* Levellers

INDEX

Henry I, 1, 2, 3n, 12n, 17n
   Charter of Liberties of, 2, 3n, 6n, 17n
   Coronation Charter of, 12n
Henry II, 1, 12n, 19n
Henry III, 4, 5, 11n, 18n, 23, 24
Henry IV, 23n
Henry V, 23
Henry VII, *139*
Henry VIII, 129-30, 232, 281, *286*, 344
Henry, Patrick, 38, 265, 302, 335
High Commission, Court of, 56, 63, 76, 129, 132-34, 136-37, 191, 226-27, *245*, *246*, 303
Higher law, 23, 26-29, 57n, 117, 264n; *see also* fundamental law; natural law
Hobart, Sir Henry, 37n
Hooker, Rev. Thomas, 115-17
Houston, William, 400
Hudson, William, 126n, 129

Impeachment, 257, 344, 355, 409, *414*, *415*
Independents, 55n; *see also* Puritans
Ingersoll, Jared, 263, *417*
Inheritance, 12-13, *14*, *16*, 34, 35n, 157, 258, 392
Innocent III, Pope, 2, 4, *12*
"Instructions of the Town of Braintree" (1765), 10n, 267-68
Intolerable Acts, 72, 278-84, 323; *see also* Quebec Act; Quartering Act of 1774; Boston Port Act; Massachusetts Government Act

James I, 32, 37n, *39*, 48, *53*, 60, 82, 133, 265
   and established church, 55
   parliamentary grievances against, 63, 130-31, 132, 234-35
James II, 4, 180, 181n, 194, 222, 230, 233, 237, *248*, 255
   parliamentary grievances against, 223-28, 236, 239, 240-41, 245-46, 426
Jamestown colony, 47
Jay, John, 291
Jefferson, Thomas, 28, 168, 291, 292, 293, 303, 317, 318, *322*, 388, 391
Jeffreys, Lord, 226, 236n, 238
John, King, 1-9, 11, 12n, 13n, 16n, 23, 191n
Johnson, Isaac, 77
Johnson, Thomas, 291
Johnson, William Samuel, 266, 403, *416*
Johnston, Samuel, 352
Jones, Hugh, 50
Jones, Thomas, 352
Judgment of peers: *see* Trial by jury
Judicial review, 28-29
Judiciary
   discipline of, *150*, 195, *349*
   guardian of liberties, 125, 132
   independence of
      in colonies, 242, *286*, *327*, *340*, *349*, *353*, *377*, *385-86*
      in England, 63, 64n, 225, 228, 242, 345

Judiciary, independence of (Cont.)
      in United States Constitution, *414*
"Just Defense of John Lilburne, the": *see* Levellers

Kilty, William, 104
King, Rufus, 390, 403, *416*
King's Bench, Court of, 64, 125, *139*, *141*, 192-93, 200, 228, 235, 236
King's Council, 1n, 6, 125-28, 192-93

Lambarde, William, 8
Lancaster, Earl of, 71
Langton, Stephen, 2-3
"Large Petition of the Levellers," 134
Laud, Archbishop William, 76, 144n, 344
Law of the land
   Magna Carta as, 5-6, *17*, 64n
   phrase in later documents, 74, 126n, *138*, *312*, *325*, *339*, *348*, *355*, *366*, *376*, *384*, *416*
Lawrie, Gawen, 181
Leach v. Money (1765), 304
Lee, Richard Henry, 263, 293, 316, 317, 322
Lee, Thomas L., 335
Leighton, Dr., 131
Levellers, 134-35, 333-34, 371
   the "Agreement of the People," 135, 334
   the "Heads of the Proposals," 134-35
   the "Just Defence of John Lilburne," 136
   the "Large Petition of," 134
   the "Petition to the House of Commons," 135, 334
Lexington, Battle of, 231-32, 290, 291, *298*, 314
Licensing Act of 1662, 243, 305
Lilburne, John, 131, 133, 135-36, 334, 371; *see also* Levellers
Lisle, Alice, 236n
Livingston, Robert R., 317
Livingston, William, 291, *417*
Locke, John, 103, 167n
London Company, 33-34, 37, *39-45*, 48, *52-53*, 56, 406
Long Parliament, 70, 134, 146n, 165, 227
Louis of France, Prince, 4
Lucas, Nicholas, 181
Ludlow, Roger, 116n, 117

Macaulay, Lord Thomas, 189, 228, 243-44
McHenry, James, 335, *417*
McKean, Thomas, 324
Madison, James, 302, 335, 390, 400, 403, *417*, *421-24*, *425-26*
Magna Carta, 1-10, 25, 36, 64n, 65, 74, 104, 125, 126, *138*, 192, 204n, 207, 227, 240, 343, 406, 427, 428, 429
   in American law, 5, 8, 9-10, 101, 103, 143, 145, 146, 147, 165, 183, 333, 342
   genesis of, 1-3

461

INDEX

Magna Carta (Cont.)
  later confirmations of, 23-24, 25, *30*, 67-68
  myth of, 2n, 7
  reissues of, 4-5, 11n, 13n, 14n, 15n, 18n, 23, 24
  as restriction on executive power, 5, 9, 23, 69, 130, 228, 426
  text of, *11-22*
Maine, Charter of 1639, 35
Mansfield, Lord, 229n
Marbury v. Madison (1803), 29
Marshall, John, 29
Martial law
  in colonies, 36, 47, *110*, *175*, *348*, 361, 377, 385
  in England, 62, 65, 71, *74-75*, 240
  in United States Constitution, 71-72
  see also Due process of law
Martin, Luther, 403
Mary, Queen, 253-54
Maryland
  Act Concerning Religion (1649), 100-1, 166
  Charter of 1632, 35, 77n, 97-104, 205
    text of, *105-113*
  Constitution of 1776, 104, 341-45, *346-51*
  Declaration of Rights (1776), 332, 335, 341-45, 353
    text of, *346-51*
Mason, George, 302, 303, 335, 336, 390, 405
Massachusetts
  Administration of Justice Act (1774), 282, *286*, 289
  Body of Liberties (1641), 10, 80, 143-47, 165-66, 253, 333, 371, 427, 428
    text of, *148-61*
  Charter of 1691, 28on, 368
  Circular Letter (1768), 276-77, 279-80, 281, 283, 301
  Constitution of 1780, 232, 345, 368-72, 373-78, 380
  Declaration of Liberties (1661), 80
  Declaration of Rights (1780), 335, 368-72, 380-81
    text of, *373-78*
  Government Act (1774), 280, 282, *286*, 289
  Laws and Liberties (1648), 146
Massachusetts Bay Company
  Charter of 1629, 35, 76-81, 118, 143, 163
    text of, *82-96*
Matlack, Timothy, 324
Mayflower Compact, 55-59, 118, 371, 406
  text of, *60*
Mead, William, 204n
Mecklenburg Declaration of Independence, 314n
Mecklenburg Resolves, 314
Militia, 230, 310, *312*, 339, 348, 385, 393, 405
  in United States Constitution, *411*, 422, 426-27, *432*
  see also Standing armies
Milligan, ex parte (1866), 71-72
Milton, John, 243
Monmouth's Rebellion, 236n, 238
Monopolies, 48, 145, *149*, 342, 350, 356, 419

Morris, Gouverneur, 195, 336, 390, 403, *417*
Morris, Robert, 322, 324, *417*
Muscovy Company, 33n
Mutiny Act (1689), 71, 239-40

Natural law
  as limitation on legislative authority, 28, 264, 274-75, 277
  as source of rights, 264, 274, 275, 277, 285, 287, 303, *329*, *362*, *364*, *373*, *374*, *382*
  see also Fundamental law
New England
  Charter of 1620, 35
  Council for, 57n, 58, 76, 77n, *82-85*
  Restraining Act of 1775, 315n
New Hampshire
  Bill of Rights (1784), 335, 379-81
    text of, *382-86*
  Constitution of 1776, 379
  Constitution of 1784, 167, 379-81, *382-86*
  "Grants," 358, 359, *362*
New Haven, Code of 1656, 147
New Jersey
  Concession and Agreement (1664), 166, 180-81
  Constitution of 1776, 309, 353
  Plan at Federal Convention, 402
  see also East New Jersey; West New Jersey
New York
  Charter of Liberties (1683), 10, 147, 194
  Constitution of 1777, 232, 309-10, 345
  Declaration of Rights (1691), 167
Nobility, titles of, 327, 342, 350, *412*
Nonconformists, 55n, 77, 163n, 236n, 240; *see also* Puritans
Nonimportation, 268, 274, 277, 283, 292, 297, 323
North, Lord, 277, 278, 280, 292-93
North Carolina
  Constitution of 1776, 232, 352-54, *355-57*
  Declaration of Rights (1776), 335, 352-54
    text of, *355-57*
Northwest Ordinance (1787), 387-91
  text of, *392-97*

Ohio Company, 389
"Olive Branch" petition, 293-94
Otis, James, 28, 264, 304

Paca, William, 322, 341
Paine, Robert Treat, 322, 369
Paine, Thomas, 10, 315-16, 324
  "Common Sense," 315-16
Parliament, 6, 47, 134-35, 315, 317
  and colonial assemblies, 79-80, 205n, 262, 264-66, 268-69, 272, 275, 278-80, 317
  colonial grievances against, 262, 264-66, 268-69, 270-71, 272-83, *286-87*, *288-89*, 295, 296-99, 303n, 315, *346*, *362-63*
  frequency of meeting, 239, 247

462

INDEX

Parliament (Cont.)
  origins, 24, 25-26
  sovereignty of, 27-28, 223, 264; 272, 275-76, 277, 333, 343
  struggles with executive, 62-70, 76, 126-27, 129-30, 222, 243, 248-50, 333-34
  and taxing power; *see* Taxation
Paterson, William, 402, *417*
Peabody, Nathaniel, 380
Pendleton, Edmund, 302
Penn, John, 323
Penn, Richard, 294
Penn, Admiral William, 205
Penn, William, 181, 204-9, 251, 255-56, 259-60
Penn and Mead, trials of (1670), 204n
Pennsylvania
  Charter of 1681, 77n, 205, 208, 251, 255
  Charter of Privileges (1701), 10, 27, 167, 208, 251-54, 344n, 429
    text of, *255-60*
  Constitution of 1776, 208, 232, 323-27, *328-31*, 344n, 360
  Constitution of 1790, 327, 335
  Declaration of Rights (1776), 230, 253, 309, 323-27, 332, 342, 353, 425, 426, 429
    text of, *328-31*
  Declaration of Rights (1790), 327
  Frame of Government (1682), 167, 204-8, 253
    text of, *209-21*
  Frame of Government (1683), 208, 251, 255
  Frame of Government (1696), 208, 251
  Fundamental Constitutions of, 205-6
  "Laws Agreed Upon in England," 207
People v. *Croswell* (1804), 309
Petition, right of
  in colonies, 229-30, 266, 271, 280, 282-83, *288*, *331*, *339*, *347*, *366*, *377*, *385*
  in England, 227-29, *246*
  in United States Constitution, 230, 422, 424, 426, *432*
Petition of grace, 68n
Petition of right, 68n
Petition of Right, 26n, 62-72, 76, 192, 193, 227, 279, 427, 429
  in colonies, 103, 147, 279, 342
  text of, *73-75*
"Petition to the House of Commons": *see* Levellers
Phelpes, William, 116n
Pierce, John, 56, 57, 58n
Pilgrims, 55-58, 145n, 163
Pinchon, William, 116n
Pinckney, Charles, 195, 372, 402, 403n, 404, 405, *417*
Pitt, William, 268, 269, 275
Plater, George, 341
Plymouth Colony, 163
Plymouth Company, 33, 37, *39-45*
Popham, Sir John, 33
Poll tax, 342
Prescott, James, 369

Press, freedom of the
  in colonies, 285, 306-9, 310, *312*, 325, 326, 327, 330, 340, 350, 356, 366, 376, 385
  in England, 130, 242-43, 305-7
  in United States Constitution, 403n, 404, 405, 422, 423, 424, 425-26, *432*
Privileges and immunities, 376, *384*
  in Articles of Confederation, 399
  in United States Constitution, *415*, *436*
  see also Rights of Englishmen
Privy Council, 127n, 129, 132, 194, 205n, 208
  under Charles I, 64n, 66n, 70, 74, 77n
  under James I, 47, 63
Pro Camera Stellata statute (1487), 127-28, 131, 133
Proclamations, Statute of, 128n, 129-31
Prynne, William, 131
Punishments, *93*, *107*, 236-37, 310, *384*
  cruel and unusual
    Blackstone on, 236-37
    in colonies, 146, *153*, 237, 310, *312*, 325, *339*, *347*, *348*, *355*, *377*, *384*, *385*, *395*
    in England, 236-37, *246*, 247
    nature of, 131, 236-37
    in United States Constitution, 237, 423, 430, *433*
Puritans, 100, 163, 181, 231
  theology and civil government, 56-58, 77, 118, 143, 145, 371
Pym, John, 344

Quakers, 181-83, 204-5, 206, 310
Quartering of soldiers
  in colonies, 72, 296, 320, 327, *339*, *348*, *377*, *385*
  Quartering Act of 1765, 72, 278-79, 427
  Quartering Act of 1774, 72, 278-79, *289*
  in England, 62, 65, 67, 68n, 72, 74, 75, 245
  in United States Constitution, 72, 404, 422, 427, *432*
Quebec Act (1774), 283, *286*, *289*, *296*; *see also* Intolerable Acts
Quintipartite Deed (1676), 181

Raleigh, Sir Walter, 32, 33n, 34n
Randolph, Edmund, 302, 400, 402
Randolph, Peyton, 273
Read, George, *322*, 332, 400, *417*
Religion
  freedom of
    in colonies, 27-28, 99-101, *106*, 146, *159-61*, 163-68, *169*, 180-81, 182, *185*, 205, 207, 220, 251-52, 256, 259, 283, 309, 310, *312*, 325, 329, 332, 338, 349, 354, 356, 360, 361, 365, 374, 375, 382, 395
    in England, 1-2, *11-12*, 55-56, 162n, 223, 224-25, 228, 240
    in United States Constitution, 167-68, 419, 422, 423, 424, 425, *432*

INDEX

Religion (Cont.)
  as reason for colonization, 34, *40*, 77, *94, 105, 169*, 425
  relations between state and church, 37, *120*, 146, *154, 159*, 163, 220, 309, 310, *349, 365, 374*, 380-81, *382-83*
  see also Established church; Religious tests
Religious tests
  in colonies, 78, 115n, 168, 183, 220, 256, *325, 326, 332, 338, 350, 353-54, 360, 365*
  in England, 225, 240, *249-50*
  in United States Constitution, 403n, 404, *416*
Representative government
  concept in United States Constitution, 405-6
  development in colonies, 77-79, 98-99, 143, 165, *172*, 207, 270, 279-80, 284, 287, 310, *312, 329, 338, 346-47, 355, 365*, 375, *383*, 395
Republican form of government, 388, 389, *397*, 406, *416*; *see also* Representative government
Resolution in Anderson, the, 191, 192n
Resolutions of the Stamp Act Congress (1765), 261-69, 275, 283, 285, 426
  text of, *270-71*
Restoration, 183, 193, 227, 230, 231, 234n, 237-38, 240, 243
Retroactive laws: *see* Ex post facto laws
Revenue Act (1764), 72
Revolution settlement, 223, 241
Rex v. Gordon (1781), 229n
Rhode Island
  Charter of 1663, 35, 77n, 162-68, 180, 353, 425
  text of, *169-79*
Rich, Robert, 76-77
Richard II, 23n, *201*
Rights of Englishmen, 35-36, 47, 67n, 223, *246-48*, 266-67, 284-85
  as rights of colonists, 32, 35, 38, *44*, 47, 53, 93, 101-4, *109*, 177, 190, 206, 230-31, 261, 264, 265, 270, *284-85*, 287, 318, 342, 406
Roanoke colony, 32
Robinson, John, 56
Rockingham, Marquis of, 268, 269
Roger of Wendover, 6n
Rudyard, Sir Benjamin, 65
Ruggles, Timothy, 266
Rule of law
  in colonies, 146n, 206, 315, 371, *378*
  Dicey on, 333
  origin of concept, 1, 62
Runnymede, 3
Rutledge, Edward, 316n, 322
Rutledge, John, 195, 291, 390, 402, *417*

Saltonstall, Richard, 77
Sancroft, Archbishop, 228
Sandys, Sir Edwin, 37, 48, 49, 56
Scott, James, 269
Scrooby congregation, 55, 56

Searches and seizures
  Blackstone on, 304
  in colonies, 276, 304-6, *312, 330, 339, 348, 355, 366, 376, 384*
  English practice, 304-6
  in United States Constitution, 423, 427, *432*
Sedition Act (1798), 308
Seditious libel, 228, 229, 305-9, 327; *see also* Speech, freedom of; Press, freedom of the
Selden, John, 7, 64n, 189
Self-incrimination, privilege against
  in colonies, 153, *312, 325, 330, 339, 348, 355, 366, 376, 384*, 429
  English practice, 132-37
  in United States Constitution, 137, 422, 428, *432*
Separatists, 55, 57n, 163; *see also* Puritans
Separation of powers, 288, 310, *311*, 325-26, 345, *347, 355, 371, 378, 386, 424*
Seven Bishops' Case (1688), 228
Sherman, Roger, 317, 405, *416*, 424
Ship-Money Act, 227
Ship-Money Case: see Hampden's Case
Sidney, Algernon, 206n
Smith, Henry, 116n
Smith, John, 36n
Social contract: *see* Compact, social
Society of Merchants Adventurers, the, 33n
Sons of Liberty, 277
South Carolina
  Constitution of 1776, 310, 353
  Constitution of 1778, 310
  Constitution of 1790, 335
Speech, freedom of, 168, 307, *325, 327, 330, 366*, 422, 424, 425-26, *432*
  for legislators
    in colonies, *123*, 145, *149-50, 347*, 361, 377, *385*, 399-400
    in England, 233-35, *247*
  in United States Constitution, 235, *410*
  see also Press, freedom of the; Seditious libel
Stamp Act, 10, 28, 38, 72, 261-69, 272, 277, 278, 279, 281; *see also* Resolutions of the Stamp Act Congress
Standing armies
  civilian control of military, 310, *312, 320, 330, 339, 348, 356, 366, 376, 385*, 404
  in colonies, 230-31, 278-79, *286, 288, 289*, 303, *312, 320*, 325
  in England, 230, 231, 239-40, *245*
  in United States Constitution, 231, 404, 405, *411*
Star Chamber, Court of, 47, 63, 70, 76, 137, 191, 192, 226, 237-38, 242-43, 305, 306, 345
  act for the abolition of, 70, 103, 125-37, 192, 193, 429
  text of, *138-42*
  grievances against, 129-33, *139*
  origins of, 125-28
  powers of, 128-31, 133
  procedure of, 128-29, 428

464

INDEX

Star Chamber, Court of (Cont.)
  source of name, 127n
Statute of Westminster I (1275), 192n
Steele, John, 116n
Stephen, King, 1n, 12n
Story, Joseph, 8-9, 36
Strachey, William, 36n
Strafford, Earl of, 344
Strode's Act, 234-35
Suffolk Resolves, 274
Suffrage
  in colonies, 48-49, 326, *338*, *347*, 353, 361, 365, 370, *383*
  in England, 47
  in United States Constitution, *408*, *436*, *437*, *438*
Sugar Act (1764), 262, 264, 268, 278, 281
Suspension of laws
  in colonies, 226, 279, *312*, 326, 327, *338*, *347*, *355*, 361, *377*, *385*
  in England, 224-26, *245*, *246*
Swaine, William, 116n

Taxation
  baronial grievances against king, 1, *14-15*, 24-26, *31*
  of colonies by Parliament, 262-69, 270-71, 272, 275-78, 286, 296
  prerogative, 62, 64, 70, 73, 227, *245*, *246*
  regulation of in colonies, 50, *111-12*, 123, 181, 207, 217, 284, 303, 326, *339*, *342*, *347*
  struggles between Parliament and executive over, 62-63, 66, 68n, 70, 75, 227, *245*
  in United States Constitution, *408*, *410*, *411*, *412*, *437*
Tea Acts (1767, 1773), 277
Test Act (1673), 225
Tilghman, Matthew, 341
Toleration Act (1649): *see* Maryland, Act Concerning Religion
Toleration Act (1689), 240
Tonnage and Poundage Act, 227
  Remonstrance against (1628), 70n
Townshend, Charles, 262, 275-76
Townshend Acts, 276-78, 283, 305
Treason
  Act of 1351, 240, 281n
  Act of 1543, 281
  Act of 1661, 241
  in colonies, 280, 281, 429
  in England, 240-41, 252, 254, 429
  in United States Constitution, 241, 406-7, *415*
  see also Trial of Treasons Act
Treaty of Paris (1763), 262, 387
Trial by jury
  in civil cases, 34, *151*, 296, *312*, 325, 330, *356*, *366*, *376*, *384-85*, 404, 405, 419, 429-30, *433*
  in colonies, 34-35, 58, 145, *151-52*, *153*, *156*, 182, 185, 187, 207, 217, 263, 267-68, 275, 281-82, ,284-85, 288-89, 296, 303, 309, 310, *312*, 326, 330, *339*, *346*, *348*, *355*, *366*, *376*, *384*, *395*

Trial by jury (Cont.)
  development of in England, 5, 7-9, 132, 237-38, 240, *247*, 253, 429
  as right of Englishman, 270, 406
  in United States Constitution, 403, 404-5, 406, *415*, 419, 423-24, 429-30, *432*
Trial of Treasons Act (1696), 240-41, 252, 254, 281
Triennial Act
  of 1664, 239
  of 1694, 239

Usury, *151*

Van Ness v. Pacard (1829), 36
Vaughan, Chief Justice, 189, 238
Vermont
  Constitution of 1777, 232, 358-61, *362-67*
  Constitution of 1786, 345
  Declaration of Rights (1777), 358-61
    text of, *362-67*
Virginia
  Bill of Rights (1776), 226, 231, 233, 301-9, *324-26*, 332, 335, *342*, 353, 405, 425, 428, 429
    text of, *311-12*
  Charter of 1606, 32-38, 47, 387
    text of, *39-46*
  Charter of 1609, 37, 39n, 44, 47
  Charter of 1612, 37, 39n, 44n
  Company, 48, 49-50, 57
  Constitution of 1776, 232, 301-10, *311-13*, 318
  Ordinances for (1618), 38, 47-51, 56
  Ordinances for (1621), 47-51
    text of, *52-54*
  Plan in Federal Convention, 402
  Resolutions, 425-26
  Royal Council of, 34-35, 37, *42*
  Statute of Religious Liberty (1786), 28, 168

Walwyn, William, 333-34
Ward, Andrew, 116n
Ward, Nathaniel, 144
Warren, James, 369
Washington, George, 261, 291, 302, 401-2, *416*, 418
Weare, Meshech, 380
Welles, Thomas, 117n
Wentworth, Benning, 358, *362*, 379
Wentworth, Sir Thomas, 66
West New Jersey
  Charter of 1681, 166n, 182-83
  Concession and Agreement of 1664, 180
  Concessions and Agreements of 1677, 180-83
    text of, *184-88*
  Fundamental Laws of 1677, 166, 181-83, *184-88*
  see also New Jersey; East New Jersey
Westwood, William, 116n
William of Orange, 4, 222, 239, 243, *245-47*, 259

INDEX

William the Conqueror, 1, 7, 24, 97n
Williams, Roger, 162-65, 168, *169*
Williamson, Hugh, 404, *417*, 429
Wilson, James, 291, *322*, *323*, *324*, 336, 390, 402, *417*, 430
Winthrop, John, 77, 79, 115n, 143-44
Witenagemot, 1n
Witnesses
  false, *187*, *219*
  necessary for conviction, 183, 241
  right to summon and confront
    in colonies, 252, 253-54, *258*, 280, 281, 309, *312*, *330*, *339*, *348*, *355*, *366*, *376*, *384*
    in England, 241, 252-54, 429

Witnesses, right to summon and confront (Cont.)
    in United States Constitution, 254, 423, 429, *432*
Wolfe Tone's Case (1798), 71
Written constitution, 115, 117, 119, 135, 143, 333, 371; *see also* Fundamental law
Wyatt, Governor, 50

Yeardley, Sir George, 10, 48, 49, 52n
Young, Thomas, 324, 360

Zenger, John Peter, 307-8